Objectivity

SUNY series in Contemporary Continental Philosophy

Dennis J. Schmidt, editor

Objectivity
The Hermeneutical and Philosophy

Günter Figal

translated by
Theodore D. George

The translation of this work was supported by a grant from the Goethe-Institut which is funded by the German Ministry of Foreign Affairs.

Published by
STATE UNIVERSITY OF NEW YORK PRESS, ALBANY

© 2010 State University of New York

Gegenständlichkeit: Das Hermeneutische und die Philosophie
© 2006 Mohr Siebeck Tübingen

All rights reserved

Printed in the United States of America

No part of this book may be used or reproduced in any manner whatsoever without written permission. No part of this book may be stored in a retrieval system or transmitted in any form or by any means including electronic, electrostatic, magnetic tape, mechanical, photocopying, recording, or otherwise without the prior permission in writing of the publisher.

For information, contact State University of New York Press, Albany, NY
www.sunypress.edu

Production by Laurie D. Searl
Marketing by Michael Campochiaro

Library of Congress Cataloging-in-Publication Data

Figal, Günter, 1949–
 [Gegenständlichkeit. English]
 Objectivity : the hermeneutical and philosophy / Günter Figal ; translated by Theodore D. George.
   p. cm. — (SUNY series in contemporary continental philosophy)
 Includes bibliographical references and index.
 ISBN 978-1-4384-3205-2 (hardcover : alk. paper)
 1. Hermeneutics. 2. Objectivity. I. Title.

BD241.F4513 2010
121'.686—dc22   2009051694

10 9 8 7 6 5 4 3 2 1

This translation is dedicated to the memory of James Soden, intellectual, scholar, and devoted teacher of German literature and language at Whitman College for more than forty years.

Contents

Acknowledgments	ix
Translator's Introduction	xi
Preface	xxvii
Introduction	1

Chapter 1. From Philosophical Hermeneutics to
Hermeneutical Philosophy — 5

§	1. The Human Sciences as Problem	5
§	2. Hermeneutics of Facticity	8
§	3. Hermeneutics and Practical Philosophy	17
§	4. Origin	24
§	5. Models of Origin	29
§	6. Moments of Origin	38

Chapter 2. Interpretation — 49

§	7. Carrying Over	49
§	8. What Is To Be Interpreted	55
§	9. Setting In	61
§	10. Exterior Relations	66
§	11. Presentative Recognizing	77
§	12. Understanding	88
§	13. Objectivity	107

Chapter 3. The World as Hermeneutical Space — 121

§	14. Phenomenology	121
§	15. Space	129
§	16. The Concept of World	146

Chapter 4. Freedom — 155

- § 17. Action — 155
- § 18. Deliberation — 161
- § 19. Freedom of Things — 166
- § 20. Shared Freedom — 174
- § 21. Free Contemplation — 184

Chapter 5. Language — 191

- § 22. Based on Speech — 191
- § 23. An Individual Simple Sentence — 198
- § 24. Signs — 205
- § 25. Significance — 212
- § 26. Deconstruction of the Voice — 226
- § 27. Positions — 233
- § 28. Written Thought — 240

Chapter 6. Time — 253

- § 29. Ubiquitous and With All Things — 253
- § 30. Something Occurs — 255
- § 31. Being in Time — 268
- § 32. Time of Enactment — 273
- § 33. Temporality — 281
- § 34. Constellations of Meaning — 292

Chapter 7. Life — 299

- § 35. In Hermeneutical Space — 299
- § 36. Lifting Out and Folding — 303
- § 37. Originariness — 308
- § 38. Form of Life — 316
- § 39. Body and the Body Quick — 327
- § 40. Reason — 333
- § 41. Structure of Life — 337
- § 42. Lack and Fullness — 344

Notes — 349

Bibliography — 403

Index of Names — 421

Index of Subjects — 425

Index of Greek Terms — 441

Acknowledgments

The translator would like to express his gratitude to Dennis Schmidt and John McDermott for their encouragement, good counsel, and insightful recommendations over the course of the project. The translator would also like to thank Michael Steinmann, Constance Hauf, and Josh Hayes for their thoughtful suggestions on drafts of the English version. This translation would not have been possible without the support, patience, and critical acumen that Kristi Sweet offered each day to help see the project to completion. The translator is also thankful for the generous support of the Goethe Institute, as well as the Ray A. Rothrock '77 Fellowship program, and the Glasscock Center for Humanities Research at Texas A&M University.

Translator's Introduction

*Objectivity and Finite Transcendence
in Günter Figal's Hermeneutical Philosophy*

Theodore George

One of Günter Figal's broadest concerns in *Objectivity* is to demonstrate that the philosophical endeavor itself is oriented by hermeneutical matters: philosophy, in its character, possibilities, and limits, is animated by the tasks of interpretation and understanding. Figal's designation for philosophy so conceived—"hermeneutical philosophy"—intends not to specify one form of philosophy that might stand next to others, but, rather, to signify that philosophical inquiry itself is, at its core, hermeneutical. Of course, he also introduces the term *hermeneutical philosophy* to indicate both his philosophical debts to and efforts to advance beyond the research program most closely associated with hermeneutics in our time, Hans-Georg Gadamer's "philosophical hermeneutics." The scope of Figal's project leads him to develop a systematic view of hermeneutical philosophy and to take up a range of themes, but we may bring some initial outlines of his approach into focus with reference to this proximity and distance from Gadamer.

Chief among the debts that Figal owes to Gadamer (although certainly not only to Gadamer) is the conviction that philosophy is a distinctive form of inquiry independent of and even foundational for modern scientific rationality and method. To make good on this conviction, Figal calls for a phenomenology of philosophy—given his insistence on philosophy's hermeneutical character, this amounts to a phenomenology of the hermeneutical—that does justice to the interpretive openness and inexhaustibility of philosophical inquiry. Like Gadamer before him, he believes that philosophy aims not to establish inalterable truths, firm foundations, or certitudes, but, rather, to be open for and responsive to the matters, *die Sachen*, in their givenness and thereby to attain novel insights that put purported certainties into play.

Figal's attempts to advance beyond the context of Gadamer's thought coalesce around the central theme of his book: objectivity. In his project, "objectivity" does not pick out the character of an observation or belief that would conform to norms familiar to us from modern epistemology or from research in the modern natural sciences. Rather, his term signifies the character of objects in that they confront us as substantive matters of concern demanding our attention and eliciting interpretation. His idea is that the openness and inexhaustibility of philosophical inquiry are driven not first by us as subjects, as interpreters, with our diversity of questions, creative talents, perspectives, and needs, but, ultimately, by an unremitting wellspring of intelligibility granted to us ever anew by objects themselves. In light of this, Figal affirms, "the human being is not the measure of all things."[1] Philosophy, and likewise our lives, are sustained not of our own powers, but, rather, precisely by our responsiveness, our trust in and ability to come into accord with what confronts us from outside and remains exterior to us.

We may shed some light on Figal's conception by means of a remark on an ambiguity involved in using the English "objectivity" to translate his German term, *Gegenständlichkeit*. On the one hand, it is not hard to see that the English "objectivity" dims connotations of the German important to his work. The German word *Gegenständlichkeit* suggests the exteriority of whatever draws our attention as a substantive issue or object, a *Gegenstand*—in free translation, something that stands in opposition, in tension, over and against. Figal trades on these connotations to give contour to his belief that philosophy is conditioned crucially by whatever befalls us so as to stand out and obtrude, though not as a mute and impassible obstacle, but, rather, as something whose obduracy nevertheless betrays potential intelligibility and elicits inquiry.

On the other hand, however, the English "objectivity" is not separated from the German *Gegenständlichkeit* as if by an abyss. After all, when we associate the English "objectivity" with an observation or belief, one thing we typically wish to convey is that the observation or belief properly accords with the object under our scrutiny. Figal's point, in any case, is simply that our achievement of such accord turns not on the employment of predetermined scientific practices and methods of inquiry, but, rather, on our receptiveness to whatever intelligibility an object may grant to us. Because of this, philosophical inquiry turns not on our capacity to attain some "view from nowhere," but, instead, on our entrance into a proper rapport, a correlation, with objects. The philosophical endeavor does not need to be understood as a form of detachment from life, but, rather, as an intensification of life that results from its achievement of a heightened relation to objects.

If Figal's project succeeds, then we may suggest that it represents a sea change in an important constellation of movements in philosophy associated with the names of phenomenology, existentialism, and hermeneutics.[2] For, as diverse as research in these movements is, it may nevertheless be said that many of the figures we most often associate with them are renowned, with whatever degree of warrant, for their emphasis on the philosophical significance of the self. Certainly, figures before Figal—we think of the later Heidegger, Merleau-Ponty, and others—have in different ways helped to shift our attention from the self to our responsiveness to what lies beyond the self. Yet, as we look back onto these efforts now, we may wonder whether they appear rather as groundbreaking forays into a new outlook than as a comprehensive program of research.

Figal's *Objectivity* may be seen to take up such a challenge by calling on us to rethink the point of departure for research in these movements, and, with this, to develop a systematic picture of philosophy that arises from the question of the objective. Figal's emphasis on objectivity may thus be said to represent a new and further effort to twist free from presuppositions of the metaphysics of subjectivity of modernity.[3] Of equal importance, however, Figal's focus on objectivity also suggests that philosophical inquiry is at its best when directed and sustained by what is and remains outside of us, that inquiry into our condition is at its most vital when it focuses not solely on subjectivity and selfhood, but, rather, on what grants meaning to the self.

Although Figal's *Objectivity* no doubt builds on themes developed in his previous work,[4] he may be seen to recommend this book as a text to be interpreted in its own right. Certainly, it lies beyond the scope of a brief introduction to examine his full development of ideas in this text. Nevertheless, we may indicate the profile of his project in terms of three themes. The first theme leads us to some further comments on his interrelated notions of philosophy, interpretation, and understanding. The second theme concerns his notion of the world as hermeneutical space; he claims that this, in turn, unfolds in three dimensions—freedom, language, and time. The third theme concerns his turn to life as the aegis under which our lives in the world as hermeneutical space is to be grasped.

Hermeneutical Philosophy

What does Figal mean by hermeneutical philosophy? I would suggest that we begin to open up his conception with reference to the problem of finite transcendence. Although Figal does not develop his view of hermeneutical philosophy expressly in terms of this notion, it may nevertheless help us to put his approach into relief against predecessors often associated with phenomenology, existentialism, and hermeneutics. Indeed, because he believes that hermeneutical philosophy proves to be an intensification of our efforts to lead our lives, our consideration of his vision of finite transcendence shall also shed light on our condition.

Figal, not unlike Gadamer and Heidegger before him, elucidates his concept of philosophical inquiry in no small part as a response against the view of transcendence he sees in Husserl's phenomenology. The problem Figal has with Husserl's concept of transcendence may be discerned in Husserl's association of philosophy with the *epoché*, the idea that we can take a step back that brackets out our involvement with objects and allows us to investigate them in their noetic purity as objects of consciousness. Figal rejects the idea that human beings can attain such an autonomous and ostensibly disembodied stance. Instead, the transcendence that characterizes philosophical inquiry takes shape as a distinctive possibility of our participation in life and not a break from it. On this score, philosophical inquiry must be understood not as a "what," but, rather, as a special feature of our lives as we lead them, a "how," a view from somewhere that remains always embodied and situated.

Figal associates the finite transcendence of philosophy with what he calls its originariness, *Ursprünglichkeit*. By this, he means that philosophical inquiry involves a comportment or attitude that cannot be explained or derived from any prior origin. In contrast with Husserl, however, Figal does not see this attitude as a severance from life, but, rather, as a manner of living that involves three interdependent and interrelated moments. He discerns these three moments from a careful reading of models from the history of philosophy, but his analysis concerns philosophy in its originariness as such. For one, this originariness of philosophy is comprised of freedom as our openness to coming into relation, engaging with, and inquiring into objects. For another, this originariness unfolds in language. Third, this originariness is bound up with time.

Taken in this originariness, hermeneutical philosophy may be seen to unfold as and in interpretation. One of the passkeys to this claim, I think, is Figal's sensibility, itself characteristic of many in the heritage of hermeneutics, that interpretation is a form of mediation.[5] The mission of the interpreter is to make someone's message available to someone else; the interpreter is a third, an intermediary, messenger, negotiator, translator, who helps bring different interlocutors, disparate positions, together. On this score, Figal conceives of philosophy in its originariness, interpretation, as a form of mediation; in its interrelated moments of freedom, language, and time, interpretation pursues a heightened relation to objects, and, so, unfolds as an intensification of the otherwise more immediate course of things.

His position is distinguished by his conviction that interpretation itself is animated by objectivity. Although philosophical inquiry and, with it, interpretation belong within the context of our affairs, the need for interpretation does not arise in the characteristic flow of our everyday lives, our interactions with others and our appropriation and use of things. In light of this, we would have to say that it is not interpretation we engage in when we routinely press the button to call the elevator to our floor, reach to shake a colleague's outstretched hand, or pick up a pen and use it to write. Rather, interpretation arises in response to objects as they interrupt the steady stream of our activities.

Figal introduces a distinction important for his project to capture this difference. Everything we do involves what he calls a sense of enactment, *Vollzugssinn*—our activities are directed toward the implementation, execution, and completion of our endeavors. We recognize that Heidegger's existential analytic of Dasein in its everydayness may be one of the main touchstones for Figal's notion of this sense of enactment. Interpretation, however, is distinguished by what he calls a sense of reference, *Bezugssinn*. In contrast with other forms of enactment, interpretation involves not things we have already appropriated and know how to deal with—elevators, handshakes, and ink pens—but, rather, a referential relation to what remains as yet outside the sphere of our own abilities. The sense of reference guiding interpretation involves what Figal calls an "exterior relation." We are reminded here of the connotations of the German for "to acquire" or "to appropriate," *aneignen*, which might also be translated as "to make one's own." It may be that the sense of enactment guiding our affairs center on what we have already made our own. By contrast, interpretation is a form of enactment that has a sense of reference because it always concerns something that confronts us from outside of the sphere of what is our own.

Although he asserts that interpretation may refer to objects of any kind, Figal indicates that interpretation is exemplified in its referentiality to texts; "text and interpretation" he tells us, "are as if made for one another."[6] We may discern a general account of interpretation, accordingly, in his description of the interpretation of texts. The vision of texts at issue here is broad; texts may be found not only in writings but in any form that involves a meaningful order, a λόγος, not only, say, in philosophical treatises and literature, but also in pieces of music, paintings, sculptures, dance. Interpretation takes shape as the presentation of the text in its simultaneity. This involves both what Figal calls clarification, *Deutung*, aimed at the unity of the text, and explication, *Auslegung*, aimed at the differentiation of its aspects. The task of interpretation remains interminable in regard to texts confronting us with objectivity intense enough to elicit continued attention. Even as every successful interpretation presents the meaning of the text in its unity, each may nevertheless differ; the greater the objectivity of a text, the more interest it garners. The significance of works of genuine philosophy, literature, and the arts, as well as of the enduring themes and things they take up, can never be tapped out.

Figal associates understanding with the public arena of the consideration and adjudication of interpretations. Perhaps above all, however, he seeks to describe the phenomenon of understanding better than his predecessors in the heritage of hermeneutics. Figal's suggestion is that his emphasis on objectivity allows him to move beyond presuppositions of modernity that his forbearers in hermeneutics sought to overcome but never fully overcame. Although this idea is rich in implication, his basic claim is that the vestiges of modernity in his predecessors' thought leads them to a distorted portrait of interpretation and understanding. He tells us that in Gadamer and Heidegger, for example, the highest tasks of understanding and interpretation are ultimately self-referential; their characteristic concern is with self-understanding. And it is this, Figal asserts, that runs contrary to the phenomenon. Understanding, so he tells us, is directed not finally toward ourselves, but, rather, to what needs interpretation: objects in their exteriority. Thus, even if understanding comprises a hallmark of human life, human life is ordered not foremost by its relation to itself but rather by relations with what are and remain beyond the sphere of what belongs to it, to objects.

Because of this, understanding reaches its summit not in an inward turn of the self, but, rather, an outward gesture to a world that is larger than ourselves—or, in the term Figal will use to capture this, to life.

World as Hermeneutical Space

I have suggested that Figal's hermeneutical philosophy may be associated with the form of finite transcendence involved in our capacities for interpretation and understanding. We may take interpretation and understanding, then, as his broadest names for our responsiveness to our circumstances, for our abilities to come into meaningful relation, to comprehend, to choose among alternatives, to appropriate, and even to exercise influence over what comes our way. Thanks to interpretation and understanding, we are not simply part of and solely subject to our circumstances, as, say, an autumn leaf is subject to the strong wind that detaches it from a tree and blows it across the field. Rather, these capacities allow us to stand in relation to our circumstances and so be open to them. We also see that Figal, like many of his predecessors associated with hermeneutics, believes that the transcendence granted by interpretation and understanding remain finite because these capabilities are conditioned by features of the very circumstances they allow us to relate to and address.

Figal distinguishes his vision of finite transcendence, however, by his emphasis on hermeneutical space. Surely our finite transcendence is conditioned by myriad features of our circumstances. Yet, it may be said that, since Kant at least, many philosophers have taken our finite transcendence to be indexed to one feature of our circumstances before all others: the experience of time. We may think of Heidegger's conception of the temporality of Dasein or of the role played in Husserl's theory of cognition by internal time consciousness. Figal's approach unfolds in contrast to the views of these predecessors because he keys his description not first to the issue of time but to that of space. Figal, like Heidegger, Husserl, and others before him, maintains that our transcendence is finite because it is ineluctably conditioned. For Figal, however, the possibilities and limits of this transcendence are to be discerned from the fact that we live in space.

It is not difficult to see the rapprochement between Figal's dedication to objectivity and the shift of his focus onto space. We may cast this shift as part of Figal's efforts to move beyond some presuppositions of modern philosophy. If figures in modernity have often associated our finite transcendence with the powers of the subject, then it should perhaps come as no surprise that they often take the experience of time to be more basic than that of space. After all, time is—in an idiom taken from Kant's *Critique of Pure Reason*—the condition of the subject's "inner experience," whereas space is the condition of our "outer experience."[7] By contrast, Figal believes that our finite transcendence is animated by objectivity, by our confrontation with the exteriority of objects, by whatever solicits us as something not yet our own. It makes sense, then, that he would believe this transcendence to be conditioned above all by space as the aether in which we confront objects.

Figal identifies our finite transcendence with our capacity to achieve the distance from objects required to interpret and understand them. Of course, he conceives of such distance hermeneutically as the form of mediation that is necessary for our cognizance of things, and not simply as, say, extension. However, it is precisely this hermeneutical sense of space that guides our experience of ourselves and of objects in space. Figal's consideration of hermeneutical space builds on precedents he finds in Husserl's and Merleau-Ponty's theories of perception as well as on Heidegger's analysis of the spatiality of Dasein, and we may suspect some lines of comparison with Deleuze's notion of smooth space.[8] In Figal, in any case, the claim is not simply that we perceive things in space or that we exist spatially, but that our perception, our understanding, is itself in space. Within this context, our finite transcendence takes shape in our presentation of objects in hermeneutical space.

Figal identifies the *world* as the whole of hermeneutical space. Figal recognizes that philosophers have often used the term *world* to specify two divergent domains: on the one hand, the human sphere of meaning, values, norms; on the other hand, the sphere of things, often cast as the "physical" or "natural" order. Figal argues that his conception of world as hermeneutical space embraces both of these spheres in their tension with one another. We may see our finite transcendence as an interlacing of the world of meaning we create—sometimes he brings in the term *life-world* as an umbrella for this—and the world of things by which such creation of meaning is sustained and limited. For Figal, there is but one world, but as hermeneutical space its fulcrum is our mutual implication in life- and thing-world.

Although he gathers finite transcendence under the sign of hermeneutical space, he maintains that this space is comprised of three dimensions: freedom, language, and time. We recall that he also associated the originariness of philosophy with these same three matters. This, of course, is no coincidence. His discussion of philosophy sought to describe the shift in comportment or attitude, the heightened—because mediated—relation to our everyday affairs that comprises philosophical inquiry. Philosophical inquiry, though, turns on nothing other than the finite transcendence he associated with hermeneutical space. If philosophical inquiry unfolds in freedom, language, and time, it would seem that this is because these belong to hermeneutical space itself.

Figal, in any case, suggests that these dimensions of hermeneutical space are equiprimordial and interdependent; one does not find freedom without language, neither appear without time. He dedicates the bulk of his book to the discussion of these dimensions of hermeneutical space, and we may gain some insight into his perspective if we consider each in brief now. As we shall see, the broader gesture of his consideration of each of the three dimensions is the same. His concern with each is to show that the terms of our transcendence are given not by the subject alone but by our responsiveness to and correlation with whatever confronts us in objectivity.

Freedom

Figal's elucidation of the finite transcendence at play in hermeneutical space begins with his description of freedom. Like many in phenomenology, existentialism, and hermeneutics before him, Figal takes up freedom as constitutive of our way of being, our existence or life. It is therefore perhaps no surprise that he introduces his theme with reference to Kierkegaard's reflection on freedom as "possibility to *be able to*,"[9] or, ability, *Können*. Yet, in contrast with those who would hold out hope for an absolute expression of this freedom, Figal admits that it is and remains inexorably bound up in our relations with things and others. Freedom is never freedom *simpliciter*, but, rather, always stands and unfolds in relation with things and others.

Figal may be said to develop a general theory of a number of interrelated levels or aspects of freedom based on this. He begins with what he calls the freedom of action, which specifies the freedom of ability insofar as it is informed by intention and forethought. Although he relies on a number of concepts from Aristotle's practical philosophy, he describes the structure of the freedom of action in terms of his own distinction between reference and enactment. Action, in contrast with other kinds of activity, is guided in reference to an aim that stretches beyond the immediate aspects of the activity we are enacting. The freedom of action, then, is held open by this tension of aim-reference and activity. He uses this rubric, in turn, to describe deliberation as a pause for reflection held open by this freedom. He then describes practical understanding—it is not difficult to see that he intends his own description of what Aristotle called φρόνησις—as our more or less developed capacity for deliberation.

Figal then develops what he calls "the freedom of things" and, as we may be led to think, his turn of phrase seems to imply an equivocity of the genitive. On the one hand, he is concerned with the exercise of our freedom in relation to things; on the other hand, he wishes to motivate that our freedom hinges on the independence, or, freedom, of things themselves insofar as they may resist our appropriation of them. Our freedom involves things not only insofar as they belong to the "life-world" of what we have already made our own and know how to use, such as familiar tools, but also to the "thing-world" insofar as they harbor the potential to rebel against our uses of them. Thus, the exercise of our freedom concerns not first of all the domestication of things to our purposes, but, rather, the possibilities that may emerge when we come into proper accord with things.

Political freedom, what he treats under the auspices of "shared freedom," in turn, remains oriented by our efforts to contend with the world of things. In a discussion that draws on Plato's *Republic*, Figal suggests that justice requires the attainment of a social form that both addresses our shared needs and allows for the expression of our individual talents. Our freedom reaches its summit, however, in the speculative, or theoretical, activity of contemplation. On the one hand, he identifies theoretical life as the highest form of practice, and he suggests that contemplation continues to be concerned with the attainment of the good in life. On the other hand, however, he indicates that contemplation is freer than action because it is independent of specific practical aims. Contemplation, then, may be said to involve the sense of reference found in our relation to objectivity and not simply the aim-reference of actions.

Language

What is language? Figal's consideration may be seen as directed by his concern for the contribution that language makes to the finite transcendence at play in hermeneutical space. Within this context, his focus is on the mindfulness, the flexibility and openness, that attends our endeavors to grasp things with words and that first makes speech possible. We may conjecture that it is precisely this openness we encounter when we recognize we may say something in one way or another, when we are struck by a need to say something in more than one way, or when we find ourselves in a struggle to find the right words that would allow us to say anything at all. In this regard, his considerations are reminiscent of the "stammering" Gadamer believes we become aware of in our efforts to speak a foreign language. As Gadamer puts it, such "stammering is the obstruction of a desire to speak and is thus opened into the infinite realm of possible expression."[10] Figal's concern for such flexibility in expression, in any case, leads him to hold open a distinction between language and speech and thus to depart from predecessors who would seek the essence of language based on speech alone.

Figal elucidates this openness of language based on the claim that language itself is a form of *showing*. Figal characterizes showing as the intensification of our relation to things, even the intensification of things themselves, that is achieved when we determine something with words. He holds that this determination is reached not with reference to the thing in isolation, but, rather, requires the differentiation of something from out of a context of other determinations. Figal characterizes such a context as the fabric or "texture" within which something may achieve determinacy. He writes, "texture includes all possible determinations ... it is an infinitely enfolded fullness of differences and references. It is as it were the soil from which speech and writing unfold by raising out specific references and differences."[11] In showing, we allow some aspects of our milieu to come to the fore and others to recede in order that something determinate may show itself. This conception of showing may be understood as a theory of signification insofar as he conceives of signs as markers or leads within a texture, which gives structure to that texture. Showing, from this standpoint, aims to determine something through a specific employment of signs, which brings some aspects of a texture to the fore and backgrounds others.

Figal's view of the openness of language comes into focus in his discussion of significance, *Bedeutung*. He identifies significance with the idea that is made commonly accessible by our determination of something through the use of words. What grants significance to our words? Figal proposes his answer to this question in no small part as a third alternative to two influential standpoints within the philosophy of language. The first is the approach he finds in Frege (although, he thinks, in a comparable way also in Husserl) that significance is to be examined vis-à-vis questions of reference. The second is the position he finds in Wittgenstein (although, he thinks, also in some respects in Saussure) that significance is to be explained vis-à-vis rules governing linguistic practice. Figal holds that neither of these standpoints captures the openness of language as it is given and introduces his own alternative as a more adequate description.

In this, he identifies the significance of a word as its determinate range of possibilities for showing. It is the compass of a word's potential to determine, and, so, lift something out of the texture to which it belongs. Significance, then, concerns not the actuality or presence of an idea, but, rather, the promise of an idea that is at play in each of our uses of words to determine something. To use a word is to stand in this openness and attempt to show something; if this succeeds, then something shows itself in its significance.

Figal believes that language as showing affirms not only the openness that makes speech possible, however, but also the capacity of speech to fix the significance of things. Figal argues for this claim in rejoinder to the suspicion that such faith in the capacity of our speech to fix significance is really a self-deception driven by needs for stability and security. If this suspicion has become standard fare in the era of postmodernism, Figal nevertheless levels his rejoinder against the position he finds in Derrida in particular. This may suggest that Figal wishes to complement the hermeneutic counterpoint forwarded by Gadamer in the celebrated encounter between Gadamer and Derrida in 1981 in Paris.[12] Figal, in any case, ultimately rejects Derrida's suspicion on the grounds that the deconstruction of the voice driving it relies on mistaken phenomenological descriptions of speech and writing. And, in response, Figal develops his own concept of fixed significance by means of his own descriptions of the spoken and written word.

Figal's description of the spoken word is oriented by its role in conversation; we raise our voice to take up a *position* in hermeneutical space in relation to others. In this, he focuses on the intrinsically relational character of voice to counter the notion of voice as auto-affection, which Derrida criticizes in Husserl. On the one hand, it is easy to imagine that Figal's reliance on the phenomenon of conversation hearkens back to Gadamer's use of this motif. To the extent this is so, Figal's description of raising one's voice may be seen as a hermeneutical counterpoint, inspired by Gadamer, against Derrida's critique of the voice. On the other hand, however, Figal's approach to conversation diverges from Gadamer's in a decisive respect. Whereas Gadamer sometimes underscores that conversation concerns not foremost the discussants but the matters they discuss, Figal emphasizes that conversation never fully liberates the discussants from the interplay of their positions. What ultimately is shown in conversation are the interlocutors themselves, their postures and interests, and not only the matter under discussion.

It is the written word that allows us to shift our focus toward the matters themselves and away from the positions we take when we raise our voice in conversation with others. Indeed, Figal goes so far as to argue that our turn to the written word has the character of an *epoché* in that it puts our positions out of play. If he invokes the experience of conversation as the guide for his description of the spoken word, then he introduces the notion of *written thought*, or dialectic, to elucidate his view of the written word. In dialectic, so his point goes, we turn our attention to significances themselves, to ideas, and no longer focus on the significance only insofar as it is determined in some context or other. Figal recognizes that it is impossible to present pure significances and he conceives of dialectic in part as a supplement that fills in for their absence. Yet, in contrast to the notion of the supplement he associates with Derrida, he does not hold that it is merely a deferral, which itself requires unending further supplementation. Rather, he argues that dialectic may reach an adequate presentation of significance as a unity of a determinate diversity of expression.

Time

Figal's elucidation of hermeneutical space culminates in his discussion of time. If we may say again that the question of our finite transcendence guides his approach, then it may also be said that his concern here is with how our capacities for interpretation and understanding, at bottom, perhaps, our formation of meaning, is enjoined by time. On the one hand, then, Figal takes up the temporality of human life—the structures of our experience of time—in virtue of which our formation of meaning is mediated. In this, he may be said to build on a venerable heritage of philosophical viewpoints that includes Heidegger's account of time as the horizon of being, Husserl's approach of internal time-consciousness, and Kant's conception of the schemata of the imagination. Yet, Figal rejects the idea that the structure of our experience of time is itself somehow trans- or a-temporal. Rather, he wishes to show, the structure of our experience of time is itself dependent on and affected by another sense of time: the time governing the occurrence of things. Because of this, our formation of meanings is mediated not only by the temporality of human life, but also, more to the point, by the correlation of this temporality with the time of occurrences.

Figal's examination of time may be seen to indicate that these two aspects of time stand in a reciprocal relation. On the one hand, he turns to themes in Aristotle's *Physics* to argue that the time of occurrences is the openness of things to being experienced, and, in turn, measured by us. On the other hand, he invokes resources from Augustine and Husserl to describe the temporality of human life—what he also calls the time of enactment—as our openness to things in occurrence. In this, Figal draws on Augustine's notion of the structure of our experience of time as expectation of what is to come, attentiveness to what is now, and memory of what has passed. Yet, in a corrective of Augustine and Husserl, Figal rejects the idea that we experience our enactment of something in a present that encompasses expectation, attentiveness, and memory. Rather, our temporality is itself in time, it not only mediates our experience of time but is also subject to the time of occurrence.

The important implication of Figal's position is that the temporality of human life itself is always affected and, so, colored by occurrences in their givenness. In the idiom of Augustine's account, we may say that our expectations, attentiveness, and memory are never neutral, but, rather, always embodied in πάθη, always attuned in some manner or another, always bowed by some attitude or mood. An expectation, for example, always leans by degree toward hope or fear.

This insight may be put into relief by the contrast Figal draws with Heidegger. Figal sees a precedent of his view in Heidegger's belief that the disclosedness of Dasein is always already in a mood. Yet, Figal suggests that he goes further than Heidegger. For, so Figal's point goes, Heidegger nevertheless holds out hope for a mood—he calls it anxiety—that serves to bracket out the actuality of our ties to things and others and allows us to reflect on ourselves as possibility. Figal of course does not deny that we sometimes experience anxiety. Yet, he rejects the idea he finds in Heidegger that this mood functions as an *epoché* that dissolves all of our ties with things and others. On the contrary, Figal's view is that anxiety is only an interruption in our relations that, like all moods, derives from the fact that we belong to the world. After all, he suggests, we can only experience anxiety as a separation if we already feel ourselves to be part of the world in the first place.

Figal's discussion of time reaches its summit, in any case, in his discussion of the formation of meaning. His concern, we have said, is with the finite transcendence that arises in hermeneutical space; and, he takes up time as one dimension of this transcendence. In contrast with some before him, however, he does not identify the role of time in our transcendence solely as a function of the subject. Rather, he argues that the possibilities for meaning opened up by the structure of our experience of time remain dependent on the manner in which objects affect us in their givenness. Meaning, then, arises not from the powers of the subject alone, but rather, as a constellation that involves the accord of the time of enactment and the time of occurrence. In further elaboration, Figal considers the possibilities for the formation of meaning brought about through the experience of repetition. He turns to Proust to describe the repetition as an experience of the condensation, or enfolding, of time back from its fracturing into past, present, and future. The impetus for this experience of enfolding is not the freedom of the self, however, but, rather, the objective.

Life

Figal does not return to his debate with Heidegger about the concept of anxiety in his description of life. Yet, we may wonder whether the contrast he draws nevertheless contains, in distilled form, one of the important motivations behind his interest in the topic of life.

From time immemorial, philosophers have associated their aspirations for transcendence with a kind of death in life, the attainment of a viewpoint outside of life while still alive. It may perhaps be such a desire that drives Husserl's vision of the *epoché*, although, of course, philosophers have aspired to death-in-life long before Husserl. In this regard, Plato's familiar report of Socrates' words—"that those who really apply themselves in the right way to philosophy are directly and of their own accord preparing themselves for dying and death"[13]—may be seen as binding for much of the heritage of Western philosophy. It is not a stretch to imagine that Figal hears echoes of the philosopher's aspiration for death-in-life in Heidegger's description of anxiety as a mood that allows us to relate to ourselves entirely free from our entanglements with things and others. And, it is likewise not difficult to imagine that Figal's rejection of Heidegger's description of anxiety indicates Figal's repudiation of the philosopher's age-old ambition to achieve death-in-life. If this is so, then the suggestion seems to be that our finite transcendence comes not at the price of our involvement in life, but, rather, depends on this involvement and only arises from it. In this, Figal may perhaps agree that philosophy is not a preparation for death and dying, but a devotion to life and living.

Figal himself introduces the concept of life, in any event, in the service of his description of the character of our lives as we lead them in the world as hermeneutical space. His depiction of life may be taken as a capstone of his project. As we have seen, the world as hermeneutical space unfolds in dimensions of freedom, language, and time, and cuts across the world of meaning, values, norms and the world of things. Figal turns to the concept of life because he thinks that our involvement in this world entails more than may be captured by the notion of being. Yet, Figal tells us that in contrast with some *Lebensphilosophen* of the late nineteenth century, he does not wish to cast life as a lone principle of vitality or will that underlies all things. Rather, he characterizes life as a complex of moments that guide us in our relation to things and other living beings.

On this score, Figal distinguishes humans as hermeneutical living beings,[14] and, because of this, our interpretation of life—our presentation of life as we take up Figal's discussion—is itself a distinctive expression of life.

What is life? Figal begins his discussion with what differentiates living beings of all kinds from mere things. Living beings are distinguished by their referentiality; it is characteristic of living beings that they stand in relation, they interact with other living beings and things. It is because of this referentiality that they appear in the originariness of self-movement; they carry themselves and are not simply carried along like inanimate things. This originariness of living beings also signifies that they belong to the world of things but cannot be reduced to it. For Figal, in any case, it is precisely life in the originariness, and not foremost being, that is captured by the Greek φύσις. From this standpoint, the form of living beings must be discerned not from their fully grown appearance, but, rather, from their characteristic capacity for change, growth, and movement. Living beings are marked by *striving*, they appear in a fold of activity and passivity, of maintaining a condition or state of movement and being in a state. Implicated in this fold, living beings hold a position in and interact with their surroundings and do not merely stand at a location in extended space.

Human life is distinguished not by kind from other life but, rather, by the intensity of its referentiality in hermeneutical space, by its more mediated relations with other living beings and things. Figal develops his view based on a novel description of human beings as both embodied and rational.

In this, the life of human beings, like all living beings, crisscrosses the body. On the one hand, as being in a state, all living beings are affected and moved by other living beings and things. From this vantage, we are mere body, *Körper*, the corporeality that comes into focus, for example, in the corpse. On the other hand, however, the body—as striving—also appears as a condition or state of movement. From this angle, living beings are what I have translated as the body quick, *Leib*, the body insofar as it is ensouled and animate, quick and not corpse. As body quick, living beings hold a *position* vis-à-vis other living beings and things. Human life, for its part, is distinguished by reason, which Figal treats as a heightened form of referentiality, as our apprehension of determinate things from out of the texture we find ourselves in. For Figal, however, apprehension is only possible because the world is apprehensible; reason is not a faculty of the subject but, rather, the structure shared by human beings and the world. As such, reason appears as *placeless* in comparison to the body quick in its positionality.

What, then, is it to lead our lives as beings both rational and embodied? This question, I think, may lead us through Figal's discussion of the structure of life and what he calls "conduct directed at ourselves." We see this question of how to lead our lives come into focus in Figal's observation that the structure, or order, of life first becomes an issue for us when we experience pain as a symptom of the disruption of this order in our own respective lives. Within this context, the question of how to live our lives appears first as a problem of how to rejoin life through a restoration of order to our lives. Although Figal develops his answer in connection with Plato and Aristotle, we notice that it may also resonate with Dewey.[15] Be this as it may, one of Figal's main ideas is that human life, because its rational, quickened embodiment remains beholden to mere body and the world of things, we find ourselves always already in a condition of lack, and, so, in need of a restoration of order, of attunement and adjustment. This restoration, however, is not to be sought inwardly in a cessation of our desire, our will, for what we lack. Rather, it is to be sought in a reinvigoration of the openness that allows us to come into correlation with what is outside, that is, we may suggest, to the objectivity sustaining the creation of meaning that allows us to live.

Notes

1. Figal, *Objectivity*, 348. All *Objectivity* citations are to this English translation.
2. And, along with these, perhaps also deconstruction. Although the variety of figures associated with these movements precludes any generic grouping, I would, of course, not be the first to discern resemblances among them.
3. As a previous landmark attempt to interrogate such presuppositions, see, for example, Heidegger's fourth Nietzsche volume on nihilism. Martin Heidegger, *Nietzsche. Volumes Three and Four*, ed. David Farrel Krell (San Fransisco: Harper & Row Publishers, 1982).
4. Anglophone scholars will be familiar with Figal's pervious work from *For A Philosophy of Freedom and Strife*, trans. Wayne Klein (Albany: State University of New York Press, 1998), as well as English translations of numerous essays and portions of other books. His work in *Objectivity* may also be put in the context of his important work on Heidegger as yet untranslated into English in *Martin Heidegger: Phänomenologie der Freiheit* (Frankfurt am Main: Anton Hain, 1998), *Heidegger zur Einführung* (Hamburg: Junius, 1992). Moreover, *Objectivity* may also be seen in the context of his untranslated thematic collection on hermeneutical and related issues, such as *Der Sinn des Verstehens* (Stuttgart: Philipp Reclam, 1996). His *Objectivity* may also further be seen to draw on his extensive work on Greek philosophy, Nietzsche, Adorno, and others.
5. Here, we may think of the legend, often invoked by scholars of hermeneutics, about the relation between the study of hermeneutics and the mythological role of Hermes as mediator between the divine and human.
6. Figal, *Objectivity*, 57.
7. Cf. Kant, *Critique of Pure Reason*, trans. Paul Guyer and Allen Wood (New York: Cambridge University Press, 1998), 172–92.
8. Cf. for example, Gilles Deleuze and Félix Guattari, *A Thousand Plateaus: Capitalism and Schizophrenia*, trans. Brian Massumi (Minneapolis: University of Minnesota Press, 1987), 477–500.
9. Kierkegaard, cited in Figal, *Objectivity*, 155.
10. Gadamer, "Universality of the Hermeneutic Problem," trans. David E. Linge, in Gadamer, *The Gadamer Reader: A Bouquet of Later Writings*, ed. Richard Palmer (Evanston: Northwestern University Press, 88).
11. Figal, *Objectivity*, 203.
12. For a concise account of this encounter, see, for example, Richard Palmer's introductory remarks to "Text and Interpretation" in *The Gadamer Reader*, 156–57.
13. Plato, *Phaedo*, 64b, in Plato, *Plato: Collected Dialogues*, ed. Edith Hamilton and Huntington Cairns, trans. Hugh Tredennick (New York: Pantheon Books, 1961, fourth printing, 1966), 46.
14. For a helpful companion to Figal's conception here, see his "Life as Understanding," trans. Elizabeth Sikes, *Research in Phenomenology* 34 (2004):20–30.
15. See, for example, Dewey's examination of the interaction of what he calls "the live creature" and its environment in the first chapters of *Art as Experience*, which are collected in John Dewey, *The Philosophy of John Dewey*, Two Volumes in One, ed. John J. McDermott, 525–75.

Preface

This book has a rather long history. First outlines, which may be discerned in the contours of what is worked out here, reach back more than twenty years. In its present form, the material of the book has emerged in three years, from 2002 to 2005. In this time, I was able to test some of my thoughts in shorter pieces before they found their reconsidered formulation here. This concerns above all the essays, "Zeit und Erinnerung," "Gadamer im Kontext," "Die Gegenständlichkeit der Welt," "Leben als Verstehen," "Ethik und Hermeneutik," and "Dekonstruktion und Dialektik," all identified in the bibliography. Meanwhile, I have published a collection of essays, "Verstehensfragen" (Tübingen 2009). Some of these essays can be also regarded as preparatory for this book, whereas others develop topics, which in the book have only been mentioned or sketched.

In addition, I have also put many things into play conversationally over the years, and, through interlocutors, have been able to become better acquainted with them. To this extent, the pages of this book are also the sediments of encounters in friendship.

Present to me with particular gratitude are my many conversations with Hans-Georg Gadamer. It only intensified our closeness that he always responded to critical inquiries, objections, and divergent views with the warm-hearted sovereignty of one who knew and said that there must always be "other ways."

Without Gottfried Boehm I would know less about seeing and showing. Not least, the collaborative seminar in the summer 2004 was an important impulse.

More tightly interwoven into the history of this book than others are Damir Barbarić, Donatella Di Cesare, Pavel Kouba, John Sallis, and Dennis J. Schmidt. I owe much to their continued friendship.

I also thank my assistant Friederike Rese. She worked through the text with attentive understanding and gave many suggestions for its final version. I thank my student collaborators Christian Diem, Tobias Keiling, Sophia Obergfell, and Katrin Sterba for their committed and careful work on the production of the copy and the proofs.

I am especially grateful to Theodore George, who translated "Gegenständlichkeit" into "Objectivity." The conversations I had with him about details of my text had always the character of genuine philosophical dialogues—close to the common subject matter, and quickened by the common spirit of phenomenology and hermeneutics.

Freiburg im Breisgau, January 2010
Günter Figal

Introduction

One is well acquainted with hermeneutics also from the viewpoint of philosophy. Every introduction to the subject[1] outlines with more or less precision how the so-called art of interpretation has developed into a philosophical approach since the seventeenth century.[2] There also is no doubt as to which names are crucial here. Time and again the focus is on Schleiermacher, Dilthey, Heidegger, Gadamer, and, occasionally, also Ricoeur. It is no coincidence here that the program of philosophical hermeneutics is associated particularly closely with the name of Gadamer. It is first through Gadamer that philosophical hermeneutics received a systematically clear profile; it is first Gadamer who made his predecessors into predecessors, and assigned to them a position in the development of the program that he himself forwarded.

Gadamer's project was taken up with hesitation at first but then with great interest. The author of *Wahrheit und Methode* is counted today internationally as the most significant German philosopher of the second half of the twentieth century, indeed, already as a classical figure of philosophy.[3] This is justifiable, if one considers how much the image of philosophy, conceived even in a broader sense as hermeneutical, belongs to Gadamer's effective history. It is perhaps above all the gesture of his thought that has had this influence. His thought is convincing as an objection to a philosophy that construes its objects monologically: that is, a philosophy that moves within a field demarcated in advance, and, for this reason, despite all pretensions of an orientation of substantiveness, finds only insights admitted by the schemata foundational for it. In contrast to such a "systematic" form of philosophy, not seldom felt to be antiquated, Gadamer poses in discrete radicality the open, never conclusive "conversation," in which one actually puts certainties into play. What has won everyone over in Gadamer's thought is above all his reservation against ultimate grounds and groundings; it is openness without the demand for system and without dramatization. Philosophical hermeneutics thus comes to appear as a plea, propped up against a humanistic background, for philosophical modesty, as a "formative philosophy" in Richard Rorty's sense.[4] It could just as much be taken up, with Gianni Vattimo, as a "weak thought" that renounces the claims of the metaphysical tradition.[5] Jürgen Habermas has seen himself stimulated

1

and encouraged by Gadamer to counter the dark image of the world and of the human in the older "critical theory" with the democratic possibility of "communicative action."[6] As "post-metaphysical" thought, Gadamer's philosophical hermeneutics is connected as if of its own accord with "deconstruction" in Jacques Derrida, whose significance Gadamer recognized straightaway at the time that his earliest books were published, and with whom Gadamer engaged in debate even in his final years.[7]

If one compares the effective history of Gadamerian thought with Gadamer's own texts, however, displacements, shifts in accentuation, and abbreviations are unmistakable. Rorty's idea of a formative philosophy misses the fact that Gadamer is concerned not with formative education in opposition to knowledge, but, rather, as the title of his major work indicates, with a specifically hermeneutical sense of truth. In contrast to Vattimo's "weak thought" at the end of metaphysics, Gadamer's focus is not on a departure from the philosophical tradition but rather on the effort to motivate its indispensableness for contemporary thought. Finally, Gadamer's understanding of conversation also differs from social praxis as Habermas understands it; it is not an unrestrained, open-ended process of agreement, but, rather, a being-led by the salient matter that is operative in such a process.

Nevertheless, the effective history of Gadamerian thought is not simply an entanglement of capricious opinions and misapprehensions. It is due to Gadamer himself that the substantiveness of hermeneutical experience has stepped into the background of its emphasis on openness and its ties to conversation. Gadamer develops the idea of the hermeneutically experienced matter in such a way that even as it is supposed to sustain conversation, it nevertheless only arises in the course of conversation itself. The substantiveness of hermeneutical experience, however, belongs to its essence. Understanding and interpreting are to be more thoroughly bound to a matter, and, in a manner that may be readily experienced, to be more dependent on a matter, than in every other form of comprehension, than in every other kind access to what is. In hermeneutical experience, one is concerned with something that one himself is not, with something that stands over against [*entgegensteht*], and, because of this, places a demand. Hermeneutical experience is the experience of the objective [*das Gegenständliche*]—of what is there in such a way that one may come into accord with it and that yet never fully comes out in any attempt to reach accord. Because of this, the objective must stand as the hermeneutical matter at the center of hermeneutical thought. Objectivity [*Gegenständlichkeit*] is the principal matter of the hermeneutical approach to philosophy. If the context of Gadamer's thought and its influence cannot do justice to it, one must leave this context and say how philosophical hermeneutics, with every allegiance in the details, is to be thought fundamentally otherwise than in it.

If one looks more closely, doubts begin to arise already about the completely familiar obviousness of the signification [*selbstverständlichen Bezeichnung*]

Gadamer introduces. "Philosophical hermeneutics": that is not just any title, but instead the expression of a definite philosophical-hermeneutical program. In it, philosophy is conceived as a possibility of hermeneutics; philosophy, as such, is taken back and put into a hermeneutical context that incorporates it. If only so that the presuppositions and consequences of this idea may emerge, one must go beyond the approach of philosophical hermeneutics. The question of the relation between the hermeneutical and philosophy stands outside of philosophical hermeneutics. It is posed not without a prehistory, but without preconceptions, and, in this way, as new.

"The hermeneutical": this designation should be understood here analogously to "the beautiful" or "the just." It indicates a complex of matters that includes understanding and interpretation, as well as the intelligible [*das Verstehbare*], the interpretable, and what is in need of interpretation—precisely the objective, and, moreover, everything that can be grasped in concepts, which differentiate whatever is named. It is necessary to describe what is intended by this as impartially as possible. This occurs here in reference to the guiding question of the most forthcoming of hermeneutical activities: interpretation. Interpretation is, as shall be shown, the investigation of what is objective. Interpretation investigates what is objective by presenting it.

The hermeneutical, in the sense referred to here, would be one theme among others for philosophy if philosophy itself were not itself hermeneutical. If philosophy is hermeneutical, the clarification of the fact of the hermeneutical becomes a self-clarification of philosophy. Philosophy would founder in this self-clarification, however, if it were not also to have the possibility of finding distance from the hermeneutical. This possibility is tantamount to a hermeneutical philosophy that, even though it is not itself sufficiently determined as hermeneutical, yet does not for this reason leave the realm of the hermeneutical. Such a philosophy is, as shall be shown, phenomenological; it is a phenomenology that is thought on the basis of the hermeneutical and that philosophically opens up hermeneutical thought. As such, it is that possibility of the hermeneutical, which does not leave the hermeneutical, but which is not exhausted by it, and, thus, which makes it transparent in its possibility.

To make the hermeneutical transparent, this means to go back to the openness in which the hermeneutical becomes apparent, develops, and takes shape. It is not the openness of the hermeneutical alone, but it is a kind of openness that allows the hermeneutical to be distinguishable to the greatest possible extent. For this reason, it might be named after the hermeneutical; the openness, in reference to which the hermeneutical becomes transparent, is the world understood as hermeneutical space. Phenomenology, which is the focus here, is accordingly a spatial form of thinking; its concepts are formed on the basis of the experience of the spatial, it grasps its phenomena on the basis of spatiality. At the same time, it attempts to win the essence of this spatiality on the basis of the phenomenon, especially on the basis of the hermeneutical. It is from this standpoint that the dimensions of hermeneutical space arise: freedom, language, and time. In the investigation of these dimensions, the position of philosophy in the world shall also become evident. The description captures its own possibility without deriving it from out of the world.

Philosophy—this, too, is to be motivated here—can remain what it was since its beginnings. It is a myth that philosophy comes to an end due to its inner logic, or because of the persuasiveness of the empirical sciences, or that it must depart from the tradition. Classical concepts still obtain, better than many of the modern ones, if only one learns to use them impartially and in reference to the matter. This is tested here in various ways, but, most fundamentally, in the concluding question of the guiding concept for the description of "being" in the world, which is not a matter being, but, rather, of life.

Chapter 1

From Philosophical Hermeneutics to Hermeneutical Philosophy

§ 1. *The Human Sciences [Geisteswissenschaften] as Problem*

The formulation of the question of philosophical hermeneutics may be understood from its historical context. It arises from the nineteenth century and achieves its particular profile with the development of the human sciences. Of course, hermeneutical questions, that is, those concerned with understanding and interpretation, may already be found earlier. Such questions are posed whenever a reflective relation to practices and writings is to be found, and whenever one attempts to clarify for oneself how one is to conceive of these, and how one is supposed appropriately to relate to them. It is first with the emergence of the human sciences, however, that these questions receive a fundamental significance. No longer are they confined to the practices of reading, explicating, clarifying, and commenting, and, for that matter, no longer are they limited by the context of an "art" of understanding. With the human sciences, understanding becomes a universal problem that overarches the individual disciplines. The answer to the question of what understanding actually is, is supposed, then, to lead to the essence of the human sciences themselves; the specific possibilities of understanding are supposed to be determined, and what is supposed to be demonstrated by this is its characteristic right in contrast to all other forms of cognition.

Gadamer's project of a philosophical hermeneutics may be understood as the most distinguished of its kind. Although it is quite removed from the foundational phase of philosophical hermeneutics, it nevertheless remains marked by the problems posed in this phase. To the author of *Wahrheit und Methode* and those writings that further develop and nuance the approach of his major work, the concern is not with a universal hermeneutics in Schleiermacher's sense. A formal discussion of understanding and interpretation that aims to develop the rules of understanding "from the nature of language and from the fundamental conditions of the relationships between the one who speaks and what is heard" is far from Gadamer's concern.[1] Gadamer, and in this he takes up the bequest of Dilthey, wants to make a contribution to "self-reflection" in the human sciences. Yet, in contrast with Dilthey, who looked at the natural and human sciences as two fundamental possibilities of systematic science [*Wissenschaftlichkeit*], Gadamer doubts that the human sciences may be grasped by such science.[2] Therefore, he wants to go beyond Dilthey's "epistemological formulation of the question."[3] Whereas Dilthey "allowed himself to be profoundly influenced by the model of the natural sciences,"[4] Gadamer wants to show that the claim of the human sciences to scientific systematicity is misleading as such because it is dominated by the scientific ideal of the natural sciences. This holds for him even if one attempts to demonstrate the "methodological independence"[5] of the human sciences in contrast to the natural sciences; the comparative contrast already brings the human sciences closer to the natural sciences by subordinating them to the ideal of method. Despite all of the individual differences, "what is called 'method' in modern science remains the same everywhere"; it is simply "displayed in an exemplary form in the natural sciences."[6] According to Gadamer, however, the human sciences cannot be understood in their characteristic form if one orients oneself by the "concept of method in the modern sciences."[7] The human sciences do not follow any procedure given ahead of time by an edifice of rules that aims at the systematic deduction of a domain of objects, and, from the standpoint of certainty, the assurance of the achieved results. Rather, the concern of the human sciences is with another truth that is in principle inaccessible to the other sciences, with "modes of experience"[8] that may not be replaced by or represented in them. This is to say, more precisely: The concern is with the experience of art and history, and with the experience of a philosophy that is directed toward its own tradition and confronted by a "claim of truth" arising from among the texts inherited from the tradition, "which contemporary consciousness can neither reject nor surpass."[9] What one calls the human sciences are persuasive alone as experience of art, history, and philosophy.

Gadamer's understanding of experience is clearly oriented by Hegel, although Gadamer does not ultimately follow him. Experience is a "reversal of consciousness," a "dialectical movement"[10] in which something proves to be different than one initially took it to be. Therefore, it is "initially always the experience of nullity"[11]; it is a loss of certainty and only for that reason an achievement of insight. However, and this is the point for Gadamer, the experienced insight is not won through one's own power. It *affects* one; it *occurs* that one sees something all at once differently. And if this is accompanied by a corrective of opinions that one previously had, then an experience of truth may indeed be spoken of here: One's opinions about something comes to be corrected insofar as the matter itself affects one.

If a matter is laid open *solely* in the spontaneity of its experience, then one's own conscious attitude, or, for that matter, one's methodologically directed attitude, cannot be successful. In one's own attempt to access it, the matter becomes concealed; as soon as one believes that one has it and can hold it firmly, it disappears again. Gadamer objects to Hegel for this reason, arguing that experience cannot culminate in knowledge; experience culminates only "in that openness to experience that is freed up by experience itself."[12] Understood in this manner, it admits of no conclusion; it belongs to its essence that it time and again occurs anew. The insistence on the possibility of knowledge that is directed and aimed, then, really only forecloses experience. For this reason, the central issue is a readiness for experience that has been made possible by, and time and again makes possible, experience itself. What counts for Gadamer is not knowledge, but rather the openness to allow something to affect one.

Gadamer, it should be remembered once again, wishes to determine the essence of the human sciences with these considerations. The human sciences, however, can only be experience if experience, too, is humanistic [*geisteswissenschaftlich*]. In experience, in other words, the characteristic situation of the human sciences has to come into focus as experience. This is, in fact, the case for Gadamer: The essential difference in the human sciences between "contemporary consciousness" and tradition is the most important condition of experience; it is because the tradition is different from the present and its convictions that experiences of tradition may be had. This, in turn, demonstrates a significance of the past for the present that cannot be replaced by anything of the present. It thus also demonstrates the ineluctability of the human sciences and the historical consciousness operative in it. With this, the experience operative in the human sciences corrects both the naïvetés and the arrogance of the present: It is not possible to connect with the past of one's own power. Such an attempt—as in the architecture of the *Gründerzeit**—can only be judged as a failure of one's own possibilities.

It is well considered when Gadamer develops this conviction above all in regard of philosophy and not of the "modes of experience"[13] found in art and in history. By proceeding in this manner, he establishes the basic lines of his own philosophical undertaking and thereby also places philosophy within the perspective of the human sciences. A break stands between the "philosophical endeavors of our time" and the "classical tradition of philosophy," such that there can be "no immediate and unbroken continuation" of the tradition. Rather, philosophy today is "well aware of its historical distance from its classical models." And, a little later, to clarify once more: "the naïve innocence has been lost, with which one had made the concepts of the tradition serve one's own ideas."[14]

---

*[The term *Gründerzeit*, refers, in architecture, to the style of the period in Germany in the decades after the foundation of the new Prussian government in 1871. —Trans.]

This sounds like Hegel's diagnosis of the end of art, according to which artworks no longer make an immediate claim on us, but, rather, have become historical: "however much we would like to find the Greek divine images pertinent, or to see the Holy Father, Christ, and Mary reverentially and consummately presented, it does not matter, we of course no longer bend our knee."[15] In fact, for Gadamer the "concepts of the tradition" have not come to be of the museum, as the Greek divine images and the masterworks of Christian painting had for Hegel. In the end, however, philosophy speaks to us no differently than they do—as something whose possibilities of articulation and formation have withdrawn. Gadamer puts philosophy, just as Hegel had art, into the past. Even philosophy, then, is something one may direct oneself toward from a historical standpoint.

The concept of experience is supposed to step in to ensure that this not be understood as a renunciation of philosophy. The past is supposed to affect contemporary thought and, in this, demonstrate its substantive superiority. From this standpoint, however, Gadamer does not fundamentally differentiate the experience of truth in philosophy from the comparable experiences in art and history. As experience, philosophy, which Gadamer himself associates with reflection and conceptual comprehension of experience, remains underdetermined. It is more than the merely historical investigation of the tradition, although it cannot be conceptual thought in the traditional sense.

Gadamer's answer to the question of how to think this philosophy lies in his conception of philosophical hermeneutics. In it, he envisions an intermediary between the experience of tradition and self-standing thought: the possibility of conscious, conceptually self-articulating experience, which is, at the same time, the possibility of a determination of the essence of this experience. The task is now to make clear how a philosophical thinking of this kind is to be grasped. The concern here is above all to recognize its possibilities and limits. Through this, in turn, the possibility of a path that leads beyond these limits becomes clear.

§ 2. Hermeneutics of Facticity

Whoever wants to understand Gadamer's conception of philosophical hermeneutics must go back to the year 1923. In the summer semester of this year in Freiburg, the later author of *Wahrheit und Methode* attends Heidegger's lecture course on "Ontology," which comprises, at its core, the development of a philosophically understood hermeneutics.[16] What the young Gadamer takes in is intensified by his reading of Heidegger's early, programmatic piece: the so-called *Natorp-Bericht*,[17] the manuscript of which he possesses since 1924.[18] Heidegger speaks here of a "phenomenological hermeneutics of facticity,"[19] so as to bring together his talk of the hermeneutical, found already in his earliest surviving lecture,[20] with the concept of "factical life," which he used for the first time in winter 1919–1920.[21]

The experience of the twenty-three-year-old Gadamer continued to have an effect on him for quite some time, and ultimately comes to be productively transplanted.[22] In *Wahrheit und Methode,* he once again takes up the subtitle of Heidegger's lecture, "The Hermeneutics of Facticity." It is instructive here for Gadamer's picture of Heidegger that Heidegger himself does not later come back to the title of a hermeneutics of facticity. It shows that Gadamer reads Heidegger's philosophy as a whole on the basis of his earlier lectures. This early formulation of the program gives Gadamer the standpoint for the understanding of *Sein und Zeit* and for later Heideggerian thought.

This formulation shaped not only Gadamer's understanding of Heideggerian thought, however, but rather also put his own thought on its course—long before he would have ventured to claim any distinctiveness for his own thought. By falling back on talk of the hermeneutics of facticity as if it were obvious in its familiarity, Gadamer shows which place in the effective history of Heidegger's thought he wishes to assign his philosophical hermeneutics. As we shall see, it is also the place from which Gadamer will indicate his position in modern philosophy generally.

Initially, however, Gadamer takes the talk of phenomenological hermeneutics to capture Heidegger's decisive turn against Husserl's phenomenology. Heidegger had opposed a "paradoxical demand" with his programmatic title: "the ontological basis of the phenomenological question should be presented by the ungroundable and underivable facticity of Dasein,* existence, and not by the pure cogito as the constitutive essence of typical universality—a thought that is as bold as it is difficult to make good on."[23] Yet, for Gadamer it is a thought whose boldness and difficulty demands that one take it up and make good on it. *Wahrheit und Methode* is an attempt to do precisely this.

Gadamer's recourse to Heidegger is not to be taken as a simple continuity, however. It is in the interest of his own solution that Gadamer reinterprets Heidegger's hermeneutical approach, even if this may not be apparent on first glance. In what Gadamer writes about Heidegger in *Wahrheit und Methode* there is no indication of a debate, and not at all any explicit divergence. Gadamer takes up his teacher's thought and places himself completely within the context of that thought in his own project of philosophical hermeneutics. The decisive step beyond Dilthey's "historicism," the "overcoming" of his "epistemological formulation of the question," is first made possible through "phenomenological research" and especially through Heidegger.[24] Here Gadamer, as he allows

---

*[I have generally left the word "Dasein" untranslated unless it is clearer to put it into English, usually as "existence" or "being there." —Trans.]

himself to be understood, follows. Yet, if one looks more precisely, tensions and deviations come to the fore. Gadamer reads Heidegger so that something new emerges in the elucidation of Heidegger's program. For Gadamer, it is only in this manner that it becomes possible to make good on Heidegger's "bold thought."

Gadamer's reinterpretation of Heidegger's project begins already in Gadamer's elucidation of its title: Heidegger neither said nor meant that the hermeneutics of facticity would make an "ungroundable" and "underivable" Dasein into the "basis" of the phenomenological question. With the concept of "facticity,"[25] Heidegger in no way signifies the ungroundability or underivability of Dasein. Intended here is something different from the "immemorial" that withdraws from conception, an idea made use of by Schelling against Hegel's teleological view of the concept.[26] "Facticity," as it is identified in Heidegger, "is the signification of 'our' 'own' *Dasein*." And, as Heidegger adds, this expression indicates more precisely, "*in each case*, this Dasein," that is given "not, and never primarily, as an *object* of intuition," but, instead, is "*there* to itself" in the "How of its most own being." Here, being must be understood "transitively," as "being factical life."[27] Life, then, is factical insofar as it is lived; being has the "character of enactment"[28]; it is an enactment of life, and not something that may be captured by the "sense of reference"[29] of the "theoretical" as an "object." The lucidity and presence proper to life is a "sense of enactment."[30] It does not come to light in a view directed toward life, but is, instead, carried out in life itself.

This idea could certainly be understood as if the ungroundability and underivablity of life were emphasized here; if life essentially has the sense of enactment, then nothing leads back behind its enactment. Heidegger, however, does not have in mind a movement of life that resists the attempt to determine it and that leaves unanswered every question about its whence. The accentuation of the factical aims much more at the respective attentiveness and lucidity by which life is led. The factical being of life lies, in Heidegger's word, in *Dasein*, that is, in the presentness of life that actually comprises life. Life, for which there is presentness, *is* its presentness; it is lived by dealing with its presentness, that is, wanting to be disclosed as lucidly and openly as possible, or withdrawing from its lucidity and openness into the dimness of self-concealment.

It becomes clear on the basis of this what is at issue in the *hermeneutics* of facticity. In his early "Ontology" lecture course, Heidegger determines the lucidity of life, which Dasein is, as understanding. This is the "being-wakeful of Dasein for itself"[31] and it is realized insofar as it explicates itself, which is supposed to mean: to communicate itself and thus attain an announcement of itself. Here is the point of departure for Heidegger's hermeneutics: It is for him not an art of interpretation, but instead a philosophical articulation of life in its "sense of enactment." It is an attentiveness that brings itself to language, an "announcement,"[32] that knows itself as the enactment of life.[33] Heidegger spoke of "hermeneutical intuition" in this sense in the special war semester lecture course. This intuition, understood as communicable lucidity of life, is an "essential moment of life in and for itself,"[34] and goes "along with inner experience."[35]

Heidegger unmistakably opposes his understanding of hermeneutics to Husserl's understanding of phenomenology; as may be seen in the cited comment by Gadamer about the "pure cogito,"[36] he later takes up the opposition. Ever since hermeneutics comes into play in the early Heidegger, it is intended as an oppositional project to phenomenology of Husserlian influence. For hermeneutics, a relationship such as that between "the comprehension of an object and the object comprehended" is not supposed to be characteristic. Instead, Heidegger wishes to conceive of hermeneutics as an exceptional "how" of the "ontological character of facticity"—as if a science were to help make possible what it investigates; as if, for example, "the plants, what and how they are," were possible only "with and from botany."[37] The hermeneutics of facticity is an "exceptional" realization of facticity itself; it is an explicit illumination of a being that is in itself illuminated and is only for this reason able to darken.

Gadamer follows from here. Nevertheless, the matter at issue in hermeneutics presents itself differently to him, even though this does not become immediately clear from the text of *Wahrheit und Methode*. In a consummate act of philosophical diplomacy, Gadamer speaks against Heidegger precisely by giving the impression of speaking with him. In *Sein und Zeit*, Gadamer states, it does appear as if Dasein's comprehension of being presents a "final basis." But, in truth, he tells us, "the talk" is really about "an entirely different reason why the understanding of being is possible at all."[38] It is, according to him, only after what Heidegger called "the turn" that he set free and undertook the task he originally set for himself in *Sein und Zeit*.[39]

Yet in order to elucidate this setting free and undertaking, Gadamer does not turn to what one would expect: that is, not to Heidegger's ontological-historical discussion of metaphysics, and just as little to his later thought on language, with the questions of poetry and the work of art that belongs to it. Instead, what is decisive for Gadamer is that Heidegger "had to put the problem of history in the foreground." The problem of facticity is ultimately also the "core problem of historicism," "at least in the form of the critique of Hegel's dialectical assumption of 'reason in history.'"[40] And, furthermore, when Gadamer now speaks of "belongingness to tradition"[41] with Yorck von Wartenburg—notably not with Heidegger—to elucidate this idea, the transition to his own version of a hermeneutics of facticity is complete. Hermeneutics has come to be coined philosophically as a "historically effected" consciousness, that is, consciousness that understands itself as an effect of history.[42] Hermeneutics is a conceptually articulated "wakefulness of historically effected consciousness," which also owes its own articulation to effected history. Insofar as history experienced as tradition is, in the pregnant sense of the word, something pre-given that immemorially sets free all possibilities for articulation, the idea of an "ungroundable and underivable facticity of Dasein" is reached. Gadamer elucidates this idea later in a piece with the title "Hermeneutik und ontologische Differenz" from 1989 in reference to the notion of the incalculable, understood as "what constantly withdraws and precisely for this reason is always there."[43] It is not first here, however, but already in *Wahrheit und Methode* that the incalculable arises from out of the factical in Heidegger's sense.

That this reinterpretation could not be more radical becomes clear when one considers its philosophical consequences. Whereas Heidegger in his early lecture course had described philosophy as the possibility of Dasein "to come to understand itself and to be,"[44] Gadamer is concerned to render the pre-givenness of historical being the "ontological basis" of philosophical thought. And, whereas Heidegger had seen the philosophical self-interpretation of Dasein as the chance to pursue "the tradition of philosophical inquiry . . . .back to its substantive source" in self-understanding, and, thereby, "to dismantle"[45] or to "destructure" the unquestioned status of this tradition of inquiry, Gadamer wants to reassign tradition to its rightful place. However much philosophy might attempt decisively to penetrate and to outstrip what has been inherited from the past, it is nevertheless tradition alone that passes on the possibility of philosophical thought.

Heidegger concerns himself, in a word, with the fact of the hermeneutical, Gadamer with the hermeneutics of the factical. Philosophy is therefore for Gadamer no longer an attempt to attain an originary position of inquiry that would go back behind the tradition and to make such a possibility intelligible on the basis of the being of Dasein. Instead of this, philosophy is a conscious relinquishment of the self-presence and self-transparency that was at issue for the early Heidegger. "To be historically," Gadamer once says, means "never to attain self-knowledge."[46]

However, this consideration is in no way accompanied by a reduction in the claim made by philosophy, and, because of this, the widespread understanding of Gadamerian hermeneutics as an exercise in philosophical modesty applies only on the surface. Gadamer's critique of self-transparency directed against Heidegger's early hermeneutical project is no minor corrective. But even more is intended. At its core, Gadamer's hermeneutics of facticity is an imminent critique of Hegel's philosophy of spirit.[47] It is directed against the "hybrid assertion" of an absolute knowledge, "in which history would become completely self-transparent."[48] It takes its measure against this as a conception of "self-knowledge" and thus attains the constitution of history that is characteristic for it.

Or, as Gadamer himself formulates the decisive idea of his hermeneutical program: "All self-knowledge arises out of historical pre-givenness, which, with Hegel, we call 'substance,' because it underlies all subjective intentions and conduct and thereby also delineates and limits all possibilities to understand an inheritance in its historical otherness. This almost allows us to characterize the task of philosophical hermeneutics in this way: it must return to the path of the Hegelian *Phänomenologie des Geistes* until one shows in all subjectivity the substantiality that determines it."[49] For Gadamer, substance in this sense is history as tradition. It is, with Hegel, "*being without self*"[50] that is only "in itself." On the Gadamerian conception, however, this "in itself" is no longer thought to develop into a complete "for itself" of knowledge, but rather gives rise only to possibilities of "self-knowledge," which are seen to be sustained by substance that cannot be exhausted by them. Self-knowledge comes to be transformed from self-transparency to an insight into our boundedness to "being without self."

With this, the systematic place of Gadamerian philosophizing is identified: Gadamer reiterates, on the soil of Hegel's historical thought, critical objections to Hegel as they were first definitively formulated for all further Hegel-critique by Schelling. In Gadamer, however, this occurs not from the theological motive that was the decisive one for Schelling as well as for Kierkegaard after him. Gadamer directs himself not against the—actual or putative—dissolution of God in self-knowledge, but rather transfers the theological concern to historical life. It is because of this that a signification such as that of "simultaneity," with which Kierkegaard wished to make the immediate relation of the Christian to Christ intelligible,[51] can be brought to bear on classical texts and artworks.[52] Gadamer, and in this he remains a Hegelian, holds onto the historical possibility of the experience of truth. The true is neither—as corresponds to the Romantic view—something that has become unrecognizable through history and hidden in the depths of past life, nor is it—as it was comprehended by the radical figures of the Enlightenment—something that must first be fought for and won against historical pre-givenness and formation. The true is accessible as the matter at issue in what has been inherited from the past, though never in such a way that one could assure himself of it.[53] The true is, in the Gadamerian sense of the word, experienced. Whatever is experienced is the effect of historical substance.

The significance of Heidegger's philosophy for Gadamer may now also be determined: Heidegger's hermeneutics, on the soil of Hegelian thought, clears the way for Gadamer from subject to substance. As Gadamer states— incidentally, without reference to Heidegger's early texts—his hermeneutics of facticity aims "through a critique of Husserl at an ontological critique of speculative idealism."[54] This is Gadamer's view; for him, Heidegger's early hermeneutics is a corrective against Hegel's claim to an "absolute knowledge, in which history would become completely self-transparent."[55]

Read in this way, however, Heidegger's hermeneutics loses its center: his idea that hermeneutics is concerned with self-understanding as possible self-transparency—differently than in Hegelian thought and nevertheless comparable to it—as well as with the development of a philosophical interpretation of this can no longer arise when the hermeneutics of facticity is introduced as a corrective of Hegel. The self-interpretation that stands at the center of Heidegger's view becomes a self-illumination of historical being; self-knowledge becomes a "flicker in the closed electrical circuit of historical life."[56] Those who know themselves dissolve into a history that is liberated from the claim of self-transparency.

The image of the closed electrical circuit that Gadamer finds for historical life once more makes his Hegelianism of substance especially clear: only the interruption of the circuit allows its closure to be experienced—just as for Hegel only the "consciousness of becoming other"[57] allows the unity that had been meant by substance to become explicit. Factical life must tear open and lose its density in order to become accessible as what it is. The truth, however, lies not in the interruption, but rather in the continuity that first comes to the fore through the interruption of what it is.

Gadamer has elucidated this in an idea that is central to his hermeneutics, the "fusion of horizons." The plurality of horizons implied by this expression is meant to capture the difference of a present world from the past. This difference is the condition for historical self-reflection, if such reflection is possible only through a historicizing distance from what has been inherited from the past; only when what is inherited appears as other and alien can one relate oneself to it. It is instructive that this is the case. However, reflection on the past is only genuinely historical in Gadamer's sense when it recognizes itself as the "extension of a tradition that continues to be effective."[58] The projection of the historically other is, as Gadamer says, "only a phasal moment in the enactment of understanding," and, accordingly, the "wakefulness of historically effected consciousness" consists of bringing about, "at once with the projection of the historical horizon, its supersession."[59] In order to understand, one must be challenged by the alien. As soon as one understands, however, one slides back into the stream of historical life.

Gadamer's trust in this stream stands in stark contrast to Heidegger's critique of tradition. The contrast is so clear that one may presume Gadamer had even developed his hermeneutics of historical substance as a counter-model to this critique. As Heidegger sees it, the transmission of concepts and manners of thought from the past wears down everything about them that had comprised their authenticity; the concepts and manners of thought become round, easy to grip, like water-worn stone. Therefore, he spares no effort as it were to roughen them again, that is, "to penetrate to the originary motivational sources of explication" in a *"dismantling return [Rückgang]"* and to win back in a "destructuring"[60] the "originary expressive functions" of concepts.[61] Thus, tradition comes to be taken as the epitome of that familiar obviousness [*Selbstverständlichkeit*] against which an authentic understanding must first be won back.

Gadamer's corrective of this understanding of history and tradition is quite comprehensible. When he takes up and reinterprets Heidegger's conception of hermeneutics by directing us to Yorck von Wartenburg's view of our "belongingness" to what is inherited from the past, the issue of hermeneutical practice is raised decisively. This is ultimately sustained by the fact that something from the past can make a claim and communicate insights that cannot be achieved other than in an understanding of what has been inherited. This experience must even be undergone if one critically interrogates what has been inherited and wants to "destructure" something in it that remains unsaid. Otherwise, every "destructuring" of some inherited thought would have a result that remained detached from that same thought. The result could always be the same, and then where one might look for the forgetfulness of being would be arbitrary.

Gadamer does not pursue this idea to the consequences demanded by the matter itself, however, but rather sacrifices it for the sake of his substantialist understanding of history. Because of this, there is a decisive respect in which he does not move beyond the understanding of tradition as it had been determined by Heidegger. To Gadamer's trust in historical life belongs just as homogeneous an image of history as to Heidegger's hermeneutical suspicion against what has been inherited. The difference lies solely in how the homogeneity of history is respectively appraised, and, also, how the possibility of its interruption is differently appraised: because for Heidegger tradition is as such concealing, a moment of truth lies in the caesura that occurs with the recollection of something inaugural. However, the concealing tendency of tradition is not put out of effect by this; by getting handed down, concepts that had become transparent in the moment of destructuring once again take on their opaque familiar obviousness. Like authenticity as it is described by Heidegger in *Sein und Zeit*,[62] the illumination of tradition in his early hermeneutical program appears as a flash in the night. In Gadamer, things are at once different and similar. Because tradition is like a closed electrical circuit for him, the momentary caesura only takes on the sense of allowing this closure to become explicit. Here there is no more than a flicker, a passing irritation, which can only serve to confirm the continuity of historical life. There is in no case the possibility to *maintain distance* from what has shaped and shapes one, and to give account of what happens to us.

This, however, has been the claim of philosophy ever since Plato's differentiation of philosophy and science in the *Republic*. Whereas science, for example, geometry, proceeds from presuppositions (ὑπόθεσις), and presumes that whatever derives from them is entirely evident (παντὶ φανερόν), it belongs to the essence of philosophy to admit nothing that is obvious in its familiarity. Its purpose is to add some clarity to what one is, and always already is, familiar with.[63] In modernity, this conception of philosophy is taken up by Husserl with special emphasis and effect. The program of phenomenology he develops in the first volume of *Ideen zu einer reinen Phänomenologie und phänomenologische Philosophie* is sustained by the possibility of not participating in the "natural attitude"[64] that grants the existence and value of everyday reality, but, rather, of radically changing this attitude,[65] in order thus to achieve the constant possibility of philosophical reflection, and, with it, the possibility of describing and forming concepts. As philosophers, Husserl says, we put the natural attitude *"out of action,"* we *"switch it off,"* we *"bracket it."*[66] Although Husserl's word for this bracketing, ἐποχή, is taken from the language of skepticism,[67] the programmatic idea itself is not skeptical. What is intended is by no means a mere caution in the face of something that might be held as true, but rather a new possibility of insight. One could compare it to the proximity one first finds with the distance from situations in life, say, when one withdraws from the bustle of a festival and becomes observer or beholder.

Although the young Heidegger in fact developed his hermeneutics of facticity against Husserl's program, he did not give up the idea of the ἐποχή. The "dismantling return to the originary sources of motivation" presupposes the ἐποχή; it is equally built into the "facticity" of Dasein and thus also into "hermeneutical intuition," understood as the conceptually articulable self-presence of Dasein.[68] Yet, because for Heidegger the ἐποχή belongs to the facticity of Dasein, it is met by the contrary tendency operative in Dasein toward self-obfuscation, by "dissolution" in "everydayness."[69] It cannot be maintained, and, in fact, it remains unclear, how philosophical thought is supposed to be developed and articulated in it.

Even in Gadamer the Husserlian ideal is still operative. Gadamer's comment that experience is essentially one of "nothingness" is intended in this sense. That something "claims" and wishes to be understood is to be understood as "a fundamental suspension of one's own prejudices,"[70] that is, those convictions and manners of thought that are to be transformed by experience. Considered more precisely, however, the suspension is not a pause in Husserl's sense, but rather no more than an openness to experience. In experience, nothing is seen and realized. Rather, experience is tantamount to a readiness to let something be said, and, in this manner, to partake in the occurrence of inheriting from the past.

That the idea of the ἐποχή does not disappear in Heidegger and Gadamer may, on the one hand, be understood as a testament to its philosophical indispensability. Yet, if one attends to the privileged status of the idea in the hermeneutical projects of Heidegger and Gadamer, it becomes clear, on the other hand, why the idea cannot be elaborated in them: The distantiation suggested by the idea has as little purchase in a Dasein that is nothing other than its enactment as it does in an effective history that is nothing but occurring. Heidegger, and, following him, also Gadamer, conceive of things exclusively on the basis of movement; for them, there is nothing that eludes, respectively, the movement of Dasein and the occurrence of inheriting something from the past. The attempt to distance oneself from the enactment of Dasein or from the occurrence of inheriting something from the past must itself accordingly be seen to belong to the enactment or occurrence. But this means: it is present only momentarily, just as a moment of truth, or as a flickering in the circuit of historical life.

This allows the status of the program of a hermeneutics of facticity and no less that of a philosophical hermeneutics to become clear: Hermeneutics, in the one sense as in the other, is a philosophy that is entirely and only understood on the basis of enactment and occurrence, answerable only to movement. The critique of the phenomenological ἐποχή is grounded accordingly. The idea appears as the scarcely plausible claim that one is somehow able to position oneself next to and watch the enactment or occurrence of one's own life, not to mention one's own conscious life, as it runs its course. This claim can only come off, as Heidegger determined quite early, under the "general regime of the *theoretical*,"[71] that is, through the belief that one can recognize matters of importance in life by considering them as things. It is, he holds in contrast to Husserl, "a methodological misunderstanding simply to analogize the investigation of emotional inner experiences to cognition."[72] What belongs to the enactment or occurrence of life is not a thing, and it remains misunderstood as long as it is taken as such.[73]

The hermeneutics of facticity is not to be understood without this fundamental critique of the theoretical. It lives from the fact that it radically brings into question the possibility of a theoretical philosophy. Because hermeneutics is nevertheless supposed to be philosophy, both Heidegger, and, influenced by him, Gadamer, follow out a consequence that suggests itself but yet remains problematic: They have, with different accentuations, construed philosophical hermeneutics after the model of practical philosophy.[74] Because of this, however, a displacement takes place that is as rich in implications as it is problematic. Practical philosophy becomes in this manner first philosophy, or, building on Manfred Riedel, a "second," for which there is nevertheless no longer any first.[75] It is uncertain whether such a philosophy is in a position to carry the burden that encumbers it.

§ 3. Hermeneutics and Practical Philosophy

Practical philosophy is already in play as a model when Heidegger characterizes the hermeneutics of facticity as the "*being-wakeful* of Dasein for itself."[76] The idea may be traced back to Socrates and his fundamental principle of the *care of the self* [*Sorge um sich*]. If it is asked that one care not for one's possessions before one has cared for the self, and, more precisely, in order that one be as virtuous and reasonable as possible,⁷⁷ then it is also asked that one carry out one's life awake, and not as if in a dream, imprisoned by representations and images.⁷⁸ Heidegger is concerned with a wakeful self-care of this kind. He finds a model for it not in Plato's dialogues, however, but rather in Aristotle, more precisely, in the idea of a practical form of reason (φρόνησις). Φρόνησις, as Heidegger maintains already in the *Natorp-Bericht*, turns on a specific practical truth (ἀλήθεια πρακτική), and this is, "nothing other than a respectively present moment of factical life that is completely revealed in the how of our decisive readiness to deal with it."⁷⁹

Heidegger nevertheless finds this idea of a "readiness to deal with," or, the ability to conduct oneself toward what one is and is not, to be only insufficiently realized in Aristotle. Aristotle characterizes human life only "formally"⁸⁰ and negatively by determining it as something that can also be otherwise,⁸¹ and in this way sets it apart from what is manufactured [*das Fertige*], completed. That which is manufactured, however, forms the genuine reference point of Aristotelian philosophy. Because of this, as Heidegger puts it, it is oriented not ultimately by human life, but rather by the "movement of *production* [*Herstellen*]."⁸² Accordingly, philosophy reaches its fulfillment for Aristotle in that it attempts to grasp the "*final respects*, in which beings [*das Seiende*]* are brought to their greatest possible determinacy in regard to themselves."⁸³ Aristotle's concern, then, is with the possibility of searching for what is complete and in this way something that is—no longer coming into being and passing away—by inquiring into the aim of movement. What is manufactured, completed, however, is experienced precisely not as practical truth. It is a correlate of "*mere looking*,"⁸⁴ theory.

Like every other activity, theory is for Heidegger bound up with life. It is, as he calls it, "dealing with by purely looking," a conduct that belongs in the context of the everyday world determined by the use of things and that nevertheless wishes no longer to be such a conduct, but, rather, a pure taking-up-into-knowledge. Thus, theory is a dealing with beings that closes itself off to its own possibility, and, "in its whereupon, no longer sees precisely that life itself, in which it exists."⁸⁵ It is a disregard of life within life, and it is for this reason poorer and less lucid than practical reason.

Yet, by raising the status of practical reason in this way, Heidegger also transforms it; by conceiving of theory as a deficient form of praxis, he poses

---

*[In order to preserve clarity in English I have translated *das Seiende* with different expressions in different contexts: not only, then, with "beings," but also "what is," and in some cases, for example, "whatever is," or even "being." —Trans.]

practical philosophy absolutely. Measured against the Aristotelian model and counter-model of this revaluation, he takes the benchmark of practical philosophy that was oriented by the question of the good life. Aristotle had answered this question with a determination of human nature that was oriented by the idea of completed actuality: The proper "work" (ἔργον) of the human being is the actuality of life in accord with reason articulated in language.[86] Accordingly, a life is good when it is carried out in accord with this essential determination. It is, in this case, measured by what is possible for the human being, it is the most completed, the most actual life—not in fact unalterable, but, given the fundamental condition of mutability, at least the most persistent. However diverse situations of life may be—they will all be lived in the abiding orientation of λόγος. Aristotle reads actuality as definitive here, although, not with reference to production understood as manufacture but rather to bringing forth [*Hervorbringen*], perhaps in the sense of artistic performance; a flautist brings something forth, but produces nothing. This orientation toward bringing forth may already be seen even in the formulation, "the work of the human being" (ἔργον τοῦ ἀνθρώπου); in it, Aristotle carries over the idea that every ability, in the sense of an art (τέχνη), proves itself as such first in a result, to human life as a whole.

Yet, even if Heidegger's diagnosis is on the mark—the critical turn he gives to it is not justified. Aristotle in no way loses sight of human life with his orientation toward bringing forth. Bringing forth serves only as a model. It is supposed to indicate the priority of the actual over the possible, in the sense of ability, which may only be developed in a discussion of the concepts of possibility (δύναμις) and actuality (ἐνέργεια). The warrant for this priority no longer belongs in practical philosophy, but, rather, in that theoretical question about beings themselves (ὂν ᾗ ὄν),[87] which, in modernity, will be given the name "ontology." For Aristotle, however, the theoretical discussion first sets free the possibility of inquiring philosophically into the question of the good life. With this, Aristotle connects practical philosophy with an insight that cannot be achieved in a solely practical context.

Because Heidegger revokes this connection, he does not hold any practical philosophy back that is liberated from theoretical burdens. Rather, he burdens practical philosophy with the tasks of the theoretical. In contrast to Aristotle's practical philosophy, Heidegger's hermeneutics of facticity is not dependent on any ontology, because it *is* itself ontology. "The problematic of philosophy," as it is named in the *Natorp-Bericht*, concerns "the *being* of factical life."[88] This is not to be understood in the sense of a discussion *only* of this being. How is this even supposed to be possible, if beings, though diverse, point "toward a one,"[89] and the "meaning of '*being*'"[90] is supposed to be maintained on the Aristotelian model[91] as both one and unified? In this case, the ontology of factical life must be "principle ontology," such that "the specific, individual, concrete, regional ontologies receive the foundation and meaning for their research problems from the ontology of facticity."[92] In *Sein und Zeit*, this is grounded by the idea that any understanding of something in its being goes back to that originary understanding of being, in which Dasein understands itself.[93] Human Dasein is for Heidegger "the condition of the possibility of all ontologies,"[94] and, indeed, not only in the trivial sense that there may be no ontology without human beings. What is intended, rather, is that the self-understanding of Dasein is inherent in every ontology as a conditioning possibility, whether it is concerned with human Dasein or not. Every ontology, then, is a more or less clear self-understanding of the human being.

It is certainly illuminating of this idea that every meaning of "being" is only to be made clear by way of the understanding of being. How should this meaning be given otherwise than in understanding? It does not follow from this, however, that every understanding of being results from the understanding of one's own being. On the contrary, to grasp something in what it is, one must be able to disregard one's own being. Otherwise, the other being could be grasped always only as a modification of one's own, or in contrast to it. But this does not hit the mark: that we are, building on Merleau-Ponty, *amidst things*,[95] and, in some respects, like things, is not simply a modification of our being that is in its essence completely different. It is also not another manner of being, which is so incompatible with our proper manner of being that we would have a part in two different manners of being. Rather, our being surrounded by things only opens up when one gets involved with the being of things. This, in turn, is possible only reflectively; it is a possibility of theory that cannot be achieved from the self-clarification of human life. The hermeneutics of facticity does not resolve what is to be expected from theory.

Heidegger's ontological revaluation of practical reason is still problematic in other respects. It is tantamount to a renunciation of almost everything that is practical about this reason. Heidegger understands φρόνησις not, like Aristotle himself, as a deliberation concerned with respective possibilities of action [*handeln*], but rather solely as the openness of the situation of action itself. Φρόνησις makes "the situation of the agent [*das Handelnde*] accessible"[96]; as "carefully deliberating" reason, it is only possible "because it is primarily an αἴσθησις, an ultimately simple overview of the present moment."[97] Heidegger can in fact summon Aristotle for the thought of such an "overview." Even in the *Nicomachean Ethics* analysis, an immediate grasping lies in φρόνησις, which Aristotle calls "perception," αἴσθησις; it is a perception that is to be distinguished from the proper function of reason (νοῦς), which is concerned with principles (ἀρχαι) of knowing.[98] The perception in play in practical reason is concerned not with the unchangeable, but, rather, with each respective case, with what is respectively to be done (πρακτόν[99]) in each case. Heidegger achieves his interpretation solely because he reads the futurity of action into the πρακτόν and thus understands φρόνησις as the futural openness—in *Sein und Zeit* he calls it "disclosedness"—of Dasein. In Heidegger's clarification, φρόνησις is transformed from a deliberation about possibilities for action to a being-possible that precedes every action and first provides access to action as such, or, in Heidegger's words, a "readiness to deal with."[100]

It is not only to be objected against Heidegger's hermeneutics of facticity, however, that the possibilities of theoretical reason are not appreciated and those of practical reason are marginalized. It may moreover be doubted that it does justice to the essence of the hermeneutical. Because Heidegger radicalizes hermeneutics to a self-understanding of Dasein, what up until then had stood as its most proper subject matter is lost: the interpretation [*Auslegung*] of word and writing.

Although Gadamer does not formulate this objection explicitly, it is maintained emphatically. With Heidegger, Gadamer is convinced of the key role played by practical reason in hermeneutics. Yet, he wishes to understand practical reason differently than Heidegger on the basis of the ethical context to which it had belonged in Aristotle. By motivating the "hermeneutical relevance of Aristotle"[101] in regard to practical philosophy, Gadamer at the same time stresses the practical essence of philosophical hermeneutics.

The point of departure for Gadamer is the same as for Heidegger. For him, too, hermeneutics sets itself apart "from a 'pure' form of knowledge detached from one's being."[102] Yet, his concern is not with a philosophy that articulates the self-transparency of human existence [*Dasein*], but, rather, with the idea that philosophical thought be put fully into the service of "practical knowledge" that comes to fruition in each case individually.[103] Thus, Gadamer, with an eye to hermeneutics, reaffirms that for Aristotle ethics is concerned not with knowledge, but rather with action.[104] Decisive for philosophical ethics is "that it does not usurp the place of ethical consciousness and yet does not seek a purely theoretical, 'historical' knowledge either, but, rather, helps ethical consciousness shed light on itself through the clarification of phenomena in outline."[105] One needs only to put hermeneutical consciousness in the place of ethical consciousness here in order to find this statement a programmatic self-description of Gadamer's philosophy.

The "clarification in outline," of which Gadamer speaks, is only possible if hermeneutical and ethical consciousness agree in the essentials despite all of the dissimilarities that Gadamer himself emphasizes.[106] For Gadamer, the commonality lies in the fact that in both cases the knower "does not stand" over against "a matter of fact that he merely observes," but, rather, "is directly affected by what he sees. It is something he has to do."[107]

In this sense, Aristotle said of φρόνησις that it is directed toward "human things,"[108] that is, toward the multiplicity of possibilities for action that are to be deliberated[109] in order to reach a decision in the culmination of weighing out which good should be pursued.¹¹⁰ As Gadamer comments, this is tantamount to "seeing what the situation as it were demands of him" (i.e., the one who acts).¹¹¹ What is demanded, however, does not arise from the situation alone. It must be capable of being known as a rule in something overarching of a binding nature, for something singular and unrepeatable cannot be binding for the orientation of action. Because of this, that which is demanded, "is demanded universally."¹¹²

The universal accordingly provides the understanding of the respective situation that is binding for an action and at the same time preserves itself in this. As something universal, such as, say, the conviction that one should if at all possible stand by another whose life is in danger, it is there to disclose a situation, and to allow one to realize oneself in it in action. From a practical standpoint, knowledge that is only universal remains, by contrast, "meaningless."¹¹³

However, the relation of the universal to the particular situation does not result of itself. The universal must be found, and it is found in practical knowledge. The proper function of this nevertheless lies not in a universal that is to be known for its own sake and then subsequently directed toward a specific situation. It is in its essence "application."* Ethical knowledge, Gadamer states, must "include the application of knowledge to a particular task."¹¹⁴ This is certainly not just any particular case, but rather a situation, in which one has to prove oneself. The knowledge of the universal that is in itself directed toward one's own action is "an essential moment of ethical being;"¹¹⁵ it is, as Gadamer says with Aristotle, a knowing of the self that is a knowing what is good for oneself.¹¹⁶

All of this also holds of "hermeneutical consciousness." For Gadamer, it is a consciousness of application in the interest of one's own life. It is also supposed to hold for the human sciences and for hermeneutical practice that its "object" is "the human being," "and what he knows of himself": the human being knows "himself, however, as an agent, and the knowledge that he thus" has "of himself" does not wish "to ascertain what is."¹¹⁷ Rather, the agent discovers "where he has to intervene in action"; knowledge should "govern his *activity*."¹¹⁸ This occurs in hermeneutical practice by each time experiencing possibilities of one's understandings on the basis of the inheritance of the past that affects one and bringing them into focus in respective situations of life. In its application, what has been passed down is passed down further, one allows oneself to determine oneself in his present through it, and places oneself in this way as knower back into the tradition: "We spoke of the belongingness of the interpreter to the inheritance that he is concerned with, and we saw that understanding is itself a moment of historical occurrence."¹¹⁹

---

*[Figal cites the important Gadamerian term *Anwendung*, translated in this passage as "application," and then introduces a Latinate equivalent, *Applikation*, which I have eliminated here for the sake of clarity. —Trans.]

Compared with Heidegger's hermeneutical conception, Gadamer's is more convincing in one respect: Whereas Heidegger overburdens practical philosophy through the elevation of its status as ontological, Gadamer simply allows it to stand on its own. He remains closer to the Aristotelian model without conceptual violence and this alone is enough to make his considerations attractive. Because his presentation of "practical knowledge" is illuminating in itself, the analogy to "hermeneutical consciousness" also appears to be conclusive. And, if hermeneutical consciousness is to be demonstrated as a variation of practical knowledge, philosophical hermeneutics is consequently able to be understood on the model of ethics as "practical philosophy."[120]

The fundamental difficulty that had shown itself in Heidegger is admittedly also here: Gadamer leaves open how a practical philosophy, without its relation to the theoretical, which was essential for Aristotle, is supposed to be possible. Theory appears in his considerations solely as a counter-model. It is *scientific* theory, and, as such, the problematic model of the human sciences against which Gadamer writes. The "example of Aristotelian ethics," is summoned against the "objectifying methods of modern science,"[121] that is, against knowledge that is merely observational and detached from one's own being.[122]

On the basis of this, the conviction could be voiced that in modernity, theory is nothing other than this, and that the loss of philosophical theory, then, would have to be "compensated" for—in aesthetic experience, as Joachim Ritter[123] has attempted to show, or, perhaps, in a hermeneutical experience that, even if it encompasses "aesthetic" phenomena, is conceived on the model of practical philosophy. This answer does not put the matter to rest, however. Is Gadamer's reformulation of the Hegelian philosophy of spirit really supposed to be understood as a contribution to a "clarification of the phenomena in outline" that aims solely to help hermeneutical consciousness to achieve "lucidity about itself"?[124] Or, is it concerned with the "application" of the philosophical tradition to a current question that is guided by "knowing what is good for oneself"? If one considers that Gadamer's recourse to Hegel has not only an explanatory function, but rather, a preliminary decision reached consciously or unconsciously in favor of a philosophical approach, then both illuminate equally little. Obviously, there are questions about the philosophical discovery and formation of concepts that do not come out in the requirements of a practical, or practically oriented, philosophy.[125]

A further question remains in regard to Gadamer's—and Heidegger's—conception of the theoretical. Is the alternative between knowing what is good for oneself and cold, indifferent observation really supposed to be exhaustive? Or, is there not also that most highly interested desire for knowledge and contemplation, which, although not directed toward one's own being and in this way self-forgetting, is nevertheless just as possible in regard to sensible nature as it is to theoretical physics or to the work of art? Perhaps a knowledge that is not minted for leading one's own life is nevertheless most itself.

There is, in any case, an inevitability of the theoretical; Heidegger and Gadamer attest to it in their way clearly enough. To get distance from what is enacted or occurs does not have to be a problematic reification. And, there is no understanding without distance. Something that one had gone into in familiar obviousness up until now or something that had inconspicuously always occurred in the same manner all at once becomes questionable. If one now would like to know what it is, how things stand with it, or even how one is supposed to conduct oneself toward it, a different access is needed, for which nothing of the previous familiar obviousness matters any more as such. One does precisely what Husserl had determined as the essence of the ἐποχή in regard to one's everyday attitude: one no longer goes along with what is enacted or occurs. One finds a different vantage point and places oneself in it to oppose what earlier had appeared in familiar obviousness. A new meaning for context and belongingness belongs to this: a meaning that brings and puts together the different moments of something.

The question, then, is of the possibility of an understanding, which, differently than Heidegger's "hermeneutical intuition" and differently than Gadamer's hermeneutics of historically effected consciousness, *no longer goes along*. It would be an understanding, conceived of on the basis of phenomenology, in which something is already operative that is able to show itself as a specifically phenomenological attitude. With this understanding, the possibility of a hermeneutics in the sense of phenomenology is opened up. This would also have to be capable, therefore, of being developed on the basis of a phenomenological approach as hermeneutical philosophy, instead of being philosophical hermeneutics.

For the possibility of such an understanding there is a stark clue: the self-understanding of traditional philosophy as theory. Accordingly, it must be asked whether traditional philosophy, in its theoretical essence, can be construed as understanding, and, consequently, as hermeneutical. If this is the case, thinking that has become explicitly hermeneutical can be demonstrated as a possibility of traditional philosophy, instead of merely a retrospective or destructive view of it. First, however, one should know how a distance to what is enacted and occurs is to be conceived, one that is not a concealment of the historical, but, rather, a distance that is disclosive, and even ineluctable for the understanding of tradition.

§ 4. Origin

Something is all at once there. Possibly, it has prepared itself; conditions for its emergence [*Hervortreten*] were present, there was a favorable moment for its existence. Yet, the preparations remained unrecognizable; only now, after the new has emerged, does it become apparent what had prepared or even just anticipated it. What emerges, then, is never to be derived from the conditions of its appearance; they were there as favorable, certainly some of them even as a *sine qua non*, but they did not provide the essence of what is now there. Even the most favorable moment could have passed without something having occurred; nothing indicated what is emerging, it did not develop, such that one could have seen how it gradually achieved its form.

Whatever emerges in this way has originated [*entsprungen*], its essence is originariness [*Ursprünglichkeit*]. "Origin," as Walter Benjamin identifies it in the "Epistemo-critical Prologue" to the *Ursprung des deutschen Trauerspiels*, is in fact "[an] entirely historical category," yet it "has nothing to do with genesis." In the origin, "no becoming of what has originated" is "intended, but, rather, what originates in becoming and passing away." The origin stands "in the stream of becoming as an eddy," and swallows up "the material of its genesis in its rhythmic."[126]

The originary, in this sense, is something like an unforeseeable and underivable center, on the basis of which and in which everything else discloses itself all at once anew. Benjamin's comparison is on the mark: The originary is like an eddy in the stream. It is not explained based on a context, but, rather, first establishes a context; it does not belong in a process of development, but, rather, the originary is that which first allows what belongs to this process of development to be known. Thus, on the one hand, the originary is radically separated from formation and transformation, from dissolution and disappearance. It has, as "what originates in becoming and passing away," escaped from them. It has also escaped from becoming and passing away in such a way that it withdraws from them. It has parted from them, although not because it is differentiated from formation and transformation, from generation and dissolution, and is now itself, but rather, through its force that is effective, formative, and integrative in the stream of becoming and passing away. The originary determines what it has originated from, anew, without having brought it forth.

Thus, with the originary, it is possible that nothing changes, and, on the other hand, everything. It is possible that nothing of what had been before disappears, is transformed, or arises anew. Everything is still recognizable as what it was for itself, and everything is nevertheless entirely different, as if in a previously unfamiliar light. It has not changed, or, if it has, the change is not decisive. It enters into a new essence.

Origination is no transformation, such that one could say: that previously something was so, now it is different. Even the "other," the foreignness in which something all at once appears, traces back to origination. Origination is an *absolute change*; from among the classical concepts of change it is that of a shift [*Umschlag*], μεταβολή. The weather shifts; the transformation of the light, the looming of the clouds is not what is decisive; all of this could also belong to prevailing, stable weather conditions. One sees the quality of light first differently and assesses the clouds differently once one has understood that they belong in the context of new weather.

Following this, it would have to be intelligible why Benjamin is able to call the origin a "historical category." The originary was not always already there, it originates. One could with approximation call this an occurrence [*Geschehen*] or an event [*Ereignis*], but the concern is with an occurrence *sui generis*, which one can only describe precisely with the one word proper to it: it originates. This is no incantation—as if the matter of concern here could only be described by repeating and repeating the word appropriate to it. It may be delimited and elucidated in contrast.

It is for this reason especially important that an origination stands in a certain way orthogonal to becoming and passing away and yet is not independent of them. Origination is not a becoming and passing away. Rather, what becomes and passes away, what is able to become and pass away, is all at once determined somewhat differently. Nothing is added to what is able to become and pass away, however, that would be in itself of a different kind. What has originated and is originary is not its own kind of being that would stand outside of what becomes and passes away. It is not possible without it. The originary is not some essence that stands next to becoming and passing away, it is not something that would somehow be given for itself. It exists only in that it determines something else, allowing this something to enter into a determinate context. It is *limit*, understood as the delimitation, which provides a prominent place within a whole, and, thus, determinacy, to another that for itself remains unlimited. Limit and unlimitedness comprise an ultimate distinction, one that cannot be derived any further. In the mythic image that Plato finds for the belonging together of limit and unlimitedness (πέρας and ἀπειρία), it may for this reason be said of them that they are given by the gods, or stolen from them.[127]

Delimitation, as originary, does not simply come from outside; whether it impresses or expresses itself, it would in any case somehow already have to be given. It arises, rather, as if something entered into a new aggregate condition, through which it becomes recognizable in a surprising and yet at the same time illuminating manner. Something given in becoming and passing away had perhaps been compressed in a peculiar manner. In this case, there is a shift, an absolute change or leap, and the unforeseeable, the originary, is there.

Because the originary cannot be without absolute change, it is not necessarily of duration. The new light, in which something stands, may fade and ultimately disappear. Everything is now once again in the stream in a diffuse manner; alone the memory that something had been different may endure. There may, in this case, also be a memory of the manner in which the originary had been articulated. Things of this kind remain behind like remnants of an ancient culture; tools, of which one still knows that they were tools, but whose use is unknown.

The disappearance of the originary is, however, just as little a passing away as its origination was a generation. Something is generated *from something*, and it turns *into something* when it passes away. All generation and passing away is a *relative change*; in order to identify it, one must be able to say where it ends and where it begins, but still always think about and beyond the process. Thus, the plant arises from the seed and returns to the earth when it passes away. Or, something of use arises, for example, a bowl. It may have gained its form by means of joined, creative hands; in any case, the form must have been there so that the bowl could be formed from clay. The bowl thus arises from this form and from earth, which, as potter's clay, may be dried or fired. The bowl, in its form, could now be adapted; it could be of wood or bronze instead of clay. Something is always there, from which generation, and, certainly, transformation, proceeds. And, passing away and, certainly, transformation, always and again move toward somewhere. The originary, by contrast, is simply there or not there.

A *form of life* can be originary in the elucidated sense. It is this because the most diverse moments—convictions, manners of conduct, appearance, rules, rituals, and the like—form a context that is unified, and, in this unity, underivable. Each of these moments could also appear independent of the form of life or in another form of life, and would nevertheless be determined differently in its essence. In the form of life, the moments can vary, perhaps even change; one drops off and another comes in. The form of life is nevertheless the same. As long as it is there at all, it is independent of what occurs within its bounds.

Artworks, which really deserve the name, are also originary. They do not belong in an overarching context like everyday things, but, rather, open up contexts, which one is able to experience through them as one experiences them. Even if the experience is not directly that of the work, it remains bound to the work, for example, when one sees a sunset in nature as if in a painting by Monet, or when the experience of a memory is as in Proust. Without the painting, without the novel, the experience would not be possible as it has been had. Even the historical context that is connected with the work is disclosed anew by the work; it belongs in the work, the work does not belong to it.

In contrast to life forms, artworks are not, or, at most within very narrow limits, variable. The painting is no longer what it is once it is changed; in the poem that is a masterwork, no word is missing and none are too many. Transformations within the bounds of the work occur because it allows various things to be experienced in various ways. Whereas life forms have limits that one can transgress, the artwork is a limit that opens, not confines.

Finally, *science* and *philosophy* are originary. Both enter into an area that, taken for itself, is neither scientific nor philosophical, and allow the area to become visible in an unforeseeable, underivable manner. They investigate it as a context that, through their investigation, is a scientific or philosophical one, and determine everything that enters into this context anew. There are possibilities of clarification that are originarily scientific or philosophical. By articulating them, scientific research and philosophical inquiry differentiate themselves from other possibilities of understanding life and the world. They thus often first give these possibilities their contour; there is the unscientific, nonphilosophical only through science and philosophy.

On the one hand, talk of the originary character of "the" science and of "the" philosophy is justified. Every science and every scientific theory has the fundamental character of the scientific, just as every philosophical conception has the fundamental character of the philosophical; this allows individual projects to belong together; it makes them comparable to one another and allows them to be differentiated from other possibilities of knowledge and experience. On the other hand, there is never "the" science or "the" philosophy. There are sciences, and, each of these, originary formations that Thomas S. Kuhn has called "paradigms."[128] They are determined to a certain extent by common methods, recognized fundamental concepts, and more or less homogeneous structures of understanding. The shift from one paradigm to another is, as Kuhn describes it, absolute. This is not to say that there are no longer possibilities of comparison. Nevertheless, from one paradigm to another no *crossovers* are possible. A matter of fact is determined either from one paradigm to another.

It is the same in philosophy. There is philosophy only as philosophies, and every great philosophy is a paradigm in Kuhn's sense. Nevertheless, and this will still be shown more precisely, philosophy differs from science, in that it is only in paradigm shifts that philosophy is what it should be according to its essence. There is, in fact, also in philosophy what Kuhn calls "*normal science,*" that is, the expansion, the refinement, the clarification of a great systematic project. Yet, philosophy is not aimed at such things; when it is carried on as *normal science* it lags behind what it should be. In it, the concern is not with the achievement of schemata or the application of laws and rules, but, rather, with the originary itself. Even in work on philosophies that are already established, it is necessary to achieve originariness always and again anew, and to understand what is there in an originary context on the basis of its originariness.

Now to be made clear is what, precisely, this means. On the one hand, this turns on the formal determination of philosophy in its originariness. This must have validity for all philosophies; only in this way may it be said every time of the originating that it is philosophy. On the other hand, the diversity of philosophies must be able to be made intelligible. Why does it belong to philosophy that it time and again starts in anew, and comes to new solutions that, although comparable, cannot be reducible to one another? And, finally, there is the question of whether the originariness of philosophy can be deduced from its hermeneutical character. Does philosophy have a hermeneutical essence? And, if so, how does the possibility of an explicitly hermeneutical philosophy arise from its determination?

All of this is best made clear by orienting oneself by philosophical models. There have to be multiple models so that different possibilities of philosophical development as well as the common essential trait of philosophy stand in view. "The" philosophy only admits of being presented by means of models. It is never simply there and also does not decay in a succession of historical conditions. All of its possibilities stand for a philosophical essence that is itself a possibility and, for this reason, is given always only in possibilities.

§ 5. Models of Origin

A model is a definitive example—neither the matter itself, not an arbitrary appearance. On the one hand, the essence of the matter is present in the model; something is all the more suited as a model the more decisively this is the case. On the other hand, what one experiences as having the character of a model is not simply the essence of the matter, but rather, this essence in a certain respect. Models are, for this reason, neither compulsory nor arbitrary. They must be chosen, and the decision as to what is supposed to serve as a model may have turned out differently; perhaps another model would have been no less helpful, perhaps a different picture arises on the next occasion through reflection on a different model. However, if one is really dealing with models, it could not be an essentially different picture.

Whether something is suited as a model is not to be judged in advance. Models must prove themselves; they must prove themselves as models by allowing the matter whose models they are to be recognized. If it is, the matter does not show itself in the model immediately. It must, rather, be shown; a model is that in regard of which something may show itself. This is also the meaning of the Greek word, for which the correspondence "model" has here been chosen: παράδειγμα; παραδείκνυμι means "I show something in something and thus make it present."

Because a matter of concern is not immediately present in a model, models must supplement one another. The better they are chosen, the more this will be the case. In this case, a picture of the matter arises from their composite that allows at once its richness and subtlety to be recognized. And, it is also possible, in this case, to take the difference of the models as the opportunity for a conceptual unification. The essence of the matter may be investigated by the various models. If it is not given simply and immediately—in this case, models would be superfluous or merely illustrative—such an investigation is the only path that leads to the essence of a matter.

The matter that is of concern here is philosophy in its originariness. Best suited as models, accordingly, are philosophical conceptions that allow their own originariness to be recognized with special clarity. Models are supposed to be distinguished by their pregnancy; they must prove themselves as such by really letting something be shown in them.

Yet, something is shown through models that is not present in them alone; philosophical models stand fundamentally for every philosophy and for the originariness of every philosophy. Every philosophy is originary. A philosophical discussion that is not originary is not a philosophy, but, rather, only makes a contribution to a philosophy.

It is an indication of the originariness of philosophy that the discussion of its own possibility belongs to its essence. Philosophizing does not hold once and for all, or even for just a certain time, or for a school of thought with its established procedures, or, as Heidegger once formulates it in an early lecture course: "it is for philosophy, then, only a deficiency that it must always and again get clear about its essence if the idea of science is introduced as a norm."[129] In the philosophical question of the essence of philosophy, its presuppositionlessness is in play. Every philosophy is in essence something underivable, new. Nevertheless, its presuppositionlessness is not demonstrated by the fact that a philosophical project is developed as if from nothing and would have to be differentiated in every respect from what was already there. This is impossible; every philosophy takes up others or opposes itself to them; one finds in every one of them, more or less clearly, what has preceded and what has been inherited—figures of thought, patterns of presentation and argumentation, concepts and metaphors. When a philosophy is originary, however, it cannot be derived from what has preceded; it does not further, with more or less modification, what has preceded, it is not dissolved in getting passed down. With every philosophy, moments of the tradition are put into a specific context anew; all moments may still be familiar, but the whole of this context is new and different from every other philosophy. It is traditional and nevertheless has escaped from tradition. With the whole of philosophy, what is thought and thinkable are determined in a distinctive manner; delimited, and, thereby, opened up anew. Thought is open always only within specific limits; by opening itself up, it delimits itself.

Although the question of the essence of philosophy belongs to philosophy, philosophical thought is better able to orient itself toward a matter than to labor at self-clarification. The originariness of philosophy is first experienced where the latter is the case. This does not have to mean that it is also put into language as such. Otherwise, originariness would not have to be shown through models; it would lie in the light of day like a matter of fact. But this is not so. The originariness of philosophy obtains only by being emphasized always and again anew and more or less explicitly determined in philosophizing.

Philosophy shows itself in its originariness with special clarity through models that are quite varied. Their historical order plays no role in this; decisive, rather, is that the models can be referred to one another in their difference so that, in a formulation of Benjamin, they obtain "the status of complementary energies."[130] It is thus prevented that one bind oneself to one of them as to a presupposition, and simply overtake its respective possibilities of description. And, the probability thus grows that philosophy is able to investigate itself in its origin through them, or, more precisely: in their field of tension.

To begin with is a picture, and the picture is like a daydream; it indicates the possibility of philosophy as a journey. At the beginning of his didactic poem, Parmenides outlines how a team of horses leads him to the "much famed path of the goddess,"[131] through all cities, until he comes from out of the "house of night" into the light. There he encounters a goddess, whose divinity is demonstrated by her promise to impart the truth: He will become familiar with the "untremulous heart of well-rounded truth,"[132] although also the opinions of mortals, on which one cannot depend. As this pronouncement of the goddess who remains nameless suggests, the journey is one from out of the mortal view of the world to a truth that is divine; with this truth comes insight, whereas mortals do not understand what is. As "two-headed,"[133] they have only "wavering understanding"[134] and remain at the mercy of what is shown to them. Thought alone, as the author of the didactic poem claims, leads to something invariable, fixed.

The journey of Parmenides has precedents. Hesiod understands his writing as a journey[135]; the initiation into knowledge as it occurred through the goddess has its precedent in the inspiration of the poet through the muse, who, already for the poets of antiquity, is the one who knows and the one who announces knowledge.[136] Like the inspired poet, the thinker Parmenides simply passes on what has been said to him. It is a singular proclamation, a definitive truth; what the poet or thinker brings to language is spoken on the basis of this, itself something sent, given, and not found. Without the goddess, he who thinks and undertakes the journey would be a mortal like the others: one, who remains imprisoned in wavering, indecisive opinion.

However, the proclamation of the goddess is no revelation that overpowers those who hear it. The proclamation is just as little a doctrine that must be taken over as law. The goddess points out one *path*[137] and advises against other paths. Without her, the one who thinks would not have found this path, but he must himself traverse it. It is up to him to see the "being" [*das "Seiend"*] (τὸ ἐόν) in everything and thus no more to fall prey to the wavering of mortals between what is [*das Seiende*] and what is not [*das Nichtseiende*]. That this can be entrusted to him is demonstrated by the guiding power of his journey to the goddess: the *striving* toward truth comes from within himself; the horses draw as far along the path of thought as the life force[138] of their driver allows.

The next story of thought begins much more tranquilly. It is, first of all, told in retrospect, and this accords with its matter: the experience that it is supposed to concern lies quite a few years in the past. It already struck him earlier, Descartes reports at the beginning of the first of his *meditations de prima philosophiae* (1641), how much he had accepted that is false instead of true, and how much there is that is dubitable.[139] For this reason, it has become clear to him that, once in his life, everything must be toppled and built up anew from the first foundations,[140] should he ever wish to secure something that is stable and enduring in the sciences.[141] Because this is a monumental task, he has waited for an appropriately mature age. Now, however, things have come so far: at the right time, he has rid his mind of all worries and arranged for himself the leisure, in order to be prepared for the universal overthrow of his opinions.[142]

The experience is, on the one hand, similar as in Parmenides: The uncertainty of opinions tended to in the everyday become conspicuous, and, in fact, in contrast to the steadfastness and constancy of a truth, which one does not reach in everyday thought. For Descartes, too, everyday thought is two-headed: in it, the true and the false are mixed in an impenetrable manner. For Descartes, however, the pure truth is not *pointed out* as it was for Parmenides. It is rather *available*. Only appropriate precautions are needed, but then it is in principle no problem to find it. It is the thinking one himself who seeks out and secures in the sciences the steadfast and the enduring. His investigation also has time; until it is begun, it is still possible to live quite well with the mixture of the false and the true in all appearances. The philosopher is no longer pushed out from the double-headed life, rather, he is able to defer the foundation of secure knowledge as the establishment of stable science until the right age, until the favorable moment. The philosopher no longer undertakes a journey, but rather furnishes himself with leisure and draws himself back.[143]

The reason for the lassitude voiced in the *meditationes* comes to language in its central idea. The firm foundation that is laid bare by the assault on everyday opinion is the being of thought itself, that is, something that is never removed from the one who thinks: "I am," "I exist" —this is necessarily true, as often as I utter it to myself or comprehend it in my mind.[144] It is certain, as long as I think: "I am indeed a genuine and genuinely existing thing. But, what kind of thing? I have already said it: one that thinks."[145] This cannot be lost or missed like a truth that comes to us from outside. The truth is there, albeit not always explicitly. It is not achieved or experienced; it suffices that one lay it bare. It will not get lost. There is for this reason time to lay it bare.

There is a critical question to this approach. It comes from Heidegger and is formulated in his introduction, written in 1949, to his Freiburg inaugural lecture from 1929, "Was ist Metaphysik?" Heidegger here cites a passage from a letter by Descartes, in which Descartes compares philosophy, and, with it, metaphysics, to a tree, that is: he ascribes the search for firm foundations, through which the sciences receive stability as the task of the roots. Building on this, Heidegger wishes to know: "in which soil do the roots of the tree of philosophy find their support? From which grounds do the roots and, through them, the entire tree welcome the nourishing juices and powers? Which element, concealed in ground and soil, pervades the roots that bear and nourish the tree?" And then, in clarification of the comparison: "In what does the essence of metaphysics move and stir? What is metaphysics, seen from its ground? What, in principle, at all, is metaphysics?"[146]

Heidegger's reading of Descartes' statement is easily recognizable as subversive: The image of the tree is thought through to its consequences, and, in this way, discovered in its insufficiency. The roots that nourish and bare do not receive their power from themselves; rather, they are only organs, by means of which the tree draws nourishment from the soil, and through which it reaches into the earth that supports it. So, too, is metaphysics not the ground of philosophy, but rather arises from a ground. This ground must be questioned, if one wants to comprehend what metaphysics "in principle, at all," is. The grounding does not come from metaphysics itself, and, for that matter, does not construct metaphysics through its own power. No one constructs it. It is erected by no independent activity; rather, it happens [*es ereignet sich*].

What this means more precisely was developed by Heidegger in the inaugural lecture itself. Here, the characteristic question of metaphysics is formulated as that of "beings as a whole" [*das Seiende im Ganzen*].[147] Even if this appears at first glance to have nothing to do with Descartes' programmatic concern for grounding, it is for Heidegger nevertheless its presupposition. The dismantling of all opinions and their cloudy mixture of truth and falsity does indeed lead beyond orientation by the respective given thing, by the particular and individual; no attention is focused any longer on this, as what it respectively is, rather, the concern is solely with the question of its possible truth, which is understood as soundness—and, thereby, with the soundness and truth of everything. The journey of Parmenides, too, led to a similar experience: The truth shown to him by the goddess is that of the whole; it consists in the possibility of grasping the whole as such. Yet, for Heidegger, the focus is no longer on seeing "what is" [*Seiend*] in everything. The question is, rather, how the thought of "what is" is accessible as such. How, as Heidegger puts the question, do "beings as a whole" allow themselves to be experienced, and whereby is this experience philosophical? Heidegger gives his answer in two steps: the experience of beings as a whole goes back to a mood; and whether this is philosophical depends on the mood with which one is dealing.

The answer is sustained by a certain understanding of mood. For one, mood is involuntary, something that imposes itself, in Greek one would say: a πάθος.[148] And, for another, mood is not able to be linked to anything specific that brings joy or provokes fear. Mood is originary, it is like the weather; it colors every individual and particular thing. Heidegger illustrates this in what he calls "deep boredom"; that is, boredom that is a mood and no longer merely an affect, so that it is no longer that something bores one, but, rather, that "one is bored." "Deep boredom," Heidegger says, "moves to and fro in the abysses of Dasein like a silent fog, collapsing all things, human beings, and oneself together into a peculiar indifference." And then, as a consequence: "this boredom reveals beings as a whole."[149]

This experience, however, is not yet philosophical on Heidegger's understanding.[150] One experiences beings as a whole even in everyday Dasein; one "finds" oneself constantly in it, and in moods like boredom it emerges because at the same time what is recedes in its diversity and particularity. When one no longer has interest in anything, when nothing attracts one any more, then the "as a whole," as Heidegger puts it, "comes over" one.[151] However, it does not become explicit; it does not emerge as such. Beings as a whole envelop; it is like a situation from which one cannot get any distance.

This is different if there are moods that set at a distance; in this case, the "as a whole" would have to be connected with attentiveness to "being" [*seiend*]. Heidegger describes a mood of this kind: anxiety [*Angst*], which, as a "fundamental mood"[152] is raised above the moods that take hold of everyday Dasein and, certainly, from the fears that are directed toward specific beings. In anxiety, "it is uncanny to one;" the familiar trust in what is no longer obtains. Everything sinks into "indifference,"[153] not in such a way that things no longer matter, but, rather, in such a way that their fading familiarity imposes itself. Beings as a whole withdraw as the context of one's own existence [*Dasein*] and emerge precisely in this. Anxiety, Heidegger says, is a condition of suspension[154]; beings as a whole provide no hold anymore, and, precisely for this reason, are there in an especially pressing manner.

Heidegger sums up his discussion in the idea that anxiety reveals the nothing.[155] Nothing, *niht ihts*, as it is called in middle high German, is the "not something," the not something determinate, and, so, the indeterminate. It is a modification of the "as a whole" in such a way that now what is has become inconsequential. The nothing is not the fullness of wholeness but rather the emptiness of withdrawn meaning—it is the whole without sense and in this the whole is intensified as still only itself, the whole in and from which being becomes urgent as something that has disappeared. As the nothing, the not-being in which all being is emerges in its purity by detaching itself from what is.

Philosophy only becomes possible, to Heidegger's mind, with this experience of the nothing.[156] As "stepping beyond beings as a whole," anxiety is "transcendence," that is, it leads beyond the determinate in its context in such a way that first now beings as a whole are also capable of being asked about. Thus, anxiety is the origin of philosophy as metaphysics—that is, of the going above (μετά) what is (τὰ φυσικά),¹⁵⁷ for the sake of its conceptualization. Metaphysics is "questioning above and beyond what is, in order to get it back as such and as a whole for conceptualization."¹⁵⁸ By understanding philosophy as metaphysics based on the question, Heidegger follows a fundamental motivation of the philosophical tradition. Because Heidegger sees questioning and questionability to originate from the fundamental mood of anxiety, however, there is philosophically always only one question—that of beings as a whole. Philosophical questioning answers to the mood with which it originates, and answers only to this mood.

One sees that it can also be otherwise in a fourth and final model for the originariness of philosophy to be discussed here. The scene is a soirée. The host is a rich salesman, in old age, and inclined to the contemplativeness that is connected with this age, the time of retrospection. No wonder, then, that he enjoys conversation, especially, as he himself says, since the pleasure of talk increases the more that bodily satisfactions lose significance. This soon leads to the question of what makes old age bearable. The answer, given by the elder man in regard to the adage that there are many consolations for the rich, is unwavering and calm: The certainty to have done nothing unjust is the most important thing, that is, one must not remain in any debt, neither in sacrifices to a god, nor in money to a human being. In response it is asked whether justice, then, is to give back what one has had in one's care. To the objection that it surely could not be just to return a weapon deposited earlier for safekeeping to a person who had gone mad, the elder man responds lapidarily by agreeing. He is hardly still interested in the matter. And, why should he be? He has his affairs in order and no longer needs to tend to a question of this kind.

His son now intervenes in the conversation in his place. Certainly, he says, justice is precisely that, at least if one would be permitted to believe the poet Simonides. And, in the following discussion that takes this poet as a point of departure for the theme in question, it becomes increasingly clear that the concern cannot be with individual cases, insights anchored by life stories. Rather, it must be concerned with the clarification of what had already clearly been indicated in the inquiry made of the elder man: this very thing itself, justice.¹⁵⁹

With this question, this outlined scene from the first book of Plato's *Republic* identifies the theme that will determine the entire, long dialogue. It thus forms the nucleus for the grounding, which is realized in a thought experiment, of the most enduring *polis* (πόλις) possible, and, with it, the nucleus for the discussion of philosophy, which comes into play under the auspices of the question of rule [*Herrschaft*]. The concern is with the question of what philosophy is in its essence and this also determines its relation to politics: philosophers should rule because they are least bound up in the *polis* and for this reason have no interest in power. This is a new variation on the idea of the distance of philosophy from everyday life.

Yet, this distance must come into existence; something must interrupt the familiar obviousness of the everyday. This occurs here, in Plato's dialogue, as a shift in language. A word familiar in the everyday, "just," is all at once lifted out of the familiar context of its use. This does not occur because it had been used falsely or without sense; what the elder man, Cephalus, says is comprehensible, it makes sense. Things first become difficult with carrying the word over to another case. The elucidation given by Cephalus fails here; the elucidation was not meant for such a captiously devised case as the one brought into play. With this, it becomes apparent why linguistic expressions must be elucidated in the first place: they only have significance and can only be experienced as meaningful because they are usable in more than one situation. Universality belongs to the essence of language. What can be said belongs to no one; no word is for one person alone. Only because something cannot be said only once and only by one person is there language and a world that is communicated and is communicable in language.

This does not always have to be considered in speaking—not as long as agreement succeeds without bother or remains unnoticed in its failure. Yet, as soon as an expression is no longer able to be communicated, the expectation of universality becomes apparent. Further questions and objections are possibilities of making this explicit.

The question of the universal is not in every case philosophy, just as little as occasional doubt in one's own knowledge is. Only a possibility of philosophy is formed here. Cephalus' reflection is one such possibility that appears. Another lies in the doubt of Descartes, which leads to his retreat into the leisure of thorough reflection, another further one in the experience of the whole, which Heidegger describes. The situation first becomes philosophical in the moment of radical doubt, in the "fundamental mood," or, as in Plato's dialogue, as soon as the universal comes into view as such. This can be pointed to linguistically, for example, in the formulation that appears in the text of the *Republic*: this very thing itself, justice.

In the conversation with Cephalus, admittedly no impetus exists to pursue the matter. Cephalus gives the conversation over to a younger man, he himself withdraws. Nothing in this is to be reproached; he is able to live at peace with himself without a discussion that pursues things to the grounds, and, with this, he can do what he understands as the just. One may represent Cephalus as a just human being; his way of life [*Lebensführung*] has stood firm in the face of every test. This is clearly to be read into his conduct, in that no impetus for testing exists at all.

The impetus for the realization of the philosophical possibility exists first in the conversation with Polemarchus, his son. This one, however, is ensnared by language; he does not speak from experience, but, rather, summons what is said with authority, which suggests that one should bend to its authority.

If it is possible to draw Polemarchus into the conversation and convince him that it is better not simply to follow the poet's word, but, rather, to ask how it is to be understood, then he can come to an understanding that, because of his lack of life experience, he has not yet developed himself. For him, the discussion of the universal can be orienting, and, for this reason, it is good to use the possibility opened up by language.

Does this possibility really originate from language, however? The one who questions further in the conversation with Cephalus and introduces the formulation, "this very thing itself, justice," has not, up until now, been discussed. He—obviously Socrates—has of course, as one might suspect, directed the conversation so that it ultimately took the philosophical course. Here, then, philosophy would not have originated from language, rather, Socrates, the philosopher *par excellence* for the author of *Republic*, would already have brought philosophy with him into the house of Cephalus. The opportunity to put into play what he brought with him comes soon enough, and, ultimately, one expects this from him.

If one rereads the beginning of the *Republic* once again, and sees how deliberately the conversation at Cephalus' is directed by the question of how to live one's life, one will not be able to dismiss the objection so easily. Yet, on the other hand, the Socratic guidance of the conversation is only possible because language allows and suggests it, perhaps even demands it. That an expression does not simply stand on its own, but, rather, is bound up with others because it is concerned with the same matter, makes agreement possible and necessary—newly every time, as soon as the familiar obviousness of the everyday no longer holds. Philosophy, in this case, originates. And Socrates, or another, is the one who *perceives* it, that is, recognizes and realizes it, in its origination.

That the presented conceptions are really models is in principle supposed to have become clear. The originariness of philosophy was outlined four times; with this, philosophy was shown to be underivable in how it belongs to the essence of origin. The image [*Bild*] of ascension found in Parmenides provides the most vivid portrait of the break with the everyday. It is the archetype [*Urbild*] for all images of journey and ascent, in terms of which philosophy is presented right up to the moderns, as may be found with special clarity in Nietzsche: "Beginning of August 1881 in Sils-Maria, 6000 feet about the sea and much higher above all human things!"[160] Philosophy admittedly needs images in order to grasp itself as a whole in its characteristic attitude; the development of ideas and argumentation are written and said on the basis of this attitude, so that the attitude remains operative in them, although imperceptibly.[161]

In Descartes, things remain more a matter of the everyday, and, accordingly here, as well as in Heidegger and in Plato's dialogue, the commonality of everydayness and philosophy is also recognizable. Even before he resolved deliberately to carry out his experiment in doubt, there had already been occasional doubt for Descartes in the trustworthiness of his knowledge. According to Heidegger's description, the "as a whole" comes up occasionally in a mood without being opened up by philosophical inquiry. Justice, finally, is often the topic of discussion in political life; wherever there is to be the settlement of different interests and relations of power, the question of the justice of a conduct, a person, or a community, is always and again posed.

Yet, all of these are possible impetuses, not grounds, for philosophy. As Heidegger's critical question of Descartes brings out, even philosophy can become an impetus for philosophizing. The same text toward which Heidegger directs his question could just as easily be the impetus for an investigation in the history of ideas, or for considerations of an editorial nature. These possibilities do not proceed on the basis of the impetuses of philosophical thought.

The four presented models also do not explain the possibility of philosophical thought. Yet, they present this possibility and attempt, each in its own way, to show what it is to come to this possibility. This possibility is thereby more or less penetratingly elucidated; it is made intelligible in different respects. If one follows the presentations and elucidations, the originariness of philosophy proves itself to be a matter that is as differentiated as it is unified.

§ 6. Moments of Origin

Descartes names three things that are essential to him for the philosophical investigation he undertakes: Without leisure (*otium*), it appears that it cannot be carried out, and, in carrying it out, one must be serious (*serie*) and free (*libere*). According to this view, philosophy involves a *pause* and a *peace* that only arise when one has achieved *freedom* from the obligations and pressures of the day; the retreat to the study is nothing other than an outward expression of this. The retreat could nevertheless also be inconspicuous, disguised as a stroll, or as a wait at the train station or airport. Besides, it is not as if leisure and freedom were two distinct things, such that leisure would somehow be able to precede freedom. Leisure is not the same as doing nothing. It is less a condition than a disposition, one enabled by freedom and aware of freedom.[162] It is what first makes it possible for one to gain the kind of access to something that allows it to come into view as "impartially" as possible, that is, not colored by dependency, interests, or pressures to act. Only thus may a matter be investigated seriously, that is, not just superficially, in the sense of the common parlance and manner of thought.

Descartes made the perception of this freedom dependent on the disciplining of thought. Thought, as he determines it, should follow a "method," that is: it should be oriented by a unified complex of those considerations (*considerations*) and rules (*maxims*) that would allow it to cultivate and increase its knowledge as much as possible.¹⁶³ Even if this method were to be developed in accord with the model of geometry and mathematics—a thoroughgoing mathematization of thought is not intended. As the four principal rules named by Descartes make recognizable, the sense of his method is foremost the practice of a certain cognitive disposition. The concern is to be cautious of hastiness and prejudices in the investigation of something, and to pay attention to differentiation, structuration, and completeness.¹⁶⁴ Even one who is only partially certain of these things is able, with the lassitude described in the mediations, to do work in philosophy. It is the lassitude of a pause; it allows one to tarry on a matter and the concepts in which it is supposed to be articulated.

If Heidegger wishes to make philosophy intelligible on the basis of a "fundamental mood," then this is to be read as an objection to the Cartesian understanding of philosophy. His reference to a "fundamental mood" expresses the idea that the practice of deliberate and careful procedure is not enough for philosophy. Rather, a distinctive impetus is required for mental abilities capable of unfolding in one way or another to become philosophical. Without this impetus, supported solely by the reliability of method, the investigation of something remains science—research bound by unquestioned claims, which does not attain to the presuppositionlessness of philosophy. The distance from the everyday, the pause in regard to its familiar settings, which Husserl named with the concept of the ἐποχή, and which Descartes saw to be protected by methodological doubt, Heidegger trusts solely to the "fundamental mood."

Heidegger's idea still reverberates in Gadamer's understanding of hermeneutical experience; in this experience, too, something affects one that cannot be opened up by any method. On the contrary, the possibility of the experience is concealed by the orientation toward a method; that prejudices can only be corrected through experience remains out of view when one takes the avoidance of prejudices through method to be possible. Therefore, it is consequential when Gadamer moves toward a rehabilitation of prejudices based on his conception of hermeneutical experience: prejudices are not in principle misleading, but, rather, nothing more than the convictions always already operative—prejudgments, in the literal sense of the word,* to which experience moors itself.¹⁶⁵

This objection to the unfaltering trust in method is illuminating; it in fact belongs to philosophizing that something affects one. Otherwise, the radical break with the everyday that belongs to philosophy would not be intelligible. The doubt that Descartes takes as the impetus for his meditations must be pervaded by a deeper uncertainty, which cannot be attached to *any one* dubitable thing. Only thus is he able to find the radicality of the philosophical

---

*[The English "prejudices," is a translation of *Vorurteile* here, which might be translated literally as "pre-judgments." In this passage, then, "prejudgments" is a translation of Figal's *Vor-urteile*.—Trans.]

experiment. If this doubt becomes encompassing, something has happened that displaces one from the course of everyday life.

That Heidegger wants to understand this displacement as anxiety is, however, less illuminating; anxiety, as it is described in the Freiburg inaugural lecture as the fundamental mood of philosophy, has little to do with what one otherwise understands under the rubric of anxiety. That it bears "no opposition to joy" and stands in a "secret bond with cheerfulness and the gentleness of creative longing,"[166] barely admits of a connection with the oppressive feeling of groundlessness as Heidegger had described anxiety in *Sein und Zeit*. Wittgenstein identified how the fundamental mood is actually intended in a statement from a conversation in 1929, the same year of Heidegger's inaugural lecture. He can "certainly think what Heidegger" meant "by being and anxiety." "Think, for example, of the astonishment that something exists. This astonishment cannot be expressed in the form of a question, and there is also simply no answer."[167] The question of why there is this particular thing, or something in general, could only be understood as a question of the ground for existence; but such a question is not at all intended in astonishment. In fact, astonishment could be articulated in such a question; however, it is itself more like what Heidegger describes as anxiety: a dizziness of unfamiliarity [*Unselbstverständlichkeit*].[168] This sense of astonishment was described first by Plato.[169] It is the characteristic way that philosophers are affected, philosophy's experience of origin.

If one wanted to grasp somewhat more precisely what occurs in astonishment, one would have to think of an ungrounded and undirected attentiveness, of an awakening of a view, which was displaced toward and which comes from outside. What is experienced here is not just disconcertedness [*Befremdlichkeit*]. To be disconcerted is relative, it is connected with familiarity and is defined by it. It is more as if something were removed, and then, lightning fast, put back, brought to a distance, and, at the same time, moved into an unfamiliar present. In this case, astonishment would be a caesura in *time*. It is like a magnification of what always occurs in time: something withdraws, something is there. Only here it occurs *in the blink of an eye*; a being-there [*Dasein*] from a being-withdrawn [*Entegnozsein*]; a being-withdrawn that is just as emphatically being-there [*Dasein*].

If this consideration hits the mark, there is no originariness without time, more precisely, without the tear between being-there [*Dasein*] and being-away [*Wegsein*], between the determinable and conceivable and its negation, as which the nothing may be portrayed and which Heidegger determines as "nothing" [*Nichten*].[170] It is not a temporal tear, but, rather, a tear of time itself, comparable to the "sudden" (τὸ ἐξαίφνης) that, as the "between," (μεταξύ) holds things together whose opposition prevents them from being connected.[171]

Such a between comes into focus in the philosophical fundamental mood as Heidegger describes it; there is not an inner experience of something determinate as withdrawn—lost, past, no longer accessible—but, rather, it is withdrawal in general. This withdrawal is not emptiness, however, but is rather of such a kind that the unfamiliarity of what is disclosed, the unwithdrawn, arises from it at the same time. Heidegger saw this idea concentrated in one word, which brings accessibility based on withdrawal to language: ἀλήθεια is unconcealment, openness conceived on the basis of closedness.[172] In his inaugural lecture, Heidegger says in this sense of the nothing that it is "the antecedent that makes possible the revelation of what is in general."[173] Only "on the basis of the originary apparentness [Offenbarkeit] of the nothing" can "the existence [Dasein] of the human being approach and enter among what is."[174]

These formulations indicate an understanding of the originary that is characteristic for Heidegger's thought differently than the talk of unconcealment does: If the originary is the "antecedent," which is something that grounds, then it precedes something else. It is the *inaugural* [Anfängliche], not in the sense of a beginning that can be fixed in time, but, rather, as that to which one must return in order to experience and understand something different.

This idea is to be found already in the *Natorp-Bericht*: the "originary sources of motivation," which Heidegger here wishes to achieve through "dismantling return,"[175] are, according to the conception of the Freiburg inaugural lecture, supposed to be disclosed through the "fundamental mood" of anxiety. With this, the historical character of the originary is in fact more clearly to be recognized in the *Natorp-Bericht* than in the inaugural lecture; the originary stands here as the inauguration of tradition, which was to be freed up again through "dismantling return." Yet, when Heidegger understands the task of philosophy in the inaugural lecture as "the setting-into-motion of metaphysics," "in which it comes home to itself and to its explicit task,"[176] he is still following the same program. And, just as already in the *Natorp-Bericht*, this program is shaped by a single question: philosophy is always already the question of the being of beings [*das Sein des Seienden*], and has remained it. Therefore, it is necessary to get *behind* this question and to be open for its inauguration.[177]

The originary, however, is not something inaugural that is "displaced" by a superficial orientation toward beings, and that can only be there when we no longer "turn to our dealings with beings," and press "into the public surface of existence [Dasein]."[178] The originary is all of the sudden there amidst "what is" whenever something undergoes the radical loss of its familiar obviousness. A tear goes through the matter that one is dealing with, the matter withdraws and imposes itself; on the one hand, it is lost and yet, on the other, becomes a matter even more decisively. One will only say that it thereby attracts attention as something that *is*, however, if the description stands in an ontological perspective from the outset. Otherwise, it could also be as in the scene from the *Republic*: the question of the very thing itself, justice, is philosophical and yet has nothing to do with ontology.

The scene moreover helps make clear that the turn to philosophy does not remain in the suspension and ineffability of a mood alone. The attitude has changed, and this, in turn, is the result of a possibility of *language*. A word, which to this point, had been used more or less unquestioningly, is all at once like a riddle, and, at the same time, is like a promise. It no longer signifies, and nevertheless does not become an unintelligible sign. It is more as if the word now first really stands in for a matter: It stands in for what was always in play as something respectively encountered and thoroughly different that was signified and that one believed oneself obviously to know of as what it is. Yet, because one believed it and had still not known that he believed it, he had not inquired into it. Language sets free both possibilities and thereby the absolute, and ultimately inexplicable, shift of attitude.

One would not inquire if one were not sure that there is also here something to know. When it is philosophical, the disappearance of familiar obviousness has to do with the desire to find orientation or to overcome confusion as much as possible. It is no failure, but, rather, a new possibility: the opening of a path that was not known, but that had been sensed. That, and how, this path now unfolds before one is not something that can be derived from the everyday. Measured against the everyday it comes from outside; yet, its direction does not break into every day life, but is, rather, a possibility of stepping beyond this, which comes to this life itself, when it does not remain imprisoned within itself. The journey that Parmenides represents stands for this; it lies outside the common course of human beings,[179] a direction that one does not take in the everyday. Yet, this journey does not proceed into emptiness; it leads, rather, into the open. The goddess stands for its goal, the approaching possibility of insight.

One should take care not to be misled by the image, with which Parmenides opens his didactic poem, or by all other philosophical images of ascension and distance. Even if the talk is of "places beyond the heavens,"[180] philosophical travels do not lead beyond this world, but, rather, only illustrate the distance between the accustomed and the philosophically experienced world. With the origination of philosophy, one would in fact get out of the everyday, but not out of the world. Distance is intended here less as a departure from a place than as the shift in attitude that may be seen in Descartes, Heidegger, and Plato; what is image in Parmenides is found in Descartes as autobiographical report, in Plato as literary depiction of a scene of origin. The changed attitude entails a freedom from everyday activity—leisure—that is at the same time the freedom to investigate. It does not obtain without the fold of withdrawal and opening in the figure-ground picture puzzle of the nothing and being. And, it cannot be thought without the shift in language that leads from indication to the word itself and to its substantiveness.

The models taken up here are instructive, because, in their comparability, they make the commonality of the moments mentioned above comprehensible.

At the same time, they make recognizable that the attempt to describe the originariness of philosophy on the basis of just one moment is insufficient. The exclusive emphasis on freedom underestimates occurrence in the origin. Concentration on occurrence and being affected, in turn, allows one to forget freedom, and, with it, the responsible discipline of how to proceed. And, if one takes the scene from the *Republic* in such isolation as it was taken here, then, in this case, it also does not provide a sufficient picture.

The aforementioned moments of philosophy that are understood as originary also arise in the everyday world. Peaceful pausing, being-present [*Dasein*] and being-withdrawn [*Entzogensein*], the characteristically substantive meaning of a word, as well as doubt, the experience of the "as a whole," and the question of what something is, may be experienced in the everyday. One would also not hesitate to call an interplay of these moments philosophy. It could come upon the everyday and nevertheless be included in the context of everyday life. The interplay of these moments of origin first attains the character of philosophy, when it intensifies in a characteristic manner and, in this way, is able to be at work and exist for itself.

What precisely this is supposed to mean may be made most clear, again, in regard to the *Republic*. The discussion of justice transforms into something philosophical only once the problem is experienced to a certain degree. It could, however, lose its philosophical character once again. The philosophical question becomes unavoidable first when no everyday possibilities for a solution take hold any longer, say, because the understanding of justice disseminated in the everyday is too suggestive simply to be dismissed, and, on the other hand, is not convincing. This is how it is when the apparent forms of what one calls "justice," even in critical comparison, no longer lead to a satisfying answer, and when the consideration of the consequences of just action leads to just as little progress. In this case, the question may arise: what power does justice itself, the very thing itself, have, if it inheres in the soul?[181]

What occurs here may be signified as *intensification* of questioning and making clear. *Intensio* is the tension, *intensus* means "strong," or also "tense." In this, the concern is not, however, with some arbitrary tension of a greater or lesser scale. In order for a question or a discussion to become philosophical, a certain tension, a certain *degree of intensity*, must be reached. With this, a matter is on the one hand more clear than before, yet on the other hand the matter is no longer simply itself. The tension no longer lets it be intelligible in the previously familiar manner, and, on the other hand, a "more" of intelligibility has arisen. It is as if the matter were to enter into a new aggregate state. It does not change, and, yet, it is entirely different; the new aggregate state, which cannot be derived from the old one, allows it to emerge otherwise, and, in this otherness, to be understood better, indeed, more intensely.

The concept of this degree of intensity comes from a different context. It was coined by Carl Schmitt to determine the essence of the political. Schmitt did not determine the political on the basis of institutions or through the treatment of specific political questions or problems, but, rather, as the "degree of intensity of an association or disassociation of human beings."[182] The political can, as Schmitt states, "draw its power from the most diverse spheres of human life, from religious, economic, moral, and other oppositions"[183]; every problem can become political, and this occurs as soon as a distinctively intense consciousness of belonging together or disassociation appears.

If Schmitt sees this intensification as given in the "distinction of friend and enemy,"[184] then this is not unambiguous. Yet, although some passages of his writing are able to suggest this, he does not think that there is only politics where a group of human beings actively turn themselves against another one. Definitive for the political is the real, not merely abstract, but recognizably given, *possibility* of enmity; that a group *is prepared* to defend its economic order, its religious and moral convictions, is enough to make it political. This can be prepared and occur all at once, so that the political, too, proves to be something originary. According to the aforementioned determination, institutions are political when they are established for the possibility of danger and are geared toward it. First under the auspices of possible jeopardy to communal life is there politics.[185]

That Schmitt conceives of his concept of the political on the basis of possible jeopardy corresponds to the essence of intensity. A real clash between peoples or social groups is no longer formed by tension. A relation is tense whenever differences and oppositions fail to overcome difference and opposition—whenever they are bound together, and, in this boundedness, fail to resolve what is contestatory in its relation. In this respect, intensity always arises from an unstable peace; if whoever is different or in opposition could settle his relation, the tension would be dissolved.

The intensity that is essential to philosophy, would, accordingly, come about because it finds no conclusive answer. A moment of openness always remains, which places the answer under reservation. Nevertheless, this is grounded not so much in the inconclusiveness of every questioning and answering as in the originariness of philosophy. Certainly, every question may be put anew into a question; every further question that is identified as substantive is an impetus for a more or less fundamental revision. Just as philosophy came into view through models, however, its originary moments exclude what would be understood as a "solution" in the everyday sense. Thus, they remain in *suspension*, and allow being in suspension in being experienced.[186]

This allows to be shown how something is encountered philosophically. If this occurs in the manner of a self-giving that is in itself withdrawn, that is, with Heidegger: in the interplay of being and nothing, then it is, in this case, impossible to get hold of what one is encountering. The astonishing does not integrate into the familiar. The freedom to devote one's attention to something experienced as leisure is just as little directed toward a solution. As long as it holds, it finds of itself no end. It can cease, be interrupted, but it is not predisposed toward an end; it has no aim. Of characteristic openness, finally, is the form of language that is characteristic of philosophy. The question of "something itself" promises a knowledge of the matter that is not present in the everyday signification of things; instead of taking something into view based on respective interests in it, one allows oneself to get involved impartially in the question of what it is. It is, accordingly, not as an easy answer that this will win the day in the play of interests. One would only do it justice in the attempt to think it through anew; the conclusions that it offers are given only from the standpoint of presuppositionlessness. This does not mean that philosophical descriptions would have nothing to do with the everyday world. They simply grasp this world as if from outside; in this, they are comparable to great literature. Its comprehension is without the demand of a result. What is described is a world, in which there is also action, but the description does not unfold from the perspective of action.

If one considers the originary moments of philosophy in their relation once again more precisely, it becomes apparent that they are dependent upon one another in a characteristic manner. What is encountered in self-withdrawal is encountered only in the freedom to devote one's attention to something; otherwise it would perhaps appear in a flash, but would just as soon be concealed once again through the requirements of the everyday. Conversely, freedom to devote one's attention to something is only what it is through the astonishing; it is after all only attentiveness as attentiveness to *something*; the astonishing, by affecting one, sets the devotion of one's attention free. That one's devotion of attention to something must be articulated should be illuminating without adding anything further; if it were to remain speechless, it would have no direction toward what is encountered, and could not, then, really be a devotion of attention. To devote attention to the astonishing means: to find words for it, which are articulations of its nontransparency. Without coming to language, however, what is encountered is also not what it is. It could not unfold, but, rather, would remain a momentary impetus and would not set free any devotion of attention. On the other hand, the relation of what is encountered and the devotion of attention is not dissolved in language. The fact that something affects one does not arise solely language, and, without freedom, life in language could not be a search for nontransparent words. That the playing of language games on occasion stops and language—as Wittgenstein puts it—"goes on holiday,"[187] does not have its ground in language alone.

If the moments of origin relate in this manner, then none can be traced back to the others, and, at the same time, each of them is bound to the others. None of them operates "straightaway," simply as itself; rather, the effect of each is indirect in a characteristic manner; in this way, one's conduct, as well as what is encountered in it, is held back or bracketed, put in ἐποχή. Through this, the interplay of the moments as such comes forth. What is encountered operates through the devotion of one's attention and only in language. The devotion of one's attention operates only on the basis of what is encountered and in regard to it; it operates by coming to words, and, through this, it provides openness to language, which allows it to be philosophical. Each moment operates only through *mediation* in the others, so that the originariness of philosophy is, in its essence, mediated. It is only originary as mediated. There is not first an origin after which mediation then sets in. With the indirectness of the moments of origin, mediation is what originates, so that mediation itself is originary.

In everyday language, "to mediate" means to bring two opposing positions into conversation, to work at a settlement between them and perhaps even to reach the settlement. In an older manner of speech, it also means to reach something else through something that serves as a means. In every case, the mediatory is represented as a third between two moments that would have no—or, at least, no successful—relation without it. In contrast, mediation is here meant as the essential indirectness of something. Whatever is mediated in accord with its essence only comes into focus through others and yet does not dissolve into these others. Mediation is thus both dependency and difference in one; it is never total or absolute mediation that leads to immediacy or unity. Mediation is meant here in a *hermeneutical* sense, in the sense of carrying over [*Übertragen*]. Something is there in something else, and yet is able to be recognized in this otherness as what it is. If a text is carried over into another language, then the result is a text, which is not simply itself, but which also does not refer only to another. A translation is the otherness of the translated text; through it, the translated text is present, and nevertheless withdrawn. Now, if something is carried over not through an activity that is added to it, but is rather instead itself a carrying over, then it is never present without its otherness. In this case, every word is indirect, none is spoken on the basis of its own power or its possession of the articulated matter. In this case, every word holds for a matter which is never put into the word as itself and which is nevertheless not hidden. Like the word, the matter is also indirect. It is not withdrawn, but, rather, is given in mediation; it is not there solely from itself, but, rather, through another. What is there through the other, however, is the matter.

Mediation in this sense is the essence of philosophy, at least, according to a story told in the *Symposium*. Here, Eros, the divine power that determines philosophizing, is signified as a mediator. He carries over and transmits to the gods what comes from the humans, and to the humans what comes from the gods: from the one, prayers and sacrifices, from the other, commands and replies to sacrifices. Thus, in the intermediary between both as the one who mediates, he fulfills a whole in which he is himself bound.[188] Eros is represented here as a being that stands between gods and humans—as an in-between-being, a demigod. Yet, no mythical being of the described kind is intended. Eros is the divine in human beings, in the gods, what appears to human beings as prescriptions. Human beings are related to the gods erotically, and realize this relation in a human way: in prayer and sacrifice. In contrast, the relation of the gods to human beings is something that exceeds human measure and nevertheless appears in human life: commands and replies, divine messages.

That philosophy—even without all of the mythical pictures—is hermeneutical in its essence is up until now admittedly only a claim. It may not be unilluminating. Nevertheless, it was only achieved in models; it has not been supported by an investigation concentrated on the matter itself. The mediated and mediating character of philosophical knowing is still in need of clarification, and, to this end, one must in turn say what, precisely, a mediated and mediating knowing is.

The matter at issue here is *the hermeneutical*, in that broad sense of the word that encompasses both hermeneutical experience as well as its objects. In the determination of the hermeneutical, thought has proved itself if it is itself to be counted as a degree of intensity of the hermeneutical. By achieving clearer contours of the hermeneutical, the possibility emerges, at the same time, of a hermeneutical philosophy. This is demonstrated through the identification of where it comes from; it will appear as what it is by determining its matter.

In this sense, the task is now to inquire into something that is in an especially palpable matter a mediation of the kind that was indicated here as the essence of the hermeneutical. Mediation in its most familiar, and, for hermeneutics, most definitive sense, is interpretation.

Chapter 2

Interpretation

§ 7. Carrying Over

Interpretation is mediation, the *interpres* is the negotiator, the translator. He brings the standpoint of one home to another, and so also confirms that the standpoints are different; he formulates something that was said by one so that it is intelligible for another. Yet, there is not always a need of the third; often enough one takes on the third's task oneself. In this case, the mediation is then not an aid to help one out of a difficult situation, but, rather, a recognizing. This is the guiding question of the following discussion: what kind of recognizing is interpreting?

When one brings home the other, a *carrying over* occurs: something that is other, alien, is carried toward and to, made one's own, and, in this, recognized. The process, as the word suggests,* is determined by distance and removal; something is somewhere other than where it is, and then one fetches it here. This is something different from a rash seizure, and this could mean that not all appropriations are also carryovers. Carryovers are appropriations of a special kind; what kind it is needs to be made clear.

Moreover, one should distinguish carrying over from interpretation. Carrying over, *transferre*, μεταφέρειν, is a different word than interpretation, *interpretari*, also ἑρμηνεύειν, and so until the contrary is shown, perhaps, too, not the same matter. Interpreting could be a special kind of carrying over. Precision is thus not only a question of terminology; only when concepts are made clear in their substantive relation to one another is something conceived with them.

First, something more on appropriation: The pencil there on the table that one takes in one's hand in order to make note of an idea is appropriated—not in the sense of taking possession but rather in order to do something with it. It is recognized in a specific manner: as something for writing. This "something as something"—Heidegger calls it the "hermeneutical as"[1]—indicates an

---

*[My translation of "carrying over" from the German *Übertragen* also serves as a literal translation. —Trans.]

understanding that is in fact a mediation but not a carrying over. The pencil is in fact recognized on the basis of writing, the writing is realized by means of the pencil. Yet, it requires no special capacity to recognize the pencil as a writing instrument. Familiarity with writing implements is always part and parcel of an ability to write that has been acquired and practiced. One was well prepared, then, to recognize the thing on the table immediately as a writing instrument. Certainly, recognizing may not always be so easy; it would take a second look to recognize that this peculiarly formed thing is likewise a writing implement. Or, no appropriate tool is to be found; then one drives the nail into the wall with a stone instead of a hammer.

This, however, is no carrying over. Instead of recognizing something immediately as something, one had simply *discovered* it as something, namely, the stone as a possible tool. One knew what had to be done, and, likewise, how something must be fashioned to be suitable to drive nails. Prepared in this way, one was able to discover the stone "as something." The appropriation was possible because there was already something like a field of one's own abilities and possibilities.

Things are similar in the understanding of linguistic expressions. A sentence of one's own language, which is understood, has not been carried over into one's own usage, and, if interpretation is a special case of carrying over, then the sentence was not interpreted, either.[2] It was simply understood. The failure of understandings is not an indication that one is dealing with a carrying over here either. It is just that the unquestioned assumption is not fulfilled, that the other speaker uses the expression more or less exactly as one himself. This also may be experienced in the conduct of persons: a gesture that one understood as a greeting was only an attempt to take out and look at a wristwatch. The error is possible because the two look similar enough to mix up and because a gesture like this belongs to the repertoire of common possibilities of expression. Where there is such a repertoire—as in every language and in every shared life—what is one's own and what is other are not fundamentally separated; they belong together in what is had in common.

By contrast, distance always remains when things are carried over; something that already belongs to one's own domain of life does not have to be carried over into it. In carrying over, familiar obviousness is absent; sometimes it may appear as risky or even as inappropriate, say, in the case when one carries over insights, which someone achieved in regard to one matter, to a completely different one, and, thus, applies the insights of another person in one's own, clearly different, context.[3]

What one makes one's own in the sense of carrying over is, in principle, *recognizable*, as something other. As long as the carrying over is conscious, the appropriation remains under reservation; because carrying over refers to where it comes from, it remains in suspension itself. The sense for this otherness may become weaker or disappear so that one no longer recognizes a carrying over as such. The insight can, however, be won back; one had taken something for one's own that had actually been carried over, and the error is now corrected. The sense of distance that belongs to carrying over is awakened anew.

Yet, something could also be transformed so much in its being carried over that it would no longer be recognizable as what it is. The only indication that one is still dealing with a carrying over would then be the process of carrying over itself. Nietzsche generalized the concept of carrying over under this assumption and wished to understand every instance of knowledge—more than this, every substantive reference—as carrying over, or, the same in Greek, "metaphor," and also "interpretation."[4] In his early, in some regards programmatic treatise, *Ueber Wahrheit und Lüge im aussermoralischen Sinne*, he projects a picture of knowledge in which it appears as a succession of discontinuous carryovers. First, a "stimulation of the nerves [is] . . . carried over into an image," then, the "image is reconstituted once again into a sound." And, "every time," there is a "complete leap across spheres, right into one completely different and new." Nietzsche illustrates the idea in regard to a physical experiment in which a thin layer of sand on a plate is displaced by vibration in such a way that it forms sound waves.[5] Just as a deaf man who "had never had a sensation of sound and music" might assert "that he now had to know what human beings call sound," so it is "for all of us with language:" "we believe to know something of the things themselves, and yet posses nothing but metaphors of things that correspond not in the least to the original essentialities."[6]

Against this description it could first of all be objected—in a repetition of Hegel's critique of the "thing in itself"[7]—that even though their inaccessibility is asserted the talk is of "things" and "originary essentialities." In Hegel's signification for the things in themselves, these are ghosts[8]; by speaking of them, one suggests an outside apart from representational image and language that does not exist for them.

Yet, Nietzsche does not have to feel struck by this objection. He also thinks that things in themselves are ghosts. It is not his concern to distinguish "metaphors" as the mere appearance of things from their inaccessible substantiality. He is interested, rather, in the "leap" from one "sphere" into another; one "metaphor" follows upon another, and reality exists, then, in this exchange of metaphors; "carrying over," or "interpretation" is the one thing that exists at all. Nietzsche later challenges "positivism" on the existence of facts in this sense—"no, there are simply not facts, only interpretations"—and, he objects to subjectivism, the subject, too, is an "interpretation," "not something given, but a fabrication that has been superadded to, stuck there behind."[9] "Finally," he suggests, however, it is completely unnecessary "to pose further interpretation behind interpretation."[10] Since there are not even any "facts," the world is nothing other than a mixture of "interpretations" that have effects on one another as "forces." As "force throughout, as play of forces and exchange of force," the world is a "monster of force," "a sea of raging and flooding forces." It is, as Nietzsche puts it with the leading concept of his that replaces the concept of force, "will to power—and nothing else."[11]

With this totalization of carrying over, or, "interpretation," however, the point of departure has changed: If carryovers are supposed to be nothing other than forces with effects on one another, then they are no longer really carryovers. Every carrying over, which is recognizable as such, must be able to be *traced back* to its point of extraction; even if this may, for its part, be understood as a carrying over, it would have to be distinguishable for the later carrying over as something, from which it comes. *Insofar as* this something is to be carried over, it is no carrying over, but, rather, something that is of *substantive* significance; whether it can be determined as a carrying over in other regards is not important for its status *in* a carrying over. Thus, an idea can be carried over into a new context. What is carried over is, in this case, *this* idea. If it should itself come about through a carrying over, this is, for the later carrying over either unimportant or it is an integral moment of that idea, which is the point of departure for it, and, therefore, a moment of the matter to be carried over.

That Nietzsche does not consider the point of extraction of a carrying over and, with this, its substantive significance, is already to be seen in the early writing on truth and lies. What he signifies here as "metaphor" is a "complete leap across spheres," not, to wit, a carrying over, but a break. In his later idea of the "will to power,"[12] he takes up the earlier idea of "metaphor" once again. A will to power is a center of force that is directed toward only its own possibility. It does not refer to something else as this center of force, however, but, rather, finds in others only impetuses for its own enhancement, or, as Nietzsche himself once says: "a something that wants to grow . . . which interprets every other something that wants to grow on the basis of its value."[13] Even if "will acts on will"[14] in this way, and other wills are appraised solely from the standpoint of "value," this occurrence of willing is no carrying over; and if interpretation is a special case of carrying over, then it is also no interpretation. Nothing is taken up and taken over that remains distinguishable as such. Rather, everything is posed only as a matter of "value," that is, as "condition of preservation and enhancement."[15] Everything that is suitable to these ends is taken up into the will's field of force, in order to multiply the will's development of forces and its force. What Nietzsche calls interpretation is in truth assimilation, the "incorporation of the outside world," as it is once called.[16] Even though a will to power is able to develop its dynamic solely through its own challenge to what is exterior, there is no outside for it.[17]

This is different for carrying over rightly understood; there is always something that does not dissolve in its result. Precisely because the point of extraction is preserved in its process, a *reference* arises though it. Yet, the reference is often formed so one-sidedly that Nietzsche's understanding of carrying over as integration is comprehensible. The relationship of two moments, which have been referred to one another through a carrying over, is, indeed, not always constituted as it would be in the carrying over of a method to a different specialized area. Here, the relationship is symmetrical; the two specialized areas can be compared to one another, and it is for this reason possible to decide whether carrying over the method makes sense. Things are different when, for example, one carries over the insights of another to one's own situation in life. This may in fact be an application in the sense of Gadamer's elucidation of practical knowledge as a matter of knowing what is good for oneself. Even if the motivation for this carrying over is substantive, however, it still remains shaped completely by the one who is carrying over. What is carried over, and how, is, in its possibilities and motives, predetermined.

Nietzsche named this the "perspectival character of existence,"[18] and did not see this as a mere qualification; in another passage he signifies "the perspectival" as "the fundamental condition of all life."[19] The idea goes back to Leibniz; he introduces the concept of perspective into philosophy, and, in fact, in a manner that remains binding for Nietzsche. In the *Monadologie*, Leibniz employs the image of a town to illustrate the essence of the simple—that is, not compound—substances, the "monads" out of which the world is formed: just as one and the same town, looked at from various sides, appears differently and as if in multiple perspectives, so too, by reason of the infinite number of simple substances, it is as if there were just as many different worlds, which, nevertheless, are nothing other than perspectives on a single world, according to the different viewpoints of every monad.[20] "Perspectival" in this sense refers to a limited view onto the world, whose limitation is fixed by its respective point of view (*point de vue*). Every view, then, is holistic: Everything that is seen is joined together with a world—just as every city view is a view of this city, even when one does not see the city completely.

The perspectival concerns not only what is seen, however, but also and above all the one who sees. Perspectivity is not a quality of a "simple substance" that would be determined independently of such a quality. Rather, perspectivity constitutes the being of the simple, that is, not compound,[21] substances; these substances are determined by nothing other than a unified view. Accordingly, the multitude of substances is to be grasped as the diversity of "perception," *perception*.[22] A simple substance is a "soul" (*âme*)[23] and is determined solely by its unified openness to the world, itself enacted in diverse ways. Therefore, it is not a contradiction when Leibniz says that they have no windows.[24] On the contrary, it is consequential: If something could get into or come out of the monads, there would be a difference between them and their world, and then they could no longer be determined as respectively complete perceptions of the world. In accordance with this determination, the world is always restlessly present in the perspective of every single monad. Every monad is a living, perpetual mirror of the universe[25]; every resident of the city is, in his own way, the whole city.

Nietzsche appropriates this understanding of the perspectival and makes it more dynamic. The place of the simple substances is taken by the many wills—"resolutions of the will that constantly increase or lose power."[26] Also for them, however, just as for the monads, there is no difference from the world. There is will itself and *its* world only according to how it succeeds in taking hold of the world—in an "interpretation" whose "essence" is "to overpower, to push into shape, to abbreviate, to omit, to pad, to elaborate, to fabricate."[27] Yet, on the other hand, *there is* a world outside of a respective will to power; without an opposition against which it can be realized, a will would be impossible. In this, however, a will to power is not concerned with *how* the world is outside and other.

If, by contrast, there is a difference between will and world, perspectivity is not thereby removed. In this case, however, it is not an inalterable view of the world belonging to a respective life, but, rather, an ever possible, limited view in the world; reference may be made perspectivally to what is there and occurs. If one *is* not a perspective but rather *has* perspectives then they may be changed. One always has a perspective, although not always the same one; every reference is perspectival, but it can be directed toward what is different, even to what is different in the same. Because one is not "his" world there is here a spectrum of possibilities and selection: devotion of attention, disregard, concentration and absentmindedness, focusing of attentiveness.[28] All of this is grounded in the attitude that one has toward things. However, this attitude is not established through one's own being, but, rather, alone through the circumstances and possibilities of a *respective* attitude. It is in fact the case that every individual has a certain view unto the things, in which one thing draws attention rather than something else, things are "colored" differently, and some, because one has "no sense" for them, stand at most at the edge of one's field of vision. This does not exclude, however, that one can take on thoroughly different viewpoints and that some, which one did not know, can be brought closer or make an impression on him. The possibility of different perspectives entails that one is not "his" world, but, rather, is *in* a world. This may not be investigated without a change in attitude.

That one takes on different perspectives has to do, conversely, with the intentions of one's investigation. It is not a symptom of a general relativity, according to which something is only as it respectively appears,[29] but, rather, a condition of *substantiveness* [*Sachlichkeit*] for a being that experiences perspectivally. Nietzsche, thoroughly in contradiction with his monadology of the will to power, once put this in an especially striking manner: the "more affects we put into words about a matter, the more eyes, different eyes, we know to commit to the same matter, the more complete our 'concept' of this matter, our 'objectivity' [*Objektivität*] will be."[30]

What Nietzsche indicates here is a complex program of investigation that would not be feasible without methodological discipline. Nevertheless, it would hardly unfold in something that can be planned as a process. Different affects cannot be put into words about a matter without impartiality and sincerity; it is not easy to look at the substantively productive sides of something against which one has reservations. This is only possible when ahead of time a fundamental attitude of substantiveness has been found. That one is always somehow dealing with matters and matters of fact is not enough; it would have to be specifically concerned with what is substantive.

In the intention to investigate something, this is still not unambiguous. The investigation could stand in the context of a "knowing what is good for oneself." In this case, it would in fact concern a matter, but central would be that it means something to one himself. It would be a matter in the sense of a *causa*; this is what one has to carry out and achieve. And, in this, it is one's *own* matter, the matter that one pursues for one's own sake. By contrast, a different orientation to a matter is in play when one attempts to grasp something as clearly as possible in order that it would come into focus as what it is. Only this is true substantiveness and no longer something bound to respective interests in a matter. If the concern is with the *matters themselves*,* a mere reference or indication is not enough; the more differentiated the summoned possibilities are, the greater is the outlook of success. Substantiveness, accordingly, does in fact have to do with shutting out one's own interests, although not with the neglect of one's own possibilities. It does not remain imprisoned in the perspectivity of one's own view, and, in this way, in a "discussion of standpoint,"[31] although it is also not fulfilled in some sort of represented, immediate, and detached appearance of the matter itself. Its achievement lies solely in the mediation of the matter so that it is necessary "to leave" "the last word to things themselves and the work on them."[32] The mediation of a matter, in which the concern is specifically with the matter, is a carrying over of a special kind. It is interpretation.

§ 8. What Is To Be Interpreted

Putting together substantiveness and interpretation may be disconcerting, on the basis of Nietzsche's view it certainly is; the conviction that interpretation

---

*[Although I have translated *Sachlichkeit* here and throughout as "substantiveness," I have put *Sache* into English as "matter" and sometimes as "matter at issue." Accordingly, I use the phrase "matters themselves" here as a translation of the German, *Sachen Selbst* —Trans.]

is concerned with "values" excludes substantiveness. This conviction, however, runs contrary to an experience: Interpretation is most held to be necessary when something is not sufficiently clear in one's inner experience. This may be just as much the conduct of a human being as a historical occurrence, for example, the collapse of an empire. Interpretation is the clarification that is wished for here, although, only under two conditions: It may not be restricted to bringing into play the clarification of as yet unknown or unconsidered facts; likewise, it must be more than the attempt to derive the conduct or occurrence from a universal law, and, in such a way, to "explain" something in the sense of the natural sciences.[33] These two things have nothing to do with the task of interpretation. Its characteristic task is posed first when the question of the facts no longer plays a role—be it that all relevant facts are already known, or be it that explanation has to be achieved on the basis only of those facts available. And, it is posed in such a way that one attempts to clarify what lies before one *in itself*; it turns on the belonging together of its moments, on how they form a whole. This is how things are in regard to the conduct of a human being that, on first glance, is confusing, or with a historical event that one barely has a view of. This is also how things are in regard to a scientific theory. When such a theory makes good on its claim, facts may indeed be explained based on the laws it erects. The theory itself, however, may still be interpreted.

In need of interpretation and interpretable, then, are contexts, whose unity is, despite all complexity, not in question, and, in whose complexity order may be discovered, questioned, and, in whose complexity an order is not in fact recognized on first view, but may nevertheless be discovered. Order and unity must somehow be there, in order that it can be discovered in interpretation. If both stood in the light of day, however, they would not have to be discovered.

This initial characterization in outline of what is in need of interpretation and what is interpretable is perhaps suited to nothing as well as to *texts*. However, this means neither that it applies to everything that is fixed in written form, nor does it mean that only pieces of writing are interpretable. Texts, which are at the same time writings, form only one, although an especially clear, way in which the essence of the text is developed; they make it especially easy to recognize, though if they are thought to represent it exclusively, then they serve to conceal it as well.

The word *textus*, the fabric, the weave, denotes not a writing, but, rather, the *order* of talk[34]; its Greek equivalent is λόγος, which means talk, and, in fact, in the sense of a multiplicity that is linguistically articulated, gathered and grasped together in a unity.[35] Linguistic articulation is concerned less with the annunciated saying than with what is said, or, too, what is written down. This makes it clear why λόγος can also mean "relation," "proportion," "rule," or "calculation." The result of a calculation, to wit, a number, is also a unity of a multiplicity.

It is nevertheless no coincidence that talk about texts is most often about them in the sense of writings. It is true that the unity of a λόγος that is in itself structured and potentially complex also can be developed in talk. To fix it in written form, however, is an essential condition of being able to *conduct* oneself toward it. Seen in this way, the writing that fixes the text would be not only a convenience, but rather, a condition for the accessibility of texts. As soon as the concern is with the inner order of the text, this fixing is indispensable. This also holds for a score of music in regard to the λόγος of music. The "dumb logos"[36] of visible things is disclosed alone by fixing them in drawing and painting.

Text and interpretation, then, are as if made for one another. The expectation of the text belongs to the attitude of interpretation; interpretation is only to be realized by fulfilling the expectation of the text. This does not exclude the interpretation of manners of conduct or of occurrences; what it sets into motion is the expectation of an unwritten text, an order to the matters of fact that as such lets them be grasped and identifiable.

It is once again clear on this basis that interpretation is not something secondary, which steps in as temporary help for writings or works that are difficult to understand. There is interpretation not only in regard to works and writings. In general, these are themselves interpretations, and, in parlance that is not philosophically forced, are often referred to in this way. A painter provides a certain interpretation of his theme in a painting, philosophers interpret the world, and are supposed to have done nothing else up into the nineteenth century.[37] Accordingly, there are interpretations of interpretations. No infinite chain of indirectness arises due to this, however, in which one refers linguistically to something else linguistic, that, in turn, is referred to something else linguistic and is dissolved in such references. That there are interpretations of interpretations has to do—as shall be shown—with the substantive essence of interpretation and its quality of knowledge.

The concept of interpretation as it is supposed to be developed here is broad, although not for that reason unspecific. Interpretation is rather a particular kind of recognizing, which may be grasped conceptually in its particularity. That, to this end, the interpretation of written texts is offered time and again as a model, and that the interpretation of works and writings come more often into view, has a simple ground: Interpretations of this kind are more easily comprehensible. They are dealing with something that is already made for being interpreted, at least, when the writings are not mere substitutes for talk, but, rather, as Gadamer puts it, "eminent texts,"[38] and when the works are not mere products of handicraft, but, rather, works of art.

With this, a significance of interpretation may be brought into play that until now has not been considered. Interpretation is not only a particular kind of clarification, but, rather, can also be performance. The recitation of a poem, the production of a play, the intonation of a piece of music are interpretations in this sense. It is necessary to emphasize this aspect generally, that is, beyond performance. In a certain manner, every interpretation has a moment of performance; whatever an interpretation clarifies is also always made present as what it itself is.

One quickly sees that both aspects of interpretation—clarification and performance—belong together; if one does not involve oneself in making the inner order of a work clear, a satisfactory performance will hardly be possible, and, likewise, every clarification of a work refers back to the performance, at least in the manner in which it is comprehended. To wish to clarify a text—this also always means: to read it, and, in reading, the text is performed.

The belongingness of performance and clarification is moreover demonstrated by a fundamental trait that both have in common. Every interpretation emphasizes, it lifts up out of contexts of life determined by conduct and occurrence. The sound of a piece of music stands just as much for itself as the interpreted historical event or the conduct of a person that has become enigmatic and needs to be made clear. Such an emphasis is only possible, however, because what is emphasized somehow elicits interpretation or even demands it. Only because it has stepped out and stepped in the way is it able to be emphasized interpretively. The complex unity that it is necessary to interpret does not belong in the more or less continuous context of life. Although it has a history that one can recount or reconstruct, this has nothing to do with the fact that it is in need of interpretation and is interpretable. What is in need of interpretation and is interpretable has leapt out from and so escaped the flow of life. It is there *simpliciter*, originarily.

This becomes as clear in little else as in the contrast of written text and spoken word. The latter is never simply for itself. It is always an *answer*,[39] a counter-point in the precise sense;* it is a reply,[40] even when it is meant to indicate agreement. Even the question is an answer whenever it takes up something that has been said, and it becomes recognizable as an answer when the question aims to check into or follow up. Yet, the answer does not remain as counter-point over against the other. It is directed toward the other and, if it is successful, is taken up by this other. It is communicated with the other. Every spoken word is communication and thus belongs to a *conversation*, if one would understand under it not only the exchange among a few persons and moreover take the edifying sense of the word "conversation" that at times surrounds it. "To be in conversation"—this is not in every case a good thing, and it also need not be pleasant or friendly. Political talk, too, is tied to conversation; it is conversation even as polemic, provocation, or riposte.

---

*[The English "counter-point" is, here, a translation of *Gegen-wort*, in literal translation, "counter-word." —Trans.]

In conversations, what is spoken has its place. Although there would be no conversation without what is said, conversation is of course always more than the said. Intention plays in, also expectation, and, always, also the things that go beyond the intentions of the conversation partners. A conversation is not an exchange of words, it cannot be reduced to the expressions made by those who participate in it. In this sense, Gadamer emphasized that, contrary to common parlance, a conversation is not "led."* Especially, and, for this reason, "authentic conversation" is "never something that leads where we wanted"; the "more authentic" a conversation is, the less "the direction of it" lies "in the wills of the one or the other conversation partners."[41] Every conversation is a commonality that is not first established by the conversation partners. They must already be there so that commonalities can be discovered.

In the context of the "authentic" conversation that Gadamer has in mind, it is the common matter that has "always already" bound the conversation partners as an "a priori perfect."[42] Things that belong to the atmosphere of the conversation cannot be said to play a small role in it—mood, the impetus for it and its expected outcome, the favorability or unfavorability of location and time. Decisive, however, is the familiarity or foreignness of the conversation partners. How openly and without inhibition one expresses oneself depends on this, for example, whether one admits that he does not know, and, accordingly, inquires further. In what measure this is possible certainly also has to do with the experience of the conversation partner, his education and customs; it moreover depends on what, in one form of life, is typical, and what is not. Yet, in conversation, it remains in principle possible to inquire further. As long as one is able to ask, he does not have to interpret.

The difference between conversation and text can admittedly remain hidden, above all when what is to be interpreted is a document and looks like recorded talk. Then there appears to be no more than an interval between conversation and text, and not a caesura. The caesura, however, obtains nevertheless: upon a question, the text refuses an answer.

The situation is described in Plato's *Phaedrus*. The audaciousness and dangerousness (δεινόν) of writing (γραφή) lies in its similarity to the art of painting; it is, as the Greek word for the art of painting, ζωγραφία, literally says, a writing down of the living being, although of one in which the life is lost. A writing cannot put down its offspring as alive, but, rather, only feign their life. Should one ask them something, they fall still and silent with sacred solemnity.[43]

---

*[Gadamer's point makes use of a feature of common German usage that differs from English usage. In common German usage, a conversation is not "held," as is typically said in English, but, rather, "led" (i.e., *geführt*) —Trans.]

The critique of writing, as these ideas are usually taken,⁴⁴ actual comprise a critique only on one assumption: that writing is measured against talk. In the *Phaedrus*, precisely this is warned against. The warning may be especially appropriate for a writing that is dialogical and poses persons as if they were speaking. Yet, it applies universally; one does not do justice to the written if one has not recognized it in its essence.

The difficulty with writing as it is here outlined rests on a disappointment that, in turn, traces back to a confusion: What is written is treated as a person who is able to complete, vary, or elucidate what he says. Its silence thus appears as a lack; it is tantamount to an inability to provide desired information; compared to conversation, what is written is, as it appears, deficient. Yet, in truth, its silence is a refusal like that of the gods who do not intervene in human conversation and certainly do not allow themselves to be drawn into this conversation; it is for this reason that the silence of the written word is one of sacred solemnity (σεμνῶς). Writings do not belong in the context of human life; they are not persons. One who would like elucidating information from them must fall back on the extant writing, on what stands there before him.

The λόγοι are now compared to writing in the sense of the discernable sign that is written down. One is able to believe that they said something as if with intelligence. But, if one is desirous to learn something from what is said, they always just indicate one and the same thing.⁴⁵ The λόγοι do not exist without a writing, but they are not identical to it. Whereas a writing is the sensible surface of the λόγοι, these are the complex unities that have their material record in writing—that is, written texts. They refuse one as a writing does, but they refuse differently. Whereas a writing simply falls silent, texts do what, according to Heraclitus' word,⁴⁶ the lord of the oracle of Delphi does: they indicate.* They say something, as if with thoughtful intelligence, but they do not think. It would be senseless to inquire into the thought from which they proceed. It is after all gone, and what stands there is not its relic; it is not a reference to the fact that there was once thought here.

Texts "say" something—this does not mean that they speak. They are indeed present only in writing, but this falls silent. There is something in them, however, which belongs so much together with thought that one could take it for thought. It is outside of thought, but it is not separated from thought as by a wall. It is the *exterior* [*Äußere*], which is *for* thought—exterior, because not thought itself, and *for* thought, because it belongs together with it. Texts are

---

*["Indicate" in this context is a translation of *zu verstehen geben*. In the English translation of Heraclitus by Kirk and Raven, the fragment at issue here reads, "the lord whose oracle is in Delphi neither speaks out nor conceals, but gives a sign." Kirk and Raven *The Presocratic Philosophers*, 209. The author's comparison of texts to the pronouncements as things that "indicate" may be taken in this sense. —Trans.]

nothing, toward which thought can direct itself as toward some arbitrary matter. Texts offer something to thought, and, with this, they draw it out, outside of itself.[47] They give it something that it cannot find in itself or by itself: a *meaning* [*Sinn*], which is not its own direction. Meaning means direction—one might think of the [German word for "clockwise," *Uhrzeigersinn*, that is, the] "meaning of the clock hand"—it *directs* a movement, indeed, allows it to be meaningful. In its reference to texts thought is *displaced* into reference. It no longer proceeds on its own toward something it grasps, and it just as little turns toward itself; this is the case only in the first moment of confusion, in which one takes the text for "thinking." In truth, it sets it into a reference that allows thought to become aware of its possibilities for understanding. Thought only learns about "itself" when it is outside and learns something other.

This occurs because texts "indicate." They indicate what one has to understand without the purpose of communication and without the purpose of refusing something. Their writing is simply just there, readable; they stand outside of living thought. Through them, through everything that is a text in the narrower or broader sense of the word, thought comes into an *intensive exteriority that is discernible as such*. It is the intensive exteriority of the hermeneutical. It is the originary scene of hermeneutical thought—of a thought, which has a hermeneutical character, and, likewise, of a hermeneutical philosophy that is concerned to investigate it.

The question now is, how does thought realize its intensive exteriority? It occurs in interpretation. However, this is no answer; what is asked is how interpretation occurs. To this, it must first be said how one enters into the intensive exteriority of the hermeneutical. This is the question of the beginning of interpretation. Interpretation, however, does not begin, it sets in.

§ 9. Setting In

One first gets into some matter when one interprets. Nevertheless, this "first" is a caesura; one must turn one's attention to what is to be interpreted. A text—picture, book, or musical score—is like a promise that, in the moment one turns to devote one's attention to it, one believes can be fulfilled. It is a promise for thought, but not for thought alone. It must be accompanied by seeing or hearing, by representing, for the text is not beyond the lines and surfaces or the sounds, not beyond the words. It is their fabric, the openness between them as well as their connection.

One opens up a book. Even before the first sentence, something is different; things become quiet. If conversations are being held in the surrounding area, they now recede. They remain only a droning sound, a tapestry of voices, like murmuring water or distant traffic noise. The inner conversation of thoughts and representations also ceases. The silence of the written word has worked and has brought the foregoing conversation to a standstill. One concentrates, one collects oneself, but, in truth, this means: one devotes one's attention. There is also tension, expectation in this. It arises from the silence, which proves to be an open possibility—like the silence before the first note of a song is performed. Just like this singing, the seeing, hearing and reading must *set in*: all at once, one is into the matter, in a relation between reader and text that is once again originary every time it sets in.

The first word, however, does not arise of its own accord. It does in fact stand there, but it must be spoken, either in silence or out loud. The inauguration of this process may go awry. One then does not find the language of the text; it remains inaccessible, like a melody that is alien, perhaps too complicated, and then it remains so obtuse that what is written goes over one's head. The risk of the moment of setting in is even clearer in reading aloud. Every word that one recites may be correct, while the register is inappropriate, the tempo is off, the "tone" misses the mark.

In cases such as these, something does not fit together; the contract between reader and text that was made upon setting in to read does not get ratified. The reasons for this are various, even incidental. They concern not the relation between reader and text, but, rather, solely the possibility of the failure of this relation. It was the wrong book for this reader at this time. However, it is no less the case that this is the wrong reader. Only the book is not able to get angry with the reader.

Even if one fails to achieve a reading [*Lektüre*], the possibility of devoting one's attention remains open. Perhaps one tries again, and, as is often the case in repetition, more consciously. Possibly reflection [*Nachdenken*] now first takes place. It is less a reflection about the text than one directed *at* it; the devotion of one's attention found in the moment that one sets in to read is not reneged, nor for that matter even interrupted, by this reflection. Rather, the endeavor to achieve a reading is now *reflected* [*reflektiert*]; its possibilities are seen as such, weighed out against one another, and, on the basis of this attentiveness, brought into focus. The interpretation, insofar as it is a performance, and the process of interpreting that, as reflection, enacts the prospect of the text, are not in essence separate. They do not operate beside one another, but, rather, supplement one another. No reflection has existence unless it is achieved in reading; reading that is devoid of reflection can hardly do justice to its matter. The reflection does not have to be articulated. It can be like a delay, an interval, during reading: a brief interruption, a deliberation, and then one finds one's way back into the ongoing effort to achieve a reading. Clearly, those interpretations that are performances in the pregnant sense, that is, that are recitations, should not be interrupted in this way. Reflection must be inserted into, must have as it were penetrated, the performance. Often a text does not open itself up. It must be unlocked.

In texts, which are writings, the manner in which performance and explanatory reflection belong together is especially clear. They belong together in the same way, namely, that in reading and reflecting, one *puts* the text *into language*. The belonging together fractures slightly in regard to the visible and the audible, but it remains preserved: Here something is expressed in language that suggests a difference from language and yet remains allied with language. The hearing of a musical piece may be played out against reflection just as little as the observation of a picture. There is a reflective seeing and hearing, a reflection that looks at and listens to, even a reflective playing and singing. All of this has the task that putting-into-language has in regard to literature: The text is supposed be brought to the fore and brought into focus.

To put into language, this means here: to put into a language, which does not of itself possess what is supposed to be put into language. The writing is reticent, the text does not articulate itself in thought; there is thus a need here for another voice, one that approaches from the outside, for thought that—in listening to and looking at—devotes its attention to the text. This is a voice that speaks neither of itself nor from out of itself. This thought is, despite all of the power it can have, not one concerned with its own matters. Something is put into language and grasped in thought, something, which is not immediately the matter of this speech and thought.

This does not have to be recognized in every case. Possibly, one who recites something is taken for someone who simply speaks on his own behalf. The more reflective an interpretation is and the more its reflectiveness is recognizable, the less probable such a confusion will be. Whoever explicates a text takes up this relation, and, typically, makes it explicit: in the naming of the title or the author, which then stands for the text.

It is only possible to *put* something into language that differs in some respect from the language used to put it into language. A piece of music is also not identical to what is made loud in its performance. Otherwise, it would be a different one with each performance, and, with this, it would no longer be what it is; it would be dissolved in its performances, which, consequently, would also no longer be performances. Music, which is made loud, is only interpretation, when it is not made loud immediately and inimitably, as is in the case of improvisation. *Something* is always interpreted, or, more precisely: something that is recognizable, and, accordingly, determined on its own. It is for this reason that the interpretable can be familiar. Even before a performance, it is possible to know what will be performed, and, in fact, one generally does. Sometimes one actually knows the piece quite well from other performances.

This allows the tension before a setting in to become still clearer in its essence. If the piece about to be heard is familiar, the tension has nothing to do with surprise. The uncertainty about whether the piece will be manageable is also really only seldom in play. The tension is also there when no doubt about the interpreters' ability exists. And, it is just as present when the interpretation involves no performers, as on the way to a picture that one has not seen in a long time, or, as before the first sentence of a book one is about to reread. Yet, it is certainly clearest in regard to performances in the narrower sense.

One could compare this tension to what occurs before and also during an artistic production. What captivates here is the unresolved tension between ability and danger. A ropewalker puts himself on the line to a certain extent without taking an incalculable risk. He is a master of his art, and it nevertheless remains an open question whether his summersault will be successful. This is what constitutes the tension.

In the interpretation of music, things are similar and at the same time completely different. If there is no reason to doubt in the interpreters' ability to interpret, failure is improbable; for the most significant interpreters, in fact, the tension is at its greatest precisely when no slip is to be feared. Besides, the artistic performance, with all of its difficulties, does not have the character of a piece of art; one presupposes that good interpreters will have mastered the technical demands of their trade. Success and failure nevertheless stand as something that remains undecided. This, however, turns not only on what is under the interpreter's control. Every note could have been played properly, however, the performance had no luster. "The right tone" was not struck. Something decisive was missing.

What was missing here was the work itself. One had, as it appears, expected this; in this case, the tension before the setting in had been focused less on the interpretation than on the question of whether the interpretation would be "more" than just a respectable production. The question was whether the activity of the interpreters would shift, turning into an occurrence of the work.

This is less enigmatic than it perhaps sounds. One need only bring to mind that performances can always be spoken of in a twofold way: the performance itself can be emphasized, or be neglected in favor of what has been performed. Both are equally appropriate to the matter. One is always dealing with an interpretation of something and, in the interpretation, at the same with what is interpreted.

Accordingly, talk of the "work itself" and of the occurrence of the work is not intended in the sense of a "real presence"[48] of the work or text—as if the interpretation has to draw itself back, put itself wholly in the service of the work, and, renouncing everything it has contributed, simply prepare the way for the arrival of the work. The work does not arrive without the activity of interpreters; to experience it in its presence is always only possible through interpretation. There cannot, then, be anything like a real presence that breaks into the world in the manner of an event. Interpretation prevents this because it is always also present as interpretation; without the presence of the interpretation, the work is not present.

This is not meant reductively, however—as if interpretation was actually to aim at real presence, and yet, in the end, were to remain "always only" interpretation. The mediated presence of the work or text is precisely how interpretation is fulfilled. The activity of interpreters is not supposed to be just activity, without there being something other than activity; when interpreters no longer participate, the presence of the work ceases as well. It is rather that something is supposed to occur *in* the activity: the occurrence does not supercede or break through the activity. It is supposed to be nothing other than the other, as such recognizable, side of the activity.

Here, in the example of musical performance, occurrence means: the way that it sounds no longer makes one think of intention and not at all of exertion. The activity is as it should be. It has reached fulfillment, and this is so when the matter it was concerned with is present in it. In this case, something in the activity is over and above the activity, and nevertheless not beyond it, as if it could be put beside the activity. An activity that remains beside its matter cannot reach fulfillment, although, on the other hand, a matter is never dissolved in the activity. The matter occurs in the activity; the matter sets itself in. What comes into focus here as the matter in such a way that it occurs in the activity of the interpreter is the text, the fabric, the complex unity, which the activity of interpreting was after. It is the exterior over and against one's own activity, which, accordingly, cannot be fulfilled as incorporation or assimilation. The activity is fulfilled solely in an effect that would not be possible without the activity, but that also cannot be attributed to it alone. And, this fulfillment remains provisional. Even if the text is present in the interpretation, it is not dissolved by any interpretation. An interpretation can therefore set in anew, or a new interpretation can set in. Thus, its exteriority not only remains preserved in the activity but is rather intensified. The occurrence, and, with it, the self-setting-in [*Sicheinstellen*] of the matter, is the exteriority of the activity itself.

Experience, as it is when it succeeds, is more familiar than the description of it. Yet, on the other hand, experience is made clear first through description. It is the same here: When a musical performance is successful, one's enthusiasm holds not only for the activity of the interpreters, but, rather, always also for the respective presence of the work; otherwise, things would be the same as they are at the circus. The joy in the discoveries that one makes in a careful reading of a text is always also a joy of being into the matter. And, when one succeeds in devoting one's attention to a picture in peace and with open eyes, one is rewarded for it with the special pregnancy of the visible. One would not come upon the idea of judging this pregnancy only as the result of the acumen of one's own powers of observation. The matter disclosed by the reading traces back just as little to one's own ideation. And nevertheless, the picture would not have emerged from a less impartial perspective, one would rather only have registered it, taken note of it, and it would have remained one picture among others, a part of the collection in which it is preserved. The matter of the text only becomes present in a thorough and nonreductive reading. Otherwise, what is read will remain an insipid sketch of ideas, which does not concern one.

Yet, what is done and what happens when an interpretation that sets in is still not sufficiently clear. How is it to be conceived more precisely that something is brought into focus in activity and nevertheless retains its exteriority? What does "exteriority" mean here, and how is the relation to it to be more precisely grasped?

§ 10. Exterior Relations

Exterior is a word of contrast, it indicates what is not interior. The interior is what is closed in. One must penetrate through the surface or through the wrapping to get to it; conversely, the surface or wrapping is what protects against such penetration. It encloses what is interior; what it excludes is what is exterior. A context, something to which one belongs or in which one participates, a society or circle, for example, can also be enclosing. Exterior is in this case what is excluded, something is exterior when it does not belong.

Texts, however they may be given, remain exterior because they do not answer. For this reason, they do not belong in conversation. That they do not answer means they communicate nothing and also withhold nothing. *Intention* belongs to both, and texts do not have intentions; only persons can have intentions. Sometimes persons communicate their intentions in written form, for example, in letters. In this, intentions can also be withheld. The recipient can set in on it—to judge the communicated intentions more or less skeptically, and to wish to glean from the letter what is withheld.

Interest in the intentions of others usually proceeds from one's own intentions, be it that one, in order to pursue one's own intentions, would like to know the intentions of the other, or, be it because one can be struck by the intentions of the other, and, in the pursuit of his own intentions, be hindered or aided by them. In these cases, one reads written communication on the basis of one's own intentions. Reading belongs to the pursuit of one's own intentions and in this way in the enactment of one's own life. Posed in Heidegger's concept, it has the *sense of enactment*.

Heidegger, one will remember, plays this concept against Husserl; if human Dasein has a sense of enactment, then it also cannot appropriately be taken as a thing to which one refers in reflection.[49] The relation to a thing, as it is taken here as a model of reflection, is moreover problematic for Heidegger because it does not appear in the sense of enactment of Dasein. As Heidegger wishes to show, what Dasein initially encounters belongs to its dealing with the "useful thing"; it is recognized in the sense of enactment of everyday conduct.[50]

Accordingly, *immanence* belongs to the sense of enactment: Although there is much that is there besides oneself in it, it does not stand out as something exterior since it belongs to the context of one's own life. What can no longer be understood in this way emerges as something exterior. It has fallen out of the sense of enactment and one can now only refer to it. It discloses itself only to a *sense of reference*.

The experience of exteriority may be disconcerting. Something is different from what is normally encountered—irritating, enigmatic, impossible to put into the order of the familiar possibilities of one's surroundings. Yet, the sense of reference cannot be clarified solely in contrast to the sense of enactment. This would be to suppose that life in its context—what counts as interior to one's life in the broader sense—were normal life, and, by contrast, that the discovery of the exterior were a kind of depreciation or loss. In this case, however, the proper, irreducible, and by no means "deficient" possibilities of life that are connected with this sense of reference would not come into view.

This impression nevertheless has a basis in the matter at issue. Although the expressions have the same construction, their meaning is quite different: enactment is implementation, performance, an action in which something, for example, a juridical ruling, becomes effective and an actuality. Reference, by contrast, is the existence of a relationship; something stands in a relation to something else. The impression is thus able to arise that the sense of reference is abstract, as it were no more than a mere gaze unto something, which—when measured against life in its enactment—would no longer appear to belong to such a life.

In interest of a reevaluation of this sense of reference, one would have to show, then, that the reference to something exterior could be fulfilled completely on the basis of life. As a question of exteriority, the discussion of interpretation is meant in precisely this sense. The exterior over and across from the activity, which appeared in the first consideration of interpretation, is indeed not the correlate of a viewpoint now without context and orientation, but, rather, is something, which is there and at the same time is supposed to occur; it is there and is predisposed to arise with the activity. The activity, conversely, is predisposed for this occurrence; at least, the characteristic tension before the setting in of interpretation suggests this. In this case, interpretation is an activity, which lives *in reference* to the exterior. Insofar as interpretation has the purpose of bringing the exterior into focus, it is not the mere existence of a reference to something, but, rather, the implementation of a reference. Interpretation is an enactment that has its purpose in a reference, but that nevertheless remains in existence as such.

From this standpoint interpretation may be grasped as *presentation* [*Darstellung*]. Presentation is the mediated presence of something, brought about by a presenter, that is in itself given although not in this presence. It is the possibility to give something a presence that it is not able to have on its own accord, and, at the same time, to make it recognizable as a bestowed presence. This would not exist if what is presented were not, of its own accord, predisposed to its mediated presence, and if one were not capable of recognizing what it is in the mediation. Taking orientation from the concept of presentation thus has the double advantage that it makes it just as possible to clarify interpretation in its structure as it allows the consideration of different ways in which interpretation may be developed. The clarification of a work, just as much its performance, is presentative. The activity of art by which something is made recognizable is also presentative.

A classical discussion of presentation may be turned to in order to understand this more precisely. It is found in Plato's *Republic*, and, in fact, as a discussion of μίμησις. The word names in one both the process of presenting and with it the manner in which it is enacted. Mimesis may, then, be translated both as presentation and as imitation, *imitatio*. These two possibilities of translation are not alternatives but rather supplement one another. Together they capture the process that is signified by the word mimesis.

In the *Republic*, the discussion of mimesis appears in the context of the question of the possibilities and limits of poesy.[51] Socrates distinguishes two possibilities of poetic language (λέξις): either the poet speaks himself and does not at all wish to give the impression of someone else speaking; this is called "simple narrative" (ἁπλῆ διήγησις). Or, the poet wishes to direct our understanding (δίανοια) elsewhere and speak as if someone else were speaking.[52]

The model is thereby introduced by which Socrates achieves his determination of mimesis: to speak like another person. The determination itself is given by saying how it occurs: To liken oneself to someone, in voice or in looks, this is indeed the enactment of mimesis in regard to that one, to whom one wishes to liken himself.[53]

This determination first of all provides guidance about how the word μίμησις is to be translated. If one were to translate the formulation μιμεῖσθαι ἐκεῖνον with "imitation of that one," then the sentence would be a tautology. μιμεῖσθαι and ὁμοιοῦν ἑαυτόν would simply signify the same thing, and then no consideration would be given to the aim that is to be served by likening oneself to another. The attempt to make oneself similar to another could, after all, have a different purpose than the one discussed in the *Republic*: It does not have to be poetic or otherwise to be enacted in an artistic intention. One might wish to learn something; for example, the pronunciation of a foreign word, or one might desire to coordinate one's own conduct with that of another; dance or gymnastics would be examples of this. Yet, here, the imitative conduct would have a purpose in its own right, and, in fact, the same purpose as the conduct that had served as a model for it; it would be a conduct *of the same kind*, and, as such, successful when it becomes as similar as possible to the model and be able to stand next to it.

In mimesis things are different. Here, as Socrates says, the concern is to direct our understanding elsewhere; not the conduct itself but rather something different, a different conduct that is only present in one's own conduct, is supposed to stand at the center of attention. One's own conduct stands not for itself, but, rather, for something that is outside of what is one's own.

As the broader discussions of the third book of the *Republic* proceed, not only the recitation of the poet is supposed to be understood as mimesis, but also the performance of a drama, as well as the recitation of the epic by someone other than the poet. With this, it would certainly be assured, that interpretation in the sense of performance might be understood as mimesis. The question of whether this also holds for clarification, by contrast, must remain open for the moment. It can only be answered once the structure of mimetic conduct has emerged more clearly.

To this end, the example of the reciter mentioned by Socrates may be considered. The conduct of this figure is—in a manner different from poetic speech—thoroughgoingly mimetic; the difference between simple narration and mimesis would arise here only if the one who recites were to step out of his role and supplement the narration or modify it on his own authority. Only, in this case, he would speak himself in order to communicate something as he himself. This, however, is not intended in mimesis. That conduct is mimetic which draws attention to itself in order to bring something else into one's attention. The concern is only with the conduct itself because it stands for something. It is such that it itself, in itself, *shows* something else.[54]

Mimetic conduct is differentiated from other possibilities of showing like pointing out and exhibiting. In it, something is not brought into one's attention, as in pointing out, because one directs oneself or refers to it, and, in this way, lifts it out from others. One also does not lift something out of its context and keep it, as in displaying, so that it is easily visible for others. Something is shown, rather, because one does something, without doing it in one's own name. One *carries over* the conduct of another to oneself; one does not take it over, but, rather, remains at a distance from it; one does not take over a conduct so that he would behave in just this manner, but, rather, conducts himself in order to allow the conduct as such to be brought into focus. The concern is not that one conduct oneself in this way, but rather with the conduct.

Mimetic conduct is not yet sufficiently determined solely by this. A tennis instructor could hit a backhand stroke in order to show how to hit a backhand stroke. Here, however, what is done is nothing to which he would have to "make himself similar," because it was already familiar as his own possibility of conduct. It is only if the tennis instructor hits a backhand stroke as incorrectly and awkwardly as his pupil that he would have "made himself similar." His intention in this would now be to demonstrate a conduct not his own so that this conduct would emerge with clarity as what it is. The instructor's intention would now be to make something present by means of this conduct, namely, a different conduct. If, however, the pupil attempts to hit a backhand stroke exactly as the instructor, he does in fact imitate something and attempts to conduct himself in a similar manner as the instructor. But his concern is not with the conduct of the instructor insofar as it is the *instructor's* conduct and not his own conduct. Here, the similarity is only an intermediary stage, in which the pupil adapts the conduct of the instructor. He does not wish to show this conduct but rather to learn something in order then to do it himself without taking orientation from another.

Showing, as it was described on the example of the tennis instructor, is in fact presentative, and, accordingly, mimesis may be understood with it as presentation.[55] However, in activity such as that of the tennis instructor, presentation remains restricted; it is guided by an overarching aim, and, for this reason, is for the most part not even recognized as presentation. This is different in a theatrical play, or, for that matter, in parody. Here, one conducts oneself as someone else, makes oneself similar to this other, so that the other becomes present in one's conduct. The example of parody moreover teaches which sense is found above all in a presentation of this kind: a more precise recognition of the one who is presented. The conduct of this person emerges in its distinctiveness much more clearly in the successful presentation than it does in oneself. In oneself, it is simply only this specific, more or less conspicuous, conduct. In presentation, one's attention is drawn to the conduct because it is now separated from the person to whom it belongs. In this separation—that is, in its indirect, because mediated, presence—one recognizes the conduct much better than in a direct encounter. One expressly assigns it to the person, and, in this way, one has recognized the person in his conduct.

How this is possible may be elucidated in regard to parodic presentation as well. This only reaches its goal in a manner comparable to caricature by accentuating and even exaggerating, concentrating, then, on certain traits that are to be emphasized and leaving others out in the bargain. The conduct or kind of conduct must be something characteristic for the one to be presented, something that suggests the intended person immediately. In this case, one recognizes not the presentation based on the person by understanding who is intended, but, rather, the person based on the presentation: The emphasized pattern of conduct is so pregnant that one is able to grasp it as a fundamental trait in the conduct of the person. Presentation does not lead to recognizing once again [*Wiedererkennen*],[56] but, rather, it is an intensification of recognizability [*Erkennbarkeit*]. Something is recognized in presentation, and, because presenting is added to something, it is, at the same time, emphasized as recognizable to an exceptional extent. Thus, it has made the presented person recognizable in a certain manner.

Because presentation is concerned not with the duplication of a person, but, rather, with recognizability and recognizing by means of presentation, it lies among its consequences that the person, in regard of whom a certain pattern of conduct was achieved, can become unimportant. The presentation of the pattern then increases the scope of recognizability to *many* persons, or, indeed, shows fundamental traits of human conduct in general. In this case, what is shown is the *typical*. Type comes from τύπτειν, "to strike"—intended is the imprint, the clear contour, such as one stuck into metal. Aristotle saw the characteristic capacity of mimesis in this power to form types, and called dramatic poetry, to which his discussion refers, "more philosophical and more serious" than historiography: As "mimesis of actions and life,"[57] it leads beyond factically realized action to the universal.[58] The typical is the universal that has been developed; something that concerns not only this person but also what becomes superpersonal in this person.[59] Thus, in Molière the presentation of a miser can lead to knowledge of miserliness just as that of one who imagines oneself ill can lead to knowledge of hypochondria.

The typical does not emphasize itself. It must be emphasized, and, to this end, one must "make it out" from the diversity that one has before one's eyes. One could comprehend this seeing as the first step to a mimesis; following on this, what is seen would in this case need to be carried over into one's own conduct. Yet, the carrying over does not occur in such a way that something is transposed immediately and on a first glance. In presenting, rather, seeing and doing belong together in such a way that one's view already pursues the presentation; something is seen as presentable and to be presented. It is only because of this that the look unto something to be presented can guide the presentation, although it also is sharpened in the presentation and becomes more precise. Accordingly, the typical, with which the presentation is concerned, is not simply given to the first look. Rather, the carrying over achieved in making-oneself-similar will generally unfold as a process of forming the typical; one tests out a possibility, corrects it, and works until he is able to achieve the impression that, now, the typical has been reached.

In this case, carrying over may also be recognizable as a capacity of the one who presents: what is shown is, in contrast with the diversity that one is concerned with immediately, that is, without presentation, a simplification; instead of a multiplicity of possible perspectives, presentation offers an established, and, for this reason, clearly outlined picture. And, this picture is supposed at the same time to be so differentiated that it is able to refer to something clearly identifiable as what is intended. Important for presentation, then, is to be simplifying and at the same time differentiating. With this, the relationship of these two possibilities is not simply fixed, and it is also not to be fixed once and for all. How it has to be in each case is determined through the intention of the presentation; at one time, this may aim more at simplification, at another, more at differentiation. However, the presentation may only be realized at all if it is predisposed to a balance between the two.

Every interpretation is presentation in the discussed sense. No matter whether the concern is to interpret some conduct or a historical event, whether a musical piece is performed or a literary work read, the interpreter carries over something to himself, and so, at the same time, "makes himself similar to," in order to bring it into focus in its recognizability. The conduct or historical event is not simply described. Rather, one gets involved in it descriptively; one as it were creates a place for it in one's own thought, in order to make it accessible in its complex unity. In the performance of a piece of music, the concern is not to transpose the score musically into sounds, but, rather, to make recognizable what resounds in the resounding. Just as it is in reading, the concern here is with a text that must be lifted out from the signs of the score, out from the sentences of a book written down and printed, and displaced into recognition. There is a book even without interpretation; centuries may pass without anyone tending to its text. The piece of music could be heard in a reproduced form day and night without the slightest attention being paid to its text. It is first through interpretation that this changes.

By presenting something in an interpretive manner, one also changes oneself. In getting involved with something, one becomes in each particular respect different than otherwise. Initially, everything that one is able to involve oneself in is external. None of it belongs to habitual conduct or in the vicinity of the world that has become familiar through this conduct. Only for this reason must one comport oneself to and involve oneself in it; one must make oneself similar to it by carrying over the possibilities of thought and conduct that are pre-given in it into one's own conduct. As in the presentation of something by an actor, this carrying over occurs for the sake of the matter to be presented. One does not wish to adapt new possibilities of thought and conduct, but, rather, to recognize and to make recognizable, and to open up access to something that is not accessible other than through making-oneself-similar.

Nevertheless, one is changed by presentation. Presentation means to have experiences; and experiences, as Gadamer has stressed, put the power of acquired notions and manners of thought out of effect. The manners of thought and conduct to which one has made himself similar also leave their mark, so that they, like what is now put out of effect, becomes habitual.[60] As is maintained in the *Republic*, the concern is therefore also to decide what is and is not appropriate to present, and not to involve oneself, or, if one does, only under reservations, with texts that are problematic because they articulate untruth.[61]

The idea has weight even beyond its context in the pedagogical considerations found in the *Republic*. It reaffirms that interpretations, as presentations, are not mere assimilations of something at the caprice of the interpreter. Rather, interpretations, and, with them, interpreters, are also always subject to the force of the matter that is presented. Whether they succeed or fail would, then, depend foremost on whether the force of this matter is able to unfold in the interpretation.

Gadamer understood mimetic knowledge in this sense; for him, it is in fact determined exclusively on the basis of the matter. For him, a matter comes into focus as itself in mimesis and, in this respect mimesis constitutes "knowledge of the essence."⁶² This is grounded in reference to the elevation of presentation out of the context of everyday life; what is presented emerges, "as if illuminated, from all the contingent and variable circumstances that condition it"⁶³; through this, it is supposed to be recognizable as what it actually is. First through presentation is there a clearly outlined whole, which stands for itself, whereas in the context of everyday signals and references something remains diffuse; here, it stands not as "itself," but, rather, drowns in a complex, perhaps even chaotic, play of perspectives and forces.

On first glance, the idea may be illuminating: Something becomes apparent as what it is first when one experiences it in a narrative, brought on stage as drama, articulated musically or put into a picture, that is, experienced in a presentation. It is only possible to experience miserliness or hypochondria so often in the everyday—one recognizes them as what they are first when one finds them presented. Nevertheless, the idea is problematic; it neglects the fact that there are always many and often clearly different presentations of a matter. How, though, are these, in their difference, supposed each time to capture the essence of the presented matter, which, however, must always be the same? How are they, as different presentations, supposed to be equally illuminating when the concern is always with the same essence? It is true that different presentations of a specific matter are only recognizable as such because something the same is experienced in each of them. One only notices them as presentations, however, when their difference emerges and they are not encountered as the more or less varied appearance of some same thing. Because they are carryovers, presentations do not have the character of different circumstances that share an identical underlying "essence."

Gadamer resolves this difficulty through a kind of preemptive strike by understanding every presentation as the self-presentation of a matter in its essence. The purpose of the presenter's activity is, for him, only to see to it that this self-presentation of the matter is achieved, and, in the service of this end, completely to recede into the background. In the performance of a theatrical play or piece of music, though also in "epic and lyric recitation," it is crucial that the performance itself not become thematic, "but, rather, that the work comes to be presented through it and in it."⁶⁴

Certainly, the realization of a work must not itself be allowed to become "thematic"; for Gadamer, if this occurs in the process of the realization, and the spectator or listener takes critical distance, this is just an indication that the realization is unsuccessful.⁶⁵ That a presentation does not become thematic, however, does not mean that it would dissolve, as, for Gadamer, an actor "disappears" completely "in the recognition of what he presents."⁶⁶ Even if one does not reflect on the presentation critically or affirmatively, it is there as such, and the work is only present for this reason. One would have no idea what one would be dealing with if one were not to grasp what occurs as presentation, as the mediation of the work into presence.

Gadamer would not contest this; for him, the "reproduction" of a work is also a mediation. Yet, for him, mediation is "total," and by this he means, "that what mediates is superceded as a medium."[67] The successful presentation is no longer conspicuous as such, but, rather, succeeds precisely because it provides the work and the matter to be experienced in it the opportunity to be present on its own. Analogously to this, Gadamer also understands the presentation that is a picture based on what is presented, which, here, is determined as an "archetype" [*Urbild*]. In this sense, the essence of the portrait lies in the fact "that the one who is presented in the portrait presents himself and is represented by his portrait."[68] The picture, which is distinguished from the one who is presented, nevertheless belongs to him; it expresses an "*increase in being*"[69] in him, an expansion of his own presence, which lives from the always already given mightiness of this presence. The portrait even allows the one who is represented to be present where he is not able to be present in the flesh. The archetype of the portrait is accordingly the portrait of the sovereign. Inasmuch as this is displayed in civic offices, the sovereign presents himself.

One understands these ideas and the difficulties connected with them still better when one remembers on which models Gadamer orients his understanding of self-presentation. Play and festival serve him as models for self-presentation. Whoever plays loses himself in play. Playing, as Gadamer understands it, is a getting involved in the characteristic movement, which the play as such is. With this, everyday interests lose their meaning. One no longer follows any purposes that are understood and taken seriously as one's own. There are of course also purposes within play, but they are not followed for their own sake. Rather, they serve only as the impetus for play.[70] Relief from "playing oneself out"[71] lies in this, in which an occurrence comes from activity: because play goes on "as if on its own,"[72] all playing is, in truth, a being played.[73]

The forgetfulness of the self that is characteristic for the players is supposed to hold just as much for the spectators—that is, even when a "theatrical play" arises from the play.[74] The spectator, too, should be able to "forget his own purposes in the face of a matter before him," and, "be present to" [*dabei sein*] it completely.[75] Gadamer finds the model for such a being-present-to in the forgetfulness of the self in the "sacral communion" of the festival; the proper spectator has his archetype in the Theoros, in the participant in a festival's legateship, and, then, also in an understanding of philosophical theory as the "rapt attention of looking at.'"[76] Gadamer at the same time turns to the festival to make intelligible the self-sameness of what is always and again newly realized, that is, presentation: The recurring festival is "neither a different one, nor, for that matter, the mere remembrance [*Rückerinnerung*] of one that was originally celebrated." It is true that it changes from one time to the next and that different things are always contemporaneous with it; it is always in different situations that it is celebrated. However, it still remains "one and the same festival also from this historical perspective."[77]

Taken on its own, this would have to be illuminating, no less than Gadamer's emphasis on the forgetfulness of the self in play. Except, one would say neither of an instance of play nor of a festival that it is presented. To play or to celebrate a festival is in fact an activity, in which something comes into focus that constitutes this activity; and, indeed the concern is more with this than with one's own activity—the play or festival have a priority over and against one's own contribution. What is encompassing, embracing in the play and festival, however, is nothing, to which one has to make one similar in order to let it become present as something differentiated from one himself. Instances of play are played and festivals are celebrated, neither is performed, and, accordingly, they are unsuited as models for an understanding of presentation. Seen on this basis, the concept of self-presentation documents a genuine embarrassment: It is supposed to connect the simple self-presence, which is what matters to Gadamer, with the occurrence of its presentation through an other, in order thus to make presentation plausible as "knowledge of the essence." The word itself resists this, however, when someone or something presents him- or itself, the presentation also has to be brought about by him or it.[78]

Gadamer's intention is nevertheless comprehensible: Only its elaboration is problematic. Gadamer wishes to defend the experience [*Erfahrung*] of art against its reduction to an "aesthetic consciousness." For him, this consciousness is nothing more than the inner experience [*Erlebnis*] of an aesthetic quality, which is to be distinguished from both the matter that has been set into a work of art, and the mundane "conditions of accessibility"[79] for such a work. Against this abstraction of "aesthetic differentiation," Gadamer wishes to rehabilitate the "knowledge," which art as such is, and, once again, to bring into focus art's "claim to truth, which is certainly different from that of science, but just as certainly not inferior to it."[80] This, in turn, allows him to take up Hegel's *Ästhetik*, and follow Hegel in the conviction that art may only be adequately understood in the context of religion, while things come to an end for it, once it is taken out of this context. Yet, differently than for Hegel, for Gadamer art is not possible only as "religious art." It does not have to be religious art—as long as it retains the structure of religious occurrence, and this just means: the structure of "sacral communion" and of the festival. "An artwork," Gadamer once says, "always has something sacral about it."[81] Yet, the converse is rather the case. When artworks appear in a cultic context, the performance of art always also belongs to the cult. Because of this, cult and performance may be confused with one another, although their substantive difference is not thereby refuted.

Gadamer's intention may be worked out much more convincingly in another manner. In order to be able to understand art as knowledge, and, even before this, to ascribe to mimesis a "cognitive function"[82] at all, one does not have to trace back the knowledge of concern here to the self-presentation of an essence. Rather, it lies in the essence of presentation itself. Through every presentation of a matter, this matter is recognized and made recognizable in some respect. It comes into focus, albeit only in some respects and in varying degrees of clarity and pregnancy. Admittedly, these various respects, various perspectives, are needed to do justice to a matter that is not presented only once; the mimetic knowledge that sets in always and again anew corresponds to its richness and complexity. The great themes of world literature may be as infinitely presented as those of painting, and no successful presentation is ever replaced in every respect by others. However, they do supplement and correct one another in such a way that, in regard to the matter they treat, they are connected more in the manner of family resemblance[83] than by something that could be determined with uniformity. The great themes of literature and art are diverse and are connected to one another in complex ways. Every presentation puts them in a new light and, at the same time, in all clarity allows latencies to be sensed and undeveloped possibilities to be recognized. Because of this, no presentation is absolutely convincing, not even if it arises from a fabric of complex possibilities and proceeds toward the clear development of a determination or figure. The power of a presentation to be convincing does not simply persist, but, rather, must be achieved presentatively each time anew.

If this is the case, every successful presentation makes things all the more recognizable the more marked and distinctive it is. Presentations are not simply subject to the power of a matter, which is pressing toward presence and is self-manifesting, but, rather, achieve their substantiveness through the intensification of their presentative character. A presentation is all the more convincing, the more differentiated its own possibilities are. A presentation that is guided by a consciousness of its own possibilities does more justice to its matter than one that recedes and wishes to be nothing other than the medium of its matter.

Until now, it is admittedly still unclear how such a differentiatedness and reflectiveness develops itself. In order to make this clear, one has to turn again to the enactment of presentation, and, with this, describe it not only itself, but also in its connection with making reference to a matter. With this, the backside of making-oneself-similar is also to be considered: How is presentative activity at the same time an occurrence, namely, the emergence of a matter? And, how does the matter achieve clarity and pregnancy with this, how does it arise in the course of the presenting? The concern, to formulate it in another way, is with the question of how, with presentation, the text is *developed* in presentation. One may understand this in the sense of photography; presentation bears its text out of what is to be presented like the chemical process in the photo laboratory bears the picture out of the exposed surface of the photographic paper. Presenting is like making visible. In this, it is recognizing.

§ 11. Presentative Recognizing

Every interpretation is an achievement of the interpreter. However, it is a presenting that is specifically the enactment *of something*; whoever presents gets involved in something. The text does not actually speak by itself but must rather be put into language. For this to be possible, though, it has to be able to attract interest. It has to bind one's attention and one's will to interpret in such a way that its silence continues to hold in reading. It is this silence that allows one to find a way out of the stream of conversation and to linger in reading.

One gets away from oneself in this way and breaks out of the imminence of one's own intentions, notions, and feelings; only because this is so, in fact, is reading able to provide a diversion or be relaxing. If setting in to read goes well, then one finds oneself elsewhere, outside, completely into the matter that constitutes the text as what is said in it. This is the experience of reading, the simplest possibility of performance; it is a performance only for oneself, so the question of its effect and power to be convincing, and, along with it, of possible alternatives, does not yet arise.

One reads, silently or at most quietly—generally without forming words—and what is written nevertheless comes to language. It is as if one follows path marks, even anticipates some of them; one takes a path, and, in so doing, experiences what kind of path it is. If the concern is to achieve a first reading, what is written is like unfamiliar terrain, which proves to be accessible. One is outside, but not in the wilderness; there is a possible path that runs through the writing, and one takes it.

The further one reads, the more easily things go. The sentences link from one to the next, obstinately or effortlessly, although usually as if on their own. They suggest a direction, as well as a way to move in this direction. One is able to catch on to this movement just as in music. When it succeeds, one has found the tempo and rhythm as he reads. Now, it is perhaps as if one is carried along by the writing. One is *in* what stands there before him, and, because of this, into what is said [*das Gesagte*].

This effortlessness of reading brings Gadamer's concept of self-presentation once again to mind. And, in fact, even if this concept is not adequate, what it is supposed to capture does exist, at least in one respect: When what is written does not simply refuse its reader, it finds the actuality of a language as if of its own accord. Things are only otherwise if one does not find one's way into what one reads, or does not want to find one's way, due to reservation or ressentiment. In such cases, what is written remains alien, the sentences individuate themselves, one does not make any headway. Yet, at the latest when one is distracted or pauses, one understands that the language of the reading is not that of what was written; nothing comes to language any more, and the writing recedes into silence. Nothing had occurred on its own after all, and, nevertheless, what was experienced did not have only to do with one's own plans and desires. What was experienced was something intermediary, a mediation. One was elsewhere without losing himself; one conducted oneself without being of one's own mind. One was in an intermediary position: away from himself with another, yet, with this other, one was himself, with his own capabilities and possibilities, which he as it were brought along with him. One had made himself similar to the other. This did not occur as a disguising or impersonation in such a way that one conducted himself as another. It was rather like finding one's way into the course of a movement, which one wished to become familiar with and bring into focus.

The fact that writing is exterior comes to consciousness when what is written becomes alien. Whenever the setting in of reading is successful, however, one experiences it differently. One is elsewhere and one forgets the exteriority of what is written, so that here there is not the experience of a distance. The earliest experience of having a reading can confirm this: one was completely into the narrative, sharing the hopes and fears of its heroes, as well as their fortunes in their continuing adventures. One had become so similar to what had been written that one got lost in it.

To get lost in a narrative means to *follow* it—not simply as a sequence of sentences, but, rather, as the binding continuity of a portrayal, and, with it, the continuity of an occurrence. One goes along with this occurrence. However forgetful of the self reading may be, though, the continuity that it is enacted in does not arise of its own accord; it must be *maintained*—to retain and anticipate what has occurred and what will occur: One expects that what is to come will link up with what has been until now, and this expectation may only be met if what has been until now has been retained. This is all the more effortless, the more similar one is to what is said in the writing. The story is in this case as if transparent, so that one would be tempted to say it is enacted or occurs and does not need to be retold by the one who reads it and not at all reconstructed.

This changes when the continuity of the text is disturbed—for example, because a person in the narrative can no longer be identified immediately, or because a situation is unclear. One had not noticed the person in his first appearance and had not made note of his name; or, something that occurred earlier in the story had been forgotten and now one no longer knows how the situation arose that is presently of concern.

The difficulty usually does not lie in the story itself; the person did not *have to* appear, and in a different reading or in someone else's reading, he does not appear. The difficulty lies in the one who reads, and, accordingly, he is the one who must overcome it. The possibility to do so is offered by what is written: If one's memory does not serve, one may leaf back through the pages and attempt to reestablish the continuity of the story. This continuity no longer arises of its own accord, but, rather, must be produced by the one who reads.

In reading more complex stories, this is a normal, and, precisely for this reason, remarkable process. This makes clear that a text is not disclosed in a steadily unfolding reading; it is different from and more than a continuous sequence. This may also be illustrated on the model of narrative: The coherence of a story is constituted not as a conclusive succession of events, where each one of them would be determined only by what immediately precedes and follows. In order to be able to follow a story, one must rather be able to keep connections present that stand outside of immediate succession. Something that is named right at the beginning can be of significance for the whole and this does not have to be shown at the beginning; something that is introduced only later can give a story a new turn, and, indeed, perhaps one that first allows the story to appear as coherent. The story may thus be followed not only in the *enactment* of a reading; it must rather also come into focus as a complex arrangement [*Zusammenhang*]; one must apprehend the moments of this arrangement in regard to the text, and grasp them for one's reading. The fact that one also goes through a story backward, the fact that one can relate motives to one another that appear at various points in it, shows that it is coherent only as a whole, as a rationally recognizable weave of references.[84] This whole, however, is present with every narrated event, in every moment of reading. It is not continuous, but, rather, *simultaneous*.

That this is the case may be discovered in repeated reading. When one recalls the course of a story, one will recognize allusions, foreshadowing, which had remained unnoticed in the first, perhaps even in a second, reading. The more fundamentally one is familiar with the story, the more clearly he will see how the persons, motives, and events are mirrored in one another and how they gain their significance in the whole. The individual moments of the story are no longer linked together only successively, as in the first reading. When one is familiar enough with a story, one no longer has to recall what is read by reading it, and to allow himself to be guided by his expectation of how it moves along. One has the story as a whole in his head, and so could reconstruct it from each of its moments. One could open the story to any arbitrary page and would have a point of reference for it as a whole. In fact, the story still has its course; one must read it from front to back to experience it as a story. What makes it meaningful, however, is the structure of connections that gradually discloses itself in the process of reading. It is its *text*, understood as logos.

The relationship of continuity and simultaneity is, accordingly, not one of two determinations of equal rank. Every attempt to follow a story is maintained within its text. Without simultaneity, there is no meaningful succession. What is retained in reading only appears as a sequence of events from the standpoint of one's efforts to achieve a reading. In truth, it is the text, to the extent that it has been disclosed in the reading up to this point; seen in this way, what one anticipates is not that which is yet to come, but, rather, the still undiscovered text; the concern here is for the blank patches within the whole, the passages that remain open, but whose discovery stands within the horizon of one's expectations. Or, put in another way, in the continuity of enactment, the concern is with a simultaneity, which one moves toward as toward a whole.

What has been described here leads one to think of a celebrated issue in the context of hermeneutics: the hermeneutical circle.[85] With this, what is intended in general is the state of affairs that something particular must always be understood on the basis of the whole to which it belongs, and that the whole is not disclosed except through the particulars. This can refer to the particular moments of a text and its unity, though also the text as a moment of an overarching arrangement, that is, context. Considerations of this are found in Schleiermacher and Dilthey.[86] Yet, it is first in Gadamer's concretization of this circular structure with reference to Heidegger that it becomes definitive as that of the experience of the text. The concern is to "project" [*entwerfen*] a meaning that then gradually pays out in the enactment of a reading. "Whoever wishes to understand a text," Gadamer says, "always makes a projection. He forecasts [*wirft voraus*] a meaning of the whole as soon as an initial meaning appears. Such an initial meaning appears, in turn, only because one already reads with certain expectations of a specific meaning."[87]

What Gadamer describes is the interplay of the expectation and fulfillment of meaning, in which a partial fulfillment of meaning sets free an expectation of meaning for the whole of the text, and, conversely, in which the fulfillment of meaning had always only been possible in the context of an expectation of meaning. Here, the expectation of meaning goes back to the reader himself; it is, in a concept taken over from Heidegger, a "project,"[88] that is the establishment of a framework of possibilities that can be realized through concrete activity just as the architect's blueprint can be realized through construction. However, what for the architect is more the exception proves here to be the rule: The project must be corrected repeatedly in the course of being realized. He thus adapts himself to the experiences had in reading and thus in the end leads to an understanding of "what stands there."[89] The "constant task" of the reader is, Gadamer says, "the working out of proper and appropriate projections, that, as projections, are anticipatory, and can first be confirmed only 'by the matters.' "[90]

This description is given completely from the perspective of the enactment of reading, whereas the simultaneity of the text plays no role in it. It therefore captures the circularity of the experience of a reading only one-sidedly. In fact, it is generally the case that the whole of a text becomes clearer when one enacts a reading. And, when one has read the text to the end, nothing more of this whole needs to be anticipated but is rather there, at least for the reading that has just enacted. This does not mean, however, that it would arise in the enactment of a reading and count as its result. This may only be said if one understands the presentation of the wholeness achieved in the enactment of reading, as Gadamer does, as its self-presentation. Yet, the whole of a text can only stand at the end of a reading if it was there from the beginning. Nevertheless, it is possible that at the end one is left confused and at a loss. And, it is also possible that one believes fundamentally to have grasped the text, although particulars are still not integrated.

In short, the wholeness of the text is not realized through the enactment of reading. In order that this wholeness can in fact become clearer in a reading, it must already be there as guiding for it. That this is the case becomes clear at the latest by the second and every subsequent time that one gives a reading. Here, a prehensive projection of the whole becomes superfluous; one is after all already familiar with the whole and simply comes to know it better. From the standpoint of its presence, the reader does not anticipate wholeness as something that gradually pays out in enactment. It is rather *discovered* as a simultaneity of the text that is always already given, and is thus able to sustain the enactment of the presentation.

"Discovery" has a double meaning here: The wholeness is only revealed because one uncovers it and *puts* it *forward* in reading; without reading, it would remain undiscovered. Accordingly, it is respectively given only as one is able respectively to put it forward; it is always only there in a respective perspective, through respective attentiveness, concentration, and synthetic power. At the same time, however, one *finds* the wholeness in reading; it is present as soon as one has begun to read, and, in this regard, recognizing plays a role in reading itself. This recognizing, in turn, is not an initial grasp that is transformed with each further step. Rather, it provides orientation for the enactment of reading, it provides the context, in which every new detail is integrated. The reference to the text proves itself in the enactment of reading, just as this enactment is sustained by its reference to the text. This is the circle of interpretation.

How the enactment of reading and the reference to the text belong together may be made quite clear in regard to lecturing and recitation. Here, it is unambiguously knowledge of the text that carries the performance; it is communicated, in the most favorable case, in every accentuation, in every embellishment of voice, it is just as operative in the tempo of the lecture as it is in the attitude of the one who reads, whether it be animated, distanced-substantive, pathetic, or however else. The lecture is sustained by the text, the text is able to be in the lecture only for this reason. What is to be experienced in the lecture based on the reference to the text exceeds any given sentence or section followed by the listener. The better the whole is recognized, the more pregnantly the whole is there in each spoken sentence. However, this knowledge of the whole must be *realized*, and it may only be realized in the enactment of reading. The whole of the text is not to be established and determined like a matter of fact in the world. The text is recognized only in interpretation. This, in turn, is neither the application of knowledge acquired independently of it nor an enactment that as such constitutes knowledge. Presentative recognition, which interpretation is, always also has the character of recognizing presentation. In this it is comparable to the kind of knowledge used in production, which also does not stand on its own, and is only confirmed in the production of something. What it is as knowledge may not be grasped at all without the enactment of production. Just as little is it realized in the enactment of production, but, rather, is sustained by the recognition of an order that first prescribes the possibilities for the arrangement of materials used in production.[91] Like production, presentation is a recognizing in activity, and an activity based on recognizing.

In straightforward reading, this all remains indistinct, for here text and enactment of the text are not differentiated. Here it is as if the order, which the text is, is completely filled out by reading and reading further. The text is experienced solely in the continuity of what is read; it lies in retention and expectation and does not stand out. Although the text is even now differentiated from the enactment of reading, the difference is still not—in the dual sense of the word—noticed: One does not experience it and therefore does not make anything of it. Things become different as soon as the enactment of reading falters. The wholeness of the text then emerges as such. When a name is suddenly missing, or when an event important for understanding what one is reading is no longer present, this wholeness then becomes a task: The wholeness now has empty patches, like a fresco that has become worn; the whole of the references, as it was previously present in the course of reading, is no longer conclusive. So one attempts to produce this whole once again, to close up the gaps, so that the reading is once again enactment without disturbance.

A reading that only wants to be enacted without disturbance does not keep the wholeness of the text in consciousness, and, because of this, it remains unaware that it is itself a presentation. Therefore, it also completely fails to understand that a task is posed and that, in regard to texts, the concern is with presentation. Perhaps some sense of the difference between wholeness and enactment of reading surfaces after the conclusion of a reading. Now nothing is enacted, although something lingers. Depending on how memorable what was read was, it now becomes clearer than it was while one read—this is, to be sure, something one has experienced. By reflecting on what one has read, it emerges ever more clearly as such.

This would not be possible, if the text were given only in the enactment of reading; if this were the case, the text would have its strongest present in reading, although this would come at the price of a loss in pregnancy. Reflection on something one has read, however, is no mere recollection of one's reading; if it were, reflection would be no more than a more or less complete comprehension. The only remaining explanation is that the text is also accessible in some other way than simply by reading. By reflecting on it, one has begun, perhaps without noticing, to interpret it other than performatively.

It is consequential that this reflective interpretation can develop in this manner in reflection on the text. It shows, namely, that it is not merely an intermediary phase of reading that serves to ensure its continuity, but, rather, a possibility in its own right. In it, the concern is to grasp the text more clearly and precisely. On the one hand, reflective interpretation has more distance than reading; it does not follow what is written, but, rather, proceeds what is written from specific viewpoints that may be clarified methodologically. However, reflective interpretation is nevertheless "closer" to the text. What the text is in each case comes better into focus. It is another possibility of presentation, which can retrospectively influence a reading and performance, whereas new viewpoints arise for it from readings.

Two fundamental forms of reflective interpretation may be distinguished: *explication* [*Auslegung*] and *clarification* [*Deutung*]. The two rarely appear separately; they supplement one another and only in their interplay produce insight that could be entitled reflective knowledge. That they are nevertheless different is revealed by the fact that in reflective interpretation generally either explication or clarification predominates.

The word "explication" already indicates what is meant by it.* It is to be understood in the sense of laying apart, which corresponds to the Latin *explicatio*, itself containing the verb *plico, plicare*: to fold, to unfold apart, such that in *explicare* this meaning is strengthened. In explication, one lays apart what is read. This means the discovery of the text, which one achieved in the carrying over of reading, is made explicit through the differentiation of the many and the particular.

Yet, because the text leads one to deal with a wholeness, the concern is not only with the multiplicity of possible aspects and connections, but, rather, always also with unity. The discovery of unity cannot, if one is oriented by the precise understanding of the word, be explication. It is a *clarifying* [Deuten]. On the one hand, this word means that same thing as "to point"; to point out something, this is the same as to clear up.† On the other hand, it means as much as the exposition of the actual meaning of something that has not been brought to light. Dreams and riddles or oracles are not explicated. Rather,

---

*[*Auslegung* may be translated literally as "laying out." —Trans.]

†[In order to retain the author's point, I have had to diverge from the original slightly, which reads: "...auf etwas hinzeigen, das ist dasselbe wie hindeuten." —Trans.]

one clarifies them. One clears up how they are to be understood, and this is possible because one carries over a meaning onto them. One clarifies a story, for example, by taking them into view on the basis of something that is not said in the story itself and that cannot be developed—in the sense of explication—from out of what is narrated. When the chief cupbearer of the Pharaoh dreams of a vine with three branches whose juice he presses into his master's cup, this is a story that is clear in itself that one could simply take as it is. Something is added to it when Joseph says: "This is its"—the dream's—"clarification [*Deutung*]: the three branches are three days."[92] The clarification has found a viewpoint on the basis of which something said may be *said differently*. It is, translated into Greek, an ἀλληγορεῖν and, in the precise sense of the word, in fact, an *allegory*. Allegory synthesizes what has been laid down. It points to what has been said on the basis of something else and thereby allows it to emerge as a unity. Clarification is therefore also able to synthesize a number of texts in one text. One thus points to groups of works or collected works.

This determination of clarifying is not meant to suggest that the unity of everything read is like that of an oracle or riddle. Not every story has to have an underlying or hidden meaning; meaning and significance often arise from the story itself. In this case, there is need only of a viewpoint from which its unity can be grasped and characterized as what it is. It is a motive or an idea, through which everything else is held together. In this case, however, a clarification is only possible because the motive or idea is specifically emphasized and related to the story in order thus to make its unity recognizable. This is also a saying otherwise, only it is less radical.

Because a clarification approaches what is read in this way from outside, it is not seldom held to be arbitrary. The more allegorical it is, the more the suspicion will set it. This is especially the case for clarifications that follow what Ricoeur calls the "hermeneutics of suspicion,"[93] and wish to unlock texts on the basis of something that does not itself appear in them. Usually the basic conviction here is that the meaning of a text is concealed by this and must be brought into focus against it.[94] This, in turn, allows the clarification not seldom to arise in an authoritative gesture; either one follows it, or one finds oneself guilty of the same concealment that is assumed in the text.

Even for decipherings, destructurings, and psychoanalytic or socioscientific discoveries of an underlying meaning, it nevertheless holds that they can only be maintained if they are comprehensible, that is, if the multiple moments of the text are submitted to an explicit unity through them in such a way that this relation to one another confirms the explicit unity. The unity of the text is given not first through clarification. However, without clarification it does not come out; it remains bound up in the explication or merely in the comprehension of what is read.

If it is possible to confirm clarifications in this manner, then there are also paths directed out of multiplicity toward unity. Whoever, for example, retells a story without losing himself in the particulars to the point that one no longer knows what the story actually is, is involved with the unity of the story; the concern is with what constitutes the different events and persons that appear in it in their belonging together. What one had already experienced in reading is now specifically grasped. The more concise the retelling is, the clearer the unified character of the story becomes in it. Detail that is seen as more incidental is in this case left out; one directs oneself synthetically toward just the conclusiveness and coherence of what is read. The unity itself, however, cannot be identified in this manner. For this, there is need of a view that achieves distance and clarifies.

In a comparable manner, the unified character of what is read also plays a role in explication. Its aim is not, after all, simply to treat the many aspects of what is read rhapsodically. When only this occurs, things do not get to an explication, rather, one restricts oneself to isolated elucidations; one explains the meaning of expressions and sentences, works out allusions, and proffers isolated historical references. If this is carried through for a whole text, then one is dealing with a *commentary*: a more or less loose succession of remarks and references. *Commentarius* is a succession of notes and outlines; *commentor, commentari* means to prepare considerations, also, to engage in the study of something, usually, a preliminary study. Commentary first attains the status of explication when the elucidations, references, and remarks are condensed in such a way that the inner connectedness of the text comes into focus. The more clear and dense this structure of the various moments of the explication is, the more it does justice to its claim. If it is successful, it is the presentation of the text in its wholeness that is brought about based on the individual and the multiple. It develops the text such that its different moments emerge as in agreement.

Every step of explicating, then, must be guided by the conviction that the text is unified. Even here, however, the unity of the text is not captured as such. It may be intended, but it does not come to language itself; it is only indicated by the coherence of the multiple.

Just as explication as it were does legwork for clarification, so too clarification approaches explication. A clarification, which would be restricted only to naming the unity of a text, would remain abstract. It can only be convincing if it succeeds in demonstrating that its granted oneness is actually that of a multiplicity. A clarification is successful when it shows how the multiplicity of the text actually is integrated into a unity based on the standpoint, which has been brought into play.

Precisely in their belonging together, explication and clarification prove to be fundamentally different. Because of this dissimilarity, the one cannot gradually become the other, but rather, can only shift all at once from one into the other. Nevertheless, it will often be difficult clearly to classify the reflective interpretation of a text as explication or clarification. Both are concerned with the whole of the text, and the direction from which this is presented needs not always to be clearly recognized—not by the interpreter and not at all by an outsider. What appears as an explication can be directed from the standpoint of a unity, without this unity being named. What sets in as a clarification does not necessarily have to be carried through as such to the end. The standpoint of unity may one again recede in favor of the many; that other, on the basis of which the unity is named, no longer stands in view as such, but, rather, remains effective only by organizing the discussion of the many. Or, this unity becomes doubtful, and the clarification then suddenly shifts into explication.

Despite their complementarity, explication and clarification are not of equal rank. Clarification is *more* presentation; it allows what is read to become clearer, in the literal sense of the word.* One no longer only moves within it by following its inner connections, but, rather, achieves clarifying distance from it. Explication remains closer to reading. It in fact also deals with the whole of the text, but, because it is concerned with the multiple and the particular, its tendency is to strive for enactment. Characteristic of it, with its re-reading and referring back, however, is a manner of enactment that no longer follows what is written but that is rather determined by the simultaneity of the text. By contrast, clarification is referential; it is a pointing out and, in this, an explicit intent.

Clarification and explication remain complementary, however, in their unequal rank. Clarification does not stand above explication such that it would be in a position to sublate it within itself. Explication is not negated by clarification, lifted up to a higher level, and, at the same time, done so as something that one holds on to, preserves. In this respect, there is no educative history [*Bildungsgeschichte*], construed on a Hegelian model, of interpretation. Interpretation does not reach fulfillment in clarification, instead, clarification again refers back to explication: The explication of a text that has already been clarified on the presupposition of a certain unity is nothing short of a test of whether this clarification is really convincing. Once the experience of clarification has been had, explication is no longer able to be the self-movement of a transparent unity, but, rather, only lets this unity hold under the reservation of other possible clarifications. The possibility of other explications, which deviate not just in detail, is actualized solely from the standpoint of clarification.

In the complementarity of explication and clarification, the issue is to produce the whole of the text, and this means finding a mean between unity and diversity. The unity is not supposed to be abstract, and the diversity is not supposed to be unorganized. Where this mean lies cannot be determined once and for all. A renewed reading of the explicated or clarified text can displace it: Particulars are noticed that do not conform to what one had previously

---

*[The English "clearer" is a translation of *deutlicher* here. —Trans.]

thought. In this case, it may also be possible that the unifying standpoint of the clarification as it has been given no longer holds: The corrective that has been formed by the explication achieved in the new reading makes it necessary to grasp the unifying principle differently, that is, to clarify the text differently. It can also be that a new standpoint of unity found in a new reading makes it necessary to take the diversity of the text differently into view. In this case, one presents the whole of the text differently.

A new reading can be pursued at one's own liberty; a change of interpretation is justified solely because one reads many times, indeed, always and again. Or, a new reading is put into motion through *another interpretation*, explication, or clarification. In this case, the coherency of the interpreting comes to be revealed in the context of other interpretations given by others. This goes along with an intensification of reflectiveness; because interpretations are developed in contrast with others, whether explicitly or not, its interpretive character emerges more clearly.

Other interpreters are always in play, more or less explicitly, in explication and clarification—initially, not any specific ones, but, rather, "others," in the indeterminate plural. The reason for this lies in the essence of the writing of the text. Writings are of themselves *public*; not everyone may find access to texts, but it is not limited and, in this sense, is universal. Writings are fundamentally, as Nietzsche captures it with the subtitle to *Also sprach Zarathustra*, "for everyone and no one." This can come to consciousness, because one attempts to restrict access to them—say, by means of a censure or exclusive publication; such attempts show that those whose access is denied actually already have it.

As long as one is only a reader, others can remain indifferent. In reading, one is alone; that others also read does not matter to one. Yet, as soon as one explicates or clarifies a text, one enters into the public domain of interpreters. In the effort to further the wholeness one had discovered in reading, there are other clarifications and explications to consider, which is not to say that one would have to mention or quote them all; they may remain marginal if they are not essential for the profile of one's interpretation. Yet, when they are considered, one should aim to capture the unity, which provides them with the standpoint for a discussion of their diversity. It is possible, however, that this unity will be a different one in the others, and this, in turn, also makes it necessary to think over the presentation of the oneness, which one had himself given.

The reason for this, however, does not lie in one's relationship to the others. Over and against them, one could appeal to the fact that one pursues a different intention with one's own presentation, so that the different interpretations could exist indifferently next to one another. Yet, the issue is not the intention alone. The furtherance of an interpretation would be idle if the concern were not to make it better. Seen in this way, the reason to consider other interpretations lies in the matter alone: unless one more or less explicitly engages the other interpretations, it remains unclear, whether one has himself adequately interpreted the text. This question, in turn, may not seriously be dismissed: Interpreting is only able to be a recognizing when it provides criteria for whether the matter of concern was actually grasped by it, or, whether such a grasping is only putative or pretended. The question of such criteria is that of the fulfillment of presentative recognition. With it, the question of understanding is posed.

§ 12. Understanding

Understanding is a word that has been used time and again here without being made clear. This was unavoidable because it is impossible to avoid the word if the talk is going to be about interpretation. To proceed in such a way lies in the essence of language: The clarification of linguistic expressions is possible only in language; it does not precede speaking and writing, and not everything may be made clear at once. Like language itself, its clarification also has a context of its own. Therefore, it is necessary to wait for the moment at which a specific word may best be brought into thematic focus. Until that point, one may allow it to remain in the familiar obviousness that every word possesses and must possess in order for one to be able to use it at all.

It is often difficult to delimit the significance of "to understand" from that of "to capture," "to grasp," "to apprehend," and even "to know." One nevertheless senses that it has a meaning all its own whenever an attempt to replace it with one of the others appears as inadequate. It is one thing not to know something, and another not to understand something. Of a person's conduct, it may be said that one understands it, but not that one apprehends it. And, if one says to another that he now grasps what this other is doing, this is something different than saying that he understands it. Something similar holds for capturing and catching on. One does not capture a poem, but one does understand it.

The fundamental meaning of understanding arises on the basis the common usage of the word. It often has to do with linguistic expressions, and, in fact, in various respects. One has not been able to understand what someone has said because the expression had not been articulated loudly or clearly enough, or, likewise, because although one could hear the expression well, one cannot tell what was meant by it. Lastly, it can be unclear *how* an expression is intended—whether, for example, it is something of a rude joke or an insult. In all of these cases mentioned, regardless, in fact, whether the concern is with the wording, the significance, or the meaning of an expression, the difficulty is fundamentally the same: when one does not understand, one is not in a position to *follow* the talk. This is because one misses the context in which one could place the expression, or because the expression does not fit within the context that is present to one. This can also be the case when one does not understand a lecture or a book or even how to play a game; one has no context and just does not get something. The difficulty can also refer to others. It could be that one does not understand what someone is doing because one does not know what this person's activity aims at. If one were to know, then one could follow this person's activity, and comprehend the individual steps.

The example of play helps explain how "to understand" can also mean as much as "to understand how." Here, "to understand" is equivalent to "being able to" do something. It is, following the distinction introduced by Gilbert Ryle, a *knowing how* and not a *knowing that*.[95] Considered from this standpoint, "understanding" refers to a form of *knowledge of enactment* [*Vollzugswissen*], whereas the previously mentioned usage indicates a capacity for *comprehension* [*Nachvollzug*].

The word also elicits philosophical interest above all in the latter significance. This interest comes quite late, although then in a manner that guarantees the word enduring attention: in being used to give profile to the human sciences, which are to be legitimated as sciences and delimited from the natural sciences. Since that time, the word has come to refer philosophically above all to historical life in that broad sense encompassing what is inherited from the past. With this, it falls into an opposition with concepts that are valid only for knowledge of nature. Thus, understanding—and not interpretation—has become the central concept of modern hermeneutics. This alone is enough reason to take up the concept on the basis of its historical and systematic context. Only in this way, too, is it possible not simply to follow the presuppositions and familiarities of this fundamental hermeneutical conception, but, rather, to be impartial in regard to it and independent of it.

The aforementioned determination of understanding goes back to Droysen, although above all to Dilthey. According to Droysen, only "historical material"[96] is understood, and Dilthey summons his conception of understanding in *Ideen über beschreibende und zergliedernde Psychologie* with the pregnant, and not least of all for this reason often cited, proposition: "we explain nature, we understand inner life [*das Seelenleben*]."[97]

With this idea, an immense preliminary decision is reached; that in understanding the concern is supposed to be with "inner life" establishes philosophical hermeneutics in a consequential manner: In everything that is understood, the concern is ultimately with the understanding of persons. This idea may be traced back to Schleiermacher, who had determined hermeneutics as "the art of properly understanding the talk of another, preeminently, in its written form."[98] The understanding of inherited writings as written *talk* forms the picture of hermeneutical activity and activity in the human sciences. To understand a writing, this means to understand what is in it and how it is intended, and, to this end, one goes back to the "inner life" of the author.

The idea that, in understanding, the concern is always with "inner life" still remains in effect, where the conception of it given by Dilthey is criticized as insufficient. In his hermeneutics lecture course from summer 1923, Heidegger, without mentioning Dilthey's name, takes up Dilthey's determination of understanding as a "cognitive relation to another life." For Heidegger, however, this formulation merely points to "what understanding is usually called." Understanding is "completely incomparable" to this, insofar as it must be grasped as—the formulation has already been cited above[99]—"being awake of Dasein to itself." This understanding no longer has to do with the inner life of *others* and their expressions, and, therefore, it is also no longer a "conducting oneself toward . . ." but, rather, the "*how of Dasein itself.*"[100]

Heidegger worked this idea out in *Sein und Zeit*. Here, understanding is determined as a manner of *disclosedness* of Dasein, and Heidegger elucidates this not without reason as an ability. Only here, "what is able to be done" in understanding is "not a what, but rather, being *qua* existing."[101] Understanding as it appears in *Sein und Zeit* is the enactment of the knowledge of Dasein; it is a self-understanding, which, at least in one respect, is at the same time the being of what is understood: as the disclosedness of one's own possibility of being, the understanding is not only the comprehension of this possibility of being; as the openness of the possibility of being, it is this possibility of being. Understanding is tantamount to the possibility of being oneself in the immediate perception of the possible, which one is, and the possible, which the world is for one's own being.

Heidegger's narrowing of understanding to self-understanding, in the sense of a being that understands itself, may appear to be implausible in comparison with Dilthey's considerations; that nothing other than one's own being is ever understood is, at least, not obviously illuminating. Yet, considered more closely, Heidegger's radicalization is not a counterposition to Dilthey; rather, Heidegger critically develops Dilthey's considerations further by determining existential enactment of knowledge as a condition for understanding in Dilthey's sense. In order for us to be able to capture something as an expression of an alien "inner experience,"[102] [*innere Erfahrung*] we must at least in principle be able to discover it as a possibility of our own lives. Understanding is grounded, as can be thought, in self-understanding: in understanding something, we discover something as a possibility that is not completely alien to us. It is only possible to "re-live"[103] [*Nacherleben*] what can count as a possibility of one's own life. One understands something because one can or could be this something, or, in any case, one understands something on the basis of one's own ability to be.

This result finds further support when one takes into consideration that it is not possible to comprehend something without one's own standpoint, however inexplicit this may remain. When one says that he understands the conduct of another, one not seldom expresses that he himself might have conducted himself in this way, or, at least, is able to imagine conducting himself in this way in a comparable situation. One who understands does more than just take notice. Often, approval comes with it, though even disapproval is not possible without comprehension; it is first by imagining for oneself how another acts that one's distance from his action is demonstrated. With the possibility of comprehension, one is in any case himself in play.

The consideration shows, on the other hand, why Heidegger's emphasis on one's own possibility of being is one-sided in comparison to Dilthey's conception; it leaves out an aspect, which, according to the everyday use of the expression, belongs to it essentially. That one, along with one's own convictions, is in play in understanding, does not have to mean that one's concern in this is with himself. Yet, when one's concern is not with himself, the determination of understanding as the disclosedness of the enactment of existence is an implausible reduction.

One could once again point in the spirit of Heidegger to the sense of enactment in understanding and motivate that comprehension without enactment is not possible; in order to comprehend something, one must be able to realize it. However, this does not hit the mark; a historian could attempt to comprehend the decisions and actions of a head of state without being suitable to the business of politics. And, even if "ability" were the fundamental meaning of understanding conceived as the enactment of knowledge, it would not follow from this that such ability has to concern oneself. The ability that constitutes an understanding always has the character of an *acquirable* skill; no one would say that one understands how to see or hear. Besides, in discussion about one's capacities to understand, more is at issue than just the capacities. What is emphasized, rather, is the condition of having mastered them in a particular manner; one knows how to do something, this means: One has actually mastered them or has mastered them especially well. Here, the concern is not with one himself, but, rather, what one is able to do.

Such an emphasis on ability also appears in other contexts. One actually only says that one understands a game if one had previously not understood it—now one understands what up to this point had remained unintelligible. And, what one has already understood may, generally, be understood better. This is just as true of linguistic expressions, of the conduct of others, of lectures and books or works of art. Communicating that one understands something only makes sense in conjunction with the possibility of not understanding. Not understanding can, in turn, refer to the matter in general, so that one simply "does not know where to begin" with it. But, it can also be relative; in such a case, one does not understand something as well as he could or would to understand it.

A first clarification of what understanding is arises on the basis of this: Understanding is the successful conclusion of an occupation with something or someone, sometimes, also the conclusion of an effort. "Understanding" is a *word of success*; when one understands, something has come off, and, with this, come to a conclusion. This also holds when one now successfully carries out what he has come to understand; in this case, success is a matter of being in a position to do something that one had not been in before. Because it belongs together with success, what is understood [*das Verstandene*] is distinguished from what is already understandable [*vom Verständlichen*] and certainly from what is in *familiar obviousness* [*vom Selbstverständlichen*]. The latter has been understood or acquired through practice at one time or another, and, because of this, has gradually been made familiar. Yet, now this is forgotten; one has adopted what had to be understood at an earlier time, and now it has come to be clear in an unquestioned manner. Wherever everything is understandable and, for this reason, in familiar obviousness, one does not have to understand anymore.

An understanding of Dasein as Heidegger conceives of it can neither succeed nor fail. As disclosedness, it is at most a condition for the possibility of what can be experienced as successful. The fact that this condition is supposed to be an understanding, however, is not obvious from the literal sense of the word. In order to have the character of success, a *determinate* possibility of one's own being would have to be grasped and approved in understanding in the sense of ability. Precisely this is excluded, through, if one follows the conception of *Sein und Zeit*. Determinate possibilities are, according to the terminology introduced there, not understood, but, rather, arise through "explication."* First in explication, which Heidegger conceives as the laying apart of one's own possibility to be into various individual possibilities, "understanding appropriates what it has understood in an understanding way"; explication is above all "the development of possibilities projected in understanding."[104] Here, explication is—as it already is in Dilthey's approach[105]—derivative of understanding. Because it is the development of understanding, in explication one is always already concerned with understanding and the possibilities projected by it. These possibilities may accordingly neither be born out nor proven unrealizable; in contrast to Gadamer's conception of the projection of something that is to be understood in its wholeness, projection as it appears in *Sein und Zeit* is incorrigible: The concern here is not with something to be understood that is anticipated in a probative manner, but, rather, with the immediate openness of one's own possibility to be. This, however, is always as it is. It may in fact

---

*[In both the Stambaugh and the Macquarrie and Robinson translations of *Being and Time*, *Auslegung* appears as "interpretation." In order to remain consistent with my translation of the distinction the author makes above between *Deutung* and *Auslegung*, however, I translate *Auslegung* here, too, with "explication." —Trans.]

be foreclosed by one's "flight" in the face of it or it may "disclose" itself in the negation of this foreclosure but it cannot prove itself.[106]

Accordingly, a paradoxical situation arises with Heidegger's conception of understanding: Never before has the concept been philosophically so central, for never before has ontological and indeed "fundamental ontological" meaning been conferred to it; the self-understanding of Dasein here becomes the crux of the understanding of being in general. However, the revaluation of the concept comes at the price of its everyday sense and, because of this, its intelligibility: If one understands oneself alone, and, insofar as one is, has always already understood oneself, then there is nothing more to understand.[107] Self-understanding is not central, and certainly not, if it is taken in the sense of the concept of understanding used in the everyday. In this case, it proves to be a special case of the understanding of the alien. One must have become alien to oneself before the attempt to understand oneself—that is, an earlier stage or a different aspect of one's own life—can be undertaken. In the familiarity of one's own life, by contrast, one does not have to understand oneself. In this respect, Dilthey is right when he wants to signify "the comprehension of one's own circumstances . . . only in an improper sense as understanding."[108]

It is necessary, then, once again to conceive of understanding on the basis of that "conducting oneself toward . . ." which Heidegger had reproached. Even in ability, one conducts himself toward *something*; there is always something that one understands how to do, and, accordingly, the success belonging to the essence of understanding becomes all the clearer the more clearly the "something," toward which one conducts himself, is recognizable as something different from himself. This traces back, initially at least, to Dilthey. Based on his considerations of understanding the alien "inner life," it may be made clear how the sense of success of understanding is to be grasped more precisely.

For Dilthey, understanding is[109] the "process, in which we recognize an interiority"—indeed, it may be added, the interiority of someone alien to us—"on the basis of signs that are given sensuously from outside."[110] In understanding, one always has to do with the "comprehension of alien persons,"[111] who, as such, are not directly accessible. Their "interiority" is given only through their expressions, and so the task is to grasp them as those of another life. In understanding, one wins indirect access to something that remains inaccessible to one directly.

Dilthey attempted to describe this more precisely as a "spiritual process," "which is equivalent to drawing an analogy."[112] It is possible to understand an expression because it is taken up as a possible expression of one's own, though, at the same time, in regard to an alien life; one "understands" it as an expression of an alien life in analogy to how one takes himself to be able to realize this expression on his own. One recognizes something by means of the orientation provided by one's own activity, but, in such a way, that one does not conceive of one's own activity as one's own. What Dilthey calls "putting oneself in the place" of the other proves to be a "carrying over of one's own self into a given epitome of life expressions."[113]

Dilthey believes the possibility of such a carrying over to be grounded in the commonality between the individual who understands and the individual who is understood. But, how great must this commonality be? Just because "the same human spirit" speaks "to us"[114] from all human expressions does not, for Dilthey, ensure it. He believes that understanding reaches a limit when something alien "deviates" from "one's interiority not merely quantitatively, or is differentiated through the absence of something that is present in one's interiority."[115] In understanding, in fact, every individual proves to have "possibilities within him," "which reach beyond what he is able to realize as his own life."[116] However, this possibility must be anchored in the commonalities of a "spiritual world" in such a way that the difference between the individual who understands and the one who is to be understood is no longer decisive. In the success of understanding, this difference disappears completely, so that the alien character of what is to be understood proves to be only relative. Carrying over one's own conduct to the alien one's is only successful when both manners of conduct are actually of the same kind. They are of the same kind due to their belongingness to a common spiritual world. In this world, understanding is "a rediscovery of the I in the you."[117]

It is only one more step from Dilthey's considerations to Gadamer's conception of a totally self-mediating and self-presenting historical substance. When the commonality between the one who understands and the one who is to be understood becomes substantial, understanding is "to be thought not so much as a subjective act, but, rather, as participation in an occurrence of inheriting from the past, in which the past and present are constantly mediated."[118] Since the one history, the one spiritual world, is itself brought about in understanding, however, understanding ceases. In the "fusion" of the horizons of past and present, it goes under. Here, the otherness, which initially characterized what is to be understood, had only been a "phase in the enactment of understanding."[119]

Certainly—if what is to be understood were to remain as alien as it previously had, then understanding could not succeed. Yet, neither would it be a success if the difference were entirely to disappear. One would, in this case, no longer be aware of what he had in fact gained access to. The success of understanding only remains present when it is clear afterwards as before, *what* or *whom*, and, in what respect, one had understood, and this is only possible if what is to be understood is lifted up from what is one's own. What is indicated by expressions like "comprehending" or "re-living" is only possible as the bridging of a distance, which, as such, remains in existence. As Gadamer once formulates it, understanding has its place "between foreignness and familiarity."[120] This formulation captures the matter precisely—presuming it is not intended, as Gadamer himself had intended it, in the sense of a movement from the alien to the familiar that reaches its enactment on the basis of something that was previously familiar. What was understood is neither familiar nor alien. One has found access to it, although it does not belong to what is one's own as something familiar. It is outside, accessible only with distance, and understanding arises when this access at a distance succeeds. In this case, what is understood is, in the respect in which it is understood, no longer alien, although it remains what it always already was: independent in regard to the one who understands and, if only for this reason, different from him. As a consequence of this difference, understanding is neither an appropriation nor a dissolution in another, nor a fusion with it. No sure path leads to understanding, and it produces no result that is guaranteed for all time. Understanding arises, it sets in.

In this sense, Schleiermacher has determined understanding as *divination*; it is a capacity comparable to one of the prophetic gifts, *divinatio*, to grasp something about an alien individuality that is actually inaccessible. The divinatory power of understanding is "the one, which seeks to comprehend an individual immediately, by allowing one as it were to transform oneself into another."[121] Divination is a disregard of the self, which is an unconditional and presuppositionless openness. In it, what is different from oneself is able to be there without any mediation, simply as itself.

For Schleiermacher, understanding is not possible other than as divinatory, although it also cannot be exclusively divinatory. Divination must be supplemented and secured by a second, "comparative" method of understanding. In this kind of understanding, one posits the individual to be understood "as something universal" and then attempts to grasp its specificity in comparison with other individuals that fall under the same universal.[122] However, taken for itself, a comparison of this kind would not concern the individual that one aims to understand. As Schleiermacher states, the comparative method grants "no unity."[123] It does not reach the indissoluble connection, in which the universal and particular are found in the individual. Here, every universal is particular and the particular is always also universal. Accordingly, they may not be separated in understanding; to do so would be to dissolve the proper matter of understanding itself. "The universal and the particular," as Schleiermacher summarizes his consideration, "must penetrate one another, and this occurs always only through divination."[124]

It is a strength of Schleiermacher's considerations that the difference between the one who understands and the one who is understood is taken so seriously in them. He in fact once examined how divination is possible, and, by way of clarification, pointed to the "susceptibility" of every individual "to all others."[125] This, as he adds, appears in turn "only to rest on the fact that everyone bears a minimum of everyone else within him."[126] However, the affinity of individuals cannot explain divination itself, but, rather, only its motivation. It is only "excited through comparison" of the other individual "with one himself."[127] Comparison, however, is still not an understanding; it does not reach the goal, because it turns away from the challenges of individuality.

Schleiermacher's conception of understanding is convincing, furthermore, because it does not reduce understanding to the comprehension of an alien "inner life." Despite all of the determinations of his thought that point in this direction and that are taken from Dilthey, and also despite his hermeneutical orientation toward "talk," Schleiermacher takes into consideration that the task of understanding is not only the individual behind the text, but, rather and above all, the text itself. Seen in this way, the text is not an "expression," which has to be pursued back to the movement of expression that produces it,[128] but, is, rather, itself an essence of the kind that is to be understood: The text is individual.

Schleiermacher elucidated this idea with the concept of *style*.[129] This concept concerns not only "treatment of language," but, rather, the interplay of thought, language, expertise, and composition. "Idea and language," he explains, "interpenetrate one another thoroughly, and the proper way to capture the object involves arrangement, and, consequently, treatment of language."[130] In order for a work to have style, the notions brought into focus in the text must in fact have "proceeded from personal particularity"; otherwise, the work does not have style, but, rather, only "affectation," "and bad style is always affected."[131] However, if treatment of language and composition are essential moments of style, they achieve no actuality without artistic or literary works. From the viewpoint of style, the individual cannot be grasped except in works and their textuality. Texts are individuality, which it is possible to understand, and which demand understanding.

This result makes it necessary to revise Schleiermacher's conception of understanding. The connection of divinatory and comparative methods, in terms of which Schleiermacher wishes to conceive understanding, does not do justice to the essence of texts. Texts are disclosed neither in an immediate apprehension nor in comparison with other texts, but, rather, alone through interpretation. The fabric of its moments cannot be immediately grasped as a unity, but must, rather, be clarified, and the question of how a text relates to other texts may only be developed in a sound manner in the context of its interpretation. As in Dilthey and Gadamer, the decisive concept is also missing in Schleiermacher.

Schleiermacher's motive for his conception of understanding as "divination" does not thereby lose its value. If texts are exterior in regard to interpretation, then their unsublateable difference from interpretation remains an essential moment. However, the experience of this difference no longer has to be conceived as an immediate grasping on the model of a mantic intuition. Something different, which has been interpreted, is indeed accessible to interpretation; it is presented, and, with this, recognized. In the case of this recognizing, difference has to play a role; in this case, its experience is not itself a recognizing, but, rather, something *in* this recognizing, which is solely understanding thereby. What understanding is becomes clear in regard to interpretation—with this idea one simply draws a consequence from Schleiermacher's considerations of style.

It is not said by this that understanding would appear in interpretation alone. To claim this would be implausible; in understanding a linguistic expression or a manner of conduct one does not generally interpret. This simple or elementary understanding may be much better determined, however, when one beforehand clarifies his understanding through interpreting. Whatever comes first in elementary understanding becomes clearer through a richer and more complex development of the matters at issue. The more that has to be done for the success of understanding, the better one sees the success itself; as a "phasal moment" in everyday talk and conduct, by contrast, the success is rarely profiled.

The question of when an interpretation is successful has already been discussed. The presence of what is interpreted must be added to the activity of the interpreter; the interpretation must be of such a kind that the "work itself" is present in it. When one gets this impression, one would say that the interpreter has understood the text of the work. In judging in this way, one may himself be said to understand the interpretation of the work and the work in its interpretation. When it is clear to one that the concern is with a performance, one differentiates the two from one another—not necessarily such that one would be able to lift the one away from the other. However, one knows that there can be, or, for that matter, already have been, other performances of the same work. One likewise knows that the performers can dedicate, or have already dedicated, themselves to other works, and that these are therefore similar, if perhaps in a difficult manner to determine. One does not, then, experience the difference of work and interpretation by holding the two next to one another. How is this supposed to be possible, since works, in their textuality, are only there in interpretation, and interpretations can only be those of works or of other texts? One recognizes interpretations as a possibility of a work, though, just as one recognizes a work as a possibility in interpretation. It is not a stretch to think that this recognizing is an understanding. In order to determine understanding with more precision, however, one must clarify the relationship between possibility and actuality discussed here. What succeeds in understanding is, by all appearances, the ever-specific insight in this relationship.

An interpretation is a possibility because it never has the character of a conclusive solution. As presentation it is in fact the actuality of the work, although it does not reach its completion in this. It is not the definitive production of the work, but, rather, is sustained by the work; it is *an* actuality, and, precisely for this reason, a possibility, to which alternatives can always be conceived. Such alternatives are generally also factually given, and solutions other than those given will always be possible. Every interpretation, however successful it may have been, is only one among others.

A work is also a possibility, albeit in a different manner. It is, taken for itself, nothing actually but is rather in need of interpretation in order to become actual. The actuality of such an interpretation is a realization of the possible work, which does not itself exhaust the work; the work does not come completely into focus in any one interpretation of its text. Rather, the text is always more than it is in any respective case. The work is possible not because it stands only under the reservation that other alternatives are possible, but, rather, because the text is richer than its presence in each respective case. It is not something that is delimited by its difference from other possibilities, but, rather, something inexhaustible, and, for this reason, unlimited possibility. Taken for itself the work is the undeveloped fullness of the possible.

As possibilities, work and interpretation are always determined in themselves in specific manners. An interpretation is shaped through the skills of interpreters—their technical ability and acquired knowledge, their experience—as well as through their more or less consciously reached decisions that bring about the interpretation. With the corresponding knowledge, an interpretation may be described as such, in its specific character; it can, as interpretation, be conclusive in itself, and it not seldom has its own "signature"; it has its style, which one recognizes in comparison to other interpretations of the same work, although also to interpretations of other works by the same interpreter. In their own determinacy, interpretations can be in themselves conclusive and coherent—even in the case that one finds them problematic as interpretations of the work that they present. One thinks, for example, of Glenn Gould's Mozart recordings.

The determinacy of a work is given with its text. The task of every interpretation that wishes to be convincing as one of this work is posed by the fabric of its moments. If only portions of the text were presented, the interpretation would remain incomplete; if moments and connections that are of significance for the whole of the text were not recognized, it would be insufficient or even just a failure. However, every determination of the text nevertheless leaves open a more or less wide range of variation for its realization. None of its moments are fixed in such a way that they could not also be read otherwise. It is true that every moment is identifiable as a determinate one only in connection with others. Yet, differentiations are always possible, the order of the text in its self-sameness is always shown to be a little bit different when one opens it up from a different point of departure. As a complex order, it sets free unlimited possibilities for interpretation. That this is the case may best be established in comparison with other interpretations, although the work itself would never emerge from this as the sum of its interpretations. It is true that the task of every interpretation is to be as just to the text of the work as possible. However, this can only mean always to bring the text into focus from a limited perspective as a unified fabric, in its wholeness and coherence.

The experience that one has in interpretation is on the one hand, then, that of two possibilities: the possibility of the work and the possibility of interpretation. However, the two possibilities are, on the other hand, in one actuality, and this actuality cannot be some independent third thing in contrast to the two possibilities; there is nothing beyond the interpretation and the work or text that is in play in the facts of the matter. The actuality, which one experiences must be that of both possibilities, then, and, in fact, not of both at the same time or in the same respect; that would annihilate the experience of the possible, without which there is no experience of interpretation. One experiences both, actuality and possibility, in such a way that only one of the two possibilities is seen as actual. If the interpretation appears actual, the work remains possible; if the work appears actual, the interpretation retains the character of possibility. With actuality, the experience of interpreting always also brings into view a possibility, which relativizes actuality.

This may be shown in a description of the relationship of interpretation and work. An interpretation is actual as the presentation of a work, a work has its actuality as what is presented in an interpretation. Yet, viewed on the basis of the possible work, an interpretation in its actuality also remains a possibility; as actuality, which it is, it is given an index of possibility, based on the fullness of the possible, which the work is. Interpretation is the presentation of something that cannot be exhausted by any presentation.

The actuality of a work is given only with an interpretation. If this is realized consciously and reflectively, the actuality of the work retains an index of possibility based on the interpretation. Thus, the actuality of the work that one experiences in the interpretation is not complete, neither as the finished product of an activity, nor as the completion of the activity itself. It is, in Aristotelian terms, neither ἔργον nor ἐνέργυια.[132]

The actuality of the interpretation and the actuality of the work never coincide. They are never one and yet are not able to be without one another: as two sides of the same matter of fact, they cross over one another chiastically.[133] What one experiences is the actuality of an activity and the actuality of a matter, the matter in activity and the activity in the matter, without the two reaching concordance. This is the case because the actual is disclosed on the basis of two different possibilities. If one knows that one is dealing with an interpretation, both sides are present in an interplay; the one emerges, and then again the other. The experience that is characteristic for interpretation forms in the interplay of this actuality that is in itself doubled. With this, interpretation proves itself once again to be circular. It is a *circle of reflection*, and it is all the more clear the more clearly it turns its actuality back toward its possibility. One enacts an interpretation, or comprehends it as actual, in *reference* to the possibility of the work and therein recognizes it as presentation; and, one experiences the work by recognizing it in the possibility of interpretive *enactment*, or, comprehension, as something presented. The interpretation, as this possibility, is recognizable in turn based on the work; its possibilities and decisions are there for its never complete realization. The circle of reflection in which the issue of interpretation is disclosed has its focus in reference to text of the work.

The insight that arises in this circle of reflection is the insight of understanding. Accordingly, understanding is a recognizing based on something. Something is not there as it is given in the course of activity and inner experience but rather in the illuminating brokenness of a reference to something that stands outside of this course. There belongs to understanding an enactment that is put into a reference; it is at the same time that experience of the reference which makes it intelligible as its respective possibility. Understanding is a recognizing in this relation of reference and enactment—a recognizing that is intensified in presentation.

This may be made clear in regard to interpretation from the moment that understanding sets in: that an interpretation is at issue in something is revealed in grasping the relationship of presentation and text. One understands an interpretation by enacting it or comprehending it, and, in this way, experiences which matter are disclosed in this enactment or comprehension. And, one understands what is disclosed in presentation by experiencing it in the possibilities of its presentation. One understands, that is, how an interpretation unlocks a text through presentation. And, one likewise understands what has been unlocked in its actuality by paying attention to what is special about the presentation. Through this, the matter of the interpretation is once again opened; by recognizing the respectively specific possibilities of presentation the matter may be presented and understood anew. This awakens appreciation [*Verständnis*] for the unique character of the work as well as for the presentation in its individuality, in its possibilities and limits. One does not understand the style of the work, its distinctiveness, without its presentations. This style is what endures distinctively in all of its presentations.

Even elementary understanding stands in the tension between reference and enactment. When one has not understood what someone articulates, this is something different than when one says that he has not heard something properly. That could also apply to a sound. Yet, because something that one regards as a sentence immediately gives rise to the expectation that something is meant, listening stands in reference to the context, in which what is said could stand.

When one understands the expression and so is able to follow what is communicated, one understands this based on the context of meaning, in which it stands; one recognizes the expression as a possibility of the realization of this context of meaning. Things are similar when one understands a game. In this case, one knows how one is able conduct oneself—how, for example, one is able to move one's game pieces—because one sees the individual moves on the basis of the context of their significance. Things are also similar when one understands what another does; in this case, one is in a position to see this person's conduct based on his aim and to grasp the conduct as a possibility of the realization of this aim. Understanding means, accordingly, to have a reference for an enactment and always to be able to realize a reference in an enactment.

In the cases mentioned, the sense of reference nevertheless remains as it were in the background; the context on the basis of which something is understood is itself not explicit. Rather, the concern is with the possibility of conduct. Things are different in interpretation; here, the sense of reference has priority because the concern is with the context itself, on the basis of which a conduct is possible. It is after all the task of interpretation specifically to present it, that is, the text.

Production is closer to presentation than conduct in a context is. If production must be grasped, following the determination of the Platonic *Gorgias*, as the manufacture of something by means of a view of its inner order,[134] so that something in itself coherent comes into existence, then the concern here, too, is with a recognizing based on something, that is, with an understanding. The concern is also not with the enactment of the manufacture alone but rather with bringing into focus the order that comes into view in the result of the production. Seen in this way, production [*Herstellung*] is not only manufacture, but also always a "putting forth [*Her-stellen*]" or a putting in prominence [*Her-ausstellen*] of the definitive look, that is, of the εἶδος. As Heidegger expresses it, something should be put [*gestellt*] "in that which it is . . . in sensuous visibility and tangibility." It is "not actually the individual table, then" that is produced. It is rather "the essence" that is "put forth [*her-gestellt*] and put into [*hin-gestellt*] visibility and tangibility."[135]

Even if a presentation is at play in production, however, it must be distinguished from production. Production is supposed not only to bring the essence or idea of the table into visibility, but, rather, to have a usable table as its result. Heidegger's identification of production and presentation comes at the price that this result is marginalized and that manufacturing production becomes putting forth. On this presupposition, conversely, mimesis may also be elucidated as "making, fashioning, producing."[136] Yet, as if in objection, Greek also has its own word for production. Had Plato wished to speak of ποίησις instead of μίμησις in Book X of the *Republic*, to which Heidegger refers, he certainly would have, not least because the argumentation here touched on the difference between the two activities.

The distinction between production and presentation is consequential for understanding in still another respect. Because the concern in production is with the manufactured result, understanding, here, is always fundamentally the same. Experience accumulated in the course of time may, in fact, contribute to more secure manufacturing, but only the manufacturing itself is altered by this; the understanding is not disturbed through it. By contrast, in presentation the concern is always also with a *development* of understanding. If no presentation is final, and if it moreover lies in the essence of presentation that it is not schematically repeated, then, with every presentation—or interpretation—understanding becomes different. It is true that the momentary success of understanding does exist; something can become intelligibile "all at once," understanding illuminates "in the blink of an eye." Yet, once something is understood, it may be understood more fully and better. Understanding is predisposed toward this without becoming an endless self-surpassing that always and again annihilates its own results. Something that has been understood before is not necessarily put out of effect by a new understanding, but often, rather, refined, elaborated more pregnantly. In any case, it is enriched, and, in this respect, the possibilities of understanding that arise out of the reflective forms of interpretation—that is, from clarification and explication—are consequential realizations of what lies in understanding itself.

It is not possible to understand more or better, however, without understanding every time anew. However much an understanding may be enriched—no new understanding of the matter comes about unless every understanding commences anew. Notwithstanding all familiarity with a text, the repetition of a reading of a book must set in every time, and, accordingly, the question of the relation between presentation and text that guides understanding is posed anew. From this viewpoint, too, understanding proves to be a recognizing of a special kind. It is a realization without conclusiveness and without provisionality at once; neither is there a result that one could maintain once and for all, nor is there always something yet to come that relativizes all of the achieved results. The reason for this lies in the essence of understanding, because, that is, it is the recognizing of the actual on the basis of the possible as well as the experience of the possible in its actuality. It thus leaves the actual and the possible in suspension without any skepticism.[137]

Understanding could not commence anew if there were not always something else to understand. This means, however, that in every understanding there is something one does not understand. The more clearly one emphasizes the difference in the relation of understanding, the more strongly one will emphasize this not understanding. The task of interpretation only poses itself because the text of the work is differentiated from its interpretation. Whoever poses this task for himself has not yet understood and wants to understand.

Gadamer believes that this desire to understand goes back to an "impetus," to an irritation, with which the "difference" between "usage familiar to us and that of the text" becomes apparent.[138] However, because one allows oneself "to be told something"[139] by the text, and because this plays "its substantive truth against one's own pre-established opinions,"[140] the difference is once again dissolved. Insofar as the text is brought into focus in Gadamer's sense, what becomes of understanding is an enduring familiarity that is confirmed time and again. It is true that one experiences how projections of a meaningful whole are corrected through the self-presentation of the text. But this is only possible because the "pre-established opinions,"[141] or "prejudices"[142] on which the projections rest, are themselves moments of the tradition experienced in the text. The difference of the text is here only a "phase in the enactment of the text."[143]

By contrast, Schleiermacher emphasized that understanding rests "on the fact of not understanding"[144] and intended this as the essential determination of understanding. Not understanding is no mere point of departure that one leaves behind in understanding, but, rather, a condition of understanding itself. Understanding must always be achieved on the basis of not understanding; this is all the more clear, as Schleiermacher thinks, the greater the challenge posed by what is to be understood. Only when one principally "concerns oneself with something insignificant, or, at least, wishes to understand only for the sake of a specific interest and thus sets readily defined limits" is it possible to come to the idea "that understanding arises on its own."[145] Otherwise, it is necessary to develop the possibilities that lead to understanding as such, or, as Schleiermacher formulates it: one must take one's refuge in "art," that is, in the proficient, even methodologically guided, development of possibilities of understanding.[146] This, however, and, with it, the "stricter praxis" that is opposed to an orientation toward something insignificant, "assumes that misunderstanding arises of its own accord and that understanding must be desired and sought at every point."[147] All desire to understand arises from the expectation of an emergent understanding. It is only for this reason that the possibility of understanding may be developed, only for this reason that seeking "refuge" in art, as Schleiermacher says, lies in the desire to understand.

Gadamer does Schleiermacher an injustice when he criticizes the artificiality of the desire to understand as an aesthetic impulse,[148] and, at the same time, as a plea for "method absolved of all contents."[149] "Art," here means neither fine art nor method, but, rather, ars, τέχνη; it is not a medium of aesthetic experience and also not an organon of procedural rules in the sense of a modern empirical science. What is intended is rather an ability, on the basis of which one knows to avert the misunderstandings that arise "on their own" through initial misunderstanding—a circumspection and attentiveness in the treatment of texts acquired through experience and practice. This is different in Schleiermacher's so-called "more lax practice": Here, not understanding does not appear, and, because of this, possible misunderstanding remains unnoticed. Not understanding first leads into the possibility of explicit understanding.

What, and how, one fails to understand is something different from case to case. It depends on experience, say, the erudition of the reader or interpreter, also, on his attentiveness and concentration. Something in the text may be unfamiliar or be passed over in reading, disturbing the continuity of the story. However, it must be possible for a partial not understanding of this kind to arise; if such a partial not understanding were not constituent in everything that is able to be interpreted and understood, interpretation for the sake of understanding would not set in. Even attentiveness and concentration in reading would be inexplicable. The expectation of an understanding is at play here of which one still knows nothing as long as one has not yet had the experience of not understanding. Nevertheless, not-understanding is reckoned with unpredictably. The text, in its essence, can release not understanding in every moment.

What not understanding [*Nichtverstehen*] makes possible is *the unintelligible* [*das Unverständliche*]. With this, neither the uncomprehended [*Unverstanden*], nor the unfamiliar [*Unbekannt*] is intended. The uncomprehended is only some *each time* unintelligible thing or other, which, as such, can emerge and hinder or prevent understanding. It can, however, also become a respective challenge for understanding, and, to this extent, it is something still not understood, which is supposed to become intelligible [*verständlich*]. Yet, something that still has not been considered in regard to its possible intelligibility at all is also unintelligible. The unintelligible does not specifically have to stand out as this particular unintelligible thing. In this, it is comparable to what is unfamiliar. For a finite knowing, there is always the unfamiliar. Yet, it first emerges each time when one becomes aware of it through something familiar connected with it; one is only able to know that the author of a writing is unfamiliar to one when one knows of the writing itself. This is also how it is with the unintelligible, which, for this reason, becomes something uncomprehended.

That the unintelligible is nevertheless of a different kind than something unfamiliar can be made clear on the model of literary works: The central figure of a drama may be clearly identified, and everything that about him, which can be brought into experience based on the plot of the piece, is also familiar. His actions and even more so his motives for acting remain unclear, however, despite all attempts at interpretation. The figure is not integrated, or least, not seamlessly, into the text. He is unintelligible. Or, the abundance of allusions of a work can be recognized in reading and—with the proper education—can even be extensively classified; nevertheless, the interplay of motives and figures is not conclusive and to be reconstructed once and for all. Or, a narrative offers a number of observations in such a way that, simple as they may be, they can always be regarded from further new viewpoints, and, moreover, so that even the consideration of all these viewpoints is not adequate to grasp them entirely.

In Shakespeare's *Hamlet*, in Goethe's *Faust II*, in Kafka's parable *Vor dem Gesetz*, one is dealing in this way with the unintelligible. One experiences the unintelligible as the indeterminate or vague. However, it is also the complex and the inexhaustible. It is the polysemic, which no interpretation, no understanding integrates without remainder.

The most effective plea in hermeneutical discussion for the unintelligible originates from Friedrich Schlegel. His essay, "Über die Unverstandlichkeit"[150] is readily read as evidence for a radical critique of understanding.[151] Yet, Schlegel does not wish to demonstrate the impossibility of understanding; the experience of the unintelligible is for him no reason for hermeneutical skepticism or for the assumption of a total anarchy of discourse. His sole intention is to make clear the significance of unintelligibility as of a corrective and of a necessary supplement to intelligibility. In this sense, he stresses the significance of the unintelligible for the value of all that is brought about through art in the widest sense. "States and systems, the most artificial works of human beings, often so artificial that one cannot wonder enough at the wisdom of their creator," are only protected against the assault of "the sinful understanding" when a portion of the unintelligible, small as it may be, is "genuinely and purely preserved" in it. Even "the most precious thing that the human being has," namely, "inner contentedness" depends, as everyone can easily know, "ultimately somewhere on a point that must be left in the dark, yet that for all of this bears and contains the whole, and that would lose this power in the very moment that one would wish to resolve it in the understanding."[152] The effect of literary works is likewise ensured across the ages through the unintelligible: "a classical writing does not ever completely have to be understood. However, those who are educated and educate themselves, have to wish always to learn more from them."[153]

Schlegel says this on the presupposition of a concept of understanding that is also found in Schleiermacher. One understands when one can "construct" something.[154] Constructing something completely would be tantamount to bringing it forth oneself in building it up. It would be entirely the work of one's own understanding, founded without remainder in one's own possibilities. This idea, which became prominent through Kant[155] and which was radicalized by Fichte, forms the folio for the image of horror evoked by Schlegel of a world that "would in all seriousness be thoroughly intelligible."[156] The reason that this notion is horrible is already found in his piece, *Über das Stadium der griechischen Poesie*: "nothing contradicts the character and even the concept of the human being so much as the idea of a fully isolated power, which could be effective through itself and in itself alone."[157]

Schlegel did not develop this insight so that it would lead to a different concept of understanding. The reference of his to the unintelligible could thereby have been further elevated. If understanding arises not in construction, but, rather, in presentation, then the unintelligible is more than a mere corrective; in this case, it is an integral moment of understanding itself. It is the openness in understanding, in which understanding sets in anew and is able further to be developed. This openness is the unresolved tension of something different, which is resolved for this moment in the success of understanding and nevertheless remains in existence, by allowing for the expectation of a more differentiated, more precise or in some other way better resolution.

This openness of understanding derives from its essence. When something is enacted on the basis of something else, the enactment is never exhaustive; it remains a possibility that could also be otherwise. Moves of a game are thus always only *one* way of filling out the rules based on which they are understood; what is intended by a linguistic expression could also have been said otherwise. Things are certainly this way if the enactment in question is a presentation. A presentation is supposed to bring something into focus as such, on the basis of which it is intelligible, and, insofar as this is never given fully in any presentation, the openness of understanding lies in what itself is to be understood.

What is to be understood, that is, the text, is open in two respects. It may be presented as something whole, ordered, and so must itself be whole and ordered. However, in no presentation is it finished as a whole, in none is its order actualized with finality. This is not the case because this order would withdraw in presentation; when a presentation is successful, its actuality is also that of the text in its order, be it determined in this way or that. Rather, the order is not purely recognizable as order. Even if it supposed to be as unambiguously established as a musical piece is in sheet music, possibilities of tempo, phrasing, accent, and tone remain open. The sheet music does not communicate the order, but, rather, only indicates it, so that it must always be put into sound "differently" than it appears on the page. And, even if in a poem there should be no doubt about sentence construction and significance, possibilities of explication and clarification remain available. Even if a text is clearly structured, its elements are still not unambiguously determined. Each of them can, in its variations of significance, be differently accentuated, and, with this, referred differently to other elements. Whether an episode in a novel is more or less important for a narrated story may be judged differently, and, depending on the judgment, the story would be presented differently. One would nevertheless recognize it, in the different clarifications, as the same. Because the text says nothing, it can always only be said otherwise; yet, in return, it leaves itself a space of play open. Every text, then, is on the one hand ordered, structured, *limited* in relation to its moments; and, on the other hand, incomprehensible, not fixed, that is, *unlimited*, at the same time. For texts hold what, in Plato's *Philebus*, is developed as a determination of beings in general: unity and multiplicity, and, with them, limit (πέρας) and the unlimited, (ἄπειρον) belong together in beings as things grown together.[158]

Written, drawn, or composed texts are not, however, simply like other beings. They are in need of interpretation, and this sets them apart from all others. Their neediness of interpretation brings with it, in turn, that limit and the unlimited are encountered differently in them than in other beings. In order to realize the order within their limits, one must involve oneself with the unlimited that allows them to be open; in order to have the experience of the unlimited, one has to be concerned with order. Indeterminacies of the text are to be used for the presentation of order, this order is of such a kind that it is realized in something that it does not ascertain. Because limit and unlimitedness point to one another in this way, they meet in special intensity. This, in turn, goes back to the texts themselves. They bring this intensity with them, and, in fact, through the manner in which they meet.

This meeting, then, must now be discussed with more precision. It is first with this that the issue of interpretation and the understanding that belongs to it is made sufficiently clear. Because the exteriority of its matter belongs to the essence of interpretation, it cannot be determined only on the basis of the reference of interpretation to it. Rather, it is necessary to grasp it as exteriority on its own. What is exterior for interpretation shall prove itself to be the *objective*. Texts are met objectively. What must be made clear, then, is what the objective is, and, just as much, how it finds form, by becoming *objects*.

§ 13. Objectivity [Gegenständlichkeit]

The word itself says what an object [*Gegenstand*] is: It is what stands over against [*das Entgegenstehende*], what is across from [*gegenüber*] and remains standing across from. In older parlance, the word can also indicate the condition of things that stand over against one another, say, in talk of the "opposition [*Gegenstand*] of planets."[159] This allows what an object is to be expressed with particular clarity: not some arbitrary thing, but rather, something *insofar as* it is over against. An object is something standing in the way [*im Gegen-stand*].*

Modern philosophy has had difficulties with the objective. This gives a critical edge to the hermeneutical rehabilitation of it. As soon as the objective is

---

*[Although the English "object" properly is a sound translation of the German word *Gegenstand*, it misses important connotations of the original that are emphasized by the author. The word *Gegenstand*, if translated literally, would appear in English as something like "what stands against," or, "what stands opposite," suggesting, as the author points out, that an object is not understood best as something in isolation, but something that stands in a certain relation. In fact, this suggestion may not be so foreign to the English word "object," if one bears in mind its etymological relation to the Latin as something thrown to, set before, thrown against. —Trans.]

discovered in modern philosophy, the question of how it may be overcome is posed. Its overcoming becomes such a decisive philosophical task that modern philosophy as a whole appears as a large-scale enterprise of de-objectification.

To this enterprise belong the different notions of increased dynamism and of fluidity, which wish to admit nothing that is steadfast, standing on its own, and which wish to displace everything into movement. This comes to expression most clearly in Nietzsche's idea "that something in existence, something, which has somehow come to a stand, is time and again interpreted to new ends, seized anew, transformed and redirected to a new use by a power superior to it."[160] "Interpretation," understood as continual carrying over, by which all "previous 'meaning' and 'purpose' must necessarily be obscured or entirely obliterated,"[161] is a dynamic in the flux of passing away and becoming that tears away from everything objective, "what has come to a stand."[162]

To this enterprise belongs no less the notion that one can withdraw into conduct and language games and leave behind all philosophical objectification. To dive into life that is simply to be lived—this is what Wittgenstein's conviction stands for, that one notices "the solution to the problem of life ... upon the disappearance of the problem." Whenever "another person wishes to say something metaphysical," one must in response make clear to him "that he has given no meaning to certain signs in his sentences."[163]

More consequential still are two other patterns of thought, because they move the object and objectification to the center of discussion. For the one, the objective presence of things counts as a symptom of failed self-actualization; while, on this view, the manifestation of human life in the world proves to be impossible without objectification, it only succeeds through an overcoming and integration of the objective. For the other, the objective presence of things appears as the objectification of one's own life; it counts as a consequence of the recognition that all life finds its place in the world through objectification and thus leads to a loss of self.

The pattern first mentioned may be pursued back to Hegel and Marx. In Hegel, it finds expression in his conception of "spirit," which brings itself into actuality through its own products in the "merely exterior, sensuous, and transitory,"[164] and, thereby, strives to close the cleft between itself and the exterior world. For a spirit that is understood in this way, externalization is an overcoming of exteriority, the exterior always comes into view only in order to become known as what is proper to the interiority. Building on Hegel, Marx develops the idea of living labor, which, with its products, is supposed to transpose even its own social character into the exteriority of the "world of goods" and to overcome its loss of self through the appropriation of production.[165]

To be sure, this pattern emerges with particular pregnancy in George Simmel's diagnosis of a "tragedy of culture." In a recapitulation of a line of tradition that goes back to Hegel, it is said with special trenchancy how the emancipation of things affects a life enacted as self-actualization.[166] A life that essentially must "objectify" itself and carry this out in the establishment of institutions, in the erection of buildings, and in the production of works comes to be confronted always and again, as Simmel emphasizes, with the "characteristic independence,"[167] the "autonomous development"[168] [*Eigenentwicklung*] of its products. This belongs to the essence of production, for what is produced is never determined solely by the intentions of those who produce.[169] For this reason, the attempt to actualize human life as culture also never leads to a complete actuality of human life. This makes culture become a "tragedy," an incorrigible error, by which "annihilating powers directed" against the essence of culture "originate from the deepest strata of this very essence."[170] Human life becomes alien to itself precisely in the attempt to win its own actuality.

Simmel's central idea of an "autonomous [*eigene*] logic of the object" [*Objekt*] is intended not merely diagnostically, however.[171] Simmel is at the same time a radical critic of the dialectical figure of thought according to which the relationship of subject and object is the movement of a self-consciousness, one that, according to Hegel's definitive formulation, posits "*itself* as object," "or, the object as itself for the sake of the indivisible unity of *being-for-self.*"[172] The "object," as Simmel understands it, may no longer be mediated with this as the other of the subject. The objective absolves itself of the subject and its self-consciousness; it is no longer the objectivity of consciousness, but, rather, simply stands over against.

Nevertheless, Simmel's idea is sustained by the dialectic that he opposes; if the objective were not intended as something posited by self-consciousness, its emancipation would also not be tragic. In its problematic position as standing over against, the objective continues to point back to the subject, and, at this point, to the subject's incapacity for self-mediation. Because Simmel does not cast off Hegel's approach, he opens himself to contradiction, if not exactly with Hegel, then certainly in the sense of Hegel. The impossibility of a total mediation of "subject" and "object" does not have to be tantamount, then, to a tragic failure of self-actualization. If this objection is convincing, the difficulty is dissolved, if not exactly as in Hegel, then nevertheless in the sense of Hegel.

Ernst Cassirer has stood up in this way for a less dramatic approach to the problem described by Simmel. To this end, Cassirer builds on Hegel without committing himself to Hegel's idea of a form of knowing that is clouded by nothing alien in its self-transparency and, in this sense, absolute.[173] Culture is itself "dialectical," because it is not a one-time reification, but rather "an activity that must continually set in anew"; cultural developments cannot be alien in regard to a developing life[174] because these developments are not conclusive results but "bridges"[175] across which an I passes along his cultural possibilities to others.

Cassirer's revision, however, fails to take into consideration something decisive. Even if works of culture can always be integrated into life again, they are nevertheless removed from the lives of their producers, without immediately coming to belong to the life of those who take them up. Cassirer did not consider this—and it is only momentary—emancipation, even though he must presume it: cultural products can only be "mediator between I and you"[176] by belonging to neither. If this is the case, however, then something that has been produced and become independent no longer comes to be realized in any integrative activity. Things stand in accord with their essence for themselves; only for this reason are they able to be appropriated.

The second pattern is articulated definitively by Husserl. It turns on a discontent with the self-description of the human being found in or oriented by the natural sciences. In the conscious life of the human being, according to Husserl's critique, science sees nothing other than a sequence of spatio-temporally identifiable, empirically describable events.[177] This leads to the fact that contents of consciousness could no longer be appropriately understood. What Husserl objects to in science is taken up and radicalized by the young Heidegger. It also holds, he thinks, in regard to philosophy, which has developed the model for science with its theoretical attitude toward the world. As "objectification," the theoretical attitude toward human life amounts to a "devitalization," which conceals originary inner experience.[178] Wherever life is encountered as an object, it is, to Heidegger's thinking, lost; under the "general rule of the theoretical,"[179] one no longer regards life for what it actually is.[180]

For Husserl and Heidegger, the conviction that the scientific self-description of the human being is perilous for human life forms an important, perhaps even the most important, motive of their philosophy. Despite all differences between their projects, both wish to achieve freedom over and against science. The path to this is the description and analysis of nonobjectified life in its enactment. Both wish to go back to original inner experience, the meaning opened up in it, and thus also show how self-objectification is possible on the basis of this inner experience, and, at the same time, misses its essence. It has been shown how this is realized in Heidegger's program of a hermeneutics of facticity in an orientation taken from the model of practical philosophy.[181]

Husserl's and Heidegger's attempts at de-objectification do not succeed, however. The formulation of the question that asks of the conditions of the possibility of science and that therein is transcendental does not prevail upon the possibility of objectification and self-objectification. Husserl and the early Heidegger do in fact achieve distance from the dogmatic commitments of science. They release themselves from "objects" and go back to the "region of pure consciousness," or, respectively, to the non-objective enactment of life or of Dasein, in order thus to free up a context of meaning, on the basis of which the meaning of putative objectivity is first actually disclosed. However, they leave the question of the possibility of objectification itself unanswered; no path leads from out of the immanence of consciousness, or, respectively, of life or of Dasein, to what is intended by objectification. However, that something is "outside" cannot, on the other hand, be disputed.

Husserl admits this himself when he speaks of a relation to the object that cannot be imminently understood as a "relation of consciousness to its intentional object."[182] The trigger for this was the question of "what the 'pretension' of consciousness actually to 'refer' to something objective, to be 'convincing,' really means."[183] Husserl answers the question by ascribing to the content of consciousness, or, "noema," an objective reference. Every noema has "its meaning" and refers "to 'its' object through it."[184] This object is "the pure X in abstraction from all predicates"[185] and is to be distinguished as the "object *simpliciter*" from "the object in the how of its determinacies."[186] In a comparable manner, the talk in the *Cartesianische Meditationen* is of the transcendental object as "transcendental clue."[187] "The point of departure," Husserl adds in elucidation, is "necessarily the object that is simply given in each case, on the basis of which reflection goes back to a respective manner of consciousness."[188]

It is, in its honesty, impressive that Husserl speaks of "curious structures" in regard to the issue just outlined.[189] The issue is, from the standpoint of Husserlian phenomenology, in fact disquieting. Obviously, consciousness' reference to the outside is so resistant to all attempts to dispense with the reality of objects that Husserl sees himself compelled to ascribe an objective reference to the noematic correlate of consciousness. After all, consciousness appears as consciousness of something, that refers to something. This is not consistent with the immanence of consciousness that is taken advantage of in phenomenological analysis; there is something of which consciousness is essentially in need: the object, the exterior, which, as such, is more or less clear. In fact, Husserl never contested the existence of this outside, and, in this regard, he is not an "internalist."[190] But, according to his understanding of the ἐποχή, exteriority is inessential for consciousness; it can be bracketed out, such that things appear phenomenologically alone in the view of a consciousness, to whose immanence belongs being directed toward something. The claim of an objective reference of noemata is in a peculiar way at odds with this.

Heidegger is no less in the clear about the limits of his approach. At the end of *Sein und Zeit*, he maintains that the question of the essence of "reification" has remained unanswered. The difference between the "being of existing Dasein" and "the being of what is not like Dasein" is only "the point of departure for the ontological problematic, but nothing that philosophy" could "get over."[191] What reification means, from whence it originates, why it "leads again and again to mastery" and is still inadequate to the "being of 'consciousness,'" remain open.[192]

If one compares this result with that of the dialectical approach, a concordance arises that is perhaps surprising in view of the difference of the approaches. The attempt to overcome the independence of thingliness proves to be problematic both times for the same reason. Both times, the attempt leads to an immanence, which would put out of effect both the autonomy of things and, at once, thingliness itself, if the things, in their autonomy, do not resist. Taken as a cultural product in Cassirer's sense, the thing becomes, on the model of Hegel, an intermediary stage of in a cultural occurrence—an idea that is found quite similarly in Gadamer's dialectic of historically effective consciousness.[193] And, taken as something that in Husserl's and Heidegger's sense belongs in consciousness, or, respectively, in life or Dasein, the thing is transformed into a moment of its givenness in "life," "Dasein," or "consciousness," although the exteriority associated with objectification or reification can no longer be grasped. Nevertheless, the thing remains as "mediator of I and you" just as autonomously as an object that no longer adheres to any normal intentional relation, or as beings that are examined beyond the fundamental ontology of Dasein. Left alone from dialectical and transcendental reflection, things simply remain standing in their exteriority.

This does not mean, however, that one would also experience them in this exteriority. As what is simply just there, things do not for the most part come into focus, but, rather, are hidden by the enactments in which they stand. Even if things are not placed in the immanence of Dasein or of consciousness, they are experienced solely by the acts of consciousness that grasp them. In the enactment of this relation they are then "something thrown in the way," obiectum, ἀντικείμενον. ἀντικείμενον is what lies across from consciousness, insofar as it stands in a relation conceived by consciousness, for example, the perceptible over against perception, the rationally apprehensible over against the apprehension of reason.[194] Objects are bound to consciousness, even if one grants them exteriority. Or, things are useful things and, as such, are conceived on the basis of how they can be taken in hand, their "handiness."[195] They are also able to have significance as mementos, such that one sees them on the basis of the one who has used or surrounded himself with them.

Even if the exteriority of things here remains unexperienced, however, it is somehow there. Really, it sustains acts of consciousness that are directed toward things and the conduct that has to do with them. If what is perceptible were not present for perception as something exterior, then what one calls perception would be a self-enclosed dream. And, however much a useful thing may be experienced on the basis of its uses—use is nevertheless a relation that grasps at the outside. Something can only be done with something, and this latter has to be there.

The motive for the "tragic" constitution of culture and the critique of reification, of objectification,* rests on this. Behind these concepts lies the worry that

---

*[The original German reads, "Verdinglichung, Objektivierung, Vergegenständlichung...," I provide a slightly elliptical translation in order to avoid redundancy. —Trans.]

in reaching out toward what is exterior, one is at its mercy and can lose oneself in it. If something other, something different from oneself has to be there in order that one may conduct oneself, then the conduct is not controllable in every respect. Instead of bestowing significance on things from a safe vantage, this conduct itself is placed among things, and this, in turn, makes one at least like a thing among things. Without a commonality with things, however it is to be thought, no effect could be had on them, and one would just as little sense the resistance they put up against this attempt at affecting them. As soon as one experiences oneself in relation to something exterior, one is himself outside. One discovers that one can observe oneself like an arbitrary thing.

Discontent toward exteriority is based solely on the sense of enactment. When things are not held as objects of consciousness or when, in conduct, significance as usability or usefulness does not befit them, they fall, so it appears, outside the sphere of the human and are merely exterior. They are the nonhuman that merely stands or lies there, something that has become useless, something that no longer has any value or significance. This is how Heidegger described it for things of use. A "useful thing"* can lose the inconspicuousness that is essential for it. In this case, it is no longer simply at hand or in its place so that it as it were awaits being at hand. It is observed, though this observation has nothing to do with its possible or factical use, or it is missing when it is supposed to be handy. In the first case, it has become "conspicuous" [auffällig], in the second, "obstinate" [aufsässig]. And, if it hinders what is presently to be done, for example, because it is lying around in the way, it is "obtrusive" [aufdringlich].[196]

Heidegger investigates the outlined situations because the essence of the thing of use, its inconspicuous handiness, becomes experienceable and determinable in them. Here, something that is handy "forfeits its handiness in a certain way." This handiness, however, "does not simply disappear, but, rather, as it were bids farewell in the conspicuousness of what is usable." It "shows itself once again," and, in this, in the tension of presence and withdrawal, actually first shows itself.[197] One knows what something is first when one knows how it has been.

The experience that something is no longer integrated within this ensemble of now familiar things can also be completely different—that is, determined not by this ensemble and the conduct that grants significance to it. Heidegger also gives an example of this, in describing something not as a thing of use, but, rather, in a particular manner as a "thing." The example is a jug, whose

---

*[The original German reads, "Ein Lebrauchsding oder 'Zeug'..." because both 'Lebrauchsding' and, following Stambaugh's transation of *Being and Time*, 'Zeug' may properly be put into English as a 'useful thing,' I left my translation here slightly elliptical, in order to avoid redundancy or confusion. Cf. stambaugh, 64 —Trans.]

bulbous, at once enclosing and opening form, emerges into view so that it then appears as the coming together of openness and closure. Now, it is moreover able to be thought of as a vessel that human beings use to express their devotion to the gods in sacrifice. Here, the devotion of attention occurs not with the jug, as if it were a thing of use, but rather in the pouring that as such is experienced on the basis of the jug. This activity stands within the precinct of things experienced as such.[198]

With this description, Heidegger discovers that there is a reliance on things, which does not arise in use.[199] This occurs in such a way, that things are determined in their essence. The thing, as such, is "thing,"* collection, which leaves the human being in referential relations that are due neither to the care of the self nor to one's own conduct. But, this collection is only possible if something is there that draws attention to itself. Only if the thing is experienced in itself does it call attention to the references that Heidegger commends as essential. The thing must be *objective*. This objectivity is, in Heidegger's determination, presupposed as if it were in familiar obviousness.

In objectivity, the exteriority of things no longer comes into focus on the basis of conduct and its context. It also does not show itself due to the fact that something falls outside the scope of one's conduct and its context. Rather, it steps across from. The objective is what steps across from, and then, at least for a moment, *stands over against*.

This standing over against constitutes the essence of the objective. If the objective were only an emergence, it would dissolve in an occurrence. It would be something surprising and overwhelming, as Heidegger reads into Goethe's turn of phrase, "over against each other." The "over" is here to be understood in the sense of "to come over one,"[200] and thus as a reference to a sudden advent of something that draws the attention of one's thought and yet can barely be grasped at all. The essence of the objective would be "presencing"[201] and only this. This, however, does not capture the objective; one misses it by dissolving it in movement.

It is true that the emergence of the objective is an occurrence. Something steps over and against and is all at once there. Yet, determinacy belongs to the objective; *something* steps over and across from and remains. This remaining is like a waiting; it is also a promising. It indicates and thereby releases the possibility of the desire to understand.

Insofar as the objective has stepped across from, become apparent all at once, one has not referred to it. There was no expectation, no interest, and also no need, thus also no initially searching, then fixed, view. It puts itself into a reference, rather, because what steps across from also steps over against. It is comparable to a person who happens upon one such that it is through this

---

*[The author uses the English word "thing" in his original German writing. —Trans.]

person that one comes to relate to him. One could turn away, though perhaps his standing across from has an effect precisely in this case. This is intensified when a person, or even a thing, remains standing there. The encounter is only now experienced in its meaning: namely, it is necessary to take up what steps over and against by standing up to it as it remains present. In regard to a person, this is tantamount to answering to his claim.[202] For something objective, one will attempt to bring it into focus in its objectivity. One presents it.

This occurs, for example, when a sketch artist or painter holds out in the face of something and takes it as his subject. Erhart Kästner reports of this. The concern is with one of Caspar David Friedrich's sketch pages, which presents a fir tree and contains a note in the corner: "5½ hours." This, according to Kästner, could not refer to the time required for the composition of the sheet. No practiced sketch artist needs five and a half hours for a hand-sized sheet such as this one. The only thing that could be intended is "that the sketch artist held on, waited, hoped before the tree, before the thing. Hoped? But of course, that the tree show itself to be stronger than he."[203]

Stronger in what manner, and in regard of what? The answer lies in the relationship between technical ability and deliberately protracted realization: the sketch artist does not want to have it easy; he wants that something, which stands across from him, would hinder him in his well-versed practice of his art. Waiting runs contrary to the all too common grain; it is a resistance against the skillfulness that is always a danger for the success of art. The danger of this signals the end for an artistic piece. The tree, to wit, the thing, should be stronger and foil the artistic piece. Like Friedrich, there is also another, Paul Cézanne, who spent hours before his subject, pausing, without coming to any rash conclusion. His painting is for this reason, as Merleau-Ponty puts it, a paradox: he sets his sights on reality and forbids himself the means to reach it.[204] This is no failure, however, but rather respect in the face of objectivity. One does it justice only by assuming it as the measure of presenting. The objective is accessible; it is not of such a kind that one would experience what it is only in failure. In this respect, it is to be distinguished from the "nonidentical" that Adorno understands as the limit "of spirit in all of its judgments."[205] However, like the nonidentical, it cannot be grasped in its accessibility. Whoever wishes to step in quickly and determine something would perhaps capture something of it, but not the objective. The objective is across from, that is: at a distance. The success of presentation is also possible only due to remoteness. Presentation is substantive to a special degree; it is founded not in one's own ability and knowledge, but, rather, is sustained by the across-from, in which, with its matter, one's own ability and knowledge is also intensified.

In principle, anything can become objective, without the least thing about it being changed. Casper David Friedrich's fir tree, Cézanne's "Montangue Sainte Victoire" are not objective in themselves. Often it is banal, everyday things that sketch artists and painters take as a subject; someone else might have thrown into the trash the same bottles and cans that formed a challenge for Morandi. Nevertheless, the objectivity of things is not granted arbitrarily. It is not always given and not for everyone, although it is always there as a possibility. With it, the exteriority of things is intensified.

Conversely, it is important that it is the exteriority *of things*. If only something like "exteriority in general" were discovered of things, what is decisive would be missing; an exteriority that is indeterminate and therefore ultimately concerns nothing would not lead beyond the immanence belonging to the sense of enactment. It would remain unnoticed that these same things that come into view as objects, or under the aspect of usability and usefulness, at the same time *condition* these possibilities of reference. In this case, there would be no possibility of coming into a relation to what is conditioning, and, in this case, the perspective of enactment would also remain unclear. By contrast, a context is opened up by the experience of the objective [*das Gegenständliche*], in which recognition directed toward objects [*Objekte*] and conduct oriented by usability and usefulness is only a moment. The context of things, as it appears based on recognition directed toward objects and on conduct, portrays this context in a characteristic reduction. The concern, therefore, is to investigate it still otherwise, namely, presentatively.

Visible things allow what objectivity is to be experienced especially impressively. The across-from of a subject matter, which may be put into a presentation and nevertheless remain across-from, is, in the literal sense of the word, viewable. Visible things make especially clear the manner in which the objective stands over against. The visible thing stands there at rest, whereas an occurrence cannot reach and retain the degree of intensity required for objectivity without memory or recollection. However, in principle, everything can become objective, for example, the conduct of a human being, insofar as it cannot be explained by previous association and familiar forms of association. Matters are similar for an expression in a conversation. If it becomes objective, it is like a caesura; one listens further, and nevertheless a peculiar contrary power is at work in one's hearing. As a lecture proceeds, a sentence remains standing and leaves one to ask: "What does that mean?" If one holds no hope of an answer to a question directed toward the speaker, then objectivity is there.

By becoming objective, something does not in fact mutate into a visible thing, though it does become thingly in a certain manner; it becomes *something*, a matter that no longer belongs in enacted life but rather stands for itself. It is something that has become exterior to the enactments of life and therefore recognizable as a moment of the context, in which even the enactments of life stand. It belongs to the *conditions* of recognition directed toward objects and of conduct, which aims at usability and usefulness, indeed, of everyday enacted life in general; because it is what is not everyday, what is not integrated into life, the everyday may be understood as what it is on the basis of it. Everything is of this kind that can emerge as a complex unity of life from out of a context that is lived—that is understood based on the enactment of life—into its own: affects and moods, attitudes and dispositions, situations and types, conflicts and powers, in short, the great themes of literature and art in general. The more often a theme can be treated without thereby being exhausted, the more intense is its objectivity. The matter remains across-from, it does not lose its hold on presentative recognition.

What does not lose its hold, here, is admittedly often enough not the matter itself, which has become objective, but, rather, its presentation. One is held at such a presentation when the concern is to recognize aspects of the world and of life, which have come to need explication and clarification. The presentation as it were steps in for the matter, which is presented through it. This is only possible because the presentation itself is objective. In this case, the objectivity that was initially experienced is taken up in the presentation, shaped, and, in this, strengthened. A presentation of the objective, to which this applies, is intended as objective. In this respect, they are not only objective, but, rather, *object*.

The objective character of presentation is revealed most clearly in fine art; with this, fine art proves once more its paradigmatic value for hermeneutical thought. What the painter takes as his subject is objective because it is picturesque [*Bildhaft*]. It stands out from the diffuse fullness of appearances as form, as color, in its material structure. This picturesque thing is determined ahead of time to become a picture [*Bild*]. The activity of the artist, by which the corporeality of presentative recognition may be demonstrated,[206] is significant only as an intermediate stage, as a "phasal moment," as a path from picturesque to picture. The picture, like the picturesque, stands as a thing before one's eyes. One recognizes it as a picture only by understanding it as an object. It is nothing but appearing, and, insofar as it is in its appearing presentation, it vouches for the appearance of what is presented. The picture presents by being form which is removed and raised, that is, carried over, from what is presented, and because it itself has color or material structure. It is not a copy [*Abbild*], which goes back to and can be compared with an original image [*Urbild*]. However, even if it cannot be mistaken for a copy because it is "abstract," it in truth has the character of presentation. In this case, it is dynamism become form, occurrence made visible, or rest carried over into form. In every case, however, it allows something to be there in it in a more mediated, and, for this reason, more intense presence. The picture brings something to stand against [*Gegen-Stand*], because it is itself an object [*Gegenstand*]—through surrealistic defamiliarization, through the emphasis on materiality in the collage, or also through a reduction to basic form as in Morandi's still-lifes. This is how things are even if the picture is nothing but a deep blue surface. In this case, the picture is blue, and it shows blue. The blue, which is shown, is not a quality of the painting. Rather, the painting is a static performance of blue, just as it could be the performance of a perspectival insight or of a look.²⁰⁷

It is this performative character, which for its part is in need of performance, that allows not only the picture, but every artwork to become an object. In the work, a text stands over and against, which is offered *as* text, whereas in the objective character of the world and life, a text remains bound to thing, activity, and occurrence, and for this reason had to be made free for itself. The narrated story provides the text of what has occurred, or, it provides a text as 'fictive,' on the basis of which what has occurred or is occurring may be understood. The poem, which appears only to name—"over all the hilltops / is calm . . ."*—provides the text of things, the expanse of the earth, the calm that breathes through the forest and the world of animals, which, finally, encroaches upon the word itself and puts it in the middle of things. Objects are something objective that is nothing other than objective; in them, what is objective in world and life are intensified. The objective, therefore, also is experienced in objects more intensely than otherwise.

With this, works of art are objects to a special degree. That they are object is constitutive of their essence, whereas they share workliness with every produced thing of use; they fulfill their objective character such that one is mistaken if one takes them as something other than object. Artworks, deserving of the name, are, more than everything else that is intelligible, determined through that dense and at the same time open textuality, which Schleiermacher wished to point to with the concept of individuality. Every attempt at its clarification, therefore, leads back to its indispensable standing over against. Comparisons, classifications, or general determinations must be bound to the individuality of an art object or they fail.

It may suggest itself to see the fundamental texts of religions similarly. Like artworks, they are presentations of something that has stepped across from and was not to be recognized other than in presentation. As sacred texts, they are irreplaceable; they are original announcements of revelation, what first endows religion with existence. As soon as it is there, the cult determines itself on the basis of it. They are performed in cult-like artworks, although here the question of the quality of the performance would be inappropriate; performance belongs to the cult, although the cult itself is not a performance.²⁰⁸ As is the case for artworks, a tradition of interpretation and commentary also follows upon sacred texts. Nevertheless, the individuality of a sacred text is less decisive. The tradition of interpretation and commentary also has its own power for religions that are concentrated entirely on scripture. Interpretation can also determine the religion's forms of representation and thought, although not exactly as the fundamental text, nevertheless in such a way that, without them, the religion

---

*[The poem referred to here is of course Goethe's "Wanderers Nachtlied." ("Wanderer's Nightsong.") whose first lines given here in translation run "Über allen Gipfeln / ist Ruh." —Trans.]

would not be what it is. Christianity has not been shaped by its sacred texts alone, but rather, likewise by church fathers, mystics, by scholastic and modern theologians, and also by art, to the extent that it contributed to the continued existence of the tradition in painting, music, or poem.

Clearer still is the difference between art and philosophy. It is true that great philosophical writings unequivocally have the character of an object. In them, too, the objectivity of what philosophical reflection initiated is intensified, and here, too, the matter is often more accessible in reference to the text than when it comes to stand out from and over against the context of the everyday. One will be able to discuss and answer the question of what justice is, for example, in only a much less convincing manner without Plato. Ethical projects are, for the most part, maintained within a contestatory field of texts that are guided by Aristotle, Kant, and the representatives of utilitarianism. Philosophical texts, too, are such that one is able to understand something based on them. Yet, the understanding they allow is less bound to its text than in the case of artworks. Whereas the understanding of a matter through art is always and again referred to the text of the work, it belongs to the essence of philosophy that it detaches itself from the texts, which are its objects. In philosophical thought, it is necessary always and again to depart from the objective itself in order to grasp it presentatively. With those disclosive possibilities of texts, which are objects, one also recognizes their limits.

Philosophy, then, is, in its essence, presentation in a double respect: it deals presentatively with the objective and with objects. Not least important, this shift is able to draw attention to the presentative character of philosophy. To reflect this belongs to the essence of philosophy, if it can really only be what it is in the presuppositionless clarity of its activity. In this sense, presentation must be considered still more fundamentally than it has been up until now. It must be made clear how the objective and objects are given, and what it is that makes possible reference to the objective as well as its standing over against. The question here is of the *space*, in which presenting, together with whatever is able to be presented, belongs—to wit, the space of the hermeneutical, which does not contain this as something arbitrary, but which, rather, is itself of a hermeneutical essence. The question here is of hermeneutical space.

If in principle everything is able to become objective and to be presented, then everything belongs to this space. The space itself is, in this case, no particular one; it is not differentiable from other spaces, but, rather, the openness for every reference and conduct, the openness for every across-from. The space is the *world*, in which presenting belongs—not as something that simply appears in the world, but, rather, as something that is a possibility of the essence of this world.

It is only possible to inquire into this without presupposition, if the approach of the consideration is made clear ahead of time. It must be a consideration that is not only hermeneutical, but, rather, a conceptual explanation of the hermeneutical on the basis of its possibility in the world. Such a consideration is, as shall first be shown, *phenomenological.* In it, the concern is with a phenomenology of hermeneutical space as world that is oriented by presentation.

Chapter 3

The World as Hermeneutical Space

§ 14. *Phenomenology*

Interpretation, understanding, and objectivity belong together. Only what is objective has to be interpreted; it is disclosed as what it is through interpretation alone, because only presentative recognizing preserves the exteriority of its matter. It reckons with it and gives it prominence; its difference from other forms of access, which are directed toward an object, lies in this. And, when a presentation is understood, the difference of presentation and matter is also present along with the matter brought into focus. To understand something is thus at the same time always to understand how it is given. One understands not only something, but rather, always also the relation of interpretation, that is, of presentation, and object. What one understands in this way is the *structure of presentation* [*Darstellungsgefüge*].

The philosophical discussion of the structure of presentation does not have to explain what presenting and understanding are as if they were in themselves completely prejudicial. There is no need for that characteristic turning, περιαγωγή spoken of in the *Republic*.[1] It is not that in understanding an appearance is mistaken for the matter itself, so that a turn to what is appearing, what is being projected on the cave wall is needed in order to experience the status of something already recognized. What the cave dwellers must first learn is always already recognized in understanding. Likewise, the consciousness that one interprets belongs to interpreting. Otherwise, an interpretation could not be put into relation to other interpretations, it would not be integrated into the play of interpretations, which together and yet each on their own labor at their object. Without consciousness of interpreting, one does not interpret, but rather, articulates dogmatic convictions about a text. Understanding and interpretation are, in themselves, reflected. Philosophical reflection, therefore, can set in in the middle of them. Yet, if philosophy does not arise, but rather, originates [*entspringt*], reflection of the structure of presentation does not become philosophical reflection gradually. A certain degree of intensity is needed in order that simple hermeneutic reflection switches over into a philosophical reflection, one that that allows the hermeneutical to be seen in a new way. The question is when this occurs.

Every level-headed interpreter is able to give an account of his activity—many of the considerations that have been proposed here about interpretation, explication and clarification, about the objective character of the text, could be those of a hermeneutically guided science. Whatever philosophical determinations were in play arose from the overarching question of a hermeneutical philosophy; it was due to the fact that the discussion of interpretation stood in a context. Insofar as this was already the context of philosophy, the manner in which reflection becomes philosophical does not become intelligible through it.

Considered from the standpoint of a hermeneutical science, philosophy comes into play as soon as the framework of the science loses its familiar obviousness. This could occur through provocations: How do the explicating and clarifying of literature, for example, relate to other forms of recognizing? What does it have to do with human life, and how does it belong in the context of this life, in which it is one possibility of life among others?

These questions also may be posed from within philosophy itself, namely, if philosophy is understood hermeneutically. In this case, philosophy is interpreting—presenting—and understanding, although not as these are established in an art or science of hermeneutics that is focused on a specific domain of matters or objects. Philosophy also does not simply move between arbitrary domains of matters and objects; it is not a diffuse investigation of this or that, not an accumulative knowledge of everything in sophistry as Plato characterizes, and, surely, caricatures it. If philosophy does not presuppose any substantive limits, then it deals with the whole of life and its context. In this case, however, the question arises as to how its presenting and understanding is able to refer to the whole of life and its context, as to how such a reference belongs in this whole.

In order to answer this, one can no longer stay at the structure of presentation itself, although one may also not leave it. Otherwise, philosophical reflection would no longer be an intensification of hermeneutical reflection; it would no longer have anything to do with the question, in regard to which the intensification was established, and, in this case, would also lose the insight into the hermeneutical character of philosophy once again.

The only possibility that remains, then, is to open up the structure of presentation, that means making it transparent for the context in which it belongs in order to consider it and put it into language based on this context. Here, one no longer concentrates on the structure of presentation itself and no longer stays at its moments, but, rather, lets these be included in and appear on the basis of their context. One watches *how they show themselves*; the focus is solely on this self-showing, on the how of being included and going forth.

With this, the moments of the structure of presentation have become *phenomena*. Viewed superficially, this word says nothing new; φαίνομενον is the self-showing, and, in this respect, the word is dispensable. Yet, on the other hand, it places the discussion of the structure of presentation into a context that allows its philosophical status to be determined: The philosophical contemplation of the structure of presentation is phenomenology.

The concept of phenomenology is no less full of presuppositions than the concept of hermeneutics; if one wishes to take it up, it is in as much need of clarification as the latter. It was only possible for a hermeneutical philosophy to take shape after the concept of hermeneutics had been made clear in its philosophical significance and made concrete in the discussion of the structure of presentation. In order that this philosophy can now be shown to be phenomenological, one has to develop how this is meant. This is all the more important as phenomenology here is supposed to have the character of an intensification of hermeneutical reflection.[2] This is not found in the classical elaboration of phenomenology in Husserl, and also not in its revision by Heidegger, who all the same was at labor to demonstrate an inner belongingness of hermeneutics and phenomenology. Still, as has been shown,[3] Heidegger restricted the hermeneutical to the announcement of the phenomenological intuition, in which Dasein is transparent to itself. And, he conceived of hermeneutics based on a phenomenology that was revised after the model of practical philosophy instead of allowing phenomenology to proceed from hermeneutics itself. No point of reference for a hermeneutical understanding of phenomenology is found in Heidegger's debate with Husserl, neither any for a phenomenological solution to the philosophical claim of hermeneutics; the model of practical reason does not do justice to this claim. One must, then, go back to the concept of phenomenology itself and to Husserl's phenomenological program.

One should remember here, first of all, that the concept of phenomenology has a critical edge: It signifies the philosophical intention to re-evaluate what was previously seen to hold a secondary status. Namely, phenomena are above all what *only* show themselves, something that is there although not understood in what it is. In the *Republic*, artistic presentations, the products of μίμησις, are signified as φαινόμενα in this sense and distinguished from what is in truth—the ὄντα ... τῇ ἀληθείᾳ.[4] Here, pictorial presentations and poems are not grasped so as to be distinguished from what is "real," as it is in truth—as if one could thus hold them as copies next to what is copied. Rather, they are mere appearances, nothing other than the surface of what one comes across. The painted bedstead has nothing to do with what a bedstead is in its essence; the picture provides only the sheer appearance, what appears simply as it is immediately there, and, for this reason, itself also wishes to be taken as it appears.[5] Understood in this way, appearances are the unbroken givenness of something mediated by knowing of no kind; they offer no access to what something is in truth.

Aristotle's verdict on phenomena is somewhat friendlier. They are counted among the things that come up in common intuitions (ἔνδοξα)[6] and among what, as something familiar, can serve as a point of departure for the investigation of what is familiar in its nature.[7] This may only be thought, however, if what appears is what shows itself *first of all* and, as such, is the beginning of knowledge. In this case, an adequate understanding of the matter may be achieved in departure from it. Yet, considered on its own, the phenomenon is also here the unbroken existence of something still unaffected by critical discussion.

The first use of the title "Phenomenology" by Johann Heinrich Lambert is still completely circumscribed by this sense. The subtitle of the work, whose fourth part is called "Phenomenology," already says what is decisive: the *Neue Organon* [*New Organon*] (1764) contains *Gedanken über die Erforschung des Wahren und dessen Unterscheidung von Irrthum und Schein* [*Ideas on the Investigation of the True and its Distinction from Error and Appearance*].[8] Accordingly, phenomenology is the discussion of this appearance as the mediator between truth and error, with the aim of examining appearance in its possibility and its effects in order thus to contribute to its overcoming. Yet, when Hegel names his first major work a "phenomenology of spirit," the intention is already different. As "science of the experience of consciousness,"[9] as the original title reads, phenomenology is supposed to indicate those manners in which spirit appears that form the respective figures of the experience of spirit. And, insofar as spirit is only what it is through experience, phenomenology proves to be the manner of philosophical presentation that is completely adequate to spirit.

It is in the philosophy of Husserl, itself definitive for the modern understanding of phenomenology, that the revaluation of what appears is conclusively made into a program.[10] The decisive idea is formulated quite early in Husserl's work, namely, in the introduction to the second volume of the *Logischen Untersuchungen* (1901): the discussions announced here belong, Husserl says, to an "objective theory of cognition and, what most intimately belongs together with it, a pure phenomenology of thinking and cognizing inner experiences [*Erlebnisse*]."[11] This phenomenology, Husserl continues, is, "like the pure phenomenology of inner experiences in general that encompasses it, it exclusively has to do with those inner experiences that can be grasped and analyzed in intuition, in the pure generality of their essence, but not with empirically apperceived inner experiences as real facts, as inner experiences of experiencing [*erlebenden*] human beings or animals in the world that appear and are posited as facts of experience [*Erfahrung*]."[12] When phenomena are understood as "essence" or *Eidé*, as it is then called in *Ideen I*,[13] they have the same status as what in Plato was named "what in truth is."

What appears, or, what shows itself, is in this way determined radically differently than in the tradition. What was once called "appearance" is opposed to what is real, or, the factical, as it is encountered in the "natural attitude." Not appearance, but the factical now has the character of the accidental, that is: "it is such that it can, in accord with its essence"—as something, which can factically be in various ways—also "be otherwise."[14] For example, an idea could be factically different than it is now, where it is conceived by this specific person, under these specific circumstances. As an idea, it is nevertheless this specific one, it is simply as it is. As an idea, of this Husserl is convinced, the concern is not that it is conceived here and now by this human being.

With this, one of Husserl's most important motives is reached. His phenomenological program is directed against the identification of "inner experiences" with their actual appearance in the inner life of a human being or an animal, and, in this sense is directed against "psychologism." However, the program is likewise a critique of the empiricist view that ideas and perceptions essentially refer to something in particular, to something factically discoverable in the world, and are only for this reason ideas and perceptions. Ideas and perceptions primarily have to do with phenomena, and these are, in contrast to what is factically discoverable, "irreal." This does not mean that they are fictions, but, rather, they do not belong to the order of the real world.[15] They have essentially nothing to do with the "world posited as fact of experience."[16] Experience [Erfahrung], in which inner experiences [Erlebnisse] are taken as such a fact discoverable in the world, determines only "natural cognition,"[17] which is enacted only in the "natural attitude."

In order to move from the natural into the phenomenological attitude, what is needed is that change in viewpoint, mentioned earlier,[18] that Husserl indicates with the concept of ἐποχή. The factical aspect of experience and of what is experienced must, as Husserl says, be put "out of action," switched off, bracketed. With this, the natural attitude is not contested or doubted; Husserl explicitly dismisses a negation in this sense.[19] Rather, Husserl describes the ἐποχή as the possibility of becoming the observer of oneself. As he says in the first of his "Pariser Vorträge (1929)," I achieve with the ἐποχή "the conceivably last standpoint of experience and cognition . . . at which I become an impartial spectator of my natural-worldly I and I-life."[20] I abstain from "all worldly interests"[21] and thus move into the possibility of discovering them "as themes of description."[22] It brings about "a kind of I-splitting": the "transcendental spectator," that is, the observer, who takes leave of himself but does not arrive any real place beyond himself, separates himself from the "I given over to the world,"[23] and looks at it. He no longer refers directly and immediately to what is perceived, thought, or imagined, but, rather, to the enacted thought of the "I given over to the world," and, in regard to the ideas of this latter, has "the world only as phenomenon"; he has what is perceived, thought, and imagined "as the appearing of the respective appearances," or, as Husserl adds in elucidation, "as mere correlate."[24]

This concept is especially consequential for Husserl's approach. It binds something perceived and recognized to the consciousness that is recognizing, although it no less binds the consciousness to that which it is referred or directed. With intentionality, consciousness has the "fundamental trait... of being consciousness *of* something."[25] This fundamental trait first comes into focus as such in the ἐποχή. Referentiality to what is factically discoverable is coincidental. One did not have to see the tree, which one now sees, one could close one's eyes or turn away. It is true that this would generally be tantamount to one turning one's attention to something else. Nevertheless, it remains hidden that referentiality to something is essentially immanent to consciousness in every case. That being in reference is concerned with a fundamental trait of consciousness does not come in view so long as one is "given over to the world" and interested in whatever respectively comes before one's eyes and into consciousness. Even the attempt to grasp what is perceived universally does not lead beyond the natural attitude. It leads, on the contrary, to precise self-description [*Selbstaufkunft*] of the natural attitude: "I find continually present as my across-from something of a spatiotemporal actuality, to which I myself belong, like all other human beings who are discoverable in it and who refer to it in the same manner."[26] First, when this interest is bracketed, put out of effect, does the referentiality itself become clear, and, in fact, in its reciprocity, as correlate: Consciousness is directed toward something, and, for consciousness, this something is there.

Just this is indicated by the concept of phenomenon. The "word phenomenon," Husserl once says, is "ambiguous by the power of essential correlation between *appearing* [*Erscheinen*] and *appearance* [*Erscheinendem*]."[27] The word signifies not only what appears, but rather, also its appearing; it names what is there at the same time in its existence. This, in turn, first allows the meaning of the ἐποχή to be understood. Insofar as phenomena as such are disclosed in it, the ἐποχή is not at all an observation of the self—as if one were to look at oneself in thinking and perceiving from a higher vantage point. It is rather *a return into the correlation of the phenomenal*; instead of being referred to something as to this determinate thing, one pays attention to its appearing and is thus able to see it as an appearance. Husserl's concept of the "phenomenological reduction"[28] is therefore more helpful for the elucidation of the ἐποχή than the image of self-observation he offers. One draws back from something that is correlated into the correlation itself and observes the correlates based solely on the correlation they belong in.

The correlates at issue here are already named in the self-description of the natural attitude: I myself and "temporal-spatial reality [*Wirklichkeit*]" or "the world posited as fact of experience."²⁹ The latter is differentiated in experience, such that one only deals with it piecemeal, under specific aspects. What is experienced, however, always belongs in the context of the world and is recognized on the basis of it. Here, things are such that something is given to me and I in some way or other direct myself toward it. To focus on the correlation means, by contrast, that one disregards oneself as well as the fact that appears over and against one. The concern is no longer with "me" in the sense that I determine myself as something belonging to "temporal-spatial reality." Phenomenologically reduced, I am no longer even a being-directed that has to have something as a point of departure for its direction, namely, "me." What is left of me is the appearing of the appearance, and, thus, the correlation proves to be the phenomenality of the phenomenon; it is itself the appearing, the suspension between what appears and being directed toward it. The kind of thought that not only holds itself in this suspension, but, rather, considers it as such is concentrated on appearing itself and is, in this, phenomenological.

It is quite revealing for Husserl's understanding of the phenomenon, however, that he understands appearing as a "subjective phenomenon"³⁰ and, for this reason, is able to interpret whatever appears as a moment of appearing. The "fundamental trait" of intentionality, namely, being "consciousness of something," here means "bearing, as *cogito*, its *cogitatum* within it."³¹ On the one hand, the idea is comprehensible: Without consciousness, there are indeed factically discoverable things, although nothing that appears; what appears is, as such, always for a consciousness. On the other hand, however, appearing is not to be identified with consciousness; although what appears is there for consciousness, it may not be ascribed to consciousness. What consciousness "bears within itself" does not belong to it in such a way that it would be a moment of its being directed and being referred. Appearing is a peculiarly suspended process; it may neither be assigned to what appears nor to the one for whom something appears. It is a correlation in the sense that it connects its correlates, although it cannot be determined by way of the correlates. The correlates are as they are alone through the correlation.

Husserl does not, however, push through to an understanding of the correlation that has been made clear in this manner. The idea remains undeveloped, because Husserl identifies appearing with consciousness and on this basis takes as the domain of phenomenology a "context of being closed for itself,"³² which "in principle" is in need of no other matter to exist³³ Nevertheless, the attempt to conceive of the correlation of the phenomenal as such is elicited in consequence of Husserl's program. Husserl, as has been seen, in no way provides the idea of a referentiality to exterior "objects."³⁴ Moreover, it is no longer possible to see the natural and phenomenological attitudes as they have been discussed here as alternatives, if the experience of the phenomenal is no longer reserved solely for philosophy. In this case, it is necessary to grasp the natural attitude and the attitude oriented toward phenomena as two sides of the same thing, and this is only possible to the extent that one does not determine a difference between the natural and phenomenological attitude based on the correlation. It is, in this case, no longer to be grasped as a simple change of attitude; it may be conceived solely as a different degree of correlative intensity. The degree of intensity characteristic of phenomenology is reached when one no longer asks about what appears, but, rather, wishes to explain what appearing itself is.

What is asked about here, however, rebuffs the question. It is characteristic of appearing, which is no longer understood in contrast to a "being" or to the unquestionable "reality" of the natural attitude, that it is unquestionable. It simply is what it is. Appearing may not be derived from anything. It has natural conditions, though even if it were possible to consider and describe them all, this would not lead to any understanding of what appearing is. Appearing itself, however, may be described; one experiences it, and, so, it is possible to say what one here experiences, without asking back behind it. The unquestionable, the nonderivable, may only be determined on its own basis; it is only given hermeneutically in conceptually guided description. It has to be mediated as what appears, and this mediation is phenomenological when it is guided by reflection on appearing itself.

It belongs to appearing essentially that it occurs at a distance. One must thus step back from something or hold it in front of oneself, away from oneself in order that one sees it. In distance there is a separation, but it occurs for the sake of reference. The separation here is at the same time a connection; something is away from me, therein "withdrawn," and only therefore there for me.

This relationship was present in the discussion of objectivity, though the talk had not been about appearing itself. It also came out in the self-description of the natural attitude in Husserl: "I continually find something that is a spatiotemporal reality as my counterpart [*Gegenüber*]."[35]

This reality can only stand across from me as such, however, if I "myself belong" to it, as even the natural attitude knows. In this case, my having *of* something across from me is an experience *in* something, and, in this case, in turn, the distance of something that appears must itself belong to this reality. There belongs to reality what one could signify with a word used philosophically by Heidegger as "clearing" [*Lichtung*]. Heidegger determines the clearing as the "openness that affords the possibility of letting appear and showing."[36] In elucidation of how this is to be understood, he points to the significance of the word: "clearing" has nothing to do with "light" [*Licht*], but, rather, with "ease" [*leicht*][37]; intended is the open space in the forest that allows for a vista.

This image is, however, limited in its power of elucidation. One does not conceive of the reality that one experiences as a dense stand of things that open spaces break into now and then and so once again always allow one to refer to something. On the one hand, what is there is a dense stand; everywhere, something *is*, and even a clearing that one comes upon in the forest is *something* in this sense. The idea of the "is" makes everything dense; everything is, as Parmenides has it, whole, unitary, imperturbable and not incomplete[38]; everything is connected, what is pushes against what is[39]; everything is like the mass of a well-rounded ball.[40] There is, however, in all of this the possibility of making reference from something that is over to something else. Everywhere there is something, and nevertheless one thing steps back in favor of another.

Now it is clear why one is not permitted to conceive of what has been cleared [*das Gelichtete*] in terms of individual open places. Everywhere that there is something is at the same time open. One passes through it and overlooks it just as one walks through the forest clearing, also as one moves in the thicket of trees and sees light on the edge of the forest shining through.

This experience is connected with the idea of *space* as if of itself. Where there is space, there is openness, there is passage and open view, sound carries; in space, there is removal [*Entfernung*]* and expanse. This could all be a sign that one has to conceive spatially of the openness of what is. In this case, the correlation in which something appears for someone would also have to be spatial; an understanding of space would be the key to an understanding of phenomenality. This warrants being developed. The next question, then, is how one can conceive of space and spatiality.

§ 15. Space

The experience of spaces is of confinement and expanse. Where there is too little space one feels confined, restricted not foremost in activity, but even in one's feeling of life.[41] The open country stands in contrast to this; that one's view does not come upon limits can be enlivening—it goes on forever, and this is like a promise. Sometimes, however, expanse is also frightening, no less so height and depth. One cannot stand the openness, it is as if it could devour one. Too much confinement or expanse would not be conspicuous if there were not also spaces in the right measure. In them, limitation and openness are held in suspense. Limitation first brings the unlimitedness of openness to the fore; openness holds limitation at a distance from one—it is there, without being too close.

---

*[In this discussion and throughout, I generally translate *Abstand* as "distance" and *Entfernung* as "removal." I am indebted to Joan Stambaugh's English rendition of *Being and Time* for my translation of *Entfernung* as "removal." In what follows, I am also indebted to her for my translation of *Entferntheit* as "remoteness," and "Ferne" as "remove." Also, I have typically translated *in Entfernung* as "at a removal" and the adverbial and adjectival form *entfernt* as "at a remove." —Trans.]

Confinement pushes one back onto oneself. What is still there outside of one, namely, what is, becomes too dense. In an expanse as well as in the depth of an abyss and at a height that has become uncanny, one loses oneself. In both instances, the possibility of reference is missing; requisite for this is both an expanse and at the same time the possibility of reaching something. The experience of space, therefore, is balanced when it is connected with the certainty that references are possible, or when it is given in the multiplicity of references. In this case, there is space enough to approach something, and also enough to consider it from different sides; nothing comes too close and nothing that one is focused on is unreachably far in the distance. One does not recognize everything on first glance, hardly anything is recognized in a single look. Perception and cognition are built up by grasping what they refer to from different sides.

This fact is of special interest in regard to a more precise understanding of space. Husserl granted it repeated attention. He thus made clear, on the example of a cube—he himself says "Hexaeder"—that something "is given" not immediately, but, rather, "continuously, as an objective unity ... in a multiform and determinatively coherent multiplicity of manners of appearance."[42] The object is built up first in different respects, which are no "unconnected succession of inner experiences"[43]; it is thus first "posited," "ascertained," in Husserl's word, "constituted." In order that this can occur, the inner experiences of perception must pass "in the unity of a synthesis, such that in them there is an awareness of one and the same thing as appearing."[44] This does not occur in a sort of accretion of individual, in themselves isolated inner experiences of perception, so that the unity of the perceived thing arises first at the end. Rather, every inner experience has "an intentional horizon of reference ... from the *actually perceived* sides of the object of perception to the *co-intended* sides, which are not yet perceived," but "anticipated."[45] Every perception is "interpenetrated ... by an intentional empty horizon"[46]; the expectation of a whole thing is at play in it in the manner of an "outline, which proscribes a rule for the transition into new, actualizing appearances."[47] Moreover, every inner experience of perception has "horizons of other possibilities of perception that we could have if we were actively to direct the course of our perception differently"—that is, say, by moving our eyes differently or moving to a new position.[48] In every perception that is "cognizance"[49] and not merely optically registering something, the perceived thing is there as such, and it nevertheless comes into appearance in what it is first in the course of perception, in a discovery, which is steered in this way or that.

The course of perception, as Husserl describes it, has a remarkable structural similarity to the course of interpretation. Husserl himself speaks of "presentation" in regard to perception by maintaining that we have the unity of a perceived thing always only as a "unity on the basis of presentation."[50] This is not a presentation in the sense of performance or of explication and clarification; for this, consciousness is missing the exteriority of the object as well as the certainty that its concern is with the text of an object, which it is first possible to make present through one's own activity. How one is to grasp the openness of presentation is, however, nevertheless indicated through this structural similarity. This openness of presentation is spatial, and, in fact, in such a way that it is intensified in the openness of space. By contrast, perception is an "inner experiencing"; one is perceivingly into the matter and if one were to walk around it in investigation and discovery one will not see the spatial.

What is elusive here is *remoteness* [*Entferntheit*]. Nevertheless, remoteness is there. It is indicated by the fact that what is perceptible never comes into focus completely,[51] just as no interpretation, differentiated as it may be, exhaustively presents the text of its object. Remoteness finds its correspondence in the *distance* that one has in perception from what one perceives. This becomes explicit in the perspectival regard of what is perceived; the perspective may be changed, and this shows that it is up to the one who perceives. In observing something, one walks around it or one brings it before one's eyes time and again in different manners, for example, by holding it in a different light. Or, one experiences it as a building that one takes into view from a remove, and then looks at from different sides, in order finally to enter it and look at it from inside. All of this has to do with distance, and, at a distance, with space.

Yet, one also does not perceive this in every attitude toward what is perceptible. In a few perspectives, something withdraws from view because one is too close to it or because one has too much distance from it. This shows that there must always be a certain *removal* [*Entfernung*] between oneself and what one perceives in order that it can be seen at all and show itself in perception.

It is no coincidence that the moments stressed here do not appear in Husserl's analysis; he does not take into consideration a spatiality of the situation of perception as a whole. He certainly does not pursue the question of whether there is a common fundamental trait that is at play in remoteness, distance, and removal; it might be signified as at a *remove* [*Ferne*]. For Husserl, only what is perceived is spatial, not, however, perception itself. What is perceived, for example a building, is always only there in the "space of the embodied world of perception."[52] One does not experience it other than "on the basis of various standpoints"—"in a changing orientation, according to various ... perspectives, appearances, profiles [*Abschattungen*]."[53] For Husserl, however, the being of spatially given things is to be differentiated from the "profile"[54] in which it is given. The profile that one is concerned with, say, when a building appears first from the front and then from the back, is "inner experience" and, as such, "not possible as spatial"; by contrast, what is profiled is "in principle," "spatial in its essence."[55]

This idea is, on the one hand, comprehensible: Husserl does not wish to localize inner experience in space as he does the thing thus had in inner experience;

the assurance that an inner experience takes place here, at this position, obviously does not do justice to the essence of inner experience. Yet, on the other hand, Husserl himself always emphasizes that inner experiences of perception are bound to space by speaking of "various standpoints," changing orientations, and "various perspectives." In order to experience the profile of things of perception, however, one must move himself and have moved in space. This, too, Husserl takes into consideration when he speaks in the *Cartersianischen Meditationen* of "possibilities of perception,"[56] or in the *Analysen zur passiven Synthesis* of "kinaesthetic motivation," and—once again taking remarkable orientation from the fact of presentation—of the "movements of the body," which "set the stage for" perception.[57] This suggests a consequence that Husserl himself does not draw: if perception is possible only in space, both in its perspectival character and in its perception of things in their profiles, then everything speaks for calling inner experiences of perception themselves spatial.

This consequence has been drawn by Merleau-Ponty. Building on the analyses of embodiment that was carried out by Husserl himself,[58] Merleau-Ponty replaces the thinking subject, the "cogito," by which Husserl orients his analyses, with life in its quickened embodiment. The result is an entirely different picture of the experiences of perception and thought. Merleau-Ponty understands these experiences as dependent on movement in space. Because of this it is forbidden to conceive seeing as an operation of thought that projects before the mind a picture (*tableau*) or a presentation (*représentation*) of the world,[59] and, in fact, of a world of immanence and ideality. The one who perceives does not appropriate what he sees, but, rather, only gets closer to it through the look and opens himself onto the world.[60]

In his description, Merleau-Ponty is admittedly not so far from Husserl at all. Husserl would have thoroughly agreed that in order to perceive a *specific* profile, one has to see the perceived thing from a specific standpoint that one can move into and leave. Yet, precisely this possibility gives him good reason not to reduce inner experiences of perception to "kinaesthetic motivations." There are not only movements of the body that "set the stage for" the perceiving thing, which of course belongs to the same world as things perceived.[61] There is also a setting of the stage for the movements of the body itself, say, in the inspection of a building. In such experiences, the "system of movements of the body" proves to be "characterized by consciousness"; it is, as Husserl says, a "subjectively-free system,"[62] and, in this, an "ability of consciousness," which first builds up, that is, constructs, spatial inner experience.[63]

This does not, however, speak against the idea that inner experiences of perception are spatially bound. The inspection of a building is after all not planned as if by a director who stands before a stage and directs an actor, but, rather, is itself spatially bound. The selection and coordination of various perspectives presupposes a sense for space and spatial relationships, and this, in turn, is given only in space. How else is it supposed to be developed and realized? One may in any case no longer conceive of space based only on things. It has more to do with inner experience and recognition than Husserl had thought.

Merleau-Ponty conceived of space in this spirit as a lived space in his early *Phénoménologie de la perception*. Space is not some kind of aether that things bathe in but rather the medium through which the position of things is possible;[64] it is the universal power of their connection, of the connection of things.[65] Space is conceived on the basis of spatial relations, which are not alive without a "subject" (*sujet*) who represents and bears them.[66] What is intended here is a system of localization and orientation, which is indicated by expressions like "next to," "in front of," "behind," "below," "above." On the one hand, it concerns the referentiality of things to one another; something stands "next to" something else, something finds itself "above" something. On the other hand, however, this can always only be experienced and articulated from a specific standpoint. Accordingly, localizations of this kind are bound by the possibility of a "subject" locating himself. That something stands "next to" something else may only be said if one himself stands "in front of" both and looks toward both. If one were to walk a little bit around the two things, then what was up until now "next to" the other would stand "in front of" or "behind" it. It belongs to the system of relations, which is how space is understood here, that a modification such as this one is possible and is understood. If one did not know that "next to" is able to become "in front of" or "behind" with this change of perspective, one would not be able to orient oneself. One himself belongs in the system and at the same time, realizes it, like the rules of a game, which, on the one hand, one belongs in as a player, and which, on the other hand, cannot be played without players who have mastered its rules. And, as rules of play become explicit in their transgression, the system of spatial relations appears to consciousness above all when it is interrupted. This is why Merleau-Ponty extensively discusses psychological and psychiatric studies in his investigation.

Merleau-Ponty does not describe space only in the outlined sense as a system of localization and orientation. He also observes that localization and orientation are not possible without distance from things. Something is only able to be "in front of" or "above" me and, in this, localized "next to" or "under" something else, if I have the distance from it necessary for a reference. Without this distance, seeing is not possible; one does not see what is directly before one's eyes. Distance, however, is not achieved in the kind of removal that may be measured. If one follows Merleau-Ponty, measurable removal separates and distance connects. Beyond the physical or geometric removal that exists between me and all things, there is a lived distance, which counts and exists for me, that binds me to things and that also connects things with one another.[67]

Yet, Merleau-Ponty does not make clear enough how this lived distance is to be conceived. In order to do so, he could have reached back to Heidegger's relevant analyses. Even though Merleau-Ponty consults *Sein und Zeit* in the *Phénomélogie de la perception*, he clearly did not see that a determination of "lived distance" is found in it, and, moreover, one in which the relation between this lived distance and physical removal is determined.

Heidegger already provides direction for his analyses by speaking not of space but instead of the "spatiality of Dasein." This is distinguished from "insideness." As a consequence of this distinction, Dasein is no "extended being," which is "enclosed by the extended borders of something extended"[68]; Dasein is spatial, but it is not in space. Heidegger understands this, in turn, not in the sense of a strict distinction between Dasein and things not Dasein-like, such that one could say of them that they are in space. As "inner-worldly," things are also spatial, although in another sense. Their spatiality goes back to that of Dasein.

For Heidegger, the spatiality of Dasein is determined through "the character of *removal* and *directionality*."[69] In this, "de-removing"* is to be understood on analogy with "dehabituate" and "disenchant"; what is intended is a supersession or elimination of remove. It belongs essentially to Dasein, then, to want to bring into proximity, and, in fact, to want to bring what does not—yet should—belong into its ever-familiar world.

If this is a fundamental trait of Dasein, a certain experience of remove belongs to it. Remove is as such not simply noticed, it is disquieting. It is unfamiliar, missing proximity; it is there as something that should not be. It is only for this reason that remove is disquieting and releases the impulse to de-removing, that is, to gather up, integrate, and appropriate. What, by contrast, is in proximity generally remains unremarkable. It belongs in the proximate surrounding in which everything is at hand and, in this, "handy." It is first because of remove that the proximate surrounding loses its familiar obviousness. As soon as this kind of experience of remove is had, one comes to be concerned with proximity by means of de-removing.

This does not mean that proximity first takes on a spatial character through remove; it is already spatial for itself. What is handy, that is, the useful thing that one uses in the everyday, has its "place" in the "area" in which it belongs.[70] The spatiality of the "area," however, remains unfamiliar as such. What is supposed to be at hand does not, after all, have to be "de-removed"; an easy reach such as the reach toward a pencil and notebook on a writing table is enough for much of what is in proximity; at the most, a few steps are needed, for example, to take a book from the shelf. The spatiality of the proximate surrounding

---

*[*Ent-fernung*. Cf. Stambaugh's translation as "de-distancing." —Trans.]

is demonstrated solely through remove. Proximity is that, toward which de-removing is *directed* and where it as it were arrives. "Dasein," as Heidegger summarizes this idea, "is, in accordance with its spatiality, initially never here, but, rather, there, from which there it comes back to its here."[71] Spatiality first comes into focus in the expanse between the there and the here.

It is only on the basis of this expanse, Heidegger thinks, that removal in the sense of spatial distance [*Distanz*] may be made intelligible. The idea is illuminating: to measure [*messen*] a removal is to traverse [*Durchmessen*] an expanse so as to give it a determinacy calculated in one unit of measure or other. A removal may not be measured unless one has a sense of the expanse, that is, of the stretch from there to here, from out of a remove into proximity. With this, expanse exists not only in one's imagination or consciousness. If it did not exist, nothing could or would have to become de-removed. A fundamental trait of spatiality comes into focus here in regard to the spatiality of Dasein; space in which there are distances [*Distanzen*] is what is experienced in the spatiality of Dasein. Heidegger's analysis leads beyond the diffuse nowhere of pure inner experiences of consciousness. There is spatiality not only in regard to things. In Heidegger's view, Dasein itself has and experiences it; it is "spatial in an *originary* sense."[72]

Nevertheless, Heidegger's analysis remains unsatisfying in a number of respects. It does not make sufficiently clear the status of what is spatially discovered and discoverable, and, due to this, the character of space itself also remains underdetermined. This, ultimately, leads to the fact that the spatiality of Dasein also comes into view only one-sidedly.

As to the first issue, Heidegger does not resolve the central determination of his analysis. The remove, in regard to which the experience of spatiality is established, is neither determined in its status nor described in its particularity. It is true that Heidegger dedicates some attention to the spatiality of "inner-worldliness."[73] However, he restricts himself to the analysis of "inner-worldly handy things," and, because of this, leaves open how that from which de-removing takes its departure is itself supposed to be understood. This is hardly a coincidence, but, rather, an expression of genuine embarrassment. In *Sein und Zeit*, only two kinds of things are differentiated. There are things of use, which are held in "inconspicuous familiarity,"[74] and there are beings [*das Seinede*], which have lost this familiarity so that they are no longer "handy" [*zuhanden*] but only "present" [*vorhanden*]. These beings are no longer encountered in "concernful dealings," but, rather, merely stand in view and are able to be made the theme of an expression. What is to be de-removed is integrated into this distinction. As something only present, it would be insignificant for one's own existence [Dasein]; it would have lost its "significance." But why must it be de-removed, brought closer, and integrated into the familiar surroundings? Obviously, there is something that is not handy, although also not simply without significance; obviously, what is handy stands in a context that reaches beyond it.

Heidegger finds no concepts for this context, and neither does he describe it. Even when he nuances the distinction between what is handy and what is present, and sees "multiple intermediate stages" between the two, he finds no place for remove. He treats only different possibilities of speaking of something so as to avoid simply associating it with the "extreme opposite case"[75] of everyday familiarity, namely, with impartial theoretical expression. Heidegger names here "expressions about occurrences in the world, outlines of something handy, 'descriptions of the situation,' the taking up and fixing of a 'fact of the matter,' descriptions of a state of affairs, narratives of what has happened."[76] None of these forms of speech lead beyond the "surroundings" in the Heideggerian sense, that is, beyond proximity; nothing brings something at a remove closer, or, indeed, preserves it as the remove, which it is, in bringing it closer. For Dasein, as Heidegger determined and describes it, there are neither things nor objects. There is nothing that one may make reference to that is significant for him but does not boil down to a concernful dealing. Something remains unconsidered in this whose consideration could only confirm the analysis of spatiality: Ultimately, what is handy only can be in proximity because something else is at a remove. What is handy thus belongs within a horizon of things and is only encountered on the basis of this. Things are that which are far away. There is no proximity of the "surrounding world" without remove.

That Heidegger develops no determination and description of far away things has a parallel in his understanding of remove as it can be experienced in regard to things; he also does not go into that removal, in which far away things stand. Without removal, however, de-removing is not conceivable, and, in this respect, the concept has not been made sufficiently clear. Here, the character of the distance of de-removing and, with it, removal, is implicitly there when, say, Heidegger remarks that "an 'objectively' long path" can be shorter than an " 'objectively' very short one that is perhaps quite a 'tough road' and appears to one as unendingly long."[77] It is illuminating that the paths one has to take are not primarily determined by their measurable length. Heidegger's idea that the characteristics of one's conduct and of the beings one encounters in its course must be connected back to the being of Dasein is also not fundamentally mistaken. How one experiences removals lies not seldom in the significance they have in the context of being-in-the-world and of the world; the concern is always with how important or urgent something that is supposed to be brought into proximity is. The importance and urgency, in turn, is measured in such cases by what one is and wants to be. It does not follow from this, however, that the remove at issue for Dasein is "never" to be grasped "as distance" in the sense of removal.[78] Regardless of how short or long a path appears to one, a path must still be taken, and, thereby, space is to be traversed. The concern is certainly not always with the measurable length of the path as in the stretch of road. It may well be, however, that the effort necessary to bring something into proximity plays a role. Whether something "is at a remove in an average length of one's reach, grasp, and view"[79] or not has less to do with the quality of it than with what lies between oneself and it—that is, with removal.

Heidegger's reservation against ideas of removal can nevertheless be explained based on his formulation of the problem. In his analysis of spatiality, he attempts to avoid any semblance of the going, but on his conviction abstract, conception of space. According to this, space is determined through "the pure manifold of the three dimensions,"[80] and is to be grasped more precisely as "the pure wherein in which things are ordered by measurement and the location of things is determined."[81] Heidegger lets this determination be given by Descartes: Extension in length, width, and depth[82] is "*the* constitution of the being" of what is in the world, insofar as the world itself is understood as "all of what is [*das Seinden*]"[83]: as the world of *res extensa*. Heidegger, however, does not take this as a derivative understanding of the world that for this reason may be justified. Rather, it is just the presupposition for "passing over the world as well as the being of inner-worldly beings initially handy."[84] Heidegger's declared intention to demonstrate that "extensio as the fundamental determinacy of 'world' " in its "phenomenal right"[85] is accordingly also to be understood as the announcement of a radical reformulation. Heidegger gets evidence for taking spatiality as a determination of the being-in-the-world of Dasein through Kant's considerations of orientation in space[86] and its consequence that every orientation requires a "subjective principle."[87] It is not possible to see, however, how the "fundamental determinacy" of extension is supposed to be preserved in this. What distance and remove actually are is not explained by the de-removing character of Dasein, and, in this respect, the announcement of a rehabilitation of extensio remains still unresolved.

The spatiality of Dasein also remains underdetermined here. If de-removing cannot be conceived without removal, the relation of the one who de-removes and what he is directed toward cannot be described solely from the standpoint of familiarity and foreignness. If something is at a remove from me, I am also at a remove from it, and, because of this, I am not only "spatial" in the Heideggerian sense, but, rather, *in space*. De-removing would otherwise not be plausible; after all, the attempt to bring something closer is not a matter of fetching something back over in which one remains unmoved but, rather, often a matter of going toward something. One is also brought closer to the building by going around a building or taking it into view from different positions. To be in space, accordingly, is not tantamount in every respect to that "insideness" that Heidegger sets off against the originary spatiality of Dasein.

A possibility of alleviating the shortcomings of Heidegger's analysis without opposing his philosophical intention comes into view, however, on the background of Heidegger's debate with Descartes: The factual matter of remove, that is, of removal, of distance and its overcoming, have to be grasped so that the abstract idea of a metric space plays no essential role. If this is possible, then one arrives at an understanding of space that takes the spatiality of human Dasein into account though without reducing it to this spatiality.

In order to develop this idea, one can once again take orientation from the presentative structure of interpretation. All of the discussed moments of spatiality may be recovered in regard to the remove that characterizes something objective as it is presented in interpretation. As the exterior that it is, something objective is at a remove, and, in fact, not necessarily and not essentially in the sense of a measurable distance. Rather, it is at a remove because it does not belong to the proximity as something of one's own or as something familiar. It is not everyday; its objectivity dwindles as soon as I recede into the usual course or routine of the everyday surroundings. It belongs to objectivity that something is not "at hand," and, in a certain manner, remains untouchable. There belongs to something objective an "aura." For Benjamin, this is "the singular appearance of a remove, however near it may be."[88]

Remove, or, more precisely, the remoteness of the auratic, shows that one's concern is not with an object [*Objekt*] already known as what it is, and, for this reason, already conceptually in or brought into proximity. Interpretation, however, is also a "de-removing"; one brings something at a remove near by presenting it; one performs even a painting that one contemplates by helping to bring it into the actuality of appearance. Here, however, the "de-removing" does not have the character of integration or appropriation. The picture is not consumed by one's contemplation, but, rather, is left at the remove essential to it. Contemplation, and, likewise, explication and clarification, are manners of bringing something into proximity that confirm remoteness.

The removal of something at a remove is indeed not a measurable distance [*Distanz*], although it does not exclude such a distance in every case. There is not such a distance in literature, but certainly in music and in fine art, as well as in architecture. Pictures may only be viewed by maintaining a distance [*Abstand*] to them and, in this way, preserving a removal. A painting by Monet—for example, a pond of water lilies in which the sky is mirrored or a haystack in the winter light—blurs into a diffuse mixture of colors, to a jumble of brush strokes, if one comes too close to it. The "right" distance, which the viewer must have from the picture, would in fact be measurable, although this measurability is inessential: Decisive, rather, is the removal that allows the picture to appear. The picture is there in this removal alone. This does not mean, however, that it would only be *visible* in the removal that belongs to it. It is also visible as a blur of brush strokes, even the backside of the canvas and the stretcher belongs to the visibility of the picture. Yet, the picture is *to be contemplated* only as something at a removal; it is only in removal that the text of the picture is revealed, its fabric of line and color that emerges to comprise its significance. Things are similar in a work of music. Its sound can only unfold at the "right" distance; without this, it becomes indistinct in its text or too loud.

One is accordingly not in space here so as to be together with the picture one contemplates as an "extended being" "surrounded by the extended boundaries of something extended."[89] It is true that the viewer as well as the picture may be localized in this specific room of the art exhibition from another standpoint. This, however, would only be a determination of the spatiality of the one who is contemplating and the picture abstracted from the contemplating and appearing of the picture. It is essential for this that the viewer allows the picture to stand across from him and that he is himself interpretively referred to the picture. His distance from the picture, the measurable removal between him and it, belong to the spatial essence of his contemplation and interpretation. They are determined on the basis of their belongingness to this essence. Although it is secondary here that they are measurable, this could be of importance in other contexts of experience. What matters is this context, not measurability as such. To take orientation from measurability is misleading if, in doing so, one disregards the everyday contexts in which it stands. Things are similar in perception generally. Seeing and hearing, the "senses of remove" as Heidegger calls them,[90] are not initially sensorial in order then to become connected supplementally with significance. They refer to what is heard in its respective determinacy. Accordingly, the experience of space had with them is that of a "real" space and, at the same time, always filled in a more or less developed manner with significance and meaning.[91]

If this is so, then remove itself must also get determined as the common trait of remoteness, distance, and removal. Remove is in each of these moments, it does not revolve around any one of them. It is what holds apart and at the same time connects remoteness and distance as two aspects of a relation. And, it allows an—always specific—removal to obtain between them. The relation of presentation and object, although also that of perception and what is perceived, may be conceived as such on the basis of remove. This does not, however, occur as if from a neutral standpoint, from which both may be taken into view and localized in space. As the fundamental trait of remoteness, distance, and removal, remove itself is indeed space. Accordingly, one understands the relation of remoteness and distance in such a way that one disregards the specifics of the moments and so, at the same time, sees how they are positioned spatially to one another.

The two moments set themselves in together; as soon as there is the one, the other is also there. Distance goes along with remoteness, what is seen at a distance is in truth at a removal, one always sees something at a remove only from a distance. What is seen at a distance does belong to one; what is at a remove cannot be seized and is thus always somewhere else, away from the one who experiences it.

Remove also is at play in removal. Here, it finds a determinacy that is neutral in regard to remoteness and distance. It does not matter whether removal is determined from the perspective of distance or on the basis of what is at a remove, in both cases it is the same; one is at just as much of a remove from something as it is at a remove from himself. In this neutrality, removal provides a first possibility of experiencing the relation of distance and remoteness; it makes possible an investigation of this relation so far as it is always a specific one in the various forms and degrees of removal. Because removal leads to spatial relation, it is the initial appearance of remove.

If this is the case, remove itself may best be understood on the basis of removal. On the one hand, removal holds apart; it allows one to experience how much of a remove there is to something, and, likewise, how much distance one has to something. On the other hand, removal also thereby connects; the size of the distance and the measure of the removal would not matter if the concern while at a distance were not to preserve or overcome it and if what is at a remove was not to be brought closer or left at a distance. In this connection, however, the one is not brought into line with the other or put into relief in its commonality with the other. The connection is of such a kind that separation is not overcome; it only ensures that the separation is no indifferent adjacency. The connection allows what is separated to be connected as something separate. The more intensive the connection, the more intensive, too, the being separated; when the connection becomes weaker, removal diminishes in significance, distance no longer has any meaning and fades. The essence of remove lies in this tension of connection and separation.

The tension that comprises the essence of remove may also be grasped conversely. The connection, which is to be experienced in removal always as a specific one, exists in its specific manner only because what is connected remains separated. Only because neither of the two may be derived from the other is the relation of the connected moments as it is. If what is perceived were a moment of perception itself, one would not speak of perception; if presentation could be grasped as a manifestation of what is presented, there would not have to be any talk about it as a matter of fact. Perception and presentation obtain only because both are *exterior* to the moments belonging to them. What they allow to be exterior in relation to one another is *exteriority itself*. This, however, is only another, differently accented, word for remove. Remove is exteriority that neither is indifferent nor has fallen apart into the chaotic; exteriority is what is irretrievable, insuperable about remove, and, in this, exteriority belongs to the essence of remove itself.

Remove and exteriority are given not only in removal. With different accentuation, they are likewise at play in remoteness and distance. They are at play in all spatial relations. Remove, to whose essence exteriority belongs, is the essence of space.

The determination of space developed here also agrees with conceptions of space that have not been considered up until now, and, for this reason, played no role in how its determination was developed. Kant already saw that space, in its essence, is disclosed by the idea of exteriority, although he understands space as something subjective. "By means of the outer sense (a characteristic of our mind)" so it goes in the *Kritik der reinen Vernunft*, "we represent objects as outside of us and these altogether in spaces."[92] This is not intended to mean that things are as if in a container. It is true that a room may be conceived of as a container that has furnishings in it. One understands the room as space, however, only if one grasps it not as a container but rather in its exteriority; it is a specific space, in which things prescribe how they stand at a remove. Space itself, in turn, is not put together from spaces. Rather, every specific space is subject to the essential determination of space. Outside of one space there may be another. From the standpoint of removal, however, space may always be experienced in what has previously been experienced as a specific space. Thus, a house, which is a space, is spatially at a remove from other spaces. Space is "ubiquitous," wherever there is a space, each space provides the experience of space. In this respect, one is able, as Kant formulates it "to represent only a little bit of space, and, when one speaks of many spaces, one understands by this only parts of one and the same sole space."[93]

Because of its uniqueness, space is not one thing given among others. It is, with Kant, "not an empirical concept that has been derived from experiences,"[94] that is, not something that is given with exterior things, that can be focused on discretely next to them. "For," Kant offers as grounds, "in order that certain sensations be referred to something outside of me (that is, to something in another region of space from that in which I find myself), and similarly in order that I may be able to represent them as outside and *next to* one another, therefore not only different but in different places, the representation of space must already be in place."[95]

According to these determinations space is the *representation* of exteriority. It is, once again with Kant, "a necessary representation *a priori*, which underlies all outer intuitions,"[96] or, as it is also identified, "the form of all appearances of outer sense."[97] Kant, however, provides reason to doubt what the representational character of space is about. When he elucidates reference of sensations "to something outside of me" with the suggestion that "something" is "in another place in space than the one I find myself in," he gives away that "I myself" must be spatial in order to understand something as outside of me. This spatiality, however, may no longer be conceived *a priori* as mere representation. If the concern is with space insofar as it is to be traversed—and Kant discusses only this—then one must locate himself in order to be able to understand something as outside of himself. I can only estimate and overcome the removal to that wall over there, as Heidegger had grasped it with the concept of de-removing, by starting out from me and returning to me. If one must belong in space himself in order to experience something as outside, however, then space is no longer only a representation of exteriority, but, rather, as has been shown, exteriority itself.

This also holds for space as Kant describes it. The "little bit of space" is exteriority because there is always yet another outside—beyond the room, beyond the house, behind whatever appears as the horizon from a certain line of sight. Hegel treated space in this spirit under the concept of quality in the *Wissenschaft der Logik*, and determined it as "absolute *being outside of oneself*," as "a being-other and again other, which is identical with itself."[98] Exteriority, as the reference to its 'identity with itself' might be discussed, is that of an unrestricted remove at play in all relations of space.

Yet, even if the essence of space is adequately determined as remove—the determination, as it has been developed up until now, is still not sufficient. Insofar as it was achieved in an orientation by the structure of presentation and by perception, it may be richer in content than the formal determinations given by Kant or Hegel. What remove itself is nevertheless remains unclear, however, as long as one always refers to it only in relations whose fundamental trait it is. It is thus merely thinkable, but not yet thought; determinative thought is not realized without description. Such a description that would realize the concept of the essence of remove is still wanting. It is, however, indispensable for the phenomenological purpose of this investigation. Only with such a description does it become possible to grasp spatial relations based on the essence of space, only with it, then, is a phenomenological consideration of the structure of presentation possible.

It is worth returning once again to removal to begin this consideration. Removals are not dependent on whether one gets across [*zurücklegt*] them or not. However, one only recognizes their significance when one asks what it takes to get across it. While underway, it is generally not solely the length of the path that plays a role here. Of significance, too, is whether the path is laborious or not, whether it is easy or difficult to find, and whether it is perhaps associated with danger. What matters, then, is how passable the path is and how the removal at issue can be *traversed* [*durchmessen*].

"To traverse" means, initially, "to pace out" [*ausmessen*], however, moreover, "to wander through," "to walk through." The two can belong together—by ascertaining a removal in accord with a certain measure when one walks through it, for example, in indicating the number of steps. Yet, in order to be in a position to do this one has to have an awareness of the distance that one wishes to traverse. One has to be able to *estimate* [*ermessen*] what is to be paced out or walked through.

What is estimated is removal, but, in it, also remove itself. There lies in estimation a sense for remove and for how it is to be traversed. In enclosed spaces, one experiences confinement and expanse in this way; one knows whether there is enough space to allow one comfortably to stay in it. This is not always clear on first glance; in this case, one has to be in the room, stay in it, in order to be able to estimate its expanse or confinement. Even the estimation made on first glance was, admittedly, a possibility of one's stay; one was in the space and had, estimating it, more or less clearly grasped the possibility of traversing it. Because space is an openness that one stays in, estimating belongs together with traversing.

What can be traversed and, as such, is estimated, is a *dimension*. The word names both of these; *dimensio* is traversing, understood as proceeding, as well as the extension to which this proceeding belongs. Dimensions are remove in ever-different respects; they provide possibilities of traversing and are, as such, able to be estimated as possibilities. In this way, length, width, and height or depth are dimensions of space. In an enclosed space, one may go forward, one stretches out one's arms to the side, and, as concerns height, one estimates it through one's own height alone. Directions, which are given in this way, may be checked; one establishes, which length, width, and height the room has.

Little is said by this, however, from the viewpoint of the significance space has for one himself. The size of a room is always of significance or of import only as size for a specific manner of stay; what matters is the furnishing of the room, what one wishes to do with the room and what is supposed to occur in the room. Estimating and traversing must correspondingly, then, be different. They not only have to do with the perceptible confinement or expanse but also arise from a sense for the openness proper to the stay. This is a sense for how one can conduct oneself, a sense for the possibility of setting something up so that it comes sufficiently into focus, and, likewise, for the room that someone needs to enter. In this, different viewpoints than length, width, and depth and height are at play. If things are nevertheless measured out, this is subordinate to these viewpoints; in this case, it is no longer determinative for the estimation of the room.

If this is so, then a sense for space not only has to be richer than and different from how it appears when one measures it out; its dimensions also have to be determined differently. The space of a stay has dimensions that, as such, are not to be grasped through the dimensions of length, width, and height. These determinations only emerge when all significance of the stay is disregarded and only the most simple relations of space are left over: steps forward, lateral stretching of the arms, a look up to the heights or down to the ground. That something one wishes to reach is "behind there," that one stands in reference to something that makes him "behind there," no longer appears here. To measure something out is now the single experience of remove with which, admittedly, hardly an everyday conduct is content.

The experience of space, however, is for the most part nevertheless only little formed in everyday conduct; it hardly comes up in the context of conduct. By contrast, presenting is an essentially reflective activity, and, because of this, the meaning of space may be intensified in it. If this is the case, then the dimensions of space also come out in regard to the structure of presentation with special clarity; they could then be identified in orientation from the structure of presentation and discussed in general. What would come into view in this way could be named after the experience that it opens up. It would be *hermeneutical space*.

The first thing that belongs to presentation is that it comes into existence through decisions reached more or less consciously by the one who is presenting; it stands and is developed in the openness of alternatives. Because of this, it is determined through *freedom* in terms of an understanding that still remains as yet unrevealed but that is nevertheless harbored in linguistic usage. Moreover, it belongs to presentation that it bring into focus the text of what is to be presented, and, thus, moves within *language* in a sense still wholly unspecific and broad. And, finally, the moment that work and presentation meet together is an occurrence. At a certain moment, the presentation meets up with the work, so that it is moved into the context of other presentations. From the standpoint of the work, the presentation is generally a repeated one, whose enactment is of a certain duration. Insofar as a presentation occurs in this way, it is in *time*.

The triad of freedom, language, and time, has already been encountered, namely, in the discussion of philosophy in its originariness.[99] This could indicate that it, too, lies in the nature of the hermeneutical. It is obvious that all three moments can be experienced in multiple activities and occurrences. This also makes it probable that they involve determinations that allow the structure of presentation to be put into a larger context and thus be considered phenomenologically.

It is true that the understanding of freedom, language, and time as dimensions of space could appear disconcerting, perhaps because the arrangement is not illuminating, perhaps, too, because one asks oneself what of all things they are supposed to have to do with space. The answer can only be provisional before the three are discussed as dimensions. Yet, provisionally, it is the same in regard to both questions: *Remove is at play in freedom, language, and time.*

To be free from or for something always also means to have distance from it. Whoever is free in his decisions or in his activity has distance to his possibilities and does not simply get completely engrossed in his respective activities; the activity remains reflected and can, for this reason, be shaped. Things are similar in language. What one speaks about always remains at a remove; it is not seized or used or consumed, but, rather, remains in existence for itself and remains what it is. One can also put oneself at a distance from something by speaking of it. It is thus when one succeeds in putting situations in life into language that they appear as such; matters of fact get loosened from the proximity of everyday conduct and may be evaluated. Finally, time, too, cannot be conceived without removal. Something is at a remove because it is futural, or it is removed in passing away with time. Whatever is present arrives from the removal of the future and withdraws in passing away; insofar as this arriving and passing away belongs to whatever is present, it does not simply exist, but has come into proximity. It moreover remains determined by the possibility of being removed.

This outline alone suggests that freedom, language, and time, are difficult to separate from one another. The freedom to decide is often accompanied by the possibility to name the alternatives one has as such. Freedom also comes into focus in the possibility of putting something into language. There is also freedom in regard to what is said, however; one does not follow it straightaway, but, rather, remains at a distance. Freedom from something often sets in with time; one's inner experience of the passage of time is different, in turn, when one has a free relation to it than when one is subject to it without distance. Language and time are also connected with one another. Time is arranged linguistically; in the use of expressions of time like "soon," "now," and "once," temporal relations are not simply ascertained but turned into something that it is possible to experience. On the other hand, speech is a process in time whose purpose is to make something present to mind. In language, it is possible to retain something in presence that passes away in time and would be lost without language.

The outlined connections would have to be supplemented with others; here, the concern is not with completeness. More important is to see each of the determinations of freedom, language, and time on their own together with their connections. Connections may only be referred to based on something determinable in itself, even if it is factically never experienced alone. Both their factical belongingness and their determinacy as such support that it is appropriate to conceive of freedom, language, and time as dimensions. The abstract modes of the dimensions also always appear together in the experience of space. It is only because one is familiar with all three dimensions in one's experience of space that one may ever say something is missing one of them and is only two-dimensional. Just this is claimed of human life here. This life is spatial, insofar as it is in a space, whose dimensions are freedom, language, and time. In respect of this, human life is always determined through all three dimensions.

With this, the addition is important that spatiality is tantamount to being *in* space. If freedom, language, and time are to be conceived as dimensions, they are not characteristics of the human being, and they belong just as little to the apparatus of a transcendental subject, however it might be conceived. They are that, *wherein* we are, in such a way that we are amidst things and at the same time encounter whatever is thingly as something different from ourselves. Even things are in freedom, they are in language; that they are in time is immediately obvious. This of course does not mean that things are free in the same manner as we are or that they are linguistic and temporal in the sense that they have language or are in a position to experience time. It does mean, however, that life in freedom, language, and time can neither be led nor described adequately without them. Freedom, language, and time are dimensions of space, in which conduct belongs and in which *everything* is. Understood on the basis of this totality, hermeneutical space is the world.

This could appear as an arbitrary equivalency. Why should an adequate understanding of the world be possible based on the discussion of hermeneutical space? This may only be justified by taking up the concept of world and discussing it in regard to the concept of hermeneutical space.

§ 16. *The Concept of World*

Talk about the "world" is usually in two senses: "World" is either the entirety of what is or the characteristic context of human life. The latter can be intended in contrast to religious life, so that the world is the context of only human life, turned away from God, and, in this, also sinful. Or, the concept is specified by signifying a particular context of life, for example, the world of art or the scientific world. Thus, talk of religions or cultures can also be as that of "worlds."[100] Here, the world is the context that accords with a specific "picture of the world" or "worldview."[101] World, understood in this way, is the "spiritual world"; it is the epitome of a life lived, and, at the same time, modified and always newly developed in forms and institutions, in "values and goods," as Dilthey puts it. World is the "effective context" of spiritual life.[102]

The concept of world owes its central position in hermeneutically and phenomenologically oriented philosophy to this understanding of it. In the development of this concept of world, the other, first-mentioned understanding of the world has served more or less openly as a background contrast. As the entirety of what is, the world appears underdetermined, and in fact conclusively so when the focus is on the *context* of what is. It is no longer enough, here, to supplement the idea of an entirety of what is with a "spiritual world"; what this concept indicates must rather be conceived such that it makes intelligible whatever is in its context.

Heidegger developed the concept of world in this sense in *Sein und Zeit*. If everything that is may be explained in its being only through the being of Dasein, then its "inner-worldly character" may only be made intelligible in regard to the "worldliness" of Dasein.[103] "World" is, and in fact is exclusively, a "characteristic of the being of Dasein."[104] With this understanding of world, Heidegger combines the two concepts of world, which can be counted as the predecessors of the one distinguished here. By understanding the entirety of what is based on the "significance" [*Bedeutsamkeit*] opened up in Dasein, that is, based on its significance [*Bedeutung*] and importance for Dasein, he brings back into play that understanding of the world as an ordered state that was intended by the Greek word for "world," namely, κόσμος. And, by conceiving of this context on the basis of *human* Dasein, Heidegger goes back to the understanding of κόσμος found in the New Testament, that is, to the understanding of the world as "state" or "condition" of the human being.[105] In regard to the matter at issue itself, Heidegger hereby reacts to the nominalistic revocation of what Hans Blumenberg has called the "cosmic conservatism," which grew from an "arrangement of Christianity with ancient metaphysics."[106] If it is no longer possible to motivate the world as order from creation, there remains only the possibility of finding the order on the basis of the human being. One possible answer as to how such an order can be conceived is the world of useful things and work as it is described in *Sein und Zeit*.

Heidegger was not satisfied by the concept of the world as he developed it in *Sein und Zeit*. This is comprehensible: as world of useful things and work, the world is grasped too narrowly. In this regard, the concept of world conceived on the basis of meaningfulness cannot replace the understanding of the world as the entirety of what is. As if a corrective of the conception from *Sein und Zeit* were intended, Heidegger turns in his treatment "Vom Wesen des Grundes" to Kant's determination of the world as the "absolute totality of existing things."[107] His focus here is foremost on the tension between the two moments of this determination, that is, on the fact that the totality of existing things can only be grasped as a transcendental idea—in the sense of a representation necessary for, but not realized in, experience—in opposition to its infinite multiplicity. As Heidegger expresses it, the world understood as such a totality "transcends" [*übersteigt*] "appearances," and, in fact, in such a way "that it is *referred back* to them as *their* totality."[108] With the world as a totality, a viewpoint that lies outside of appearances is achieved that allows one to conduct oneself toward appearances as a whole.

Heidegger wants to move beyond this idea. His point is to draw a consequence from Kant's "transformation" of the understanding of world in "inherited metaphysics"[109] that Kant himself did not draw. That the issue of world no longer turns on the "all" of things[110] but rather on the possibility of such an understanding is realized for Heidegger in the idea of a totality of what is that is always formed historically in Dasein. Dasein's "transcendence" in regard to what is lies in the fact that Dasein is "world-formative," that is, Dasein lets world occur as totality because it "provides an originary look (picture) [*Bild*], which does not grasp specifics, but nevertheless functions as the pre-picture [*Vor-bild*] for all revealed beings, among which the respective Dasein himself belongs."[111]

Heidegger elucidated how this is to be understood in detail foremost in his 1931–32 winter semester lecture course.[112] Here, the talk is of a "projective binding" of Dasein, and of the fact that Dasein, with the projection of a world, gives a "bond," "which remains binding from the outset in advance, so that all following conduct, down to the details, first becomes and is able to be a free one through it."[113] World-projections of this kind occur in science, history, and art. Understood in this way, natural science is not only empirical research, but, rather, the preliminary delimitation of "what . . . in the future is supposed to be understood by nature and natural process."[114] History worthy of the name projects "the anticipatory understanding of the *occurrence* of what we call history."[115] In art, the "concealed possibilities of what is" are brought into "a work," so that a completely new look can be given to "what actually is" [*Wirklich-seindes*].[116] In each case, the totality of the world is always discovered anew because what is, including "the respective Dasein himself," is *clarified* under a unified viewpoint. World-projection and world-formation are clarifications of what is from the standpoint of the "absolute totality" of the concept of world.

Heidegger's conception of world-formation belongs in the effective history of Nietzsche's understanding of interpretation. That the world is not contemplated but rather created had been emphasized by Nietzsche, for example, in the *Fröhlichen Wissenschaft*: the "entire eternally growing world of appraisals, colors, weights, perspectives, ladders, affirmations, denials," are brought forth as "poetry" by "thoughtful-sensitive individuals" and are "memorized, habituated, translated into flesh and reality, indeed, everydayness by the so-called practical human beings."[117] Yet, even if Heidegger takes this up in his idea of world-formation, the difference between his understanding of world and that of Nietzsche's is considerable. Nietzsche understands the world—"eternally growing"—as a chaotic occurrence of the will to power. Because of this, the whole of it cannot not be circumscribed in an "idea." It lies in each respective moment of a manifestation of the will—just as for Leibniz, every monad contains the picture of the world in a specific abbreviation.[118] The world, as Nietzsche conceives it, is a finite "quantity of force,"[119] whose state is a different one in every moment due to the dynamic of the will to power, but which, on the assumption of infinite time, recurs eternally in every moment.[120] By contrast, Heidegger wishes to conceive of projecting the world based on a "preview" of its totality and unity. Otherwise, the projection that constitutes the transcendental movement of Dasein could not be a projection of *the* world.

The two conceptions lead to different difficulties in accord with their difference. If one follows Nietzsche, then the world is always given only perspectivally, although one could not name a whole as such in which the perspective belongs; in this case, the world is always only given as different worlds.[121] If one follows Heidegger, then the world is always projected as a totality, although the result is always only a possibility of the world. Nevertheless, only one of the two can be: Either there are worlds that rise and fall and remove one another, or there is *one* world that is interpretable in various ways. If the projection of a world presupposes the idea of the world as totality, then the alternative is decided. From the hermeneutical standpoint, this is the better solution: It is possible to mediate between different interpretations of the world, they may be connected in new interpretations. Between worlds, by contrast, there always lies an abyss.

Neither Nietzsche nor Heidegger can do without the concept of world in the Kantian sense; the idea of an absolute totality is as operative in the attempt to conceive of the world in terms of a chaotic play of wills to power as it is in Heidegger's conception of world-formation and world-projection. This holds, in fact, in a twofold respect. The conviction or claim that everything eternally comes again can only be held in a given moment in virtue of grasping one experiences as a totality; *everything* that belongs to this moment comes again, however confusedly and unclearly this may be conceived. And, the idea of finite quantity of force by which Nietzsche wishes to ground the possibility of eternal recurrence cannot be grasped without the concept of an absolute totality; it is itself only a version of this totality. In Heidegger it is obvious how Kant's determination of world entered into his conception; he takes up the idea of an absolute totality and reformulates it so that it no longer operates as a representation or concept but rather as a projection or world-formation. Yet, Kant's determination is also operative in still another respect: the beings [*das Seinde*] that are brought into the unity of a world by an "originary look"[122] have to be experienced in their totality in order for them to be clarified in the manner Heidegger describes. The "as a whole" of what is that Heidegger speaks of in his Freiberg inaugural lecture is nothing other than the absolute totality of existing things, a totality which is accessible not in the manner of an epitome but rather in the disclosive mood.[123] Thus Heidegger himself provides evidence that there is one world and not worlds.

On the other hand, it is comprehensible that Nietzsche and Heidegger did not wish to be satisfied with Kant's determination. The concern for both of them is with a determination of world that takes into account its ability to be experienced; world that is supposed to be more than only an "idea." The experience nevertheless remains bound to the idea in both cases, however. Only if the idea of finite quantity of force is presupposed is it possible to conceive at any given moment that "everything" recurs; only on the assumption of a concept of world is it possible to say that a new clarification of beings achieved by a science or by an artistic discovery of the possible is a projection of the world.

Nietzsche and Heidegger conceive of the world based on the enactment of life as experience of *the world*: thus they cannot get loose from Kant's determination of world and on the other hand cannot explicitly accept it.

The solution is already marked out in this description of the difficulty: The issue is to conceive of the world without the expectation that it refer to the world as such, so that the concept of world may freely come into focus once again as totality. The experience of the world has to be experience *in* the world; one may not expect experience to stand and vouch for the concept of world. On the other hand, the concept of the world must be able to take experience of the world into account. The absolute totality is not only to be conceived as an epitome of existing things but just as much as an epitome of its possible experiences.

Probably almost no one has come so close to such a solution as Husserl in his late considerations of the concept of world. According to the self-description of the natural attitude as it is recounted in *Ideen I*, the world understood as spatiotemporal reality is something to which "I myself belong like all other things found there and all other human beings referred to it in the same manner."[124] As Husserl will refer to it in the *Crisis*, the world understood in this sense is "the all of things."[125] Yet, here Husserl makes a consequential differentiation by determining the world not only as the world of things or thing-world, but, moreover, as *life-world*.[126] As such, it is "the domain of something subjective that is completely and utterly self-contained, that has its own manner of being, ubiquitously and inextricably involved in all experience, all thought, functioning in all life, yet never beheld with the eye, never seized and grasped."[127]

An echo of the talk of "immanent being" in *Ideen I* cannot be ignored here; what is intended is the immanence of consciousness achieved through the ἐποχή. Now, however, the immanence of consciousness is understood as anonymous-collective, operative in spheres of meaning in various circumstances of life. Meaning is now experienced at the level of the life-world, advanced, changed, enriched through innovation. In the life-world, things and matters of fact are significant and can be experienced, confirmed or discovered in their significance. In this respect, it is comparable to the world as Heidegger describes it in *Sein und Zeit*;[128] except that Husserl's understanding is neutral enough to avoid being reduced to a world of useful things and work.

The life-world in Husserl's sense is in any case distinguished from the world in *Sein und Zeit* in a decisive respect: It is not a world in which one can "fall" into a "flight" from the openness and indeterminacy of one's own Dasein.[129] "Being" in the life-world is no "inauthentic" existence [*Dasein*]; Heidegger could have found a model for his understanding of inauthenticity as the press toward what is already actual, assured, in the "natural attitude"; but he could have found no point of reference for inauthenticity in Husserl's idea of the life-world. The life-world is prior to the natural attitude as well as Desein itself in its world-fallenness. To state it with Heidegger's concept, the life-world is Dasein *as* world, or, to put it in Husserl's own formulation, as "the domain of something subjective that is completely and utterly self-contained." The life-world is thus the world in which everything is *phenomenal*, without being recognized phenomenologically as phenomenon. It is "the universe of the ... subjective,"[130] in which "the world," understood as "the all of things"[131] first "comes to its simple existence [*Dasein*] for us." The life-world even makes possible the "universality of synthetically connected abilities,"[132] which lie in the "subjective." The life-world is what Husserl calls "constitution" as world. One could therefore also call it the world of phenomena; it would be the world of appearance and not only of what appears taken as real.

This would of course mean that it cannot be further phenomenologically reduced, taken back into appearance. Indeed, it is the pre-given "horizon,"[133] in which something is appearance. The theme of the "life-world," as put by Blumenberg, stands "for the insight that reduction" may "not be carried over from things to world": "one pulls back from experience as from being involved; one is not able to do this from one's immersion in the world."[134] Even so, one's "immersion in the world" may still be made explicit. The ἐποχή in fact finds a hold in it; it brings the life-world in its "pre-givenness" to consciousness. It illuminates the "world with pure and complete conclusiveness *as which* and *how* it has meaning and ontological valence and always achieves new figures in the life of our consciousness."[135]

The concept of life-world accordingly does not replace the concept of the natural world that is experienced on the basis of things. Because of this, one has to determine the relation of the two worlds to each other. If one follows Husserl's considerations, it is not that there are two worlds next to one another—not, then, that the world is experienced as the "all of things" in the natural attitude based on the life-world. This is impossible if the life-world in itself is distinguished by something like a pre-phenomenological reduction. As Husserl sees it, both worlds belong together: Just as the world of things appears in the life-world, life-worldly subjects appear in the world understood as the "all of things." Husserl holds this "togetherness" of "subjectivity in the world as object," and "subject of consciousness *for* the world"[136] to be in special need of clarification, because he sees a "really serious difficulty" here.[137] This difficulty is supposed to lie in the fact that the abilities of the life-worldly subject to constitute meaning cannot be reconciled with its boundedness in the world: "how should a portion of the world, its human subjectivity, constitute the whole world, namely, constitute as its intentional structure?"[138] Husserl's solution of this "paradox"[139] lies in his understanding of the subject of consciousness as "an 'other' I"[140] and, so, always determines the human being in regard to the two distinguished worlds differently.

This solution, itself reminiscent of Kant's distinction of a "visible" from a "moral" and under this aegis intelligible world,[141] is clearly only necessary if the world conceived as the all of things has to be *traced back* to the subjectivity of the life-worldly subject and its ability to constitute meaning. The problem falls away if the world is understood as hermeneutical space. Then the world is life-world and thing-world in one, the totality of the epitome of experience and the epitome of what it is possible to experience. Experience appears in the totality of what is, and what is appears in the totality of possible and factical experience. Regarded in this way, the fear that the "existence of the subject of the world" engulfs the "entire world and, with it, itself,"[142] is also groundless. Just as little do "subjects" become submerged in existing things. There are both: the thingly, which is as such exterior, and the meaningful, which is disclosed from out of us in the context of our attitudes. Life-world and thing-world are chiastic, crossed over in one another. They relate to one another like two sides of one matter.

That this is so is especially clear in regard to the structure of presentation. Interpretation, presentation—this is something that appears in the world not only in cases that stand out and are therefore easily recognizable. Objectivity may be only barely formed or reach the degree of intensity required for the formation of an object, for explicit interpretation. The structure, though, that comes to appear as the structure of presentation is always there; this is why whenever one aims at, directs oneself toward something and whenever one is affected by something, this can be investigated from the standpoint of correlation, that is, investigated phenomenologically in the sense established here. The investigation, as it is now to be undertaken, thereby pays attention to remove itself in order thus to make clear the status of the structure of presentation. It is thus possible to show *what kind of world it is that reaches its most intense form in the structure of presentation.*

It is of central significance for the understanding of world that this occurs in a threefold respect, namely, in the investigation of the three dimensions proper to hermeneutical space. If the totality, which the world is, is arranged in three dimensions, the totality is more than an idea in the Kantian sense. Because the dimensions of world are determinate in their essence and can be experienced in their determinacy, the world as such may be described in a conceptually structured manner.

The description that is now in store does not begin from scratch as if it were preceded by nothing. Freedom, language, and time are philosophically central themes. Accordingly, they may not be adequately discussed without taking up classical discussions of them, or, at least, the ones relevant to furthering them. Yet, none of these discussions grasp freedom, language, and time precisely as they are understood here; this alone suggests that there is good reason for the investigation of the matter, which is itself the principal concern here, to keep at a distance from them. The fact that this avoids a mere affirmation of the eternal verity of the classics, however, does not mean that the conceptions drawn from them would be "destructured" in reference to something that unwittingly motivates them. Talk can only be of destructuring insofar as the conceptions taken up are put into a new context, and that this new context functions as the measure for the assessment of their possibilities and limits. The concern, then, is less with the explication of the conceptions drawn upon than with their clarification based on the systematic context developed in this treatise. They are read in the context of a phenomenology of the hermeneutical. In this, phenomenological contemplation catches up with itself because in reflecting on hermeneutical space in its dimensions, it is also reflecting on its own possibility at the same time. It is the most extreme degree of intensity of what it contemplates and presents. It is in this way originary.

Chapter 4

Freedom

§ 17. Action

One does and does not know what freedom is. At some point, one experienced something one perhaps only later learned to bear the name "freedom." The designation, however, also appears in other contexts. One then asks oneself whether the matter at issue is the same or at least something comparable. As soon as this question receives a certain, namely, philosophical, intensity, it is the question of freedom itself.

On the one hand, what is to be understood as freedom is given ahead of time: It is a dimension of hermeneutical space, that is, the world. On the other hand, however, this determination is anticipatory; how it is to be understood must first be achieved. To this end, there is no other possibility than going back to an understanding of freedom that is perhaps elementary, although in any case as impartial as possible. If one were now to orient oneself only by the structure of presentation or by the philosophical experience of freedom, the purpose of the discussion would not be reached; it is what is intensified in presentation that is supposed to be captured, but this does not get recognized in presentation itself.

The word "freedom" is only enigmatic when one isolates and stares at it as if it had to reveal its meaning. By contrast, the meaning becomes clear, as with all words, based on the context in which the word belongs. "Free" is a word that suggests *relations* [*Verhältnisse*]; one is free *from* or free *for* something. A free man is someone who has no master, that is, who is free from having to follow commands. Thus, he is free to decide for himself and possibly even to issue commands. In the broad sense, one is free from something when one is not ruled, imposed on, oppressed, or restricted by it. In this case, one is often enough also free *to* relate to it.

One is free, but what is above all free is his relation to what had previously ruled over him. One is no longer bound by it, nothing is stipulated any longer. Seen in this way, the freedom of the self is what Kierkegaard described as the experience of the dream of freedom: the "possibility to *be able to*."[1] One has to do something, however, with this possibility. It is first in this that free relation proves to be what it is, and, in this respect, freedom again concerns one himself. One must perceive it, although in doing so one will discover that not only he himself is free.

If freedom is the "possibility to be able to," then it is possible to understood what freedom has to do with conduct [*Verhalten*], more precisely, with the possibility of conduct. The experience of freedom concerns the "also otherwise": One had been able to conduct oneself otherwise, and, in this, one is free. However, the question of the "also otherwise" is not always a question of freedom. If one has slept poorly, this could also have been otherwise, although it has nothing to do with freedom. That one has slept poorly is an occurrence; sleep, so it appears, is not conduct.

The experience of freedom, however, certainly does not become apparent in all conduct. One could have gesticulated otherwise than one did, one's facial expressions could have been otherwise. Things of this kind do not occur to one as do sleeping or getting a chill or coughing. They are an expression of what one feels and how one feels, but the question of the "also otherwise" does not usually appear here either. This question is posed first when gesticulation and facial expression are supposed to be controlled, whether because another expects this or because one demands it of oneself. Often, this has to do with the structure of relation to others, although also with whether a certain gesticulation and a specific facial expression would be beneficial or a hindrance to what one is doing and wishes to do. There must be *planning* involved in the conduct, and this generally has to do with the fact that one wants to *reach* something. One has to take orientation from this kind of conduct, then, if one wishes to find access to what freedom is.

Conduct, in which one wishes to reach something, is an *action*. Action is referred to an *aim*. What one does stands in a relation to this aim; the concern is to realize something that was named as the aim and, with this, was designated as something that is wanting. Everything that is intended as a contribution to this realization, then, belongs to action; if the aim were supposed to be realized through something that was not intended in this way, one does not attribute it to action. The aim makes action what it is. It gives *meaning* [*Sinn*] to what is done, that is, determinacy and direction.

As soon as one knows the aim of an action, it is generally determined sufficiently enough that one does not necessarily have to clarify its impetus and motive. Things are different in aimless conduct. If someone paces restlessly back and forth across the room, for example, one comes to understand this conduct first when one learns that this person is waiting for someone else and cannot bear his restlessness sitting still. There is of course impetus and motive in action, but neither of them is essential for the understanding of action as such. Just as inessential is everything done in the course of an action that is not done in reference to the aim. The aim makes it possible to recognize such things as inessential, for example, the fact that one lingers or lets his thoughts wander.

It is not only actions that have aims; a process can also be directed toward an aim. However, the directedness of actions toward an aim is different from that of natural processes. The growth of a plant also has an aim, namely, the complete development of what the plant is. However, this growth occurs *of itself*; the aim resides within it, and, accordingly, the process of growth is *predisposed* toward the aim. It is only in regard to the aim, in fact, that it is possible to say that the process could be interrupted, even broken off. But this can only be ascertained from the outside. In action, things are different. The aim has to be *realized*, and this is only possible if the one who acts is in some way conscious of acting. Actions are processes directed toward an aim, whose enactment is guided by the more or less clearly developed *knowledge* of this aim.

This concept of action is admittedly still vague. It may be grasped with more precision if one further delimits and differentiates it. Action is not the same as production [*Herstellen*]; the latter is determined by the fact that its goal is the independent presence of a work. Closer to action is bringing forth [*Hervorbringen*], if meant by this is the actualization of something, for example, the performance of a piece of music. Here one would not speak of action without hesitation; the attention focuses on what comes into actuality and less on the aim-oriented process itself. In action, it is less of significance that something comes into focus as an activity than that it occurs *through someone* to whom the result can be attributed. In this sense, the question of who was responsible for something belongs together with action; as soon as the question is posed, producing or bringing forth becomes action. Accordingly, in action it also counts more whether and how others are affected by the result of an activity. If someone builds a house in order to provide accommodations for his family, then in respect to the result that is available as a work, it is a production, though, in respect to the aim of this work, an action.[2] If attention is directed toward the fact that *someone* wishes, say, to actualize or effect a specific purpose, then producing and bringing forth can also be called an action. In this sense, every activity directed toward an aim is an action so long as it is not restricted to the manufacture of something or is concentrated on the actualization of something.[3]

In action, one wishes to reach something. But there is also a kind of action, in which what is supposed to be reached is already reached. Aristotle even understood it as action in the proper sense. As movements (κίνησις), actions whose aim is not present in them are not themselves what they are supposed to be, namely, aim.[4] Such actions are incomplete—as, for example, losing weight, which occurs for the sake of slimness although slimness itself is not given in losing weight.[5] According to this, only incomplete actions can have an effect in the discussed sense; they are directed toward their aim as toward a specific result that is first reached with the end of action. They have this in common with production. By contrast, actions that are complete in themselves are a *work* [*Wirken*]. In this kind of action, the *actuality* that the action is concerned with is present in every moment. It is "in the work" that it has and is therefore ἐνέργεια,[6] a work that is actuality in itself. This is also the case in bringing forth; both work [*Wirken*] and actualization [*Verwirklichung*] are "in the work." The difference is just that a work does not have to be of a specific duration, whereas actualization, say, the performance of a work, reaches its conclusion when the work as a whole has been performed.

However illuminating the Aristotelian distinction between incomplete and complete actions may be, one cannot support it without differentiation. When Aristotle names seeing (ὁρᾶν), sensibleness (φρονεῖν), and appreceptive thought (νοεῖν), indeed, even the good life (εὖ ζῆν) and happiness (εὐδαιμονεῖν) as examples of complete action,[7] one should not deduce from this that he wishes to signify the whole of life as a single action; if so, the concept would lose all precision. The good life, for example, is certainly complete in that it does not have an aim but rather is aim. It is only action, however, if it is always again realized in terms of different aims. If the good life is not supposed to be a state but rather an action, then one has to deliberate each time about what has to be done in order to reach the aim of the good life. This goal always lies in front of one anew whenever one directs oneself toward a limited goal.

Based on this consideration, what is common to both incomplete and complete action becomes clear: Both are *referred* to their goals, and therefore both also involve a *removal* between an activity and the aim of the activity. This can be the case for a limited activity, such as losing weight up until the aim of one's desired weight is reached. Or, one can remain referred to an aim that one must always reach anew even when one has reached it.

The issue here, in any case, has less to do with the distinction than with how the concept of freedom may be developed based on the aim-reference of such aforementioned activities. Here, the aim-reference establishes once again that removal belongs to the essence of action. There is a reference at play in the enactment of action that leads beyond whatever is done and, thus, first gives direction to this enactment. The characteristic reference of action is aiming at, εφίεσθαι, as Aristotle names it in his language.[8] The *tension* of action lies in the removal experienced in aiming at. On the one hand, this tension is a matter of stretching. In stretching, action is always more than its respective activity; it stretches itself by aiming at its aim, and, because of this, it is based on its aim that an activity may be identified as an action. On the other hand, the tension [*Spannung*] is tantamount to that tenseness [*Anspannung*] present when something is unsolved or unresolved. This expresses the idea that reference to an aim exceeds the enactment and, thus, that an enactment may remain unfulfilled even in a completed action.

This tenseness of action may be more or less great, barely perceptible or forcefully, as gnawing uncertainty, as doubt in one's own abilities. In every case, it allows the characteristic *openness* of action to be experienced. It becomes perceptible in the slightest pause and new beginning, as a hiatus between what is done now and what is still supposed to be done. The tension of action makes it vulnerable; it can be dissuaded from its aim or in some other way fail to realize its aim.

This possibility of failure is connected with the conviction that an aim is essentially supposed to come into existence *through one himself*. Even if action is effortless, it does not proceed of its own accord. One can and must keep a firm hold on his aim and realize it himself as it were step by step; if one were to interrupt and finally give up the realization, then it would be conclusively clear that the problem here lies essentially with oneself. If, by contrast, one brings something about without keeping a firm hold and without striving in this way, then although it does not occur without him, neither is it due to one's own action, any more than it is when one is dissuaded from an aim or is forced to realize an aim.

The experience of freedom comes into play in situations such as these. The freedom of action is its openness that was revealed as the tension between enactment and aim-referentiality. It is the openness one *perceives* in action, that is, it is there for him and he himself realizes it. It is traversed and in this remains open as long as one acts; it was possible to do "also otherwise," at least so as to interrupt or end his activity. Without this—that is, without the span [*Spanne*] between activity and aim—action is not possible. Accordingly, action is always concerned with this span in greater or lesser intensity. It is in acting that one attempts to preserve and also to increase the freedom that lies in action.

The attempt to preserve freedom presupposes the experience of jeopardy, and, likewise, the experience of the possibility of failing to achieve something. The jeopardy lies in the *unclarity of the point of departure*; whatever does not simply obtain but is brought about or is supposed to become more actual can also be foiled or fail. As soon as something steps in to impede one from reaching his aim, the openness of action is closed; the relation of the enactment of action to its aim is disturbed. Freedom misses the mark because one no longer holds firmly to his aim amidst the tension and directs his activity toward it but instead does something that has nothing to do with the aim. One does something, the effects of which remain unclear. Here, too, one loses the openness of action; one operates blindly and one notices first upon the result what he has brought about. In Aristotle's terms, freedom stands in opposition to what comes into being through force or through ignorance.[9]

Both of these, however, may only be experienced in freedom, and they are determined as such only on the basis of freedom. In the context of action, not everything that affects one so as to form an obstacle is a matter of force, but, rather, only something that hinders one from the realization of a goal that he is referred to. Here, ignorance is not simple unfamiliarity, but, rather, an inability in the realization of an aim. In both instances, one is not free for his aim. This stands in contrast to the activity that is what it is due to *foresight* about its aim. In this foresight, one perceives freedom as the openness of action. It is only thus that something one does can be *intentional*. "Intentional" means: determined through an open, this is, free reference to an aim. This freedom comes into focus when nothing prevents it and no ignorance obstructs it.

The intentional determinacy of activity, however, is never simply given; rather, it is realized by the fact that an activity is subordinate to an aim; it is intentional *based on an aim*. Conversely, what one is referred to proves to be an aim solely through the intentionality of the activity. Aims are not future matters of fact, whose possible presence one awaits; it is in their essence that one only has them as one who acts, that is, as one who strives to reach them through one's own activity; what another person is able to reach or does reach is no aim for one himself.

This is of significance for the understanding of freedom itself; the interplay of aim-referentiality and intentional activity determines how one experiences both of these in action. As the openness of action, they are the removal of what one is referred to. In action, this removal is as such neither realized nor experienced as an occurrence, but, rather, is traversed in the interest of diminishing distance. Action is, as Heidegger puts it, de-removing. Action does not, in fact, necessarily aim to bring something at a remove into proximity in order to have it at one's disposal or to change it. The concern in every case, however, is to bring the aim from out of the possibility that it is into actuality, no matter whether this occurs in a one-time effect or perpetually anew, that is, in work.

Even if action is de-removing, its enactment remains determined through reference to an aim. This reference, however, does not appear as such unconditionally; action can be completely occupied by the effort to reach its aim, and, in this way, be absorbed in enactment. In this case, the one who acts presses on toward an aim that is perhaps really more sensed than known. There are also actions based in need or strong inclination. Aristotle therefore even maintains that the conduct of very small children and actions of children are free.[10] This corresponds to a broad understanding of action, by which any striving whose aim may be reached by different paths is an action; here, the fundamental condition that enactment and reference must be able to be distinguished through the "also otherwise" is met. One could call this sort of action "elementary." If one were to dispute the possibility of elementary actions, one would have to assume that action would have to be learned at a specific stage in the development of a human life. But how should one be able to learn action in the narrower sense if it were not pre-given in an elementary manner? It is clear that elementary actions do not meet the expectations that one places on developed actions. The reason for this, however, is not as obvious. It lies in the fact that freedom in elementary actions remains as if shrouded. It is there, although it is not perceived—in the double sense of the word, it is not seen and not realized as such. What is missing is that by which an adult and mature human being's action is distinguished from that of a very small child: Like animals, very small children do not reflect while acting, although unlike animals, they are able to learn this reflection. This reflection is at the same time an experience of freedom in which this freedom is determined more richly than before.

§ 18. Deliberation

The reflection at issue here does not come from the enactment of action itself nor does it come to this enactment as something alien. It develops as it were in an intermediary position by taking hold in removal from an aim and perceiving this removal—that is, recognizing and realizing it—as freedom. This reflection is a *deliberation*,* a discussion with oneself. It is a pause that holds one's reference to the aim and the enactment of its realization apart and thus holds removal open. It counters the press toward realization and, in this respect, holds it up.

Action does not, however, come to a standstill through this hold up. It is not a cessation but rather a delay, which does not revoke one's reference to a goal but rather confirms it. In deliberation, the press forward toward an aim is broken. Yet, precisely in this way a more transparent orientation toward the aim is reached. By being momentarily [*innehaltend*] free from the enactment of action, one achieves freedom for his aim. Thus, orientation toward an aim is *freer* by comparison to elementary action. The openness that freedom is comes into focus in it more strongly.

As Aristotle stresses, deliberation (βουλεύεσθαι) is concerned less with an aim than with what is taken into consideration for the aim.[11] The aims

---

*[In the present discussion and elsewhere as appropriate, the English words "deliberation," "to deliberate," and so on, have been used to translate *Überlegung*, *überlegen*, and the like, in order to capture the sense Figal gives to the word as a term of art. This translation also helps capture the author's association of *Überlegung* with Aristotle's use of the term "βουλεύεσθαι," itself often translated into English as "deliberation." Elsewhere in the book, however, Figal also uses the word *Überlegung* in a nontechnical manner and in these cases I have translated it with "consideration," "to consider," and the like. —Trans.]

themselves, by contrast, are counted as a form of discovery that Aristotle names βούλησις. This means something that oscillates between willing [*Wollen*] and wishing. Even something that is not humanly possible, such as immortality, can be desired in this manner, also things that only others can accomplish, such as the victory of competitors that one wills or wishes as a spectator.[12]

It would be false, however, to think here of a clear division of tasks between two abilities. Both are restricted by each other. Thus, Aristotle stresses that deliberation has to do with what is up to us and is able to be done.[13] It holds only for what is of significance in regard to an aim, and not then, for what always is as it is or for what, as unchangeable, cannot be influenced and also not for what one happens upon by coincidence and therefore eludes planned activity, such as finding treasure. Neither does deliberation arise for what concerns only others.[14] All deliberation must be referred to an aim; it concerns how and through what something can be reached.[15]

Yet, even if the aim is not made the theme of deliberation, deliberation only has meaning when what is willed or wished is actually an aim. It cannot be unreachable like immortality or the victory of a competition for a spectator. It must rather be reachable as something that has an effect or as something that does work.

It becomes clear whether this is the case in reflection on what is required to reach an aim as soon as this reflection runs toward a decision. In this case, it is concentrated on a preferred choice and, insofar as the choice is at the same time the initiation of action, to decision (προαίρεσις).[16] As soon as decision determines action, there is no longer any uninterrupted willing or wishing. What is willed or wishable is, rather, judged from the standpoint of its realizability and in regard to its realization.

It is because of this that προαίρεσις appears closely together with βούλησις[17]; it is only together that each of them is what it is; neither of them can be thought without the other. βούλησις has "more" to do with the aim[18]; it connects deliberation in its directedness toward an aim and concentrates it as a choice [*Auswählen*] that selects something [*auswählendes*], that is, one that comes to a determinate possibility of action. Only when there is an aim is there a need for decision. By contrast, what an aim of *an action* can be becomes clear solely through προαίρεσις. It is only in regard to an aim of action that one can decide on a specific possibility of action; if something that is supposed to be does not lead to a decision, then it is not an aim of action but rather something that one merely wishes. Decision for Aristotle thus proves to be the intermediary of action; in it, deliberation in its referentiality to an aim and the enactment of action in its directedness toward the realization of an aim meet. In this respect, it is the common ground of thinking through and striving,[19] it is a striving that can in itself deliberate.[20] From the standpoint of decision, it belongs to striving toward an aim, to thinking through the possibilities of activity. And, by thinking through these possibilities, what one is referred to remains an aim. An act of deliberating that runs toward a decision is in itself already a striving toward an aim; it is only employed to reach an aim.

This makes it possible to understand that Aristotle signifies decision as something free, without identifying it with "the free" (τὸ ἑκούσιον); the free applies to more than only decision.[21] The free is also supposed to refer to elementary actions; these are free without decision. For Aristotle, however, decisions are free in the same sense as the elementary actions; they are a striving that can be enacted without being hindered by force and that is not in danger of leading to unintended effects through ignorance. Although one's orientation toward an aim is more transparent with deliberation and decision, action, for Aristotle, is not any freer because of them.

The reason for this is easy to identify: Aristotle understands deliberation from the standpoint of decision and sees this, conversely, as a specific form of the enactment of action toward an aim—namely, one determined through deliberation. On the one hand, this is illuminating: if deliberation were not determined through the enactment of action, deliberation could also not guide action; it is practically effective because it is practical deliberation. Yet, on the other hand, action is transformed by deliberation in a manner that cannot be grasped solely from the standpoint of decision; the fact that deliberation comes to be concentrated in each decision does not mean that it comes to an end. Insofar as it is a pause and a delay, it involves the possibility not only to traverse the removal from an aim in the enactment of action, but also to estimate [*ermessen*] it. In the openness deliberation is in, deliberation is *more open* as estimation than action that is being enacted. Accordingly, deliberation is also freer.

Estimation first occurs because deliberation opens up a circle of reflection; possibilities of activity and aim are always understood based on one another. Because an aim stands before one's eyes, reflection goes back to the possibilities of its realization. The clarification of it, conversely, brings the aim as such more precisely into view and makes it possible to recognize whether it is an actual, that is, realizable, aim. In deliberation about possibilities of action, an aim, which is itself only possible as a projection, as a presupposed unreality, receives an anticipatory—although by no means merely contrived—determinacy. This determinacy, conversely, only has meaning in regard to the aim.

What is described here is not a relation of presentation, however similar it may be to it. Here the aim lacks objectivity and the deliberation lacks a mimetic essence. The aim is not something exterior for which one then supplies a mediated presence, but, rather, a possibility of action always one's own that is projected outside into remove. Yet, the structure of presentation comes through in deliberation about action; practical deliberation belongs as it were in the prehistory of presenting; it can be intensified to presentation.

There is an understanding at play in deliberation insofar as it is a circle of reflection. If deliberation is successful, then one recognizes something based on it. Without this understanding, there would be no decision; the tension referred toward an aim must be successfully brought to a close in order that a possibility of action directed toward an aim be chosen and in order that the aim can be recognized in regard to it as something capable of being realized. Decision is thus the intermediary of action; it is the openness [*das Freie*] in regard to which the freedom of action that is guided by deliberation may be ascertained. What is concentrated in it, however, is an estimation of freedom in the open reference to an aim that is achieved in understanding. Possible activity is understood based on an aim, the aim is understood as something that it is possible to realize in one's own activity. Viewed in this way, the freedom of decision does not lie only in the enactment of action that is unhindered and is not misguided by ignorance. Action from decision is freer than an elementary one can be in virtue of the openness of the reference that comes into focus in the circle of reflection. It is more intentional.

The priority of open reference before decision may be recognized in yet another way: Even if the estimation of freedom achieved in understanding is concentrated in the decision, it does not come to an end with the decision. Deliberations held in the context of an action do not lose their meaning as soon as one has come to a decision. Clarifications that have already been achieved and are not forgotten are the foundation for new clarifications; they contribute to them or bring something new to attention by contrast. They are supplemented, differentiated, adapted, and sometimes also discarded. In this, even the possibilities one has chosen against are in play. What was once discarded can prove to be useful on another occasion. If this does not happen, one develops an awareness of the potential of what one is and is not capable of based on the horizon of possibilities one has discarded and passed over. In this way, one experiences one's own limits and, thereby, himself, insofar as he is one who acts.

This also concerns possible intentions and wishes. In the investigation of possibilities of action, one gets clear about what one finds worthy of striving for and what one is able to reach. This clarity is determined by Aristotle as φρόνησις; it is practical reason, or, understood from the standpoint of understanding, practical understanding [*Verständigkeit*]. φρόνησις is no mere capacity, but, rather, a disposition for deliberation that is prepared for action, one that has arrived at clarity about what the good and the bad are for the human being.[22] In this respect, it is the "true disposition," ἕξις ἀληθής. Aristotle also mentions that it involves language and its characteristic substantiveness; it is μετὰ λόγου. It is nevertheless determined not through the essence of language, but, rather, that of freedom. Because of the openness of practical understanding, freedom is its dominant dimension, although it also stands in the dimension of language. It stands no less in the dimension of time, for that matter, since it has to do with what can be otherwise.[23]

Practical understanding is freer than a particular deliberation and decision. More is estimated in it than only the span between what is to be done and an aim. In practical understanding there is a sense for the openness of aims and for what it is possible to do in general.

Although Aristotle does not signify practical understanding itself as free, he takes this into account insofar as he assigns it generally to the domain of "the good and bad for human beings."[24] And, he adds in elucidation, we hold Pericles and those who are constituted like him for sensible ones because they are capable of contemplating what is good for themselves and for human beings.[25] It could not be a coincidence that the word "contemplate," θεωρεῖν, appears here; he could just as well have said βουλεύεσθαι, that is, "deliberate." Had he done so, he would have in fact held more narrowly to the determination of understanding as a practical one. Yet, he does justice to the matter precisely through his putative inconsistency. The disposition that allows someone to be called a sensible one (φρόνιμος) prepares one for action precisely because in it, one maintains the distance of contemplation from particular actions and aims of actions, from what the good and the bad are for the human being. With this distance, a removal to aims arises that is no longer determined by the tension between one's possible activity and what is supposed to be reached. In the disposition of the sensible one, freedom is at play as that openness of reference in which actions themselves are put in remove. One is free from them, and, in this, also free for them. Because of this, the intentionality of action is once more intensified in comparison to deliberation; the intention here is no longer only a reference to an aim, but, rather an aim-reference in the selection of aims.

One should not think of the disposition of the sensible one, though, as a disposition of contemplation that as it were occasionally comes to an action. As Aristotle describes it, sensibility is for all of its contemplation still practical in its essence. For all of its distance from particular aims, it remains subordinate to one aim that Aristotle refers to variously as happiness (εὐδαιμονία), good life (εὖ ζῆν), and good action (εὖ πράττειν).[26] If all of these indicate "the best"[27] and "the highest of all goods to be done,"[28] then this can no longer concern a particular aim among other possible aims, and, consequentially, this aim may not be reached in a particular action differentiated from others. This aim must rather be intended in every action; in reference to this aim, all other references to aims and likewise all enactments of action are subordinate.

In one regard, this aim is closest; once it is discovered one is always concerned with it. On the other hand, it is the most removed of all aims; the removal to it is such that all aims and actions are intelligible in their priority based on it and can be understood based on it as a measure each time.

Since the concern here is with the integration of aims of action and action into one's own life, the measure can only exist in the disposition of sensibility. The decisive question is therefore whether a specific aim and the action that realizes it conform to the freedom of sensibility. The disposition that brings freedom into focus is the best possible formation of practical reflection and, as such, one of the best possible formations of reflection in general[29]; it is ἀρετὴ διανοητική. In it, practical freedom is the greatest because the openness that comprises freedom determines the entire domain of action. From the standpoint of praxis, everything that is practical can be perceived, seen, and realized in freedom.

Everything that is practical—so far, this has admittedly only meant: all aims and all possibilities of action. Yet, scarcely an aim affects one alone and action as good as never has an effect or does work that concerns oneself in isolation. It is true that one can have the aim to lose weight or to learn something. In the realization of these aims, it is only one himself that is different than before; one's own weight is different after losing some, and after learning one knows something he did not know before. Yet, in both cases, one is dealing with things—with means of sustenance that one has chosen or avoided, with the books that one has consulted and the writing instrument one uses. If the realization of an aim leads things to be intentionally altered, then they also stand within the purview of being referred to an aim. In the one case as well as in the other, things stand in a relation to freedom; if freedom is a dimension of hermeneutical space, this is indeed called for by the concept of freedom: Hermeneutical space is the world, and this is as much life-world as thing-world. Things, then, must also belong in freedom; freedom must be determined such that it does not exclude things.

§ 19. Freedom of Things

What often leads one to pause and deliberate in action are things. All at once, one cannot get any further with what one is doing. Something resists; something does not submit to use or something gets in the way as a hindrance. One then has to rethink the issue and search for a new possibility that will lead to the aim.

This experience says something about planning itself. To plan means: to project possibilities, and this, in turn, means: to think of schemata for action and to arrange individual steps of action as well as to connect and coordinate various schemata of action with one another. A schema of action is a more or less precise picture of an activity—not only its signification such as "furnish a house," but rather a representation without much detail of what the furnishing of a house is and what belongs to it. Kant elucidates the concept of the schema in this sense; a schema is a conceptual picture, that is, not a factically given intuition but rather a representation unspecific enough to accord with the universality of the concept and specific enough to lead down a path from it to a respective action in a respective context.[30]

Certainly, intuition, or, in general: experience can fulfill the schema. The factical activity of writing a letter, then, is approximately as one had expected it to be. There can, however, also be deviations; in these cases, something no longer fits into the schema. Perhaps the schema was too detailed, that is, too much intuitive picture and not enough schema, or it was so unspecific that the experience would likely have to be surprising or irritating. In both instances, one got into trouble with things.

Surprise and irritation may not be ruled out and can never be avoided completely. Even if the things that one is dealing with are so standardized that they correspond to one's schemata for action, they can, perhaps due to circumstance, always be different than one had expected. The tension that appeared in action between factical activity and aim appears here, too. There is an openness of action toward things. Action is also free in its relation to things.

Freedom is understood here precisely as it was in the tension between enactment of action and referentiality to an aim. It lies in removal, and not primarily in the fact that one can conduct oneself toward things "also otherwise." It is first in intentionality that the possibility of the "also otherwise" relevant for freedom attains prominence, and this intentionality is given in relation to things through the projection of a schema. The schema of action is always also a schema of things; it is a representation of how an activity is enacted as a manner of dealing with things and how things of this kind belong in activity. The schema remains at a distance, however, over and against the things as they are factically there and encountered in experience; it does not anticipate them as they factually are. It is only because of this that a view [*Sicht*] of things may be an intention [*Absicht*].

One's intention is realized in dealing with things, that is, in using or transforming them. If one's schema is not fulfilled here, but one's intention does not have to be given up, then this is not ultimately a failure, but rather only a test of the "also otherwise"; one has to adapt to things in a way that was not anticipated in the schema.

What occurs here is different from deliberation about how an aim could be realized. In deliberation, various schemata of action are taken into consideration and weighed against one another only in order to decide in favor of one of them. To adapt oneself to things is different: here, the schemata of action are themselves put into question; they must be modified and corrected, sometimes also discarded and replaced by others. One's intention emerges in proving itself against things. Here, the independence [*Eigenständigkeit*] of things, which intensifies in objectivity, first makes itself apparent.

The necessity for this proof and for the revision of plans in which this proof occurs makes it clear that things do not dissolve in the context of action. Conversely, the fact that schemata of action are able to prove themselves and that the revision of plans is possible shows that the world of things is not completely and utterly alien to that of action. If this were the case, then action, insofar as it has to do with things, could never be signified as free without skeptical reservation. This consequence, drawn by Kant,[31] arises only on the presupposition that actions are carried out in a world completely and sufficiently described under natural laws. Here, actions belong in a context that excludes freedom; they are in truth not actions, but, rather, occurrences in the world of things and are only regarded as actions. If one does not wish to sacrifice the idea of freedom under this presupposition, then this freedom can only be the origin [*Anfang*] of action in the rational determination of the will. Viewed from the standpoint of action, however, this origin must be understood as a pure, "transcendental idea."[32] There is no empirical reference for it. Freedom thus becomes a condition of action that must be established outside of the world of action, such that in the end it is unclear how freedom should still condition action at all.

The concept of the will that is supposed to save freedom in the face of the representation of a world able to be described completely under natural laws thereby also loses its meaning. The will is not "something unconditioned" outside of action, through which action is only initiated[33]; there are no acts of the will, in the sense of some capacity in "mind" or "spirit" or wherever.[34] Rather, willing proves to be in action itself, and, indeed, because it is for the sake of an intention that action is enacted; otherwise, it would only be a wish. If this is the case, however, then willing is conditioned in the literal sense of the word.* There is not any willing without things; willing is the persistence of one's intentional action in its influence on things.[35]

Willing understood in this manner has limits: persistence at any price is rarely successful, nor is it free. Successful action also requires that one is able to recognize the possibilities and limits of one's influence; one has to recognize which kind of influence things are susceptible to and which they are not—both here and now and in general. Otherwise, one stiffens up against something that despite all efforts will not yield and thus misses the possibility of rethinking things and adopting a new plan.

This, however, means that the essential remoteness of things belongs to the freedom of action. Only because they do not dissolve in action does the "also otherwise" become necessary in influencing them. Not only this; one can only

---

*[The English "conditioned" here translates *bedingt*, which, transposed into English, might be rendered as "bethinged." —Trans.]

successfully have an influence on them if one at the same time lets them be. They may only be used and transformed by reckoning with what each of them is and with their compositions. It is only possible to take hold of them by approaching them with a letting. In letting, one remains free over and against the things; every time one takes hold one also keeps at a distance and things remain at a remove. Because of this, however, things are also free; they remain free from being beset by rash action.

The idea that things are free is no anthropomorphism. One does not ascribe the possibility of willing and acting to things; that they are free—or, more precisely, in freedom—does not mean that they could perceive their freedom. It means only that in their remoteness from action they are determined by the same remove that determines action. One may nevertheless continue to think that this remove is ascribed to or conferred on things only from the viewpoint of action. On this view, things only appear free because one perceives freedom while engaged in action. Things would not be free in themselves, but, rather, placed into freedom by us.

The question of what is really going on here may best be discussed in reference to Heidegger. In his determination of our relation to things developed in his analysis of the useful thing, he opts for the answer outlined. A few years later, in supplementing and revising his conception, he sought a contrary answer. In the tension of his two solutions, Heidegger offers the possibility of making still more thoroughly clear an idea of the freedom of things.

In *Sein und Zeit*,* Heidegger determined the essence of the useful thing as "reference" [*Verweisung*]. He means by this determination a special kind of referentiality [*Bezogenheit*] of something to something else: In the use of something one may "refer" [*verweisen*] to something else if one finds the significance of the thing one is using in that other. Accordingly, one's attentiveness focuses on not what one is using but rather what it refers to. For example, the writing instrument is "for writing"; it refers to writing. One accordingly discovers it in its essence when one directs one's attention not to it but to the text that one is writing.

Reference is a special case of the possibility of understanding something based on something. One does not return to something based on another thing but rather remains directed toward the other thing; one understands something by overlooking it. Heidegger captures this with the concept of "relevance" [*Bewandtnis*], the ambiguity of which he puts to good use. On the one hand, "relevance" means as much as "constitution"; if something has a certain relevance, then it is constituted in such and such a way. On the other hand, one

---

*[In my translation of the following discussion, I have consulted and relied on Stambaugh's English version of *Being and Time*. Cf. Stambaugh 64ff. —Trans.]

can "let" something "have its own relevance" [*sein Bewenden haben lassen*];*
one no longer tends to it, but lets it be. On Heidegger's analysis of the useful thing, both of these moments must be taken together: one only experiences the constitution of a given useful thing by letting it be.

This is not all, however; Heidegger gives the outlined analysis an "ontological" turn by tracing the essence of the useful thing back to a "previous" or *a priori* form of letting something have relevance [*Bewendenlassen*]. Just as one lets a given thing in a given use have its relevance, the useful thing is in general "previously" left "*as* it is and *in order that* it is such."³⁶ This is the "previous freeing"³⁷ of what is based on relevance. In this case, what is would be "freed" in such a way that it can be accessed and encountered in its relevance. Heidegger summarizes this idea in his signification of "having always already let something be freed for relevance" as an *a priori perfect* "that characterizes the kind of being of Dasein itself."³⁸

As "*a priori* perfect," this freeing is prior to all experience, it has always already been; no experience ever gets hold of the accessibility of beings in terms of their relevance. And, the fact that this accessibility is founded in a freeing should not be taken to mean that it goes back to some conception or other of a resolution [*Entschluß*], back to a primordial action that first constitutes a being as a useful thing. Freeing is after all not an activity but rather a letting, and, in this respect, it can only be understood in terms of an openness of Dasein for the openness of what is. If one lets something stand or leaves it unhindered, this is an abstention from transforming it, and, so, a confirmation of its independent being from one himself. Consequently, it belongs to the "way of being of Dasein" that within it beings are always already "discovered"³⁹ as something handy. Dasein entails a dependency on things as well as the possibility of discovering things in this dependency on them.

As Heidegger develops this idea, however, it remains ambivalent. On the one hand, the freeing of beings is understood ontologically as a "letting be"⁴⁰; it is tantamount to taking or even accepting what is simply as it is. Yet, on the other hand, in Dasein something is added to what is by freeing it. Freeing [*Freigabe*] involves a *giving* [*Geben*]; something that comes from Dasein comes into what is. This, conversely, is due to the fact that Heidegger determines freeing in the ontological sense based on relevance. The concern is not simply to accept what is as such, but rather to discover "something that is already a 'being' in its handiness."⁴¹ Through Dasein, what already is takes on a way of being that

---

*[My use of the English 'relevance' for Bewandthis' follows Stambaugh. Although my use of the English 'have its own relevance' for 'sein Bewenden haben' has the advantage of picking up relation of the German 'Bewandthis' and 'Bewenden,' it nevertheless misses some connotations of the verb's usage in German. For a fine discussion of the difficulty in translating these words, Heidegger, *Being and Time*, trans. John Macquarrie and Edward Robinson (San Francisco: HarperCollins, 1962), 115, translators' note 2. —Trans.]

it does not have on its own; freeing, and so the Dasein who does the freeing, is "the condition of the possibility of encountering what is handy."[42]

Heidegger elucidates this a little later by taking the being of Dasein as the basis for understanding the possibility of the use of something. Dasein has always already been "referred to an in-order-to based on an explicitly or inexplicitly grasped ability to be, for the sake of which it is, which can be authentic or inauthentic." And, in elucidation, he continues: "this marks out a what-for as the possible whereby of letting something be relevant, which structurally allows for relevance *to* something. Dasein is always already referred based on a for-the-sake-of-which to the with-what of relevance. This means that, insofar as it is, it always already lets beings be encountered as something handy."[43] To summarize the idea once more: the useful thing can only be discovered in its being, in handiness, because Dasein is "primarily a possibility to be" in the sense of "being-able-to." It does not discover itself as continued existence. Rather, it can be or not be, it can be as it is or otherwise; in considering and seizing on possibilities, Dasein is, for as long as it is, its own possibility. This being-possible not only concerns Dasein himself but also the world that Dasein is in. The world communicates itself in regard to useful things and, indeed, because Dasein "refers" himself to the world in its ontological structure.

Heidegger develops this idea in an ontological reformulation of Aristotelian determinations. If it is said that Dasein is referred "based on a for-the-sake-of-which" to a with-what of a relevance, then it is easy to recognize the teleological structure of action described by Aristotle in it. "For-the-sake-of-which," as literal translation of οὗ ἕνεκα, is tantamount to aim (τέλος).[44] Accordingly, referring oneself to things of use could be understood as a return from a set aim of action to the possibilities of its realization; if Heidegger had not blinded out deliberation, one could say that it would be connected with deliberation and decision. This teleological structure of action is carried into a determination of the for-sake-of-which, which Heidegger derives from the Aristotelian idea of a highest aim. Heidegger, however, understands the supreme for-the-sake-of-which not like Aristotle as the most possibly complete actuality of life in the sense of the good life or happiness, but, rather, as comportment to one's own "ability to be." As the being that "is concerned in its being *about* its very being,"[45] Dasein is the "for-sake-of-which" of itself. Because of this, for Heidegger Dasein is also the "for-the-sake-of-which, to which all for-what ultimately goes back."[46] If all conduct is concerned with nothing other than the possibility to be, as Heidegger thinks, then the structure of the context in which conduct belongs must be understood based on this possibility.

Heidegger's analysis is convincing in one respect. Things form a context of action only insofar as there is action. And, if action can in turn be understood as the enactment of Dasein itself, then the context of action is disclosed solely on the basis of Dasein. This accords with the experience that everything encountered in action is understood based on action. Something is applicable or not, it is advantageous or detrimental, of significance or a matter of indifference for the realization of an aim. Understood in this way, action alone belongs in the life-world, and so, with Husserl, in the "domain of a subject [*Subjektive*], which is completely and utterly locked within itself."[47] On the paradigm of dealings with things of use, Heidegger develops a conception of a "life-world," without using the concept.[48]

Precisely this, however, becomes a problem with regard to the idea of freeing. Because the ontological version of letting something be relevant is constituted purely in terms of life-world, it does not achieve what it is supposed to achieve; it makes the usefulness, but not the accessibility, of things for Dasein clear, and, because of this, misses their ontological claim. The life-worldly world of Dasein is given only together with the world of things, only both together are the world. Things can be discovered as handy only because they are also free from life-worldly ties and, in this way, accessible. The talk, however, can then no longer be of an ontologically conceived freeing. One would free things in that one would release them from their life-worldly ties of action and thereby let them be at as much remove as they are on their own.

In a later version of his idea Heidegger comes very close to such a consideration. Terminologically, the talk in *Vom Wesen der Wahrheit*[49] is no longer of "freeing," but rather solely of "letting be." What this means is now developed without any echo of the discussion of the useful thing, completely independent of a life-worldly understanding of the world. "Letting be" [*Seinlassen*] signifies "entering into [*einlassen auf*] the open [*das Offene*] and its openness [*dessen Offenheit*],* in which all of what is stands." The open is the "unconcealment" of being; it brings whatever is "as it were along with it."[50] Because it is the open that ushers in beings in this way, they are "beings ... as the beings that they are."[51] Heidegger answers the fundamental ontological question that Aristotle had formulated in terms of beings as beings (ὄν ᾗ ὄν)[52] based on the idea of the open itself; beings are as they are because they belong in the openness of being. Letting be is the experience of beings from out of this open.

Heidegger leaves no doubt that this experience is only possible at a distance. Letting be unfolds "by stepping back in the face of what is so that what is comes to be revealed in what and how it is, and so that the representation of what is comes into line with it by taking it as its proper measure."[53] In comparison with the idea of letting be as it had been developed in *Sein und Zeit*, the relationship here is reversed: what is no longer gets discovered on the basis of Dasein, instead, Dasein is now determined on the basis of stepping back in the face of what is. Letting be is the "freedom" of Dasein[54]; Dasein is no longer free in

---

*[Although I have used "the open" as a translation of *das Offene* in the context of this discussion, I have otherwise generally used "openness" for *das Offene*. —Trans.]

its possibility to be, but, rather, in its being "ex-posed, ek-sistent."[55] It is now the "openness of the open"; in it, the open of being is "there," because Dasein "safeguards" the "deconcealment" of what is in "ek-sistent involvement [*Sich-einlassen*]" with the open of being.[56] If one follows these considerations, then the freedom of the "there" cannot be thought without things, or, as Heidegger puts it, "what is." Dasein can only come into focus as openness by taking the "proper measure" from what is; it is the openness that it is by getting involved with the open of what is and letting this—what is—be.

Unlike the openness of Dasein, the freedom of things cannot be lost. Insofar as this freedom is determined as involvement with the open of being, however, it depends on the occurrence of this open in Dasein—as Heidegger described it in the Freiburg inaugural lecture, in terms of the mood of anxiety. This occurrence, the "event," as Heidegger himself calls it, is nevertheless once again concealed by the sense of the everyday and by habit. The human being, Heidegger says in *Vom Wesen der Wahrheit*, "indeed constantly" conducts himself "in relation to what is," but "for the most part always" only lets what is have its own "relevance in this or that being and in its respective openness." He keeps himself "in what is practicable and masterable even where the first and the last" are at issue,[57] that is, in the experience of being itself that first moves him into his "there." But "what is practicable and masterable" are also at play in the freedom of things, and, in this respect, dealing with things is never possible without freedom. The freedom of Dasein is never the freedom of Dasein alone. Therefore, even one's failure to appreciate one's own freedom is dependent on the open that is the remoteness of things.

Heidegger describes this failure of appreciation as "insistence"; what he means is a reversal of "ek-sistence," in which the human being insists "on the protection of himself through what is accessible to him in each case as practicable."[58] Involvement in the open becomes an "ek-sistent turning away"[59] from it; instead of taking the open as a "measure," the human being now takes his measure from his own "intentions and planning."[60] In doing so, he "misses" himself all the more fundamentally "the more exclusively he takes his measure from himself as the subject for all of what is."[61]

The insistence that Heidegger speaks of here does exist. It involves the urge to bring things closer at any price. They should be understood solely on the basis of one's intention and planning and action. Human work [*Wirken*] becomes the foundation, that is, the ὑποκείμενον or *subiectum* for all of what is. For Heidegger, this turn from the open of being to subjectivity forms the fundamental trait of modernity. It is enacted as the "hasty tossing aside of all removals,"[62] which can be recognized as much in the acceleration of transportation as in the omni-presence of information and ostensibly entertaining images that make the world into the illusion of a life-world, as well as in the standardization of things designed to be at one's disposal.

"Moving things together into distancelessness"[63] would require only a modest urge, however, if it were not always refuted anew by removal itself. The "insistence" on giving oneself power and having things at one's disposal is only possible because the open is there not only in the "ek-sistence" of Dasein, but, prior to this, and always already, as the remoteness of things. It is only because things do not submit [fügen] to human plans and actions that there is the possibility of putting them at our disposal [verfügbar machen].

"Insistence," as Heidegger calls it, obviously then has to be understood differently, as well. It cannot have anything to do with the fact that the open of what is—the remoteness of things—falls out of view and thereby gets lost. Rather, remoteness can only become a problem because one's action has become so involved in its relation to things that one simply is unable to let them be. It is the freedom of things itself, and not planning and acting, not even directing oneself toward "what is practicable and masterable," that leads to one's loss of a sense for the freedom of things. It is from *them* that the possibility of unfreedom arises, which itself exists in bringing closer, in the desire to annihilate remove. It is an unfreedom that is not to be overcome in the event of an openness for the open of things, but only through the limited preservation of possibilities of acting amidst things. Without the freedom of things there is no freedom for them. The freedom of things, however, is shared with others. It is in this way a condition for the free presentation and contemplation that is the perception of freedom *for* things.

§ 20. Shared Freedom

No one acts only on one's own and only for oneself. Others have always already begun to act. They have arranged themselves in a world that has been reconfigured from arrangements taken over by others in order to preserve, to protect, to improve, or, after destruction, to attempt to reproduce it. Or, they have destroyed the arrangements passed down to them in order to put their own—or what they take to be their own—in their stead. One has others in front of him and around him. For them, one is an other or "one of us."

Because one is not alone, one does not have to do everything oneself. And he would not at all be in a position to anyway. This is the case in the first years of life and does not become fundamentally different later. One always fails to master something in one's dealings with it, one does not have the knowledge, the skillfulness, or the opportunity for possible access. Even if this were not so, one could not do everything oneself. One remains dependent on others, in varying respects and in varying degrees. The dependency may be kept within limits, it may not fundamentally be abolished. It is always and again the case that one has no choice in his dependency on others. In this, as it seems, one is unfree. Yet considered more precisely, dependency indicates that there is no freedom without bonds [*Bindung*]. Freedom is not an indifferent openness for one's own caprice, but rather the remove in which something binds us precisely because it is removed, and in this bond preserves the "possibility of being able to."

The fact that bonds belong to the essence of freedom goes back not least of all to the freedom of things. In their remoteness, things are never all reachable; countless things always remain beyond one's reach, many that are accessible to others remain inaccessible for one himself. The remoteness of things sometimes allows what remove itself is to be sensed: an openness that is never filled out by any conduct. That the world is not only a life-world but also a thing-world reaches all the way into the most inconspicuous moments of everyday life. We need things, but the things do not need us; they are free from us, and this binds us to them in freedom. Above all, however, we may have bonds to the freedom of others, even though this could never supersede our free boundedness to things. It allows us to be dependent on others, although this could not free us from our dependency on things.

This fact of bonds with others, however, is not a second-best solution, better than which can be conceived. It is an essential determination of the human being that follows from the determination of the world. The sociality of human life is explained based on the remoteness of things in a world, which is not cut to fit for human beings. This does not mean that one could explain the origination of social life in this manner; no research, however conscientious, leads behind its givenness back to the "state of nature" of an individuated life.[64] Rather, our dependency on things is a fundamental motive at play in all sociality; it is its primary sense. At least, in the thought experiment Socrates and Adeimantus carry out, they find no other explanation for the foundation of an elementary community of human beings, the most simple *polis* possible, other than that no human being is self-sufficient [*Selbstständig*] and needs much,[65] obviously more than he would be able to obtain alone.

The foundation of the *polis* in ideas by Socrates with his interlocutors Glaucon and Adeimantus confirms not only the neediness[66] and, with it, the dependency of everyone on each another. It makes equally clear that the freedom of action is not to be conceived other than in this dependency. Each individual can only perceive his freedom because all get reciprocally involved in their neediness and thus realize their bond to one another as freedom. Bonds to others exist only in freedom just as shared freedom cannot exist without these bonds. The elementary community is really more of a "system of needs."[67] Without others, everyone's own action in freedom would not be possible. The others do not cause one's own freedom; they of course also act and, with this, conduct themselves in freedom. No one causes anything here, instead, something arises; the freedom of action comes into focus insofar as the freedom of action is perceived and thereby *shared* in the mutual dependency of those who act. It is *shared freedom* in a double sense: freedom that one shares in with others in that it is shared out into the freedom of individuals.

The freedom of action can accordingly always be only the freedom of a specific and limited, although not isolated, action. This concerns above all the *conditions* of what one does. One could no more act without things of use and materials provided by others than without other actions that precede one's own activity; no one begins completely from scratch. Action is thus always possible only in the context of means already at one's disposal and those actions that have already been taken; one takes up and continues; one picks up and moves forward.

Moreover, others play a role in the *ability* one has for one's own activity. One does not learn without others; upbringing and education, as well as training, precede every action.[68] And, insofar as others do something themselves, they put aside and rule out occupations that they have taken for themselves. They thus give themselves the possibility of restricting themselves to a specific activity. It is only by means of this that one is able to learn, practice, and then correctly do what one has chosen to do. As Socrates maintains, one will act "more beautifully" (κάλλιον), that is, in a manner also clearer to others, if one restricts oneself to one matter.[69] To put the point in a way that would have to be supplemented by Aristotle, one only arrives at even passable decisions if one is limited to a matter that he has experience in. It is only when one is seriously dedicated to his aim and makes its realization his own concern that one reflects seriously on what leads to the aim.

There is no deficiency in this restriction, nor any forcible constriction of freedom, because human beings are unequal in their abilities; because not everyone is gifted in equal measure for all things,[70] one should not try to do everything. Besides, no one can bring about everything, because everything to be done must be done at the right moment (καιρός); there is no luxury of waiting until the person responsible for it finally gets to it.[71]

The interdependency of one's own action with the action of others does not affect one's experience of freedom in every case. What others do could be like a surrounding for one's own activity. In this case, the others' willing and activity remain insignificant; they recede into familiar obviousness like a house that first gives the workroom its place and status and that for the one working is hardly there anymore. Others, in this case, have withdrawn. That they are there only still speaks from what they have brought about—like the writing desk one sits at; or, from what belongs to one of them, say, the borrowed book over there.[72] Or, more precisely, that there are others who would speak from these things if one would consult them instead of simply just using them or letting them rest.

One's own experience of freedom also does not have to be affected when one himself does something for another. In the case of "concern" [*Fürsorge*], as Heidegger names the referentiality to others in *Sein und Zeit*,[73] the life of others appears above all as that toward which one's own action refers, either mediately, by producing or preparing something for them by supporting others, or directly, by "dealing with" them in one manner or another. This makes it clear enough that the others are not the aim of one's own actions, but rather, that they themselves have aims and strive to reach them in action. Precisely for this reason, one equips oneself mutually with things of use; one exerts oneself to promote the reciprocal ability to act or, if it is impaired, to reproduce it. There is, however, no cause to refer to the others' goal setting or action in the aforementioned cases. This occurs first when different aims are to be coordinated with one another.

Socrates makes the status of such a coordination intelligible in his thought experiment on the foundation of the πόλις. It is natural that the aims of those who live together [*Zusammen*] are somehow assigned to one another; it lies in the essence of social life [*Zusammenleben*] itself. Socrates can thus also signify a community in which the assignment is successful as ἀληθινὴ πόλις, the true city.[74] It is the city as it is supposed to be in its essence, the city in which its essence comes into focus undisguised, without impairment. The well-ordered city is "as if healthy."[75] Its sickness, however, is not the disturbance of a pre-given order, and because of this the well-ordered city can really only be compared with the healthiness of a living being. Conflicts of aims and action in a city are lapses that lie as much in the essence of social life as its well-orderedness. If Socrates inquires precisely into whether it is better that each perform "his own work,"[76] this indirectly indicates precisely the alternative that the thought experiment on the foundation of the *polis* is directed against: against the attempt to bring everything about by oneself that is necessary or putatively necessary for oneself. Here, one would not only have nothing to do with one another but also overestimate one's own possibilities and entrust things to himself that he either cannot do at all or do only poorly. Since one would feel independent of others, there would be no impetus to take one another into consideration. Asociality and presumptiveness are the two dangers of social life. Either social life breaks apart into the indifference of merely being adjacent to one another or conflict arises between those who would entrust everything to themselves and attempt to assert themselves against others.

One could see the achievement of an absolute form of freedom in this, although it is in truth a hindrance to freedom. Through asociality and presumptuousness one is pushed back into the unfreedom of mere neediness. One cannot get past oneself—in the neediness of mere survival as well as in bearing out an unrestricted and therefore completely unspecific ability; it is concerned not with an action that is directed in deliberation toward an aim, but instead only with the preservation and intensification of one's own existence in terms of the "will to power."

If this is so, then the well-ordered distribution [*Verteilung*] and assignment [*Zuteilung*] of aims has to do with freedom not only insofar as it enables action. Insight into the difference between one's own affairs and the affairs of others also belongs to the experience of freedom because there is no freedom of action without restriction to one's own affairs. From the standpoint of action, this determines one's free relationship to others: It is the relation of a distance that holds as the intermediary between indifference and infringement; it is a matter of being at the right removal. The order that allots aims is not only supposed to secure survival in the community, but also aims at this removal as the fundamental condition of the "true city," that is, to the freedom that is between those who act.[77] It is the openness of life with others, of a being-with-others, that otherwise does not exist.

The removal between those who act is measured differently than is the distance between one who acts and his aim. Here, the concern is not with causing and having an effect but rather with the limits of effectiveness. Someone who can and wants to act differently from oneself remains unaffected by ability and will that comes from outside, for the ability and will to differ cannot be taken from anyone; the very factical success of attempts at this in subjugation or disenfranchisement confirms that what it wants eludes it. Subjugation, after all, presupposes the ability and will to differ. Subjugation reveals this ability and will in resistance; subjugation oppresses and stifles something that one would resume if given even the slightest opening.

To take the others as they are in freedom means to be *just* to them. Initially, this occurs in the restriction of oneself to one's own activity, itself the determination of justice in the *Republic*.[78] However, this restriction does not simply obtain; it has to be practiced, demanded, and implemented. Jurisprudence [*Recht*] and law exist to prevent infringements on the domain of others, although jurisprudence and law receive their meaning based on possible restriction and in general also actual individually practiced restriction. The freedom, with which jurisprudence and law are concerned, has its individual correlate in *freeing*.[79] This is not to be understood here in the ontological sense that Heidegger focused on, but, rather, literally; here, the freeing of others has the sense of a letting go and letting be free that corresponds to a holding back in one's own action.

Here, too, there is what was described as a pause in regard to action realized through aim-oriented deliberation.[80] Here, however, this pause does not have the sense of a delay that keeps apart one's reference to an aim and the enactment of its realization. It is not a halt *within* one's own action, but, rather, a halt of this action itself. The press toward an aim is broken in order to give others room. This break is not a one-time incident. One can, of course, accomplish it specifically in a particular situation of action, but it is usually carried out when those who act have an upbringing that allows them to hold back before others' freedom and to help others be freed while they pursue their own aims. Much of what one calls "virtues" is the ability for this.

Whether in the upbringing of others or in one's action, in both cases action is seen from the standpoint of others; it comes from beyond one's own action, although it is reflected in the context of this action. Others are not beyond being, but, rather, beyond one's action, even when one pursues a goal together with them or carries out conflicts to victory or defeat with them.[81] One lets the removal between oneself and others *be*; this allows a freedom to arise that is to be measured as the experience of action in its context.[82]

Kant attempted to grasp the fact that one who acts is beyond action by means of a limit-concept, by which this agent is determined as an "end in itself."[83] Agents are not sufficiently captured by the aims or ends posited by others. Rather, as Kant formulates it, they have "an absolute value"[84]; they are of significance in themselves, not just because something is to be brought about in regard to or with them. In their "rational nature,"[85] agents do not have "merely relative value, that is, a price, but rather an inner worth, that is, dignity."[86] For Kant this leads to the moral imperative that one deal with "humanity" equally in one's own "person as in the person of every other, always at the same time as end, never merely as means."[87] Accordingly, it is not reprehensible in principle to want to have an effect on others or to enlist their service for the sake of one's own ends. This is only reprehensible when one "does something to" others and, with this, injures their dignity. There is, then, a limit of one's own activity. It is not drawn like a line of demarcation, but, rather, exists in removal.

Yet, because Kant's formulation of the "end in itself" grasps others from the standpoint of action, it provides, as has been said, only a limit-determination; it determines the limit of action with a concept of action. Others only come into view insofar as they are not wrapped up in action that is referred to them; action cannot be directed toward them as it is toward something that is supposed to be realized, for they exist [*sind da*] already "realized"—on their own. Just how this "existence" [*Dasein*] can be understood, however, remains open if it is seen only from inside the perspective of action. This is only different if one understands others based on the remoteness in which one encounters them.

Here, too, one initially remains oriented by action; others appear as free in the sense of the freedom of action. They could also have conducted themselves differently; the aim that is recognizable from their action or through communication and indication could also have been another one. However, this "also otherwise" has a different status than when one has it himself. It is not an "also otherwise" that one can realize for himself. One can in fact attempt to assess, comprehend, or even imitate the action of others. One can follow what others say in description or elucidation of their action, and—one way or another, more or less penetratingly—one generally does just this. One quickly finds one's limits, however, because the deliberations of others are not familiar at all or not familiar enough. Even if one knows something of these deliberations, what one is familiar with still belongs to a context that one does not himself comprehend and that is in any case never completely familiar. In fact, the latter holds just as much for one's own action-guiding deliberations. The unobtainability of the action of others, however, stands *over and against*. This does not mean that they have to be alien. *As* others they are, despite all intelligibility of what they say and do, *unintelligible*. It is this unintelligibility that one experiences on the basis of action as the remoteness of others. The answer to it is the freeing of others. Even the attempt to deny this remoteness and to bring others into proximity can only confirm the remoteness. It is only because the freedom of others is, despite all community, always their own, unavailable to oneself, that one can want not to admit it.

Remoteness exists reciprocally. One is at as much of a remove from others as they are from oneself. One also has the possibility to become more or less familiar with the impetus and motive of one's own activity. Deliberations that guide one's own action do not have to be communicated, and the explanations of others that refer to one's own activity may more or less clearly be rejected. One moves to a distance and draws back in attempting to withdraw his availability to others. Thus, remoteness is not simply noted, but, rather, *lived as removal from one another*. It is only in this removal that there is proximity; one comes toward each other and thus confirms the open, in which coming into proximity occurs. What kind and how great the removal, the "between us," should be is settled in conduct toward one another each time. Conduct works out the tension that exists in the freedom residing in removal.

Helmut Plessner was the first to see the essence of human sociality in this relation of tension.[88] By developing the tension itself as the oppositional play of the preservation of distance and the longing for relation, Plessner draws attention to possible conflicts in shared freedom and considers, moreover, how this freedom can be absent. When Plessner develops the question of human sociality as a question of the "limits of community," it is not simply because of time constraints, but instead because of the character of the matter under discussion. The idea that human life is not realized in communalization does not have to be stressed only against nationalistic and communistic elevations of it to the absolute; this claim also warrants attention if one wishes to grasp such an elevation to absolutes in the first place.

Plessner believes that the possibility for this lies in the radical individuality of human life, that is, because it is impossible to determine someone in their conduct or action—or, in terms of the matter at issue, because of freedom. In regard to the unfathomability of the individual, Plessner speaks of an "independent inwardness, which is incomparable in depth and richness of quality," and of the "possession of a soul."[89] What is meant here is the unintelligibility—the unobtainablity of ideas, feelings, motives, and possibilities of expression, the insufficiency of every carryover into comprehension. Precisely this, however, elicits the reciprocal desire to comprehend, the discovery of the related and similar, of commonality and, ultimately, alignment with one another. As long as the attempt at alignment is guided by the experience of the individual, its inevitable failure is generally known, at least, sensed. Alignment, however, can also be asserted against the individual toward whom it is directed. In this case, it is, as Plessner has it, formed by the "ethos of absolute uninhibitedness"[90]; life is to dissolve into accessibility.[91] The assertion of unconditional proximity is developed against the experience of remoteness.

The sacrifice of individuality required here and often forced is, on the one hand, a temptation, and, on the other, directed against the essence of the individual. On the one hand, it belongs to the essence of the individual to want to be recognized by others; individuals want to be there in the eyes of others. On the other hand, it belongs to the essence of the individual to protect himself against the presumption of being recognized and to withdraw his recognition. It is true that we want "to see each other" and that we want "to be seen as we are," yet we just as much want "to veil ourselves and remain unknown."[92] For Plessner, this constitutes the "ambiguity"[93] of the individual.

This veil not only provides protection, however, but also self-protection, indeed, it is the only possible existence of the individual. Individuals who express themselves directly and wish to be there as they are lose the authenticity to which they aspire. As Plessner puts it, the individual steps "under the law of appearance."[94] Here, "he becomes one-sided and loses his depth and fullness, without which he cannot at all be what he wishes and deserves to be taken as."[95] The expression that one intends as immediate and uninhibited carries the "risk of being laughable,"[96] and just as much, it might be added, of banality. Therefore, the individual as such can only be there indirectly; it needs "clothing of form, in order that it remains on the surface what it is in its invisible depths."[97]

Plessner's idea can be made still more convincing through further refinement. The thesis that every uninhibited expression stands in danger of being laughable is not illuminating. Deep pain or sadness etched in a person's face and disposition can be genuine and, in this, moving, just as the unbridled expression of joy can be. These kinds of expressions, however, are to be distinguished from the kind of expression that one wills. Precisely when moods and feelings are genuine, this is often accompanied by a tendency toward concealment and shutting oneself off, in any case, by discretion. The more directly one attempts to grasp moods and feelings in words, the greater the danger is of cliché and banality. In this respect, the indirectness of an expression belongs to its believability; it has to have found "clothing and form" in order that it actually be able to reach others. The more it is "form," the more intelligible it is. It is not without reason that the articulation of moods and feelings reaches its consummation in art.

The indirectness of individual communication can be made intelligible in terms of the remoteness of the individual. It is only if the remoteness at play in communication is not overplayed that it is convincing. Because the individual himself is something at a remove, the measurement of removal belongs to his essence. His unintelligibility is not locked away in him; it is rather just at a removal. The individual is always what he is only in exteriority.

Viewed on this basis, the opposition between individual and society appears abstract. Individuals are able to supply value for their individuality first by taking over "functions" and "roles"[98] as forms of presentation that are as such not individual. Plessner calls this existence of the exterior individuality a "Nimbus"[99]; it is the appearance that an individual "simultaneously" can "maximally make visible and veil."[100]

Despite the great value he places on indirectness, Plessner does not overlook that forms and roles can also become rigid. In fact, they have an intrinsic tendency toward rigidity insofar as in them the relation between individuals becomes a "constant relation [*Relation*]." Plessner introduces the concept of "distance" to discuss this idea as if it were obvious; functions and roles require "a distance, which can become neither too broad nor too narrow, because" this would prevent "the rigidity of the given significance" that a role or function has.[101] Faced with a person who holds an office, one conducts himself as the office requires; because of this, the conduct does not change essentially when the one who holds the office is someone else. As is also the case in ceremonies and rituals, the focus is not on individuals. In this respect, the "unassailability of individuality" that they have achieved with indirectness is "purchased at the price of representative [*stellvertretende*] significance."[102] Considered from the standpoint of the individual, it has the character of an "irreal compensation"[103]; the human being "masks" himself; he relinquishes "being considered and respected as an individual in order at least . . . to have an effect and to be respected in a representative manner."[104]

It is a strength of Plessner's project in social philosophy that he holds this observation together with the idea of the inevitable indirectness of individuals. Even rituals and regimentation that have become rigid still belong to possibilities for individuals to bring themselves out into the open. The possible alternatives to this are implausible. One would fall back into the opposition of individual and society and would conceive of the individual either on the model of actors, for whom their roles are generally exterior, so that these roles are arbitrarily able to change. Or, individuals would be like coat hooks that only serve to hold up social roles.[105] Yet, Plessner leaves open how the appropriateness and inappropriateness of functions and roles is to be grasped more precisely. The concept of play, which he—in fact, building on Schiller—introduces in this context,[106] provides no convincing answer. Not all societal relations can be playful; that a society is sustained "by the spirit of play alone"[107] is not illuminating. The individual appropriateness or inappropriateness of social forms is to be recognized on the basis of freedom alone. The more freedom an individual has in filling a social form, the more appropriate it is to him.

The appropriateness is measured by how mobile an individual is in receding from view and in traversing removals to others, as well as by how much his remoteness may vary. An individual who does not have to recede from view in the fulfillment of a function or in filling a role but instead has possibilities of the "also otherwise" is more free than one who enacts an action in such a way that the various possibilities of enacting it are of no significance. Cultic actions are often of this kind; although they are actions, their concern is with an occurrence. Freedom, however, is the dimension in which the focus is, as Aristotle puts it, on *us*; freedom [*das Freie*] is given to us and it is up to us to enact it.

The connection of roles with individuality succeeds at first in *representation* [*Repräsentation*].[108] This is a preliminary form of presentation in which an individual has to bring more than his individual aims of action into focus even though he does this in his individual action. This gives one's individual action form and emphasis and at the same time allows it to come to light in its individuality. Someone who is a representative is more than the bearer of a function, he is no functionary; neither does he take over any role, but, instead, stands in for a matter that is essentially not his own. Insofar as such a matter—for example, the matter of the sovereignty of a nation-state—is in need of representation, it can come into focus alone in representative action. Conversely, the representative owes his characteristic authority to this matter. It is precisely because representation is bound to action that it is distinguished from presentation. Someone concerned with the presentation of a matter does indeed conduct himself freely, yet he no longer acts. Presentative activity accordingly stands outside the context of agents, whereas representation is concerned with this context. As an agent, a representative stands, ultimately, for shared freedom. It is up to him, not only to perceive this shared freedom, but, rather, to make it visible and to investigate it within the limits of action through action.

The inevitable need for such an investigation obtains for action generally, but under normal conditions it does not deal with shared freedom as such. Because individuals are at a remove from one another in their essence, how close one may come to someone is not fixed; in this respect, tact, which Plessner treats extensively, is not only the *sine qua non* of sociality, but also at the same time a perception of freedom. The same holds for the "logic of diplomacy,"[109] which sees to it in the "decision of violence"[110] that the "the dignity of others" remain "unoffended" in conflicts of interest.[111]

In his treatise *Zur Kritik der Gewalt*, Benjamin drew attention to another aspect of diplomacy that is even more important here. For Benjamin, diplomatic regimentation and all forms of "civil agreement"[112] in general are of a special kind because they are not employed for the accomplishment of one's own ends. Rather, they serve the clarification of relations that first make the pursuit of one's own ends or aims possible. Because they are not conceived as means to ends, Benjamin calls them "pure means."[113] Moreover, it is essential to them that they hold not "immediately for the settlement of conflicts between human being and human being" but rather indirectly "on the way through the matter."[114] Diplomacy involves undertakings that do not have to do directly or even at all with mutually conflicting aims of action; they belong, say, to sociality in the broader sense and provide the possibility of relating to one another beyond mutually conflicting aims. And, when there is success in directing attention to a common matter, the conflict is at least relativized. What is absent in "pure means" is the de-removing and taking hold of that is characteristic of aim-directed action. People are involved with one another though they are not directed toward one another. Remoteness thus remains in force, although the relation does not lose its connectedness and tension.

Yet, what Benjamin attempts to grasp by the concept of "pure means" is nevertheless an action; in diplomatic activity, too, something is supposed to be reached, it, too, has an aim. Mediatory activity is, however, an action of a special kind. It is an action characterized by pausing, that is to say, an action whose purpose is freeing; an attempt at freeing by means of action, or, to work so as to give rise to a freeing. Action that frees in this manner comes closest to what otherwise operates as a delay in action. It is an attempt—often successful—to bring freedom into focus through action as it is shared by those who act. This attempt, however, remains bound up in action; it only unfolds in the tension of different aims that come into agreement in their difference. Something can only be genuinely held in common if it is disclosed in free contemplation.

§ 21. Free Contemplation

There is also contemplation, θεωρία,[115] in action; for Aristotle, we recall once more, it is the matter at issue for the sensible person who wants to get clear about what is good for the human being.[116] If there were no contemplation in action, then what is experienced in action could only be radically alien for contemplation; everything would come into view from an estranging attitude—as if one were to look at the earth from another star. Back on earth, one would in fact not forget the view from outside, although it would have nothing to do with the life one leads. The world of action and the world of contemplation would be different worlds. Things, however, are not so. There is only one world, and what differs is only its accessibility. Different accessibility means:

this same world can also be experienced otherwise. Thus, freedom in regard to the world offers itself as a development of freedom in the world.

As concerns contemplating and acting, the "otherwise" is not like a mere change of viewpoint. Different lines of sight can belong in the same conduct, for example, if one looks at a building from different sides; the concern is always to investigate the building. In the shift from acting to contemplating, everything remains on the one hand the same, assuming that a contemplating, at least a deliberating, was already operative in acting. On the other hand, everything nevertheless changes; because one no longer acts, the reference to an aim, which is essential for acting, ceases to apply. One no longer wants to reach anything but continues rather only to look.

There may be motives for the shift in attitude; they may be the same or similar to those that were shown as models for philosophy in Parmenides, Descartes, Heidegger, and Plato.[117] Perhaps the question of what one should do leads to no answer because one does not get an overview of the alternatives to be considered. Perhaps one all at once feels dislodged by a mood from aim-reference, perhaps the shift is a change in position brought about consciously because contemplation is a methodologically driven process. Yet, regardless of how the shift is motivated, it is a shift into freedom; one becomes free from the orientation of action toward an aim and achieves freedom for a viewpoint that is no longer biased by an orientation toward an aim.

This alone is not enough to guarantee that this viewpoint is unbiased; one could have exchanged one kind of bias for another. Yet, one thing already speaks in favor of the idea that being unbiased is possible: If there is contemplation even in action, then there is no exchange of one attitude for another with the shift to mere or pure contemplation. Rather, something that was already there earlier is dislodged, and, with this, set free from a context. Contemplation goes to the ground of action, namely, to freedom, and perceives specifically this. Earlier, contemplation was locked up as reflection and as practical intelligence in the tension of action, now it has come into the open air [*ins Freie*].

The picture is the oldest of the freedom of contemplation. Plato made it visible as a picture of the cave of the *polis* from out of which one comes into the freedom of the light of day through philosophical education.[118] The fundamental significance of the picture is clear; what there is to see is first to be seen correctly outside in the open air; only once outside the cave is one involved with the things themselves and no longer their appearances. However, the diversity of what is seen arises first through distance from the earlier attitude. For the cave dwellers, there is nothing but shadows, because they, tied down as they are, can only look at the wall of the cave. They first recognize that they are seeing shadows after they are turned around and have left their earlier place. Now they see the things carried past a fire, which illuminates the cave so that the shadows of things fall on the wall of the cave. With the shift of their attitude, the cave dwellers can refer what they now see to what they saw before; they understand what they see now based on what they saw earlier by putting their present seeing into relation with their earlier seeing. The two belong together inseparably, for, taken by itself, the seeing is the same both times—the simple sensuous awareness of what is there. An insight that stretches beyond mere seeing only arises with the shift in attitude. One achieves the insight with distance from the earlier attitude and the insight operates at a removal from this attitude. The "based on something" of understanding is only thus possible. There is no insight, understanding, without freedom.

Freedom and insight are first realized when a standpoint is reached that one can no longer experience based on another standpoint. There was freedom even in the cave; otherwise, the path outside would have been impossible. Yet, one no longer finds any distance to the open air that is outside the cave; there is no further possible attitude from which one can still experience this open air. It is true that there is the path back into the cave. One's residence in the open air, however, may not be experienced based on the cave, one rather always experiences one's residence in the cave based on the open air. That one enters into the restricted view once again is a diminishment that one only recognizes as such based on what is unrestricted. Also, the insight achieved may not be reversed. Some product that one sees in the cave is designed in accord with what exists on its own because the manufacture of the product presupposes it. And, the shadow is cast by a thing, not the other way around; even if one takes the thing into view based on the shadow, one understands the shadow based on the thing. One is in the position to do this because one's view of things is less biased. It is broader; one understands the view that is more biased along with the view of what is disclosed without bias.

It has admittedly not been stated why unbiasedness lies in a contemplation that stands at a distance from action. The end-orientedness of action could still determine the insight even in its unbiasedness; in this case, the insight would be a matter of work understood as completed action in the Aristotelian sense. Theory would be the highest form of practice.

Aristotle draws a clear distinction here: Although contemplation is actuality (ἐνέργια),[119] it is no action (πρᾶξις); rather, contemplation is what is left over when one removes action, and, more still, production, from a living being.[120] Moreover, the gods, as he put it, do not act, although they do contemplate; everything that concerns action is low and unworthy of the gods.[121]

The reason for this is independence, self-satisfactoriness in a completed, unqualified sense (αὐτάρκεια). It is true that the necessities of life must be there[122]; but insofar as they are provided, contemplation itself no longer has anything to do with them. Although this may also be true of certain actions, these remain shaped essentially by neediness—that is, by what was determined as the ground of social life in the *Republic*: Even the just person, as Aristotle says, still always needs that by and with which he can act justly. Contemplation, by contrast, is independent; it is given simply as itself.[123]

One should not take this as a theoretical solipsism; Aristotle does not exclude the idea that contemplation is shared. The one who contemplates is simply not dependent on others and precisely for this reason is free in regard to them. The relation to others is determined neither by the bonds of one's own activity to another's activity, nor by a good that Aristotle upholds as the highest of public or political life: regard, honor (τιμή).[124] Even if honor lies less in those who honor than in those who are honored—ultimately, one of course wants to be honored only by sensible ones, thus leaving sensibleness higher than honor[125]—honor only obtains when it is granted to one from others. In action, one wishes to stand in the public.[126] In contemplation, this would be an irrelevant motive. It is predisposed simply to let removal to others exist. The connection here turns on whatever is disclosed in contemplation. It belongs to no one, no one can with right reclaim it for himself alone. If contemplation is shared, this is not restrictive but rather leads to greater differentiation. Contemplation is intensified by the various points of access.

The independence of contemplation also lies here, that is, in regard to the matter contemplated. One does not want to change or shape it, but, rather, leaves it as it is. Accordingly, one is independent regardless of whether the things conform to one's own purposes or not. The freedom of things is not threatening to contemplation. In contemplation, one may rather come into accord with them. Where there is freedom from things, one is also free for them.

This freedom actually constitutes contemplation. It belongs to the essence of contemplation that one no longer sees things within the horizon of the life-world alone. On the contrary, in contemplation something that belongs to the life-world can and even should become thingly. It becomes objective, and, with this, the possibilities for presentation that are already contained in action become free.

Because contemplation loses this life-worldly bond, it is *placeless* in the life-world. This makes it uncanny sometimes, it gives it the appearance of disinterested coldness. Yet, the view from outside gives rise to a special kind of participation: the intense interest for something to show itself without disguise. For contemplation, everything has the freedom to be objective, and, with this, to be *binding* in freedom. In this sense, something is binding that one is bound to and that nevertheless is permitted to exist, to stand over and against, as something at a remove.

This binding character is demonstrated by the fact that contemplation is not mere looking. It befits something objective to be presented, and, so, contemplation belongs together with presentation. This is clearest in the activity of a painter or sketch artist: Here, looking and realizing stand in a reciprocal reference such that the one brings the other into focus. Painting and drawing are activities for the sake of contemplation; they are activities in which contemplating is intensified, and, at the same time, the transposition of the visible into a more intense visibility, intensification of what is there, into a raised, emphatic appearance. The same thing is possible in every presentation, as well as in description and in the philosophical work of the concept.

Contemplation and presentation remain different in their belongingness. Although neither is possible without the other, their relation to one another is not fixed. The accent can lie more on presentation or more on contemplation. In the first case, the issue is more to realize the reference to the object, in the second case, the realization is rather a matter of bearing out the contemplative relation to something objective.

Both contemplative presentation and presentative contemplation are nevertheless in agreement in the intensity of the experience of freedom. In presentative activity, the removal to the objective or the object is reflected; presentation, therefore, is not possible at all without posing the question of the "how" of presentation, and this equally means the question of its possible "also otherwise."

Here, the experience of freedom one has in action comes to be modified in a characteristic manner. It is true that presentative activity has an aim, namely, to bring what is to be presented into focus as adequately as possible. The realization of this aim, however, is included in the reference to the objective or the object in such a way that it cannot be de-removing. The status of the "also otherwise" changes because of this: a possibility of presentation is not determined by its exclusion of other possibilities. It is true that only one possibility may ever be respectively realized, but the possibilities not realized remain in play. In contrast to action, presenting is not subject to the need for unambiguousness in choice and projection by the situations in which it is enacted. In contrast to action, in presenting one may experiment without a loss of seriousness[127]; to realize later a possibility that was initially projected does not have to be inconsequential. If it is in keeping with the essence of presentation, it is also not arbitrary but instead in the interest of the matter. In presenting, the sense for the "also otherwise" is more awake, the realization more free. This goes back to the substantive character of the presenting.

Conversely, it belongs to contemplation that it cannot come about without the experience of freedom; Plato's image of the cave provides a visible testament to this. Contemplation does not arise without liberation from the biases of action and the concern for appearances in relation to others. Moreover, it lives from its open relation to its matter. Only what does not overpower may be contemplated. Contemplation itself, therefore, can be a free letting-exist. Devotion of attention and distance, connectedness and remoteness are in free relation in contemplation; it is an open play of distance and removal. Contemplation measures remove by adjusting to the play it is included in. In this respect, it not only belongs in freedom, but also is always an experience *with* it. In contemplation, philosophical attentiveness to freedom itself, therefore, is free.

This attentiveness must admittedly be realized; it must be presentation. Its possibilities of realization are in fact not conceivable without freedom, yet they are themselves not a matter of freedom. They can only be made intelligible in terms of another dimension of hermeneutical space. Presentation belongs essentially in language. Language shall now be contemplated in regard to the status that presentation, also presentative contemplation, have in it.

Chapter 5

Language

§ 22. Based on Speech

Language is more than intimate, it is there even in silence. If language is there, a life without language can no longer be imagined. One knows that animals do not speak, though no one who speaks any longer understands how it is to be without language. Nevertheless, language never quite attains complete familiarity. Although language is omnipresent, a consciousness of language belongs to language; to live in language means always and again to come upon the limits of one's ability to say something. Language just as much involves an exertion of effort that is required to use language; what is said but not understood can be said differently. One really comes to experience language in regard to another language that one does not at all understand. One knows that something is being spoken here, but not what is said.

Another language is *a* language, this individual one, and can be differentiated from others as such. One does not initially understand this other language, although even before one learns it one can be in a position to recognize it. Languages sound different, the script looks other. There is the possibility of differentiation and comparison for any description no matter how precise, thus allowing a language to emerge in its determinacy.

One's own language also becomes *a* language through other languages. One says something that others do not understand—this becomes clear then at the latest. This insight, however, remains abstract. One cannot know how it is not to understand one's own language. It is too close, in its proximity it belongs to one's own life. Speaking one's own language is like breathing or walking; its characteristic sound belongs to a person himself, almost like his skin color, like the line of his face. One often recognizes foreigners by their looks, but always by their language.

Although one's own language is so near, it does not belong to a person himself in the same manner as his looks. One has the looks that one has; changing them is either a masquerade or a forcible operation. Yet, other languages may be learned without going against the nature of one's own; and there is no language that one cannot learn. The experience that speaking is like breathing or walking is not completely lost here. In learning pronunciation, learning another language is also an embodied process and, in this, is comparable to practicing how to walk in another manner.

As soon as it becomes clear that languages belong together, the question of the essence of language appears as if of its own accord. However different they may be, the many languages have in common that they are language, and, so, there is something like language in general. This is the essence that inheres in every particular language and allows it to be language. It is common to all languages, however different they may be. That this is not an empty abstraction is revealed by the fact that every language is translatable into every other. The most obvious corroboration of the idea of language in general, however, is the acquisition and speaking of other languages. That something is language is revealed in speech. Grammatical description is secondary to this, even when learning begins with it. This grammatical description refers to speaking as the description of dance steps refers to dance.

This standpoint makes it easy to understand the conviction that the essence of language, and in this sense language in general, can be grasped based on speech. Wilhelm von Humboldt formulated this conviction in an especially pregnant manner. The "true definition" of language can "only be a genetic one," and, in this sense, language is "the eternally repeating work of spirit of making the articulated sound capable of the expression of the idea." It is "not a work (*Ergon*), but an activity (*Energia*)." Humboldt then adds the decisive point: "taken immediately and strictly," this is "the definition of every instance of speech." However, "in the true and essential sense," "one" could "only as it were look at language as the totality of this speech."[1] Understood in this way, the essence of language is *linguistic enactment* [*Sprachvollzug*].

Humboldt grounds his idea by referring to the power of speech to form unity. In the "diffuse chaos of words and rules we customarily call language," "only the individual item brought forth in speech" is "present, and this without completeness, even with a need for new work to be able to recognize the kind of living speech from it and to give a true picture of the living language."[2] Without speech, words and rules are not there as moments of language. They are like stones of a mosaic whose determination is fulfilled only in the context in which they are placed. The dictionary is not a language, and the rules do not form a rigid, closed system but are rather combined anew with every expression; the rules, just like the words, are first made into meaningful moments of a complex whole in the unity formed with speech. As Humboldt adds, "precisely the highest and finest" may "not be recognized in a particular separated element."[3] A word's shades of significance are always shown only by being posed differently in the whole of an expression. The word itself appears in its possibilities solely through the difference of connection, in such a way that they may be ascertained only as possible connections in speech. This also holds of rules; rules—for example, rules of sentence construction—only come into play in speech in a way that allows them to be recognized in their meaning. This gives Humboldt reason to reaffirm "that proper language lies in the act of its actual bringing forth."[4]

It is only with difficulty that one will elude the suggestive power of the Humboldtian idea; it accords with linguistic usage and the conception that has been formed through it,[5] and it is confirmed by experience. It is illuminating that dictionary and grammar are, in contrast with speech, subsequent compilations and, in light of this, abstractions. It is just as comprehensible that the "elements" of language become senseless when one does not see them in context. A word becomes more and more alien the longer one contemplates it and attempts to fathom it for itself. In the end, it becomes detached and is dissolved as an element of language. It thus becomes linguistic rubble.[6]

Yet, despite all of its suggestive power, Humboldt's idea does not stand beyond doubt. Heidegger engaged in debate—incidentally, as the first to do so—with Humboldt along these lines.[7] Heidegger's attempt to think against Humboldt has a still greater weight because it is connected with an almost unsurpassable esteem for Humboldt's thought about language. Heidegger elucidates this thought in three respects: for him, in Humboldt the conception of language oriented by speech comes to conceptual clarity as it is indicated in expressions like "tongue"*—lingua, langue, language, also from the Greek γλῶσσα.[8] Moreover, the "contemplation of language," which "commences and is striven after in multiple ways in Greek antiquity," is gathered "at its peak" in Humboldt's "consciousness of language."[9] And, finally, Humboldt's later treatise determined, "the entire subsequent science of linguistics and philosophy of language up to the present day in for or against, in name or in silence."[10]

Heidegger's judgment of Humboldtian thought about language may be exaggerated in its universality,[11] but it is indisputable that it is essentially on the mark. That Humboldt could appeal to an understanding of language determined by linguistic usage for his fundamental idea is shown with the reference to the conception of language as "tongue" in various languages. There is even a point of reference for what Heidegger says about Humboldt's significance for the philosophy of language and science of linguistics; thus Ernst Cassirer goes back above all to Humboldt in his determination of language as "symbolic form." And even if it is not always easy to ascertain the influence of Humboldtian thought about language in the science of linguistics with precision, it is undoubtedly marked by Humboldt.[12]

---

*[The original German word, which Figal points to here, is *Zunge*; it belongs to the same etymological family as tongue. —Trans.]

From a philosophical standpoint, the most important of Heidegger's elucidations is his reference to Humboldt's boundedness to the tradition. Heidegger does not develop this, although he makes it clear that he sees in Humboldt's idea a later concentration of a determination of language that goes back to Aristotle. This may be verified. When Aristotle characterizes language by determining "what is in the voice," that is, sounds [*Laute*], as symbols of affections of the soul,[13] this is the basic pattern for Humboldt's understanding of language as the "eternally repeating work of spirit to make the articulated sound capable of an expression of the idea." Language is not a tool made accessible from outside but rather something that belongs to the human being like the hand and eye. And, in elucidation of this idea, Humboldt adds that the "intellectual activity" becomes "exterior and perceptible for the senses through sounds in talk." In this, sound and language are "unseverable from one another." If intellectual activity did not enter into a "connection with enunciation [*Sprachlaut*]," then thought could "not reach clarity, representation [could] not become concept."[14] Aristotle means precisely this by the word σύμβολον. The word σύμβολον, token of identification, emphasizes that the "impression" that has affected a person becomes accessible for others in the figure of sound. Taken for themselves, the two are fragments, like the two halves of a shattered disc of clay. The intellect can only be actuality in the exteriority of speech, and this is also how it is for what affects one.[15]

If one remembers that Heidegger saw thought about language in the tradition to reach its "peak" in this idea, he formulates his objection with disconcerting brevity. Humboldt's conception of language in no way stands under the "direction of the human being,"[16] and he certainly does not understand it as "*one* kind and form of worldview that is worked out through it in human subjectivity."[17] For Humboldt, there is no "subject" "before" language. Rather, language understood as speech is itself the "work of spirit." It is not a "special case" of the "universal" that is signified by expressions like "energy, activity, work, spiritual power."[18] If this is so, then Humboldt also does not conceive of language based on the subject. Rather, for him the human being is to be conceived solely on the basis of language. Unlike Hegel, Humboldt conceives of the process of experience and education indicated by the concept of spirit as language and, with this, he takes into account the respective cultural specificity of this process at the same time. Compared with Hegel's only remotely linguistic philosophy of spirit, Humboldt's thought is a powerful step ahead on the way to language.[19]

Heidegger's reservations about Humboldt's idea are nevertheless justified. What remains unthought in Humboldt emerges in Heidegger's attempt to "put into language" "language as language" and not as speech[20]; it becomes clear that there is something based on which speech is to be understood. Heidegger's central idea is summarized in one sentence: "We not only speak *the* language, we speak *from out of* it."[21] Here, as also in Humboldt, what is meant must always be a specific language; one cannot speak a language in general. To do this means to speak in a specific way—to form specific sounds, to use specific words, to hold to specific rules that, if one follows Humboldt, are always brought into the unity of a saying in speech. It should be illuminating that just this happens in speech; it is also not refuted by Heidegger's statement. Yet, Heidegger doubts that the formation of unity can be traced back solely to speech or spirit that is active in speech. To speak *from out of* language, this means always already to be in language and to form sentences in accord with the possibilities pre-given by it.

Humboldt also takes into account that something is pre-given in every act of speaking. For him, the pre-given is what has been previously spoken; it is the historical legacy of a "nation." This legacy either obtains in the familiar obviousness of speech or it is material in regard to which the work of spirit can prove itself. Here, familiar obviousness comes with the development of the language: The "further a language" is "advanced with its grammatical structure," the less it is in need of new decisions concerning linguistic structure. The "struggle to express ideas" becomes weaker; the more "spirit" attends "only to what has already been created," the more "its creative drive and, with it, also its creative power" slacken.[22] Language becomes an impetus for new linguistic formation insofar as language loses this character of something pre-given. Every language, Humboldt says, has "already received a material from earlier races of a prehistory unknown to us," and, therefore, "productive spiritual activity," is "always at the same time directed toward something already given, not by generating, but, rather, by transforming."[23]

In order that both familiar reiteration and transformation are possible, what has been spoken before has to be taken up as "structure" or "material"; one has to have understood it as something spoken. In this case, however, there belongs to speech an ability to receive and a readiness to receive that no longer allows language to be conceived based on speech alone. Every act of speaking is, in this case, at the same time reception, it is, Heidegger says, "listening to the language that we speak."[24] This is to be taken in the strict sense. Heidegger does not mean that speaking stands in an exchange with listening, so that one first listens and then speaks. Rather, speaking is "of its own accord a hearing," it is "*previously* a hearing"[25]; speaking is enacted *in* a hearing that belongs to it and nevertheless always precedes it.

It goes without saying that for the kind of hearing intended here the concern is not with the sensuous awareness of sounds. Hearing is, as Heidegger says at another point, a "gathering of oneself which composes itself on hearing the pronouncement and is claim."[26] One experiences the characteristic attentiveness in speech that is of concern in this "gathering of oneself" as the search for words. If one wishes to bring an idea to language, one does not draw from a stock of words and rules in order to bring forth the idea in its linguistic form as from a material. Neither, however, does one hold to a fixed "structure" reproduced without mental effort. Rather, one finds possibilities of expression—perhaps just as one finds possibilities to make a move in a game of chess. One moves in language as in a game; here, too, a move does not always arise from out of the previous ones. Rather, one is attentive to the openness in which it is possible to continue. There has to be, as Heidegger puts it, a "gathered" attentiveness—concentrated on the matter and yet not directed with the expectation of a specific solution; it is once a person puts a specific intention in play that a solution will no longer occur to him. The search for and finding of words[27] belongs with the fact that one *wants* to say something. There is a subject matter, a theme and with this perhaps a first formulation, a word, that is open for attracting, eliciting others.[28] But these things have to transpire; if they could be derived from the formulation that one had begun with, then one would not search, risk, wait for a possibility, that, if one has luck, is there all at once. It has come from language.

It is only because something sayable comes from language in this manner that speech is possible. Humboldt's formulation of the "eternally repeating work of spirit" at least leaves this possibility open. One step further and the incompleteness that makes such repetition possible and necessary could be understood as an openness that precedes speech. It would be understood as the openness of *language itself* as it is distinguished from speech, it would be openness as the essence of language.

Heidegger's idea that every act of speaking comes from language addresses this openness. Yet, Heidegger does not adhere to his idea when he assigns to the "listening to language" a speaking of language. Hearing is only possible for him because "language speaks."[29] Certainly, this is not intended in the sense of an enunciation any more than the "listening to language" is intended as the sensuous awareness of sound. Nevertheless, in this formulation Heidegger's attempt to extricate himself from Humboldt's understanding of language is reneged. It is true that language is now no longer an activity, although it is—incidentally, just as for Gadamer[30]—an occurrence. It is understood no less than in Humboldt on the basis of speech thereby; Heidegger's idea thus does not lead beyond Humboldt.

If one wishes to rescue Heidegger's idea there is only one possibility: One must insist on the difference of language and speech and develop it as such. To this end, one does not have to give up the considerations that are tied to Heidegger's formulation of the listening to language. It is enough to get clear about the problematic consequence of his formulation and not adopt this consequence. If language does not speak, then it is also not possible to listen to it. The gathered attentiveness that holds of language in speech can in fact also be there in listening. The attentiveness itself, however, is not a matter of hearing. It is rather a mindfulness [Sinnen]; the wakeful sense for the openness of language lives in it.

This idea may only be developed by determining the openness of language as such. This openness must be understandable as *linguistic* openness, as openness that is given only with language. The path to this openness leads across speech; following Heidegger's idea, speech must indeed be in language and thus must be determined through language and in the openness of language. It is necessary to look precisely at what appeared in the experience of the search for and finding of words in order to make it clearer.

For this, in turn, it is necessary to grasp the individual, more precisely: *the individual speaker* and, from this, *the individual sentence*. The sentence is the most elementary thing that can be said. The single word is either an abridged sentence or it is simply pronounced, but not *said*. It is recited [*hergesagt*] or blurted out [*dahingesagt*] without *something* getting said [*gesagt*] by it, for example, in a practice session to acquire elocution, or in the compulsory ritual repetition of the word to the point that it ceases to be a word and becomes a mere sound. One does not need to understand what is blurted out; one only wants to understand when something is said, such that understanding focuses on speech in its referentiality toward something substantive and its substantiveness. The individual sentence, however, is already said *to someone*. That one speaks "to himself" does not make the other or the others disappear; the definition of thinking as it is developed in the *Theaetetus* and in the *Sophist* arises from the normal case of speaking to others. As it is identified in the *Theaetetus*, opining (δοξάζειν) is saying (λέγειν), except that it is carried through not in regard to another and not with the voice, but, rather, silently for one himself.[31] Yet, everything said silently in this manner could also be vocalized and said to someone; it is only for this reason that it is something said and recognizable as such. Language connects three "elements": an I, a you, and a he (she) or something—someone speaks to someone about something.[32]

The three "elements" of speech belong together. No one is a speaker without having something to say to someone; no one is spoken to without something being said to her or him. And nothing is said, unless it is said from someone to someone. The whole of an instance of speech, however, may be described with shifting accentuation; one can direct attention toward any of the three "elements" and let the others recede. Nevertheless, the "elements" are not equivalent: Speaker and the one spoken to are, as such, determined by saying; the "something," which is spoken about, is encountered here. In this respect, saying is the point of departure for our consideration.

§ 23. An Individual Simple Sentence

No sentence stands alone. Even if sentences are not a part of a conversation or a longer discourse, they belong in situations. If taken on their own, sentences that are supposed to show something, sentences expressing models or examples, often for this reason have a laughable or banal effect. Although a sentence that is singled out, picked up, or contrived still has an order, it no longer has meaning; one does not say anything with it any more, and, as a listener, one can no longer get anywhere with it.

One must imagine a situation, then, in which a simple sentence can be uttered. While on a walk on the castle mount, someone says that the minster tower lies in an especially glorious light this morning. One could call this an assertion. It may be assented to, or the assent may be refused. Of course, both would depend on whether one has understood the sentence; one must be able to connect something with it. Moreover, one would have to allow oneself to be addressed by the sentence, that is, voluntarily or involuntarily to connect something with it. When this has occurred, one turns to look at the city and, with it, at the minster tower. In this case, one has followed the sentence; one has turned to what the sentence says. When one has been able to follow the sentence, one will, with the words "minster tower," turn toward it.

To follow the sentence means, then to allow oneself to be *directed* toward [*sich hinweisen auf*] something by it. By following this directive [*Weisung*], one understands what a sentence *intends*. "To intend" originally means to direct its meaning toward something.[33] This is only possible when one follows a sentence because this sentence itself has a direction. This direction is the *meaning* [*Sinn*] of the sentence. One follows its direction, that is, one allows oneself to be *shown* [*zeigen*] something by the sentence, in the given example, the minster tower and the especially glorious light in which it lies in the morning.

Under the presupposition that this example is serviceable, then, saying may be understood as a *showing*. Accordingly, saying may be further determined by determining more precisely what showing is. In this, it should also be made clear how saying relates to showing; whether it is a possibility of showing alongside others or its single possibility; whether, conversely, all saying is a showing or not. If there is no showing without saying and without saying no showing, then the two belong together in such a way that one cannot understand the one without the other. Even the showing in mimesis, which has already been addressed, would in this case have to be understood as a saying. Something may be said not only with words.

A first answer has already been given to the question of what showing is: Showing, as was illuminated by the example, is directed toward something, and, for this reason, one is able to follow this direction. This, however, is still too imprecise. The orientation toward or away from an aim that one has to deal with in action also has a direction. With one's decision for an aim among many possible aims, one gives oneself a direction, and by deciding for appropriate possibilities of action, one pursues this direction.

Precisely therein, however, lies the difference between action and showing. In action, one strives to reach what one directs himself toward. Things are different in showing. The direction one gives oneself in showing *keeps* its distance; it *remains* at a remove from what is shown. Showing is a reference that is impossible without removal from what is shown. This becomes quite clear in gestural showing: One can only point out [*zeigen auf*] something that one has not seized and does not hold in one's hand. What one shows is something one does not have on him.

This does not appear to be the case, however, for all showing. One can not only show something, but also *exhibit* [*vorzeigen*] something—something that one wants to draw someone else's attention to or that someone else would like to see. In this case, one has what is shown in one's hand. This does not appear to involve any distance. Yet, one holds something that one exhibits differently than something one uses, also differently than when one wants to hold on to something tightly, keep it in one's possession. Rather, one holds something one exhibits so that it may easily be seen, that is, more or less clearly away from oneself. One offers it, although not in order to give it to someone. If one understands that something is being exhibited, then he—as the one who is being shown something—is able to connect a specific activity with the exhibitive gesture; one knows that he is not supposed to grab what is being exhibited and take it into his possession. Something that is exhibited also stands at a remove from the one who shows it as well as from those who contemplate it. It is found as it were in the "intermediary position" between the two, in a position that should be understood as ungraspable in the literal sense.

Things are similar if something is shown even though the one who is showing it does not make an appearance. This is the case, for example, in exhibitions [*Ausstellungen*]. The owner separates himself from what is on exhibit, temporarily or for the duration, yet it remains in his possession; events of this kind often do not occur in the private rooms of the owner but rather in rooms that are accessible to the public. What is on exhibit, for example, an art object, is given as such for contemplation and is understood to be given in this manner in that one restricts oneself to the contemplation of it. It remains in its essence "in ob-jectification" [*im Gegen-stand*], over and against. Things are also similar, when someone exhibits something that one cannot give away, for example, his residence. In this case, one holds oneself back as resident and, conversely, may expect that the visitors only look at everything instead of conducting themselves as if they were "at home."

One has to deal with a special case of exhibiting when someone shows how something is done. A tennis instructor can show how to hit a backhand shot. Here, the instructor's distance to what he exhibits or demonstrates is not visible, although it can nevertheless be understood. One can also get distance from what he does—in "not really" doing it, but rather in just doing it in order to show it.

There is a third form of showing. Here, nothing is shown that is itself accessible like the minster tower, nor is anything held and thereby put into relief as occurred in exhibiting. Rather, something is not given, or not yet given, but at the same time is not inaccessible, because it is *indicated* [*angezeigt*]. An illness can thus be indicated by specific circumstances and manifestations; a gong in the theater can invite one to go back into the auditorium. The advertisement of an event by means of a placard or an oral announcement is also an indication.

Distance is also characteristic of indication. What is shown is there in the showing and is at the same time withdrawn. An illness that is only indicated is not identical with its symptoms; the gong requests a specific conduct, but one that still remains ahead; the placard only fulfills its indicative function if one does not already find oneself at the event indicated by it. Indication is a showing that goes beyond what is present in the showing.[34]

It may be ascertained for all three forms of showing, then, that distance from what is shown is essential for showing. Accordingly, showing only remains what it is insofar as the distance is preserved. Considered anthropologically, it may be that this experience of distance developed from grasping, and was initially an abortive, and then relaxed grasping motion. This may at least hold for pointing to something.[35] Yet, the pointing motion cannot be traced back to a grasping motion; it is something completely and utterly different. No animal, as Cassirer puts it, proceeds "to the characteristic reformulation of the grasping motion into the ostensive gesture," and, in this respect, there lies in pointing "a trait of typical, universal-spiritual significance."[36]

Wherein this significance lies may be discerned in the outlined forms of showing. In showing, one finds a relation to something at a remove. This something remains in a removal, outside of one's own sphere of influence, and in showing one has no intention of bringing it into this sphere. Nothing is supposed to be "shaped" or otherwise changed. Showing is not de-removing. It leaves what is shown there, where it is, and just as it is; in showing, the concern is with what is at a remove as such; showing is animated by such a removal and in showing one adjusts to it.

Not everything, however, remains the same as before when still nothing had been shown. By pointing something out, exhibiting it, or indicating it, it becomes the focus of attention. This is not seldom the meaning of showing; One shows something in order to awaken attentiveness for it. Sometimes it has previously been there, perhaps even noticed. It is first through showing, however, that it is lifted out and emerges. In this, the emergence is not *caused* by showing; showing does not change anything about what is shown. Certainly, the awakening of attentiveness has an effect. However, it is no guarantee that the showing will succeed. In showing, one can only *see to* the emergence; what is pointed out has to emerge of its own accord. Conversely, the reference to what emerges in this way can only be a showing; if one wished to seize it or to cause something with it, it would no longer be what it still just was.

A correlation exists, then, between showing and what is shown: One shows something, and it shows itself; it shows itself and stands in a reference that is nothing other than showing. The latter can only hold for the moment of self-showing; showing, in this case, is fulfilled through self-showing. Or, the self-showing is preserved through the showing; a showing that lasts or that is always newly initiated confirms and fixes something that shows itself in what it is. Something that shows itself is φαινόμενον, phenomenon in the literal sense. The concept is not meant here in its phenomenological significance, although also not in a significance completely different from it; rather, it signifies what gets intensified in phenomenology.

Attentiveness to a phenomenon can be of the shortest duration. Something is phenomenon for only a moment, then it again already becomes a "fact of experience" or something in regard to which one discovers possibilities of action. If something only becomes phenomenon in showing, its phenomenality lasts only as long as the tension of showing is maintained. This restriction of the phenomenal can in fact be desired, say, in cooperative action when one draws someone's attention to something that should be noticed. One brings it to attention only in order that action is adjusted to it.

The attentiveness to a phenomenon in this is more or less great. It can be in passing and, as such, barely come to consciousness, it can also be chosen as an attitude and be consciously sustained; in this case, showing is an explicit activity. This is how things are, for example, when someone acts as a guide through a building or through a collection, and certainly, this is how it is in every presentation. The performance of a music piece or a play is an exhibition, the explication and clarification of a picture or a poem is an exhibition and pointing out. Here, the correlation of showing and self-showing does not in fact have to be thematic; when this occurs, it more likely disturbs one's attentiveness to what is showing itself. In presentation, however, the correlation has a characteristic intensity; it emerges as a tension because showing is pursued alone for the sake of self-showing and because self-showing allows the possibility of showing to become explicit as such. Here, showing appears in particular clarity as an *activity that moves away from itself*; it is through showing that what shows itself is *preserved in self-showing*. Thus, the two refer to each other. Their correlation emerges as such in the tension-filled difference of showing and self-showing. Presentation is an intensification of the phenomenal.

This leads back to the question of the relation between showing and language. In quite a few of the aforementioned examples, showing is not speech. This holds for the performance of a musical piece and likewise for the exhibiting of an art object; even showing someone how to swing a backhand stroke can occur wordlessly. Indication also requires no words, although it can also be enacted in speech; the gong, which indicates the end of the break, is wordless, just as is a high body temperature that indicates an illness. This does not mean, however, that this showing is not linguistic. In speech, it is not the articulation of sounds that makes what is articulated a showing. Something, for example, the minster tower, has to be *intended* [*gemeint*], and there may be no intending without language. Intention does not exist in a nonlinguistic gesture, to which saying is only added.

Such a gesture, for example, pointing with one's finger,* can in fact be helpful in certain circumstances. The gesture, however, is not the "essence" of showing, as if the sentences and the expressions contained in it could be given direction and fixed on something by the gesture. On the contrary, the gesture itself shows nothing. It could be a mere stretch of the arm—say, in order to look at one's watch, or a movement in order to pull a jacket that had slipped back up onto one's shoulder, or something else. Even if the gesture were intended as a showing, however, as mere gesture it would remain helpless. Although it would reach across to the things at a remove, this is not a showing, not even a reference. For the gesture that is nothing but this gesture, there is fundamentally only *one* possibility for putting it into words; what it intends is said with the word "this," also "this there." This expression, however, only reinforces the helplessness. It intends all things and everything that is "there"; it does not intend anything specific but rather simply "something," or, as Hegel expresses it in his discussion of "sense certainty," "being in general."[37] It is true we may believe that we show what we have immediately before our eyes with that word. In contrast with this intention, however, language proves—as Hegel puts it—to be "more true." By putting sense certainty into words, "we ourselves immediately refute our intention, and since the universal is what is true of sense certainty, and language only expresses this truth, it is thus not at all possible that we can ever say a sensible being, which we intend."[38] Said is always only "this" or "this there."

The effort to reach across to things is fulfilled first by reaching something determinate. The gesture only has the character of showing when it refers to *something*; there is first a reference with the determinate "something." In this, something has to be explicitly or inexplicitly distinguished from something else. In other words, the gesture has to be sustained by something determinate,

---

*[The German for "pointing" here is 'Zeigen,' the same word that means "showing." —Trans.]

which, for its part, belongs in the context of different expressions that supplement each other in one manner or another. Thus, one may only point out the minster tower to someone when one is in a position to differentiate it from the nave of the minster and the minster, in turn, from other buildings. Certainly, the one who is being shown something can understand that the minster tower is intended solely through this gesture. In this case, he understands what is intended without a single word. This is how things are in every showing that does not involve speech. In these cases, the determinacy of what is intended is not explicit. Exhibiting is only intelligible, however, when what is supposed to be exhibited is clear. One always understands indication based on something familiar as such. For this, in turn, it must be determinate.

Nothing has determinacy solely in itself; every determination belongs in the context of other determinations. The minster tower has to be distinguishable from other towers and other high buildings; what a building is only becomes clear in the context of and in its difference from such things that are not built but grow or that have come into existence in some other manner like the mountain range behind the city. The determinations within which a showing belongs are connected with one another in multiple ways; they supplement one another even where they are objective. They form a fabric, one could also say: a *texture*. Texture is to be distinguished from text.[39] In contrast with text, texture includes all possible determinations in it and is in this way a thickly woven fabric; it is an infinitely enfolded fullness of differences and references. It is as it were the soil from which and on which speech and writing unfold by raising out specific references and differences.

Showing is possible solely in texture regardless of whether or not it is enacted as speech. Showing is itself reference to something in its determinacy; something determinate is there to be brought into attentiveness. The directive gesture by which showing becomes apparent is an expression of this reference. The gesture lives in a texture. In this texture, the gesture wants to move toward over there, toward this determinate item, which it emphasizes as this determinate item. The gesture arises from the texture; without this texture, the gesture would be a diffuse reaching out, but not a showing. And, the gesture stretches into the texture; something determinate that is supposed to be shown by it stands in the texture as this determinate item and at the same time beyond it. When something shows itself, it is as if a material whose pattern had remained unnoticed were to take on a precise form at a place. When something shows itself, the texture comes into focus and yet at the same time recedes as texture.

Texture is accordingly the source of possibility for all determination and determinacy that gets developed and can be developed. The gesture—and certainly the sentence that it sometimes replaces and sometimes accompanies—arises from the possibility of determination and it is intended as a determination in being directed toward "this there"; "this there" is to show itself as "this determinate item." If showing succeeds, the gesture arrives at the determinate thing, which, for its part, has emerged from the source of possibility for its determinacy. In the actuality of the gesture, the possibility of determination is connected with the source of possibility for all determinacy. Yet, both are texture. With the gesture, the texture is traversed. In its inconspicuous, enfolded thickness, texture is the openness of showing and self-showing because it allows for things to be raised up and unfolded. It is the openness of determination and determinacy. Its openness is, conversely, that of showing and self-showing. In this way, as the openness of the phenomenal, texture is the language in which and from out of which there is speech.

The textural essence of language itself comes into focus in speech, although it is not disclosed straight away in the character of speaking. As it were, it shines through in speech, and this, in fact, because speech always connects and differentiates and as such *points out* [*Aufzeigen*]. This is first seen in Plato. In the *Sophist*, the connective character of speech is developed in regard to the observation that we give something, for example, human beings, many different names by attributing to them colors, forms, sizes, vices, and virtues.[40] Because not everything may be connected with everything else, however, the issue is to know what may and may not be connected with each other, such that one has to separate them from one another.[41] Aristotle takes up this idea and, upon developing it, takes it over himself. He understands indicative speech [*das aufzeigende Sprechen*] based on the indicative sentence [*vom aufzeigenden Satz*] (λόγος ἀποφαντικός),[42] in order then to distinguish two fundamental forms of the indicative sentence: it is affirmation (κατάφασις) and denial (ἀπόφασις), and, as such, a connection or separation of determinations: Something is of a certain composition or it does not have this composition. This is not, however, an insight into language in its distinction from speech. Aristotle understands language completely based on speech, it is φωνὴ σημαντική.[43] Aristotle sees no fabric in λόγος, λόγος is for him not a text that belongs in texture and stands out in it. Because of this, the essence of differentiations and connections also remains unclear in his view.

The Aristotelian position continues to shape Heidegger's attempt to conceive of language as language. The idea that language "speaks" goes back to the claim that language itself is to be grasped as the λόγος that inaugurates, first moves each respective instance of speaking. Heidegger finds the word "saying," also "index" [*Zeige*] for this λόγος.[44] By this he means the inaugural showing that allows everything "present" to show itself; it is the speech, itself unpronounced and prior to any specific pronouncement, that it is necessary to hear in speech. For Heidegger, it is only in this hearing that the meaning of presence as a self-showing is revealed.

Heidegger does not consider here, however, that every showing already reckons with the possible presence of what is to be shown. Even with the referential gesture, a "this there" is intended, and in this respect, even it is in the openness that allows showing. Heidegger considers the possibility of self-showing based on language, yet not the possibility of showing. It is only possible to take both into account if one conceives of language based on the correlation of showing and self-showing and conceives of the possibility of this correlation as language. Language is not an occurrence characterized by showing, it is a dimension.

In Heidegger's understanding of language, moreover, determinacy does not make an appearance. The idea of a preserved presence alone does not make clear how showing can be determinative and how self-showing can be determined. Language is a dimension insofar as it is texture; only for this reason is what is shown more than and different from Hegel's "being in general." However, the texture of language has still not become clear; what may be conceived by this word remains vague and preliminary. Therefore, it is necessary to make clear with more precision how language may be understood in its textural essence.

To this end, a point of reference may once again be found in the sentence with which something—for example, the minster tower—is shown. The sentence is more than a hopeless extension of the arm because something is said, and conversely the saying is recognizable as such because the sounds that one hears are intelligible as linguistic expression. The voice that announces is, as Aristotle puts it, not a mere voice but rather a sign-giving voice,[45] φωνὴ σημαντική.[46] It is the signs, then, that comprise the linguistic character of what is heard, and, accordingly, one would have to say that the determinative showing in speech is signification [*Bezeichnen*]. If this belongs in language, then it is possible that language itself may become clear in regard to signs.

§ 24. Signs

A sign is something that shows. This would have to be illuminated with signs that are encountered in the everyday. A traffic sign—for example, the straight white arrow against a blue background—shows that one may only drive in one direction, namely, straight ahead. The sign fulfills its function by itself. No one is doing any showing, although such a person would be conceivable. If the regulation permitting only one-way driving had been instituted on short notice and obtained for only a limited time then a police officer could take over the task of showing. In this case, the sign would be something that takes the place of the police officer. It would replace him, as this is more convenient, especially for permanent regulations.

Signs, as this idea may be generalized, first have to be granted the function of showing. In this regard, they are conventional and arbitrary. One could exchange and change them without impairing their function. Therefore, as one might think, they must be traced back to showing. Even if showing were not to be carried through without signs, signs remain dependent on it because by the signs a specific showing is intended. As this specific one, the showing is always the same. If a sign replaces it, different formations of the sign are nevertheless possible. One has to have understood the showing in order to understand the showing of the sign. Here, understanding a sign would mean rediscovering the showing in it.

Linguistic signs, that is, both the enunciated and also the written words of a language, have always stood under suspicion of arbitrariness.[47] The multiplicity and diversity of languages allows this suspicion to arise all but on its own. The idea of a showing that goes back to the one who is showing, therefore, is quite attractive if one wishes not to be at the mercy of this arbitrariness. Given that the understanding of language as a complex of signs first came to be generally accepted in late antiquity—the Aristotelian determination of λόγος as φωνὴ σημαντική is singular[48]—this solution is also first proposed here. This occurs in Augustine in the *Confessions*, in the context of an autobiographical report about the acquisition of language, which has become familiar not least because Wittgenstein cites and discusses it in the *Philosophischen Untersuchungen*. Here, Augustine traces the learning of words back to the conduct of the one who speaks. If adults named some matter or other and, corresponding to their talk, moved their bodies toward something, then he had seen and retained that the matter was named by the adults through what they had enunciated because they wanted to refer to it. That they wanted to do this, however, was shown by the movement of their bodies, through the natural words of all peoples that are generated by facial expressions and looks, through the action of the rest of the body parts and the tone of voice, that recognizably indicate (*indicante*) the affection of the soul, whether it desires, possesses, rejects, or shuns something.[49]

The point of departure for Augustine's description is the claim that the expressive sounds, gestures, and looks may be understood as *verba naturalia*. Under this presupposition, they are signs in a double sense: On the one hand they are indications, in regard to which the affection and movement of the soul, the *affectio animi*, are to be read. On the other hand, they are signs that point to something; the movement of the soul arises based on something that causes it. One is referred to precisely this in his affection. As their name says, the *verba naturalia* belong to human nature, and they are therefore also common to all peoples. It thus lies close at hand to explain languages that are not natural and that change in the course of their history based on them. Their words are intelligible initially only because they accompany the *verba naturalia*. If they are later to take the place of the *verba naturalia*, then their assignment to the *verba naturalia* must be clear.

Augustine's idea is by no means nonsensical. The expressive sounds, gestures, and looks, which Augustine understands as *verba naturalia*, are not like that helpless desire to point that characterizes sense-certainty as Hegel describes it. Every mimetic or gestural expression is rather determined; it is more or less clearly distinguished from others, with which they stand in a context. From the various situations of expressions, it moreover comes out that they point out various things. If the soul is transposed into fear by something threatening, the *verba naturalia* are different than in joy, desire, or sadness about something.

With his idea, Augustine quite recognizably varies the Aristotelian determination of enunciations as σύμβολα of what affects the soul by putting "natural" expressive sounds, gestures, and looks in the position of enunciations. He thus separates the "interior" and its language from the various—and, in their diversity only conventional—"exterior" languages; the natural language is the exteriority of the interior, and, in this, authentic.

Yet, on closer inspection, Augustine's idea is not convincing. Its weakness is the doubling of language and the distinction between natural and conventional signs. As Wittgenstein fittingly formulates it, Augustine describes "the learning of human language as if the child came into a foreign country and would not understand the language of the country"; it is "as if he already had a language, only not this one."[50] That is, Augustine provides no illuminating presentation of the first acquisition of language; he already presupposes the language, the learning of which he wishes to make intelligible. The presupposition is moreover problematic because the depiction of the presupposed language is not illuminated. If one considers it more closely, its naturalness dissolves, and it is like all other languages.

This affects first of all the assertion that mimetic and gestural expression is immediately intelligible. Augustine overlooks that in human beings with different temperaments, say, the expression of joy can appear very differently. This is certainly the case for different cultures; one culture does not have to be very distant from another at all and still its language of expressions has to be learned just as the language of purportedly arbitrary words does.

Moreover, it is by no means clear that the sounds accompanying one's mimetic or gestural expression refer to what produces one's affect. The sound could also be like a shout of joy or a sigh, that is, itself only the expression of the affect. Even if a respective expression were to make the affect operative in it recognizable, one would have to be able to understand the sound accompanying the expression as a sign, in order to recognize its "direction"; one would have to know—or, what is probable, to learn—what it signifies in the respective case and how its quality of signification is to be differentiated from other sounds. If this is so, one also learns the purportedly natural signs like the other purportedly arbitrary ones.

If this is so, however, there is no essential difference between natural and artificial signs; even the forms of expression have the character of signs. All signification and expression plays out in signs. There is no "behind" the signs, nothing that the signs merely stand in for, like traffic signs do for the police officer. The very suggestion of this example leads to error: considered precisely, the police officer stands not "behind" the traffic signs, not even when they replace him. He also gives signs. In his gestures, what plays out in his "interior," in his consciousness, may in some manner or other come into focus. He can only communicate it, however, by showing it. Moreover, no one who is supposed to have understood the gestures of the police officer has access to his consciousness. No one is able to think the thoughts of another; no one knows immediately how the feelings of another are.[51] In the attempt to understand these, one is directed to the exterior, to the signs, and, in fact, to these alone. What needs to be made clear, then, is how one understands signs—how one knows that something is a sign, and, moreover, what it signifies.

There is a point of reference for this attempt: Signs appear in order that they be noticed. This noticing, however, does not occur for its own sake but instead has a function. One is supposed to understand something: that one is only allowed to drive straight ahead at this intersection, or that one has to stop now where the red light is to be seen. Even if one has no idea how signs fulfill this function, one is nevertheless able to say what their function is. They provide, as Heidegger expresses it in *Sein und Zeit*, "orientation within the surrounding world."[52]

As the aforementioned examples suggest, signs are orientating. Therefore, it is not convincing to understand them with Heidegger as useful things because of their "serviceability." Heidegger's ascription of signs to useful things goes back to his conviction that one has to determine everything that is thingly in terms of the life-world, namely, in the structure of "reference" [*Verweisung*]. Its essence is supposed to lie in the fact that it "refers" from itself toward something else because it exists not for its own sake but for the sake of another, ultimately, for the sake of the highest aim in the sense of human Dasein. This structure is realized with particular clarity in the useful thing: the useful thing is "something in order to . . . ," a means to ends, and it accords with this particularly well in its characteristic inconspicuousness. The useful thing is all the more a means, the less it occupies one's attentiveness, which is itself supposed to be referred entirely to the end.

Signs like traffic signs, however, are not used like hand tools. One *heeds* them or *takes notice of them*, among other reasons in order that one can use something in a specific manner or all the better to realize an aim. Heidegger does in fact take into account that signs are only able to fulfill their function through "conspicuousness."[53] But he misjudges the proper meaning of conspicuousness. By rising up out of their surroundings, signs emerge *as thingly* and thus outside of the connection of effect and cause. It is only in this way that they are able to fulfill the function Heidegger ascribes to them, namely, to raise "a complex of useful things explicitly into circumspection."[54]

In response to the question of how this occurs, one gets a familiar answer from Heidegger that does not lead anywhere; signs are useful things whose "specific character as useful thing" lies "in showing."[55] If, however, showing is only intelligible by way of signs, then what a sign is does not become clear through showing. One has to continue to work on this idea of showing and hope that one will be guided to it by another idea achieved in the interim.

Signs orient. But how, precisely, does this orientation occur, for example, through a traffic sign? Not, as one might think, because signs point in a specific direction. This is again bound to a purportedly clear idea of signs, and, moreover, misleading: By no means do all signs point in a direction; for example, a No Parking sign does not do this. However, not even the straight white arrow on a blue background may be understood in this way. In terms of direction, the sign points upward and this has nothing to do with how the sign is to be heeded. Rather, the sign is orienting because it indicates a possibility of conduct and, with this, discloses others; it commands that one is here only permitted to drive straight ahead. But even this one command does not stand on its own; it is intelligible only together with the inexplicit prohibition against turning right or left. The single sign thus lets a context be known. Signs—traffic signs, for example—orient how one has to conduct oneself in a context.

Because signs stand in relation to a context, their multitude is not coincidental. The orienting function of signs can only be fulfilled because they themselves form a context; it is only in this way that they lay open* a context. Signs let the context be known as such, perhaps in the way that signs such as traffic signs suggest what one's own possibilities are and in which regard one has to reckon with the conduct of others. Warning signs have this function in a particularly pregnant manner. Whereas a deer that steps onto the road *poses* possibilities for action and immediately requires conduct, the sign on which a leaping deer is depicted brings a possibility to consciousness so that one can *adjust* oneself to it as a possibility. Clearer still, finally, are signposts, indications of direction and removal. They allow city and country to be overviewed.

Overview is not possible without distance; one does not overview a context that one belongs in. It is true that one could investigate it successively and thereby achieve an idea of it, but one would not achieve a complete picture in this manner. In order that something present itself as a context, one must contemplate it from a removal, for example, a landscape from an airplane. In this case, one sees the context of the townships and highways *simultaneously*, in one view. In this case, the landscape is a more or less clear fabric; it is like a text.

---

*[The verb "lay open" is my translation of *aufschließen* here. Cf. Stambaugh's translation of this word in *Being and Time*. —Trans.]

Not every context may be grasped as such like a landscape from above. Removal has the further disadvantage here that it displaces one from the context; removal could only be helpful for orientation if one retains the complete picture that one has achieved and then later has it present like a map inscribed in one's memory. The laying open of a context through traffic signs is different. Traffic signs bring one to a distance though they do not leave the context of traffic; the context is brought to a removal through the signs themselves.

This occurs because the signs are thingly. Because they stand in as things in the life-world in contrast to what is useful and applicable, they remain at a removal. They reflect the context of the life-world by interrupting and doubling it. They are contexts of the life-world, although reified and, with this, emphasized. They thus give one the possibility to *refer* to the context in which one had previously circulated.

The experience outlined here does not depend on specific signs being posed in the life-world, that is, things that draw attention to themselves. Everything that is encountered in the life-world may itself be taken as a sign. This occurs, say, when something becomes a marker. One does not take it as what it is but rather lifts it out and lets it stand for something else. The furnishings of a house can have the character of a sign in regard to the temperament and lifestyle of those who live there, the clues that someone leaves behind in a house are signs for the reconstruction of a crime. The revolution of the heavens, as in astrology, can have the character of a sign for the destinies of human life. Even the mantic interpretation of signs means to recognize a context of life to which one would himself have no access. In each case, the concern is with connections of how something agrees with other things, in a word: with the world in ever-different respects insofar as it does not have order and structure as a life-world. Contemplated from this standpoint, signs are like entries on a map; even on maps, not everything in the landscape is recorded. A map that would take into account every path, every tree, and every topographical feature would ultimately have to as comprehensive as the landscape itself. In this case, it would have become like the life-world and no longer orienting for it.

Signs, as these considerations may be summarized, are things that are established with more or less permanence in the world insofar as it is texture. Conversely, texture is the context that may be established through signs and that are always disclosed when established in this way. Signs mark the texture in various respects, in different densities, and thus make the interweaving of moments and connections transparent. They as it were loosen it up by keeping a firm hold on certain moments and connections and thereby allowing the texture to be permeated and experienced. Through signs, the density of the texture is structured; it is *articulated* such that one is able to traverse it in specific manners.

This occurs by taking notice of the signs and following them. In order to understand signs, one has to be able to *read* them. This means: one has to be capable of capturing them in their context and taking the context that arises here as the context of something, which is itself not, or at least not in this respect, a sign. One has to be able to *carry over* the context that has been read to something not first given through the context of the sign, even if it is not accessible other than through it. The brainwaves of a living being cannot be directly observed but rather only measured and recorded. To be able to read the recorded curve means to recognize the brainwaves in its course.

Heidegger drew attention to this characteristic double sense of reading in an elucidation of the word λέγειν.⁵⁶ On the one hand, reading [*Lesen*] is to be understood as gathering; it is gleaning [*Zusammenlesen*], which is still current when one speaks of vintaging grapes or gleaning corn [*Wein-oder Ährenlese*]. On the other hand, reading is "to lay." Its meaning is to bring things "to lie in that it lets things lie together before us."⁵⁷ One may understand it as letting come to appearance.

If this is so, signs are what properly show. One shows something when one, in reading signs, uses signs. Such a reading is at play in every use of the sign; every use grasps the signs together, and thereby lays open a context or even just something in its context. This also holds for speech. It has the power of showing because it occurs in the context of signs. Signs stand for language itself in its distinction from speech.

This idea is hinted at by Aristotle when he speaks of the σύμβολα in the voice also as σημεῖα, sign. It is carried out with consequence admittedly first in Ferdinand Saussure's "structuralist" conception of language.⁵⁸ Saussure takes up the distinction between language and speech in order radically to tip the scales in favor of language. Language (*langue*)⁵⁹ is a system of signs (*signes*), which are determined solely by means of their difference from other signs. This is not intended as an establishment of different elements—as if there were specific linguistic unities, which could then be recognized in their difference. Saussure expressly opposes this misrepresentation. There are no "*terms positifs*," between which a distinction is then struck. Rather, linguistic unities are given through this distinguishing and through nothing else. As Saussure summarizes this idea: In language there is nothing but differences.⁶⁰

This idea may be illustrated especially well with regard to enunciations. That a sound is an enunciation may only be decided by testing whether it belongs in a system of differences or not. The answer will always have to be referred to a respectively given language; click sounds, for example, do not appear in the differential system of European languages. Moreover, the answer will always be referred to a type and so admit of modifications in expression. Such modifications always remain unproblematic as long as they do not offend against established differences of the phonetic system.

Saussure's idea that there is nothing in language but differences, however, also affects the "content" side of language. The fact that linguistic expressions show something and are intelligible because of this, as Saussure thinks, cannot be traced back to an "idea" that merely finds its exterior form by way of signs. Thought without linguistic differences is formless and undetermined; it is solely through language understood as a system of signs that thought is more than a diffuse heap of impressions.[61] In this respect, thought—or, with Humboldt, spirit—is not capable of forming signs. Their modification, reformulation, or new construction always already presupposes the sign-system of language.

On the one hand, Saussure's analyses may be counted as a breakthrough to an adequate understanding of linguistic signs and of signs in general.[62] Saussure is the first to determine signs in all consequence without recourse to the signifying activity of spirit. In this respect, his analyses are on the way to a refined understanding of language that is differentiated from speech and that is not conceived based on speech—precisely language itself, as Heidegger discovers it in his way but then misses it once again with the idea of a language that speaks.

Yet, language itself remains insufficiently determined by the idea of a system of signs as Saussure develops it. Although signs stand for language itself, they may not be identified with it. Besides established signs, there also belongs to language the characteristic openness of texture; it is in this openness that the demarcations of signs stand and in terms of it that their context is open, and this openness is itself demonstrated through the signs in their openness and made available for investigation through the signs inscribed in it. Texture is demonstrated through the signs posed within it in language; it is first revealed as texture through signs, although it is itself not of the order of signs. It lets signs be what they are. Even in the understanding of language as a system of signs, the sign-character of signs still remains unclear. Even if signs are what they are only through "differences," they do not become signs through differences. Signs lay something open. In this, they first have a *significance*.

Saussure stands before the question of the significance of linguistic signs as before an unsolvable riddle; how something can be formed in the domain between thought and sound that is neither materialized idea nor a spiritualization of sound is, for him in a certain way a mysterious matter of fact.[63] Indeed, in his unpublished notes, Saussure considers giving up the understanding of signs as an ideational-audible unity in favor of adopting elements that remain determined only contextually.[64] This idea, however, is only an answer to the question of how the sign is to be conceived as a material-spiritual unity. It does not say how signs signify. In order to make this clear, one has to take more into view than only them.

§ 25. Significance

Signs lay open a context. Yet, with this too little is said about their function. In the context that the signs themselves form, their value is always different;

on Saussure's view, they are nothing other than this difference. So, they must also stand in relation to different moments of the laid open context. What is different is their significance for this context.

"Significance" can be a "signification," that is, an "intention" and signifying showing. In this case, the significance of a linguistic expression would be what is "signified" by it. One signifies something by naming it and, in this way, distinguishing it from other things that appear within the same context. If everything that appears somehow or other has the character of a thing, then what is signified would be the thing intended with a linguistic expression.

Gottlob Frege has forwarded this idea in a manner that is definitive for recent philosophy. Frege develops his understanding of significance* [*Bedeutung*] oriented by "proper names," distinguishing the significance of the name from the "representation" that accompanies its use and its "meaning" [*Sinn*]. Here, the representation is "completely subjective"[65]; our representations are very different from case to case when a name like "Aristotle" is named. Whether one thinks of the sculpture in front of the main entrance to the University of Freiburg, of some reproduction or other, or only vaguely of a bearded man in Greek garb always depends on one himself. In contrast with this, the significance is "the object itself"[66] that we signify with a name, that is, what gets represented in many ways, but gets conceived as what is commonly represented. Of "meaning," Frege says that it lies between representation and significance; it is "no longer subjective like the representation, yet also not the object itself." It is, as one may add in a first elucidation, the direction of a name or, more precisely, the direction of naming; the name would have its meaning, in this case, in intending.

The field of these considerations is drawn quite narrowly; they apply, if at all, only to the significance and meaning of proper names, and, as regards significance, the names of fictive persons cannot be treated. Frege elucidates this idea in saying that the question of the significance of "Odysseus" is first posed when one does not consider the *Odyssey* as an artwork.[67] Accordingly, the sentence, "Odysseus was set ashore in Ithaca while in a deep sleep" certainly always has a meaning, but only a significance if there is someone or something with the name "Odysseus."[68]

---

*[Here and throughout, I have used the English "significance" for the German *Bedeutung*. It is true that the English word "reference" is often used to translate the term *Bedeutung* as it appears in Frege's classic piece, *Sinn und Bedeutung*. And, indeed, the English word "reference" may be said to capture nicely Frege's particular definition and technical use of *Bedeutung* in his essay. I have chosen to use "significance" for *Bedeutung*, however, because this translation accords better with the standard German usage of *Bedeutung*, on which Figal relies in the present discussion. As Figal himself will point out, in fact, Frege's technical use of the word *Bedeutung* is rather idiosyncratic: Frege's discussion is indeed in part about what in English may be called "reference," but this is not captured well by the German word *Bedeutung*. —Trans.]

One could admit Frege's terminology and understand significance solely in his sense. In this case, one would have to accept that only proper names have a significance, or, accordingly, clear identifications like "the author of the 'Nicomachean Ethics,'" and clearly identificatory descriptions like curricula vitae and biographies. What one generally understands by the concept of significance would then be shifted to what Frege calls "meaning." What "meaning" is, however, remains unclear in Frege's considerations; it is even contradictory. Frege provides two elucidations of "meaning" that cannot be unified with one another. On the one hand, as he has it, meaning is that "wherein the kind of being given" is "contained."[69] According to this, an expression only has meaning when something that can be put into language in a determinate manner is factually "given." On the other hand, in the sentence cited above about Odysseus, a meaning is granted to a linguistic expression in every case, even, then, for the case in which it remains undecided whether or not there is actually something with the name "Odysseus."

It becomes clear that this is not just a matter of inadvertent carelessness when Frege formulates the same alternative once again differently, and, in this, betrays his uncertainty. Perhaps, as he puts it, one could "grant that a grammatically well-constructed expression which stands for a proper name always has a meaning"; it is just not said "whether a significance corresponds to this meaning."[70] Shortly thereafter, however, Frege clarifies the relation of representation, meaning, and significance such that he excludes a meaning without significance. As an example, he mentions the observation of the moon through a telescope and then compares "the moon itself" with its significance; the moon is "the object of observation, which is mediated by the real image projected by the object-glass inside the telescope, and by the retinal image of the observer."[71] The image in the telescope is comparable to the meaning, the retinal image of the observer "to the representation of intuition." The image in the telescope is not simply one's own, but, rather, a possible standpoint; it is certainly "one-sided" and "dependent on one's location," although "objective, insofar as it" can "serve numerous observers."[72]

If one follows the logic of the comparison, then there cannot be any image in the telescope—and of course the one on the retina—without the "object." As Frege fittingly puts it, the telescope "mediates" what the observer observes. Without this mediation, the "object" could not be seen in this—for it, characteristic—manner. That it should nevertheless accrue "objectivity" [*objektivität*] is grounded by its universal accessibility. The look through the telescope is in principle open to all; the mediation is shared with others.

Frege calls this universally accessible thing the "idea," and not, in fact, in the sense of a cognitive act, but rather of its content. The act would always be individual, "subjective," as Frege would say, but the content is "capable ... of being the common property of many."[73] The idea is, then, tantamount to the meaning. It is, put in still another way, the *said*, that is, what signs make intelligible and what can be understood with them or in regard to them. In a less restrictive use of the expression, one would understand the idea as the "significance" of the signs. And, in this case, one could say of sentences about Odysseus that they had significance, regardless of whether a human being of this name exists or not.

Based on this consideration, it would seem reasonable to put aside the distinction of "meaning" and "significance" in Frege's sense and to solve the question of significance taking orientation from the "objects." Husserl made the case for this in the *Logische Untersuchungen*. The allusion to the fact that the distinction is not even made in everyday language, however, is not illuminating. Philosophical refinements of linguistic usage are always possible and often also defensible. It is thus possible, as occurs here throughout, to distinguish the meaning of an expression from its significance; the meaning lies in *how* an expression—or else a conduct—is intended and can be understood, the significance in *what* is intended and can be understood. Two expressions can have the same significance, but different meaning; sometimes an expression is significant and at the same time meaningless.

The latter point may be justified with Husserl. For him, it belongs "to the concept of an expression" that it has significance. An "expression without significance" is for this reason "no expression at all," but, rather, "is at best a something or other that awakens the claim to or the appearance of being an expression,"[74] for example, a succession of sounds that appears as word but does not exist in any language.

Husserl's answer to the question of significance is not at all so distant from Frege's answer. Husserl, however, does not get entangled in the difficulties of Frege's position. He took up the two moments, which Frege calls "meaning" and "significance," and combined them in one sound concept of significance. "The reference to the object" is constituted in the significance, where the focus is on the *reference* and not on the factical givenness of the "object." For Husserl, in fact, "to use an expression meaningfully and to refer to an object in an expression" are "one and the same." But, a reference is already given when the object is only represented. Whether "the object exists or whether it is fictive, if not entirely impossible," plays no role in this.[75] The significance of the expression lies in the *intending of something*, in the intentionality, which is enacted in saying. It lies "unrecognizably" in the "essence of the acts in question."[76]

In contrast with Frege's conception, Husserl's is in itself sound because it resolves the contradiction that Frege had been entangled in due to his understanding of "meaning"; if the reference to an "object" is not bound to the factical givenness of that object, then the "meaning"—or, in Husserl's terms, "significance"—can be given solely on the basis of the constitutive structure of the reference. Husserl can understand what Frege calls "significance" as the enactment of significance; here, "the possibility of a unified visualization"[77] corresponds to an intention, that is, what has been intended and, in this, perhaps also represented, is factually given.

Husserl's conception is nevertheless problematic in other respects; it varies on an idea that is already familiar from Humboldt. Just as Humboldt accepts a spirit that makes "the articulated sound" capable "of the expression of the idea,"[78] Husserl makes the supposition of the possibility of a form of intending that first enlivens the signs with intention, and, in this way, makes them into signs. It is an intending that precedes significant signs. The pretense of this is, with Jacques Derrida, the attempt to preserve for inner experience an originarily silent, pre-expressive layer.[79]

Even if intending remains silent, however, it cannot "lend" any significance because it is itself sustained by significances; it is enacted in significances, which may possibly remain unspoken, but which are not there without signs. How could they be differentiated without being demarcated, how should they be able to comprise the determinacy of intending without differentiation?

That there is no intending without significances may be seen in regard to gestural showing. The gesture would remain a helpless reaching out if it were not conceived in regard to something determinate, that is, to what can be said with another expression fulfilling the "this" or "this there." Only when one knows that *something* is there, and, in fact, that it is determined in such and such a way, does one get *over there* in showing. The remoteness from which showing is sustained must be marked; otherwise only a diffuse openness that cannot be traversed in showing would be there.

Even the expression "this there" has a significance. One should not say here that it has a meaning. It has meaning when the process of showing has a meaning, for example, that of warning someone in the face of something that is approaching him, or of making him aware of a view that is felt to be especially beautiful. The expression names nothing; there is no "object," through whose "unified visualization" it could be fulfilled. Whoever is able to show has understood, however, what the expression or another expression corresponding to it stands for. What is that which is understood other than its significance?

Considerations such as these can justify Wittgenstein's conviction against Frege and his own earlier position "that the word 'significance' is used in a manner adverse to language if one thereby signifies the thing that 'corresponds' to the word."[80] It also suggests Wittgenstein's answer to the question of how significance is to be grasped differently. The answer is lapidary: "The significance of a word is its usage in the language."[81]

By usage, its *respective* use cannot be intended. In this case, the significance would change every time; the word would have the significance that one respectively gives to it. Usage, then, is to be understood in the sense of common practice. The significance of a word lies in how it is used *in general*. Whoever is familiar with the word has thus also acquired the capacity to use the word correctly, that is, to use it in its meaning in common practice, regardless of how different the situations and contexts of its use may be. It is not that one anticipates this in the use of a word such that one first lends it significance. Rather, the use is determined through the significance of the word itself; it is a conduct *in* the language.

Wittgenstein's model for this conception is *play*, insofar as one understands by this a complex of rules, which do not establish everything that can be done in obeyance of them, but, conversely, first open up determinate possibilities through the restriction of activity. Chess may only be played because there are rules for how one is permitted to move the figures; these rules are that through which the figures are essentially differentiated.[82] However, within the limits of what is established by the rules, one is permitted do what one wishes with the figures. In this, one is not supposed to understand the rules as abstract prescripts. They may in fact be formulated in this manner, yet what is grasped in them is only something generally binding for conduct. Rules, as Wittgenstein treats them, determine conduct, and they only come into focus in conduct.

Wittgenstein's conception of the significance of linguistic expressions does not exclude naming or identifying things or "objects" in Frege's sense. Here, too, however, the significance would be neither the named "object," nor the reference to it that is enacted with the expression. The significance would exist in that one refers to "objects" with an expression of this kind. To refer to "objects," this is something that one masters like moves in a chess game and that belong together with other "moves" in the language that are not references to "objects."

The outlined definition of significance may be well integrated with Saussure's idea of the constitutive difference of linguistic expressions. The differences, as it may be put with Wittgenstein, do not primarily have to do with the sound figures of the words, just as little as the differences of the chess figures has to do with their appearance. They are given with the rules of use. In the chess figures, however, these are in turn determined through differences, such that the use of a figure may be elucidated by delimiting it from other uses.

Despite its strengths, Wittgenstein's conception of significance is not really satisfying. Wittgenstein describes language as if it is a context, in which there is nothing to understand outside of play, but, rather, only something to do correctly. Whoever is practiced in the game and, accordingly, "trained,"[83] conducts himself so as to correspond to the respective "language game" as a whole "of language and the activities interwoven with it."[84] Here, significances are not determined fundamentally differently in language than in the games that orient Wittgenstein's considerations.[85] This is in fact how things are for the acquisition of a language and the ability to speak it; there is no essential difference between the use of a linguistic expression and that of a chess figure. It may be said just as much of a chess figure as of a word that it has a significance—and, in this case, there is no longer any significance that is specifically linguistic. If, by contrast, one wishes to remain true to its givenness, one cannot understand language only as a game. For it is indeed also more than a game: It has the capacity to lay open, and, for this reason, the significance of every linguistic expression is disclosed on the basis of the essential capacity of language to lay open. Linguistic significance, then, has everything that belongs directly or indirectly to the essential capacity of language to lay open.

This is not a plea to turn back to Frege's or Husserl's approach. One should not relinquish Wittgenstein's insight that the significance of linguistic expressions cannot lie in "objects" or in reference to "objects." Yet, on the other hand, the orientation toward "objects" in the question of the significance of linguistic expressions is no coincidence. It is suggested by the showing character of saying, just that here only "objects," that is, things, are considered as what is showable and shown. This, however, is not necessary. That which can be shown does not always have to be a thing, and so showing is not always fulfilled through "unifying intuition." Indeed, more that this; that which shows itself is not a thing at all but rather a phenomenon. Because of this, it is necessary to develop the question of linguistic significance on the basis of phenomena. In asking about the linguistic exhibition of phenomena, the essence of language should also emerge more clearly. This is a further step to the understanding of language itself.

For this, let us once again consider an example. One points to something, and something simple is intended. Normally, showing is more complex; in this case, much is intended at once, and, accordingly, the showing is more refined, or, like what is shown, can be refined. Yet, every refinement presupposes something simple, and, likewise, everything that has been refined can be addressed as something simple. One points to this book there, neglects everything else and says only that it is red. This could have been motivated because someone had named something else "red," for example, the curtains, and one wishes to contradict him. The curtains are not red but violet. It is rather this book there on the table that is red.

The expression "red" signifies the color of the book here. The book *has* this color, at the moment this is not in doubt; no one whom one asked would call the book anything but, in German, *rot* [i.e., "red"]. This assent is only possible, however, because one can compare the color of the book with something else that is red; one must be able to *continue on* [*weitergehen*] with the same word, "red," to *pass over* [*übergehen*] from this thing to the next one. In this case, besides the book, still other things show themselves to have the same color; conversely, color shows itself as such only because one has gone on. The power of the word to show is confirmed here. If the book—and nothing else besides it—had a particular color, then it could not be signified with this word, indeed, with any of the familiar expressions for color. One could invent a name for it or attempt to circumscribe it with familiar expressions for color in various manners. Everyone, however, has an equal right to do this, up until one word prevails. As concerns the color of the red book, however, one can also point to something else, for example, to this round pillow there. Under the presupposition that one has learned what color is, one would immediately understand, in going over from book to pillow, that the form of the book is not intended and, just as little, its determination as something to be read. As concerns its form, the book is rectangular, as the picture there on the wall is too, though there is nothing red on it at all. As concerns the possible uses appropriate to the book, it belongs together with the newspaper, which may likewise be read. The white plate over there next to the book is, by contrast, round like the pillow.

Insofar as the concern is with the red book over there on the table, the expression "red" signifies the color of the book. However, the color *of the book* is obviously not the significance of the expression. The word "red" does not change its significance, when, instead of the color of the book, the color of the red pillow is signified. One could attempt to do justice to this by seeing the significance of a word like "red" in the fact that it can be correctly used for everything that is red. The significance of the word would not, then, be something particular, given respectively with it, but, rather, *the universal*.

But how, conversely, may the universal be grasped as the significance of an expression? May the universal be maintained at all as such, or is "the universal" nothing other than an expression for the sum of the individual cases? The universal is understood in this way for the first time by Aristotle. His word for "the universal" in German*—καθόλου, literally, "directed toward the whole"—is determined by him as "what, according to its nature, is present in many."[86] The stress here lies on "being present," ὑπάρχειν. The red color, though also something universal like "living being," is given only in something respectively present—the color in the respective red thing, the living being in the individual human being or in the individual horse.[87] As Aristotle adds, however, it is clear that one grasps the universal and can determine it in what it is linguistically; there is "something like a determination" of it (τις αὐτοῦ λόγος).[88] Even if the universal does not exist for itself it may be captured as such in the experience of it in respectively given things. What one has experienced in all of the given things may be brought to the fore: for example, "red," or "living being."

The Aristotelian consideration rests on the idea that the givenness of something is to be grasped exclusively as an independent presence. In this sense,

---

*[I.e., "das Allgemeine." —Trans.]

there can be no universal; it is not independently present. This, however, does not make it necessary to understand the universal as the result of an abstraction and then in consequence "nominalistically" as a mere construct of thought. The difficulty in ascribing an original givenness to the universal holds only if one takes orientation in one way or another from the Aristotelian idea of being as presence. This orientation misses what is decisive, for the universal of concern here is not after all supposed to be a being, but, rather, a phenomenon.

The difficulty mentioned remains even in Husserl, who is no doubt the most decisive critic of the nominalistic supposition in modern philosophy. When Husserl dismisses the accusation of being a "Platonic realist" with the argument that the understanding of the universal as "something" need not be intended in the sense of a "real" or actual thing,[89] the "objectivity" of the universal is thereby reaffirmed. The universal is, as the individual, originarily given in the "look onto the essence," although this givenness depends on the spontaneity of consciousness;[90] it is not present in existence but is rather only there in consciousness. In the *Logische Untersuchungen*, Husserl had already reinterpreted the process referred to as "abstraction" in intuitionistic terms and signified this process as the act by which an "abstract content . . . although not cut loose, nevertheless" becomes "one's own object of a concrete representation that is directed toward it."[91] This objectification does not change the fact that the content at issue is "nonindependent" because it cannot be "in and for itself" but is rather "possible only in or in regard to concrete contents."[92] Here, the Aristotelian orientation toward what is present remains determinative, though it is connected with the idea that the universal, insofar as it comes to consciousness, is also an "object" like other objects. For Husserl, the question of the status of the universal is solved by the distinction of independent and nonindependent objects—of such objects that can become objects *simpliciter* or only together with something else and "funded" by it.

When one is dealing with it, however, the universal is not always intended on the basis of something else. If something is signified as "red," the idea of "all possible red things" is not at all in play. Accordingly, one would not have to point out all possible red things to someone whom one is supposed to explain the significance of "red." It suffices to draw attention to the fact that not only this thing here is red but also that one over there. Other things are also red and one can pass over to them with the word. One only has to show that with the expression "red" one is not restricted to the respective case of its application. The word is something like a vehicle that allows one to traverse the range of what it is possible for him to show. This is the range of the word's significance. Significance is a determinate openness; it is a determinate possibility of the phenomenal, which is marked by a word, although not necessarily by this word alone. The word and every other one tantamount to it ascertains openness and makes it measurable. It is an openness that connects what can be shown in it with the capacity of the word to continue on and pass over. Insofar as what is shown is not only something red it may, at the same time, be at a remove from something else. Every significance is, in its determinacy, a determinate range of showing.

The "universality of the word" was also determined by Husserl in this sense. The passage in the sixth of the *Logische Untersuchungen* is thoroughly remarkable. For here, Husserl achieves an understanding of significance as it were in passing that differs from his considerations discussed up to this point. The determination basically leads beyond the orientation of acts of consciousness that grant significance.

The universality of the word implies "that one and the same word, through its unified meaning, embraces (and, when it is nonsensical, "pretends to embrace") an ideally, well-delimited manifold of possible intuitions, in such a way that each of the intuitions can function as the basis of a nominal act of cognition with the same meaning."[93] The word, then, does not have its significance—as Husserl puts it instead of "meaning" on the presupposition that meaning and significance are equivalent—because it belongs together with an act that grants significance and intends something but that does not necessarily arrive at its aim. In the first of the *Logischen Untersuchungen*, it was still said that "reference to the object" is constituted in significance, and, for this reason, "using an expression with meaning" is "the same thing as referring expressively to the object (representing the object)."[94] As Husserl now sees it, however, the word itself first announces the respective act of intending something and the possible enactment of this intending in an intuition; it "pretends," that is, it provides the pretense of determinate possibilities of intentions and their possible enactment. In fact, Husserl ties this pretense to the "possibility of referential cognitions."[95] But this just means that the "pretension" is not yet realized simply by the word. If one takes the word in its significance for itself, it is only a promise. It is only when one uses it that one enters into its significance and can recognize something in it, just as one can investigate the range of significance through use. When something is recognized it emerges in the context of the world as if it were intended in the context of signs. Showing and self-showing are connected under the yoke of the significance that is demarcated by signs in the texture of things.

To use a word like "red," means to show something red in the delimited range of its significance. Insofar as this succeeds, the significance of the word *shows itself*; red emerges. Significance no longer only enables the continuation and passing on of the word, but, rather, is fixed to something. This something, for example, the book, could also be shown differently than by the word "red"; first of all, one could, taking up the word "book," point and say, this is a book. Yet, when "red" is said, all other determinations recede. The very fact that this red something is a book may be unimportant; for a painter, for example, this fact could recede behind the color. With this receding of the other determinations, the red comes to the fore. This may be carried out methodically in painting, in such a way that the red alone or the increasing effect of color is set down. One thinks of Barnett Newman's pictures with the title, *Who is Afraid of Red, Yellow, and Blue?*

Both—coming to the fore and receding—belong together in such a way that one does not occur without the other. The receding determinations form the ground for the determination that comes to the fore; this one stands out against the others like a color against the ground of the picture. It is this emphasis that is intended in showing; the "this" or "this there," in which showing becomes explicit, aims at making significance apparent. The word, by which significance is demarcated, pauses [*hält inne*] and thus ascertains [*hält fest*] significance. It is ascertained through the pause of the word; in being ascertained, it is phenomenon.

Now, one should not think that showing concerns something present or a thing in order to ascertain one of its qualities. Considered solely on the basis of appearance, the determination of "something present" is a determination like any other. "Book" or "pillow," just like "red," are expressions whose significance is demonstrated in their capacity to continue on and pass over. Just as one can say that this book there is red, one could have named this red there a book. One can also continue on with the word "book"; what is shown in continuing on is not some individual thing, but, rather, a significance with other significances. Of course instead of always showing something in this significance, one could also concentrate on estimating its nuances, variants, and valences. The concern in this case is not with books, but rather with *the book* [*das Buch*], just as instead of *red* and *red* and *red*, the concern can be with *the red* [*das Rot*].[96]

Showing does not concern something present in every case, but, rather, reaches into the texture of possible determinacy, that is, into the *texture of significances*. It belongs in this texture and estimates its range by ascertaining something in it such that it can only be stressed in this texture. Because this occurs in the receding of other significances, that which shows itself remains at a remove from showing; it remains over against showing in its belongingness to what recedes. Every showing concerns a complex of significances but never shows everything that belongs to this complex. Some of them show themselves more or less clearly along with shown significance or significances, others remain on the edge and fade there like something co-perceived on the edge of one's field of vision.

What ultimately recedes with self-showing is not this or that significance. It is texture. This becomes recognizable in showing and self-showing as the fabric of significances that reaches beyond every act of emphasizing. This texture involves not only delimitations that are as if enfolded in it. It is rather also always unlimited and is thus something that always keeps itself in reserve, never completely shows itself. There are not enough words to demarcate texture completely; texture can therefore be openness for showing and self-showing, it is that which, from the perspective of showing, remains always and again at a remove. Texture is likewise that in which one maintains oneself and which one investigates by holding onto the demarcations of signs. Whenever this happens it is as if the texture crystallizes. In this case, something becomes phenomenon.

The essence of texture is disclosed in the significance that is determined. The word, and with it, showing, has significance. What shows itself, too, has significance; what shows itself is based on precisely the significance that the showing circulates in by holding firmly to a word. Significance *is* the ever-determinate correlation of showing and self-showing; it is the connective, the correlation itself in contrast to the correlates. Significance is correlation in the manner of phenomenality.

There is a word in Greek for what is common to a respective saying and what is shown and shows itself in this saying: εἶδος. What is intended by this word in pre-philosophical linguistic usage is something that is seen, and, based on this, a visible shape, that is, the *look* that it offers to a person. If in philosophy the word no longer indicates something visible but rather something conceivable, then it is no stretch to understand thought as a spiritual conceiving that is analogous to seeing. This analogy is already found in Plato.[97] In more recent philosophy, it is taken up with emphasis by Husserl in that he assigns "the sight of an essence [*Wesenserschauung*]"[98] or "originally given intuition [*Anschauung*]"[99] to the "eidetic object" or "essence."

On the one hand, this analogy is comprehensible, especially if one understands it from the standpoint of significance. That something shows itself as something determinate does occur in language, but it is no linguistic process in the strict sense. Rather, something garners our attentiveness as this determinate something and is simply there for our attentiveness—as if something simply stands in view. On the other hand, the serviceability of the analogy may be doubted, and, in fact, again from the standpoint of significance. What shows itself is indeed shown, and this suggests the suspicion that it always only shows itself as one shows it. In this case, the talk of spiritual seeing would be a self-deception; the self-showing would prove to be an effect of the fact that something can be said in such and such a way. The fact that looking at something and realizing it belong together[100] could be a reason to doubt in the possibility of proper looking.

This doubt is reminiscent of what Nietzsche calls the "perspectival character of existence,"[101] only that this character is not thought of on the basis of significance. This gives renewed weight to Nietzsche's idea. Namely, if there is something like a perspectivism of significance, then the objection against his conception of the will to power—that there would be no outside for it—no longer hits on what is decisive. For then the perspectival is outside, then it is itself installed in the exteriority of language, which is a manner of exteriority as a dimension of hermeneutical space. With every significance, a view would arise that is fulfilled only in that significance, such that with the next significance, the view would change. If one moreover takes into account the possibility of the combination of significances, then the view arising within such a combination could hardly be controlled; one would never know what all is in play in showing a demarcated significance, such that, strictly speaking, every showing would be unique.

This idea is not to be applied to the conception of significance developed here. Rather, the idea arises from the concept of texture. With this idea, the ungraspable, inexhaustible character of texture is taken as the point of departure for the understanding of showing and its significance; texture now appears in a dynamic or "fluctuation"[102] that ultimately determines the essence of saying that shows something.

Certainly, the fact that there are texts stands opposed to this idea. Yet there are texts, understood as fixed unities of significance, only in texture, such that the ambiguity of texture could also be that of the texts. In this case, every reading would be an unrepeatable trial run woven into the fabric of significances: although obligated to the text, never able to grasp it in its wholeness, although a manner of presentation, always only as a reading, summarizing for itself without ever reaching the text as an identical order. The text would keep in reserve like the texture.

Whether or not this is the case remains to be tested. The issue is *whether* there are fixed significances, and, if so, *how*. A positive answer as it is intended here would have to be developed by saying how fixed significances can be discovered in texture. Only in this case are there also presentations that allow the text itself to come into focus instead of what one refers to as the presentation of the text, thus appearing only like a disturbance on the surface of the water. Only if there are fixed significances in the texture are there writings that, in their significance, are not merely labyrinthine play but objects whose constancy is to be recognized in the presentation.

The question of whether there are fixed significances, however, concerns not only writings and everything comparable to them. It concerns life in language generally. Without fixed significances, the freedom of linguistic usage would only be restricted by habit, by social bonds, and by virtue of the fact that changes are generally slow and never concern a language as a whole. Nevertheless, the arbitrariness of linguistic usage would not be marginal. This arbitrariness would not simply concern individual deviations from what has been said previously or from what others say. In addition to this, the possibilities of translation would be so restricted that what is said or written could never be reproduced, except in a given nexus of significance that would once again be different in the next reading. And, finally, there would be nothing binding about how the concepts definitive for understanding and leading life are to be understood. Fundamentally, everything beyond convention and voluntary or compulsory social bonds would be permitted.

Just what this means is shown more precisely in the first two books of the *Republic*. The question of what a just life is and how a community can be constituted justly may only be posed meaningfully if the word central to the question has a binding and not merely a functionally determinable significance. Otherwise, as Thrasymachus asserts with a directness unaccustomed for even a sophist, the word is a label with which something conducive to respective interests of power is to be designated.[103] Every attempt, even every philosophical attempt, at a substantive determination would remain unclear about its proper status.

That one can employ a word like "just" in the service of his interests even when it has a substantively fixed significance is not prevented. Talk that is oriented toward the achievement and preservation of power probably determines public life on the presupposition of fixed significances no less than if there are not fixed significances. Yet, what is decisive is whether or not one must give the last word to the sophists. The debate with them only has sense if the objection against arbitrariness and the apology of it are grounded.

A fundament for this debate would be easier to achieve if one could call on an insight that is independent of language. If there is not such an insight—say, a kind of spiritual seeing—linguistic relativism first receives its full weight. Nevertheless, one does not have to capitulate in the face of such a relativism; the assertion that there are no fixed significances is neither evident nor trivial. This assertion is challenged by the assertion that things are otherwise, and, so, the former assertion is only to be held up as convincing if it refutes the assertion that challenges it; one would have to be able to show why it is self-deceptive to hold the conviction that there are fixed significances.

The philosophically most ambitious attempt to show this has been undertaken by Derrida. His undertaking is obliged in many respects by the orientation of Nietzsche's thought toward dynamization and fluidity.[104] Yet, whereas Nietzsche explains the opposition of self-deception and "sovereign becoming"[105] solely based on the need for stability and security,[106] Derrida further wishes to shed light on the *process* of the self-deception; he wishes to show how it occurs that one intends to hold on to fixed significances and that one fails to appreciate language as what Nietzsche calls an "army of metaphors, metonyms."[107] This occurs as the "deconstruction" of a certainty that Derrida understands as that of "voice." The question of speech, of the relation of speech and language returns again, then, in the debate with him. Now that language has been clarified from the standpoint of signs and significance, however, this question may be posed—and for this reason, also answered—with more refinement.

§ 26. Deconstruction of Voice

"Deconstruction" in Derrida's sense is, just like its model, intended as the dismantling of what has become fixed through force of habit. Like Heidegger's destructuring,[108] it aims "to break up" purported certainties in terms of "hidden motives, inexplicit tendencies and paths of interpretation and, in *dismantling return*, to penetrate to the originary sources of motivation of explication."[109] Yet, whereas Heidegger's concern is with the destructuring of received "representations of the being of human life,"[110] Derrida inquires into the hidden sources of the understanding of the significance of signs, which has fallen into familiar obviousness.

This occurs in departure from Saussure's conception of signs. Insofar as Derrida is convinced that this conception offers the possibility for positive development as much as an impetus for critique, it presents an ideal point of departure for him; it at once merits and requires deconstruction. Therefore, Derrida describes Saussure's achievement in its strengths and weaknesses.[111] Saussure clarified the inseparability of the signified (*signifié*) from signifier (*signifiant*), that is, from signs, in a convincing manner; signified and signifier are two sides of one and the same production.[112] Saussure furthermore "desubstantialized" the content of signs with the idea that signs are determined alone through their difference from one another.[113] But the concept of the sign nevertheless remains problematic because ambivalent. Saussure has taken it over from the metaphysical tradition and used it against this tradition, but nevertheless remained unable to free himself from the metaphysical implications of this concept.[114] Saussure, as it is put in another passage, stops at the limits of metaphysics: within metaphysics and beyond the metaphysical concept of the sign that he nevertheless uses.[115]

This is not intended as a critique of a lack of consistency. Derrida rather emphasizes that such a consistency cannot be achieved once one has decided in favor of a concept such as that of the sign; it is impossible to take up a concept and not, at the same time, remain bound to the implications that are inscribed in its system.[116] For Derrida, the central "metaphysical" implication of the sign obtains in the distinction between signifier and signified. This leaves the possibility of conceiving of an idea that is signified in itself,[117] and, because of this, the possibility of accepting something that is simply present for thought and thus independent from a system of signifying signs.[118] On the presupposition he takes over from Heidegger that the philosophical tradition from its beginning in Plato and Aristotle has conceived of beings as something in the proper sense present,[119] Derrida sees something in the sign that eludes the sign. For him, the concept of the sign as it were refutes itself because it releases the idea of something that is not signified and nevertheless present. Derrida calls it a "transcendental signified."[120] It is, as would have to be added, that for whose sake the sign is properly there: its significance.

Derrida cannot assign the metaphysical effect of the sign outlined here to the essence of the sign, however, and at the same time still take an anti-metaphysical strategy like Saussure's to be fundamentally intelligible. Therefore, he does not turn against the structure of the sign as such, but, rather, solely against the pretense of a transcendental signified. This, in turn, leads him to the philosophical critique of the distinction in which the structure of the sign is articulated; this is problematic insofar as it does not exclude the ossification of what is being distinguished. In the course of his critique it appears as if what is being distinguished can be maintained for itself in such a way that something perceptible and something spiritual were to comprise the two sides of the sign.[121]

Deconstruction begins from this ossification of the structure of the sign. It is supposed to show that the signified is not *in principle* distinguished from the signifier, but rather, is always already in the position of the signifier.[122] The sign then does not signify something beyond signs, but rather something that would itself have the character of a sign. What one refers to as significance would then be nothing other than a play of signs.[123] This still does not explain, though, how the "metaphysical" veneration of the signified comes about. One may only assert the no-longer "metaphysical" understanding of the sign as illuminative once this veneration is proven to be a problematic ossification and, in this, an effect of self-deception.

For Derrida, the veneration of the signified arises from the priority of speech over language. This priority determines Saussure's conception of language,[124] and not in fact coincidentally but rather because it is integral in the concept of the sign. The concept of the sign in itself entails the necessity of giving priority to phonic substance[125] because as signifying substance it provides consciousness with what is most intimately connected with the idea of the signified representation.[126] Phonic substance is *voice* (*la voix*). It is what, in virtue of its proximity to consciousness, signifies with the greatest precision and without appreciable deferral or carrying over. It is the signifier par excellence and, thus, the key to the understanding of the sign.

But more still: Insofar as the voice provides the idea of an actuality that is not separated from it, it can, as Derrida believes, be understood as consciousness itself.[127] The voice proves to be an instance of that inner experience of a spontaneous and underivable activity that is completely and exclusively the presentness of my representations, which are my own and thus at the same time unalienated. If I speak, as Derrida elucidates his view, then I am not only conscious that what I am thinking of is present to me. Moreover, I have the consciousness of preserving a signifier that is quite close to my idea or my representation. I hear what I utter and this appears to be dependent on my pure and free spontaneity. I need no instrument, no aid, no power that would be taken up in the world. The signifier and the signified not only appear to unite. Rather, in this confusion, the signifier appears to disappear or to become transparent so as to allow the representation to be present as what it is by itself in such a way that it refers to nothing other than its presentness. The exteriority of the signifier, as Derrida concludes this consideration, appears reduced.[128]

For Derrida, the experience of voice is therefore also the fundamental experience of metaphysics. It has, as the confusion (*confusion*) and illusion (*leurre*) that is it, determined the tradition from Plato up through Husserl. In order to illustrate the boundedness of "Logos"—one may certainly also say here: reason—to the experience of voice, Derrida also goes into the beginning of *De interpretatione*. The "Logocentrism" of Western thought is "phonocentrism," reason is an effect of speech.[129] If what is in the voice[130] is understood as a symbol of the states of the soul,[131] then the voice is thereby distinguished as the producer of the first symbols[132]; the voice signifies the state of the soul that for its part mirrors or reflects things because of its natural similarity.[133] In illustration, Derrida could also have referred to Humboldt and his understanding of language as an in itself complete and nevertheless unfinished work of spirit. Derrida sees the most recent epochal form of phonocentrism in Heidegger's elucidation of conscience as that of a "call"[134] and likewise in the idea that the human being is called "by the voice of being."[135] Heidegger is thus also placed into the metaphysical tradition, whereas only Saussure, as thinker of language at its limits, prepares the "closure"[136] of metaphysics with which Derrida is concerned. This closure is enacted with the deconstruction of the sign however interminably metaphysics may endure as the "epoch of the sign."[137]

Derrida's talk of the "phonocentrism" of the philosophical tradition is not unambiguous. Derrida of course does not wish to show that the tradition has taken orientation from the experience of the voice, but, rather, that the experience of the voice is the truth about the "metaphysical" constitution of *thought*. In this respect, precisely the *forgetfulness* of the voice would be metaphysical in Derrida's sense. The Aristotelian determination of language in *De Interpretatione* is in fact evidence for the priority of speech over language, but not for the understanding of reason based on speech. In Aristotle, the talk is not of the characteristic transparency of the sign in speech as Derrida emphasizes it. For Aristotle, the names of things, understood as signs, are "by agreement,"[138] that is, they always already belong in the world; they are shared and are thus able to serve communication.[139] It is not Aristotle's concern "to reduce the exteriority of the signifier."[140]

Such a reduction is there, however, when linguistic expressions are not only spoken to "announce" something, but rather, appear "in the solitary life of the soul." In this case, as Husserl has it in the first of the *Logische Untersuchungen*, the focus is not on "the word itself" at all: "the expression appears so as to direct interest from out of itself toward the meaning, toward this"—and this means "to point" toward the intended object insofar as it is intended. In this, the "nonexistence of the word" does not disturb us; "the focus is not on this at all" for "the function of the expression as expression."[141] Seen in this way, thought appears as a state between speech and nonspeech; one in fact deals with expressions, though one does not make anything known. This would be, as Husserl emphasizes, "wholly without purpose"; the acts of thought "are indeed in the same moment had by us in inner experience,"[142] so that we do not have to communicate them to ourselves.

These considerations are the point of departure for Derrida's discussion of voice as it is carried out for the first time in *La voix et le phénomène*.[143] One easily sees here that in Husserl himself the voice cannot appear at all. The focus is precisely not on the spoken word for expressions in the "solitary life of the soul." It is put out of effect and because of this one's attention can be directed toward what is expressed in an expression and not toward the expression; when there is nothing audible, the intentional content of what is in "inner experience" comes into view. Considered on this basis, there is already a deconstructive point lying in the replacement of the "solitary life of the soul" by the voice. Derrida wishes to show that consciousness is only purportedly with itself in silence and that this impression is in truth due to the experience of speech.

Derrida develops his idea in an analysis of the Husserlian distinction between "indication" [*Anzeige*] and "expression." In this, he understands the indication (*l'indice*), which points to something itself not given, as the proper sign, and supposes that Husserl also thinks so.[144] There are grounds for this. Husserl is of the conviction that "all expressions in communicative talk function as indications; they serve as signs for the one who hears the 'ideas' of the one who speaks, that is, for meaning-giving psychic inner experiences of this speaker, as well as for the other psychic inner experiences, which belong to the communicative intention."[145] By contrast, expressions in the solitary life of the soul are not "perceived" as "in existence."[146] As Derrida expresses it, they are nonexisting signs that show ideal significances, that is, significances that are nonexisting and specific because present in intuition.[147] They are signs in suspension, neither manifest nor completely extinguished. They have become as if transparent for the matter shown by them. This matter is no longer experienced as given in reality, but rather, only continues to be there for the activity of expression. With the consideration of expressions in the solitary life of the soul, the step is factually taken—a step tantamount to the phenomenological reduction—into the "sphere of ownness"[148] of consciousness that is independent[149] of everything exterior.[150] Yet, even if this comes into focus solely in a silence [*Schweigen*] that is a concealment [*Verschweigen*] of its linguistic character, speech proves to be the truth of concealed consciousness. The voice as it were reverberates in silence, it fills the silence with its reverberation, and, then, consciousness as such is transposed into exteriority.

In order to show this, Derrida initially develops the idea of the characteristic self-referentiality of the voice, which he elucidated in *Sémiologie et*

Grammatologie: something, an intentional correlate as something meant, finds expression in the voice such that the voice itself is at the same time for itself present. The voice *hears* itself without any requirement that a subject go out beyond himself, and, in this, the subject *understands* himself in what he hears. "*La voix s'entend*"[151]—this sentence, in virtue of the double meaning of *s'entendre*, contains both hearing and understanding. Consciousness understands itself only by hearing itself. In this respect, consciousness, which exists in "speaking-hearing-itself" and in "speaking-understanding-itself" (*s'entendre-parler*),[152] can be described as "self-affection."[153] This is pure, it is not an effect of consciousness mediated by something exterior, and because of this, as Derrida says, "without doubt" what one calls "subjectivity" (*subjectivité*) or "for-itself" (*pour-soi*).[154] Heidegger had already understood self-affection in this manner.[155] Conceived on the basis of voice, this self-affection is in any case a for-itself that owes itself to a doubling into an instance of speaking and hearing that can only appear as pure self-presence by means of the concealment of perceptible hearing. As soon as one gets clear about this and thus understands that the for-itself is given alone by a difference (*différence*) in self-presence the purported independence of consciousness becomes problematic. For with this difference, the exteriority that is supposed to be excluded from consciousness is there once again.[156] Consciousness does not refer to itself in what it hears, but rather refers to a sign that belongs in language. What is in consciousness points beyond consciousness. Consciousness does not have itself but rather a supplement that points toward outside.[157] Consciousness is dependent on this supplement for the suggestion of its self-presence, and, in this respect, the supplement is that of a lack[158]; consciousness proves to be an originary nonpresence of itself.[159] The voice, itself the ground of the self-presence of consciousness on the one hand, reveals the exteriority of consciousness on the other. It turns out that the voice belongs in the context of a language that is alien to it and that is appropriated as if with intimacy only in the moment of speech. It belongs, as Derrida says, in *writing*.[160] What has always been seen as the disadvantage of writing in the tradition: Its secondary status in contrast to oral expression,[161] now proves to be its advantage. This is one of Derrida's most significant insights: Writing is not a belated fixing of talk, but instead language itself in its exteriority.

This exteriority is insurmountable because what is signified by the voice is only apparently a content of consciousness. The conviction that there is such a content arises with signification because signification is enacted as a conscious act. It becomes connected with the impression that one also has the content of the signification, that is, with Husserl: its intentional correlate. Such a correlate is only there with the sign, however, that is, only as something indicated. If one wished to grasp it, one would have to name it, that is, signify it again, so that it escapes anew. Every sign is a *trace*[162]; the signified is always already withdrawn in such a way that it is "always in the position of the signifier."[163] Whoever seeks contents finds new signs.

It is this characteristic occurrence of exteriority that withholds, which Derrida signifies with his celebrated neologism *différance*. *Différance* is the "operation of difference and deferral"—the verb *différer* means both—"that at once tears open and defers presence and thus subjugates it in one stroke to the originary separation and the originary deferral."[164] Insofar as the occurrence of *différance* concerns not only the relation of a signification that wants to express itself[165] to an indication in its exteriority but rather every transition from one sign to the next, Derrida can determine *différance* as the "systematic play of differences."[166] Language is play as a consequence of infinite substitutions in the enclosure of a finite context.[167] With every sign or complex of signs one always comes into the context of signs anew and differently because significance never becomes manifest with any sign. The "deferral" (*retard*) of which Derrida speaks does not open the possibility of a reference but rather prevents the significance from being grasped. Speech may be intended as a showing but nothing shows itself in it; everything remains unshown. The essence of writing is indication. In every attempt to signify "something" that one wishes to get hold of, in every attempt to signify it differently so as to grasp it more precisely, something is added to what is said. The addition does not enrich the picture of a matter, however, but instead steps in always in a different manner for what the one holding onto a signification takes to be the matter.[168] Because "the matter" is not simply given, the play of significances is infinite in the finitude of every language. Accordingly, every attempt to determine something is "bricolage" (*bricolage*) as Derrida puts it in a concept from Claude Lévi-Strauss. *Bricolage* is the movement in language that can never be sure of language as a whole because there is no Archimedean point for the reconstruction of language in its totality.[169] Language is an arrangement whose elements always reorder themselves anew as elements. These elements are not given in such a way that one can determine them for themselves and, then, establish their differences. Rather, what one refers to as "elements" is nothing other than the play of differences that is always and again forming anew. *Différance*, this is the occurrence of the distance through which the elements of language are referred to one another.[170] In *différance*, for Derrida, language has its openness, that is, its dimensionality.

The question, however, is whether the dimensionality of language may be understood as Derrida describes it. This question is concretized as that of his understanding of voice; this is the presupposition for his understanding of writing. The idea of *différance* as the idea of a removal between signs that always and again defers significance is conceived on the basis of the certitude about significance accompanying the voice, and, with this, is conceived on the basis of consciousness. The experience of the "trace," the escape of significance, can only be had in the expectation of a transcendental signified, of a *signifié transcendental*. The trace is given only for a consciousness that both wants to grasp a significance as significance itself and then has the inner experience of the disappointment of its boundedness in the chain of signs.

If Derrida had not taken his point of departure from Husserl's conception of consciousness and its "sphere of ownness" then he could also have taken up Saussure's concept of the sign differently and more properly. Thus, the dynamization of the difference of signs that is indicated by the concept of *différance* comes at the price of obscuring the idea central for Saussure. Saussure had after all wished to show that signs have the determinacy that makes them suitable as signs in their difference from one another. Precisely this determinacy dissolves in its dynamization. According to Derrida's description, one passes through signs in an incalculable play that makes every sign always and again different through new constellations. *Différance* is not only the postponement [*Aufschub*] of significance, but, also the deferral [*Verschiebung*] of signs. Because of this, it is not possible to understand why signs are still recognizable as determinate ones. Accordingly, it remains open how the play of signs can be what Derrida says of it: a "systematic play,"[171] that is, a play whose elements form a whole, a plan with rules and order.

Derrida's answer to the question of the essence of the connectedness of signs is aporetic. On the one hand, he refuses the concept of structure,[172] which derives from the context of architecture and, in this way, is static; the idea of *différance* is incompatible with the static, synchronic, taxonomic, ahistorical, and so on, motive for the concept of structure.[173] On the other hand, he does not hold this motive for the only one that can be used as the basis for defining structure; rather, *différance* produces systematic and regulated transformations.[174] Only the dynamic character of the system is decisive; the focus is on "the *production* of a system of differences,"[175] and, by contrast, it is of secondary importance that this can be presented through abstraction and in accord with the aforementioned motives as a structure. There is a difficulty, however, that Derrida does not resolve here: How is *différance* able to produce differences and, at the same time, be incompatible with their systematic description? If the description is not to be an abstraction it has to accord with its matter, and then it is not at all possible except as "static, synchronic, taxonomic, and ahistorical." But then, conversely, language may no longer be made intelligible based on the idea of *différance* alone. It is dynamic and static at the same time.[176]

The question of how to understand this more precisely may be posed with Derrida's concepts; it is the question of the relation of voice and writing. The attempt to answer it can begin with the voice, and, in fact, initially with the description that Derrida gives of it. According to this description, it accords with the essence of voice that it is for itself. Its elocution, however, does not properly match that silent solitude of the life of the soul with which Derrida associates it. It rather accords with the essence of voice that it is oriented toward communication; the exteriority, which it also has for Derrida in its dependence on signs, comes to expression in communication. For the voice, speaking with others is not an interruption of self-affection, but, rather, normalcy. It only appears otherwise if the voice is understood based on the idea of a spontaneous—and, in this, also pure—self-reference. Derrida imposes this idea on the experience of the voice and, because of this, isolates it in a manner inadequate to it. This does not mean that Derrida's conception of voice is completely mistaken. There is the experience of voice as he describes it; one always experiences himself along with his own voice. Yet, it is only possible to describe the experience of the self adequately if one takes up the communicative essence of the voice. What the voice is can only be shown by describing it in its exteriority. The focus is on how it is positioned in its exteriority.

§ 27. Positions

One perceives one's own voice as soon as it resounds. One hears it, and those who are deaf feel the resounding in the vibration of the sound. One knows that one can be heard solely by hearing. Whoever wants to be undiscovered or unnoticed is quiet. It is possible to contemplate, to smell, to feel in secret. To raise one's voice in secret, however, is nonsense. Whoever makes himself heard is hearable; one knows this because one hears oneself.

There is thus what one could call with Merleau-Ponty[177] a chiasm, that is, a fold, of the voice, and this chiasm is clearer in the voice than in any other corporeal activity. Seeing and being seen, touching and being touched, also belong together: One not only sees, but, rather, is visible even for oneself; this is attested to not first by the mirror but rather by every look down at oneself. One not only touches something else, but, rather, can also touch even one's hand that is touching. Seeing, however, can be forgetful of itself, giving itself completely over to something that stands in view. In this it is comparable to touching. There is not this self-forgetfulness in the voice. It is possible to hear oneself when one speaks to oneself under one's breath, even in unnoticed humming, moaning, or singing. By raising one's voice, one is outside and nevertheless does not get free from oneself.

This also means: by hearing oneself, one experiences oneself not as if from outside, as if from the perspective of someone else; one hears oneself, one does not listen to oneself. In order to listen to oneself one's own voice would have to be recorded and reproduced. To hear one's voice in this way is disconcerting, at least initially. Something resounds there that is alien, and one is aware of its characteristics with embarrassment. This shows that exteriority is to be distinguished from what is alien. The voice is always exterior, whereas it is only alien under certain circumstances. The voice is not a "self-affection." Rather, one is in the world as in no other way when one raises one's voice. The experience of one's own thingliness does not lie in seeing oneself, however; touching one's own hand is not yet the experience of how other things in the world are touchable. In order to experience oneself as a thing among things, as Merleau-Ponty puts it,[178] one always has to disregard how one experiences oneself. Even if one rests one's own hand on the desk or sees one's hand lead a pencil across paper, for him it is not the same as pencil, paper, and desk. One would never say of it: It is *something*. It would always be: That is *I*. It is precisely the same way with one's voice. *One himself*, and not only something of himself, is outside; in hearing oneself, one knows in every moment that one is effective and perceptible. Whoever raises his voice is never for himself alone, but, rather, also always for others. One is voice and hearing at the same time—and, in fact, in such a way that one *knows* of his own elocution that is outside. This knowledge is often only a thoughtless, incorporated certainty. As such, however, it sustains the voice and determines its resounding. By raising one's voice, one wishes, more or less explicitly, to be for others. One does not see in order to be seen. Touching is possible without occurring for the sake of being touched, and, for the most part, it is carried out in this way. Raising one's voice, however, this means: wanting to be heard.

The fact that it is one himself who raises his own voice and the fact that one wants to be heard—these belong together. The sound of one's voice is not supposed to be like a sound or noise among others; one wants to make himself heard, to make himself heard as unmistakably as one hears himself. Hearing oneself carries this desire; in the certainty that one can be heard, one's striving to be heard is initiated and bolstered.

Whoever wants to make himself heard does not have to speak. Even the scream, say out of joy, fear, or distress—all the more the scream while under attack—is supposed to be hearable. The scream is supposed to reveal what one wants and how one is, it is a cry for help or is supposed to shock an opponent.

What the voice is as such is thus already recognizable in the scream: The voice is *expression*, a conduct, which wants to be nothing but outside, recognizable for others. This distinguishes it from facial expressions and gestures. These, in fact, let one read how someone is doing. Because they are not immediately present to the one whose expression it is, however, they are missing what comprises the essence of the voice. It does not belong to the essence of faces and gestures that they are intended as an expression; in general they are involuntary, and indeed they are supposed to be; it feels uncomfortable when someone who is not an actor uses them in a recognizable manner as possibilities of expression. What goes without saying for the voice is not readily accepted in regard to faces and gestures. This only changes when they step into the role of the voice, say, in the case when one can only make himself heard through a gesture because the sound of his voice cannot get across.

That the voice is in its essence an intended expression does not mean that what it wants to express is clear. It is possible to misinterpret screaming as well as groaning. It is unambiguous, however, *that* the voice is an expression. It is only for this reason that one engages in raising one's voice. As soon as a human voice resounds, *someone* is present—his voice or the person himself. One is only able to put this aside when one recognizes that it is not he but someone else who is intended. Otherwise, hearing is only overhearing. One can turn one's glance away, but if one has not forcibly closed one's ears, the voice still reverberates even when one looks away. It calls after the one who attempts to flee into indifference.

That the voice is an intended expression holds for every instance of speech and is communicated in every instance of speech. The voice itself is the expression here, as it is in unarticulated sound, and this means: not what is said [*das Gesagte*]. What is said could be said with a very different expression; it is not bound to an expression even if one automatically connects a certain expression with it. What is said can substantively come to expression in this way, but it first becomes an expression because someone *communicates himself.*

To communicate oneself means being there for others as oneself. Even if this is possible through any arbitrary sentence uttered in response to other sentences because the focus is not on what is said as such, there are nevertheless words that make the expression itself intelligible. The fundamental word of the expression is "I." Even if the word is generally countered among the indexicals and so taken together with words like "here," "now," or "this," it is different from them in the decisive issue. This word does in fact always signify the one who uses it, just as "here" always intends the place at which the word is used, and "now" always the time at which one uses the word. Likewise, "this" belongs in the context of the respective showing, in which what is respectively shown is referred to. "I" is nevertheless different, however, because with this word speech itself is made intelligible.

"I" is the fundamental word of the voice. Whoever says a sentence with "I" puts himself into play, not as this specific "I" but as speaker. One does not simply point something out, but above all shows himself as the one who sees, conceives, or assesses something in such and such a way. One shows how one positions himself toward something, and with this how he, in this respect, is positioned; one takes up a position [*Stellung*]. Whoever says "I" moves into *position* [*Position*]. "I" is a position-word [*Positionswort*] more than an indexical [*Indexwort*].

It obviously only makes sense to say I when it occurs *for someone*, and so taking a position is also always an *address*. In addressing someone, one turns to someone[179] who is at a remove from oneself as someone else. The address traverses this removal, it establishes a connection that only exists at a removal because it leaves the other in his remoteness; the other can answer but is never compelled to answer.

Because one's voice is an address, its fundamental word "I" belongs together with another fundamental word, namely, with "you."[180] With this word the voice finds its direction, or, as one can say: its intention. One's voice does not intend something, but, rather, someone. In elocution, it goes into the openness of speech toward someone and wants to reach him. Someone who is addressed should do what one does himself: hear. What one only experiences as the exteriority of his own voice himself, however, is supposed to be realized by the one who is addressed as he turns his attention to it. Someone who is addressed is not only supposed to hear—this occurs of its own accord if normal conditions for it are in place; the issue for the one speaking is, rather, that the one who is addressed *listens*. The resounding of the voice is thus not primarily an acoustic process; only when one does not recognize the voice as such can it be one sound among others. The voice has the direction of the address of its own accord; listening to the voice perceives this direction and is attentiveness simply by virtue of the fact that it discerns the voice from all other sounds. It is in its essence different from the collected attentiveness that, with Heidegger, would have to be understood as the essence of "listening to language,"[181] even if it would be determined through such attentiveness. Listening to the voice is a hearing of a *claim*. The face of the other does not make us responsible; one is able to turn away from the face. It is rather the voice that calls one into responsibility; one ought to [*soll*] answer to the voice.[182]

To listen, this means to take up what the other says. More important still is the intention of communication; in listening one is supposed to take up what the other *wants* to say, and how, in speaking, he positions himself toward what he says. In a word, one is supposed to perceive the position of the other. This always involves cognizing [*Erkennung*] and recognizing [*Anerkennung*] that it is a position in the first place. Recognition obtains only in the removal between voice and hearing[183]; it is not an *a priori* process, but rather something that takes place anew in every understanding. Recognition, however, is not a special kind of devotion of attention distinguishable from others. That one recognizes the position of someone speaking has no consequence for how one positions oneself toward that speaker. Recognition refers to the positional as such; it is the opposite of disregard as it comes into focus in ignoring [*Überhören*], and, so, already lies in listening itself. Once cannot listen without at the same time also recognizing. In this, recognition is guided by understanding; one's own position is reflected based on the other's, the other's based on one's own, although the positions need not thereby necessarily come to agreement or be settled. Understanding is not a normative concept; one has to have understood even what one wants to reject, and, in this, one's rejection can indeed grow with understanding; without understanding, one does not reject, but simply refuses to consider.

Recognition concerns not only the other but also the one recognizing. The agreement to get involved in the *play* of positions belongs to it. It is play in the sense Derrida ascribes to signs, that is, the kind of play that is always only determined as a respective ensemble of positions. One is able to open up the play by raising one's voice. The one who is speaking, however, will very soon have to adjust to the positions of the others who are challenged by his speaking. Positions are not as rigid and fixed as the word could suggest. In its belongingness with other positions, a position can be modified, also relativized and revoked, and this immediately influences the other positions belonging to the play.

A position is always only given, then, together with other positions. For this reason, the resolution of positions requires listening, in whatever form. Up to a certain degree, one has to give credence to the other and accept what he has said. Unity is required even in dispute; one must at least be in agreement concerning what the dispute is about. If one were not, however, elementarily in agreement with the other, even reflection on one's own position could no longer succeed.

In its reflexivity, every position belongs together with other positions; as soon as an address succeeds and has been turned to and recognized, positions are in *conversation* with one another.[184] The conversation does not have to have a common "basis"; its commonality often only arises through the reflexivity of positions. Even a debate [*Streitsgespräch*] is conversation [*Gespräch*], except that in debate the reflexivity of positions reaches a tension, in which what is unacceptable, sometimes irreconcilable, presses apart even as one remains unable to get loose from the other position. As long as one remains in a conversation of this kind, the openness between the voice and hearing will nevertheless always be what determines the relation to one another. The conversation thus remains a play between expectation and fulfillment or refusal, between agreement and demarcation, inclusion and exclusion. The play is interminable; the one who is excluded belongs no less than the one whom we take to be "one of us" in the exteriority that play is. Regardless of what position one has—one always remains at a remove *from one another*.

The latter especially comes into focus when "I," as the fundamental word of voice, is modified to "we," and, accordingly, "you" [in the singular] to "you" [in the plural] or to "they."* In this, the "we" is not said in unison, its realization is not the matter for a choir. Usually it is one person who says "we"

---

*[In original German: "...*das 'du' zum 'ihr' wird oder zum also Mehrzahl verstandenen 'sie.'*" — Trans.]

and, with this, includes others in order to be included. By contrast, "you" [in the plural] is excluding, "they"—like "he"—puts someone outside of the conversation. This often occurs for the sake of an inclusion; the point is to make clear that the excluded position cannot be unified with one's own. It is also possible, however, to turn to "the others" in order that they take up and share one's own position.

Like all speech, speech in the play of positions is a showing. What is shown, however, is not in the first instance something, but, rather, someone. By raising one's voice, one shows *oneself*; one claims attentiveness and attention, and, in this, one lets oneself be recognized in some manner. Speech is always also a *self-identification*. This includes the account of what one has done and does, the elucidation of one's own activity and the attempt to put this in the context of the activity of others, the elementary or complex autobiographical narrative; in these things, however, the concern is less with the outlined matters of fact as with one himself.[185]

Expressions of this kind are moreover usually connected with an expectation that goes beyond that of listening. One expects that the other adjust to one's own position, and this expectation is shown in an *instruction*, say, in the form of a request or a command. To call this a speech act or a communicative action[186] does not in every respect do justice to the matter. In fact, command and request have the character of action insofar as something is supposed to be achieved by them. The expression of a request or of a command is neither a cause nor an effect, however, because the other can withdraw from both of them. One does not cause anything, but, rather, expects that the other cause something. Things are the other way around when one, say, makes assurances or a promise in answer to a request. This, too, may only be understood as an action with qualification. On the one hand, one has an intention, for example, that of retaining or earning the trust of the other. Yet, on the other hand, one does not act but rather only points out that one intends or at least wishes to endeavor to act in a certain manner. Linguistic action is the attempt to cause something through showing. The ambiguity of the attempt makes it clear that showing may be integrated into the context of intentional activity, but that acting and showing are accordingly different in their essence.

Finally, identification and instruction must in one manner or another accompany an *assertion* of a matter of fact. If one says he is not well and he requests help, this includes the assertion that he will not come to grips with the situation he is in by his own power. The assertion itself can already be the indirect formulation of an expression and an expectation. In no case is it "neutral"—as if one only ascertained a matter of fact and was to arrive at moments of expression and expectation like overtones. The assertion will always be "colored" by the intention of identification and the intention of instruction; it is not the simple ascertainment of a matter of fact but rather an intention of assertion. One often only sees that things might be different than one had asserted when one reflects, that is, when one can consider identification and instruction based on the asserted matter of fact anew.

In the play of positions, however, this is always only possible within limits. Even if the assertion is not dominated by one's interest in making himself intelligible and if the expectation made on others also recedes, it remains an assertion, that means an ascertainment that is in play together with other factical or possible ascertainments. The assertion stands over and across as well as over and against these other ones. This, and not an always-individual will of assertion, is the reason that the deployment of the power to convince belongs essentially to assertion. To be convinced by something means: to have taken a position and to take a position. Assertion, too, is positional.

Because the focus of raising one's voice is on the generation and reinforcement of positions, the possibility of *rhetoric* lies in speech; speech is predisposed to being developed as a kind of craft concerned with convincing.[187] The rhetorical is one possibility of the voice itself, and this possibility is given solely through its resounding. Someone's voice can address one so that one not only hears its claim but also cannot withdraw from its sound. The voice speaks from out of trustworthiness, enthusiasm for a subject matter, the voice awakens sympathy or understanding, and it can represent "our" interests against others so that one feels a sense of belonging to the party, group, or community represented by it. The skillful arrangement of talk, the clarity of sentence construction and expression, are answerable to the presentation [*Vortrag*] itself. They have to prove themselves here, and they are of little use when one's voice does not carry the presentation [*Vortrag*].[188] Talk is like a resounding river that carries and sweeps one along so that one asks less about what is said. The most substantive talk thus still has a fundamentally nonsubstantive trait.

This changes with the shift from the voice to writing. Writing has the effect of deferring; it favors pausing. Whoever wishes to read and understand looks more precisely and questions. The impression of evidence as it belongs to the voice is put out of effect here. The position from which one has spoken loses significance, and, likewise, as reader one is no longer transposed into a position. The position from which speech has arisen loses in significance, and likewise one, as reader, is no longer transposed into a position. What is read does not address, it demands nothing; one is no less free to read than one is to interrupt reading. Writing is language outside of the voice; it is the exterior, withdrawn from wanting to say and to be heard, and, in this way, the "pure" word.[189]

In a conversation that endeavors to be substantive, it is necessary to take back the positioning of one's voice; one brackets it and puts it out of effect. Through this ἐποχή what is said stands for itself; even if it is articulated in conversation, it no longer holds only in the enactment of speech. The voice retreats, it enters into the service of what is said. This shows that what is said is not in its essence something said in the sense of something spoken, but rather that what is said can also exist in language in a different form: in language insofar as it is not speech and, in this way, *nonlanguage*, that is, writing. In writing, what is said is indeed more what it is; it is free of every positioning, and a voice in retreat wants to preserve just this. Writing is closer to substantiveness; it is always the written that was what was substantial under the surface of the voice.

That the voice is put into the service of the written occurs in presentation, already in a presentation that is performance. In recitation and lecture, the voice is not there for its own sake, but rather for the sake of what it speaks. In this, the voice is no longer an address, but rather speaking that has become free of conversation; it is in fact heard, but does not demand that one turn one's attention to it. The voice is simply there by reason of what it presents; this is the case in song even more than in speech.[190]

It is true that in performance, one labors for the sake of a matter and not for the sake of one's own substantiveness. The matter does in fact have to be shown in order that it can show itself. But what is supposed to show itself is clearly outlined; as a text that is put down in writing it is well determined and stands as object. This is also how it is in the explication and clarification of objects. This provides a model for substantive speech, but it does not fill out its possibilities. The substantiveness at issue now is a counterweight to the positionality of the voice. It is demonstrated in the presentation of something that, although there in the voice, nevertheless remains hidden and displaced as long as it remains in the life-worldly grip of positionality—distorted through interests, needs, power struggles, and compromise. It is the presentation of the significances that sustain speech and no less writing oriented by speech without being taken into consideration. These significances become free as such when they become grasped in writing, transposed as something objective in the freedom of things. Written thought corresponds to them. In Plato this is called "dialectic."

§ 28. Written Thought

The word "dialectic" has to do with conversation. διαλέγεσθαι means "to have a discussion," so that διαλέκτικὴ τέχνη would be the art of holding conversation. As soon as the expression is used philosophically, however, the focus is hardly still on factical talking with one another. The concern is now no longer with the exchange of words and, in this, the exchange of ideas and opinions, but, instead, with speaking thoroughly about a matter. Saying no longer counts as expression, even if it of course still is expression. Expression retreats in favor of a matter.

The matter at issue in it, therefore, also is completely of its own kind. It is not a case of conflict that is at hand and, in virtue of this, pressing. It is also not a problem that has to be resolved now for the sake of the possibility of further action. What is of interest is not a particular event of interest only in its particularity. Thus, dialectics in its substantiveness is not only an illuminating interruption of action and positional speech; it is not a mere pause but rather speech that refuses what is pressing, what requires clarification in the situation, and, with this, what is given only here and now—the this-there. In all of these respects, it is abstention, ἐποχή, and it is originary: rising out of everyday speech and escaping it.

In dialectic, one turns away from the natural direction of saying. Here, the turn that Husserl wished to understand as a reflective one of consciousness toward itself occurs in language. But how is one supposed to direct oneself toward ideas, if not in such a way that one comprehends them linguistically? And how can one reflect on them other than through concentration on their linguistic composition? That the phenomenological ἐποχή is a turn in language is hidden as long as consciousness appears as if free of language. As soon as—with Derrida—its linguisticality is made apparent, the fundamental movement of phenomenology presents itself differently: It can only be enacted as dialectic, that is, in written thought.

One sees how to understand this more precisely in the so-called "analogy of the divided line" in the *Republic*. Here, being in language is described in regard to the example of geometry. In this, a distinction between two fundamental dispositions is made clear and, thus, the possibility of dialectic is introduced. When geometers make their calculations, their concern is not with the circle drawn with chalk on the blackboard, with a foot in the sand, but rather with what is mathematically determinable. But they nevertheless refer to the visible. They convey what they say by way of visible figures, although of course they do not think about this but rather about things that are similar to the visible figures; when they speak, their concern is with the quadrilateral itself and its diagonals, not with the quadrilateral they draw.[191] Geometers accordingly find themselves in a half-dreaming state as concerns language. They intend something other than what they put into language, and this is the basis of the confusion concerning the similarity of the two. They remain biased by what is demonstrated [*dem Aufgezeigten*]—which something visible stands for here—even though their actual concern is with what they ascribe to what is demonstrated, namely, significance, understood as εἶδος.

This bias is problematic because it prevents a clarification of significances. If a view is cast toward something respectively given even if only to grasp something that is not merely given in regard to it, the significance remains as it were in the shadows. For geometers it is the foundation of demonstrating, more precisely: something that they allow to be the foundation in that they disregard it in the normal direction of speaking. In this it is possible to be thoroughly aware that the significance exists as such. In the half-dreaming state of the geometers this is indeed openly admitted; geometers are not, as can also happen, in any way biased by demonstration, that is, caught unawares about significance. Rather, they relate to significance by "putting" the significance "underneath" [*darunterstellen*] their demonstration. They *suppose* [*unterstellen*]—in a neutral, not at all pejorative sense—the even and the odd and geometrical figures and the three kinds of angles and other related things in accord with a respective procedure. By supposing this as if they knew it, taking it as ὑπόθεσις, they do not regard it as worth proving, neither to themselves nor to others, as if it were entirely obvious.[192]

This state of geometers is instructive in numerous regards. It is the state of the type of cognition that one must understand as that of the "arts" (τέχναι).[193] This state makes it clear that there are significances, as distinguished from respective things with significance, even in cognition that is guided by the everyday life-world. Ideas are no invention of philosophers; the claim that there are ideas is in fact quite trivial,[194] an art like geometry would be impossible without them. For geometers, it is in fact only half-clear what ideas or significances are because geometers do not move among significances as if it were their natural element. Rather, they suppose them. Significances are not familiar and obvious. Rather, they are *posited* in familiar obviousness—as something that on the one hand is supposed to function as obvious and that, on the other hand, cannot really be. Geometers thus experience what has significance not simply in this or that particular case. They know that what has significance stands as something demonstrable, for they do not intend this or that particular case but rather what remains the same in all of them: the significance, the εἶδος. This does not become clear to them, however, in the suppositional character of their procedure.

The state of geometers also makes it clear how the dreaminess essential to them could be overcome. To awaken, this means: to arise from the half-obviousness of supposition. This may at first be like a shock, as, say, when someone whom one had not noticed turns on the light in a previously dimly lit room. The shock is a movement from out of the dimness into the brightness of clearly distinguishable contours. For the half-dreaming state of geometers, this awakening would be tantamount to a possible shift of attentiveness; what was previously posed in obviousness can now gain full attention.

This does not actually occur in the manner that the images of light and of looking in the *Republic* suggest. Because the state of geometers is a state in language, the shift has to occur as a shift in language. This, in turn, is not to be thought of solely or principally as a shift in attitude—in such a way that one takes the word differently than before. Rather, the word itself turns around; it becomes an object and, all at once, it is no longer significant of anything but instead remains only significance. What can be conferred is no longer determined on the basis of conferral, but, rather, simply stands there for itself in the word.

In the *Republic* the possibility and power operative in this turn-around is determined as that of dialectic. What is meant by this is not a power of reason or of spirit that partakes of the word, but, rather, the characteristic power of the word. It is the word itself—αὐτὸς ὁ λόγος that, with dialectical power, fixes on a significance in the sense of an εἶδος;[195] the word shifts over into the possibility of dialectical thought by emerging as "pure word" and making significance as such accessible. Its comprehension is distinguished from going through something demonstrated (διάνοια) as a "perceiving" (νόησις).[196] This, however, has nothing to do with visible evidence. What is decisive, rather, is that the νόησις is grasped as λόγος. Even if one should resolve to render this word in the aforementioned passage as Schleiermacher did with "reason"—how can one not read along with λόγος the linguistic essence of such reason? A thought without intention, that is, without direction toward something respectively given, which is supposed to show itself as something, is given only in language and only because one perceives it as a linguistic possibility.

The pure word stands in contrast here to given spoken words. The pure word is not linguistic in the sense of the voice. Even if it is spoken, it receives its sense from writing, which simply puts down significances and lets them stand. Putting down a significance in this manner is embodied in the step from using a word to referring to its significance. Conversely, putting down a significance is not possible without the word. If one were not concentrated on the word, one would refer to something demonstrated in a determinate significance, that is, to "this there"; it would always be something that showed itself, but not its significance. In order to grasp ideas or significances, one has to flee into the λόγοι,[197] that is, into what is ascertained in nonlanguage.

The significance that is put down in, written down with, the word does not have the character of a supposition. The word is taken without any intention to point something out and no longer has any direction to its significance but rather only significance *simpliciter*; it has significance and stands for the significance. Taking the word as something that is completely non-suppositional, it is possible to pose the unbiased question of how to understand significance itself. Now the significances are no longer the beginnings (ἀρχαί) of demonstration, but rather, "genuine suppositions,"[198] as it were entry ways and trial runs,[199] that allow one to reach what is nonsuppositional at the beginning of the whole.[200]

Earlier in the *Republic*, this beginning of the whole had been discussed as the idea of the good. What the good has to do with the turn from what is demonstrated to significances proceeds from its elucidation: With the good, no one is satisfied to grasp what appears but rather seeks what is and, in this, despises appearance.[201] Understood in this way, the good is "that, which every soul purses and that for the sake of which it in fact does everything, sensing through divine inspiration that it is something, about which, however, it is at a loss, and which it does not always sufficiently know how to grasp in practice and does not know how to use through a firm trust as it does with other things."[202] The good as such closes itself off from the familiar obviousness of supposition; it is in its essence something nonsuppositional. The question of the good leads beyond all connection to what is familiar, also to what is only conventional, so that with it, the openness of the divine, which is to be conceived as something without appearance and deception, steps into human life. If one at all asks himself what he should do, implied in this is the interest in a sincere answer; otherwise one could not even ask, and if one is satisfied only with a superficial answer, with what is comfortable, obvious, esteemed, and expected by others, this is an evasion of the point—not only of the perhaps uncomfortable answer, but of the question itself.

In action—and, connected with this, in positional speech—the unfailing character of the good remains like a light that is remote and always easily confused. Due to insecurity, weakness, or obsequiousness, though no less due to assertiveness, obstinacy, and narrow-mindedness, one gives up the question. One wants to do something and thereby pull through, one wants to assert oneself. The pause for questioning often lasts only for a moment.

Accordingly, one's interest in the sincere answer may only be protected if one wants to grasp what should be done in its essence. Whether one's plans can succeed, whether it would be prudent, courageous, or just can only be decided if one has discovered what prudence, courage, and justice actually are. Thus, the interest in the good that belongs to the structure of action leads as if of its own accord to contemplation. Conversely, this movement is sustained by an orientation toward the good; whoever turns one's attention to significances has been oriented by the impulse toward truth that belongs to the good and he has come to know, however unclearly, that appearances are not everything.

Nevertheless, the relation of the good and significances, that is, the εἴδη, is not circular. The good can lead to the explicit question about the εἴδη because it is itself eidetic in a *preeminent* sense. Because the good may only be recognized from out of the openness of the question, it is ἀνυπόθετον, something nonsuppositional; it not only stands outside of the trust in givenness (πίστις) that is characteristic of everyday action and positional speech, it also does not admit of being made into an obviously familiar point of departure for knowledge bound to appearance. Because of this, it must and can lead to overcoming the half-dreaming state toward which, for example, the geometers are biased. It is not from some other source that the good is realized in the turn to significances but rather of its own accord. It can only be the impulse to truthfulness because it is eidetic through and through, concentrated, εἶδος refusing every appearance of itself, pure significance. Accordingly, in the question of the good the concern is always with something itself.²⁰³

It is in this sense that the good can also be named τοῦ πάντος αρχή, the beginning of the whole. It is a more truthful—because nonsuppositional—beginning²⁰⁴ and not a supposition of something in familiar obviousness that then serves to enable some results-oriented process or other (μέθοδος).²⁰⁵ It is also not the kind of beginning one goes back to, however, but rather the possibility of a completely different access to what can show itself, and, as such, one that concerns everything, "the whole." It is by the power of the good that everything is significance; as pure εἶδος, the good lets everything be eidetic, just as the sun puts everything into the light and, with this, into visibility.²⁰⁶ This gives the good a priority before all the others, although it would not thereby be fundamentally different from them. Just as the sun gives visibility to what appears for the eye and at the same time can—albeit with difficulty—be seen, so too is the good the openness of the eidetic and the same time eidetic in kind. It is differentiated from the other εἴδη by the fact that it does not allow itself to be involved in any demonstration and does not correspond to anything demonstrable. This position of priority is expressed in the *Republic* by the fact that talk about the good always concerns only an ἰδέα and never an εἶδος. As idea, the good is the illuminating character of language itself. In this way, it is the possibility of dialectic, the beginning that determines dialectic and holds it open in its transparency, its essential independence as the origin that presides throughout it. If one has grasped the good, then one has what is had by it,²⁰⁷ that is, the εἴδη, and one can now, without additional need of something visible,²⁰⁸ make use of the εἴδη by going from one to another, and, thus, concluding the investigation with the εἴδη.²⁰⁹

This research program, which is concerned with nothing other than significances, may only be exemplarily realized, that is, beginning with a significance whose clarification one is concerned with. It is because of this that it has the character of a "genuine supposition"; it is τῷ ὄντι ὑπόθεσις because it leads into the dimension of significances. Supposition, ὑπόθεσις, in this sense can in principle be anything: the approach to a matter that is to be made clear, such as—in the *Republic*—justice, or—in the *Sophist*—sophistry, and equally something as general as—in the *Parmenides*—the one, which is explicitly introduced as the supposition of the dialectical practice of the dialogue.²¹⁰ It is then necessary to lead what is supposed into the range of significances, that is, to develop in which respects the one is to be found in the multiplicity of significances. If one would not approach what is dialectically supposed as one,²¹¹ the investigation would have neither point of departure nor aim; it would not be an investigation, but, rather, a planless leap from one meaning to the next. If one would not unfold the one in the many, it would remain unclear whether one's concern is with a significance at all or rather just a word—a word that only feigns a matter that is determinate in its significance. "Sophist," "Statesman," and "Philosopher"—as is admitted in the *Sophist*, these can be three words that all have the same significance, or three "figures" based on which each can be made clear in its significance.[212]

With the tension of unity and multiplicity, the attempt to make a significance clear has the same structure as reflective interpretation in its differentiation into clarification and explication. Yet, whereas interpretation can never be definitive, the clarification of significances can be conclusive, at least for matters of more limited complexity; the necessity of revising a clarification of significance arises only due to a radically different understanding of the same word, which must admittedly be measured against an already given clarification of significance.

That the clarification of significance is carried out in the tension between the one and many in this way persuaded Plato to understand *number* as the fundamental figure of dialectical thought. Number, ἀριθμός, is understood here not as a determinate enumeration of something, not as the size of a calculation or measure, but rather in its "nature,"[213] that is, as the belonging together of one and many. We experience number when all at once the same thing is to be seen as one and as a multitudinous unlimited many.[214] Understood dialectically, the concept of number refers to the structure of significances and thus focuses our attention on the fact that in dialectic we are concerned solely with significances.[215]

The *Philebus* shows more precisely how this it to be grasped, and, in fact, in such a way that the development of the idea is connected with a more precise determination of the numeric character of significance. The determination of number given in the *Republic* is corrected by this in a decisive respect. Number now no longer holds simply as the belongingness of one and many; rather, this claim is given up with reference to the notorious difficulty it leads to; whoever says that one is the same as the many cannot avoid the peculiar assertion that the one is as many and as unlimited and that the many are only as one.[216] This difficulty is avoided by understanding number dialectically now as *determinate enumeration*. Compared with the considerations in the *Republic*, which were directed toward the "nature" of number and disparage given dealings with number as unphilosophical, this is an about-face—away from the undifferentiated opposition of unity and multiplicity and toward a conception that does justice to the determinate, substantive results of a dialectical investigation. One should not confuse this by an analogy between dialectic and the arts (τέχναι) as they are elucidated in the *Republic* on the example of geometry. On the contrary: Dialectic now genuinely becomes for the first time what was only intended by the *Republic*, an investigation of pure significances that is in the position to preserve their purity.

This occurs because in the *Philebus* the determinations of unity and multiplicity are supplemented by the determinations of limit (πέρας) and unlimitedness (ἀπειρία). In this, number is understood as something "between" unity and unlimitedness.[217] It has this intermediary position as limit (πέρας), that is, as a determinate enumeration of significances that first make intelligible what was supposed as one, and, on the other hand, what is possible in unlimited variations. Insofar as something may be understood, it is not simply a one that can be given in an indeterminate, broad variation of aspects. In attempting to comprehend something in this way, the thing eludes us, for comprehending is a differentation; we name the significance of a word only by adding other words that belong with it. If this differentiation is enacted without limits, however, it leads to a flurry of determinations that no longer have anything to do with one another. If the one has eluded us and always and again eludes us, the many determinations cannot be held together and held on to. If we take our point of departure solely from the one and many, we do not, then, reach the pure significances that the dialectic is concerned with.

The dialectical process as it is proposed in the *Philebus* to solve this dilemma aims to determine pure significances in a different manner, namely, in a determinate enumeration of significances that necessarily belong together. One always has to presuppose and search for one idea (ἰδέα) for all things—one will find the idea, for it is in there. If we have grasped the one idea, then we must examine whether there are indeed two, and, if not, then three or some other number. We should proceed in the same way for each of these unities until we see not only that the one we started with is one and many and unlimited but also how many it is. We should not apply the idea of the unlimited to multiplicity before we grasp its number in everything that is between the unlimited and the one. Only then are we permitted to let each of the "ones" pass out of the whole into the unlimited.[218]

It is decisive for this consideration that the talk of the one and many is not given up, but rather, formulated in a new way based on "determinate number." The one and the many in the sense of the unlimited are explicitly made intelligible as ideas and, with this, protected against the suspicion that they are a matter of empty words. The expressions "one" and "many" have significance. However, their significances do not hold for themselves alone. In order to understand what a given, initially supposed one is, we must let the many step into the position of the one and *replace* the respective significance it stands for with other significances.

This formulation can—and should—recall Derrida's talk of "supplementation." The concern here, however, is not with the replacement of an expression with an indication and so also not with the dismantling of a pretension held to be problematic, but, rather, with a gain on the same level; a significance is not dismantled, "deconstructed," but rather, comes into its own first through its replacement. Accordingly, the steps from one significance to the next here do not form a chain of disappointments, either. To understand a significance means: to be able to hold it together with the significances that step in for it. The significance and the significances that step in for it offset each other. The plurality introduced had not been arbitrary, but rather, a limited one, and this means: the newly introduced significances were not lined up without relation but were rather intended *in their connectedness with one another*. The significance supposed at the beginning is indeed not supposed to be elucidated exemplarily by each of the newly introduced ones; rather, what was intended was its replacement with a determinate number. The significance supposed at the beginning is intelligible because the significances introduced on its behalf supplement one another in their difference. What makes a significance intelligible is not an enumeration of relationless other significances, but, rather, a *complex of significance*.

The significance supposed at the beginning does not just become intelligible, however, with the establishment of a complex of significance. It has at the same time lost its character as a supposition. This holds as much for *what* was respectively grasped as one as for the one as such. What was respectively supposed no longer counts as something simply given; it could only appear in this manner so long as one accepted it in diffuse intelligibility and did not consider its determinacy. As soon as it becomes clear that the one may not simply be understood as one, however, it has also been demonstrated that the one belongs together as such with the determinate number. It proves itself as significance in terms of the complex of significance.

This also holds of the many in the sense of the unlimited. Insofar as it is understood on the basis of determinate number,[219] it is, on the one hand, another possibility of comprehending what is determined in this; in this case, what is determinate appears in its infinite variation. Every further determination is a modification in regard to the complex of significance of determinations that grasp something as what it is with differentiation. On the other hand, however, this is less a shift in viewpoint than an expansion in the dimension of significance: That one can understand determinations as modifications is as if one puts them under a new sign; one assigns them to the complex of significance and at the same time carries them into a significance that cannot be achieved by them—in the idea of the unlimited.

The complex of significance of a determinate number thus stands for its part in an essential relation to significances that do not belong to the complex itself. In the *Philebus* this is expressed in reference to the complex's intermediary position.[220] Yet, the significances between which the determinate number stands—that is, the one and the unlimited—are bound to this. The determinate number alone allows them to be accessible in their essence: As the still undifferentiated beginning of what can be brought to explicit determinacy as significance and as the unlimited range of possible further determinations in which a significance can be connected each time with an infinite multitude of other ones suitable to it.

Although the one and the unlimited are just as accessible from the determinate number as from its intermediary, their status is thoroughly different. The symmetry that might be suggested by the intermediary position of the determinate number does not hold for their relation to it. The one initiates and fixes determining; with the one, we bind ourselves to a significance for which we inquire into a complex of significance. By contrast, the unlimited is the range of the texture that it is possible to experience through the significances themselves. As the possibility for further determining, the unlimited makes it possible to experience the determinate number in its delimitation; this delimitation comes to stand out from the unlimited significances excluded by it as a constellation stands out from the star-strewn Milky Way. At the same time, however, the possibility for further activity of determining allows the limited complex of significance to be put within a range and thereby provides a determinate indication of how this range can be experienced. As a determinate number of significances, the matter at issue does not just stand there enclosed within itself in rigid refusal but rather holds determinability in reserve in its possible modifications. Conversely, insofar as the infinite multiplicity of significances is disclosed based on a complex of significance, it is not a chaos, and that means that it is disclosed as a diversity of modification. As something that remains the same, something identical, the complex of significance is like a pattern that allows those significances suited to it to step to the fore from out of the infinite multiplicity of significances.

The *Philebus* shows more precisely how the idea of determinate number is to be understood on the example of the relationship between voice and writing[221]; this occurs in a manner that lets Plato's dialogue appear as an anticipation of Saussure's conception. Voice is in fact *one*; *it* is what allows all vocal sounds to resound. At the same time, however, the voice is unlimited in the sense of an infinite multiplicity as concerns the enumeration of the different sounds; there are here infinite modifications, such that no sound sounds exactly like another. One can only understand what resounds and can only describe it, however, by distinguishing the sounds in which one's voice is articulated. To this end, the number of sounds must be determined; only in this way, in their determinate number, can they be established as different and be lifted out from their multiple modifications in speech. It is only in determinate number that there is definite difference, for, in the determinate number, every sound taken up is determined in itself in its difference from others. Conversely, its determinacy may be elucidated in regard to its difference from others. There are enunciations solely in this way; there is no more any such thing as "the" enunciation than there is "the" body part.

The determinate number of enunciations is, however, not recognizable if one orients oneself only by speech. One's voice articulates sounds in infinite diversity; if one keeps only to them, then it is not certain whether something is a modification, variation, or independent sound. Insofar as a voice articulates something at all, that is, insofar as it speaks, it has to be certain about what is supposed to count as a sound. Determinate number gives a structure to what one calls language. Without this, there are only unarticulated sounds; without it, voice cannot be speech.

Yet, what gives certainty to the structural form of language would have to be ascertained at a distance from the voice itself. In the voice itself, it is forgotten; the voice simply articulates itself, it does not pay attention to what makes this articulation possible. The voice passes over it in speaking. It is first recognized in being fixed in writing. One achieves knowledge of language through this and is γραμματικός. The study of language, γραμματική, is actually the study of writing, it is "grammar" not simply in the sense of a study of what is fixed in writing, but also a study through writing.

In this, writing is to be taken quite literally. In order to capture the structure of voice, there is need of established, distinctive signs, of an order, which remains in existence in its material persistence and wants to be enacted, that is, read, as order. In contrast to something spoken, which is gone as soon as it is made loud, with writing there is a structure that is independent of every context. The more something is writing, the less it has to be this determinate sound articulated in one's voice, which could also be otherwise. It has detached itself from speech and for this reason provides the order of speech.

One may assume that the author of the *Philebus* is clear about the aforementioned point of the word γραμματική. Otherwise it would hardly have occurred to him to ascribe, in mythical play, the invention of grammar to the Egyptian god Theuth—the very same God who is represented as the inventor of grammar in the *Phaedrus*.[222] What is true of speech and its sounds is true generally. First, writing lifts something up from out of the flow of speech and allows it to be fixed. It presents structures, lets connections be revealed. And, with writing, the succession of the said is turned into the simultaneity of something that is only what it is in the difference of one thing from another. Writing captures in simultaneity what is supposed to hold as the structure of the said.

It should be clear by now that writing is not a temporary exteriority of language to be surpassed; it is not an intermediary stage, not a "phasal moment" that only comes to life again once it is removed from its fixity and transformed into living talk. That exterior signs are only what they are in relation to one another becomes the key of every order, every ordered fabric. The significance of the world, texture, appears in signs; it appears only insofar as it is ascertained in signs. And, insofar as signs are in themselves closed complexes, they have a tendency in themselves to become text. Texts are unified fabrics, collections of structure, that is, λόγος in the literal sense.

Texts can serve to put *emphasis* on structures or to let structures *emerge*. The former holds above all for philosophical and scientific texts, the latter for those of art. Theological texts have a proximity to philosophy, religious texts a proximity to the artwork. Emphasis originates in the experience of the objective. Here the focus is not so much on the modifications and variations of the structure, that is, the unlimited. The text is based in the unlimited, remains open for it, yet it is generally taken up only for the sake of illustration; the unlimited is as the unlimited diversity of sounds whose structure, which always already governs speech, needs to be worked out in presentation. By contrast, the artistic text—and this can also be a painting or a musical score—brings out the structure from the unlimited, as if this structure were to arrive from out of the unlimited. In the artistic text, the unlimited itself is revealed with the structure, in such a way that seen from the standpoint of the structure it is *pregnant*.[223] A painting, for example, does not in fact have the quality of being blue but rather shows blue; this only occurs, however, because over there where the painting is—is blue. In the picture, blue is transposed into readable significance as this particular blue in the tension of its hues, as elementary structure. Pregnancy can also be reached through an increase in complexity; with the density of references, the structure together with that from which it arises is intensified, and both in their tension are increased phenomenality.[224]

The structure gathered into texts is accessible only through presentation; the more complex the structure or the greater the pregnancy, the more they demand explication and clarification as objects. This succeeds basically as the explication and clarification of the objective succeeded—that is, in the attempt at a presentation of structure that is as unified and sufficiently differentiated as possible. Here the criterion for its *truth* is also designated; this criterion turns on adequacy. Interpretations are not isolated expressions that are, in a simple alternative, true or false. If they really are interpretations, they cannot miss the objects they are concerned with any more than attempts to describe the sound-structure of a language can pass it by. The question of an interpretation's adequacy is generally not a question of the yes or no but rather a question of comparatives. There are, as Nietzsche once said, "levels of apparentness"[225]; from the perspective of the showing-character of language, one should say rather levels of phenomenality, levels of appearance. Here, specific levels are not always reached in one stroke; it is possible to work on the presentation of a structure in repeated attempts, and there is always the question of how an attempt that goes to the whole of the text holds up in comparison with other attempts. Presentation always belongs in a language, which does not make the world accessible like a key, but rather, is the accessibility of the world itself from the standpoint of its "readability." The presentation of the objective is a probe into this readability of the world.[226] It is confirmed in the objects, although in such a way that it always has to be probed again. Even if texts endure in writing they cannot be fixed. They put themselves at a remove and come anew to their presentation. They are in time.

Chapter 6

Time

§ 29. Ubiquitous and With All Things

Time is ubiquitous, and for this reason it barely can be grasped. It is not even unlocked by the attempt to measure it, for this attempt presupposes an understanding of time. Otherwise, the glance at the clock would be at sticks that senselessly rotate and move along numbers or markings. Initially, this barely graspable yet nevertheless understood issue leads to the observation that everything is of a restricted duration, that everything arrives and passes away. Time, so it appears, is the restriction of duration through passing away and through the arrival of the new, that is, the restriction through something that is itself unrestricted; *always*, as long as there is time, something passes away, and always something new arrives. Thus, duration itself belongs to time as restricted through arrival and passing away. Something that lasts resists passing away, although it does not resist forever. One of the earliest statements that has been understood as philosophical and passed down to us speaks of this: "whence beings come to be, therein too occurs their passing away, in accordance with their debt to one another. Because of the injustice they do to one another—by driving one another out—they must then pay penance, in accordance with the order of time."[1] Thus, Anaximander of Miletus in the sixth century before Christ. According to his sentence, time is the order of everything that is. It orders by letting everything arrive and exist for a while as something that is; it gives everything its passing place and lets it then go. In coming and going, it is the order of things.

Even if, as Heidegger suspects, the formulation of the "order of time" should be a later addition,[2] time is Anaximander's topic; the kernel of the inherited sentence also concerns it. Although time is not named here, time—and precisely this immediately sheds light—has to do with becoming and passing away. Consequently, what is, insofar as it is, may only be conceived on the basis of time; as duration and remaining, it is what may only be determined in relation to becoming and passing away. The question of "being and time," which Heidegger turned into a book title, has its basis in this matter.

The information that time has something to do with becoming and passing away, however, is not yet an answer to the question of what time itself is. One cannot identify time with becoming and passing away. Time is more than this, for example, it is the possibility of dividing up becoming and passing away and—in both senses of the word—reckoning with them. To have time, to take one's time, this is to be distinguished from the fact that something becomes and passes away, and nevertheless it has something to do with time. By reckoning with time, one positions oneself toward something that occurs to everything, that is, to all things. Whether one knows it or not, one is put into the order of time. Of course, it is only because one always already stands in the order of time that one must comport oneself toward things, no matter whether one works on, deals with, forms, or, once they become objective, interprets them. Together with things, one belongs in time and is subject to its order.

But where and how is there time as this order? Is it also there when no one perceives it? Becoming and passing away always are as long as the world is. But do becoming and passing away occur in time also when no one experiences it? The question is not easy to answer. On the one hand, one cannot imagine time without the experience of it; if one does not "have" time, then where and how is it supposed to be? In order for time to be "given," one must, it appears, somehow be conscious of it. Yet, on the other hand, this consciousness is that of something inevitable; one either "has" time or does not, one has "no more time"; one's lifetime itself is limited, and, so, time is given not only in consciousness. Time appears to be something mediatory, a peculiar both-and. On the one hand, it appears to be bound to experience; without beings who experience time, the universe would be timeless. On the other hand, one experiences time as something that is there without one's own assistance; the experience of time would have to be of such a kind that something merely comes into focus that is also there without it.

If there is time, there appears to be nothing without it. It creeps into action, nestles itself into the succession of one's ideas, pounds as the motor of feelings and moods; there is no impatience, boredom, fear and hope, there is also no mortifying anxiety, despair about lost time, without the loss of something. Moreover, language is interspersed with time; without verbs and tenses,* language cannot be conceived. Time is, as Aristotle says, "ubiquitous and with all things."³ Is it at all possible, then, to understand it as something in particular, or is it, as Heidegger wished to show, "the horizon of being"?⁴

What is to be shown here is that both are correct: Time is ubiquitous and with all things and, at once, something in particular, in such a way that one

---

*[Note that the German words for "verb" and "tense" are, respectively, *Zeitwort* and *Zeitform*—in literal translation, respectively, "time-word" and "time-form." —Transl.]

can say what it is, and in fact, so that one distinguishes it from other things that are comparable to it. In this thoroughly particular sense, it is the "horizon of being," however, as shall become clear, also of nonbeing, of becoming and passing away. If both answers are correct, then something specific has to be addressed by being and nonbeing. In fact, as Parmenides discovered, it may be said of all things, however diverse they may be, that they are, and there thus appears to be nothing outside of being. It is not everything, however, to say of something that it is. Being—or becoming and passing away—can recede to the point of disappearing. The fact that it can be thought and said along with every experience of something does not mean that it is foundational for this experience. If one says of something that it shows itself or that it is experienced as a possibility of action, other aspects are touched on, namely, those of language and freedom. Or, formulated more generally: There are experiences of something, in which time plays no role. This does not mean that they now are no more. It means only that the experience could also be formed otherwise than temporally, and, in this case, even the experience of time is such that it can be described in its particularity. In order to become familiar with this particularity, one has to describe the experience. The possibility of gaining access to the "known without qualification" thus arises from the "known to us."[5] In order that the question of the relation of time and the experience of time is not already answered in advance by the examples, the examples should be as simple as possible.

§ 30. *Something Occurs*

The maple in the garden turns color; the greenish-brown of the leaves becomes a radiant red. A train passes by; one hears it coming, the clatter and noise rises as it passes, it is only just there and again becomes weaker. There is a knock at the door, and one can hardly answer it before someone enters. One is surprised, delighted, perhaps also indignant because one has been disturbed; in any case, one is affected, has been touched, because someone comes. All of these are things that occur.

It is not difficult to make the temporal sense of the occurrence clear in all three examples. One needs only to introduce expressions of time into the description of what occurs. In this case, one would perhaps maintain that the leaves of the maple "now" have begun to turn color; they change their color "gradually," so that they have "finally" become red. One knows that this red is not their single possible color, because in the consideration of the red foliage one can "look back": "earlier" they were greenish-brown, "now" they are red. "At that time" one could have been able to "look ahead," "still" without discerning the first trace of the turn in color. One would have known that the leaves of the maple are in fact "now still" greenish-brown, although "later" will be red.

One had perhaps not heard the passing train right from the start. The sound of it coming had rather slipped into the silence, but "now" the train is there and with it the experience that it is becoming louder. The "moment" it passes by the house that one is staying in can be "expected." "Now" it has come, and one follows how the train moves off into the distance. "In just a moment," "soon," it will no longer be possible to hear it, and "now" it is gone. For a "while," it is still as if the sound of it "lingers."

The knock on the door occurs "suddenly," and just as suddenly the visitor enters. One had not "expected" him, his arrival was not "gradual," but, rather, "in a trice," like an assault. Also, between the knock and his entrance was "hardly a moment." Yet, it did not occur "at once"; one will remember even more clearly later that the visitor had knocked and "then" had entered, admittedly without waiting to see whether his knock received an answer.

Through this description, which is more detailed and precise because it uses expressions of time, something has also become clearer that might initially have been only a vague impression. Time does not have to do with the experience of an occurrence only incidentally, but, rather, concerns the *occurrence-character of the occurrence*. First by the introduction of expressions of time can an expression concern an occurrence as such. If one were to say a train passes by this house, an occurrence is not necessarily intended; one could also wish to say the house lies near the train tracks. One first emphasizes an occurrence when one says the train is passing by "now." Moreover, it becomes clear through the expressions of time that occurrences are thoroughly diverse. Their diversity emerges through the introduction to expressions of time, and this suggests that the diversity exists above all in regard to their temporal character.

The first example stands for a process that begins sometime and ceases sometime. The occurrence is determined by beginning and end; it may not be grasped other than on the basis of the two states that demarcate its beginning and end. These states, in turn, are held together because they are states of *something*. This, for example the foliage of the maple, gives the occurrence its unity. On the other hand, the foliage of the maple is itself encountered in two different states that are connected with one another through the occurrence of the turn in color. There is thus a fold of something to which something occurs and of the occurrence that allows this something to be revealed as the same and yet in different possibilities. Here, the occurrence is such that *something changes*. This change can be, although it need not be, visible. It can also be due to the fact that, after a while, someone sees something differently than before.

The occurrence of the passing train may be differentiated from what was just described by the very fact that the train is moving. The tree whose foliage shifts color remains at the same location, whereas the train in fact remains the same but shifts its location. It goes from one location to another and in this traverses a stretch, on which locations are or could always be marked again. Such markings would also be possible for the foliage's shift in color; one could establish various states of the turning color. For the train this is only possible, however, if one takes the train or otherwise enacts its movement. In this case, one would experience that the focus here is above all on the *course* [*Verlauf*] of the occurrence. If one were to move on one's own and were able to interpret his movement whenever he wished, then the focus would be less on the course than on the *enactment*.

One experiences the course [of this occurrence of the train passing by] even when one only hears the approach, passing, and disappearance. It is true that to the one who hears the train come and disappear, the silence, in which the sound of the train arises at first almost imperceptibly and then becomes ever louder, might not draw attention. Once one listens to the ever quieter and then disappearing train, however, the silence it leaves behind will draw attention. Nothing occurs in this silence any longer, and nevertheless something remains behind: the openness for the fact that something has occurred and can occur again. This is not an indeterminate emptiness but rather the characteristic *openness of occurrence*, in which even the arrival and passing of the train had already belonged—that is, the openness for an arrival, being there, and disappearance. It is an openness in which there is a "not yet," a "now," and a "no more," as well as an "ever still" and a "then again." Yet, in each case something is there and other things are not there, such that one knows of what is not there together with what is there. Here, being there and not being there are held together by the expressions of time. "No longer" belongs together with "now" or "still," as much as "not yet" with "now," "then again" with "not yet." In their belonging together, the expressions point out a span, that is: a removal. The expressions separate something in what is occurring from some other thing in such a way that without them neither could be held onto as it is held onto: as put at a remove from one another by an occurrence or in an occurrence.

The openness of occurrence was also there before someone suddenly stepped into the room. Here, the openness does not linger as after the disappearance of the train, but, rather, is confirmed by someone's *entering*, also by the entrance of something. That something enters means that something occurs "all at once." There were antecedents that were either perceived or not, but now something is different. A season of the year can enter, hot or cold. A new moon enters. And, when a lecture sets in, this is at the same time also an entrance of the text.

On the one hand, an entrance is in fact a particular kind of occurrence; something enters by occurring suddenly and surprisingly. Yet, on the other hand, there is an entrance in every occurrence—in the first turn in color of the foliage and even when the approaching train is all at once audible. Conversely, an entrance might be so sudden—it is never experienced solely for itself. Essential for every entrance is that, with it, *something* becomes different and then has become different. One only experiences and understands this, in turn, if one takes what is entering or has entered together with what is changed or taken away by it. It is first in this way that its entrance is perceived. "Now," as one says in this case, something has entered; "previously" things were different. Or, formulated differently, "earlier" things were this way or that, "later" something entered by which the situation is transformed.

The expressions of time say it clearly: One experiences time in the experience of an occurrence as change, in the course [of an occurrence] or as entrance. This, however, is trivial; one does not yet know what time is through the expressions of time. Something can enter without ever being noticed. In a solar system that could not be observed from earth, two heavenly bodies could race toward one another and smash each other to bits. "Beforehand," "earlier," they had been there, "then," that is, "later," they were no longer in existence. If no one were to observe them and follow the occurrence, however, then by all appearances it would not be apportioned into an earlier and a later. As soon as one represents the smashing of the heavenly bodies, it is after all integrated into our possibilities for experiencing an occurrence. Without this representation, it would be null and void; concepts that we always connect only with our representations crash against whatever we put outside of our representation due to its character as unrepresented. If this is how things were, "earlier" and "later" would prove to be concepts of order or representations of order with which we structure changes, or, better: with which we always already have structured, and so experience as, changes. The collision of the two heavenly bodies in a remote solar system would then be timeless in the sense that we would not even be able to conceive of its temporal character. This is just how things are for the collision's timelessness, however. In order to conceive this timelessness, we must think ourselves away. We cannot, however, get behind our thought and our representations. As soon as we fiddle with something like the smashing of heavenly bodies even just as an example, we put it in time.

One can call on Kant's understanding of time as it is developed in the *Kritik der reinen Vernunft* for these considerations; this understanding found its classical formulation in the determination that time is "pure form of sensuous intuition."[6] Time, as Kant elucidates his idea, can neither "exist for itself," nor belong "to things as an objective determination." In the first case, time would be actual even if there were nothing besides it, and this—as Kant's argument might be supplemented—is a nonsensical idea if time may only be spoken of in regard to something that occurs. In the second case, if time were a property of things it could not be understood in distinction from things as the order of things, which is patently how it functions.[7] On the presupposition that we always have only appearances of the "objects," time can be "no determination of external appearances."[8] We do not experience time as we do things or occurrences *in* time. Rather, time determines "the relation of representations in our inner states,"⁹ that is, it is nothing but the order of representations in accord with the possibilities of before, after, and at once.

Things cannot be so. One can easily make it clear that the before and after always concern the things themselves. A while ago the apples were still enjoyable, now they are putrid. Whoever establishes this has not ordered his representations only in a transcendental manner belonging to perception itself, but, rather, taken note of something verifiable. The apples have *undoubtedly* shifted their state. This might have occurred relative to certain things one is accustomed to or to one's needs, and one has experienced the apple in a certain perspective; enjoyability is not an "objective" property that simply accompanies apples but rather a property that presupposes living beings to whose foodstuff apples belong. On the presupposition of this living being, however, enjoyability is something that accompanies the apples themselves; they actually are eaten. This actuality also holds for the shift in which the apples lose their enjoyability. The order that is expressed with "before" and "after" or "earlier and later" concerns not representations alone but rather what is represented itself. It is in accord with this order that what occurs to—or with—this represented thing is enacted. Different states are not only distinguished by us and thereby separated from one another such that it is only for us that they are put at a remove from one another. The removal actually exists.

Aristotle had determined time in this spirit and in doing so passed down something like a foundational determination for all philosophical reflection about time. Now it must be said that it belongs to the destiny of its determination that its leading concepts were thoroughly misunderstood. Consequential in this regard was above all Heidegger's assertion that Aristotle provides a determination only of measured time, and this means: of the "vulgar" understanding of time, which remains in the familiar obviousness of the "natural" attitude.[10] This understanding of time, according to Heidegger, is "what is counted, showing itself in following, making present and counting the moving hand of the clock."[11] To be sure, Aristotle does foster such a misunderstanding through the wording of his determination of time. Time, so Aristotle puts it concisely as if in a formula, is number of movement in regard to earlier and later.[12]

If Heidegger's clarification is a misunderstanding, then the expression it latches onto, that is, number, cannot be intended in the sense of an enumeration of counted units of time—minutes, hours, days, or years. What there is to enumerations of time in this sense is to be considered later; it is only possible to arrive at a determination of the measurement of time based on a substantive foundation. To this end, however, the dispute with the Aristotelian determination of time is an important step.

Number—Aristotle says himself—has a double significance: It is to be understood as what is counted (ἀριθμούμενον) or as that by which we count (ᾧ ἀριθμοῦμεν).¹³ In this, the latter is what is countable, to wit, that by which one indicates the enumeration in counting it. As Aristotle elucidates this distinction, we know the quantity by the enumeration, say, following the example Aristotle chooses, a quantity of horses, using one horse as the basis for the number of horses.¹⁴ In order for an enumeration to be ascertained, there always must be something whose enumeration it is. This is taken as one and belongs as the "by which we count" together with the enumeration that ascertains something uniformly determined in a respectively given multiplicity.¹⁵ Multiplicity is always multiplicity of something; something, understood as something uniformly determinate, is always only determinable in multiplicity as determinate number.

Of time Aristotle says that it is to be understood as number solely in the sense of enumeration.¹⁶ It is not something uniform, then, that gives multiplicity its respective determinacy, but, rather, multiplicity itself. But, multiplicity of what? At stake in the answer is whether and in which respect time has to do with things.

Aristotle gives his answer in multiple steps. The first step is determining that "by which we count" in regard to time as "now" (τὸ νῦν). If this is not intended in the sense of a measurement of time, that is, counting off units of time—minutes, hours, days, years—one has to say more precisely what it is supposed to mean. The word νῦν signifies "now" in the sense of "presently"; οἱ νῦν ἄνθρωποι are human beings presently alive. According to this, νῦν appears to be an expression of time, and this would lead to the disconcerting view that time is counted with time. When Aristotle says that time is number in the sense of what is counted and not in the sense of that by which we count, however, it is clear that the νῦν itself cannot have the character of time. As that "by which we count" the νῦν functions rather as the determinate thing whose number one names. It forms the unity for a multiplicity, which is time as something counted.

Aristotle proffers how this is to be understood in his formula of time by determining time as the number of movement (κίνησις), whereby the word is intended in such a general way that it includes every occurrence. Aristotle does not wish to identify time and movement with one another. Movement, Aristotle maintains, exists only in what moves itself, time, however, exists ubiquitously and with all things. Moreover, whereas movement can be faster or slower, time cannot. Rather, the fastness or slowness of movement is determined through time by establishing how little or how much movement eventuates in a certain time; a movement is fast when something moves a lot in a short time, slow when something does not get anywhere in a long time.¹⁷

If time and movement have to be distinguished in this way, the only thing that can be intended by the formula of time is that time and movement belong together in their difference. If this belongingness is essential, then there is no time without movement. Because of this, Aristotle emphasizes, one also does not perceive time without movement. If nothing moves or if the movement escapes us, then for us there appears to be no time.[18] Aristotle—even in the aforementioned formulation—leaves no doubt, however, that the concern here is with a deception. The fabled Sardinian sleepers, whom he takes as his example, do not perceive what time it is; it escapes them because the movement enacted while they are asleep escapes them.[19] For them, there *appears* to be no time, although there is time. In any case, time does *not* exist *without* movement, and for this reason we also perceive it only with movement.

The "not without" is not to be understood here as a condition or even a cause, not, that is, in the same way as there is no smoke without fire. Rather, time is not without movement like action is not without freedom and language is not without signs. Just as action is not what it is without freedom, so too freedom is the openness that proves to be in essence openness for action; also the freedom of things, the freedom of contemplation, are not conceivable without action. Likewise, signs are possible alone in language; but language would remain empty—and then it would no longer be language—if it could not be understood as the removal and remove at play in signs.

Aristotle himself gives an example for how the relation of time and movement is to be elucidated more precisely. It is remarkable for its vividness in a number of respects and, for this reason, can stand for all of the kinds of movement that Aristotle considers from the standpoint of time: passing away and growth, change, and movement from one place to another.[20] And the example is of this latter kind: A young man Coriscus, let us assume, goes from Lyceum, a district northeast of Athens, to the marketplace. It is the same person who was initially in Lyceum, then passes through the streets, and finally reaches the marketplace. There is movement only as movement of something or someone, in this case, Coriscus; the movement is "in him," in so far as it is *he* who moves. From the standpoint of time, however, the focus is less on this and rather on the movement itself; what is decisive is how the movement is to be experienced in its unity and diversity.

This is possible in the double experience of the now. Insofar as the now is just as much unity as multiplicity, it forms the number of movement. *Now* Coriscus is in Lyceum, then he gets under way and *now* he has reached the marketplace. The first now is earlier, the second is later. Thus the number of the now forms the number of the movement in regard to earlier and later.

The number, as it is illustrated in the example, is the smallest possible, namely, the two.[21] One is not a number in the sense of enumeration, but, rather, simple unity, in regard to which there is no counting. But, of course, the number could be higher than two. Instead of saying "now" only in Lyceum and the marketplace, one could mark every station that Coriscus reached and leaves along his way with a "now." This is what Heidegger gets out of the

Aristotelian conception of time in regard to the clock. Coriscus would in this case be like the second hand, whose movement may be described by the commentary, "now and now and now" and so forth. Time, as Aristotle conceives it, is thus for Heidegger "now-time."[22]

In this, however, an important aspect of the Aristotelian conception is suppressed. Aristotle understands time not as a succession of countable nows, but, rather, as the multiplicity of *a* now, which is likewise the unity for a multiplicity of phases of movement. As Aristotle says, the now is on the one hand the same, on the other hand not the same. Insofar as it passes into another one and again another it is different; what the now is as something without determination in time and in this sense something that is extant at any arbitrary time, however, is the same.[23] It is the same, as Aristotle says, insofar as it follows (ἀκολουθεῖ) what moves (τῷ φερομένῳ), or, as one could also translate: insofar as it accompanies what moves.[24] When Coriscus goes from Lyceum to the marketplace, Coriscus is "now" during the entire movement; Coriscus's being-now is itself not temporally marked by supplying it with an "earlier" or "later." Coriscus is earlierlessly and laterlessly *now*. He is not the now; the now may not be identified with what currently is.[25] Rather, the now stands for the simple presence of Coriscus, for the fact that he *is*—without any further determination of, although nevertheless at a determinable, time. The formula, ὅ ποτε ὄν, which Aristotle uses to indicate this,[26] is therefore most appropriately understood this way: πότε means "at any time," as much in the sense of "always" as in the sense of "at an indeterminate time," "whenever." It signifies a presentness that can be resolved temporally, and, in this respect, is relative to time, although likewise indifferent to time, or, one could also say: a simple being there [*Dasein*]. On the one hand, whatever has this kind of being does not have the character of something that is absolved of time, and, in this sense, timeless. Considered for itself, on the other hand, whatever has this kind of being is not temporal because it is *indifferent* in regard to a specific time but can become temporal "at any time." If there were only the ὅ ποτε ὄν νῦν, then time would as it were rest; it would be like a path that no one ever travels or takes into view as a path. What rests in temporal indifference here, however, is as it were made for what Aristotle calls "time"; it can—as something different than earlier and later—be divided into and earlier and later and stretched out. In it, there is removal through the earlier and a later; it is itself that in which there is removal.

This removal becomes explicit when the now is demarcated by the expressions of time "earlier" and "later." In this case, the now is duplicated and divided and a now is thereby differentiated from at least one other. The difference may be articulated solely in the relation of *earlier* and *later*; there is the present now, which is earlier or later than this present is, or earlier than the earlier one, which is then the later one in relation to this one. In order to signify it more precisely, however, one would have to say *what* it is the present of. It does not suffice to call the present the presence of Coriscus. Rather, this present has to be determined as the present and be determined more precisely so that it can be distinguished from other presents of the temporally indifferently present Coriscus: To wit, it has to be determined by "Coriscus in Lyceum" or "Coriscus at the marketplace."

Coriscus is always *somewhere*; accordingly, significations of this kind are always possible. They are really only important, however, when the concern is not with *Coriscus himself*. One could identify him without much trouble—say, as the son of X and born in Athens—without making reference to where he is at a given moment. The focus here is on identifications that are always applicable to Coriscus. Even if he is no longer alive and one still wishes to know of him, he will remain the Athenian born son of his father and, as such, be identifiable. If, by contrast, the talk is of Coriscus at a certain place, or even in a certain situation, in a certain state, then the concern is with something changeable, which is actually changed in movements of one kind of another. When Coriscus goes from Lyceum to the marketplace, he enacts the movement himself. He could also let it occur on its own, however, say, when he traveled by ship from Athens to Crete. And, changes affect him even without his assistance: above all, by aging and finally dying.

Coriscus is only an example; the issue is not that he is a human being, he would not even have to be a living being. What became clear with him in regard to time might have been shown in regard to all things, and, in this respect, Coriscus is in time, as it comes into view with Aristotle, a thing among things. All that is presupposed is that there are *individual things* that endure as identical in a shift of states. As these identical things, they must at the same time be "somewhere," in some respective state or other. Aristotle takes the individual thing understood in this manner as something underlying, and, in underlying, as something found in things, ὑποκείμενον; it is graspable as "being in there," materially given form.[27] One can refer to it in its recognizable identity in order then to follow the course of a movement that is unified by this identity.[28] The Aristotelian conception of time is made only for individual things in this sense, for "substances," as they are later called.[29] A diffuse, or "elementary" occurrence,[30] such as the gathering of a storm or the play of colors on the water in the sunlight, may not be grasped with the concepts that Aristotle has developed. There is nothing to bear the load here, nothing that one can latch onto in order to provide a description; there is nothing that endures in the course of a movement such that one can understand this course based on it.

In Aristotle's discussion of time the concern is admittedly less with what remains the same than with mutability and change. This is why he attaches so much importance to the belongingness of time and movement. Through movement of whatever kind something changes; even if something might be identifiable as enduring, it is nevertheless not outside of time. In this respect, time is the accessibility of change and of what underlies change. Insofar as something underlies change, it is not *simpliciter*, but, rather, *it is at each time*. Something respective, in turn, proves to be respective by standing in the order of time as it is given with the distinction of "earlier" and "later." Something is temporal insofar as it stands in reference to something else that has been for its sake. In this sense, Aristotle—thoroughly in Anaximander's sense—determines the essence of time as the cause of passing away;[31] it is indeed the number of movement, and movement changes what underlies it.[32] It melts everything, everything is made old and condemned to oblivion through time.[33] Time assaults even what is underlying.

Without what underlies, however, the stretch between earlier and later would not be conceivable. If forgetfulness and pastness were complete, there would no longer be any experience of time. There is only time insofar as what has passed away remains present. Aristotle speaks of an earlier *now* in this sense. The earlier that is "melted away" remains as the earlier present. The later now can only be understood as such because of this. The fact that there is time involves that Coriscus at the marketplace and Coriscus in Lyceum can be referred to one another in their removal from one another through time.

It is true that on closer examination talk of an "earlier now" is by no means as clear as it can appear if one takes orientation from the course of movement. The now could be intended in the sense of a now that was given and said earlier but that later passes away; as Coriscus still stayed in Lyceum, it was "now"; it was the present, and this present would then later be past.[34] But how should the present pass away? What passes away is not the present itself, but, rather, something that is initially present and then in the past. The Aristotelian formulation cannot, however, refer to the presentness of this thing of the past as the presentness of an earlier thing in the "current" present; Aristotle speaks unequivocally of an "earlier now."

But the formulation is not senseless. It only appears so if one thinks that it intends an earlier state, a thing of the past, which has occurred at a certain point and then later is over. A punctuated now in the sense of a row of moments—now and now and now and now...—can do nothing but pass away. By contrast, something earlier remains present when one thinks of it on the basis of movement. A movement that, as such, may be followed and determined, always goes from one respective state to another—Coriscus from Lyceum to the marketplace, the turn in the color of the maple's foliage from greenish-brown to red. When the movement is enacted, point of departure and aim remain present in the movement because it is this determinate movement—from here to there, and the one is earlier, the other later. Likewise, in the course of the movement the point of departure remains behind and the aim stands ahead. Even if the aim is reached, the movement that led to it remains graspable as this determinate movement, and the point of departure remains present with this movement; otherwise the aim would not be what it is.

This determinacy holds for the movement itself, not only for the experience of it. It is definitely not uncommon that the point of departure and the aim of a movement remain in obscurity for an observer; whoever sees Coriscus going through the city does not necessarily know that he comes from Lyceum and wishes to get to the marketplace. But precisely this is the movement he enacts. It is only because point of departure and aim are themselves in the movement that it is a movement in the first place. It belongs to movement that there is an earlier as well as a later of its terminus—both *simpliciter* and as long as the movement is still in its course.

Such a course, however, can only be grasped on the basis of something that moves itself. In the course of the movement, the earlier and later prove to be *now* through the temporally indifferent presentness of what moves or is moved. It is its existence that is differentiated into an earlier and later now in this course. The earlier and the later now are only given, then, in the folded belongingness of temporally indifferent existence and the stretch of movement. This belongingness is, with Aristotle, time. Understood as the number of movement, it is *the possibility of the occurrence of movement*. Time is removal that is filled out by something when this something disperses itself in movement. Movement, conversely, is an existence that occurs in removing.

Aristotle backs up this consideration by ascribing the earlier and the later to movement itself and seeing its temporal significance given first in connection with the now. The earlier and later are initially a matter of place (ἐν τόπῳ), and, in fact, in the sense of location or position (θέσις), but then also in magnitude (μέγεθος) and, because movement is to be understood as magnitude, also in movement.[35] The former is intended simply as a clarification of words: πρότερον and ὕστερον can also mean, respectively, "in front" and "behind." Concerning magnitude, what is to be thought of is extension or stretching; if one considers a line, then the end lying closer is the front one, the end lying farther away is the one behind. The temporal *earlier* and *later* come into pay, however, first when one *traces over* the line.

Based on this, it is also possible to understand why Aristotle determines the earlier and later as what movement is without determination of time and, in this sense, at any arbitrary time.[36] The path from Lyceum to the marketplace exists without anyone traveling it. The path may be described; if one has a vantage point to do so, it may be shown, and it can likewise be recorded on a map. In each of these cases, there is always its point of departure, Lyceum, and there is just as much its aim, which is given with the marketplace. Yet it is only when someone is taking the path that the point of departure becomes an earlier now, the aim a later now—presently in the movement and likewise in what is left behind or in what lies ahead. Someone has brought his existence along with him on the path and thereby transposed his temporally indifferent being into something respectively given. There occurs in the time of the movement both the duration of its enactment, and, in it, the leaving behind and standing ahead that belong to what is respectively given.

The time of movement is, on the one hand, *a* time. It is the time that a movement lasts and with this the time in which the movement is fast or slow. Time, however, does not come to an end with the end of the movement. In this regard, movement does in fact last for a time, but it occurs in time. Time is always "longer" than that of a respective movement because every aim, as something respectively given, is the point of departure of further movement. Because the "in time" is like an "in number," it is, as Aristotle says, possible to grasp a time that is greater than everything which is in time. Therefore, what is in time has to be encompassed by time.[37] It is thereby conclusively shown that time may not be identified with movement. There is always already time before the onset of a movement. It is only in time that something can occur.

This "encompassing" time only plays a role for the Aristotelian understanding of time, however, insofar as it can be established in regard to a specific movement. The question, therefore, arises of whether time is not indeed dependent on someone who realizes it. Movement understood as a path that one can take does not have any temporal character, and what is merely there as a determine form has just as little temporal relevance. There is time only insofar as both come together, that is, only insofar as something is in movement—as if it were taking a path. Although Aristotle does not understand time as an ordering addition to movement, and, so, not "subjectively" like Kant, Aristotle nevertheless has cause to take up the question of whether or not there can be time without a soul, more precisely, without thought (νοῦς) that enumerates.[38]

The question is refined and also conclusively answered within the framework of the Aristotelian conception: On the one hand in favor of a time that is independent of the soul, on the other hand so as to bring into focus the significance of the soul that enumerates for time. Aristotle presents the solution of the problem as follows: If there is nothing besides the soul whose nature it is to enumerate, then without the existence of the soul there could be no time, unless time is without any determination of time and in this sense at any arbitrary time as if there could be movement without the soul. The earlier and later are in movement, and just this is time, insofar as it is countable.[39]

As was already the case in the discussion of the now and that of the earlier and later, it is the formula ὅ ποτε ὄν that becomes the key to the question of the dependence and independence of time on the soul. Here, it indicates time itself—and in no way movement, as one is led to understand in connection with the formulation that the earlier and later are as if in movement. Movement is enlisted by Aristotle only for comparison, as the formulation "οἷον εἰ ἐνδέχεται κίνησιν εἶναι ἄνευ ψυχῆς" unequivocally verifies. Just as a path is also a path when it is not being taken, so too there is also time although no one counts it, that is, although no one orients himself by the presence of something that moves or is moved and in doing so distinguishes an earlier from a later now and refers both to one another. Time that is counted in this sense is time as it is experienced in regard to a respective movement; it is the time of this movement and, in this sense, respective time.

This formulation, and no less the talk of what time is without determination of time and at any arbitrary time (τοῦτο ὅ ποτε ὄν ἔστιν χρόνος), may awaken the impression of a paradox. But it is only an impression: With the idea that time may be established in regard to a respective movement, time is not subordinate to time. If something occurs and is ascertained in regard to its respective character, then it occurs at a determinate time. But even if it is not ascertained it would be ascertainable, for it occurs in time. By ascertaining the time, one relates oneself *to* it; following a movement, one conducts oneself *in it*; one as it were goes along with the movement, and this can occur only in time. The one is not, however, without the other; following a movement in time, one conducts oneself toward it in different degrees. This is only possible because time is open and can be measured in counting. It is only because time is the openness necessary for movement that one can conduct oneself in it and toward it.

The Aristotelian answer is not unproblematic, however. It is in reference to the answer that the difficulty of the Aristotelian conception of time as a whole is revealed in concentrated form. The one who counts, the one who follows a movement, may easily be imagined as an observer: Someone stands at the window and sees Coriscus walking from Lyceum to the marketplace. In this, he "counts" the presences of Coriscus there and here and there. Certainly, Coriscus could himself also take note of his earlier and his later now and hold both together. In this case, he would understand himself as the one who simply exists, who enacts the movement from Lyceum to the marketplace. Here lies the difficulty: Coriscus, according to the Aristotelian conception of time, would see himself just as the person at the window sees him, that is, from the perspective of the observer. He would have to think of himself as an individual thing; how he had experienced time in walking would not appear in his "counting."

On the one hand, this disregard for the perspective of enactment has a basis in the matter; in regard to time there is no difference between Coriscus' walk and the course of a stone that rolls off an inclined place. In this respect it would be appropriate to see himself as a thing among things in regard to time, or, within the framework of Aristotelian ontology, as a substance among substances. In this case, there would be time only as *time in its course* [*Verlaufszeit*]. Yet, on the other hand, Coriscus knows more of time by walking than when he steps outside of himself in thought and sees himself simply as something that moves itself. Namely, he knows that in walking he changes, however insignificantly. Even if he does not have the concepts, it is clear to him that time, as Aristotle says, assaults even what is underlying. Insofar as he conceives of himself as substance, he disregards this. He would have to determine himself in what he is with temporal indifference as form (εἶδος) and view the time of his path from Lyceum to the marketplace as a stretching and division of the temporally indifferent existence of this form. It could thereby become clear to him that the Aristotelian conception of time determines this based on something temporally indifferent. It equates the temporally indifferent phenomenon given in a designation with the νῦν of a present and understands time based on this present. If, however, even what is underlying is assaulted by time, this present—every present—belongs in time. Time may not be understood based on what does not belong in time. On the contrary, a person presupposes time: this happens insofar as one does not any longer contemplate something shown as a phenomenon, but instead transposes it into time in view of the fact that something is now actually occurring to him.

It appears, then, that one knows more of the reality of time from the purportedly "subjective" perspective of the enactment of the experience of time than if one disregards himself in time and sees himself as a substance among substances. One also knows more clearly then that time actually passes away and that one, too, succumbs in this passing away like a thing among things. In the life-worldly experience of time, the time of the thing-world comes into focus better than when one disregards the life-world. Yet, all time is ultimately thing-worldly time. Knowledge of time arises out of time and belongs in time, and this may only be ascertained insofar as one is in it oneself. This holds even when one only follows a movement, and in this regard the relationship of soul and time may also be considered conversely: Although there is never a time without the enumerative soul, the enumerative soul is given only in time. What this means more precisely is now to be discussed.

§ 31. Being in Time

Something occurs, but it occurs to someone or by his own means. It is possible for both to go together, indeed common: One can do something and in doing so changes. Or one does something and changes without prior intention to do so; it is only in retrospect that one realizes that he has become different. Like every movement, what one does occurs in time and has its time. Yet one thereby always experiences time and one experiences himself in time. Activity proves to be temporal.

There is a classical example that indicates how this is to be understood. It derives from Augustine, and his introduction and analysis of it brings into focus the experience of time neglected by Aristotle. Augustine takes for his example a performance: I sing a song that I know—*dicturus sum canticum, quod noui.*[40] This, too, is a movement, although its enactment is fixed: The singer has to enact it himself and what he enacts is the movement. What one refers to as "the experience of time" is disclosed only if one takes getting involved with this idea under consideration and exchanges the perspective of observation for the perspective of enactment. The example that Augustine places at the center of his consideration is intended in this sense: The movement at issue, that is, the singing, is given only through a self, and one has inner experience of himself in this. The enactment of the movement, however, is not arbitrary. Whatever is to be decided in the singing of the song, its time is at least in principle pre-given. The speed of what is sung could not be completely and utterly arbitrary. Besides, the song is long or short. It needs its time. In this respect, what one does is at the same time an occurrence; the perspective of enactment is at the same time the perspective of a course. It is the perspective, in which something occurs both by one's own means and to him.

The concern here is no longer only with the time of movement, but above all with the time of one who is moving himself. It is a time that *is experienced* by this individual *as his time*. As such, however, time is not merely the divided, respective present of something present that is stretched in movement, as it would have to be understood with Aristotle. Rather, for the one who is moving himself, time lies ahead at the beginning and during enactment and time lies behind as what has already been enacted. What is present, by contrast, is the enactment itself in its respective phase. As soon as the concern is no longer with the temporally stretched movement alone, but, rather, with enacting or also only co-enacting this movement, the temporal determinations of an earlier and a later now no longer suffice. Outside of them, *future*, *past*, and *present* now come into play.[41]

Augustine has described this connection very clearly and in doing so introduced a few concepts that are indispensable for the experience of time and likewise for the attempt to grasp it in presentation. This occurs in the elucidation of his model example: Before I begin to sing, the entirety of the song is stretched into my *expectation* (*expectatio*). After I have begun, what has been sung stretches into *memory* (*memoria*). What has just now been sung, by contrast, is there for my *attentiveness* (*attentio*). What was futural passes through this attentiveness, in order thus to become something of the past.[42] The song in its being thus passes through time as it respectively unfolds. The openness that it passes through, however, remains in existence as such. This openness was already in existence before I had begun to sing, and it is only for this reason that the singing was possible at all. The song was not there as something sung, yet it stood in my expectation; after the end of the singing, it is no longer present in singing, yet it stands in my memory.

What may sound completely obvious and not very exciting here is, for Augustine, the key to the understanding of time. Namely, because expectation and memory are taken into account, a problem is solved that Aristotle had already seen: How can something that is not there at a given time nevertheless be there? Aristotle answered the question by his understanding of time from the standpoint of the temporally indifferent stretch of movement and the temporally indifferent presence of the one who is moving himself: Point of departure and the aim, taken in the sense of something given, are present in determinate movement through their determinacy. And, it is the duration of the one moving himself that bears the enactment of the movement; its nowness differentiates itself into states of the earlier and the later now and in this way holds together the stretch of the movement in respective being. Time had thus proven to be the unified duplication of the present of a respective being in regard to the stretch of movement. Augustine thinks otherwise: Neither does he go back to the temporally indifferent stretch of the song, which has beginning and end and is this or that long, nor does the temporally indifferent presence of the one who is moving himself give him sufficient assurance for the fact that an earlier now and a later one belong together. The givenness of the song, which, as Augustine says, is familiar, plays just as little a role as the continuous presence of the one who sings. Rather, it is solely through the experience of time itself that the earlier and later are sublated. Who would want to dispute, Augustine says, that the future is not. And yet, in the spirit (*animus*), there is the expectation of the future. This holds, accordingly, for the past and even for the present: what is present, the song verse resounding just now, has, in resounding, already passed. What remains, however, is the attentiveness, which always holds for whatever is respectively passing.[43] The condition for the fact that something temporal is there lies solely in the experience of time.

This idea has formed the point of reference for the idea that Augustine is to be understood as the father of the modern philosophy of time.[44] Husserl takes up the discussion of the eleventh book of the *Confessions* as the foundational "analysis of time-consciousness" with special emphasis.[45] Of course, in Augustine there is not the phenomenological concentration on an "inner time-consciousness" revealed through a "bracketing of objective time," of "world-time."[46] The talk cannot be of a "return into the immanence of the spirit, which understands time."[47] Rather, with the experience of time, it is the being of the one who is in time itself that is addressed, and this, in turn, in a twofold sense: On the one hand, what is not yet, what is just now, and what is no longer have their accessibility solely in the experience of time. The song that is to be sung, that is just now resounding, and that has been sung, exists solely in the "three times" of future, present, and past. On the other hand, for Augustine expectation, attentiveness, and memory *are* the three times; there is no "objective" or "external" time in contrast with it that may be "bracketed."[48] Rather, human life is itself temporal in the three times. Augustine understands his example of the sung song as representative generally for this life that is led in the present, that lies ahead and that has also always become past.[49]

Because human life is in time in this way, Augustine holds that it cannot be a whole enclosed in itself; rather, it stretches itself, *tenditur*,[50] into the different directions of expectation and memory, it is "distended," *distenditur*.[51] Distension, *distensio*, is the fundamental trait of spirit and, with it, of human life. *Distensio*, however, is the essence of time. Time is nothing other than the distension of human life.

In order to understand this result, one must notice that Augustine achieves his understanding of time from the analysis of the experience of time itself. That time has to be understood as distention is in no way certain from the start. Augustine's central concept is passed down from the stoic and Neo-platonic tradition. As translation of διάστασις, *distensio* would admittedly signify above all "extension"; with this concept, the stretch between an earlier and a later now would be intended. The concept is also introduced in this manner in the treatment of time in the eleventh book of the *Confessions*. That time is "a kind of *distensio*"[52] is said immediately in connection with a consideration of different "spans" of time. This does not entail, however, that time should be grasped as *distensio* in the sense of a dispersion and splintering of time into multiplicity, that is, into the three times of spirit. Only after this has arisen from the analysis of the experience of time may it also be said that the *extension* of time is to be grasped as the *distension* of human life.[53]

Based on the twofold significance of *distensio*, the status of Augustine's determination of time may now be still better understood: Regardless of whether Augustine was aware of it or not, he reverses the Aristotelian idea of temporally occurring movement by understanding human life as a movement in time and emphasizing the incompleteness of this movement. This incompleteness is essential to human life, and, in fact, in such a way that this life is not only incomplete, but also can only be led in the knowledge of this incompleteness as determined by expectation and memory. It is above all this that comprises its incompleteness; if, in leading one's life, one were not conscious of this incompleteness it could be a matter of indifference. Augustine's interest in the incompleteness of human life understood in this manner directs his consideration to the forms of the experience of time, that is, expectation, attentiveness, and memory; the essence of the movement that the human being is can only come into focus in them.[54] Accordingly, the character of time as number is now also determined differently: Time is no longer number as a present that is divided in movement but temporally indifferent for itself. Rather, time is the triad of the "times" that can find their unity solely in the eternity of God, to which the Christian knows himself to be referred in faith.

Because Augustine understands human life insofar as it is enacted and thereby occurs as the *single* movement by which time may be elucidated in its essence, he thus cannot distinguish between an "objective" time and a "subjective" one conceived on the basis of the experience of time. The fact that he does not make this distinction is the point of his treatment of time. Augustine does not take even a first step in the direction of a "subjectivization" of time, as Kant and Husserl do, and in this respect one will not be able to criticize Augustine's analysis of the experience of time as inconsequential.[55]

One can nevertheless doubt that Augustine actually does justice to the relationship between a movement that is enacted in time and the experience of time. One does not have to go beyond basic tenets of his treatment of time in order to articulate this doubt. It suffices once more to consider more closely the model from which Augustine takes his orientation.

I sing a song that I know—Augustine describes this process solely from the standpoint of the question of how that, which is not yet, and that, which is no longer, can be there. By contrast, it remains unnoticed that expectation and enactment of movement, enactment of movement and memory, do not always have to coincide. Rather, expectation can lift itself up from the enactment of movement; it then reaches beyond it and reaches further. This is the case, to wit, in impatience; one cannot wait until one has sung through all the verses of the song. Because it nevertheless takes time to sing it through, the expectation goes beyond the enactment of movement. Things are similar in regard to memory. There is more present in memory than what belongs to a respective enactment of movement; memory puts this enactment in a context that emerges more or less clearly and that can thus determine the movement just now enacted in one way or another—say, because this song is especially dear to me due to the situation in which I learned it. In this case, one reaches back behind what is just now remembered into the more or less clear remove of memory. Attentiveness, finally, can be more or less developed. Perhaps one strays from what one does just now; one fails to concentrate—one is not into the matter as is demanded by oneself or by others; in this way, too, one reaches beyond whatever is to be enacted in his referential possibilities.

This consideration casts a light on Augustine's conception of time; it makes clear why Augustine cannot account for the divergence of the enactment of movement from the experience of time: According to his conception, memory and expectation are always "filled"; they "contain" the parts of the song, or, if one understands the song as a model, the parts of life that are not currently present. One's entire life is given only in expectation, memory, and attentiveness, and, in this way, never as a whole but rather "dissected" or "scattered." Nevertheless, the three "times," as Augustine calls them, are three presents that make it possible to speak of life as a whole and of its dissection. The three times that Augustine distinguishes are the present of what is past, the present of what is present, and the present of what is futural.⁵⁶ Like Aristotle, then, Augustine clarifies time based on the present. Only for him it is not the idea of a temporally indifferent, stretched and divided present, but, rather, the idea of a whole that is actual only in God, whereas it is split up in human life. Time is this splitting understood on the basis of the present.

The difficulty of this idea is documented in Augustine himself; he cannot get around the assumption of two presents, one of time itself and one in time. In this, his analysis shows that only the present in time is covered by experience. It is necessary, then, to repeat the analysis of the experience of time so that it is not eclipsed by the idea of a time-encompassing present. One has to describe the experience of the enactment of movement in time differently than Augustine in order that the divergence of the course of movement from memory, expectation, and attentiveness may be made intelligible.

§ 32. Time of Enactment

The example given by Augustine may be carried further. I sing a song that I know. Whoever does this or something like it is normally into the matter completely. Otherwise, such things are quite difficult to do. One would lose the beat or would fall into confusion about the text. To be into the matter, this means here: to become completely engrossed in the activity. Questions of interpretation—say, the question of the tempo of the musical recitation—should have been made clear as much as possible before hand; otherwise they are just an irritation. Whoever is into the matter in this way, however, does not generally refer to what is already sung or reflect on the verses of the song that lie ahead. The movement, which singing is, is simply *enacted*, and, in fact, in time.

In answer to the question of how to understand the temporal character of this enactment, Husserl has achieved the most helpful contribution.⁵⁷ According to Husserl's analysis, in hearing or singing—and, singing, as the expression of one's voice, is of course always also hearing—one only has present what just now resounds. The sound that has ended is nevertheless not simply gone, however, and it is also not remembered as something that has been once before. One does not think of it as one thinks of an earlier, long past inner experience that has no bearing on what one presently has in inner experience. Rather, one holds on to it in the enactment of singing or even just in hearing—even once a new sound rings out. Husserl names this holding on to "*retention*."⁵⁸ The word *retentio* is also in common usage in classical Latin. It is formed from the verb *retineo* (*retinēre*) and signifies holding back, for example, a sum of money, or also holding up a carriage.⁵⁹ One does not let something out of one's hand, one does not let it go. Precisely this is intended with the word in regard to what passes away. Although something is no longer there, it is still not so far in the past as something lying further back. It is still preserved and has nevertheless made room for something else.

Because what is held on to in this sense is no longer immediately there, Husserl sees only one possibility for determining what retention is; it must, he thinks, be a manner of memory. It is "primary memory"[60] and, as such, to be distinguished just as much from "secondary memory," "recollection"[61] as from the "original impression," that is, from the actual hearing of a sound, which Husserl also signifies as the "sound-now."[62] As soon as a sound has rung out and another follows it, the perception of the first tone goes into retention and makes room for the perception of a new sound. The more sounds that ring out, the more complex the retention. With every passing tone, a new retention comes into play, which, however, does not simply stand for itself, but, rather, holds together "its" sound with those that have preceded it. In this sense, as Husserl says, every "now-apprehension" or original impression is "as it were the core of a comet tail of retentions."[63]

Husserl does not assign the retentions each to a sound, but, rather, emphasizes that every sound that one holds on to belongs together with the sounds preceding it. In so doing, he would like to take into account the characteristic flow of the experience of movement and time. "Impressional consciousness" crosses "continually, flowingly over into an always new retentional consciousness." Moreover, every retention is in itself a "continuum"; the sound begins and steadily continues. This continuation is itself held in retention. Every retention is "in itself a continued modification," which bears "the legacy of the past in it in the form of a series of shades."[64]

Husserl's description is impressive if only because it lets the dynamic character of the experience of time come into focus—much more than this occurred in Augustine's description. Whereas Augustine, on the presupposition of a present that encompasses time as such, conceives of *memoria* as a receptacle in which something passing away is taken up,[65] Husserl not only works out the difference of primary and secondary memory, but moreover takes into account that memory itself changes with the progression of experience.

Nevertheless, Husserl's description is not satisfactory in every respect. Husserl describes the course of the experience of time as if it proceeded like the leap of the second hand of a quartz watch.[66] The reason for this is the conception—which remains unquestioned in its familiar obviousness—of every present as a "now point." Husserl describes the "flow" of time as a series of nows; each respective perception always coils back into retention so that a new perception can follow. Like Aristotle and Augustine, Husserl also understands time based on the present, only that the present has become the now punctuated moment of a respective perception. That there is an inconsistency here becomes apparent even just in the metaphors Husserl uses: the metaphor of the flow, which he enlists throughout for his description of time, and the metaphor of the point are not suited to one another. Either: What occurs flows from the present on into the past continuously. In this case, even its passing is had in inner experience. Or: What occurs steps from the "original impression" into retention such that one only ever has the experience of its being-past. It was just still there and now it is only held on to.

It is possible to achieve understanding based on Husserl's description, however, despite the discussed difficulty. The difficulty arises, as one might be led to think, from the description of the matter itself—more precisely, from what can be called the *negativity of time*: now something occurs; it lasts for a while, and then it gives way to something else. One sound follows upon another such that the one that rang out before is no more. It is because this is how things are that one has to distinguish as clearly between perception and retention as Husserl does. Retention is, in this case, a "distinctive intentionality,"[67] that is, not an immanent modification of perception. Because of this, as Husserl stresses, one may confuse it neither with the perception of a sound that now rings out nor with the lingering of a sound.[68] Even the lingering of a sound is still perceived, whereas the sound that has rung out is "not actually [*reell*] present in retentional consciousness."[69]

This is indisputable, and yet the description does not do justice to what one experiences in enacting or co-enacting music. The sounds being made or followed do not leap about, but, rather, flow—even when they are played staccato. They do not follow upon one another as discrete unities, but, rather, *arise from one another*. In enacting or co-enacting, the clear distinction between current perception and retention does not emerge. What the matter at issue demands that we distinguish, however, is not thereby blurred away. Current perception and retention are not two different phases of the experience of time but rather *aspects* of this experience that play a role in every phase. Perception that has a temporal character is current and just as much *in itself* retentional; retentions of what has been perceived belong in perception. The foldedness of the two are what first comprises the experience of enacting or co-enacting.

This appears in regard to perception itself. Perception in an occurrence—differently than in the contemplation of a picture—is not the experience of something present, but, rather, of something coming and going. In the contemplation of a picture one can forget time. The one-after-another plays no role. It is true that here too the contemplation is in time; one looks at the whole, and then over here and over there. For what is contemplated, however, the enactment and course is itself unimportant; it is there "all at once" as a whole, and one attempts to come into accord with this in that one subordinates its course to the viewpoint of possible simultaneity; the picture is text and writing.

By contrast, an occurrence such as music that is ringing out is in time. The sound never "is," but, rather, it becomes and passes away, more precisely: it only is in becoming and passing away; every phase of its ringing out is arriving and fading. Arriving and fading are there as such, and arriving and fading are in what is there. This also holds for the melody or for the musical work as a whole. Insofar as a work rings out it is in its existence nothing but occurrence. Its textual structure is there in the movement of ringing out and fading; it is recognizable in the continuum of the sounds as well as in modification, variation, and repetition. One has to take up this occurrence in its unity and division in order to hear the piece as such. What one hears is not something that is only there for a moment and then binds itself with memories and only thus joins into a whole. Rather, it is this occurrence.

Up to this point, one might think that the description would still be consistent with that of Husserl. Husserl, too, takes into account the outlined experience of fading insofar as he goes into the possibility of lingering sound or reverberation. He does not draw the consequence from this, however, that the current perception is itself to be conceived as temporal. The perception or "original impression" has a present sound that can be stronger or weaker. With every change of sound there is a new now—now one still hears it, now it can barely still be heard. If the sound is not simply present but rather arrives and fades, and if precisely this is perceived, then perception itself must be in time. Only in this way can passing away itself be heard.

It is only possible to speak of a fold of the perception with the retentions, however, if not only what is just now passing away but also what has passed away can be experienced in hearing. The fact that things are this way becomes clear in an experience that has already been mentioned. A train passes by, the sound of its passing becomes weaker and weaker, and then things are silent again. With Husserl, one would have to say that, now, nothing is any longer present and that the sound of the passing train can rather only still be accessed retentionally; it is remembered. But, hearing by no means breaks off when there is no longer any sound to be heard. What is now heard is the *silence*. This silence can continue to be completely filled by what was audible even once nothing acoustically discernable is occurring any longer. The silence is different depending on what has just passed away. The perception of silence is not possible as such unless there was something to be heard. This perception is not coupled with a memory but rather lingers currently from out of what is no longer there. Thus, what has faded away reaches into hearing itself. Where it reaches in from is time.

The same process may be described from the standpoint of retention. In hearing a piece of music, retention is no memory enacted for itself that follows upon a respective sound. Rather, retention is a matter of holding-on *while* the sound rings out or during the silence that itself still belongs to that sound. This holding-on is enabled by what rings out or by the audible silence. In what rings out or in the silence, hearing reaches into the lingering sound and, in this, finds its characteristic tension. Without what rings out or the perceived silence, the lingering sound would simply be gone. One could not hold it. Rather, it would have to be remembered—in the manner Husserl names "recollection" or "secondary memory."

Retention can be just as little conceived without perception, then, as, conversely, perception without retention. In hearing the passing away of a sound, the whither of the lingering sound is there with the perception itself. Conversely, the whither of the sound that lingered, and with it the sound that lingered, belong to the openness of perception itself. And, just as the inner experience of the whither of the lingering sound is only possible based on the sound that rings out, it is also at play in perception. The perception of something that occurs is in itself retentional, because time is at play in perception. Because time is this characteristic openness of occurrence and perception, retentions belong in perception, presuming that perception is more than the punctuated registering of an acoustic signal.

There are considerations in Husserl in which he comes quite close to this consequence. He admits, for instance, that one can describe a melody as a whole as something perceived. Yet, it becomes clear in his rationale for this that his concern is with a perception only in a figurative sense. A whole melody may only be signified as perceived, namely, "because the extension of the melody is given in an extension of perception not only point for point. Rather, the unity of retentional consciousness still 'holds on to' the passing sounds themselves in consciousness and progressively produces the unity of the consciousness, which refers to the unified temporal object, to the melody."[70] What here appears as perception goes back to the constitutive capacity of consciousness. This holds together being and nonbeing, perception and "nonperception," in such a way that they—as they look in the flow of inner experience—can "go over into one another."[71] In the interplay of perception and primary memory, the difference of the two no longer stands out. Yet, if one follows Husserl it is necessary to hold on to them as moments of the experience of what occurs. But then there is admittedly no perception of an occurrence but only a complex consciousness of it, and in this respect it is consequential when Husserl wants to speak of the "perception" of a whole melody only in a figurative and superficial sense.[72]

That perception itself involves the mutability of what is perceived: This is nevertheless confirmed by an aspect of the time of enactment, which, up until now, has not been taken into account. Enacting or co-enacting an occurrence involves not only a stretching into things of the past, but also the readiness for something to occur. Husserl names the forms of this readiness "protentions" or "intentions of expectation." Their function lies in the fact that they "blankly constitute and collect, bring to fulfillment, whatever is coming as such,"[73] that is, protentions first make it possible for something that occurs to arrive in perception. Put another way, they are different forms of *readiness of perception*. "Seizing upon the new now" comes through them, as Husserl once said.[74]

This idea is illuminating: The perception of something that occurs is only ever possible if what occurs can *arrive* and *commence*; in order for something to be able to enter, there has to be an openness for what enters and its entrance. It is also illuminating that this openness is always a specific one: Sitting in the concert hall, one expects that after the curtain is raised, it will be precisely the piece on the program that will begin. If one is already familiar with the piece, one will also have a more or less developed representation of what is now about to be heard. One does not know precisely how it will sound, however, and in this respect the "intention of expectation" is always determined by an openness that is grasped in this way or that, that is more or less extensive.

This openness belongs to the perception of something that is occurring and to what occurs in this perception. This openness is an essential moment of enacting or co-enacting, likewise of the occurrence that is enacted or co-enacted. Therefore, one will not be able to follow Husserl's characterization of an expectation, even when it is very specific, as an "intuitive representation of a future event."[75] In order to put it this way, one would have to disregard the fact that enacting or co-enacting has the character of occurring. Even if, as Husserl says, we "have a precisely determined plan, and, intuitively representing the plan, take it so to speak lock, stock, and barrel as a future actuality,"[76] this is only more than a neutral play of ideas if the incalculability of what occurs grounds the representation itself. It is part and parcel of the tension of entering that such a representation has the character of an expectation. This tension first makes protentions into what they are. Husserl gives his idea of a "prophetic consciousness,"—for which "every character of expectation, of what is coming into being, stands in view,"[77]—its orientation toward the intuitively given presentness of a "being" simply by transposing this presentness into the future. But one does not experience the futurity of an enacting or co-enacting in this manner. This futurity does not belong in an independent capacity of consciousness that joins the experience of something present. Rather, it belongs as an openness for what comes to the perception of something that is occurring. A perception of this kind does not "have" its content, but, rather, this content *comes to it*. The content enters and passes through. And, what is enacted is not fulfilled but is rather always also open for something to enter. This forms the experience of duration; one only knows that something lasts by sensing it become different or pass away, or by experiencing how it remains while something different—always and again something different—arrives and goes by.

This consideration may be illuminated especially well by examples that would seem to speak for the contrary, that is, for a clearly determinate and intuitive expectation. Augustine's example, I sing a song that I know, is an example of this kind. Here, one appears to know quite precisely what will occur, and appears to be able to anticipate the occurrence in representation, such that the course of singing would be only a transposition of what is to be expected. What is more, one is oneself the performer; it would seem that what will occur lies solely in one's own hands. Nevertheless, this is not how the performance is; it is fundamentally incalculable. It lacks the certainty of knowledge and ability, and even if such a certainty is supposed to be there it recedes with the leap into occurrence. This is the experience of "stage fright." It appears when one stands just before the leap into occurrence. It is not just that disturbances can arise which one has not previously reckoned with; even when everything was well prepared and goes "according to plans" irritations are possible, say, because something suddenly sounds different than one had ever imagined it. And now, in this moment, the meaning of a line of verse in the song being sung can dawn on one so that its expression takes shape in a manner that could not have been planned.

This is all because every activity is also always an occurrence. Disposition, practice, and intention cannot as such sublate the character of occurrence. The reason for this is time: Everything that is done is in time and therein respective, arriving, and going by, and, therefore, determined by the fact that arriving and passing by are not at our disposal. Never can everything be done all at once; only successively can it occur, in arriving and going by. Everything that is done thus stands in expectation of the next step; it is open to how this next step arrives in activity, and, because of this, whatever is done is never only activity but also waiting. Moreover, what is done is determined by what has just been done and was done. Activity is thus open to the inalterable, and not only changes things but also lets things rest. Both belong to activity itself; there could be no activity without the arrival of the new and passing away into inalterability. Activity is always also an occurrence; in this it has a temporal character and is not free.[78]

Not everything that occurs, however, is also done; some things simply occur. It rains, wind picks up, and then dies down again. The day begins and takes its course until it becomes evening and night. In the shift of the seasons, the days become longer and shorter, warmer, brighter, and then once again cool and grey. All activity and action as such rises from this occurring; all activity belongs to it insofar as it is itself occurrence. Time is the *dimension* of occurrence, that is, it is the openness, in which everything that is, is an occurrence. In coming and passing away it is thus also the whence and whither of everything that occurs.

The fact that this is how things are could be seen in terms of the time of enactment. Here it appeared how, in playing music or listening, a performed work can arrive and pass away as what occurs in perception and thus how, in activity, the openness of occurrence is also always at play. The occurrence in activity can remain unnoticed; the freer one feels, the more it will recede. But it can also completely occupy one's attentiveness. This does not have to make freedom disappear, as is the case when one loses control, or is someone being hunted down, driven out, someone for whom life merely still occurs.[79] It is also possible that one pays attention to occurrence and the time of occurrence for the sake of his ability to act. One's paying attention to time becomes quite clear if the difference of activity and occurrence emerges and one thereby sees oneself put into a relation to the temporal character of occurrence. In this case, one's effort to pay attention to time comprises a reckoning with it. One takes time into account, one counts on it, even if one does not measure the time itself, and, so, does not count in minutes, hours, days, and weeks. To be in time, this now means having time or having no time.

Occurrence becomes even clearer in its temporal character when one compares it, and, in this way measures it, with another occurrence. One knows how long or how briefly something lasts. Plato represented the order of things, the κόσμος, in this sense in the *Timeaus* as a great clock. Here, the creation of time is connected mythically with the order of the heavenly bodies, of the heavens. There can only be the experience of time if the heavenly bodies are "in accord with number,"[80] that is, complete their course at a fixed distance; time, however, is not the movement of the heavenly bodies itself but rather only comes into focus in regard to it. It is "the has-been and the will-be"[81] in the revolution of the heavenly bodies, that is, the openness of arriving and going by. The determinate revolutions—days and nights, months and years—are "parts of time,"[82] times in the sense that arriving and going by may be established in regard to them. Every occurrence has "its" time; an occurrence that is enacted in accord with time in an ordered manner, in fixed revolutions, however, provides a measure for the respective character of occurrence. The sun has completed its course and it becomes dark; that was a day. Something else that occurs, a journey for example, lasts seven days. That was its time. What one calls the measurement of time is nothing other than the depiction of something that occurs in regard to an occurrence of as much constancy as possible. In this way, one puts one's own activity into an occurrence; one gives oneself a determinate time in which something is to be done, and, measured by this, the activity can be quicker or slower. Often, one does not take the time that the activity would actually require, and, in this way, subordinates himself to a determinate time. The time one "has" or "does not have" is not the occurrence one measures himself against, but, rather, what is open in the difference between the definitive occurrence and one's own activity. One lets something arrive, for example, the next hour, and undertakes to do something in the determinate openness given with this arrival. In this, one continues to direct oneself by the order, which, according to the *Timeaus*, is the order of time. The clock is a model of the heavens, a presentation of heavenly revolution.

Being put into time becomes intuitive in the measurement of time; with this measurement, one knows that one has a determinate time not only for a specific activity, but also in general. In our difference from heavenly rotation, the tension between "the time of life" and "time of the world" breaks open.[83] If the tension is intensified, the possibility of the enactment of life can itself be put into question; when the time of life and the time of the world "appreciably gape apart from one another,"[84] life loses its "meaning," that is, it loses its "direction" in the openness of arriving and passing away, so that it may no longer be "led," but, rather, just occurs. Everything now appears to be put into unavailability and inalterability.

Because of this, time, or, *pars pro toto*: "the day," can also be understood as what burdens and plagues human life. Pindar can say in this sense that time hangs over the heads of human beings and coils around their course of life.[85] It leaves the course of life inestimable and puts it at the mercy of whatever is respectively given, so that based on this time becomes what controls human beings. Time, as Michael Theunissen formulates it, is "the preeminent way that the whole of the world lords over us."[86] A variant of this idea is found in Nietzsche's *Also Sprach Zarathustra*, where time is put into language from the viewpoint of the inalterability of the past and finds its concrete expression in the "spirit of gravity." Here, the talk is of the "it was" as "the will's gnashing of teeth and loneliest sorrow"; the will is "helpless against what has been done," "an angry spectator of all things of the past."[87]

It is only possible to talk of gravity, of burden, or even of the lordship of time, however, if time not only comprises the dimension of occurrence but also opens a possibility of relating to occurrence and its "lordship." But in this case the experience that time "burdens" is not extra-temporal or timeless; it is a temporal experience *with* time. It would only be necessary to refer to time as such as alienating, as alien to the essence of the human being, however, if there were a possibility of time that led beyond its burden.[88] Yet, whether this is how things are may only be judged once experiences with time have emerged more clearly; the considerations of the measurement of time were only a preparation for this. The concern now is with the *temporality* of human life.

§ 33. Temporality

In the time of enactment [*Vollzugszeit*] and time in its course [*Verlaufszeit*], as they were just described, there is the simplest experience of time. Something occurs, and one is oneself that by means of which it occurs; or, it occurs and one co-enacts what is occurring. One is in the flow of occurrence and experiences this as arriving and passing away at once. Something can only arrive insofar as something else passes away; something passes away and lets something else arrive. One thus experiences time in the course of occurrence.

Time becomes more conspicuous when one is no longer taken up in the flow of occurrence. This is how things are when something *accelerates*, that is, occurs too quickly, or *slows*, that is, occurs to slowly. Here, things are such that one no longer follows or can only do so with effort, or that one is "ahead" of the occurrence. In the first case, the retentional moment is intensified, in the second case the protentional, and in both, it comes to an incongruency of occurrence and inner experience. The experience of time as such is intensified with it.

It is also possible for something to become untethered from an occurrence. In this case, it no longer belongs in the movement that occurs and is enacted or comprehended, but, rather, stands in a *reference*. A decision that one reached could become conspicuous in this manner, say, because it proved to be disastrous. One does not, as is said in such a case, get past it. The mistake is inalterable; one had gladly done it otherwise, but now it is too late, and precisely for this reason one cannot free oneself from the matter. Or, one listens to a lecture and does not get a certain expression at issue in it. The one who speaks went over it too quickly or expressed oneself unclearly. Now one remains in suspense—because this indispensable sentence, as one believes, is lost, and then with it the development of the whole.

Something comparable is possible in reference to something that arrives. What is expected as the furtherance of whatever is occurring is slow in coming—say, the answer to a question in conversation. It remains absent, so that it becomes urgent as something imminent. Nothing is now more important than the absent answer.

Finally, there is likewise an experience of this kind in regard to something that has arrived but has still not passed away. In listening to a lecture, a formulation makes a special impression. It takes hold and steps out beyond the occurrence of the lecture. As for the lecture, one loses track of the further development of the idea. Because one cannot let something go, the possibility for the arrival of other things is barred. What has been held on to thus loses its context. It remains unintelligible and distant by being present.

In experiences of the kind outlined something takes hold: this regretted decision, this lost sentence, the answer that remains absent, the formulation that becomes preoccupying. Despite this something continues to occur; the movement, in which whatever had taken hold belongs, goes on. For a short while, the movement may in fact recede in favor of what now draws one's attention. The movement is there, however, if only because what has taken hold belongs in it. What has taken hold belongs in a specific stage of the movement, and, because it is held on to, it comes to stand in contrast with what the movement itself is. Something further arrives, but what one remains fixated on does not come; something goes by, but what one is thinking about has simply not occurred; or, something is held on to in the occurrence in such a way that it is raised out from what is arriving and going by. One no longer experiences the flow of occurrence, as in the course of time and time of enactment. Rather, something that is as if stopped at a determinate position of the flow is lifted out from the flow. What has taken hold as not arriving is *futural*. What does not simply go by, but, rather, stands out from the flow of occurrence as something gone by is *past*. And what is there now, insofar as attentiveness holds to it, is *present*.

This sounds as if Augustine would indeed once again receive his due. What is in the future would then be present as what lies ahead, what is in the present would be present in the present, and what is in the past would be present as what no longer is. There is no time-encompassing present, however, that divides itself apart into the present of what is in the future, in the present, and in the past. What is in the future is not present but rather something experienced from the standpoint of arrival but that does not arrive. It is *something* that is represented and determined in this way in distinction from everything that belongs in the flow of occurrence. It *is* not, however. Rather, it is possible. It can arrive, and can even be grasped already in its arrival without thereby belonging in an enactment. As long as it is in the future, however, its arrival remains *withheld*. It is similar for things of the past. Something in the past does not pass, however: for it, too, it is not the case that it *is*. Rather, it is *withdrawn*; it is irrevocably gone. In time it lies further and further back, but as something in the past it remains in its "no longer." By contrast, what is in the present is what *is*. It exists and is ascertainable because it *lasts* in time. Nothing that flashes only for a moment is present; the momentary is rather like a caesura of time; it is an interruption, and, in fact, because something enters. Yet, being present and, in this way, being, means: being more or less constant; whatever is stands in time. Everything else belongs in the flow of time; it arrives and goes by.

It is true that on the one hand, what is in the future and in the past are lifted out from arriving and going by, yet, on the other hand, both are determined based on the being of what is present. Both are *something* and, in this, grasped as it were on the model of what is. Both are, if in always different ways, at the same time the refutation of it: not simply nothing, but, rather, nonbeing, negation of being as withholding and withdrawal. Both, in turn, can thus only be grasped on the basis of arriving and going by. It is only possible for something to be in the future that can be present and then can become a thing of the past; it is only possible for something to be a thing of the past that was once present and before that in the future; and it is only possible for something to be in the present that is no longer in the future and not yet in the past. Something that can never be present and then past is not in the future. It is a mere representation of something that cannot be and is not. There is in time only what can be, respectively is, or has been.

What is in the future and in the past are not as Augustine thought, then, present in a modified manner. But neither is his determination of their givenness refuted here. What is in the future and in the past are given not simply in themselves, but, rather, for expectation and memory. This does not mean that they would be mere representations; otherwise, what is in the future could not enter and what is in the past could not have been. Of course, as what is in the future and in the past, they are there always only relatively. What is still in the future today can be past tomorrow; what is in the past today was in the future yesterday. The same is true of what is in the present; even what is in the present is not simply there but rather can be only when it actually lasts and draws one's attention to it. Likewise, what is in the future is first there not *through* expectation, and what is in the past not *through* memory, but, rather, *for* them. The two, as Augustine says, are not "in the soul,"[89] yet neither do they exist as they are without it.

It is only in this belongingness of something with the reference that it has toward its possible experience that there is what Augustine already took to be the enactment of an occurrence: three times, that is, fundamental possibilities of time, in which experience of time may be had in regard to something that has a temporal character. It follows from this that "future," "present," and "past" are expressions that can be equally well ascribed to *something* as to *someone*; something belongs in the future, and the future belongs to someone who is able to expect something. Future, present, and past are openness in that they enable something to be there for someone in an ever-particular manner. In them and in them alone is there ever a specific *correlation* between something and the possible experience of it, precisely the correlations of expectation, attentiveness, and memory. If success is achieved in grasping these correlations more precisely, the times shall emerge more precisely as well.

The first thing to notice here is that expectation, attentiveness, and memory are not neutral possibilities of reference. They are always positively or negatively colored, more or less clearly perceptible—even seeming indifference tends toward the one or the other. Expectation is always hope or fear, attentiveness always being attracted or repulsed, and memory is either relief that something is over or the regret of a loss.

All of these attitudes can appear in different intensities. Hope can be a scarcely detectable, calm approval; it is fine with someone when what is expected comes. Or, it is urgent; in this case, according to one's own understanding, all of one's fortunes, perhaps even one's bare life, depends on what comes. The possibilities of fear reach from uneasiness to mortal anxiety. There is a comparable scale for the two forms of attentiveness; being attracted goes from being lost in devotion to something to a more incidental cognizance, being repulsed from quiet resistance to disgust or to panicked horror. The regret of a loss can be equanimity or likewise take the form of the deepest sadness. Relief exists as the satisfaction that something burdensome or tiring is over up to the thankfulness that one has escaped once again.

The different forms of expectation, attentiveness, and memory are thus not directed toward something determinate that they "intend" as something given for itself. They are sustained by *how* something is seen to be arriving either in possibility or probability, how one has the existence of something or its having passed away in inner experience. There is—and, indeed, each time in the two forms—calm as well as impatient expectation, attentiveness, and memory, and these, again, in different degrees of intensity. How one's attitude is from this standpoint each time depends on how remote it is and also on how one stands toward its arriving, its duration, and its having past. It depends, in other words, on how what is in the future, present, or past is *referred* to the one who experiences it by the fact that something can occur or occurs. The different forms of expectation, attentiveness and memory are, moreover, *attitudes* toward how it is to be in time; something is kept out of the occurrence that has been untethered from it. It is *near* or *far*, taken to be something constant nearby or to be something inconstant in the possibility of removal. What has not as yet occurred can be urgently hoped for as something that is occurring soon and is already announcing itself in its arrival, but it will only be possible to fear it less acutely than something that stands immediately before one. Attentiveness to a constant existence can be calmer than that to an inconstant one; however, something enduring can also burden, inconstancy can be an impetus for hope. Relief and regret are directed according to how far something has already been removed into the past. It can therefore happen that sadness actually only becomes deep sometime after a loss. Shortly after the loss, one was still completely unable to measure it because the existence of what was lost still stood before one's eyes all too vividly. Right after the misfortune, avoidance was still possible and by contrast relief was in fact most intense. As what transpired recedes into a removal, relief decreases, regret increases. It appears clearly here that time is a remove.

More careful consideration of these attitudes makes it clear why they are, according to their essence, attitudes in time. However they may be, what is essential for them is *that in them something occurs to someone*. Each of them is a πάθος in the precise sense of the word: Something that affects one. This is not to be taken in the narrow sense that something factically happens to someone. This is only possible in the present, only, that is, when something comes and concerns one in his present; it strikes him and changes his state, possibly his life. What affects one, however, does not have to be anything in the present; it is also possible that something withheld or withdrawn, that is, in the future or the past, affects one.

Being affected is no simple matter of making reference to something; one does not decide for it. Rather, one finds oneself put into a reference to something, and this also means that what affects one guides the position and attitude in which one finds oneself. What is withheld, withdrawn, or what is there puts one into time in such a way that it determines the removal at which it is encountered. It imposes itself or shirks back and it is given to one in such a troubling manner that one would like to get out of the way, or in such refusal that one perhaps attempts to overcome its removal from him. It is impossible to achieve these things, however, when what is encountered temporally remains what it is. In such cases, what is encountered always remains at a removal in its own way, and, in this removal, it affects one. One has come under the influence of things, and, through this removal, one is placed all the more emphatically into the preserved occurrence of things.

Aristotle determined πάθη in this sense as that whereby those to whom a change occurs make distinctions in regard to the entrance of a change attended by pain or pleasure.[90] The πάθη are the manners of one's inner experience of changes, and, in fact, such that the entrance of the change (κρίσις) is painful or pleasurable. This, too, does not have to be experienced in the sense of the factical experience of pain or pleasure. A πάθος is impairing or uplifting even when the change is confined to memory as one that has already taken place or is anticipated in the imagination.

The latter is the case in fear (φόβος), which Aristotle determines as pain or disturbance through imagining an imminent evil that is destructive or inflicts pain.[91] In this, fear is not an accompanying feeling to the fact that something is experienced as threatening. Rather, it is the concern for something that is itself threatening; if one were not to experience something imminent as threatening because one believed himself to be safe in the face of it, then one would also be without fear. But fear is just as little an anticipation that works to picture what is imminent; in fear, what threatens is concerning precisely in its remoteness, it affects one. The fact that the expectation (προσδόκημα) of an unpleasant occurrence is itself unpleasant and, accordingly, that the expectation of a pleasant occurrence is itself pleasant, has already been established in the *Philebus*.[92] It is only through time that this is possible. Time, understood as temporality, is the remove in which something is of concern.

When one thinks along these lines, however, one assumes that something *can* be of concern in the first place. The reference and attitude one is put into because something is concerning is only possible because one is open to letting himself be concerned by something. This is the guiding consideration of Heidegger's understanding of time. On this consideration, one can only be concerned, struck, in time because one himself *is* temporal. Temporality is the "ontological meaning" of "Dasein," that is, the meaning "wherein the intelligibility" of Dasein is maintained, "although it" does not have to come "into view explicitly and thematically."[93] Human existence [*Dasein*] can only be understood in its being [*Sein*] on the basis of temporality. It is only as something temporal that it, as Dasein, is as it is. Yet, as Heidegger thinks, Dasein's boundedness to temporality may also be reversed. Just as Dasein is temporal according to its essence, likewise time—understood as temporality—belongs exclusively to Dasein. Heidegger goes a step further: only temporality is time proper; only when time is understood as temporality is it grasped in its essence.

Time is, according to its first and essential determination, the temporality of Dasein.

Heidegger's idea may not simply be rejected. This holds even if one wants to understand time not like he did as temporality, but rather wants to understand temporality as the conscious form of time. Precisely in this latter case, one has to test how far Heidegger's idea leads in order to put the workability of an alternative conception of it to the test. If it turns out that Heidegger's idea leads of its own accord to a conception of temporality different from his own, then one may take up his intention without following his own elaboration. Of special interest here are Heidegger's discussions of the relationship of being affected and time. This relationship can be made even clearer in taking orientation from his discussions and, thereby, at the same time an even sharper light can fall on our understanding of temporality. For Heidegger, temporality is not only an experience of time in the sense developed thus far. Rather, he wishes to show that there is an experience of temporality in which temporality stands out against time insofar as something occurs in time and which is revealed as what makes time possible. The experience of time would, in this case, be the key to a comprehensive determination of the essence of time itself.

Heidegger's understanding of temporality may be developed in connection with the Aristotelian determination of fear. He takes this up as an example[94] in order to clarify the possibility of fear based on Dasein and the imminence of something threatening based on Dasein's temporality. The decisive idea of his discussion is that one can only fear something determinate because Dasein himself is ultimately threatened with everything that is threatening. If it does not matter for Dasein himself, then one would simply investigate what stands in front of him without being concerned by it in some manner. As Heidegger says, fear refers "not only to 'what is in the future,' in the sense of what first arrives 'in time.' Rather, this referring is itself futural in the originarily temporal sense."[95] The referentiality to something in the future could not be fear other than in this way. The characteristic openness of Dasein that is fear is only there because not-yet-being belongs to Dasein. Something that can occur enters into this not-yet-being. By entering, it can be of concern.

For Heidegger, however, the possibility of fear may not be made intelligible based on the futurity of Dasein alone. Rather, one's futurally directed "awaiting" in fear lets what is threatening "*come back* to one's factically heedful ability to be."[96] This is immediately comprehensible from the situation of a threat: something can only be threatening by appearing as detrimental for a given state; one fears what impairs one's own person, his form and circumstances of life. To be afraid of something is, as Heidegger expresses it, always also "fear for. . . ."[97] One fears for his own life, even if this is not threatened as such but only in a specific respect—say, in its directions, convictions, or possibilities. As Heidegger formulates it, in fear the concern is with the "factically heedful ability to be," or, as it is also called, with the "thrownness" of Dasein. This, conversely, is not simply given. It comprises what one has been, which is always one's own, and can therefore only be experienced in the temporal openness of what Heidegger refers to as "having been." Fear is only possible, then, insofar as Dasein as such is equally past and futural.

The decisive idea of Heidegger's analysis of temporality, however, has not yet been named. Fear does not put into focus the fact that future and having been as they were outlined are forms of the temporality of Dasein, as Heidegger thinks. This only happens when one succeeds in achieving distance from the occurrence that, say, determines the fear. Whenever something threatening comes at one in such a determinate respect that one comes back to one's past being, the characteristic openness of temporality remains unexperienced. To Heidegger's mind, this openness quickly becomes covered over, and, indeed, because one attempts to *conduct* oneself in regard to the threat as the fear discloses it. Temporality as such only comes into focus if future and having been are not covered over by the present of the conduct. This is only possible, however, when what stands in front of one and is occurring becomes unimportant.

The fact that it is in the character of conduct to cover over temporality is also elucidated by the example of fear. By attempting to find a way out of the threat one forgets oneself and leaps "from one thing to the next, without grasping any specific possibility."[98] This, in turn, closes off the thrownness of Dasein insofar as one no longer knows one's way in the world, which alone can allow possibilities of conduct to be familiar and graspable. The "forgetfulness of confusion" that is supposed to rule over the mindless conduct of the one in fear likewise modifies the future; it is just the "depressed or confused awaiting" that is characteristic of fear and distinguishes it "from a pure expectation."[99]

This description is conspicuously one-sided. Certainly, in fear things can come to a mindless conduct of the kind Heidegger outlines, but the idea that this is the only possible conduct is not illuminating. And, although Heidegger summons the Aristotelian determination of fear for his description, one will not be able to hold this responsible for his one-sidedness. If Aristotle determines fear as ταραχή, he does not intend a spiritual confusion by this, but, rather—as even the parallel to pain already indicates—a disturbance; something that is standing in front of one threatens either to be painful or to upset the order of one's relations of life. It is possible to react to such threats, however, in a thoroughly considered manner; one then takes the appropriate precautions to protect oneself or attempts to fend off the disturbance or at least to keep it within limits.

If Heidegger does not take this possibility into consideration, this is due solely to the intention of his description: he wishes to describe the situation in which something determinate is imminent as self-forgetfulness so that the experience of temporality can be emphasized all the more clearly by it. It is only if nothing determinate is imminent that time is demonstrated as temporality and thereby as the time proper to Dasein.

It is revealed as such in *anxiety*, which Heidegger describes in terms of fear and in contrast with it.[100] Anxiety, which unlike fear is not an affect but rather a mood, brings "Dasein before its own most thrownness" and reveals "the uncanniness of being-in-the-world, which is familiar in the everyday."[101] This is possible, as Heidegger wants to show, because there is nothing determinate in anxiety that is threatening. "Actually nothing" is frightening.[102] Anxiety, in Heidegger's sense, simply rises up for no specific reason, such that one is unable to act in it. Anxiety immobilizes one and, as long as it lasts, excludes all hectic pursuits. In anxiety, nothing specific comes up for one, and, so, one is also not referred to the "factical ability to be" in a determinate regard. In anxiety, nothing is threatening, rather, one feels "uncanny."[103]

Uncanniness, as it is indicated here, is no construct. It may be elucidated by a number of examples. Uncanny is what is unfamiliar, say, an abandoned building lying in the dark, a situation that one does not feel himself to be a match for, perhaps also the sudden experience of something alien about people with whom one up until then knew himself to be connected. In anxiety, one as it were loses the ground beneath one's feet. This would not be the case if one could ascribe the experienced uncanniness to something or other. The building lying in the dark is not threatening, and just as little is the situation that tests one; one can prepare as best as possible and nevertheless be anxious. Also the others from whom one all at once feels separated have not initiated the estrangement through their conduct. "It is actually nothing," and precisely this is the uncanny.

Heidegger interprets this state of affairs by determining anxiety as a relationship to the world. Insofar as the world slips away as the familiar context of everyday being and conduct, "the world as such" may be understood as "the before-which of anxiety." The "innerworldy being" is "completely inconsequential"; although one still knows completely what it would be used for, one is separated from it as by a glass wall. It has no significance for one anymore and precisely "on the basis of this insignificance," it is the case that "the world in its worldliness imposes itself still more."[104] With this, however, the possibility of being in the world and of conducting oneself in it likewise imposes itself. Insofar as what is becomes uncanny and thereby also insignificant, only this possibility remains; this possibility finds no answer in plans, perspectives, and manners of conduct. Since one no longer knows how one should and can be in the world, "being-in-the-world itself" proves to be the "about which" of anxiety.[105]

Anxiety is accordingly a radical experience of being possible that arises from impossibility. The experience of one's possible impossibility[106] throws Dasein back on itself and on its dependence on the world. Correspondingly, as Heidegger thinks, temporality is also no longer displaced as it is in fear. One does not take action and because of this the moment remains open; it remains, as Heidegger says, as "the moment... in wait."[107] Because one's conduct remains focused on its possibility, past being cannot form the context of familiar obviousness that alone makes conduct possible. It thus comes into focus as being possible; it is regained from its lostness in conduct as what it always already was. This does not mean, however, that one gains a possibility of conduct from the context of the world, and because of this, the future of one's being-possible also remains open. Anxiety takes one "not only back from 'worldly' possibilities, but, rather, "at the same time" provides "the possibility of *what is one's own*"* in Dasein: an "ability to be" that is conceived solely based on one's Dasein itself.[108] Understood in this way, anxiety is like a pause in Dasein. One is removed from the enactment of existence [*Dasein*] and this opens the temporality of Dasein, just as a street draws one's attention as such when one stops driving it. Temporality comes into focus, as Heidegger thinks, because past, future, and present remain empty.

On the one hand, this is illuminating: the fact that there is no Dasein without having been does only show itself insofar as one is not reminded of something determinate that one has been; one becomes attentive to the presentness of one's conduct by learning that one could conduct himself "in the moment" and not completely abandon himself to the course and enactment of a determinate activity. And, finally, the futurity of one's own Dasein first comes to the fore when the question of how one can or wants to be remains in suspension.

Yet, on the other hand, one never experiences the possibility in isolation. Anxiety does not displace one into pure being possible; it is only an interruption, and it would not be what it is if what it is blocked from were completely out of play. The insignificance of the world only brings about anxiety in so far as it is still known in its significance. The impossibility of conduct is only of concern insofar as one would like to act, but feels himself to be peculiarly immobile and, for this reason, unable to do so. The openness of the ability to be is, in this case, like the opening of an abyss, if possibilities, plans, and intentions are still there, but just no longer mean anything. What Heidegger describes as anxiety is the feeling of how it is to be excluded from the world. For the one in anxiety, however, the occurrence of the world continues on. Instead of Dasein being thrown back on its original temporality here, the divide between temporality and the time of things opens up, or, with Blumenberg, between the "time of life" and the "time of the world." Without being able to separate them, one's own time and the time in which something occurs are no longer suited

---

*["One's own" is the translation for *eigentlichen* here. Note that "authentic" often is the translation of Heidegger's *eigentlich*. —Transl.]

to one another. The oppressiveness and stranglehold of anxiety lies in this, and this is something that speaks from the word itself, or, more precisely, from its relation with the Latin *angor*; *angor* is the lacing together, the strangling, the constriction of the throat. The same fundamental experience would lie in the leaden passivity of depression; here, too, the world has been lost as one in which a person is able to be, and yet at the same time remains there in a cumbersome and depressing manner. Expectation, attentiveness, and memory remain empty; there is nothing that takes hold as something in the future, in the present, or in the past. And, if one were thrust into an occurrence under the aegis of the time of enactment, one would nevertheless remain indifferent, and so, in a radical manner, uninvolved with the matter. The occurrence would run its course like a movement of things; one would enact it and yet have nothing to do with it.

Based on this consideration, the analysis of anxiety would bring to light the opposite of what Heidegger intended. Instead of disclosing Dasein as "isolated, pure, thrown ability to be,"[109] anxiety would bring Dasein's dependency on the world into focus. Anxiety would be no ἐποχή that would liberate one from ties to the world. As an epoché accompanying the experience of the "not-at-home,"[110] it would have to be located all the more emphatically in the world of things.

Heidegger has come very close to this matter of fact in another and, indeed, one of his best, phenomenological analyses. Certainly, the quality of the description is also thanks to the appropriateness of the described matter; the temporality of Dasein comes into focus in boredom better still than in anxiety. Here, the intention of Heidegger's description in his winter 1929–30 lecture course had not essentially changed when compared to *Sein und Zeit*; just as before, he wishes to show that time is to be grasped essentially as the "originary temporality"[111] of Dasein. Accordingly, he structures his analysis of boredom such that it takes him off the subject of the things that occur. For boredom proper—Heidegger calls it "deep boredom"—there is no impetus; it rises up from Dasein himself, inexplicably, through something that can be boring. It is not that *something* bores one, for example—they are Heidegger's examples—the soirée that one takes part in but does not feel comfortable at, or the wait at the train station where one somehow has to pass the time. Rather, one is bored.* Deep boredom does not concern the respective occurrence that one finds unappealing, and just as little one himself as someone who does not know what to do with himself. It is encompassing and anonymous. In deep boredom we are, as Heidegger says, "not merely relieved of our everyday personality, somehow remote and alien from it, but, with this, also at the same

---

*["One is bored" is the translation for "...'es' ist einem langweilig" here. —Trans.]

time lifted up beyond our respective, specific situation and the relevant beings surrounding us."[112] In deep boredom, an encompassing indifference prevails, in regard not only to ourselves but also to what is outside of us. This indifference makes things such, as Heidegger says, "that everything matters equally much and equally little,"[113] and, so, all of what is "as a whole" becomes indifferent.[114] When one expects nothing and when nothing fills one's memory anymore, when nothing occupies one's attentiveness anymore, temporality—empty as it now is—is brought to bear as such. In the boredom that refuses any interests, Dasein is claimed by temporality itself. Dasein, as Heidegger summarizes this idea, is "captivated" in temporality and by it.[115]

Heidegger underscores that this captivation is not to be grasped in contrast to occurrence in time. Captivating time is not "what remains at a stand in distinction from flow" but is rather the time "beyond such flowing and its standing"; the focus is on "the time that" is "always Dasein himself as a whole."[116] This rebuff—for which he provides no further grounds—is consequential, not least of all if one reads it together with a contradictory formulation found shortly before it. One's withdrawal as it is expressed in regard to what is, Heidegger says here, is only possible "if Dasein is no longer able to go along."[117] What is Dasein "no longer" supposed to be able to go "along with"? But of course: the occurrence that is in time. Because Heidegger wishes to bring the temporality of Dasein into focus as purely as possible, he does not come around to conceiving its belongingness with the time of occurrence. From here, it is only one step to the insight that life-worldly integration into temporality and no less into the time of enactment cannot be enacted without the world of things and its time of occurrence. Without the world of things and its "time of the world," the life-world does not have meaning in its time of enactment and temporality.

Conversely, this would indicate that there is meaning because "time of life" and "time of the world" are in concordance. This would not be something to cause or otherwise to be seen to; when one is affected so as to feel taken out of the occurrence of the world, the contrary also has to come by affecting one. What affects one gives or takes the possibility of meaning. Because every being-affected is an experience of time, time is what gives and takes.

§ 34. Constellations of Meaning

Meaning, it is recalled once more, is direction, say, as "clockwise" is a direction of turning. The meaning of a linguistic expression is what is intended by it, that is, what is said in regard to what is supposed to be shown. Someone speaks about the minster tower and in fact wanted to draw attention to it. It is thus that what is said has meaning. The meaning of an action, then, is the aim at which it is aimed. An action is meaningful if it serves to realize what was intended.

Even if the aims of actions are intended, what gives rise to an action does not come from oneself. It comes to one from the context of life in the world; even if one freely chooses one's aim, there is an impetus, and it is always connected with expectations; one hopes for or fears something. Insofar as it is possible, one acts "in accordance with the meaning" of an expectation colored this way or that. This gives the action a meaning.

If this is so, then the meaning of action always has to do with things that affect one. Something has to take hold in expectation as something in the future and strike one in this way in order that one can intend anything at all. Things are similar when one says something that is directed toward another. One hopes that one makes oneself intelligible, one fears that one will not have been appropriately understood; it is because of this that one searches for words. Or, one suddenly notices the light in the filigree tracery of the minster tower. It has entered into one's attentiveness, it is present, and one would like that another share this attentiveness; so one shows him what one sees. Remembering, too, can give meaning to what one is doing or saying: One does something in memory of someone whom one has lost; one tells of something that one has in inner experience and that fills one then as before with joy or sadness. This is also how things are in history in the sense of the study of history. It only has a "use for life"[118] if it is connected with an endowment of meaning, say, because it gives one's own activity a context that reaches beyond it. If nothing of the kind is in play, the activity becomes an empty gesture, what is told becomes something that one recites as if called on or that one carries out as an empty enumeration of facts. Both are then without meaning.

The meaning here does not lie in activity or in saying, although just as little in being affected. It is at play in the removal between the two. Something at a remove is passed on in being affected, it concerns one. One comes into accord with this by conducting oneself *in accordance with the meaning* of what is passed on. One directs oneself in action or in speech toward something that concerns one and, in this, one takes up the direction that this something had as it became a concern. One retraces the direction and therein comes into accord with it. By conducting oneself in accordance with the meaning of something, the conduct is meaningful.

Meaning, then, is the correlation between what is in the future, in the present, or in the past and the conduct that is always one's own. It is a relation that is always to be seen "from two sides," "in two directions." It arises, however, from what affects one and also from what is of concern; meaning is only possible because something can affect one is such a way that one can conduct oneself in accordance with its meaning.

The removal at play in the correlation of meaning is a removal in time. Something of concern is apportioned in time, and conduct, too, has a temporal character. Conduct as action or speech is always also a temporal process. This recedes if action and speech proceed simply of their own accord. In this case, it is not primarily in time but rather freedom and language. The fact that conduct also has a temporal character only comes into focus when it is no longer easily enacted and distance emerges to what one would like to cause or say; what one intends is only reached with effort, what one would like to say gets said only in repeated attempts. The correlation of meaning becomes all the more clear, then, the greater the delay of one's conduct is in its endeavor to accord with what has affected one. The intensity of experience grows with the removal of what affects one, and this also means the experience of time.

With growing intensity, what had always already held for the correlation of meaning also becomes clearer: insofar as what affects one is temporal one cannot make good on it. A conduct directed toward something in the future is possible only as long as it remains what it is, that is, something that does not arrive. As long as something in the present lasts, it outlasts every conduct that is supposed to accord with it. And, something in the past always remains withdrawn; no activity for its sake and no memory put into language ever retrieves it.

Yet in every case the correlation of meaning can also once again fade or disappear just as it had entered; something that affects one is no longer binding, it recedes or remains as if standing isolated in expectation, attentiveness, or memory. Something can therefore lose its meaning, or something that one has always done the same way or similarly all at once receives meaning or a new meaning. Meaning remains in every case instable, dependent on what takes hold in expectation, memory, and attentiveness. This may possibly be revised in the next moment through arriving and passing by. Something occurs, and it proves one's expectation wrong, takes the duration away from something in the present, or makes something remembered unimportant. Meaning, as it is shown here, then, has no anchoring in what occurs. And how is something supposed to be anchored in the flow of arriving and passing by? The correlation of meaning is actually a *constellation*[119]; something assembles in time and forms a bridge in time.

There is of course an experience of constancy in arriving and passing by: *repetition*. What this is appears to be clear: something occurs that has already occurred once or many times. For example, a day begins once again, and once again one does the same thing that one has done on the days before. Here something is repeated, one repeats something oneself although one barely experiences it as repetition. It is too uniform, there is too little tension in it. It is true that a day begins "once again," but this occurs in a familiar self-repeating change. What has become habituated does not step out of continuity of the every day. It is true that things are different when a festival or ritual is repeated. But, here, too, the repetition is barely noticed as such. Even if the same festival as the year before is thought of, it nevertheless stands completely for itself every time that it is celebrated. The *observance* of the festival or ritual is what is decisive, not the repetition.[120]

The repetition is also barely experienced as such when it is intentionally enacted. This appears to be a paradox only for a moment. When one repeats what one said or did previously, perhaps even announcing it, the novelty is predominant; more important than the "once again" is the activity. Memory provides as it were only the starting point for one's view to the aim. Kierkegaard names repetition in this sense a "memory directed forward," whereas he signifies memory as "repetition directed backwards."[121] And he adds that repetition makes the human being happy, memory makes him unhappy; repetition leads to something reachable, whereas memory always has only to do with what is past in its withdrawal. It is only for this reason that active repetition is not bound to what is remembered; in the "once again," it is not the same thing that comes again, rather, one poses a difference against it; as the one who acts, one is now different or a different person in contrast to what one was in the past. Gilles Deleuze can for this reason signify repetition as "pure creative movement"[122] and say that a "differential" is disguised in it.[123] Under the aspect of active repetition even the unrepeatable can therefore appear as repeatable. Nietzsche's thought experiment of the eternal recurrence of the same is actually an apotheosis of inimitability. If everything recurs precisely as it has already once been—"this spider and this moon light between the trees and likewise this moment"[124]—then the experience of recurrence cannot belong in what recurs. What recurs, then, cannot be experienced as such, but it may nevertheless be said that one wants what is—precisely as it is—once more.

This already indicates indirectly the conditions under which repetition comes into focus as such. There must be a clear tie to the past, not one given in the natural course of things or through habit, and there must likewise be a clear experience of the new that, however, does not belong to a deliberate activity. Otherwise, what the repetition makes possible and what is at play in it remains hidden or at least unclear, such that it is also to be experienced based on this: time. This, however, this may also be reversed: by experiencing repetition, one experiences time, and, in fact, in particular intensity. Repetition is a temporal effect in which the essence of time comes into focus as such. The constancy that accompanies it is therefore a constancy of time.

A scene from Proust's novel *Le temps retrouvé* reveals how this is to be understood with particular impressiveness.[125] The narrator is on the way to a concert in the city palace of Herzog von Geurmant. In the courtyard of the palace, he notices an approaching car so late that he has to jump to the side. In doing this, he steps on the poorly cut paving stones at the edge of the courtyard and is unexpectedly torn from his thoughts. By putting his foot on the stone that is somewhat higher than the one before it, a condition of happiness (*félicité*) [*Beglückung*] seizes him that initially remains inexplicable to him. He attempts to make his inner experience clear by putting his foot on the stone numerous times, but the test is without result.[126] The "repetition directed backwards" that is initially undertaken as if gropingly and the forgetting of the future that accompanies it offers a point of reference; in both, a promise is connected with the unevenness of the stones. The promise is fulfilled through a recollection that has nothing to do with memory in which something from the past is fixed. Rather, the paving stones in Paris are connected with the slabs of the baptistery of San Marco in such a way that they make the narrator's stay in Venice detectable again. At the same time, the stay in Venice steps into a relationship with the present in Paris.

What is sketched here is an experience that arises only in the meeting of two different and nevertheless concordant moments; it is a constellation of the greatest intensity that holds the two moments in suspension and, in this manner, takes away one's natural attitude toward what occurs factically and what is factically remembered. Without the memory of the stay in Venice, the irregular paving stones in the courtyard of the city palace would be without importance; they are significant only insofar as they stand in relation to a remembered inner experience. This also holds for the inner experience that the narrator is suddenly reminded of; during the inspection of the basilica, the irregularity of the slabs might hardly have been conspicuous. The condition of happiness that the narrator feels only comes into existence because a present inner experience points back to a past one—a past inner experience on the basis of which, in turn, the present one is experienced.

The reference, as Proust describes it, is not immediately clear. It arises, rather, initially only insofar as it brings about a sense of happiness [*Glücksgefühl*] that is at once demand and promise. With this sense of happiness, the experience has momentarily stepped out of the flow of everyday life. The experienced situation is as if put at a remove from time and again put into it, as if taken away and given again. This momentary affair could not have the character of a promise, however, if the reference to the past were not contained in it. In the moment, the constellation of meaning is as if condensed; it is not yet unfolded, it is like a bud that already contains the flower within it. If the happy moment could not unfold into a constellation of meaning, it would again soon lose is intensity and would sink back into the flow of occurrence. The moment counts only in regard to its possible unfolding; it is first realized in the remove that is time. The moment is, then, no "atom of eternity," as Kierkegaard thought[127]; it is condensed, not yet unfolded, time.

What comes into existence through the connection of these two inner experiences is no memory; memory is there *simpliciter*, namely, in the photographic snapshot (*instantanés*) that the memory (*mémoire*) of the narrator had taken in Venice.[128] The pictures are there and can be retrieved, yet even the idea of describing them leads to aversion and antipathy. They are like an exhibition of photographs[129] that has become a matter of indifference to the narrator. This only changes through the experience in which the present and the past inner experiences are connected. The one thus receives a direction from the other. The present one has this direction right from the start, before all indications, because it refers to what is in the past. The past inner experience, conversely, reflects the present one; it can only be experienced as inner experience instead of "snapshot" because the present generates its character as inner experience. The pictures of memory that previously only had a significance now have a meaning for the first time.

The formation of meaning occurs through repetition. The constellation of the two inner experiences forms itself in the "once again," without which each of them would remain meaningless. This constellation is only possible, however, through the removal produced by time. The experience Proust describes would not be brought about if one were to step numerous times on uneven paving stones one after another. What is present has to reach into the remove, which is the essence of time.

The sensuous is indispensable for repetition as Proust describes it. The "inner experiences," spoken of here are *sensations*[130]; this is to be taken literally. Without feeling, be it of the uneven paving stones, be it also of the madeleins dipped in tea that Proust comes back to in the context of the discussed scene, there would only be the snapshot of memory. Nevertheless, the condition of happiness that the narrator of the *Recherche* pours through in stepping on the uneven paving stone is not the happiness of feeling. It is this just as little as the feeling of the madeleins is primarily a matter of the taste buds. The condition of happiness is also enigmatic in the sense that the experience of happiness is that of a riddle and the riddle, in turn, that of a promise. The riddle therefore does not want to be solved but rather realized in such a way that one follows the direction pre-given with it. The riddle promises a meaning, and this warrants understanding.

Feeling is promising of meaning because it is the perception of the objective. Something is objective in that it *enters* and promises the possibility of repetition, be it, as sketched by Proust, the "repetition directed backwards" in which it is confirmed that the feeling has already been a repetition, be it as a "memory directed forwards," now, however, in the sense, that a new experience of what has stepped-in and stepped-across-from is held to be possible. The "over against" in the objective has its own temporal character; it belongs to no occurrence and does not come up in expectation, attentiveness, and memory. It stands in time by referring to futural and past possibilities.

The objectivity of what is experienced can be a moment; in the moment in which the constellation between the two feelings Proust sketches is loosened, the stones that still just gave a direction sink back into the everyday context of the life-world. Yet, with objectivity, it is revealed that feelings and inner experiences are not bound to one another solely in terms of the life-world. In time, there is boundedness in the world insofar as the world is a world of things. And with time, there is meaning in this world.

This meaning does not become clear solely through feelings. Without the "snapshot" of the stay in Venice, there would be no context that the repetition could open up. Meaning is in need of presentation and prior still to this the significances in which this presentation is held. An openness is needed that allows one to take the directions indicated in time. In this spirit, Proust calls things that leave their impression in feeling hieroglyphs that one at first believes to represent only material things.[131] Although deciphering them is difficult, only they provide a truth that is to be *read*. Compared with them, the truths that the understanding grasps directly—that is, transparently in the world of daylight without a memorable impression of things—would have less depth, less necessity than those that life imparts to us against out will in an impression, those that are material because they entered through our senses, but from which we would nevertheless be able to wrest spirit.[132] The reference to reading makes it clear enough that this is not be understood as the absolution of "spirit" from sensible impressions, that is, from whatever affects one in time. The truths that are disclosed solely through a reading of the impressions retain their connection to writing solely because they can be re-examined in it through repetition. They are in need of such examination if they are not to mutate into truths of the understanding without depth and necessity. Only the impression that is felt in time and repeatable in time is, as it is called, a criterion of truth.[133]

What this intends is the truth of the writer, that is, the truth of the interpretations of the script of impressions that itself has the character of writing. Not only written works in the narrow sense stand in time as something objective, however, but all objects. The impressions that they leave behind are still deeper than those of the objective; the constellations of meaning that written works put their reader, observer, and listener in are deeper and at the same time clearer than those of the script of feeling as it is to be read in "half darkness."[134] As intensifications of objectivity, they are at the same time intense possibilities of the experience of time. As such, they are clarifications of human life.

Chapter 7

Life

§ 35. In Hermeneutical Space

We are three-dimensional; in all conduct and experience, in everything we do and what affects us we are freedom, language, and time. Insofar as a deliberation is at play in action, it has to do with language, and the enactment of action is at the same time a course of time. Speech can belong together with action. In the play of positions one also shows oneself to be someone who does or has done something, one shows others accordingly; one lets action show itself. There is written thought only in free contemplation. Speech, in turn, has to do with time; it is a temporal process. Moreover, nothing can come to language unless something enter and occurs; everything that is encountered is in time and abstraction receives its name because it disregards this even as it presupposes it. How one experiences time does not come into focus without language. Time is arranged ahead of time in language with temporal expressions and temporal forms, such as future, present, imperfect. Expectation and memory have to be put in words; without grasping them in the word, what still lies ahead or is past is not there in a graspable manner. That time is the openness of occurrence is proven particularly in action; without the freedom of action, something affecting one could not be an experience of unfreedom.

This three-dimensionality concerns not only us, but also things; they, too, are in freedom, language, and time. They are free insofar as they are independent from us and are accessible in this independence. They are in language insofar as they show themselves, although also insofar as their indeterminacy is an appearance of texture. They belong in time because something occurs with them as with us, or because something affects us based on them.

This indicates that our three-dimensionality belongs together with that of things. If we were not in common with things in time, nothing of them could affect us; in arriving, being there and passing by, we share with them the same fate. We could also not show things if we were not together with them in language. And, they do not show themselves fundamentally differently than we; we are not only beings that show things but also something that shows itself. Finally, we could do nothing with things and have no effect on them if we were not in freedom together with them. We are with the things, in some respects even like the things, we share the world with them in hermeneutical space. Life-world and thing-world are not two possibilities that somehow exist next to one another. Life-world is always at the same time thing-world. The difference between us and things is only that although they are in the life-world, they are not life-worldly.

The question now is as follows: How is one supposed to signify, and, based on this signification, understand this three-dimensionality more precisely, that is, the life- and thing-worldliness that we are? The question has been answered time and again—just now and already earlier—with a word that offers itself; the word "life." There are two reasons for the familiar obviousness with which this word appears: First, it is rather unspecific without saying nothing. The one thing, to which the living stands in opposition, is the inanimate, and even this is only intelligible based on life. Without life, there is nothing inanimate, and not at all death; the absolutely inanimate, a universe in which nothing lived, could not even be named inanimate.

As unspecific as it is, the word proves to be preferable to others if one wishes to avoid significations with stronger and, additionally, more problematic connotations. "Subject" would be a signification of this kind, and, as a signification of what constitutes the subject, "subjectivity." One will no longer want to use the word carelessly once one has gotten clear about its origin in *subiectum* and ὑποκείμενον. Heidegger brought attention to the fact that "subject" resonates with the notion of what underlies, which Aristotle distinguished as the fundamental feature of whatever has qualities and can exist in changing states. "If it is not purified through a prior fundamental ontological determination," "every idea of 'subject'" still participates "*ontologically* in the claims of the subjectum (ὑποκείμενον)."[1] The word does not lose its problematic character, however, through the purification indicated by Heidegger. After this purification, and this means more precisely: In Husserl, it stands for the immanence of consciousness that is posed over and against the transcendence of objects.

Yet, when Heidegger speaks of Dasein instead of subject he does not actually get beyond the claim found in the subject. It is true that the "construction" of the difference of the inner and outer sphere is not supposed to hold for Dasein; it is supposed to belong to Dasein "that this being, insofar as it is, ever already lingers on something present at hand."[2] In "directing itself toward ... and grasping," "Dasein does not, say, first" go "outside of its inner sphere." Rather, it is, "according to its primary way of being always already 'outside.'"[3] However, this exteriority is, as Lévinas has stressed time and again,[4] rather a radicalized immanence; if everything that is can only be understood and is only determinable in its being based on Dasein, then it belongs to Dasein but Dasein does not belong to it. This unidirectionality comes from the fact that Heidegger is oriented by intentionality in his development of the concept of Dasein. Even if it is supposed to be "neither objective nor subjective in the usual sense" but rather "both at once in a much more originary way," the elucidation that Heidegger provides confirms once again the unidirectionality of the relationship instead of relativizing it as proposed. Intentionality, as "belonging to the existence of Dasein," makes it possible "that this being, Dasein, conducts itself in its existence toward what is present."[5] Our relationship to things, however, is different. Although it is not symmetrical, it is nevertheless a correlation.

The fact that the concept of Dasein cannot account for this correlative character turns on not only its "prehistory" in the idea of intentionality, but just as much goes back to its ontological meaning. Heidegger, it is now to be remembered once again, sees Dasein as ontologically distinctive because it involves not only the understanding of its own being, but, likewise, "an understanding of the being of all beings that do not have the character of Dasein."[6] With this, he recalls the Aristotelian idea that the question of "what is, insofar as it is what is" (ὂν ᾗ ὄν) can only be answered by tracing back the different possibilities of speaking about what is to a guiding fundamental significance.[7] Insofar as the concern is with the *understanding* of being, Heidegger's definition is trivial; everything that is can always only be understood in its being by a being that is able to understand. The ontological distinction of Dasein does not follow from this, however, if the reference to "beings that do not have the character of Dasein" cannot be determined or, at least, not solely determined, on the basis of Dasein. If Dasein is to be determined just as much on the basis of "beings that do not have the character of Dasein" as the other way around, then there is no longer any ground for the ontological distinction of Dasein.

With the correlative conception of the relationship between "us" and things, however, not only the ontology of Dasein, but also ontology in general is put out of play. The correlation is not a determination of being; it would only be such if the correlates could be determined in their being solely on the basis of one another, and this is not the case from the standpoint of the understanding of being that has resulted in the discussion of time. Being, grasped in contrast to becoming and passing away, is a matter of duration, existing. This is a neutral determination that applies to us just as it does to things. But it applies to things differently than to us. Our duration belongs in the tension of becoming and passing away. We are put into the openness of expectation and memory. Our duration is not a simple existence. The "rediscovery" of time described by Proust belongs to it, that is, the meaning that arises between present and past. When it concerns "us," then, "being" is a concept that has to be specified through another, no longer ontological, determination of ourselves. Our relation to things no longer becomes clear under the auspices of being.

These references to the particular character of our duration, although also of our becoming and passing away, lead as if of themselves back to the concept of life. Our duration, becoming, and passing away do not simply take place, but, rather, are had in "inner experience" [*erlebt*] or "lived" [*gelebt*] in diverse regards. The fact that such a diversity can be taken into account with the word "life" belongs to its strengths. Life is, as the early Heidegger aptly says, a πολλαχῶς λεγόμενον, and, for this reason, the concern is "to make" the ambiguity of the matter as well the word "an expressly appropriate and transparent one."[8] This, however, is now no longer the question of the "ontological character" of life.[9] Instead of grasping life in its "ambiguity" as being in the course of an ontological consideration in order then to determine it in regard to the oneness of a "guiding fundamental significance,"[10] it is necessary to protect the "ambiguity" as an indication of the complexity of the matter.

The intention here is not, therefore, to return to the *Lebensphilosophie* of the fading nineteenth and commencing twentieth century. The guiding concern is not with the idea of some unity or other, be it the unity of "one who demonically plays" or "one who unconsciously creates,"[11] be it of an immemorial "fundamental fact"[12] that cannot be grasped but only had in inner experience [*erlebt*] and be re-lived [*nacherlebt*].[13] The guiding concern is also not the idea of that "dark, driving, insatiable, self-craving power" as Nietzsche determines life in an isolated formulation that anticipates the idea of the "will to power."[14] Life is different; not a unified power, but rather a complex of moments, whose belongingness is only indicated, not determined, by "life," the substantive form of the infinitive verb.*

The question of this belongingness is not without orientation, however. In answer to this question, we may build on the peculiar, because not symmetric, correlation between us and things. The key to what "life" signifies about us and for us is that we refer ourselves to things and at the same time are affected by them, that we are amidst things and yet different from them.

The issue that is spoken of here as a correlation had initially shown itself as the structure of interpretation and object, that is, as the structure of presentation. This had been the point of departure for the question of the open character of the correlation, of the openness at play in it; this led to the discussion of freedom, language, and time. Now the concern is with the relationship from the viewpoint of the moments that stand in correlation, more precisely, with the question of what it signifies for one of these moments to stand in correlation with another. How—this is the question—is its essence determined in and from the correlation? This is, furthermore, a phenomenological question; it arises from the appearance of what is alive in its referentiality to something else, and thus holds what is alive in suspension instead of taking it as a fact.

---

*[That is, "to live." Figal here refers to the fact that the German noun *Leben*, life, is formed from the infinitive verb, *leben*, to live. —Trans.]

The question of life is accordingly oriented toward us. Moreover, in answering this question, the most intensive and clear possibility of the correlation that determines us stands continually in view, that is, the structure of presentation. This way of proceeding is required by a conviction Aristotle articulates, according to which the life of a living being is to be determined based on the expression of life characteristic of it.[15] The liveliness [*Lebendigkeit*] of the living being is concentrated in its thus understood ἔργον. Accordingly, the human being is a hermeneutical living being; what is characteristic of human life lies in presenting—in the ability to present as well as in being dependent on presenting and on presentations.

What already arose in the discussion of hermeneutical space also holds here: A given idea that is at issue cannot be unfolded if one restricts oneself to a consideration of the structure of presentation. That our liveliness is concentrated in this structure is only intelligible if one also discovers the correlation by which it is determined in other expressions of life. If this is possible, the correlation may be understood as a determination of life itself; by making it clear, the essence of what is alive, that is, life itself, will emerge.

The path leads, then, not from a universal understanding of life to the specification of a particular life but rather the other way around: in departure from a particular structure into the complex of determinations of the essence. These determinations become clear in distinguishing individual moments that belong to this structure. In this respect, our way of proceeding is different from that of a universal philosophy of nature that aims at anthropological clarification and first seeks to grasp the essence of the hermeneutical based on it. Plessner has formulated this program tersely: "Without a philosophy of the human being, no theory of the human experience of life in the human sciences. Without a philosophy of nature, no philosophy of the human being."[16] But the human being is an intensification of nature; what nature is comes into focus in him with special pregnancy. If this is the case, the phenomenological self-clarification of the human being leads into nature. It leads from us to the understanding of life and nevertheless does not lead away from us.

§ 36. Lifting Out and Folding

The structure of presentation, as stated, offers a point of departure for the discussion. In presentation, one lets something that stands across from one be there. This thing is undoubtedly outside and nevertheless does not have its actuality from itself. This also holds for presentation, although in a different manner; it comes to actuality by giving actuality to something else. In this, the fundamental relationship between us and things is intensified: On the one hand, if we were not amidst things nothing could stand across from us; on the other hand, it is only through us that things are there *as* things at all. By referring to things while amidst them, we at the same time lift ourselves out from them. Seen from our viewpoint, it is only because of this that there is an outside. We are always already placed among things at a distance to them. We are this distance, we live it; with this distance, our lives come into focus and with our lives, life in general.

That life may be understood on the basis of distance is also a fundamental idea in Plessner's philosophy of nature. Plessner is initially oriented by things in general in order to distinguish from them living beings by the character of their distance. Plessner's description is consequential not least because it is convincing only within limits. It makes clear that life, although it is amidst things, is not disclosed by way of things. This leads to only insufficient specifications and stops short of the decisive step.

Plessner begins from the presupposition that all of what is stands in a "double aspect." What is intended by this is the belongingness of inner and outer, or, as Plessner already clearly says with a view to living beings, of "corporeality and interiority [*Innerlichkeit*]."[17] Even inanimate things, however, have an inner and outer. They appear outside; what they offer to perception is their outer side, which can be experienced from different perspectives. It is the side of properties, as it is to be differentiated from the "substantial core."[18] In any case, Plessner gives the idea of substance an expression made possible by Husserl's phenomenology. Properties no longer count, as in Aristotle, as something that is added to the "underlying" substance and is borne by it. Rather, every "real present side" "implies," as Plessner says, the "whole thing."[19] Properties understood in this way are *aspects*; by perceiving round or red one sees *something* that is round or red. Something perceived is thus of such a kind that, based on it, one can discover other aspects of the same thing; the round or the red proves, for example, to be fragrant and, in biting into it, edible. Each of these aspects is a "segment of a structure that does not itself appear all at once, but is nevertheless concretely co-given as the existing whole."[20]

These considerations are not difficult to recognize as variations of what Husserl calls a "profile."[21] Yet, in contrast to Husserl, Plessner's focus is not on the constitutive capacity of consciousness, through which the different perspectivally bound perceptions are first connected into something unified. Plessner has clear reservations against taking such orientation from subjectivity. Rather, it is important for him that something perceived, a "real phenomenon," itself provides the "direction into the thing and around the thing." By perceiving something as an aspect of a thing, one experiences it as a component of the "concretely co-given structure."[22] Accordingly, one finds one's way into the structure of the thing based on the "real phenomenon."

This is only possible, however, if every "real phenomenon" belongs to a thing and there is a *limit* between things: Here a thing ends, and something else begins; one can enter the realm of things and also leave once again. Something belongs to the thing, something else does not; in being perceived, it leads in a different direction, into a different "inside," into a different "structure." The limit, however, is exterior to the thing. It is, as Plessner says, "pure transition from one to another."[23] It is no concern of the thing that it has a limit; properly speaking the thing does not "have" it. Rather, the limit exists between this thing and another one.

It is precisely this, which, for Plessner, distinguishes living beings from inanimate things. In regard to the living being, it not only "ensures" "the transition to the abutting medium"—that is, to what is outside of it—in such a way that one can make a transition from one thing to another. Rather, as Plessner says, the living being "enacts" the transition "in its delimitation," and it is thus "this transition itself"; the living being's limit *belongs* to it, because the living being "has, besides its delimitation, the transitional limit itself as a property."[24]

Plessner introduces a concept central for his conception for the further development of this idea: the concept of "positionality," or of "positional character."[25] A living being can only overstep the limit that belongs to it insofar as it is posited "over beyond it"; and the limit that it oversteps can only belong to it insofar as it posited [*gestellt*] "into it."[26] "To posit" should not be understood here in Fichte's sense, that is, not in the sense of a spontaneous and therein presuppositionless bringing-into-actuality.[27] Rather, Plessner focuses on the unbound positing of the living being; in regard to the living, he once speaks in this sense of the "loosening of its being."[28] This is to be elucidated in regard to the concept of positing. Positing, "as setting down" has "a having been standing, a having commenced, as its presupposition."[29] This corresponds to the expression of positing, "which" lets "the moment of commencement, being-in-suspension, be discerned," "without for this reason losing the other moment of standing still and being fixed."[30]

Plessner's intention is supposed to have become clear with this; he attempts to grasp the essence of what is alive in distinction from the being of things. Insofar as the attempt remains oriented by the being of things, however, what is alive about living beings does not come sufficiently into view. In Plessner's description, living beings appear as things that enact their thingly character and that, though indeed limited by this, are not bound by their limits. Yet, what is this supposed to mean that a living being "oversteps" the limits that belong to it? A living being, which, for example, refers itself toward something in perception, does not indeed cross over into this thing. In perception it is not "with itself," that is, dimly caught within itself. It is rather with what it perceives. It does not leave itself because of this, however, and so also does not come back to itself from what it perceives. The impression that it could be this way remains bound by Plessner's considerations of a reflection that comes from outside; in this, one can 'leave' a thing and cross over to another. Insofar as one is himself a thing, however, one cannot do this. Even if making reference to things is possible only amidst things, making reference is not simply thingly. There must be both something thingly and unthingly about it at once.

This idea has been developed by Merleau-Ponty. He gives the name *chiasme*, folding, also *entrelacs*, interlace, interlacing,[31] to the fact that making reference to things is possible only if the one who refers has the character of a thing without the reference thereby becoming thingly; this fact and concept were also brought into play in the discussion of voice, but were not thoroughly made clear. Merleau-Ponty's considerations are not in fact intended as an answer to the question of what life is but rather have the purpose of making the possibility of perception intelligible. According to the matter, however, the concern is with an understanding of life. It is of interest here because it differentiates itself radically from that of Plessner. Whereas Plessner wins what is alive about living beings in orientation from their character as things, Merleau-Ponty determines the thingly character of the living being on the basis of its living reference to things.[32]

If Merleau-Ponty says that perception has to do not only with the mere correlation[33] of respective acts of perception but rather with the things themselves, then the critical expression against Husserl's understanding of intentionality is unmistakable. This understanding is a truncation of the full correlation. It leaves open why things appear in my view at all. As Merleau-Ponty asks: How does it happen that while my view envelops things it does not cover them but, rather, veilingly unveils them?[34]

The answer sounds simple: One's view must belong in the same world as what is seen; it must be, as Merleau-Ponty formulates it, the incorporation of the one who sees into the visible.[35] Merleau-Ponty elucidates this in regard to tactical sensation,[36] of which the eye ultimately offers only a remarkable modification.[37] Here, the fundamental commonality, the affinity[38] between the two, proves to lie in the fact that the groping and touching hand is itself accessible from outside, itself touchable, for example, by one's other hand.[39] The touching hand is among the things that it touches; what it touches, then, are things.

If one thinks about this answer, which is perhaps disappointing in its simplicity, it proffers a riddle. Certainly, the example of the touching hand is in fact illuminating; touching is not an act of a consciousness that can disregard the exterior givenness of its correlate, but rather, actually occurs amidst things. Yet, the hand that touches another hand does not touch its touching. The experiment is easy to do: As soon as one folds one's hands together, one hand is always the one that touches, the other hand the one that is touched. Merleau-Ponty also speaks in this context of a "hiatus" between my touched and my touching right hand, my heard and my articulated voice, between a moment of my tactile life and the next.[40] The body is a being with two sides,[41] whereby each of them is also the other if one turns them around. It is this "reversibility" (*réversibilité*) that constitutes the essence of the body. The chiasmus of perceiving and being perceived and reversibility are the same thing.[42]

But a decisive idea is introduced with the concept of reversibility. It indicates that the same thing is in fact perceiving and perceivable, although never at once. Experience is always devoted only to one side, one never has both, and, thus, one never experiences how both are the same. It is always the case that shortly before the fusion of both sides, one of them escapes. Therefore, it also can be said of the reversibility of touching into the touched that it is never realized, but, rather, lies always ahead.⁴³

If this is so, then the perceptibility of perception must be demonstrated differently. If it is not there in perceiving itself, it must be encountered in what is perceived. Merleau-Ponty revises his fundamental idea in this spirit. The chiasmus, the reversibility, as it is called now: This is the idea that every perception is doubled through counter-perception; the idea of the chiasmus signifies that every relation to being is at once an act of taking and of being taken, the perceiving is perceived, it is registered, and, in fact, registered in the very same being that it takes.*⁴⁴

If a being-seen belongs to *every* seeing, then this being-seen must come from the seen things themselves. As one who sees I feel myself, as Merleau-Ponty says, observed by the things,⁴⁵ so that every seeing is in truth an interpenetration of seeing and being seen. This makes the unambiguous classification that is intended by talk of "subject" and "object" disappear. If seeing is at the same time the experience of visibility, then it may be said in fact that the one who sees and the visible reciprocally interchange and that one no longer knows who sees and who is seen.⁴⁶ Perception understood in this way is a fundamental narcissism of every seeing.⁴⁷ One looks at something and, without knowing it, in truth sees himself; the purported other is in truth the same.

This narcissism is "fundamental" because it concerns everything and, thus, makes every correlation a relation of exchange. Everything that emerges does and does not have itself in the other that it encounters in an indifferent, indistinct manner. Merleau-Ponty compares perception in this sense with two mirrors turned toward one another, in which "two infinite rows of interlocking images stand over against one another, which in truth belong to neither of the two surfaces since each of them is only the replica of the other and, as a consequence of which, both together form a pair, which is more real than each of them individually."⁴⁸

Merleau-Ponty wants to solve the riddle of correlation, then, by dissolving the correlates into an elementary indifference. Everything is one; everything is like the water, in which particular moments, waves, ripples, a ruffle on the surface may be fixed for a moment before they once again recede into the undifferentiated character of the element. Thus, reference to something, and likewise emergence in perception, is like a ruffle in what Merleau-Ponty calls

---

*[Note the relation of the German for "to take," *nehmen*, and for "to perceive," *wahrnehmen*. —Trans.]

"flesh" (*chair*). Flesh is element[49]; it is the world as living element, as elementary life.

The difficulty of the idea is easy to grasp. Because Merleau-Ponty traces the correlation of perceiving and being perceived back to the indifference of the elementary, he cannot shed further light on the essential difference of perceiving and being perceived that he had determined as folding and reversibility. On the contrary, the openness between the two that Merleau-Ponty indicates with the word "hiatus" is given only in this essential difference, whereas it disappears with the idea of the elementary. It emerges only because the one who refers is *different* from what merely stands in reference. Considered this way, the riddle of correlation lies in the discontinuity of making reference; only with this does something stands in reference, and only with this does it not dissolve in reference. It is necessary, then, to understand making reference amidst things as it appears in its discontinuity. Whatever refers to something leaps out from the context of things and yet belongs in it. It does not become intelligible based on things: neither, such that—with Plessner—it is a modification of the being of things, nor such that—as Merleau-Ponty wished to show—it belongs in the elementary being of things and confirms this.[50] Making reference is an expression of life in the exteriority of life; it comes from a living being that is amidst things and yet may not be derived from this, but, rather, constitutes its liveliness in the tension of reference. It is originary.

§ 37. Originariness

The originariness of life first becomes conspicuous in regard to movement. Although what is alive is also moved by something else, the essential thing is that it moves itself. This is reversible; what moves itself appears to be alive, say, the play of the clouds that reconfigures itself into ever new figures, the surge of the sea on the shore, the light on the surface of the water. But this liveliness is borrowed; it remains hidden that the movement derives from something else. The moving force, for example, the wind that drives the clouds on and thereby forms them into figures, recedes with the impression of liveliness. By contrast, something is genuinely alive when it actually moves on its own [*von sich aus*], *from itself* [*von selbst*]. For this "from itself" there is a Greek word: φύσις. One could translate the word with "nature" if the moment of significance that matters here were not precisely lost therein. φύσις indicates an occurrence; translated literally, φύσις is "growth." Growth occurs always on its own, from itself. It is the essence of what one calls "natural" without hesitation. As this essence, it shows itself in natural things, and, conversely, it is the observation of natural things that discloses the essence that φύσις is.

Aristotle, therefore, can also discuss φύσις[51] initially by asking about things that are φύσει, that is, determined through φύσις and in it. Aristotle names as things of this kind living beings or animals (ζῷα), their parts, plants, and simple bodies like earth, fire, air, and water.[52] Each of these is characterized by the fact that it has in it a beginning of movement and of rest.[53] How this is intended is then elucidated by contrast: A bed or a garment and other things of this kind have no inborn urge to become different,[54] it is because they are of stone or earthen, and, as would have to be added, in this way behave in the sense of a "simple body."

The comparison with artifacts, the works of handicraft and art, appears to be clear and is yet not easy to explain. It is accurate that artifacts are produced, joined together, put together, whereas the φύσει ὄντα come into being in a different matter, but this misses the decisive point. The φύσει ὄντα also do not arise from themselves; they have this in common with artifacts. Yet, the question of their origin is not at all the issue. Decisive, rather, is that in contrast with the artifacts they are not *what* they are through something else or on the basis of something else. Artifacts like the bed and the garment are devised and produced for use. Their meaning lies in standing or lying ready for use with as little obstruction as possible. Thanks to this, they give their use favorable and unquestionable security, and, as Heidegger expresses it in his treatment of the *Ursprung des Kunstwerks*, this comprises their "reliability."[55] The φύσει ὄντα are not reliable in this sense; it does not belong to their essence to stand fixed or lie fixed. As Aristotle says, rather, they have the inborn urge to change, more precisely: to change suddenly, that is, now to be thus and all at once to be different.

This can be more or less developed; this not seldom has to do with the slowness or quickness of a movement. One thinks of the opening of a flower and of the lightning fast disappearance of a lizard that one has come too close to. The movement of the lizard is more conspicuous because it is more surprising. The surprise is a point of reference for the experience of the "on its own" or "from itself" in movement. When one is surprised by a movement, one sees it not based on something else, but rather, in itself.

That the φυσει ὄντα have an "urge to change" in themselves does not mean that they are grasped in perpetual change. The change to which they have an inborn urge goes back to them, that is, they can be described as changes *of this* φύσει ὄν. The change has its origin in this φύσει ὄν and is also in its course *its* change. Aristotle intends this—as Plato also already does[56]—with the word ἀρχή. ἀρχή is a beginning that remains essential for what begins in it; ἀρχή is a governing beginning that never remains behind, and, in this, is *origin*. For something that moves itself and changes itself the beginning is originary, such that it is itself determined through originariness. φύσις is originariness; everything originary has the essence of φύσις.

Change is always movement. As soon as something rests, it does not change but rather remains as it is. Yet, for φύσει ὄντα the "inborn" urge to change remains essential even when they are not in movement. It is for this reason that Aristotle also says they have in themselves the determinative beginning to movement *and* rest. Something that is able to move itself rests differently than something that has to be put into movement. It *pauses*, which means its rest is always understood based on movement as also, conversely, its movement is always understood based on rest; only something able to move itself can also conduct itself restfully. Seen in this way, it is not any determinate kind of movement that is characteristic for the φύσει ὄντα. Rather, what is characteristic is the way in which movement and rest belong together in them and thus belong to them. One understands their movement and their rest by understanding both as originary.

The list of the φύσει ὄντα with which Aristotle begins his discussion of φύσις may only be appropriately judged on this basis. The "simple bodies," that is, the elements, do not move themselves in such a way that they could also pause. It is true that fire always burns upward in accord with its essence. But it always burns until the flammable material is exhausted. Fire cannot pause, and this also holds for each of the other elements. In this case, however, the elements are really not φύσει ὄντα in the precise sense. By contrast, plants, which move themselves by growing, and living beings in the sense of animals, among which human beings are also included, are φύσει ὄντα. Put more simply: *Living beings* alone are φύσει ὄντα in the precise sense. A living being is a φύσει ὄν understood in the precise sense. Aristotle expresses this by saying of the elementary that it is no φύσις and has no φύσις but rather is only "in accord with φύσις."[57] The elementary is in fact not artificial, not an artifact like a bed or garment, but rather "natural." But this only makes it all the more clear that φύσις is not nature in the sense of a domain distinguished from what is artificial. If φύσις may be grasped as the origin of the movement and rest of a living being, then it comprises its originariness. φύσις is the originariness of life. It is how what is alive leaps out and stands out from a context, in such a way that it can refer itself to something that now confronts it as exterior. With φύσις, there is the exteriority of life.

It must be possible to discern what this means in the movements of a living being. It is what is communicated in being surprised. The movement of a living being is not characterized by the fact that it begins and then takes its course. It is true that there is movement of that kind, but it is not that in virtue of which one calls something "alive." Although the movement of a parachutist who jumps from an airplane begins with him, it is not originary in the sense of living movement because there is no possibility of pausing in it.

The sense of originariness discussed here is not simply added to something as if it were a thing among things and then had the originariness of rest and movement besides. Rather, something in which there is this originariness is fundamentally differentiated from others. It is a living being and as such no mere thing. Therefore, it may seem obvious to understand originariness in the sense of φύσις as the *being* of the living being. One could think this is the only way to account for the fact that a living being is not only pervaded by its liveliness but rather—as living being—essentially is this liveliness.

The motility of a living being moreover always appears only amidst things. This is where it is to be found—just like the form of a stone or the surge of the sea. Therefore, although the being of the living being could not be that of a thing, it could also not be distinguished absolutely from the being of things.

The Aristotelian discussion of φύσις runs toward this idea. If the idea is plausible, then the discussion of φύσις would have led back from life to being. Although the concept of life and of liveliness would not be replaceable by ontological determinations, they would remain demonstrable in such determinations in order to be intelligible. If, by contrast, it may be shown that the idea is problematic, then one would have achieved an additional argument for having reservations about an ontology of life. In the latter case, it could be shown still more clearly why life in its originariness goes beyond any determination of being.

In his ontological understanding of φύσις, Aristotle begins with the living being. Everything that can be addressed as φύσει ὄν is οὐσία, being [*Seiendheit*]; it is, namely, what is underlying, and, φύσις is always in what is underlying.[58] The living being is being [*Seiendheit*] in the sense of what is underlying because like every individual thing, it can be counted as a bearer of its properties and states. That φύσις is only in what is underlying is explained based on this determination: Only as something underlying can a living being move "itself"; only as something underlying does it have the independence needed in order for one to be able to ascribe rest and movement to it. States in complex contexts, say, in the play of the clouds, do not change "themselves." Here, the change remains an open, also diffuse, process without point of reference. There is no life, then, without living beings. And, if one follows Aristotle, the living being exists only as something underlying. It is a thing among things precisely in this, for the bed as well as the garment, too, is something underlying.

Yet, because φύσις is in them, living beings are no things like other things. Aristotle attempts to determine what this means, in turn, in contrasting living beings and artifacts. In this, artifacts provide the determinations, on the basis of which living beings can show themselves in contrast to them. It is the determinations of *matter* and *form*, out of which Aristotle develops an analogy between φύσις and productive art (τέχνη), that he uses to answer the question of the being of what is alive.

The fact that for Aristotle matter and form are "craftsmanly" concepts is revealed by the very word he uses for what here and commonly is called "matter." Aristotle speaks of ὕλη, that is, of wood in the sense of lumber; for him, matter is material. Accordingly, form (μορφή) is the fashioned form that is achieved and developed in working on the material.

Based on these presuppositions, Aristotle fundamentally has two possibilities for understanding φύσις as being. Insofar as φύσις is grasped as the determinative beginning of change, it has to do either with material or with form. The former is disregarded; φύσις is not the primary material which underlies everything that has the determinative beginning of movement and change.[59] Then nothing could be what it is *through* physis; material is the possible, the malleable and, in this, the relatively undetermined; it is material for what is to become of it, that is, form. This, in turn, may be confirmed in regard to handicraft: Something does not count as an artifact when it exists solely in possibility but rather only when it is present in completion (ἐντελέχεια),[60] that is, in its form, and has the εἶδος, that is, the figure or the look, of what it is supposed to be. This is also how it is for what is composed by φύσις: Flesh or also bone does not have its φύσις before it has taken on its identifiable look that helps us determinatively say what flesh and bone is.[61]

The idea outlined here can only serve to confirm Heidegger's thesis, according to which Aristotle understands being as "being produced."[62] What is problematic about this understanding, however, may therefore be shown especially well with reference to it. It is by no means the case that the "on its own" is best disclosed on the basis of production.[63] It is possible to shed light on how problematic the analogy brought into focus by means of contrast is in a number of regards.

The first thing to stand out is that in the Aristotelian considerations, the talk is no longer of φύσις as of a beginning or origin inherent in a living being; φύσις is here no longer life that is perceptible as independent rest and movement, but, rather, an instance of production understood in analogy to craft work. The idea is one in orientation from the ability of living beings to propagate, which Aristotle then understands based on craftsmanly production. That this is not unproblematic is revealed in the very talk of the "what is composed by φύσις" itself: A living being is not composed like a bedstead, but, rather, grows. Accordingly, understanding flesh and bone in the sense of material is also not illuminating; the two are not present like tree trunks that may be cut and then, as wood, fashioned into a bedstead.

One should not assume that Aristotle did not know this. The violence of the analogy is so obvious that he probably intentionally accepts this violence in the bargain. The reason for it proceeds from the direction of the presented idea. Aristotle wishes to show that φύσις is responsible for the form of the living being, and doing this, in turn, appears to be most readily possible in the analogy with handicraft. It would, then, not be φύσις as such, but, rather, the intention of understanding φύσις based on form, that suggests the analogy to handicraft and—under the auspices of the idea of form—makes the analogy compelling.

Form is spoken of here in a twofold manner. It is ἐντελέχεια,[64] that is, completion, the being-at-the-aim of growth, which is understood in departure from the completion of a production brought about through art. And it is εἶδος κατὰ τὸν λόγον,[65] that is, the look of the living being that is determinable in its structure—that, which the living being *is* as something determinate in this way or that. As completion, the form inheres in the living being. It is what was actually at issue in production, and, at the same time, what is actually brought about; if the material had not been fashioned so that it had received a determinate form, the production would have been unsuccessful. In order for the form to be brought forth in this way, however, it has to guide the production in each moment. It already has to be there ahead of time; it is given, as Aristotle says in another passage, "in the soul" of the one who produces.[66] Things are similar when a living being comes into existence; this, too, follows from εἶδος to εἶδος. As evidence for this, Aristotle takes the fact that living beings always come from living beings of the same kind; thus, the human being comes into existence from a human being—namely, as Aristotle intends, the one who begets him.[67] The propagative power of what is alive lies in the fact that it can pass on its φύσις and that this occurs solely through φύσις. Since the result of the development of a living being is εἶδος, however, its beginning, φύσις, also has to be εἶδος. Aristotle can thus maintain that φύσις is form, and that the form is "more φύσις" than the material.[68]

Although Aristotle takes great care in his derivation of this result, doubts about its plausibility remain. These doubts concern both determinations of form that Aristotle introduces—both the determination of form as ἐντελέχεια as well as εἶδος κατὰ τὸν λόγον. As concerns the former, the idea of a procedurally attainable completion is illuminating only in regard to the production of artifacts, and, indeed, precisely if one takes up the Aristotelian idea that growth also belongs to the characteristic movement of living beings and, then, has its determinative beginning in φύσις.[69] What grows is always already what it is as soon as it is at all; it is always already this living being even if it can still develop. The ability to develop is part and parcel of its completion as a living being. This is different for artifacts; only an artifact may be more or less finished, complete, or incomplete. Yet as soon as something is there and is able to grow as a living being of a specific kind—say, as a human—it is complete. Its completeness proves to lie precisely in the fact that it can grow and again wane and nevertheless not be in an unfinished or diminished state as a living being. φύσις, however, may not then be identified with the completeness at the end of a process of development. Rather, it inheres in something that has form but is not necessarily fixed by it; one thinks of the metamorphosis of the caterpillar into the butterfly, and metamorphoses of life in general. Living beings are not completed forms, but, rather, something characteristically unfixed, that is, unfinished, even when their look is more stable than that of a caterpillar. A living being can develop, change, and this has to do with the inherent originariness in it.

The difference of φύσις and form emerges even more clearly in regard to the second elucidation of form that Aristotle provides. The formulation εἶδος κατὰ τὸν λόγον makes clear that the concern here is with the "look" of something from the standpoint of its linguistic reference. One could translate the formulation with "form in the sense of determination." Now, it is true that the determination of something in its form is always fitting and illuminating when what is determined really has this form. Yet, on the other hand, the establishment of the form is always a matter of lifting out a structure, and, in doing so, a matter of disregarding the multiplicity of states in which something can find itself. It is only possible to grasp structures by restricting oneself to a determinate number of essential moments.[70] In ascertaining them, one grasps what something always is—that is, what it has been and is now—or, as Aristotle puts it in an expression coined by him: the "what-it-was-to-be" (τὸ τί ἦν εἶναι).[71] With this restriction, however, what is decisive for φύσις is disregarded, namely, that something in which φύσις inheres is determined in every moment by the possibility of change. This remains the case even when the determination of a structure is selected in such a way that it names the potential of something for change. Although it is then developed on the basis of φύσις, it no longer remains involved in φύσις itself. In any case, it relativizes the ontological determination of the εἶδος κατὰ τὸν λόγον. It becomes clear that the determination of what is alive has to be conceived on the basis of something that withdraws from ontology, and with this, what is alive withdraws from ontology as such. A being in which φύσις inheres can no longer be grasped in its essence as a being.

It is nevertheless possible to comprehend how Aristotle can understand φύσις itself as being. He would only have to follow the linguistic usage, according to which the word φύσις, just like the word "nature," can signify the essence of a matter. What is intended in this case is the matter as it is on its own terms—as if it were to be encountered alive so as to be completely unobscured. Something is "physical," "natural" in this sense when it is as if it has grown,[72] instead of owing its existence to the implementation of a human intention or perspective and being valid only by agreement. The issue is in this sense the dichotomy of φύσις and νόμος, which was central for the sophists and the debate with them.[73]

Heidegger saw only an "echo"[74] of the originary understanding in this concept of φύσις and took the Aristotelian restriction of the concept to what is alive as that "of the specific (in itself delimited) sphere of what is"[75] to be an impoverishment. φύσις is for Heidegger being in the originary sense; it is the "essence"—understood in the sense of a verb*—of being in this sense "to bring itself out of hiding, to come up, to come out into the unconcealed."[76] Being, accordingly, is originary appearing; even understood as "essence," it is the occurrence of the accessibility that holds as toward what is accessible in every showing and generally in every relation to what is.

This sense of "being," however, is conceived on the basis of φύσις as the "essence" of what is alive. This is verified by the fact that appearance, which is how Heidegger wants to understand φύσις, occurs on its own and so is determined through the fundamental feature of what is alive; the "on its own" is familiar as none other than the essence of the living being. There also lies in this "on its own" the possibility of holding back, the "self-concealment"[77] that Heidegger understands to belong together with coming forth into the unconcealed. Heidegger himself makes it easy to go in this direction, not least because he sees his idea verified by Heraclitus' statement that φύσις loves to hide.[78] φύσις in Heraclitus is not, as Heidegger translates, "being."[79] The nature of things, in the sense of an εἶδος κατὰ τὸν λόγον, could also not be what is intended, such that Heraclitus would be saying that what something is remains hidden behind a superficial appearance. Rather, φύσις is to be understood here in the sense of the "ever-living fire"[80] that comprises the liveliness of the world order (κόσμος) in its "turnings." The world order is "day night, winter summer, war peace, satiety hunger" and it "is changed like fire, which, when mixed with perfumes, is named according to the scent of each of them."[81] φύσις conceals itself in its transformations. One holds on to the respective state and meanwhile misses the life of the world.

The question of what it can mean to understand the world as a whole as alive is not discussed further here. What matters is only that the concept of φύσις indicates the originariness of life and not "being" even in its early philosophical use. If Heidegger comes out of Aristotle to read the idea of being into Heraclitus, then he thereby also brings the ontological formulation of the question into earlier thought. Still, Heidegger himself nevertheless suggests that life is not being insofar as he reaches back to the concept of φύσις in order to achieve distance from the ontology definitive of the tradition.

Life is not being. Life—as is shown in the consideration of the living being—is the originariness of movement and rest that completely determines a living being and is thus at the same time the starting point for the belongingness of being with becoming. This means first of all that when a living being grows and

---

*["Essence" is the translation of the noun *Wesen*, which, however, even in its nominative form carries strong connotations of its verbal form, *wesen*. This verbal form admits of being translated, for example, as "to be present," in the sense of coming into presence and remaining present. —Trans.]

develops it does not simply retain its form but also does not simply become something else. Form does not stand like an island in the stream of becoming. Rather, without becoming it is not a form at all. It is not the form of a living being in the look of the living being. It is rather *form of life*, the possibility and manner of life. This, however, cannot at all be conceived based on a living being that one considers as a being. A living being is not able to be unless it is in determinate, also changing, states. It requires confirmation and supplementation from the kind of things that come to it from outside and it just as much belongs to a living being that it protect and cut itself off from what comes to it from outside. Also belonging to the form of a living being is what it is open for; only what is open to something in this manner can also close itself off in regard to it. On first glance, something can look like a thing among things. But then it moves toward something or away from something. In this, it is recognized as alive and its openness is then also there for the one who encounters it. What gets encountered here, more or less clearly, is its form of life.

§ 38. Form of Life

The term *form of life*, as it is used here, is supposed to correspond to a Greek word ψυχή. The Greek word captures what is intended even better; it holds the intermediary between the more broadly conceived concept of the form of life that may also be applied to social relations and the usual German equivalent for ψυχή, *Seele* [soul]. By not using *Seele*, one remains free from notions associated with this familiar word, a word that has even become familiar in a misleading way and that has potentially become suspect.[82] Besides, everything that could shed light here has been said in Greek. One learns what it means to grasp life as "soul" and the living being as "ensouled" not through newer philosophy, but, rather, solely in returning to Aristotle and, then, also to Plato; the newer discussions relevant here are only intelligible based on the classic ones.[83] Seen in this way, even the matter itself points back to the Greek word.

ψυχή is what enlivens a body (σῶμα)[84] that would be a thing among things considered for itself. The ψυχή is reft from the dead person who was previously alive. This is the verifiable representation of the ψυχή in Homer; ψυχή is the breath of life—ψύχειν means "to breathe."[85] Even if one does not represent the ψυχή as something inherent in the body, this determination can be plausible. ψυχή, then, is not like a breath but rather the *essence of the movement* of the body—not its current movement, but, rather this essence that enables the body to move itself and again also to be at rest. It is not the originariness of movement and rest, but, rather, the possibility of movement and rest for this determinate individual, the ensemble of its possibilities for movement and rest. It is thus form of life.

How the concept of the form of life is to be understood with more precision here is made clear once again in connection with Aristotle. Aristotle names the ψυχή the first completion of a natural body that has the possibility for life.[86] The determination is carefully constructed, it is coherent in itself like a complete verse. Because of this it is in need of explication. One has to point out its different moments and, in this, show how they reach into one another and supplement one another.

The first thing to establish is that ψυχή is *liveliness*. It is the liveliness of a body, that is, not its actually enacted life but rather its life δυνάμει, in accord with possibility. It is life as a givenness, not in the sense of a determinate expression of life but rather as the determinate order or structure in which the expressions of life belong. For a living being, ψυχή is each time the characteristic possibility of the "from itself," that which makes it possible to expect a "from itself" in the sense of φύσις in a determinate manner. ψυχή is what is originary in an ever-determinate manner. Originariness may always be experienced as a determinate possibility of the "from itself" in regard to their ψυχή.

The concept of "first completion" aims at this order or structure that is understood as the basis of possible movement. It is a concept that points to an intermediary: On the one hand, it is referred to the body, and on the other, it has to do with life, ζωή. On the one hand, ψυχή is the *completion* of the body; it is in the ψυχή that the body is what it is, namely, something in itself ordered, not produced, something, then, that has φύσις and, with this, is itself φυσικόν. It is originary in its liveliness, a φύσει ὄν. On the other hand—namely, in regard to the actual expression of life—the ψυχή has the character of the *first* completion. Otherwise the living being could not be what it is as φύσει ὄν, namely, something that is in itself originarily movement and rest. The first completion, in turn, is an originary *disposition* for determinate movement and rest.

A disposition or dispositional quality is characterized on the one hand by latency. It does not have to be actual in regard to that to which it is ascribed.[87] Yet, on the other hand, it is only on the basis of actuality, of the "second completion," that it is possible to decide whether it was rightly ascribed. The ascription of a dispositional quality is thus always something of an advanced notice. It is, with a concept used by the early Heidegger, an *indication* [*Anzeige*].[88] It is an indication that is intended as a pointing out [*Aufzeigen*], however. If the ascription is true, then the quality actually holds for that to which it is ascribed. This can only be said, in turn, because one indicates a future actuality. Pointing out dispositional qualities, then, is comparable to a promise; they are the anticipation of something futural that already has validity now. If one says, for example, that this human being is honest, one does not only say that he has always conducted himself honestly up until now. This could also be intended skeptically, with reservations. To say that this human being *is* honest means to ascribe something to him on the basis of his future actuality. Something that dispositional qualities can be ascribed to, then, is always more than it *is* factically, as it is presently to be found. It may never be ascertained as something that is such and such. Yet, precisely this comprises it as it is encountered.

Aristotle elucidates the first completion—that is, the ordered ensemble of dispositional qualities that he understands the ψυχή as—by saying that it is not like contemplating (θεωρεῖν) but rather like knowing (ἐπιστήμη).[89] It is an intermediary between the mere possibility of taking on a determination and the actuality of this determination in occurrence and activity, at once determinate latency and latent determinacy.[90]

The ψυχή proves to be a determinacy of this kind first of all in regard to the body [*Körper*]. What one so names is more than a thing among things due to the fact that a living being can conduct itself "corporeally" [*körperlich*] in accord with the possibilities given by the ψυχή. Conversely, the body must be suited for this; it must itself be determined in terms of the possibilities of the first completion. The body is determined in this way insofar as it is "tool-like," ὀργανικόν,[91] which is derived from ὄργανον, tool. It is only possible to understand what organs are based on their respective function—it is precisely in this that they are like tools. Insofar as it is on the basis of the ψυχή that the body is what it is, however, the functions have to be understood as always bounded corporeally; the ψυχή is the first completion of *a body*. The ability that one speaks of as the first completion essentially belongs to the organs. Therefore, it can be discerned through them. With the differently formed eyes and ears of a living being, with the hands or claws, fins, paws, or feet, respectively different abilities show themselves as indications of different manners of conduct.

Insofar as a living being is determined as such through dispositional qualities, it can never be ascertained as something underlying that has determinate qualities or states. *As* living being, it is beyond itself, essentially more than it is as it may be found factically. Without this "more," its essence may not be thought at all. When Aristotle nevertheless signifies this essence as "being [*Seiendheit*] that accords with an account,"[92] this is truncated; it can only be cashed out in terms of the interplay of indication and account. The concept of "being [*Seiendheit*]," moreover, comes up against a limit. The essence [*Wesen*] that is intended is no *essentia*, no longer being [*Seiendheit*], that is, no longer οὐσία but rather an essence to which the openness of its unfolding belongs.

It is thus an essence in the verbal sense to which Heidegger has drawn attention.[93] It is an essence that has remove and is in this sense a *spatial essence*. This "exteriority" of the living being is not opposed to any "interior." What is called "interior" here—beyond what is enclosed in its perceptible surface, which it has in common with every thing—is nothing other than being-outside that has been held in reserve, ability that is distinguished from its realization.[94] The interior is, in a word used by Heidegger, an "endurance"[95] in the sense of keeping one's composure in distinction from endurance in the sense of movement. Self-composure and movement belong together in such a way that what a living being is arises only in their interplay.

It is clear based solely on this that the endurance of a living being may not be understood as a diffuse and undifferentiated presence. It is rather a play of interconnected dispositions, which, supplementing one another, usually come into focus in such a way that some of them are as if ready in wait and others are actual. Some, in turn, recede in their actuality, in order as it were to give the stage to others. In their belongingness they form [*bilden*] a never completely given whole that one can call a form [*Form*] in order to grasp its determinacy.[96] It is, however, a form of a specific kind: a form of life. This term has a double meaning that is illuminating: On the one hand, it names a form of life, that is, the form that lets life be formed. On the other hand, it names a form that is for its part determined through life, a form that is only what it is in being lived.

A form of life is thus comparable to the form that the written text is. Texts, too, are never completely there but rather only as they are interpreted each time. Their structure comes to the fore only in the play of illuminating and becoming dim, and in such a way that the structure always remains in reserve and is interpretable anew. Of course, the form of life does not need interpreters who approach it from outside. It as it were interprets itself. This interpretation is life; life comes out of the form "from out of itself" and "from itself." It belongs to the form of life that it comes forth, as does the openness for this coming forth. It is true that the form may only be determined based on what emerges and thus comes "outside."[97] What comes forth, however, refers back into the openness of determinate latencies in which it belongs.

Aristotle distinguishes a series of possibilities of movement in regard to the ψυχή, but clearly emphasizes three of them: self-preservation in its two forms of nourishment and propagation (τροφή),[98] perception (αἴσθησις), and thought (νοεῖν or φρονεῖν). In addition, movement from one place to another—and, belonging to this, remaining at one place (κίνησις καὶ στάσις κατὰ τόπον)[99]—as well as passing away and growth (φθίσις τε καὶ αὔξησις)[100] are named.

The emphasis on self-preservation, perception, and thought arises from a clearly recognizable intention. Aristotle takes it as a point of departure for distinguishing different kinds of living beings in regard to its ψυχή: The life of plants exists solely in self-preservation, that of animals in this and perception. Thought is characteristic and essential for humans alone. To what extent this is a plausible division does not have to be discussed further here; the concern is not with the classification of living beings, but, rather, with understanding what life in its forms of life, what the form of life in its liveliness, is.

The first thing to hold on to here is that the movement in which liveliness is actual does not occur without something else that is over and against the living being. Aristotle describes nourishment in this sense as the ingestion of something that has been set against (ἐναντίον)[101]; it is the ingestion of something that the living being needs, which is not any part of its body and yet belongs to it. Perception is also referred to something exterior. This shows itself in the fact that perception is a being moved and a suffering,[102] for it is moved by something perceptible that comes from outside.[103] In regard to thought, a comparable exteriority is initially contested; what is thinkable is "somehow" in the ψυχή itself.[104] Yet, later Aristotle distinguishes between a reason that something affects and one that brings forth, so that there appears to be an outside for at least that reason that something affects;[105] this will have to be come back to.

In nourishment, the relation between the living being and what is exterior to it is still elemental. Water, by which the plant nourishes itself, is in fact distinguished from it; it is water that is not yet in the body of the plant. Yet, on the other hand, it is so close to its roots that these roots can simply take it up. Moreover, in nourishment, what is exterior does not remain in existence as such; the shift (μεταβάλλειν) of the other into the own, that is, digestion, constitutes the character of the movement of nourishment.[106] What is exterior is thus only there in order to lose its exteriority. It should be seized and ingested, evaluated and—in whatever is of value in it for life—corporeally assimilated.

In perception, by contrast, what is exterior is no longer able to be assimilated. What is perceived approaches the living being and affects it. It clearly comes from outside, but it also remains outside. The living being itself is thereby an exterior one; it is amidst things, but it also has more space and, with this, more play for movement and for self-composure. One may conclude from this that it is thus also more alive. Its life is more intensive than that of a single-celled organism that only ingests and assimilates what is exterior to it. What is exterior comes into focus as such in perception; as something exterior, it is undoubtedly there because it is sensuously graspable. Perception is therefore especially well suited for the description of the form of life. The exteriority of the form of life may be revealed especially well in regard to it—namely, it reveals that exteriority is a form of life, a manner of life, and, at the same time, that the living being is corporally amidst things.

A sound becomes audible, something steps into the field of vision or something comes close, obtrudes, and touches one. Taken by itself, this is admittedly not yet perception. There is only perception when a living being capable of perception is not merely overwhelmed by its effect. It must not only be moved, but must rather itself also be in movement. Otherwise, the living being would be like a technical device that registers or records something. It is only when the living being is in movement that what moves it is there as something perceived. It belongs to perception that something with an effect on the living being is at the same time there through and for it.

Perception is determinable in this sense as an actuality of the perceiving living being, an actuality, which is caused, is "brought forth," through the impetus of something exterior. The suffering that constitutes perception does not have the character of a change in which something is destroyed by the effect of what is contrary to it; it is not, then, like the cooling of something that is warm by something cold. This suffering, Aristotle says, is rather tantamount to an awakening and preservation of something for which the capacity is there and which now comes into actuality itself through something causing it from outside. What has an effect from outside is thereby like the capacity, and, in fact, as capacity is to completion.[107]

This sameness comes to expression as if it were obvious in significations that correspond to one another: The respective capacity for perception is always excited by something perceptible that is appropriate to it—sight by something visible, hearing by something audible, and so on. Yet, more still: There is only hearing where there is also something audible, seeing only where something is to be seen. Neither of the two is actual without the other.

Aristotle grasps this more decisively still, and thus captures the matter at issue precisely: The actuality of what is perceptible and that of perception are one and the same, but the being of them is not the same.[108] Perception is actual movement solely through something perceptible, and what is perceptible is actual in perception as something perceived. It is not only at work in perception. Rather, it exists in perception as something actual in a manner that does not lie in work alone.

It may be objected against this that Aristotle says the actuality of something perceived as well as the actuality of the one capable of perception lie in the one capable of perception.[109] This, however, is not intended as a plea for a "subjectivism" of perception; he explicitly opposes himself to the sophistic conviction according to which there is something perceptible only in perception.[110] Aristotle does not want to say that something perceptible is not actual, and that what one takes for its actuality is really only actual of the one who is capable of perception. His formulation is clear enough: In the one capable of perception, something perceptible has its actuality; here, it is actual as something perceptible. The sound of the bells one hears is not a product of one's ear. Rather, what rings out in one's ear are actually the bells. For this reason, the perception of a sound may be described, as Aristotle remarks, both as hearing and also as sounding.[111] Only because it is both is it the actuality that it is.

What is referred to here as "actuality" has thus proved to be something complex. It is the actuality of the one capable of perception, which is brought forth in him through the effect had by something perceptible. And, it is the actuality of something perceptible, an actuality that it finds in perception in the discussed sense. The two things that are different in being, as Aristotle puts it, find themselves in a twofold relation to one another. The relation between something perceptible and one capable of perception is not that of excitation and reaction—as if first something were to happen to the living being and then the living being were to conduct itself toward it. Rather, the one capable of perception is referred to something insofar as this something affects it. If the effect of something perceptible were to cease, perception would be over just as much as when the one capable of perception were to lose his capability momentarily or for the long term.

The actuality of perception is a *fold*. It is in itself twofold, like the two sides of a sheet of paper of which Merleau-Ponty once speaks.[112] The fold here is not that of "inside" and "outside," but, rather, a fold of two directions. Understood from the standpoint of the intention of perception, what appears is whatever allows itself to be perceived, for example, something heard. Understood from the standpoint of the effect, it is whatever may be perceived, for example, something sounding or ringing out. If one were to take each of the two as it stands, that is, in its "being," then one would miss that the concern is not with two things that are put together and thus comprise the state of affairs which one calls "perception," but, rather, with an openness in which different things belong together through connection and removal. The essence of perception lies in the fact that something which comes close to the living being, is, at the same time, at a removal. What *occurs* to the living being is, at the same time, *appearance*. It is something that is "here" or "there," even if these expressions are absent. Perception is spatial, even if in perception space would not yet have become clear hermeneutically. It does not estimate the space as such; it is still not open for language and time. Openness is solely in the form of life of the living being. And, this openness proves itself in the movement that is the actuality of perception.

In perception, two movements are folded, of which the one goes back to something perceptible, the other to the one who perceives. The first is a change that causes something and in this sense κίνησις. The other is actuality that is complete in itself and at the same time fulfills itself over and again, that is, ἐνέργεια; this is the case with such clarity that the possibility of perception in sight can even serve as the paradigmatic example for the essence of ἐνέργεια.[113] One cannot, however, conceive of perception simply as a perpetual activity that is directed toward its aim at every moment. The completeness of perception arises rather with the appearance of something perceived. Perception is actual in the appearance of such a thing; perception lasts as long as what appears is there. As movement, it is thus at the same time a state. Even if what is perceived occurs in time, even if it shifts, changes, or runs its course, as in the hearing of music, perception has its characteristic rest insofar as it comes into actuality in the sense of ἐνέργεια. It is not the rest of self-composure but rather a rest in which one is *referred* to something. In this referentiality, perception is engaged in its matter and, in this way, in its aim, however much and often it may be modified and take a different attitude toward its matter. Perception is all the more itself the more strongly this referentiality is developed in it. In the sudden flash accompanying an unexpected thunderclap, the fact of being moved is stronger than the movement. It is only in the movement, however, that perception is developed.

Insofar as there is perception only as the fold of being moved and movement understood in the discussed sense as ἐνέργεια, its actuality itself is neither the one nor the other. It is rest and change at the same time, it is a referentiality and an occurrence, but in such a way that each is always what it is in the other. This interpenetration is *motility* [*Bewegtheit*].

Heidegger introduces this concept in order to determine the belongingness of rest and movement. The "purest unfolding of the essence" of motility is "to be sought where rest" does not mean "the cessation and termination of movement," "but, rather, where the motility" collects itself "in holding still" and "this pause" opens up "motility."[114] For Heidegger, motility so understood is tantamount to ἐνέργεια. However, the concept of motility in Heidegger's sense may also be understood differently. It may then indicate the relation in which κίνησις and ἐνέργεια are as it were held together in suspension. In motility, nothing is fixed and yet not everything is in flux. It is like a ripple in the flowing water, like the hovering of an insect in the air that is not possible without movement and yet is more than and different from movement. In its reference to something, it has gotten away from, gotten out of, becoming and passing away without being static. It is originary.

Motility in this sense is the actuality of a living being as it comes to be grasped in regard to perception. It is this actuality first of all because a living being is moved and at the same time is in movement both on its own and in reference to something. It is in movement because it is moved; in being in movement, it takes up being-moved and lets this being-moved belong to it, be *its* being-moved. This is possible because something that moves a living being comes into the rest of reference; it no longer just affects, but appears. Because of this, the self-movement of the living being is also not a "reaction" to being-moved. It does not follow "automatically," but rather, from a rest of reference that takes up being-moved. Insofar as a living being moves itself and takes up being-moved, it announces its originariness, the φύσις that determines its essence. It announces the rest of motility that alone makes it possible to rest or to move on one's own.

Considered on this basis, motility shows itself to be a *state* of the living being that is realized in movement; it realizes a possibility of is form of life in reference to something. Yet, considered on the basis of being-moved, motility is also a state, *in* which the living being is. Insofar as it takes up being-moved and, in this way, makes it its own, it at the same time announces its belongingness to everything by which it is moved and can be moved. It is amidst things.

Its form of life stands out from things not as something radically differentiated from them but is rather as if inscribed in them. Its description grasps it like a text in the texture.

The—said with Merleau-Ponty—two sides of motility are only intelligible if one sees them together without asking for a unity that encompasses them. Neither does one shift into the other in such a way that it disappears with the appearance of the other, nor are the two like formations of an element. They do not have the character of something that can be described in two alternative manners, like light, as particles and waves. They also do not sink into a diffuse commonality like figures formed by the current that always and again dissolve into the river as it flows on. Rather, each of the two "sides" is only what it is based on the other. Perception can only be perception of *something* because there is being-moved; a moving agent is only perceived by getting taken up in accord with the possibilities of a form of life and standing in reference for it, without therefore having explicitly to be there as itself or, in the strict sense, objectively. In the interplay of the two "sides," the living being is open in its possibilities of reference and likewise open for that to which it refers. The openness of a living being accordingly lies in the *difference of state* and *in-a-state*, or, as one can also say, in a correlation that is the fold of referring and being affected. The more decisively the difference in the fold comes out, the more clearly the liveliness of the living being comes to the fore. Life means: a state that is determined in itself through movement, and, likewise, being *in* such a state.

This does not yet sufficiently describe the structure of life. This becomes clear if one contemplates the form of life no longer solely in regard to perception, but rather, if, with Aristotle, one sees perception in its belongingness with other possibilities of life. As Aristotle describes it, what is perceived is not only an appearance of the living being; insofar as it affects the perceiving living being, it can *matter* to this being in one manner or another. Now, it is pleasant or painful, now, it is encountered in pleasure (ἡδονή) or pain (λύπη). Aristotle stresses that this holds even for the simplest sense, the sense of touch (ἀφή), which is found in all living beings.[115] In being affected by pleasure and pain, a living being can be reached by other things like a thing among things.

It belongs to the essence of pleasure and pain, however, that they are not simply registered. Rather, they belong together with a *conduct*. Aristotle grasps this as *striving* (ὄρεξις). It is that in the ψυχή that transposes a living being into a movement in the sense of κίνησις; or, as Aristotle himself says: Insofar as a living being is one capable of striving, it is also capable of moving itself, that is, going toward something or away from something.[116] It belongs to the living being that it *conducts* itself toward what affects it.

Because conduct belongs together with affections, it is not without impetus. Without something occurring to the living being that changes its state, it would not have to strive toward a different state or toward the recuperation of its earlier state. Yet, striving is not a mere consequence of occurrences. Although it is conditioned by what occurs to the living being, it is not fixed by this. Its openness may be quite elementary, but if one can say that a living being conducts itself at all, then the conduct does not go back to a disposition that is always activated when some specific thing occurs, like the breakability of a piece of glass. As such, it does not belong to what is affected by something else, rather, it is an *ability* that is not fixed by being affected. A living being that gets cold, for example, has to seek the warmth that once again brings it into its normal state of life. A living being that is hungry seeks nourishment; it does not ingest nourishment simply as a consequence of hunger.

The ability that striving is, then, belongs *originarily* to the living being. In fact, φύσις comes into focus especially clearly in it. Conduct is always "from itself"; because of this it can be open for freedom. Insofar as it belongs to conduct, however, being affected is also originary. This belongingness lets it be an affection of *something alive*; this belongingness is what fundamentally distinguishes whatever affects a living being from other kinds of effects. Considered for themselves, effects could be the same in different cases. Things that affect something are not adapted or restricted to living beings. They are simply something that moves something without being necessary from the standpoint of the one moved. A blow, for example, can be dealt to a stone or a living being, and it is indeed possible that something similar occurs to the stone and the living being. A tortoise would perhaps be thrust aside in such a way that without a sufficient look at it one could confuse it with a stone. The blow does not matter to the stone, however, whereas the tortoise conducts itself. The tortoise will attempt to bring itself to safety and strive to reestablish a normal state. The striving here will be respectively characteristic for a living being. When dealt a blow, a cat or a human being will conduct itself differently than the tortoise. Different living beings generally conduct themselves differently even when the same thing affects them; even striving for nourishment is different in an insect than in a ruminant and here again different than in a predatory cat or a fish.

The living being does not in any case conduct itself in terms of an isolated occurrence. Its form of life provides ahead of time what affects it, what it can perceive, and how it can conduct itself. Conversely, the form of life is determined by what belongs to it in this way. A living being is not simply amidst things, but, rather, has *surroundings* [*Umgebung*]. What can occur to it is limited by the surroundings, but is open within these surroundings. It is further limited by the fact that a living being can only be moved in determinate respects. The living being cannot be affected by everything; rather, it must be open for determinate affections. Living beings such as reptiles, whose body temperature is not distinguished from that of its surroundings, cannot get cold, but only go numb. Insofar as perception also involves being affected, a living being lives in its surroundings under threat or favor, and the more it can perceive this, the more it is alert in its surroundings. This, however, always also means that it conducts itself *in* these surroundings and *toward* them in such a way that it can orient itself in them. Perception is the appearance of something that affects and the appearances of the surroundings in such a way that it can guide conduct in the surroundings. In every respect, however, it is a state and at the same time an in-a-state.

In surroundings there exists only a lose connection between affections and aims—such that both fundamentally belong together although they are not attuned to one another in every detail. Whether an aim really corresponds to the situation that has come about through being affected is not settled from the start. There is a delay here, and, through it, an openness: that which remains unclarified between conduct and success, a distance, however small it may be, to what surrounds the living being.

Living beings are spatial, although they do not necessarily understand the space they are in. Such an understanding obtains only in the widening of spatiality as it is given in freedom, language, and time. What would be understood in this, however, is the space of any living being, if the living being may be described as it is here. In freedom, the difference between being affected and conduct widens; in language, it is possible for the appearance necessary for perception to be a self-showing that is connected with showing; and time, which underlies everything that occurs, becomes widened in its experience to the openness of time in its course, of enactment, and of temporality. Freedom, language, and time are not things that the human being would bring along with him as if from another world in order to live his life in his own manner in a space that he shares with all living beings. There is no human life without freedom, language, and time; human life belongs in them and only emerges as human life through them.

Space itself, however, is thereby made clear. Perhaps one is permitted to think of a gradual emergence of contours and nuances like what happens to photographic paper exposed to light while in the developer; what was there solely through the light cast on the paper comes forth. The human being would then be a living being in which the spatiality of life "develops" in a determinate respect, even though it would not be possible to explain the development based on what is developed or to make intelligible what is developed based on the development in its possibility. The human being would be a degree of the intensity of life, just as the structure of presentation is a degree of the intensity of human life. The fold of state and in-a-state is thus there in presentation as the circle of reflection of both of the possibilities of understanding and the intelligible matter. Both stand at once in a double actuality, which is just as much an actuality of the enactment of presentation as of what is presented. Because the same basic figure is at play in perception as in presentation, presentation enters easily into perception and intensifies it so that presentation increases perception and thereby appears first to set all of its possibilities free. As in degrees of intensity generally, here the previous state is just as little a preliminary form of the later one as the later, intensified one may be derived from the previous. Yet, one can depict the different states one on another in phenomenological description so as to let a common basic figure emerge. In this, the description always has to take orientation from whatever emerges with intensification. Description has a formation of life before it and develops the structure of life based on it by investigating what lies before for this structure.

Different intensities of life may be grasped along these lines. There are different states to be considered for themselves and then also different possibilities of life in one state. The "earlier" state is not lost with every new one, but it loses its intensity because it is put into the tensional field of another degree of intensity. It is necessary to make clear precisely what this is supposed to mean. In this, the orienting concepts are concepts of state—first of all the body and the body quick, then the concept of reason.

§ 39. Body [Körper] and The Body Quick [Leib]

A living being is in a state first of all in such a way that something can affect it. It can be dealt a blow, also just touched. The living being can be concerned by these things. Or, something occurs to it that it does not notice, either because the sensation escapes it or because there is nothing to sense; the living being is perceived, it is observed or its scent is picked up. In this, it does not distinguish itself from any arbitrary thing in the world. It can be found next to or amidst things and barely raise itself out from them. Sometimes the figure of a living being is—for its advantage—actually constituted for this indistinguishability. The stick insect looks like a branch of the shrub in which it sits; the skin of the toad barely stands out from the color of the pond in which it lives. In camouflage, the belongingness of what is alive to things announces itself. As concerns perception, when camouflage is successful the living being dissolves completely into its surroundings.

What allows living beings to belong to things in this way is their *body*. In the language of physics everything that is spatially limited and therein identifiable is a body, regardless of whether the body is in the form of a solid, liquid, or gas. It belongs to the meaning of the word that it can also be used for the nonliving. This accords with the Latin *corpus* and the Greek σῶμα; both stand not least for the lifeless body. Homer only uses the word σῶμα in terms of this significance,[117] and even the German word* is first of all predominantly used in the sense of "physical body."[118] It belongs to the essence of a living being that it is corporeal, but in terms of the liveliness of a living being the body is only a condition. Corporeally, a living being is a thing among things; it is *in*-a-state and otherwise nothing. A living being is corporeal as a thing whose liveliness one either does or does not perceive, or it is corporeal as something alien, something that has become independent, which one can conduct himself toward like a thing—say, for example, when the body refuses its service in illness. A living being is also corporeal in losing its liveliness; it is something once alive, and, in this, neither a living being nor simply a thing. It is something that is reminiscent of its previous liveliness and to be understood based on it.

When a living being that was earlier like a thing among things suddenly attracts attention in its liveliness, it causes surprise or fright. The living being steps out of the circle of things and all at once shows itself as it properly is. It is true that the living being continues to be a thing among things. This, however, does not constitute its liveliness. Its liveliness comes to appearance as soon as it moves itself and so steps out of the circle of things. What had appeared earlier as body is now *the body quick*.[119]

"The body quick" is related to "life." The word [i.e., *Leib*, the body quick] could really mean the same thing as life. Even if the two are distinguished, however, what is intended by the word is the living being as such. In early linguistic usage,† *lîp* is the living person as opposed to the dead one, *wal*.[120] Although the word usually signifies human beings, it is by no means restricted to them; it is common in the description of higher animals. One confers the body quick to a living being all the more readily as its motility of life appears to be familiar to one's own, such that one believes one can "comprehend" it, "identify with" it. The body quick is the living being insofar as it is perceptibly there based on its motility of life.

This may obviously also be reversed: There is no motility of life without the body quick. A living being moves itself in a quickened manner, and it is no different even with less perceptible movements. Every perception is quickened, as is the characteristic tension and strain that belongs to striving. Nevertheless, the movement that is life is to be distinguished from the body quick. One does

---

*[I.e., *Körper*. —Trans.]

†[My translation of 'Leib' as 'the body quick' does not accord with the author's etymological considerations that follow here. Unfortunately, there is to my knowledge no English word currently in use that has the same derivation as the German 'Leib.' Indeed, as the *Oxford English Dictionary* entry for body notes, Grimm observed that the still current English word 'body' died out in German, being replaced by 'Leib' and 'Körper.' Nevertheless, the word 'quick' that I have used to form the expression 'the body quick' for the German 'Leib' carries many of the connotations of life and liveliness that belong to the original German word. —Trans.]

not see without eyes and does not hear without ears; but seeing and hearing are not eyes and ears.

It is tempting to determine this relation in accord with the scheme of end and means. Husserl names the body quick "the means of all perception"[121] in this sense, and in doing so he reaches back, intentionally or not, to a manner of thought and speech in evidence for the first time in Plato; in the *Republic*, tools that have to do with perception are spoken of.[122] Aristotle picks this up by signifying the body of the living being (σῶμα) as a whole as ὀργανικόν, that is, as tool-like; the passage was previously mentioned.[123]

The tool analogy can be illuminating in one respect: Like tools, the sense organs belong to a specific actuality; they are determined through the possibilities of this actuality. On the other hand, the analogy is not convincing. One does not see with one's eyes as one writes with the pen or pounds a nail with a hammer. Every tool is interchangeable, and now and then one can even do without tools. This does not hold of the sense organs. Without eyes, there is no sight, without ears, no hearing, whereas one can pound the nail into the wall with a stone and simply write with one's finger in the sand. In this respect, the sense organ is also not determined based on an actuality like a tool is. Rather, this actuality is bound up in its possibility with the sense organ. One does not understand what sight is without always also thinking of the eyes, and it is precisely the same with the other perceptions. Sight and the ability to see are unimaginable without eyes.

The idea developed by Heidegger is therefore mistaken that the sense organs may be determined based only on the actuality respectively assigned to them. "The ability to see," Heidegger says in his discussion of animal life, "first makes possible the possession of eyes."[124] And in clarification he adds a little later: "we may not say that the organ has abilities, but, rather, that the ability has organs."[125] In evidence of this thesis, Heidegger can refer to the fact that there are living beings that have no specific organs for the ingestion of nourishment and digestion, but rather, enact this in protoplasm that takes over different functions in the enactment of the ingestion of nourishment and digestion. It does not follow from this, however, that the "ability" to ingest nourishment and digestion is "earlier than the respective organs."[126] "Earlier" is here in fact not to be understood unconditionally in a temporal manner. What is intended is rather that which is earlier in essence and, in this sense, what is prior: that on the basis of which something must be understood. Even still, the determination remains problematic; insofar as the converse also holds and perception is not to be understood without organs, there exists more of a mutual relation between the two than a one-sided dependency.

On the one hand, this concerns that being-moved without which there is no perception. Something that affects one so as to be significant for perception is taken up through the organs. They can even be fixed to the organs; light strikes the eye, sound penetrates into the ear, odor into the nose. On the other hand, the ability and actuality of perception are not conceivable without the organs; it is not for nothing that we may say someone has "a good eye," that is, the ability to look and capture with precision, to get a good look.

This is of fundamental significance. Insofar as a living being is no longer experienced as corporeal but rather as quickened embodiment, one has a different understanding of what can be perceived of it. Its eye is not any part of a surface formed in such and such manner, it is rather viewing; its ear is not any peculiarly formed opening, it belongs rather to the attentiveness that the living being has. The organ provides a point of reference for understanding perception; the ability as well as its actuality receive a *place* with the organ. One does not understand the eye based only on viewing but also experiences viewing in regard to the visible eye. Without their place, ability and actuality are not to be conceived.

A place is itself nothing, but something is *at it*. Or, more precisely, something is a place, insofar as it is not taken into view itself but rather as something at which something is. Thus, the tabletop is a place for lain books, the marketplace a place where people can meet. Considered for itself, the tabletop is something determinate; it has a determinate form and is of a determinate material, it has determinate qualities. This plays no role, however, when it is the place of a specific book. When one needs the book, one looks for it at this place.

Something can change its place. The book could also stand on the shelf instead of on the table; people could meet at the main entrance of the university instead of at the marketplace. In these cases, what is at a place does not essentially have something to do with the place itself. Another book may be lain where this book lies now in its stead; others can also meet in front of the main entrance to the university, directly next to the statue of Aristotle. Of course, something can also be bound to its place in such a way that it is always at this place or such that it can only take place at this place. A mountain, for example, is always there where it is; even if it would be possible to carry it away and pour the masses of earth and stone elsewhere, it would no longer be the same mountain. Things are similar with the bells of the Freiburg minster. If one takes down the bells and brings them elsewhere, their rings would no longer be that of the Freiburg minster. What according to its essence cannot be separated from its place has, as Aristotle calls it, a place proper to it.[127] One can always only experience it at its place.

This is how things are for seeing and hearing and for every stirring of life. Just as there is not a text without writing, auditory or imagistic signs, so too one finds the stirrings of life always only in their "organs" and in their belongingness in a body quick. The individual living being is always only there in quickened embodiment, but this is present only as a multiplicity of capacities that complete one another. In this respect, it is an *organism*. If one does not wish to conceive of the organism on the model of a machine whose parts are coordinated with one another and form a whole in their mutual effect, however, then one can understand it as the *place of the form of life and its liveliness*.[128] To experience something as a body quick means to have an experience of a form of life and of liveliness. The form of life is not connected with the body quick such that the body quick would serve as a means for the form of life to be there. With the body quick, the form of life is itself there.

Therefore, one conducts oneself differently toward the living being in its being a body quick than toward mere things. To treat a body quick like a thing means either not recognizing it as a body quick or affecting it in its body quick by treating it as a thing, to hurt or to kill it. This, however, would be impossible if a living being were only the body quick and not also body. As long as one experiences something as a living being, neither of the two ever completely disappears. Of course, one can recede behind the other, so that one experiences more body quick or body. Perhaps in illustration one may think of those picture puzzles in which one and the same form appears, for example, first as a young woman viewed from behind and then as an old woman in profile. The change between body and the body quick is, however, not the shift in look, but, rather, a shift of state and in-a-state. One thus has to do with the spatiality of body and the body quick.

A body is encountered in space. It is perceived, it is distinguished as this body from others, such that it can show itself as this body. It is something that something may have an effect on or that may cause something. And, it is something that something can occur to such that it is changed and, in the change, endures or perishes.

The fact that things are different with the body quick is apparent from its determination as place alone. A place is not something in space. It is also not a part of space, as if space were put together out of places. A place is rather a position in space which at the same time gives space, that means: a here or there that, as here, opens the reference to the there and vice versa.[129] A place is a spatial setting that first allows the essence of space, that is, remove, to be experienced. Remove always plays out in a movement from something to out beyond it—to something else or into an expanse that is indeterminate.

The perspectivity of perception may be made intelligible as an essential feature of the body quick based on this. One always perceives something *from somewhere or other*. This would not be captured if one were to localize the perceiving living being corporeally, but rather only when one understands the localization, for example, as a line of sight. In this case, the shift in a perspective is not any "from here to there" in the sense of a temporally proceeding movement, but, rather, a "from somewhere else." The body quick is a place, and it can change its place.

A body quick is also a place of liveliness in the sense that it is a place occupied by liveliness. As a place of this kind, a body quick is not simply here or there. Rather, one experiences it only in an *encounter*. Because liveliness is there with the body quick, there is not something merely lying in front of one here but rather the ability for conduct and conduct. Because the surroundings belong to this conduct, surroundings are opened with every living being. Its possible conduct is always directed toward or away from something, in connection to something or in regard to something. One himself belongs in these surroundings as encounterer, and the encountered living being belongs in one's own. The encounter is reciprocal and thereby folded; one belongs in the state of the other living being, and one is himself a state in which the other living being belongs. One knows that one is in the state of the other living being; one experiences this living being as such.

This becomes especially clear in the reciprocal look. Where the eyes of another living being are in view, one sees with the eyes of its view. This is how it generally is: If one is referred to as living being in quickened embodiment, life comes in return. This holds even when the reference is not reciprocal. What confronts one is always the possibility of conduct. One accordingly prepares oneself for another living being. If it appears threatening, one does not perceive it as a potentially dangerous thing that may be dealt with in such and such a manner, but, rather, reckons with the possibilities of its conduct—toward which one tries, for his part, to conduct himself. Living beings are encountered as quickened embodiment in that one encounters them.

Encounters of this kind are only possible under a presupposition: The quickened embodiment of another living being may not be experienced without one's own quickened embodiment. This does not hold only in the trivial sense that without quickened embodiment there is no possibility of perception. Rather, in the encounter with a living being from the viewpoint of its quickened embodiment, one also becomes *aware of one's own quickened embodiment*.[130] Perceiving the other living being's look with one's eye, one sees himself being viewed. In adjusting to a living being from the viewpoint of its dangerousness, one has the inner experience of oneself as endangered.

From the viewpoint of the body quick, then, the living being involves being perceived in a manner all its own. Its quickened embodiment puts it in relation to other life in quickened embodiment. This referentiality is part and parcel of its liveliness. There is a removal between living beings that is not merely that of a reference to something. What is at issue is much more of a doubled intentionality. This is not simply the sum of the one and the other. Rather, there is actually the openness here that Merleau-Ponty compares with the two mirrors turned toward one another.[131] It is the openness of life in quickened embodiment itself, in the reciprocity of strivings, of appearance and being affected.

Interest belongs to the openness of life in quickened embodiment; one is as if spellbound by the state of the other living being, the mirror play of experience offers no exit. This is a fundamental trait of quickened embodiment; it also comes into focus when something, a thing, stands in view, when it moves one or is the aim of a striving. The openness, which belongs to the body quick and in which life in quickened embodiment belongs, does not come to be experienced as such; the body quick does not become cognizant of it. A caesura is required for this that goes right through the middle of experience and breaks the spell of quickened embodiment. This caesura is given by reason.

§ 40. Reason

The word "reason" has to do with "apprehending." Apprehending is registering, grasping, although sometimes in the sense of perceiving, usually in a different sense, namely, a "spiritual" one in some manner or other. This is also the case for the corresponding Greek word, νοῦς. νοεῖν can also signify "perceiving with the eyes." Seeing and apprehending do not belong together simply from the standpoint of word history, however. It is certainly not coincidence that optical comparisons come to mind when reason is to be determined in its essence. The idea that all human beings "by nature strive for knowledge" is elucidated by Aristotle with a reference to the love of perception, and, in fact, especially to perception with the eyes; of all the senses, sight lets us recognize the most and make the most distinctions.[132]

So knowing, apprehending, means perceiving differences, and this in turn means seeing these differences in their belongingness and, thus, recognizing what is differentiated as what it is. What is differentiated is not a mere jumble of multiplicity; it is what is separated out from others and, in this, connected with others. What is differentiated belongs in a web, it is in a texture. Just as sight is not fixed on the isolated individual thing but rather produces a more or less clear overall picture, so too apprehension grasps a context; knowing that is to be comprehended as apprehending lies in this cognizance. νοεῖν is also the grasping of a situation, something like a sense of the whole. Even if a whole of this kind is in need of investigation and one therefore goes through it in different respects, it is there all at once; it is simultaneous, like a text, and is apprehended in this simultaneity. Without this, the possibility of going through it would not even arise; one only knows that something is to be more precisely investigated if one has perceived or apprehended it as a whole.

Such an apprehension is given only if one does not hold fast to individual things or is held fast by them. One must have distance from individual things in such a way that one does not get concerned and involved with them. In this sense, Aristotle can say of reason that it is "without being affected."[133] Because reason takes up *everything*, it has to be "unmixed"[134] with whatever it can take up. Reason is in its essence nothing other than capable or possible.[135]

Aristotle's description here is not of the respectively enacted thinking that is thought through (διάνοια), but, rather, of its possibility in the sense of the first completion: νοῦς is also one of its formations; it, too, is not to be conceived as currently enacted contemplation, θεωρεῖν, but, rather, as knowing, ἐπιστήμη. Reason is the capacity to take up what may be thought through.

What is thinkable for Aristotle is the form (εἶδος). Indeed, the form comprises the actuality of that whose form it is because it is "the inhering form"[136] and, so, lets something appear as what it is. Reason does not register the form in this way, however—not like the "snub-nosed"[137] that may not even be conceived as form without the visible, sensible nose. The form apprehended in reason is also not what is given in perception—not this respective magnitude or this respective water, but what being is for magnitude or for water.[138] What is perceptible does not affect reason; reason takes forms from what is perceptible.

If one can understand the forms as pure significances, reason is thereby moved into language; talk of "what the being for magnitude is" is easily recognized as a variation of the formulation, "what-it-was-to-be," τό τι ἦν εἶναι. It also signifies what Aristotle identifies as εἶδος κατὰ τὸν λόγον, namely, the determination of a matter in what it is.

That reason comes into focus in determinations of this kind would have to be illuminating. The determination of a matter is complex even when the matter is understood as an individual thing and not in the Platonic sense as a moment of a complex of significance. The capacity to differentiate the moments of a complex of significance and to hold them together in their differentiation is reason. There is only significance in the many, it is determined only in structures; reason takes up structures.

There is reason not only here, however, but also in action and in time. It is at work when respective activity is held together with what is intended, that is, in the free reference to an aim. It is also at work in the constellation of meaning, be it in understanding an activity based on something futural or past, be it in the agreement of two inner experiences as Proust describes it. Here, there are no linguistically distinguished, pure significances. Rather, the correspondence of two inner experiences occurs in such a way that they supplement one another so as to be something meaningful. The occurrence is temporal; it cannot be conceived unless something sensuous affects one. It is a capacity of reason, however, that the supplementation is apprehended. It is solely through reason that the supplementation is there.

This would not be possible if the removal opened between one's current inner experience and the one remembered were not also there. The supplement, as Proust describes it, runs through time. A removal is likewise opened when what one does or deliberates stands in reference to an intention. If the removal is not there as such and is not experienced in activity as measurable, there can be no planning and, prior to this, not even the certainty of ability. Finally, there must be a removal as such in order for a significance to stand out from what is shown in it and, so, for the significance to be able to enter into a complex with other significances. Without reason, it is not possible to extend the significance of a word to something else that is to be shown; without it, there can be no carrying over, and for all of this, there must be openness itself. Reason, then, is determined by remove itself. Reason is the apprehension of what is distinguished and thereby belongs together with one another. Reason has this in front of it and holds on to it in its simple givenness. Reason is a *sense of reference* that is pure and has come into focus as such. Reason makes it possible to conduct oneself in reference, and, in this way, is the first completion of understanding.

If one follows Aristotle, the existence of remove in reason is caused by reason itself. The causal factor, however, is reason in a different regard. Aristotle determines it as actuality[139] in distinction from capable or possible reason and calls its effectiveness a production or bringing forth.[140] This is clearly oriented by the model of τέχνη: reason is supposed to be constituted in its essence just as in τέχνη there is both the material taken up and likewise the arrangement that puts the form in it.

Aristotle's intention becomes clearer when he compares what brings forth with light[141] in a clear echo of the so-called "simile of the sun" in the *Republic*[142]; light also "in a certain manner" makes possible colors into actual ones.[143] The addition of "in a certain manner" is explained by the fact that Aristotle deviates here from his determination of the relation of light and color developed in the second book of *De anima*. There, light was grasped as the actuality of what is transparent[144]; as soon as there is light something transparent such as air or water becomes apparent, whereas without light it is only transparent in possibility. Aristotle understands color, in turn, as something visible[145] that actually comes to be seen when it actually moves something transparent in such a way that this transparent something, in turn, can set the capacity for sight into movement.[146] If there is supposed to be an analogy to reason, reason would be put into movement by what it apprehends, and it could not then be "without being affected" as Aristotle had stipulated. Because reason is determined here only as a capacity, however, there must be something that brings it into actuality without being causal in the strict sense. The idea that this is something analogous to light is compelling. If one thinks of not a blinding ray of light directed at one's eye but rather of the evenly strewn brightness of the day, then it may in fact be said that light allows sight to be actual; in the light, sight is awake, whereas in the dark it rests in its possibility. Accordingly, reason would be moved into wakefulness by something analogous to light; it is the actual openness in which something can be apprehended, or, with Aristotle: reason itself insofar as it gives whatever is apprehensible.

What Aristotle attempts to grasp here is neither the relation of two different forms of reason nor the self-relation of a single reason that would "affect" itself and thereby bring itself into actuality. It is the *rational*, which reason encounters with the apprehensibility of something. Something is only apprehensible because it is rational—just as an artistically complete work belongs in art. This does not mean that one would have to go back to one's knowledge of the producer in order to understand what one encounters as artistic. Whatever is artistic stands in art and is encountered based on it. This is also how it is with whatever is rational; it is structure that comes from whatever is rational in its apprehensibility and that belongs together with apprehension in an exterior reason that encompasses apprehension.

It is beyond doubt that Aristotle thinks of exterior reason in terms of the divine; that this reason is described as immortal and eternal[147] speaks unequivocally for this. What is intended is that it continues to exist even when the respective ability for apprehension dies away with the death of a human being. The ability may come into existence again, but it always comes into the same openness that allows it to be actual. The spirit of the idea is that the actuality of reason comes from outside[148]; reason is actually reason only in its exteriority.

The idea developed here also holds for the world in the sense of hermeneutical space; in the world, there are abilities for apprehension that arrive and pass away. The world is the openness of rational life, exterior reason, which is "similar" to the ability of reason, just as—according to the Platonic *Republic*—the eye is similar to the sun as the source for the light that makes things accessible. Because of this "similarity," reason and world may not be separated from one another. Reason is the openness of the world, and world, conversely, is the actual openness of reason. Reason is not *in* the world; it is just as worldly as the world is rational in its openness such that in reason state and in-a-state are congruent. It is true that not everything in the world is apprehended, but *the* world is always apprehended, not a world and also not a segment of it; the world is always open in its three dimensions.

This entails that reason is *placeless*. It is not discoverable, not localizable, but rather always only recognizable in terms of how a living being conducts itself based on its apprehension of the world. The placelessness of reason may be recognized especially well by the fact that a rational being can take on different perspectives toward something. It is true that if perception is at issue this is always only possible in quickened embodiment; in this case, the place of liveliness changes its place. It is thanks to reason, however, that one holds a perspective together with others and that just now, in looking ahead, one is already somewhere else than one is now, and that now in retrospect one is somewhere else than a moment ago. Without reason, there is for us certainly not the whole of a building that one walks around and investigates from different sides. That we move ourselves around the building and see it from different angles of vision is a matter of quickened embodiment; that a whole arises in a sustained reference to something is rational—not in the sense of an "inner" achievement of "subjectivity," but, rather, in the three-dimensional play of freedom, language, and time.

The example also gives an indication of how reason as such can come into focus in life: because its placelessness stands out from the place-character of the body quick. The body quick only appears as place, conversely, in the placeless openness of reason. The two supplement one another, and even if it is possible to focus on pure significances and to avoid connecting them with something individual shown in them, it is nevertheless true of life that it is rational and quickened embodiment at once. Considered in this way, life is not simply form of life but rather a structure of different dispositions and formations, a *structure of life*.

§ 41. Structure of Life

One directs one's conduct at oneself when one considers himself or something of himself. This can be this hand that, leading the pen, goes across the page and strings row after row. The hand may be drawn; Eduardo Chillida has done it often. He has also taken the form that he discovered in focusing on it and carrying it over and then carried it over further, thereby varying it, for example, in the "wind combs" (*Peine del Viento*) that are mounted to the cliffs on the coast of San Sebastián.[149] Without reason, such a contemplation, and certainly the activity of drawing the hand one recognizes as one's own, is not possible. For this, the distance is needed, in which the hand is known in its form; and also needed is the caesura that itself cannot be traced back to anything, that allows something seen to be intelligible as an object of sight.

The contemplation and also the drawing of one's own hand is certainly a conduct directed at oneself. That it is a conduct directed *at oneself*, however, cannot be made intelligible solely based on the ability to contemplate and draw. The fact that one's own hand can be contemplated or drawn does not distinguish it from some other thing. Moreover, when one contemplates Chillida's drawings, one really does not know whether it is the hand of the artist that one sees. Chillida's drawings of concern here are simply called "hand" (*Esku*). And, even if it really was his hand that he has contemplated and drawn, the form of it that is carried over is of course comparable to the form of every hand. It is more or less the same form. Factically, contemplation under the aspect of form and drawing may well be conduct directed at oneself. Nevertheless, they lead away from oneself.

For things to be otherwise, something that is perceived has to remain bound to the one who perceives it. This is the case when something perceived appears at the same time as something that perceives or as something that one is able to perceive with, that is: as an organ of one's own body. The hand that is contemplated or drawn is a hand with which one is able to grasp. If one follows how the hand holding the pen goes across the paper, it is clear that it is one's own; one writes "with it" after all. Seen from this standpoint, the constitution of the hand as an organ stands in an intermediary position between distance and distancelessness; it changes between the two as between the two possibilities of considering a figure-ground picture puzzle. It is "my hand" and I can nevertheless contemplate it at a distance. This can happen only in the openness of reason because reason distinguishes the two possibilities and thereby has them in front of it in their distinctness.

The possibility of grasping one's own perceiving or ability to perceive is imparted to everything that is perceived. What is perceived is not grasped as such without a recognition of perceiving or the ability to perceive, and this, in turn, can be fixed on an organ. The contemplation of one's hand is just as much contemplation of perceiving, then, as that of something perceived. The artist who draws the hand furthermore makes clear what drawing itself is; he shows where it came from.

If one conceives of one's hand not only as something perceived of a certain form, but also as perceiving, then it appears twice: it is corporeal and at the same time it belongs to the body quick. The more strongly it is experienced as quickened embodiment here, the more it is one's own. The liveliness to which the hand belongs then appears in contemplation; the possibility of writing, touching or gripping shows itself along with it. This remains preserved in a picture he draws [*Zeichnung*] as the past of an activity of drawing [*Zeichnen*]. With the picture he draws, the artist who draws his hand thus directs his conduct at what he does. Insofar as one can see the activity of drawing in the picture he draws, the picture he draws belongs in the conduct he directs toward himself.

This conduct is admittedly still not concentrated on one himself. It is true that it is more a conduct directed at oneself than the contemplation of one's own hand in its form or composition; the hand is now seen in its liveliness and no longer as any arbitrary thing. This liveliness, however, can also appear in regard to any other person's hand as well as in regard to one's own hand. In the picture that is drawn by hand, one sees the possibility of the activity of drawing. It is true that one knows differently what touching is if one can himself have the experience of touching; one knows it differently than one knows of the flight of the gull or the silent slither of the snake. One understands liveliness, however, without having the liveliness in particular that one contemplates. Accordingly, this understanding of life is still not an unequivocal conduct directed at *oneself*. One is himself co-intended, but not specifically intended.

Things are different when what is contemplated—or, generally, what is experienced—is an actual or possible affection or an actual or possible specific conduct. Both must be specifically intended; to do this however, it is not enough to be cognizant of them, rather, it is necessary to direct one's conduct at them in whatever manner. Only such a conduct directed at a conduct is unequivocally a conduct directed at oneself. Here the concern is with an understanding of life that may no longer be achieved in regard to others. The understanding exists in one's own conduct and refers to one himself.

This is to be elucidated in various respects. First of all, the outlined structure gives rise to a more precise understanding of the reflexive "itself" [*sich*] that is necessary for the conduct that needs to be made clear here. This expression does not express anything substantial—as if one were himself pre-given in some manner and in addition to this could direct his conduct at this pre-givenness.[150] From the standpoint of conduct directed at oneself, what might be conceived as pre-given—body and the body quick—come into view specifically not as substance, but, rather, solely on the basis of conduct and affection: It is what is threatened or moved by affections, that is, being-threatened or being-moved by affections themselves. And, it is likewise that without which specific possibilities of conduct do not come into being, that by which they are favored, hampered, or suspended after they earlier came into being. In avoiding dangers that one is exposed to corporeally, one directs one's conduct not at one's body, but at oneself. And, from one's own point of view, corporeal restrictions or afflictions are not defects of an entity that can be described by the natural sciences, but rather painful affections and restrictions of conduct at which one—for his part—has to direct his conduct. With the idea of conduct that is directed at oneself, it becomes clear once again and in an especially clear way that there is nothing substantial in life. In conduct directed "at oneself," life proves rather to be a *structure of life*—a structure that involves a conduct and also a conduct directed at a conduct.

A new understanding of liveliness comes into view with the outlined structure. Liveliness no longer appears simply as the interplay of affection and conduct as Aristotle had worked it out in regard to perception. Rather, from the standpoint of conduct, liveliness appears narrowed in a peculiar manner, one could also say "internalized," such that one could speak with Kierkegaard of a "relation that relates itself to itself," or, of the fact that a "relation relates itself to itself."[151]

This does not mean that the referentiality of the living being to something else is thereby superceded or erased, however. Having an effect on something as well as having an effect by means of something else continue to exist now as they did before. It is in any case determined and potentially eclipsed by the relation that the Kierkegaardian formulation indicates. What one could call the internalization of life is to be understood as such an eclipsing. It is the possibility of conducting oneself in the exteriority of life—more precisely, in the structure of liveliness—that does not exist without an exterior. One is amidst things but hardly even sees them, for one is concerned "with oneself."

In order to show what this means with more precision, one should begin with a conduct directed at oneself that is still free of the "internalizing" that eclipses. This is the only way to make clear how conduct directed at oneself is possible in a liveliness that is according to its essence exterior. The eclipsing of the exterior essence only becomes intelligible based on this.

The description of liveliness from this standpoint can build on the *Republic*, more precisely, on the passages in which Socrates works out the structure of human liveliness in such a way that it can form the point of departure for all subsequent formulations of the problem. The discussion of ψυχή in the *Republic* is motivated by the question of its organization. In answer to it, Plato grounds what Aristotle presupposes—that one has to understand liveliness as a definite multiplicity and, more precisely, as a structure of different possibilities of life. Whereas Aristotle considers these possibilities above all for themselves, however, in the Platonic description the focus is precisely on their difference and their interplay in tension. The possibility of conduct directed at oneself arises solely with this.

The argument that Socrates makes for the organization of the ψυχή rests on the necessity of keeping all of its determinations free of contradiction: It is obvious that the same thing will never do or suffer opposites in the same respect in relation to the same thing at the same time.[152] If one does not accept this—incidentally earliest—form of the principle of contradiction, then one would have to determine something as itself and at the same time as its contrary. For the liveliness of the human being this means concretely that desiring something and not desiring something cannot be traced back in the same respect to the same possibility of life. And, if desire and insight contradict one another, for example, in recognizing that something that one takes pleasure in is harmful, this points to different "parts" of liveliness. One cannot conceive of these as separable elements of construction. The ψυχή is not something that can be discovered as a being is. The structure of life that is the ψυχή is demonstrated solely in a respective manner of being—regardless of whether someone can bring all of the moments of this structure of life into focus in their agreement or not.

The idea of a structure of life is illuminating if liveliness is in itself fundamentally laden with conflict; in conflict, the different powers of life show themselves in their difference. And, if the conflict is grounded in the structure of the ψυχή itself, the possibility of conflict remains insuperable. The agreement of the powers of life can only be an equilibrium that always remains at risk and that always has to be found anew.

It becomes clear that this is how things are in Socrates' development of his characterization of the powers of life. The first distinction, which is foundational for all further ones that Socrates makes, is already that of an opposition; it is between accepting—literally, to nod in acceptance (ἐπινεύειν)—and rejecting—literally, to lift one's head in rejection (ἀνανεύειν), that is, between yes and no. These two possibilities are different—fundamentally different, although only if the no is nothing but a no and cannot be understood as a hidden yes. This is precisely how it is understood by Socrates. The yes is an endeavor after something (ἐφίεσθαί τινος λαβεῖν) and an embracing (προσάγεσθαι), the no an aversion (ἀπαρνεῖσθαι) and a pushing away (ἀπωθεῖσθαι).[153]

This fundamental distinction as it has thus been elucidated can only be illuminated with reference to different powers of life. As possibilities of accepting, Socrates names the desired (ἐπιθυμίαι), the willed (τὸ ἐθέλειν) and the will (τὸ βούλεσθαι).[154] Opposed to this, as formations of rejecting, there stand the unwilling (ἀβουλεῖν), the not willed (τὸ μὴ ἐθέλειν), and the not desired (τὸ μὴ ἐπιθυμεῖν).[155]

These significations make it clear that the description of the structure of life is oriented by the accepting powers of life; indeed, the ones opposed to them are initially determined only negatively. Nevertheless, rejecting cannot be mere refusal: As such, it could hardly step in against the powers of life that aim at and take possession of something. It is a power of its own kind, namely, the power of deliberation (λογιστικόν).[156] It can only be effective by not following desire, but it is nevertheless only negative when one perceives it from the standpoint of desire. Its characteristic capacity is simply to hold on to a fact, say, that despite unaltered appetite it would not be good to continue eating. As soon as this insight is achieved or again comes to consciousness, it exists regardless of whether or not desire may be determined or at least irritated by it. It exists, and it is therein distinguished from that movement toward something in which the power of desire has its actuality. It lacks the enactment-character of desire. This makes it separate from desire by a strict limit.

This idea is disconcerting if one bases one's view on Aristotle. The idea here does not focus on the distinction of conduct that is rational, because deliberate, and a-rational, because impulsive. This stands in contrast to the familiar conviction that deliberation can itself be guiding in the power of life that urges forward—put in Aristotelian terms: in striving (ὄρεξις). It is in this sense that Aristotle can distinguish between desiring (ἐπιθυμία) and willing (βούλησις) and he can say that willing arises in the power of deliberation, whereas desire comes from what is without deliberation.[157] In opposition to this, it would be held in the spirit of the Platonic distinction that a deliberation operative in striving itself does indeed concern the intentionality although never the rationality of striving: A deliberation as it were inherent in striving cannot guarantee this rationality. Striving for what is pleasant, as Aristotle determines desire,[158] could be very deliberate and nevertheless be directed only toward something pleasant and ultimately, then, be a-rational (ἄλογος). Aristotle does not really refute this objection. It is true that he sees a possible conflict between desire and deliberation, but he traces this back solely to the experience of time and elucidates it as a tension between boundedness to the moment and foresight; reason commands a direction of conduct because of the future, desire because of the present.[159] It is obviously possible that something in the future be only pleasant, so that deliberation remains subordinate to desire instead of correcting it.

On the other hand, the possibility of conduct guided by deliberation, which Aristotle emphasizes, cannot seriously be doubted. That there is a difference between impulsive desire and deliberate action is ultimately illuminating. In the Platonic conception of liveliness this is also not denied. But deliberation is not subordinated to the power of life that urges forth as in Aristotle. Rather, there is here a third[160] between the power of life that urges forward and the one that rejects. This means that not only an opposition exists between the two other powers but rather a tension that, as such, is lived.

Socrates verifies his impression that there is a third of this sort with reference to a power that sometimes (ἐνίοτε) conflicts with desire. It operates as a movement of spirit, as an impulse, that turns itself against desire. This power is initially named θυμός,[161] a little later, θυμοειδές, "the thumos-like,"[162] no doubt to mark its difference in contrast to the traditional significance of θυμός as a liveliness that proves itself in severe, also fervent, excitations of life.[163] As a power of life, what gets termed θυμοειδές is only similar to this liveliness, and, in fact, in appearance. It rebels, it is an expression like rage, but it is based on a rational ground, even if it is not rational in the manner of its appearance. It comes into focus by appearing impulsively against the power of life that urges forth, and thus becomes an ally of deliberation,[164] although it is itself admittedly not deliberation. It is a power of life that *restrains*, a power whose severity stands in the service of a moment of pausing, holding back, that is supposed to and can help the conclusions of deliberation to come to actuality. This is possible because although it is a stirring of life, it is not referred to something longed for and, for this reason, does not urge us forth. Its proximity to desire just as much as its difference from it is found in the Greek words. ἐπιθυμία, this is the θυμός for something. It is θυμός with a direction.

The secret point of the whole discussion is in any case that this direction is diffuse. The positive determination of being willed, desiring, and willing are deceptive; urging forward, wanting to seize, and taking possession have no aim of their own, however intentional their enactment may be. This stems from the fact that they arise out of "affections and illnesses"[165]; they come from a disturbance, such that their strength derives from the attempt to consolidate, although they reach consolidation by themselves at best coincidentally.

How this is more precisely to be understood is developed in the *Philebus*. Here, the reference to "affections and illnesses" is resolved through a determination of pain (λύπη). Pain arises when the harmony and thereby at the same time the nature in the living being is disturbed[166]; pain is a state *in* a state; something in life falls into disorder and now one puts everything into finding the order again.

According to the *Philebus*, there appears to be a clear criterion for the success of such an attempt. If order is restored, pleasure arises.[167] The converse, however, does not hold. Although there is not pleasure without order, this does not mean that the disturbed order is restored whenever pleasure arises. This is because this restoration is not conceivable without expectation[168]; the state that is strived for must somehow be there. The expectation is in itself already pleasant, however, just as the expectation of something painful is already painful.[169] Because of this, the desire or willing guided by such an expectation can run in a direction that only promises the restoration of the ordered state. It is only under one condition that things are otherwise: One must have found the ordered state through deliberation or simply be familiar with it. It is then also possible that one desires or wants what is correct. But this is not guaranteed. The realization of what is correct can be connected with a renunciation of what is presently pleasant, indeed, with temporary unpleasantness. Because desire and will are determined by a pleasant expectation, however, they go further in the wrong direction. In the enactment that they are, they cannot diverge from this direction. A change in direction could only come from another power of life, precisely one that impulsively rebels against desiring and willing because it is penetrated by knowledge of what is correct and remains subordinate to this knowledge in its rebellion.

The structure of life as it has become intelligible in Plato may now be determined in summary. The structure of life is the belongingness of reference and enactment with a third thing that brings into focus what one is referred to in enactment. Here, reference to something moves toward something with remoteness; in it, something is ascertained or remains as it was ascertained in its structure. It has been shown and it has shown itself in the remoteness of what shows itself. By contrast, enactment has the character of a diminishment of distance; something is far away and one wishes to bring it into proximity; understood in this way, enactment is above all in time. Therefore, there is a need for the third thing that exists in enactment at a distance and, so, gives remoteness its due. This is the restraint in enactment that makes the calm work of ascertaining effective by delaying, by keeping one from being persuaded, or by simply putting things to a halt. It is sustained by the linguisticality of reference and by the temporal affect against desiring and willing. It is above all, however, the sense of freedom that lives in it, for it is not merely free like contemplative insight but rather brings freedom into focus.

This also makes intelligible what conduct directed at oneself is. This conduct arises from the harmony of the powers of life such that their structure is confirmed or distorted through the inversion of relations that accord with nature. A dissolution of the structure is not possible; this would be tantamount to a dissolution of life itself. But the order can be disrupted or impaired. A living being *is* not, but, rather, stands in the play of being, that is, of permanence and becoming, in the play of passing away and being. The realized order that the living being can be has always been; it is "being, which has come to be"[170] as it is called in the *Philebus*, although therefore always also a diminishment of being and a loss of being. This conditions the demand for restoration found in desiring and willing. In desiring and willing, one directs one's conduct at the order of one's own life, and, in this sense, at oneself.

Desiring and willing, however, are without insight; nothing is known in them alone. Because of this, they are unable to find the state they strive for on their own. They either reach it by coincidence or they go astray. The latter brings into play the power of life that restrains or puts to a halt and that arises in the sense of an insight against desiring and willing. Here, too, there is conduct directed at oneself.

By contrast, insight remains neutral in a characteristic manner. It ascertains, and, in this, it is rather like the doctor who diagnoses an illness as a disturbance of the natural order of the body and does so as one determined by this order just like the one affected. What is ascertained as order and as its disturbance does not have to affect one himself, but, rather, can be the case for anyone. The insight is painless. Only desiring and willing are affected by the pain that urges one from the state ascertained by insight and thereby directs one's conduct at the order of one's own life. It is only based on this that insight can appear to be painful, something that is sometimes revealed when one does not "want" to admit an insight as true. Yet, in contrast with desiring and willing, and also in contrast with the power of life that restrains, insight does not engage in any conflict. In insight, there is no conduct directed at oneself.

Accordingly, conduct directed at oneself is bound to the conflict arising in the structure of life. As long as the order of life is not disrupted or disturbed, one does not need to direct one's conduct at oneself. The "oneself" here has its significance solely in its brokenness; it emerges only if a tear goes through the structure of life. Conduct directed at oneself bespeaks a lack; in it, the loss or preclusion of fulfillment and fullness announces itself.

§ 42. Lack and Fullness

One's interest in the conflict of the powers of life grows with the interest in conduct directed at oneself. If one understands life *essentially* as conduct directed at oneself, then this conflict has to be a central issue for consideration. Based on the presupposition that the human being is "relation," "which relates itself to itself,"[171] Kierkegaard therefore describes the human being as if the conflict is enduring. According to Kierkegaard's conviction, nothing leads the human being beyond conflict, and it is given even when one does not have the inner experience of the powers of life as conflictual but rather when life is apparently "in security and rest." If life as such is in conflict then conflict must always already be there. This becomes recognizable, as Kierkegaard thinks, in the fundamental experience of anxiety. This makes it clear that security and rest are a lurking conflict capable of breaking out at any moment. "All immediacy," that is, every state that is still not a recognizable conduct directed at oneself, is "anxiety despite its conceit of security and rest, and, as a logical consequence, the most apprehensive anxiety in the face of the nothing,"[172] that is, "in the face of" the indeterminacy of still undeveloped conduct directed at oneself.

Although different in the manner of his presentation than Kierkegaard, Heidegger pursues the same fundamental issue in *Sein und Zeit* when he sees the strife of authenticity and inauthenticity posed as irresolute and, in this way, as enduring. Conduct directed at oneself, understood here as conduct directed at one's own being, is the effort to address the conflict of being oneself and fallenness in the world, in which the character of Dasein as possibility always and again takes flight in the purported actuality of connections within the world, and, consequently, must as it were be wrested from this flight in a "reversal." Or, in Heidegger's terminology, the disclosedness [*Erschlossenheit*] of Dasein plays out in the effort to address being closed off [*Verschlossenheit*] and resoluteness [*Entschlossenheit*].[173]

The orientation of conduct directed at oneself is indeed a necessary condition of—but not the reason for the fact that—the conflict is posed in both cases as enduring. Rather, in order to preserve its claim to being enduring the conflict has to be conceived in such a way that there is no way beyond it. This occurs in Kierkegaard as it does in Heidegger insofar as they make the will a central issue. For Kierkegaard, conduct directed at oneself is therefore "despair" because something is supposed to be brought into "security and rest" that cannot be brought into security and rest. To will this is either an attempt to control the structure of life itself or it is an urge to get beyond the conflict in the structure of life. Despair thus exists either in the fact that one wills to be oneself while full of despair, or in the fact that one wills to be free of oneself while full of despair. The one is conditioned by the other. One can only will to be to oneself while full of despair insofar as one does not will to be what one is; and one can only will not to be oneself while full of despair insofar as *one himself* does not will to be himself.[174] The flight into the purported security of the world as Heidegger describes it is also a willful attempt at not willing to be oneself. And even if this flight is interrupted by the mood of anxiety and the "call" of conscience, both pass away without consequence if one were not to want to be addressed by conscience. Heidegger in fact conceived of resoluteness in *Sein und Zeit* on the model of the Husserlian ἐποχή. But Heidegger can only conceive of the binding force of the distance to the world given by the ἐποχή as a "willing-to-have-a-conscience."[175] Even the "leap" into faith, which Kierkegaard understands as the way out of despair, is a final act of the will that leads beyond the will-to-be-oneself. The metaphor of the leap makes this clear enough.

Kierkegaard and the author of *Sein und Zeit* are not alone in taking their orientation from the concept of the will. On the contrary, they each in their own way articulate the dominant conviction of modern philosophy that Schelling had programmatically formulated for those who come after him. There is, Schelling writes in his treatise on the essence of human freedom, "in the final and highest instance no other being than willing [*Wollen*]": "Willing is originary being [*Urseyn*]."[176] This conviction has had its most influential effect through Schopenhauer and Nietzsche. The Heidegger who has become critical of the will sees it as the center of thought in the end of metaphysics and thereby as the center not only of philosophical thought but rather of modernity generally. Metaphysics, as Heidegger understands it, does not end in Nietzsche's last fragments devoted to the "will to power" but rather in the technical revolution that it is possible to grasp not least through Ernst Jünger's descriptions. As Heidegger writes in notes he devoted to the long essay *Der Arbeiter*, Jünger replaced the "title predetermined out of the inheritance of German metaphysics since Leibniz," the will to power, "with the name appropriate to our century, work [*Arbeit*]."[177]

This development is anticipated unintentionally in Schelling's statements. They are intended as formulations of the definitive insight of "Idealism," more precisely, of the thought the early Fichte, which is articulated in his concept of "action" [*Tathandlung*]. Willing, according to Schelling, is "originary being" insofar as all of the predicates that confer being are suited to it as to no others: "groundlessness, eternity, independence from time, self-affirmation."[178] Conversely, however, all predicates that hold of the will can therefore be applied to "being." What was once called "being" fell into a movement so inconclusive, so unable to be concluded, that being is no longer the actuality—complete in itself because it runs toward and arrives at itself—which it was for the Aristotelian Hegel. What one had called "being" is now an *ability* that comes into focus as such in movement and change; it is an *urge* toward something and away from something; and, because it can only be born out in ever new manifestations, it is disposed toward that *increase*, which Nietzsche grasped with the formulation "will to power."

The modern metaphysics of the will agrees with Plato in its determination of the will. It shares with him the conviction that the will is not teleological but rather, as Schopenhauer formulates it, "blind urge."[179] The agreement could scarcely be a coincidence but is rather the result of a fundamentally Platonic doctrine—in Schopenhauer as in Nietzsche, whose conception of the will to power would hardly be conceivable without the relevant analyses in the *Republic* and no less in the *Gorgias*.[180]

Yet even a thinker as critical of the will as Schopenhauer does not conclude from this Platonic determination of the will that the concept cannot serve as a guiding concept for thought which is critical of the will. Rather, he entrusts the overcoming of the will to the will itself. By "objectivizing" itself in knowledge, the will is supposed "to be able to become something that can quiet the will and cause the will freely to supercede itself."[181] Heidegger also speaks of a will of not-willing,[182] and even Nietzsche holds a self-quieting of the will to be possible with his idea of the eternal recurrence of the same that is actually an act of the will.

Plato provided the answer as to why this does not lead to any resolution with his determination of desire and will; Aristotle took it up and varied it as laconically as he did clearly. It is only possible to will what can be otherwise and this ability-to-be-otherwise does not cease with willing; what is willed can again become otherwise, that is, become an object of a willing. But then willing never comes to an end. It is only possible to will so long as something stands out from the viewpoint of the will as something changeable or as something worth seizing, appropriating. It is only necessary to will where there exists a *lack*; desire and will are determined by a defect and the permanence of the will is nothing other than the permanence of lack.

In willing, whatever can become an object of the will is simply there. It must be recognized in what it is in order that it can be approached from the standpoint of change at all. This recognition leaves it as it is, and in this gives it its due. The lack that drives the will on is not after all a lack belonging to the world but rather one belonging to a living being that has resorted to willing. Things only have to change if something is missing for "me" or "us"; taken on their own, everything could remain as it is. From the standpoint of the will everything has the tendency to become a lack of one's own life. The more that is willed, the more the world becomes an encompassing life-worldly state; it falls into the immanence of a universal conduct directed at oneself.

By contrast, all recognition leads where one always already is before any conduct directed at himself: It leads outside, into the world of things. It confirms and renews that reference that alone gives meaning to the enactment of desiring and willing. And, insofar as recognizing does not itself fall under the dominion of willing, it confirms the fullness of things. The presentation of this fullness corresponds to the fullness. In it, things remain what they are; they remain at a removal; precisely because of this, one is not separated from them.

This holds still more for the objects that are preeminently correlated of presentation, that is, of interpretation and thereby also understanding. In standing over and against, they call back to mind the originariness of life that exists in leaping out of and standing out from the context of things. One's attentiveness integrates them at the same time, however, into the context of things. In conduct directed at objects, the state of human life and its in-a-state come into suspension. Reference directed toward objects is an intensification of meaning. And, because objects are intensifications of the thing-world, this world stands in its greatest intensity with them in the life-world. Therefore, they are a corrective against the immanence that threatens this world from out of its essence. The human being is not the measure of all things. Precisely because objects themselves refuse every answer and especially a final answer, they give the measure by which the human being can become cognizant of their exteriority. Because the exteriority of life is intensified with them, they allow us to be in the world in an open manner and to discover the meaning of contemplation and presentation that is always and again at play in all human life. It is a mediating meaning beyond what is merely human.

Notes

Figal's original includes only place of publication and date, and we are translating it accordingly.

Notes to Introduction

1. Cf. Jean Grondin, *Einführung in die Philosophische Hermeneutik* (Darmstadt, 1991); Emil Angehrn, *Interpretation und Dekonstruktion: Untersuchung zur Hermeneutik* (Weilerswist, 2003); Hans Ineichen, *Philosophische Hermeneutik* (Freiburg i. Br./München, 1991); Jean Greisch, *Hermeneutik und Metaphysik. Eine Problemgeschichte* (München, 1993); Erwin Hufnagel, *Einführung in die Hermeneutik* (St. Augustin, 2000).

2. Referred to for the first time as a book title in Johann Conrad Dannhauer, *Hermeneutica sacra sive methodus exponendarum sacrarum literarum proposita et rindicita* (1654).

3. As evidence of this in the growing scholarly literature, *The Cambridge Companion to Gadamer* (Cambridge, 2002), ed. Robert Dostal, may be counted along with the volume *The Philosophy of Hans-Georg Gadamer* in the Library of Living Philosophers (Chicago, 1997), ed. L. E. Hahn. Cf. also the expansive monographs by Fruchon and Deniau: Pierre Fruchon, *L'herméneutique de Gadamer: platonisme et modernité, tradition et intérpretation* (Paris, 1994); Guy Deniau, *Cognitio imaginativa: la phénoménologie herméneutique de Gadamer* (Brüssel, 2003).

4. Richard Rorty, *Philosophy and the Mirror of Nature* (Princeton, 1979). In German, *Der Spiegel der Natur. Eine Kritik der Philosophie* (Frankfurt am Main, 1981).

5. Gianni Vattimo, *La fine della Modernità* (Mailand, 1985). In German, *Das Ende der Moderne* (Stuttgart, 1990).

6. Jürgen Habermas, *Theorie des kommunikativen Handelns, zwei Bände* (Frankfurt am Main, 1981).

7. On the relation between Gadamer and Derrida, cf. Jacques Derrida/Hans-Georg Gadamer, *Der ununterbrochene Dialog*, ed. Martin Gessmann (Frankfurt am Main, 2004), as well as Donatella Di Cesare, *L'utopia del comprendere* (Genua, 2003).

Notes to Chapter 1

1. F. D. E. Schleiermacher, *Hermeneutik und Kritik*, ed. Manfred Frank (Frankfurt am Main, 1977), 346. Hermeneutics, as Schleiermacher puts it in another passage, is "generally, the art of properly understanding the talk of another, preeminently in written form. Schleiermacher, *Hermeneutik und Kritik*, 71.

2. Hans-Helmut Gander, *Positivismus als Metaphysik. Voraussetzungen und Grundstrukturen von Diltheys Grundlegung der Geisteswissenschaften* (Freiburg i. Br./München, 1988), esp. 210–19.

3. Hans-Georg Gadamer, *Hermeneutik I. Wahrheit und Methode: Grundzüge einer philosophichen Hermeneutik*, fifth edition, in *Gesammelte Werke* (henceforth: *GW*), Vol. 1 (Tübingen, 1986), 246. [Cf. Hans-Georg Gadamer, *Truth and Method*, trans. Rev. Joel Weinsheimer and Donald G. Marshall (New York: Continuum, 1995), 241. For passages cited by Figal from *Truth and Method*, I have consulted and often followed the Weinsheimer and Marshall translation. Note that for the passage cited here, the Weinsheimer and Marshall translation, which relies not on the fifth (1986) but, rather, on the sixth (1990) Mohr-Siebeck edition of *Wahrheit und Methode*, refers not to "epistemological formulation of the question," but, rather, to "epistemological Cartesianism." More generally, I have tried to indicate with a translator's note whenever I have expressly consulted, relied on, or followed other English translations of texts Figal cites in his book. —Trans.]

4. Gadamer, *Wahrheit und Methode*, 12. [Cf. Weinsheimer and Marshall, 7. —Trans.]

5. Ibid. [Cf. Weinsheimer and Marshall, 7. —Trans.]

6. Ibid. [Cf. Weinsheimer and Marshall, 7. —Trans.]

7. Ibid., 1. [Cf. Weinsheimer and Marshall, xxi. —Trans.]

8. Ibid., 2. [Cf. Weinsheimer and Marshall, xxii. —Trans.]

9. Ibid., 2. [Cf. Weinsheimer and Marshall, xxii. —Trans.]

10. Ibid., 360. [Cf. Weinsheimer and Marshall, 354. —Trans.]

11. Ibid. [Cf. Weinsheimer and Marshall, 354. —Trans.]

12. Ibid., 361. [Cf. Weinsheimer and Marshall, 355. —Trans.]

13. Ibid., 2. [Cf. Weinsheimer and Marshall, xxii. —Trans.]

14. Ibid., 4. [Cf. Weinsheimer and Marshall, xxiv. —Trans.]

15. Hegel, *Vorlesung Über die Ästhetik* I, in *Werke in zwanzig Bände* (Frankfurt am Main, 1970), Vol. 13, 142.

16. Martin Heidegger, *Ontologie (Hermeneutik der Faktizität)*, in *Gesamtausgabe* (henceforth, *GA*), Vol. 63, ed. Käte Bröker-Oltmanns (Frankfurt am Main, 1988).

17. Martin Heidegger, *Phänomenologische Interpretationen zu Aristoteles (Anzeige der hermeneutischen Situation). Ausarbeitung für die Marburger und Göttinger Philosophische Fakultät [1922]*, in *Phänomenologische Interpretationen ausgewählter Abhandlungen des Aristoteles zu Ontologie und Logik, Frühe Freiburger Vorlesung Sommersemester 1922*, GA 62, ed. Günther Neumann (Frankfurt am Main, 2005).

18. This is expressly recorded on the envelope in which he kept a typescript of his early, programmatic piece.

19. Heidegger, *Phänomenologische Interpretationen*, GA 62, 364.

20. Martin Heidegger, *Die Idee der Philosophie und das Weltanschauungsproblem (1919)*, in *Zur Bestimmung der Philosophie*, GA 56/57, ed. Bernd Heimbüchel (Frankfurt am Main, 1987), 1–117.

21. Martin Heidegger, *Grundprobleme der Phänomenologie* (1919/20), *GA* 58, ed. Hans-Helmuth Gander (Frankfurt am Main, 1993), 54.

22. In his "Preface" to the first publication of the *Natorp-Bericht*, Gadamer writes, "when I read this first part of the Introduction to Heidegger's study of Aristotle again today, the *Anzeige der hermeneutischen Situation*, it is as if I would rediscover in it the central thread [*Leitfaden*] of my own philosophical career and were to replay my eventual working out of philosophical hermeneutics. The force of the impetus that I then received jumps out at me even in my current reading, and, I believe, it will go similarly for some readers of my own later works." Hans-Georg Gadamer, "Heideggers theologische Jugendschrift," in Heidegger, *Phänomenologische Interpretationen*, 76–86, here 78–79.

23. Gadamer, *Wahrheit und Methode*, 259. [Cf. Weinsheimer and Marshall, 254. —Trans.]

24. Gadamer, *Wahrheit und Methode*, 246.

25. Cf. also Theodore J Kisiel, "Das Entstehen des Begriffsfeldes 'Faktizität' im Frühwerk Heideggers," in *Dilthey-Jahrbuch* (1986-87), 91–120.

26. For the first time in F. W. J. Schelling, *Die Weltalter. Fragmente*. In the *Urfassungen von 1811 und 1813*, ed. Manfred Schröter (München, 1946), 211.

27. Heidegger, *Ontologie*, 7.

28. Martin Heidegger, *Einleitung in die Phänomenologie der Religion* (1920–21), ed. Matthias Jung and Thomas Regehly, in *Phänomenologie des religiosen Lebens*, *GA* 60 (Frankfurt am Main, 1995), 3–156, here, 64.

29. Heidegger, *Einleitung in die Phänomenologie der Religion*, 59.

30. Martin Heidegger, *Anmerkungen zu Karl Jaspers 'Psychologie der Weltanschauungen,'* (1919–21), in *Wegmarken*, *GA* 9, ed. Friedrich-Wilhelm von Herrmann (Frankfurt am Main, 1976), 1–44, here, 32.

31. Heidegger, *Ontologie*, 15.

32. Heidegger, *Ontologie*, 9. In *Sein und Zeit* Heidegger speaks of a logos that has the "character of ἑρμηνεύειν," through which "the authentic meaning of being and the fundamental structures of its own being are *announced* to the understanding of being that belongs to Dasein itself." Martin Heidegger, *Sein und Zeit*, *GA* 2, ed. Friedrich-Wilhelm von Herrmann (Frankfurt am Main, 1977), 50. Heidegger takes up this determination of hermeneutics again in his later "discussion of language," in elucidating ἑρμηνεύειν as "to announce" [*Kunde geben*]. Martin Heidegger, *Aus einem Gespräch von der Sprache. Zwischen einem Japaner und einem Fragenden*, in *Unterwegs zur Sprache*, *GA* 12, ed. Friedrich-Wilhelm von Herrmann (Frankfurt am Main, 1985), 79–146, here, 115.

33. Cf. also the illuminating presentation of "Heidegger's early hermeneutics" in Jean Grondin, *Der Sinn für Hermeneutik* (Darmstadt, 1994), 71–102. In addition, cf. Otto Pöggeler, *Heidegger und die hermeneutische Philosophie* (Freiburg i. Br./München, 1983).

34. Heidegger, *Die Idee der Philosophie*, *GA* 56/57, 116.

35. Ibid., 117.

36. Gadamer, *Wahrheit und Methode*, 259.

37. Heidegger, *Ontologie*, 15.

38. Gadamer, *Wahrheit und Methode*, 261. [Cf. Weinsheimer and Marshall, 257. —Trans.]

39. Ibid., 262. [Cf. Weinsheimer and Marshall, 258. —Trans.]

40. Ibid., 261. [Cf. Weinsheimer and Marshall, 256. —Trans.]
41. Ibid., 266.
42. Ibid., 312.
43. Hans-Georg Gadamer, "Hermeneutik und ontologische Differenz," in *Hermeneutik im Rückblick, GW* 10 (Tübingen, 1995), 58–70, here, 64.
44. Heidegger, *Ontologie*, 15.
45. Ibid., 75.
46. Gadamer, *Wahrheit und Methode*, 307. [Cf. Weinsheimer and Marshall, 302. —Trans.]
47. Clarifications that point in the same direction as the considerations developed here may be found in Michael Theunissen, "Philosophische Hermeneutik als Phänomenologie der Traditionsaneignung," in *"Sein, das verstanden werden kann, ist Sprache." Hommage an Hans-Georg Gadamer* (Frankfurt am Main, 2001), 61–88.
48. Gadamer, *Wahrheit und Methode*, GW 1, 306. [Cf. Weinsheimer and Marshall, 301. —Trans.]
49. Ibid., 307. [Cf. Weinsheimer and Marshall, 302. —Trans.]
50. G. W. F. Hegel, *Phänomenologie des Geistes*, ed. Wolfgang Bonsiepen and Reinhard Heede, historisch-kritische Edition, ed. Rheinisch-Westfälischen Akademie des Wissenschaften, *Gesammelte Werke* (Hamburg, 1980), Vol. 9, 428.
51. Søren Kierkegaard, *Philosophiske smuler (Philosophische Brocken)*, chapters 4 and 5, in *Samlede Værker* (henceforth: *SV*), ed. A. B. Drachmann, Vol. 4 (Kopenhagen, 1902), 171–272, here, 221–72.
52. Gadamer, *Wahrheit und Methode*, 126–33.
53. Cf. Gadamer, *Wahrheit und Methode*, 286.
54. Cf. ibid.
55. Gadamer, *Wahrheit und Methode*, 306. Cf. Weinsheimer and Marshall, 301. As late as 1989 he continues to hold that the hermeneutics of facticity aims "at the radical counter concept to Hegel's absolute spirit and its self-transparency." (Gadamer, "Hermeneutik und ontologische Differenz," 65).
56. Gadamer, *Wahrheit und Methode*, 281.
57. Hegel, *Phänomenologie des Geistes, Gesammelte Werke* 9, 409.
58. Gadamer, Wahrheit und Methode, 311.
59. Ibid., 312. [Cf. Weinsheimer and Marshall, 306. —Trans.]
60. Heidegger, *Phänomenologische Interpretationen*, 368.
61. Ibid.
62. Cf. Günter Figal, *Martin Heidegger–Phänomenologie der Freiheit*, third edition (Weinheim, 2000), 190–269.
63. Plato, *Res publica*, 511b. Plato's dialogue is cited from: *Platonis Opera*, ed. John Burnet (Oxford, 1900–07).
64. Edmund Husserl, *Ideen zu einer reinen Phänomenologie und phänomenologischen Philosophie, Husserliana* III.1, ed. Karl Schuhmann (Den Haag, 1976), 61.
65. Husserl, *Ideen* I, 61.
66. Ibid., 63.
67. Cf. Sextus Empiricus, *Pyrrhoniae Hypotyposes* I, 201 (chapter 26). Cf. also Malte Hossenfelder, *Einleitung zu: Sextus Empirikus, Grundriß der pyrrhonischen Skepsis* (Frankfurt am Main, 1968).

68. It is in this sense that Ernst Tugendhat answers the question of why Heidegger no longer participates in the ἐποχή in Husserl's sense: in Heidegger, the concern is not, as Husserl has suspected, with a relapse, but rather with "its [i.e., of the ἐποχή] own radicalization." Heidegger no longer needs the ἐποχή, because he stands "in it from the outset." Ernst Tugendhat, *Der Wahrheitsbegriff bei Husserl und Heidegger*, second edition (Berlin, 1970), 263.

69. Heidegger, *Ontologie*, 30.

70. Gadamer, *Wahrheit und Methode*, 304.

71. Heidegger, *Die Idee der Philosophie*, 87.

72. Martin Heidegger, *Einführung in die phänomenologische Forschung, GA* 17, ed. Friedrich-Wilhelm von Herrmann (Frankfurt am Main, 1994), 272.

73. Heidegger's critique is strengthened by Tugendhat. Husserl, Tugendhat maintains, had "never felt it to be mysterious *how* the cogitationes themselves are given, how, that is, self-consciousness and reflection must be understood." Instead, he has clearly presupposed "that every act can be reflected in a second act, which discovers the second act in an inner intuition just as we discover a given thing in outer intuition." Tugendhat, *Der Wahrheitsbegriff bei Husserl und Heidegger*, 209.

74. The tendency to raise the status of practical philosophy in comparison to the theoretical traces back to Kant. Kant makes the turn to the prioritization of the practical insofar as he determines "the final purpose, toward which the speculation of reason ultimately runs" as a practical one. Immanuel Kant, *Kritik der reinen Vernunft*, AKA B 826/A 798, in *Kants gesammelte Schriften*, ed. Der Königlichen Preußischen Akademie der Wissenschaften (henceforth, AA), Vol. III (Berlin, 1911), 518. What reason finds out about the three matters assigned by its "final purpose," namely, the freedom of the will, the immortality of the soul, and the existence of God, is "not at all necessary for knowledge," but rather has an importance that "must actually concern only the practical." Kant, *Kritik der reinen Vernunft*, AKA B 828/A 800, AA III, 519. The "rehabilitation of practical philosophy" fashioned after Aristotle is not only the theme of a two volume collected work—Manfred Riedel, ed. *Die Rehabilitierung der praktischen Philosophie*, Freiburg i. Br., 1972)—but also has deeply marked philosophical debate in Germany at the conclusion of the twentieth century. Even the attractiveness of pragmatism and the outline of a "theory of communicative action" intended only under the aegis of social philosophy belong here.

75. Manfred Riedel, *Für eine zweite Philosophie. Vorträge und Abhandlungen* (Frankfurt am Main, 1988).

76. Heidegger, *Ontologie*, 15.

77. Plato, *Apologia*, 36c: μὴ πρότερον . . . . τῶν ἑαυτοῦ μηδενὸς ἐπιμελεῖσθαι πρὶν ἑαυτοῦ ἐπιμελεθείη ὅπως ὡς βέλτιστος καὶ φρονιμώτατος ἔσοιτο.

78. Plato, *Res publica*, 344e, 352d.

79. Heidegger, *Phänomenologische Interpretationen*, 385. On the concept of practical truth, cf. Alejandro G. Vigo, "Die aristotelische Auffassung der praktischen Wahrheit," in *Internationale Zeitschrift für Philosophie* 2 (1998), 285–308.

80. Ibid.

81. Cf. Aristotle, *Ethica Nicomachea* VI, 5; 1140a 30–32, in what follows, cited from Aristotelis *Ethica Nicomachen*, ed. I. Bywater, Oxford, 1894.

82. Heidegger, *Phänomenologische Interpretationen*, 385.

83. Ibid., 388.
84. Ibid., 388.
85. Ibid., 389.
86. Aristotle, *Ethica Nicomachea* I, 7; 1098a 7: ψυχῆς ἐνέργεια κατὰ λόγον.
87. Cf. Aristotle, *Metaphysica* IV, 1; 1003a 21. The *Metaphysics* is cited from: Aristotle's *Metaphysics*, ed. W. D. Ross, two volumes (Oxford, 1924).
88. Heidegger, *Phänomenologische Interpretationen*, 364.
89. Aristotle, *Metaphysica* IV, 2; 1003a 33: τὸ δὲ ὂν λέγεται πολλαχῶς, ἀλλὰ πρὸς ἕν.
90. Heidegger, *Sein und Zeit*, 1.
91. Heidegger allows one clearly to recognize this model in a late retrospective. In reference to Franz Brentano's Dissertation, *Von der mannigfachen Bedeutung des Seienden nach Aristoteles* (1862), he had been moved "since 1907" by the question: "If being [das Seiende] may be said in many ways, which is then the guiding fundamental meaning? What is being?" (Martin Heidegger, "Mein Weg in die Phänomenologie," in Heidegger, *Zur Sache des Denkens* (Tübingen, 1976, 81–90, here, 81).
92. Heidegger, *Phänomenologische Interpretationen*, 364.
93. Heidegger, *Sein und Zeit*, 16.
94. Ibid., 18.
95. Maurice Merleau-Ponty, *Le visible et l'invisible* (Paris, 1964), 180: "chose parmi les choses."
96. Heidegger, *Phänomenologische Interpretationen*, 383.
97. Ibid.
98. Aristotle, *Ethica Nicomachea* VI, 6; 1140b 31–1141a 8.
99. Ibid., VI, 8; 1142a 25.
100. Heidegger, *Phänomenologische Interpretationen*, 384.
101. Gadamer, *Wahrheit und Methode*, 317. [Cf. Weinsheimer and Marshall, 312. —Trans.]
102. Ibid., 319. [Cf. Weinsheimer and Marshall, 314. —Trans.]
103. "Practical Knowledge" is the title of an early treatise that anticipates the essential moments of the conception of *Wahrheit und Methode*. Hans-Georg Gadamer, *Praktisches Wissen* (1930), in: *Griechische Philosophie I*, Tübingen 1985, GW 5, 230–48.
104. Aristotle, *Ethica Nicomachea*, I, 3; 1095a 5–6: τὸ τέλος ἐστίν οὐ γνῶσις ἀλλὰ πρᾶξις.
105. Gadamer, *Wahrheit und Methode*, 318. [Cf. Weinsheimer and Marshall, 313. —Trans.]
106. Cf. Gadamer, *Wahrheit und Methode*, 318.
107. Gadamer, *Wahrheit und Methode*, 319. [Cf. Weinsheimer and Marshall, 314. —Trans.]
108. Aristotle, *Ethica Nicomachea*, VI, 7; 1141b 8–9: τὰ ἀνθρώπινα.
109. Ibid., 1141b 9: περὶ ὧν ἔστι βουλεύσασθαι.
110. Ibid., 1141b 12: πρακτὸν ἀγαθόν.
111. Gadamer, *Wahrheit und Methode*, 318. [Cf. Weinsheimer and Marshall, 313. —Trans.]
112. Ibid.
113. Ibid.
114. Ibid., 320. [Cf. Weinsheimer and Marshall, 315. —Trans.]

115. Ibid., 319.
116. Aristotle, *Ethica Nicomachea* VI, 8; 1141b 34: τὸ αὑτῷ εἰδέναι.
117. Gadamer, *Wahrheit und Methode*, 319. [Cf. Weinsheimer and Marshall, 314. —Trans.]
118. Ibid., 320. [Cf. Weinsheimer and Marshall, 314. —Trans.]
119. Ibid., 319. [Cf. Weinsheimer and Marshall, 314. —Trans.]
120. Cf. Hans-Georg Gadamer, "Hermeneutik als praktische Philosophie," in *Rehabilitierung der praktischen Philosophie, Band I, Geschichte, Probleme, Aufgaben*, ed. Manfred Riedel (Freiburg i. Br., 1972), 325–44.
121. Gadamer, *Wahrheit und Methode*, 319.
122. Ibid.
123. Cf. Joachim Ritter, "Landschaft. Zur Funktion des Ästhetischen in der modernen Gesellschaft," *Schriften des Gesellschaft zur Föderung der Westfälischen Wilhelms-Universität Münster*, Vol. 54 (Münster, 1963). Reprinted in Joachim Ritter, *Subjektivität. Sechs Aufsätze* (Frankfurt am Main, 1974), 141–63. Cf. also Odo Marquard, "Kompensation. Überlegungen zu einer Verlaufsfigur geschichtlicher Prozesse," in *Aesthetica und Anaesthetica. Philosophische Überlegungen* (Paderborn/München/Wien/Zürich, 1989), 64–81.
124. Gadamer, *Wahrheit und Methode*, 318.
125. Even if Gadamer appears to admit this, a "praise of theory" covertly comes to form a praise of—collective—practice in his view. The "look away from oneself" aims at no matter, but, rather to the other, whose "viewpoint" one has to take into consideration. Hans-Georg Gadamer, "Lob der Theorie (1980)," in *Neuere Philosophie II, GW* 4 (Tübingen, 1987), 37–51, here, 51.
126. Walter Benjamin, *Ursprung des deutschen Trauerspiels*, in *Gesammelte Schriften* (henceforth: *Schriften*), ed. Rolf Tiedemann, Vol. I. 1, second edition (Frankfurt am Main, 1978), 203–409, here 226. [Cf. Walter Benjamin, *The Origin of German Tragic Drama*, trans. John Osborne (New York: Verso Books, 1977, fourth printing, 1994), 45. —Trans.]
127. Plato, *Philebus*, 16c.
128. Cf. Thomas Kuhn, *The Structure of Scientific Revolutions* (Chicago, 1962).
129. Heidegger, *Einleitung in die Phänomenologie der Religion*, 7.
130. Benjamin, *Ursprung des deutschen Trauerspiels*, *Schriften* I. 1, 218.
131. Hölscher translates 'Kunde-reicher' [perhaps, "much lauded" —Trans.]. Parmenides, *Vom Wesen des Seienden. Die Fragmente*, ed., trans., and elucidated by Uvo Hölscher (Frankfurt am Main, 1969), 11. [For my English translations of Parmenides, I have found it helpful to consult *The Presocratic Philosophers, A Critical History with Selection of Texts*, second ed., G. S. Kirk, J. E. Raven, and M. Schofield (New York: Cambridge University Press, reprinted 1994). —Trans.]
132. Parmenides, VS 28 B 1, 29–30. ἀληθείης εὐκυκλέος ἀτρεμές ἦτορ; βροτῶν δόξας, ταῖς οὐκ ἔνι πίστις ἀληθής. The fragments are cited from Hermann Diels/Walter Kranz, *Die Fragmente der Vorsokratiker, siebte Auflage* (Berlin, 1954), Vol. 1–3. [Cf. *The Presocratic Philosophers*, 243 (No. 288). —Trans.]
133. Parmenides, VS 28 B 6, 5: δίκρανοι.
134. Parmenides, VS 28 B 6, 6: πλαγτὸν νόον. [Cf. *The Presocratic Philosophers*, 247 (No. 293) —Trans.]
135. Hesiod, *Opera et dies*, ed. F. Solmsen (Oxford, 1970), Verse 695. Cf. Hermann Fränkel, *Dichtung und Philosophie des frühen Griechentums* (München, 1962), 400.

136. This according to Hölscher in his commentary (Parmenides, *Vom Wesen des Seienden*, 74).

137. Parmenides, VS 28 B 2, 2.

138. Parmenides, VS 28 B 1, 1: θυμός.

139. René Descartes, *Meditationes de prima philosophiae* 7–8, in: *Oeuvres de Descartes*, ed. Charles Adam and Paul Tannery (henceforth, *Oeuvres*), Vol. VII, (Paris), 17: quàm multa....falsa pro veris admiserim, & quàm dubia sint.

140. Descartes, *Meditationes* I, 17; *Oeuvres* VII, 8: omnia....esse evertenda, atque a primis fundamentis denuo inchoandum. [In the preparation of my English translation here, I have found it helpful to consult Descartes, *Meditations on First Philosophy, With Selections from the Objections and Replies*, trans. John Cottingham (New York: Cambridge, reprinted 1991), 17. —Trans.]

141. Descartes, *Meditationes* I, 17; *Oeuvres* VII, 8: si quid aliquando firmum et mansurum cupiam in scientiis stabilire.

142. Descartes, *Meditationes* I, 18; *Oeuvres* VII, 8: serio tandem & libere generali huic mearum opinionum eversioni vacabo.

143. Similar in approach, but with a different intended meaning: Damir Barbarić, "Philosophie als Zurückgezogenheit–René Descartes," in *Denkwege* 2 (Tübingen, 2001), 5–50.

144. Descartes, *Meditationes I*, 18; *Oeuvres* VII, 25: *Ego sum, ego existo*, quoties a me profertur, vel mente concipitur, necessario esse verum.

145. Descartes, *Meditationes II*, 27; *Oeuvres* VII, 21: Sum autem res vera, & ver existens; sed qualis res? Dixi, cogitans.

146 Martin Heidegger, Introduction to "Was ist Metaphysik? (1949)," *GA* 9, 365–83, here, 365.

147. Heidegger, "Was ist Metaphysik? (1929)," *GA* 9, 103–22, here, 110.

148. Cf. Chapter 6, above all, § 33, 284–92.

149. Heidegger, "Was ist Metaphysik?" 110.

150. Heidegger revised this idea in his analysis of boredom in his 1929–30 winter lecture course. Cf. Martin Heidegger, "Die Grundbegriffe der Metaphysik. Welt-Endlichkeit-Einsamkeit," *GA* 29/30, ed. Friedrich-Wilhelm von Herrmann (Frankfurt am Main, 1983). Cf. § 33, 290–92.

151. Heidegger, "Was ist Metaphysik?" 110.

152. Ibid., 111.

153. Ibid.

154. Ibid., 112.

155. Ibid.

156. Ibid., 118.

157. Cf. Heidegger, "Was ist Metaphysik?" 118, where the "wondrous title" is understood in this sense.

158. Heidegger, "Was ist Metaphysik?" 118.

159. Plato, *Res publica* 331c: τοῦτο δ' αὐτό, τὴν δικαιοσύνην. [I borrow this translation from Allan Bloom. See Plato, *Republic*, trans. Allan Bloom (New York: Basic Books, 1968), 7 / 331 c. —Trans.]

160. Friedrich Nietzsche, *Nachlaß* 1881, 11[141], in: *Sämtliche Werke, Kritische Studienausgabe* (henceforth, *KSA*), ed. Giorgio Colli and Mazzino Montinari (Berlin/New York, 1980), Vol. 9, 494.

161. Hans Blumenberg has emphasized this dependency of philosophy on image and metaphor as no other. Cf. Hans Blumenberg, *Paradigmen zu Metaphorologie* (1960) (Frankfurt am Main, 1998). Cf. also Hans Blumenberg, *Ästhetische und metaphorologische Schriften. Auswahl und Nachwort von Anselm Haverkamp* (Frankfurt am Main, 2001), and, in exemplification, Hans Blumenberg, *Schiffbruch mit Zuschauer. Paradigma zu einer Daseinsmetapher* (Frankfurt am Main, 1979).

162. It is in this sense that in Plato the talk is of one who is genuinely raised into freedom and leisure (τῷ ὄντι ἐν ἐλευθερίᾳ τε καὶ σχολῇ τεθραμμένυο) (Plato, *Theaetetus*, 175e). Cf. also Plato, *Apologia*, 36d.

163. René Descartes, *Discours de la méthode* 1, 3; *Oeuvres* IV, 3. The subdivision of the numbered paragraphs follows the original edition.

164. Ibid., 2, 7-10; *Oeuvres* IV, 18-19.

165. Gadamer, *Wahrheit und Methode*, 270-90.

166. Heidegger, "Was ist Metaphysik?" 118. [This is David Krell's translation. See Krell, *Basic Writings* (San Francisco: Harper Collins, 1977), 108. —Trans.]

167. Ludwig Wittgenstein, *Wittgenstein und der Wiener Kreis, Schriften 3, aus dem Nachlass*, ed. B. F. McGuinness (Frankfurt am Main, 1967), 68.

168. Heidegger goes into astonishment in the lecture course from the winter semester of 1937-38, but ultimately understands it as the mood in the "first beginning" of philosophy. Martin Heidegger, *Grundfragen der Philosophie*, GA 45, ed. Friedrich-Wilhelm von Herrmann (Frankfurt am Main, 1984), 153-74.

169. Theaetetus admits that looking at the previously discussed question makes him dizzy (Plato, *Theaetetus*, 155c). Socrates provides a commentary with the words: μάλα γὰρ φιλοσόφου τοῦτο τὸ πάθος, τὸ θαυμάζειν· οὐ γὰρ ἄλλη ἀρχὴ φιλοσοφίας ἢ αὕτη. (Plato, *Theaetetus* 155d). On this theme, cf. Stefan Matuschek, *Über das Staunen. Eine ideengeschichtliche Analyse* (Tübingen, 1991).

170. Heidegger, "Was ist Metaphysik?" 117.

171. Plato, *Parmenides*, 156d.

172. Cf. Heidegger, "Vom Wesen der Wahrheit (1930)," GA 9, 177-202, here 188.

173. Heidegger, "Was ist Metaphysik?" 114.

174. Ibid., 114-15.

175. Heidegger, *Phänomenologische Interpretationen*, 368.

176. Heidegger, "Was ist Metaphysik?" 122.

177. Accordingly, the not-inaugural is of such a kind that it makes way for the origin, understood as inauguration. As it originates, it runs away from the origin. Cf. Martin Heidegger, *Die Grundprobleme der Phänomenologie (Sommersemester 1927)*, GA 24, ed. Friedrich-Wilhelm von Herrmann (Frankfurt am Main, 1975), 438: "All origination and all genesis in the field of the ontological is not growth and unfolding, but, rather, degeneration, insofar as everything originating *originates*, that is, to a certain extent, sets out. [Heidegger's elucidation of his point turns in part, I think, on the fact that the German *entspringen* can also mean "to break free," or "to escape," and not only "to originate." —Trans.]

178. Heidegger, "Was ist Metaphysik?" 116.

179. Parmenides, VS 28 B 1, 27: ἀπ' ἀνθρώπων ἐκτὸς πάτου ἐστίν.

180. Plato, *Phaedrus*, 247c.

181. Plato, *Res publica* 358 b: τίνα ἔχει δύναμιν αὐτὸ καθ' αὑτὸ ἐνὸν ἐν τῇ ψυχῇ.

182. Carl Schmitt, *Der Begriff des Politischen*, second edition (Hamburg, 1932), 38. On the concept of intensity, cf. further, Ludger Heidbrink, "Intensitätsgrad als Kategorie ästhetischer Erfahrung," in *Musik und Ästhetik*, 10 (1999), 5–27. Heidbrink understands intensity subjectively, as "the increase of sensual receptiveness" and as a condition of potential "concentration and attentiveness." Heidbrink, "Intensität als Kategorie ästhetischer Erfahrung," 5.

183. Schmitt, *Der Begriff der Politischen*, 38.

184. Ibid., 26.

185. Plato has also already shown this. As long as human beings live peacefully with one another and satisfy their elementary needs, they live unpolitically, in a "city of swine," (ὑῶν πόλιν, Plato, *Res publica* 372 d), as it is identified drastically for clarity. "Guardians," whose task is the protection of common life, are needed first where life becomes luxuriant and the stable balance of needs is jeopardized. The opposition of friend and enemy is also present here—only that the greatest enemy of communal life does not come from outside or against a community from within, but is, rather, a possibility of human nature as excessive appetite. Cf. also § 42.

186. The concept of suspension goes back to Fichte, who determined the imagination as a power "that is suspended in the intermediary between determination and non-determination, between finite and infinite." Johann Gottlieb Fichte, *Grundlage der gesammten Wissenschaftslehre* (1794), in *Sämtliche Werke*, ed. Immanuel Hermann Fichte (Berlin, 1845–46), Vol. 1, 83–328, here 216. Cf. additionally: Lore Hühn, *Fichte und Schelling oder: Über die Grenze menschlichen Wissens* (Stuttgart, 1994), 122–23. About Heidegger cf. above 34, as well as: Martin Heidegger, "Die Sprache (1950)," in *Unterwegs zur Sprache*, GA 12, 7–30, here, 11. Cf. also Walter Schulz, *Metaphysik des Schwebens. Untersuchungen zur Geschichte der Ästhetik* (Pfullingen, 1985).

187. Ludwig Wittgenstein, *Philosophische Untersuchungen*, 38; *Schriften* 1 (Frankfurt am Main, 1960), 279–544, here 309: "philosophical problems arise when language *goes on holiday*."

188. Plato, *Symposium* 202e: Ἑρμηνεῦον καὶ διαπορθμεῦον θεοῖς τὰ παρ' ἀνθρώπων καὶ ἀνθρώποις τὰ παρὰ θεῶν, τῶν μὲν τὰς δεήσεις καὶ θυσίας, τῶν δὲ τὰς ἐπιτάξεις τε καὶ ἀμοιβὰς τῶν θυσιῶν, ἐν μέσῳ δὲ ὂν ἀμφοτέρων συμπληροῖ, ὥστε τὸ πᾶν αὐτὸ αὑτῷ συνδεδέσθαι.

Notes to Chapter 2

1. Heidegger, *Sein und Zeit*, 210; for the first time in: Martin Heidegger, *Logik. Die Frage Nach der Wahrheit (1925/1926)*, GA 21, ed. Walter Biemel (Frankfurt am Main, 1976), 143.

2. This does not mean that it is illegitimate to speak of interpretation in this broad sense. Donald Davidson describes the understanding of every linguistic expression, more precisely, the step from expression to expressed matter of fact, along these lines as "radical interpretation" (*radical interpretation*). Cf. Donald Davidson, "Radical Interpretation," in: Davidson, *Inquiries Into Truth and Interpretation* (Oxford, 1984), 125–39, esp. 139. The concept is used so unspecifically here, however, as not to be sensical if interpretation is to be understood and clarified as a specific ability. Oliver R. Scholz's analyses of the "presumptive" character of interpretation are also meant to concern a

more broadly construed concept of interpretation. Cf. Oliver R. Scholz, *Verstehen und Rationalität. Untersuchungen zu den Grundlagen von Hermeneutik und Sprachphilosophie* (Frankfurt am Main, 2001), esp. 147–249.

3. To this, two references in Grimm's dictionary (Grimm, *Deutsches Wörterbuch*, Vol. 11, Part II [Leipzig, 1956], columns 598–602, here, 599): "it is inadmissible to carry over laws of style from one genre of art to another," (from Hegel, *Vorlesungen über die Aesthetik, erster Band*, ed. D. H. G. Hotho, Berlin 1835 [*G. W. F. Hegels Werke, vollständige Ausgabe durch einen Verein von Freunden des Verewigten* (Berlin 1832–), Vol. 10, First Part], 379) and "I have attempted to carry over this method and type of treatment to other objects" (from Johann Wolfgang Goethe, *Goethes Werke*, ed. under the commission of Grand Duchess Sophie of Saxony, Part IV, Vol. 27, 200).

4. To this, cf. John Sallis, *On Translation* (Bloomington, 2002), 21–45.

5. The concern is with an experiment by the founder of acoustics, Ernst Chladni (1756–1827).

6. Friedrich Nietzsche, "Ueber Wahrheit und Lüge im aussermoralischen Sinne (1873)," *KSA* 1, 875–897, here, 879.

7. For example, in the *Logik*: G. W. F. Hegel, *Wissenschaft der Logik* I, historisch-kritische Edition, *Gesammelte Werke*, ed. by the Rheinish-Westfälischen Akademie der Wissenschaften, Vol. 21 (Hamburg, 1985), ed. Friedrich Hogemann and Walter Jaeschke, 31.

8. Ibid.

9. Friedrich Nietzsche, *Nachlaß 1886–1887*, 7[60], *KSA* 12, 315.

10. Ibid.

11. Friedrich Nietzsche, *Nachlaß 1885*, 38[12], *KSA* 11, 610–11.

12. On this concept, see the definitive work by Müller-Lauter and Abel: Wolfgang Müller-Lauter, *Nietzsches Lehre vom Willen zur Macht*, in *Nietzsche-Studien* 3 (1974), 1–60; Günter Abel, *Die Dynamik der Willen zur Macht und die ewige Wiederkehr* (Berlin/New York, 1984); Wolfgang Müller-Lauter, *Nietzsche. Seine Philosophie der Gegensätze und die Gegensätze seiner Philosophie* (Berlin/New York, 1971).

13. Nietzsche, *Nachlaß 1885–1886*, 2[148], 139–40.

14. Friedrich Nietzsche, *Jenseits von Gut und Böse*, 36; *KSA* 5, 9–243, here, 55.

15. Friedrich Nietzsche, *Nachlaß 1887–1888*, 11[73] *KSA* 13, 36: "The standpoint of 'value' is the standpoint of the *condition of preservation and enhancement* of a complex form of relative duration in becoming." For clarification, cf. Martin Heidegger, "Nietzsches Wort, 'Gott ist tot' (1943)," in *Holzwege, GA* 5, ed. Friedrich-Wilhelm von Hermman (Frankfurt am Main, 1977), 209–67, here especially 227–32.

16. Nietzsche, *Nachlaß 1885–1886*, 2[92], 106–7.

17. The world of "appraisals" is for Nietzsche the self-made, fabricated world. Friedrich Nietzsche, *Die fröhliche Wissenschaft*, 374; *KSA* 5, 12.

18. Ibid. no. 374, 626.

19. Nietzsche, *Die fröhliche Wissenschaft*, Vorrede, 12.

20. Gottfried Wilhelm Leibniz, *Monadologie* § 57: "Et comme une même ville regardée de differens côtés paroist tout autre et est comme multipliée *perspectivement*, il arrive de même, que par la multitude infinie des substances simples, il y a comme autant de differens univers, qui ne sonst puortant que les perspectives d'un seul selon les differens *points de vue* de chaque Monade." The *Monadologie* is cited from: *Les Principes de la philosophie ou la monadologie*, in Leibniz, *Gesammelte Werke*, Vol. 1, ed. Hans Heinz Holz (Darmstadt, 1965).

21. Leibniz, *Monadologie*, § 1.
22. Ibid., § 14.
23. Ibid., § 19.
24. Ibid., § 7: "Les Monades n'ont point de fenêtres, par lesquelles quelque chose y puisse entrer ou sortir."
25. Ibid., § 56: "un miroir vivant perpetuel de l'univers."
26. Nietzsche, *Nachlaß 1887–1888*, 11[73], 36–37.
27. Nietzsche, *Zur Genealogie der Moral*, 245–412, here, 400.
28. Cf. Bernhard Waldenfels, *Phänomenologie der Aufmerksamkeit* (Frankfurt am Main, 2004).
29. Plato, *Theaetetus*, 152 a.
30. Nietzsche, *Zur Genealogie der Moral*, 365.
31. Edmund Husserl, *Logische Untersuchungen*, 9.
32. Ibid.
33. Considered on the basis of this, the debate about "explanation and understanding" must actually be carried on about "explanation and interpretation." The reason for this shall become clearer later, after the clarification of the concept of understanding. On explanation and understanding, cf. Karl-Otto Apel, *Die Erklären-Verstehen-Kontroverse in transcendentalpragmatischer Sicht* (Frankfurt am Main, 1979); Manfred Riedel, *Verstehen oder Erklären? Zur Theorie und Geschichte der hermeneutischen Wissenschaften* (Stuttgart, 1978); Georg Henrik von Wright, *Explanation and Understanding* (London/Ithaca, NY, 1971), German: *Erklären und Verstehen* (Frankfurt am Main, 1974).
34. Quintilian, *Institutio Oratoria*, Book IV, 13; cf. the edition *The Institutio Oratoria of Quintilian*, trans. H. E. Butler, in four volumes, Vol. II (Cambridge/London, 1921).
35. Seen from this perspective, Heidegger's understanding of logos as "gathering" or "gleaning" [Lese] arrives at the decisive point. Cf. Martin Heidegger, "Logos (Heraklit, Fragment 50)," in *Vorträge und Aufsätze*, GA 7, ed. Friedrich-Wilhelm von Herrmann (Frankfurt am Main, 2000) 211–34. Cf. also Günter Figal, "Logos (philosophisch)," in *Religion in Geschichte und Gegenwart (RGG)*, fourth edition, Vol. 7, columns 498–500.
36. Cf. Gottfried Boehm, "Der stumme Logos," in *Leibhaftige Vernunft. Spuren von Merleau-Pontys Denken*, ed. Alexandre Métraux and Bernhard Waldenfels (München, 1986), 289–304.
37. Karl Marx, *Thesen Über Feuerbach*, 11. These; *Marx/Engles Werke* (henceforth: *MEW*), Vol. 3 (Berlin, 1958), 535. Cf. contributions dedicated to Feuerbach's eleventh thesis in *Internationale Zeitschrift für Philosophie* 1995, Vol. 2.
38. Hans-Georg Gadamer, "Text und Interpretation" (1983), in *Hermeneutik II. Wahrheit und Methode. Ergänzungen. Register*, GW 2, 330–60, here 348.
39. Cf. Bernhard Waldenfels, *Antwortregister* (Frankfurt am Main, 1994).
40. Cf. the article, "antworten" [i.e., "to answer" —Trans.] in the Grimm Dictionary. Grimm, *Deutsches Wörterbuch*, Vol. 1 (Leipzig, 1854), Columns 508–10.
41. Gadamer, *Wahrheit und Methode*, 387.
42. Heidegger, *Sein und Zeit*, 114.
43. Plato, *Phaedrus* 275d: Δεινὸν γάρ που, ὦ Φαῖδρε, τοῦτ' ἔχει γραφή, καὶ ὡς ἀληθῶς ὅμοιον ζωγραφίᾳ. καὶ γὰρ τὰ ἐκείνης ἔκγονα ἕστηκε μὲν ὡς ζῶντα, ἐὰν δ' ἀνέρῃ τι, σεμνῶς πάνυ σιγᾷ.

44. This holds above all for the representatives of the so-called "Tübingen School," who wish to understand Plato's unwritten philosophy as his actual philosophy, and, to this end, call not least upon the *Phaedrus*. Cf. Thomas Szlezák, *Platon und die Schriftlichkeit der Philosophie* (Berlin/New York, 1985). But, cf. also Jacques Derrida, *La Pharmacie de Platon*, in *Platon. Phèdre, traduction inédite, introduction et notes par Luc Brisson* (Paris, 1989), 257–403.

45. Plato, *Phaedrus* 275d: ταὐτὸν δὲ καὶ οἱ λόγοι· δόξαις μὲν ἄν ὥς τι φρονοῦντας αὐτοὺς λέγειν, ἐὰν δέ τι ἔρῃ τῶν λεγομένων βουλόμενος μαθεῖν, ἕν τι σημαίνει μόνον ταὐτὸν ἀεί.

46. Heraclitus, VS 22, B 93: ὁ ἄναξ, οὗ τὸ μαντεῖόν ἐστι τὸ ἐν Δελφοῖς, οὔτε λέγει οὔτε κρύπτει ἀλλὰ σημαίνει.

47. Paul Ricoeur is on the trail of this exteriority when he emphasizes that the text cannot be understood through recourse to the subject, but, rather, that the text is by contrast autonomous from it. Paul Ricoeur, "La fonction herméneutique de la distanciation," in Ricoeur, *Du texte à l'action. Essais d'herméneutique II* (Paris, 1986), 101–17, here, 111. Ricoeur does not keep to this idea, however, but rather grasps the text once again based on the subject by determining it as "medium" of self-understanding. Ricoeur, "La fonction herméneutique de la distanciation," 116. Dennis Schmidt discusses the exteriority of the text in the tension found in the character of enactment of writing and reading. Cf. Dennis J. Schmidt, "Words on Paper," in Dennis Schmidt, *Lyrical and Ethical Subjects: Essays on the Periphery of the Word, Freedom, and History* (Albany, NY, 2005), 131–40.

48. George Steiner, *Real Presences: Is There Anything In What We Say?* (London, 1989). German: *Von realer Gegenwart. Hat unser Sprechen einen Inhalt?* (München, 1990).

49. Cf. above 15–17.

50. The earliest development of this idea comes down to us from the analysis of "experiences of the environment." See Martin Heidegger, *Die Idee der Philosophie* § 14, here, 70–73. [The passage reads slightly differently in original German than my English translation. Figal writes, "... ein Gebrauchsding, ein 'Zeug.'" In order to avoid redundancy, my translation has omitted 'ein Gebrauchsding' all together, and, following Stambaugh's translation of Heidegger's *Being and Time*, I have translated 'Zeug' as 'useful thing.' See Heidegger, *Being and Time*, trans. Joan Stambaugh, 64 ff. —Trans.]

51. Cf. Günter Figal, "Die Wahrheit und die schöne Täuschung. Zum Verhältnis von Dichtung und Philosophie im Platonischen Denken," in *Philosophisches Jahrbuch* 107 (2000), 301–15.

52. Plato, *Res publica* 393a.

53. Plato, *Res publica* 393c: Οὐκοῦν τό γε ὁμοιοῦν ἑαυτὸν ἄλλῳ ἢ κατὰ φωνὴν ἢ κατὰ σχῆμα μιμεῖσθαί ἐστιν ἐκεῖνον ᾧ ἄν τις ὁμοιοῖ.

54. For a more detailed discussion of showing, cf. Chapter 5, especially § 23.

55. This is a confirmation of the thesis proposed by Hermann Koller. Cf. Hermann Koller, *Die Mimesis in der Antike. Nachahmung, Darstellung, Ausdruck* (Bern, 1954).

56. Gadamer, *Wahrheit und Methode*, 119. [Cf. Weinsheimer and Marshall, 114. —Trans.]

57. Cf. Aristotle, *De arte poetica*, 1450a 16–17: μίμησίς ... πράξεως καὶ βίου.

58. Cf. Ibid., 1451b 5–7. Cited from: Aristotelis, *De arte poetica liber*, ed. J. Bywater (Oxford, 1897.) On the concept of the universal, cf. § 25, 219–21.

59. Cf. also Ernst Jünger, *Typus, Name, Gestalt*, in *Sämtliche Werke*, Vol. 13 (Stuttgart, 1982), 83–174.
60. Cf. above 6–8.
61. This is the central idea of the so-called critique of poetry. Plato, *Res publica* 376a–98b and 395b–d.
62. Gadamer, *Wahrheit und Methode*, 120. [Cf. Weinsheimer and Marshall, 114. —Trans.]
63. Ibid., 119. [Cf. Weinsheimer and Marshall, 114. —Trans.]
64. Ibid., 125. [Cf. Weinsheimer and Marshall, 120. —Trans.]
65. Cf. Ibid
66. Ibid., 120. [Cf. Weinsheimer and Marshall, 114. —Trans.]
67. Ibid., 125. [Cf. Weinsheimer and Marshall, 120. —Trans.]
68. Ibid., 153. [Cf. Weinsheimer and Marshall, 148. —Trans.]
69. Ibid., 145. [Cf. Weinsheimer and Marshall, 140. —Trans.]
70. Ibid., 113.
71. Ibid., 113–14. [Cf. Weinsheimer and Marshall, 107. —Trans.]
72. Ibid., 110. [Cf. Weinsheimer and Marshall, 105. —Trans.]
73. Ibid., 112.
74. Ibid., 114. [Cf. Weinsheimer and Marshall, 108. —Trans.]
75. Ibid., 129. [Cf. Weinsheimer and Marshall, 124. —Trans.]
76. Ibid., 131.
77. Ibid., 128. [Cf. Weinsheimer and Marshall, 123. —Trans.]
78. Hannah Arendt speaks of self-presentation in this sense. She treats this as a reaction "to the overwhelming effect of being shown." Hannah Arendt, *Vom Leben des Geistes, Band 1, Das Denken* (München, 1979), 31.
79. Gadamer, *Wahrheit und Methode*, 91. [Cf. Weinsheimer and Marshall, 85. —Trans.]
80. Ibid., 103. [Cf. Weinsheimer and Marshall, 97. —Trans.]
81. Ibid., 155. [Cf. Weinsheimer and Marshall, 150. —Trans.]
82. Ibid., 120. [Cf. Weinsheimer and Marshall, 115. —Trans.]
83. On this concept cf. Wittgenstein, *Philosophische Untersuchungen*, 66–68; *Schriften* 1, 324–25.
84. On the concept of reason, cf. § 40.
85. Cf. in general Hans-Georg Gadamer, "Vom Zirkel des Verstehens," in *GW* 2, 57–65.
86. Cf. Schleiermacher, *Hermeneutik und Kritik*, 97. In Dilthey: Wilhelm Dilthey, *Das Wesen der Philosophie*, in *Gesammelte Schriften* (henceforth, *GS*), Vol. V, ed. Georg Misch, fourth edition (Stuttgart, 1964), 339–416, here, 334; Dilthey, *Der Aufbau der geschichtlichen Welt in den Geisteswissenschaften*, *GS* VII, ed. Bernhard Groethuysen, second edition (Stuttgart, 1958), 145; Dilthey, *Grundlegung der Wissenschaftlichen vom Menschen, der Gesellschaft und der Geschichte. Ausarbeitung und Entwürfe zum zweiten Band der Einleitung in die Geisteswissenschaften* (ca. 1870–1895), *GS* XIX, ed. Helmut Johach and Frithjof Rodi (Göttingen, 1982), 446, Remark [Anmerkung] 554. The concept also appears in Friedrich Ast: Friedrich Ast, *Grundlinien der Grammatik, Hermeneutik und Kritik* (Landshut, 1808).

87. Gadamer, *Wahrheit und Methode*, 271. [Cf. Weinsheimer and Marshall, 267. —Trans.]
88. Cf. Heidegger, *Sein und Zeit*, 193-94. See also my discussion in: Figal, *Phänomenologie der Freiheit*, 168-70.
89. Gadamer, *Wahrheit und Methode*, 271. [Cf. Weinsheimer and Marshall, 267. —Trans.]
90. Ibid. [Cf. Weinsheimer and Marshall, 267. —Trans.]
91. Cf. Plato, *Gorgias*, 503d-04a.
92. 1. Mose 40, 20, cited from *Die Bibel oder die ganze heilige Schrift des Alten und Nueten Testaments nach der deutschen Übersetzung mit erklärenden Anmerkungen Martin Luthers* (Stuttgart, 1912), (unrevised Luther-translation). [Cf. *Holy Bible*, New Revised Standard Version, Genesis 40:12. —Trans.]
93. Paul Ricoeur, *De l'interprétation. Essai sur Freud* (Paris, 1965), Chapter II, Section 3, "l'interpretation comme exercise de soupçon."
94. The assertion that a text is corrupt and must first be reconstructed again by means of clarification is a variant of this assumption, which, admittedly, can be used against the claim to universality of the hermeneutics of suspicion. Cf. Alfred Lorenzer, *Sprachzerstörung und Rekonstruktion, Vorarbeiten zu einer Metatheorie der Pscyhoanalyse*, fourth edition (Frankfurt am Main, 1995); Jürgen Habermas, *Erkenntnis und Interesse*, eleventh edition (Frankfurt am Main, 1994), as well as the discussion between Habermas and Gadamer on the paradigmatic role of psychoanalysis for hermeneutics.
95. Gilbert Ryle, *The Concept of Mind* (London, 1949), esp. chapter 3 (62-82). Cf. also Michael Polanyi, *Personal Knowledge. Towards a Post-critical Philosophy* (London, 1973), as well as Michael Polanyi, *The Tacit Dimension* (Garden City, NY, 1966); German: *Implizites Wissen* (Frankfurt am Main, 1985).
96. Johann Gustav Droysen, *Grundriß der Historik* (Leipzig, 1868), § 9, 9-10.
97. Wilhelm Dilthey, "Ideen über eine beschriebene und zergliedernde Psychologie (1894)," in: *Die geistige Welt, Einleitung in die Philosophie des Lebens*, GS V, 139-240, here 144.
98. Schleiermacher, *Hermeneutik und Kritik*, 71.
99. See above § 2, 10.
100. Heidegger, *Ontologie*, 15.
101. Heidegger, *Sein und Zeit*, 190-91.
102. Wilhelm Dilthey, "Die Entstehung der Hemeneutik (1900)" *GS* V, 317-38, here 318.
103. Dilthey, *Der Aufbau der geschichtlichen Welt in den Geisteswissenschaften*, 213.
104. Heidegger, *Sein und Zeit*, 197. [I borrow from Stambaugh here. See Heidegger, *Being and Time*, trans. Stambaugh, 139. —Trans.]
105. Cf. Dilthey, "Die Entstehung der Hermeneutik," 318.
106. Cf. Figal, *Phänomenologie der Freiheit*, chapter 3, esp. 192-94, 258-69.
107. Here I once again take up a critique that I articulated, although with other presuppositions, in my essay "Selbstverstehen in instabiler Freiheit. Die hermeneutische Position Martin Heideggers." A thesis of this essay was that Heidegger gave "the concept of 'understanding,' itself a central concept for hermeneutics, an anti-hermeneutical

turn." Günter Figal, "Selbstverstehen in instabiler Freiheit. Die hermeneutische Position Martin Heideggers," in Hendrik Birus, ed., *Hermeneutische Positionen. Schleiermacher-Dilthey-Heidegger-Gadamer* (Göttingen, 1982), 89–119, here, 91.

108. Dilthey, "Die Entstehung der Hermeneutik," 318. Cf. also Dilthey, *Der Aufbau der geschichtlichen Welt in den Geisteswissenschafen*, 86–87.

109. Cf. in general, Rudolf A. Makkreel, *Dilthey. Philosoph der Geisteswissenschaften* (Frankfurt am Main, 1991).

110. Dilthey, "Die Entstehung der Hermeneutik," 318.

111. Dilthey, "Ideen über eine beschriebende und zergliedernde Psychologie," 198.

112. Ibid.

113. Dilthey, *Der Aufbau der geschichtlichen Welt in den Geisteswissenschaften*, 214.

114. Dilthey, "Die Entstehung der Hermeneutik," 319.

115. Martin Heidegger, "Hegels Begriff der Erfahrung (1942/43)," *GA* 5, 115–208, here, 199.

116. Dilthey, *Der Aufbau der geschichtlichen Welt in der Geisteswissenschaften*, 259.

117. Ibid., 191. Heinrich Anz brings Dilthey's decisive idea to the concept in a pregnant manner when he names the "preliminary selfsameness of the one who understands and the one to be understood" the "condition of the possibility of all understanding of expressions." Heinrich Anz, "Hermeneutik der Individualität, Wilhelm Diltheys hermeneutische Position und ihre Aporien," in Hedrik Birus, ed., *Hermeneutische Positionen: Schleiermacher-Dilthey-Heidegger-Gadamer*, 59–88, here, 77.

118. Gadamer, *Wahrheit und Methode*, 295. [Cf. Weinsheimer and Marshall, 290. —Trans.]

119. Ibid., 312.

120. Ibid., 300.

121. Schleiermacher, *Hermeneutik und Kritik*, 169.

122. Ibid.

123. Ibid., 170.

124. Ibid.

125. Ibid., 169–170.

126. Ibid., 170.

127. Ibid.

128. On the idea of this symmetry of self-expression and understanding: Anz, *Hermeneutik der Individualität*. Cf. also Gadamer, *Wahrheit und Methode*, 191.

129. On the special philosophical meaning of the concept of style, cf. Manfred Frank, *Stil in der Philosophie* (Stuttgart, 1992).

130. Schleiermacher, *Hermeneutik und Kritik*, 168.

131. Ibid.

132. Cf. Aristotle, *Metaphysica* IX, 6; 1048b 18–35.

133. On the concept of chiasm in detail cf. § 36.

134. Plato, *Gorgias* 530d–504a. Cf. above § 11, 81–82.

135. Martin Heidegger, *Nietzsche: Der Wille zur Macht als Kunst*, *GA* 43, ed. Bernd Heimbüchel (Frankfurt am Main, 1985), 219.

136. Ibid.

137. Cf. above § 6, 44.
138. Gadamer, *Wahrheit und Methode*, 272. [Cf. Weinsheimer and Marshall, 268. —Trans.]
139. Cf. Ibid., 273: "whoever wants to understand a text is . . . ready to let something be said by it."
140. Ibid., 274. [Cf. Weinsheimer and Marshall, 268. —Trans.]
141. Ibid., 272-73.
142. Ibid., 311.
143. Ibid., 312. [Cf. Weinsheimer and Marshall, 306. —Trans.]
144. F. D. E. Schleiermacher, "Allgemeine Hermeneutik von 1809/10," ed. Wolfgang Virmond, in, Kurt-Viktor Selge, ed., *Internationaler Schleiermacher-Kongreß Berlin 1984*, Vol. 2 (Berlin/New York, 1985), 1270-310, here, 1271.
145. Schleiermacher, *Hermeneutik und Kritik*, 92.
146. Ibid.
147. Ibid.
148. Gadamer, *Wahrheit und Methode*, 191.
149. Ibid., 198. [Cf. Weinsheimer and Marshall, 194-95. —Trans.]
150. Friedrich Schlegel, "Über die Unverständlichkeit," in *Charakteristiken und Kritiken I (1796-1801)*, Kritische Friedrich-Schlegel-Ausgabe, Vol. 2, ed. Hans Eichner (München/Paderborn/Wien, 1967), 363-72.
151. See Luca Crescenzi, "Die Leistung des Buchstabens. Ein ungeschriebenes Kapitel zur Unverständlichkeitsdebatte in der deutschen Frühromantik," in *Internationales Jahrbuch für Hermeneutik 2002*, 81-133.
152. Schlegel, "Über die Unverständlichkeit," 370.
153. Ibid., 371.
154. F. D. E. Schleiermacher, *Hermeneutik*, ed. Heinz Kimmerle (*Nach den Handschriften neu herausgegeben und eingeleitet von Heinz Kimmerle*), in *Abhandlungen der Heidelberger Akademie der Wissenschaften, Philosophisch-historische Klasse, Jahrgang 1959, zweite Abhandlung* (Heidelberg, 1959), 31: "I understanding nothing that I cannot look at and construct as necessary."
155. Kant elucidates the "revolution in thought" in the preface to the second edition of the *Kritik der reinen Vernunft* on the example of mathematics, whose concept of construction he thus takes over as binding for philosophy: "A new light flashed upon the mind of the first man (be he Thales or some other) who demonstrated the properties of the isosceles triangle. The true method, so he found, was not to inspect what he discerned either in the figure, or in the bare concept of it, and from this, as it were, to read off its properties; but to bring out what was necessarily implied in the concepts that he had himself formed *a priori*, and had put into the figure in the construction by which he presented it to himself. If he is to know anything with *a priori* certainty he must not ascribe to the figure anything save what necessarily follows from what he has himself set into it in accordance with his concept." Kant, *Kritik der reinen Vernunft*, AKA Bxi-xii. [I have used Norman Kemp Smith's translation from Kant, *Critique of Pure Reason*, trans. Norman Kemp Smith (New York, 1965). See NKS, 19. —Trans.] Shortly thereafter, the famous sentence follows "that reason has insight only into that which it produces after a plan of its own." Ibid., Bxiii. [See NKS, 20. —Trans.]

156. Schlegel, "Über die Unverständlichkeit," 370.

157. Friedrich Schlegel, *Über das Studium der griechischen Poesie*, in *Kritische Friedrich-Schlegel-Ausgabe*, Vol. 1, ed. Ernst Behler (Paderborn/München/Wien, 1979), 217–367, here, 229.

158. Plato, *Philebus*, 16c. [The German here is *Zusammenwächsende*. Cf. the Greek in the *Philebus*: 'ξύμφυτον.' —Trans.]

159. "Gegenstand," in Grimm, *Deutsches Wörterbuch*, Vol. 4, Part I, second half, columns 2263–269.

160. Nietzsche, *Zur Genealogie der Moral*, 313. [Cf. Kaufmann, *Genealogy of Morals and Ecce Homo* (New York: Vintage, 1989), 77. —Trans.]

161. Ibid., 314. [Cf. Kaufmann, ibid. —Trans.]

162. Cf. Werner Stegmaier, *Philosophie der Fluktuanz. Dilthey und Nietzsche.* (Göttingen, 1992).

163. Ludwig Wittgenstein, *Tractatus logico-philosophicus*, Schriften 1, 7–83, here, 82.

164. Hegel, *Vorlesungen über die Ästhetik I*, 21.

165. Karl Marx, *Das Kapital. Kritik der politischen Ökonomie. Erster Band. Buch I: Der Produktionsprozeß des Kapitals*, MEW 23 (Berlin, 1962), 86.

166. The formulation in George Lukács, which is definitive for Marxist discussion, cannot be thought without Simmel. Cf. Georg Lukács, *Geschichte und Klassenbewußtsein. Studien über marxistische Dialektik* (Berlin, 1923).

167. Georg Simmel, *Der Begriff und die Tragödie der Kultur*, in Simmel, *Das individuelle Gesetz. Philosophische Exkurse*, ed. Micheal Landmann (Frankfurt am Main, 1968), 116–47, here, 116.

168. Ibid., 143.
169. Ibid., 139.
170. Ibid., 142.
171. Ibid., 145.

172. Hegel, *Phänomenologie des Geistes*, 422.

173. Cf. Günter Figal, *Lebensverstricktheit und Abstandsnahme. "Verhalten zu sich" im Anschluß an Heidegger, Kierkegaard, und Hegel* (Tübingen, 2001).

174. Ernst Cassirer, "Die 'Tragödie der Kultur,' " in Cassirer, *Zur Logik der Kulturwissenschaften. Fünf Studien* (Darmstadt, 1961), 103–27, here, 109. Cf. also Birgit Recki, " 'Trägodie der Kultur' oder 'dialektische Struktur des Kulturbewußtseins?' Der ethische Kern der Kontroverse zwischen Simmel und Cassirer," in *Internationaler Zeitschrift für Philosophie* (2002), No. 2, 157–75.

175. Cassirer, "Die 'Tragödie der Kultur,' " 110.

176. Ibid., 111.

177. Edmund Husserl, "Philosophie als strenge Wissenschaft," in *Logos*, Vol. 1, 1910/1911, 289–341. Separate edition: *Philosophie als strenge Wissenschaft*, ed. Wilhelm Szilasi (Frankfurt am Main, 1965).

178. Heidegger, *Die Idee der Philosophie*, 91.

179. Ibid., 87.

180. A variation of this idea in found in Hermann Schmitz, who emphasizes the priority of "impressions" before objectivity. Hermann Schmitz, *Der Ursprung des Gegenstandes. Von Parmenides bis Demokrit* (Bonn, 1988).

181. Cf. above § 2.
182. Husserl, *Ideen I*, 299. ["Intentional object" is a translation of *intentional Gegenständliches* here. Here and elsewhere, I have consulted and found very helpful Dorian Cairns' *Guide to Translating Husserl* (Den Haag: Martinus Nijhoff, 1973). —Trans.]
183. Ibid., 297.
184. Ibid. [I have translated *Sinn* as "meaning" despite Cairn's suggestion to reserve "meaning" for Husserl's *meinen*. See Cairns, *Guide for Translating Husserl*, 104. —Trans.]
185. Ibid., 302.
186. Ibid., 303.
187. Edmund Husserl, *Cartesianische Meditationen*, 41–193, here, 87. ["Clue" is a translation of *Leitfaden* here. Cf. Cairns' translation of Husserl, *Cartesian Meditations* (Dortrecht/Boston/London, 1993). —Trans.]
188. Ibid.
189. Husserl, *Ideen I*, 299.
190. On this debate, cf. Dan Zahavi, "Husserl's Noema and the Internalism-Externalism Debate," *Inquiry* 47:1 (2004), 42–46.
191. Heidegger, *Sein und Zeit*, 576.
192. Ibid., 575–76.
193. Cf. Günter Figal, "Die Komplexität philosophischer Hermeneutik," in Figal, *Der Sinn des Verstehens* (Stuttgart, 1996), 11–31, here, 23–25.
194. Aristotle, *De anima* I, 1; 402 a 15. Cited from *Aristotelis De anima*, ed. W. D. Ross (Oxford, 1956).
195. Heidegger, *Sein und Zeit*, 92–97. [Cf. Stambaugh, 69. —Trans.]
196. Ibid., 98–99. [Cf. Stambaugh, 68–69. —Trans.]
197. Ibid., 100. [Cf. Stambaugh, 69. —Trans.]
198. Heidegger, "Das Ding," *GA* 7, ed. Friedrich-Wilhelm von Herrmann (Frankfurt am Main, 2000), 165–87.
199. The considerations in the treatment of the origin of the work of art, in which "reliability" is determined as it were as the backside of useful things, form a preliminary stage of this discovery. Cf. Martin Heidegger, *Der Ursprung des Kunstwerks (1935/36)*, in Heidegger, *GA* 5, 1–74, here, 19–20.
200. Martin Heidegger, *Der Satz von Grund* (1955–56), *GA* 10, ed. Petra Jaeger (Frankfurt am Main, 1977), 122.
201. Martin Heidegger, "Vom Wesen und Begriff der Φύσις. Aristoteles, Physik B, 1 (1939)," in Heidegger, *GA* 9, 239–301, here, 261.
202. What this means more precisely is developed in § 7.
203. Erhart Kästner, *Aufstand der Dinge. Byzantinische Aufzeichnungen* (Frankfurt am Main, 1973), 170.
204. As it is put there: "il vise la réalité et s'interdit les moyens de l'atteindre." Maurice Merleau-Ponty, "Le doute de Cézanne," in Merleau-Ponty, *Sens et non-sens* (Paris, 1948), 15–49, 22.
205. Theodor Wiesengrund Adorno, *Negative Dialektik, Gesammelte Schriften* 6. (Frankfurt am Main, 1973), 187. Cf. my essay, Günter Figal, "Über das Nichtidentische," in eds. Wolfram Ette, Günter Figal, Richard Klein, Günter Peters, *Adorno im Widerstreit. Zur Präsenz seines Denkens* (Freiburg i. Br./München, 2004), 13–23.

206. Maurice Merleau-Ponty, *L'Oeuil et l'esprit* (Paris, 1967), 16.
207. On the latter, cf. Gottfried Boehm, *Bildnis und Individuum. Über den Ursprung der Porträtmalerei in der italienischen Renaissance* (München, 1985).
208. Cf. above, 74–75.

Notes to Chapter 3

1. Cf. Plato, *Res publica*, 515c and 518d
2. Phenomenology and hermeneutics are, then, not—as in Ricoeur—understood as two equally valid philosophical approaches, about whose commonality one can inquire. Cf. Paul Ricoeur, "Phénoménologie et herméneutique: en venant de Husserl," in Ricoeur, *Du texte à l'action*, 39–73.
3. Cf. above, 10–11.
4. Plato, *Res publica*, 596e.
5. Ibid., 598b: τὸ φαινόμενον, ὡς φαίνεται. Cf. also Plato, *Sophist* 235d–36a.
6. Aristotle, *Ethica Nicomachea* VII, 1; 1154b 3–5.
7. Aristotle, *Metaphysica* VII, 3; 1029b 7–8.
8. Johann Heinrich Lambert, *Neues Organon oder Gedanken über die Erforschung und Bezeichnung des Wahren und dessen Unterscheidung von Irrthum und Schein, Philosophische Schriften*, ed. Hans-Werner Arndt, Vol. 1 and 2 (Leipzig, 1965).
9. Hegel, *Phänomenologie des Geistes*, 444.
10. Hans Blumenberg, *Lebenswelt und Weltzeit* (Frankfurt am Main, 1986), 27–28: "What 'phenomenon' means in phenomenology has to be taken at its word. It remains the amazing thing about its origins that a philosophy which appears to invalidate Platonism with its constitution of 'significance' and 'essence' chooses for the title of its exclusive object precisely what for Plato was unworthy of theory as 'appearance.'"
11. Edmund Husserl, *Logische Untersuchungen, Zweiter Band, Erster Teil, Husserliana* XIX.1, ed. Ursula Panser (Den Haag, 1984), 6.
12. Husserl, *Logische Untersuchungen, Zweiter Band*, Einleitung, 6. [I have consulted, but not completely followed, the J. N. Findlay translation. See Hussserl, *Logical Investigations*, Vol. 1 (New York: Routledge, 2001), 166. —Trans.]
13. Husserl, *Ideen* 1, 12.
14. Ibid.
15. Ibid., 6.
16. Husserl, *Logische Untersuchungen, Zweiter Band*, Einleitung, 6.
17. Husserl, *Ideen* 1, 10.
18. Cf. above, 15–17.
19. Husserl, *Ideen* 1, 62–63.
20. Edmund Husserl, *Pariser Vorträge*, 1–39, here, 15.
21. Ibid., 15.
22. Ibid., 16.
23. Ibid.
24. Ibid.
25. Husserl, *Cartesianische Meditationen* § 14; 72.
26. Husserl, *Ideen* 1, *Husserliana* III.1, 63.

27. Edmund Husserl, *Die Idee der Phänomenologie*, *Husserliana* II, ed. Walter Biemel (Den Haag, 1950), 14.
28. Ibid., 44.
29. Husserl, *Logische Untersuchungen*, 6.
30. Husserl, *Die Idee der Phänomenologie*.
31. Husserl, *Cartesianische Meditationen* § 14, 72.
32. Husserl, *Ideen* 1, 105.
33. Ibid., 104: "Immanent being is...undoubtedly in the sense of absolute being such that it principally nulla 're' indiget ad existendum." Cf. René Descartes, *Principia philosophiae*, 51, *Oeuvres* VIII/1, 24.
34. Cf. above, 111.
35. Husserl, *Ideen* 1, § 30, 63. [I use Cairns' 'counterpart' for 'Gegenüber' here. See Cairns, *Guide to Translating Husserl*, 59. —Trans.]
36. Martin Heidegger, "Das Ende der Philosophie und die Aufgabe des Denkens," in Heidegger, *Zur Sache des Denkens*, 61–80, here, 72.
37. Ibid., 72.
38. Parmenides, VS 28 B 8, 4: οὐλομελές τε καὶ ἀτρεμὲς ἠδ' ἀτέλεστον.
39. Parmenides, VS 28 B 8, 25: τῶι ξυνεχὲς πᾶν ἐστιν· ἐὸν γὰρ ἐόντι πελάζει.
40. Parmenides, VS 28 B 8, 43: εὐκύκλου σφαίρης ἐναλίγκιον ὄγκωι.
41. Cf. also the analysis by Hermann Schmitz, *System der Philosophie, zweiter Band, erster Teil: Der Leib* (Bonn, 1965), esp. 73–89.
42. Husserl, *Pariser Vorträge*, 16.
43. Husserl, *Cartesianische Meditationen*, 77–78.
44. Ibid., 78.
45. Ibid., 82.
46. Edmund Husserl, *Analysen zur passiven Synthesis* (1918–26), *Husserliana* XI, ed. Margot Fleisher (Den Haag, 1966), 6.
47. Ibid.
48. Husserl, *Cartesianische Meditationen*, 82.
49. Husserl, *Passive Synthesis*, 8. [I have consulted Cairns' *Guide for Translating Husserl* here. —Trans.]
50. Husserl, *Pariser Vorträge*, 17.
51. Husserl, *Passive Synthesis*, 3: "An outer perception is inconceivable, which exhausts what it perceives in its sensuous-thingly content, an object of perception is inconceivable, which can be given a conclusive perception that is replete [allseitig] in the strict sense, that accords with the totality of its sensuously apparent features."
52. Husserl, *Ideen* 1, 82.
53. Ibid., 88.
54. Cf. Ulrich Claesges, *Edmund Husserls Theorie der Raumkonstitution* (Den Haag, 1964).
55. Husserl, *Ideen* 1, 86.
56. Husserl, *Cartesianische Meditationen*, 82.
57. Husserl, *Passive Synthesis*, 13.
58. Cf. Maurice Merleau-Ponty, "Le philosophe et son ombre," in *Signes* (Paris, 1960, 201–28).
59. Merleau-Ponty, *L'Oeuil et l'Esprit*, 17.

60. Ibid., 18: "le voyant ne s'approprie pas ce qu'il voit: il l'approche suelement par le regard, il ouvre sur le monde."
61. Ibid., 17: "Le monde visible et celui de mes projets moteurs sont des parties totales du même Etre."
62. Husserl, *Passive Synthesis*, 14.
63. Ibid., 19.
64. Maurice Merleau-Ponty, *Phénoménologie de la perception* (Paris, 1945) 281: "le moyen par lequel la position des choses devient possible."
65. Ibid., 281: "la puissance universelle de leurs connexions."
66. Ibid., 282: "je pense actuellement les relations qui sont sous ce mot et je m'aperçois alors qu'elles ne vivent que par un sujet qui les décrive et qui les porte."
67. Ibid., 331. "Outre la distance physique ou géométrique qui existe entre moi et toutes choses, une distance vécue me relie aux choses qui comptent et existent pour moi et les relie entre elles." Merleau-Ponty takes over the expression "distance vécue" from E. Minkowski. On the conception of lived space, cf. also Bernhard Waldenfels, *In den Netzen der Lebenswelt* (Frankfurt am Main, 1985), 183–93.
68. Heidegger, *Sein und Zeit*, 135. [I have consulted Stambaugh for my translation of Heidegger's terms and citations in this paragraph and in the paragraphs that follow. —Trans.]
69. Ibid., 140. [Cf. Stambaugh. —Trans.]
70. Ibid., 137.
71. Ibid., 144.
72. Ibid., 149.
73. Ibid., §22, 136–39.
74. Ibid., 139.
75. Ibid., 210.
76. Ibid. ["Aussagen über Geschenisse in der Umwelt, Schilderungen des Zuhandenen, 'Sitautionsberichte,' Aufnahme und Fixierung eines 'Tatbestandes,' Beschreibung einer Sachlage, Erzählung des Vorgefallenen." —Trans.]
77. Ibid., 142.
78. Ibid., 141.
79. Ibid., 143.
80. Ibid., 147. [Cf. Stambaugh, 102. —Trans.]
81. Ibid., 148. [I have consulted and relied on, but not completely followed, Stambaugh here. Cf. Stambaugh, 102. —Trans.]
82. Descartes, *Principia philosophiae* I 53, 25: "Extensio in longum, latum et profundum."
83. Heidegger, *Sein und Zeit*, 87.
84. Ibid., 127. [Cf. Stambaugh, 88. —Trans.]
85. Ibid., 135. [Cf. Stambaugh, 94. —Trans.]
86. Immanuel Kant, "Was heißt: Sich im Denken zu orientieren?" AA VIII, 131–47.
87. Heidegger, *Sein und Zeit*, 147.
88. Walter Benjamin, *Das Kunstwerk im Zeitalter seiner technischen Reproduzierbarkeit, zweite Fassung (1936–38), Schriften* I.2 (Frankfurt am Main, 1978), 471–508, here, 479. Cf. Birgit Recki, *Aura und Autonomie. Zur Subjektivität der Kunst bei Walter Benjamin und Theodor W. Adorno* (Würzburg, 1988).

89. Heidegger, *Sein und Zeit*, 135. [I follow Stambaugh here. Cf. Stambaugh, 94. —Trans.]
90. Ibid., 143.
91. As Heidegger once remarks, "a very artificial and complicated attitude" is needed "in order to 'hear' a 'pure noise.'" Heidegger, *Sein und Zeit*, 217.
92. Kant, *Kritik der reinen Vernunft*, B37, A 22; AA III, 51–52.
93. Ibid., B 39, A 25; AA III, 53.
94. Ibid., B 38, A 23; AA III, 52.
95. Ibid., B 38, A 24; AA III, 52. [Cf. NKS, 168. —Trans.]
96. Ibid., B 39, A 24; AA III, 52. [Cf. Ibid. —Trans.]
97. Ibid., B 42, A 26; AA III, 55.
98. Hegel, *Wissenschaft der Logik I, Gesammelte Werke* 21, 178.
99. Cf. above, 38, 40–43.
100. Cf. Günter Abel, *Interpretationswelten. Gegenwartsphilosophie jenseits von Essentialismus und Relativismus* (Frankfurt am Main, 1993). Cf. also Nelson Goodman, *Ways of Worldmaking* (Indianapolis, 1978).
101. Cf. Günter Figal, "Welt (philosophisch)," in *Religion in Geschichte und Gegenwart*, fourth edition, Vol. 8, columns 1390–92, and "Weltbild (philosophisch)," columns 1406–07 (Tübingen, 2005); Wilhelm Dilthey, *Weltanschauungslehre: Abhandlungen zur Philosophie der Philosophie*, GS VIII, ed. B. Groethuysen, second edition (Berlin, 1960); Karl Jaspers, *Psychologie der Weltanschauung* (Berlin, 1919).
102. Cf. Dilthey, *Der Aufbau der geschichtlichen Welt in den Geisteswissenschaften*, 153.
103. On the difference of "worldly" and "innerworldly," cf. Heidegger, *Sein und Zeit*, 88.
104. Heidegger, *Sein und Zeit*, 86.
105. Martin Heidegger, "Vom Wesen des Grundes (1929)," 123–75, here, 143.
106. Hans Blumenberg, *Die Legitimität der Neuzeit* (Frankfurt am Main, 1966), 84.
107. Kant, *Kritik der reinen Vernunft*, B 447, A 419; AA III, 289. Cf. NKS, 393.
108. Heidegger, "Vom Wesen des Grundes," 152.
109. Ibid., 151.
110. Heidegger already opposes this concept of world in *Sein und Zeit*. Cf. Heidegger, *Sein und Zeit*, 87.
111. Heidegger, "Vom Wesen des Grundes," 158.
112. More extensively on this problematic, Günter Figal, *Martin Heidegger zur Einführung*, fourth edition (Hamburg, 2003), 94–110.
113. Martin Heidegger, *Vom Wesen der Wahrheit. Zu Platons Höhlengleichnis und Theätet*, GA 34, ed. Hermann Mörchen (Frankfurt am Main, 1988), 59.
114. Ibid., 61.
115. Ibid., 62.
116. Ibid., 64.
117. Nietzsche, *Die fröhliche Wissenschaft*, no. 301, 540.
118. According to Leibniz, *Monadologie* § 60, monads are presentative (*représentative*) in such a way that their presentation is only confused in regard to the particularities of the world and is only clear in a small portion of things, namely, in those, which are either the adjacent ones or the greatest in relation to all monads ("que cette représentation n'est que confuse dans le détail de tout l'univers, et ne peut être distincte que dans

une petite partie des choses, c'est-à-dire, dans celles qui sont ou les plus prochaines, ou les plus grandes par rapport à chacune des Monades.") If things were otherwise, then monads would be a divinity ("autrement chaque monade serait une Divinité").

119. Nietzsche, *Nachlaß* 1881, 11[157], 502.

120. As it is put in a posthumous sketch (Nietzsche, *Nachlaß* 1881, 11[148], 498): "whichever state this world *is able* to reach, it must have reached it, and not once, but, rather, countless times."

121. As it is put in this sense by Günter Abel, the "talk of 'world as a whole' " is "merely a word for the entirety of specific actions and reactions by individual force-centerings in Nietzsche's understanding." Günter Abel, *Nietzsche. Die Dynamik der Willen zur Macht und die Ewige Wiederkehr*, 206.

122. Heidegger, "Vom Wesen des Grundes," 158.

123. Cf. § 5, 33-34, § 33, 289-92.

124. Husserl, *Ideen* 1, 63.

125. Edmund Husserl, *Krisis der europäischen Wissenschaften und die transzendentale Phänomenologie*, § 37; Husserliana VI, ed. Walter Biemel (Den Haag, 1954), 145.

126. This concept may belong among the most discussed in Husserlian phenomenology. Yet, the issue here does not turn on the clarification of the concept in the context of the entirety of Husserlian thought. As a new contribution, and one that discusses the literature, cf. Hans-Helmuth Gander, *Selbstverständnis und Lebenswelt. Grundzüge einer phänomenologischen Hermeneutik im Ausgang von Husserl und Heidegger* (Frankfurt am Main, 2001). Gadamer explicitly appropriates the concept for his philosophical hermeneutics, cf. *Wahrheit und Methode*, 251-52. Moreover: Hans-Georg Gadamer, "Die Wissenschaft von der Lebenswelt (1972)," in *Neuere Philosophie I, GW* 3, 147-59. Husserl's later considerations are certainly also an answer to *Sein und Zeit*. However, the word "life-world" first appears in Husserl in 1924, and, in fact, in the lecture *Kant und die Idee der Transzendentalphilosophie* (Erste Philosophie [1923-24]. Erster Teil; Husserliana VII, 230-87, here 232: "The world achieved an infinite expanse as soon as the actual life-world, the world in the How of the givenness of inner experience, was observed.") Heidegger uses the word already in the lecture course of the winter semester 1919-20 (*Grundprobleme der Phänomenologie*, GA 58, 83). That Heidegger had taken over the word from Georg Simmel's writing, *Die Religion* (Frankfurt am Main, 1912), is probable; it is more probable still given that Heidegger speaks of the religious life-world in the aforementioned passage. That Heidegger only uses the word occasionally and later no more at all fits with the fact that he replaces the concept of life through that of Dasein.

127. Husserl, *Krisis* § 29, 114.

128. Cf. Hans-Georg Gadamer, "Die phänomenologische Bewegung," *GW* 3, 105-46, above all 123 and 127.

129. For a more precise interpretation of this constellation: Figal, *Phänomenologie der Freiheit*, 182-90.

130. Husserl, *Krisis* § 38, 150.

131. Ibid., § 37, 145.

132. Ibid., § 38, 149.

133. Ibid., § 37, 145.

134. Blumenberg, *Lebenswelt und Weltzeit*, 61.

135. Husserl, *Krisis* § 39, 151.
136. Ibid., § 53, 184.
137. Ibid., § 53, 182. There is the same difficulty in Heidegger's conception of world-formation. Heidegger determines Dasein not only as world-formative, but, rather, likewise as affected by world-formation. World-formation affects "all of what is revealed ... to which each respective Dasein itself belongs" ("Vom Wesen des Grundes," 158). The difficulty, however, is not discussed by Heidegger.
138. Husserl, *Krisis* § 53, 183.
139. Ibid., § 53, 182.
140. Ibid., § 54, 189.
141. Cf. Kant, *Kritik der reinen Vernunft*, B 837, A 808; AA III, 524; cf. also A 288–89, B 344–47; AA III 230–32.
142. Husserl, *Krisis* § 53, 183.

Notes to Chapter 4

1. Søren Kierkegaard, *Begrebet Angest (Begriff der Angst)*, 273–428, here 315.
2. It may be said with Hannah Arendt in this sense that action is directed toward the "world with others" [*Mitwelt*]. *Vita Activa oder vom tätigen Leben* (München, 1981), 172. This does not, however, have to mean that in action the concern is "to make one's presence felt [*sich selbst zu exponieren*]."
3. Action and production cannot, accordingly, count as two clearly distinguished classes of activities, but are rather two possible forms of being active. Theodor Ebert argues in this direction in, "Praxis und Poesis. Zu einer handlungstheoretischen Unterscheidung des Aristoteles," in *Zeitschrift für philosophische Forschung* 30 (1976), 12–30. For this discussion cf. also Friederike Rese, *Praxis und Logos bei Aristoteles. Handlung, Vernunft, und Rede in* Nikomachisher Ethik, Rhetorik, *und* Politik (Tübingen, 2003), 51.
4. Aristotle, *Metaphysica* IX, 6; 1048b 20–22: μὴ ὑπάρχοντα ὧν ἕνεκα ἡ κίνησις, οὐκ ἔστι ταῦτα πρᾶξις ἢ οὐ τελεία γε (οὐ γὰρ τέλος).
5. Ibid., 1048b 19–20.
6. Ibid., 1048b 34.
7. Ibid., 1048b 23–26.
8. Aristotle, *Ethica Nicomachea* I, 1; 1094a3.
9. Ibid., 1109b 35–1110a 1: τὰ βίᾳ ἢ δι' ἄγνοιαν γινόμενα. On the Aristotelian conception of the freedom of action, cf. also Figal, *Phänomenologie der Freiheit*, 99–104.
10. Aristotle, *Ethica Nicomachea* III, 2; 1111b 8.
11. Ibid., 1111b 27: [τὰ] πρὸς τὸ τέλος.
12. Ibid., 1111b 20–24.
13. Ibid., III, 3: 1112a 30–31: βουλευόμεθα δὲ περὶ τῶν ἐφ' ἡμῖν καὶ πρακτῶν.
14. Ibid., 1112a 21–30.
15. Ibid., 1112b 15–16.
16. For a more detailed discussion of προαίρεσις cf. Rese, *Praxis und Logos*, 178–204.

17. Aristotle, *Ethica Nicomachea* III, 2; 111b 20: σύνεγγυς φαινόμενον.
18. Ibid., 1111b 26: ἡ μὲν βούλησις τοῦ τέλους ἐστὶ μᾶλλον.
19. Aristotle, De motu animalium 700b 22: κοινὸν διανοίας καὶ ὀρέξεως. Cited in: *Aristotle's De Motu animalium*, ed. Martha Craven Nussbaum (Princeton, 1978).
20. Aristotle, *Ethica Nicomachea* III, 3; 1113a 11: βουλευτικὴ ὄρεξις.
21. Ibid., 1111b 6-8: ἡ προαίρεσις δὴ ἑκούσιον μὲν φαίνεται, οὐ ταὐτὸν δέ, ἀλλ' ἐπὶ πλέον τὸ ἑκούσιον.
22. Ibid., VI, 5; 1140b 4-6.
23. Ibid., VI, 1; 1139a 13-14: οὐδεὶς δὲ βουλεύεται περὶ τῶν μὴ ἐνδεχομένων ἄλλως ἔχειν.
24. Ibid., VI, 5; 1140b 5-6: τὰ ἀνθρώπῳ ἀγαθὰ καὶ κακά.
25. Ibid., 1140b 7-10: διὰ τοῦτο Περικλέα καὶ τοὺς τοιούτους φρονίμους οἰόμεθα εἶναι, ὅτι τὰ αὑτοῖς ἀγαθὰ καὶ τὰ τοῖς ἀνθρώποις δύνανται θεωρεῖν.
26. Ibid., I, 4; 1095a 18-19.
27. Ibid., I, 2; 1094a 22: τὸ ἄριστον.
28. Ibid., I, 4; 1095a 16-17: τὸ πάντων ἀκρότατον τῶν πρακτῶν ἀγαθῶν.
29. Ibid., I, 13; 1103a 5-6.
30. Kant, *Kritik der reinen Vernunft*, B180-81, A 140-41; AA III, 135-36.
31. More extensively on Kant's understanding of freedom: Figal, *Phänomenologie der Freiheit*, 105-23. Moreover, the essay: Günter Figal, "Verbindliche Freiheit. Überlegungen zu einer hermeneutischen Variante der morale par provision," 105-23, in Christoph Hubig, ed., *Conditio Humana-Dynamik des Wissens und der Worte. XVII. Deutscher Kongreß für Philosophie. Leipzig 23-27. September, 1996. Vorträge und Kolloquien* (Berlin, 1997), 95-105.
32. Kant, *Kritik der reinen Vernunft*, B 561, A 533, AA III, 363.
33. On the critique of the "unconditioned will" cf. Peter Bieri, *Das Handwerk der Freiheit. Über die Entdeckung des eigenen Willens* (München/Wien, 2001), 230-42.
34. On the critique of "volition," cf. Ryle, *The Concept of Mind*, 62-74.
35. For a more precise determination of willing, cf. below § 42.
36. Heidegger, *Sein und Zeit*, 113. [Cf. Stambaugh, 79. —Trans.]
37. Ibid. [Cf. Stambaugh, 79. —Trans.]
38. Ibid., 114. [I borrow Stambaugh's translation here; see Stambaugh, 79. —Trans.]
39. Ibid., 113.
40. Ibid.
41. Ibid. [I borrow from Stambaugh here. Cf. Stambaugh, 79. —Trans.]
42. Ibid.
43. Ibid., 115. [Cf. Stambaugh, 80. —Trans.]
44. Cf. Aristotle, *Physica* II, 2; 194a 27-29. The *Physics* is cited in: *Aristotle's Physics*, ed. W. D. Ross (Oxford, 1936).
45. Heidegger, *Sein und Zeit*, 16. [Cf. Stambaugh 10. —Trans.]
46. Ibid., 115.
47. Husserl, *Krisis* § 29, 114.
48. Cf. § 16, 150, (Note 126).
49. For a more extensive interpretation of this writing, cf. Cathrin Nielsen, *Die entzogene Mitte. Gegenwart bei Heidegger* (Würzburg, 2003).

50. Heidegger, *Vom Wesen der Wahrheit*, 188.
51. Ibid.
52. Aristotle, *Metaphysica* IV, 1; 1003a 21.
53. Heidegger, *Vom Wesen der Wahrheit*, 188–89.
54. Ibid., 189.
55. Ibid.
56. Ibid.
57. Ibid., 195.
58. Ibid., 196.
59. Ibid.
60. Ibid., 195.
61. Ibid., 196.
62. Martin Heidegger, "Der Hinweis," in *Bremer und Freiburger Vorträge GA 79*, ed. Petra Jaeger (Frankfurt am Main, 1994), 3–4, here, 3; cf. Heidegger, "Das Ding (1950)," 168.
63. Heidegger, "Der Hinweis," 4; Heidegger, "Das Ding (1950)," 168.
64. Cf. here Günter Figal, "Die Rekonstruktion der menschlichen Natur. Zum Begriff des Naturzustandes in Rousseaus 'Zweitem Discours,'" in *Rousseau und die Folgen. Neue Hefte für Philosophie 29* (1989), 24–38.
65. Plato, *Res publica* 369b: ἕκαστος οὐκ αὐτάρκης, ἀλλὰ πολλῶν ... ἐδεής.
66. Ibid., 369c: χρεία.
67. G. W. F. Hegel, "Das System der Bedürfnisse," in *Grundlinien der Philosophie des Rechts oder Naturrecht und Staatswissenschaft im Grundrisse*, §§ 189–208; Werke 7 (Frankfurt am Main, 1970), 346–60.
68. In this respect, the reference to the solitary Robinson Crusoe is not a convincing objection. Without the skills, which were acquired in community with others, he would not have managed alone on his island.
69. Plato, *Res publica*, 370b.
70. Ibid., 370a–b.
71. Cf. Plato, *Res publica* 370b.
72. About this indirect presence, Heidegger introduces the "being-there-with of others" in *Being and Time*. Heidegger, *Sein und Zeit*, 157–59.
73. Heidegger, *Sein und Zeit*, 162–64. [Cf. Stambaugh 114. —Trans.]
74. Plato, *Res publica* 372e.
75. Plato, *Res publica* 372e: ὥσπερ ὑγιής τις.
76. Ibid., 369e–70c.
77. In the *Republic*, the true city is an initial model that is brought into question. As soon as conditions no longer correspond to those of the true city, the "guardian" is needed, who is not without any reason signified as the "handworker of freedom," δημιουργοὶ ἐλευθερίας (Plato, *Res publica*, 395b).
78. Ibid., 433a, 433e.
79. First considerations of this in Günter Figal, "Recht und Moral als Handlungsspielräume," in *Zeitschrift für Philosophische Forschung* 36 (1982), 361–77, reprinted as "Recht und Moral bei Kant, Cohen, und Benjamin," in Heinz-Ludwig Ollig, ed., *Materialen zur Neukantianismus-Diskussion* (Darmstadt, 1987), 163–83.
80. Cf. above, 161.

81. On the idea that the other is beyond being, cf. Emmanuel Lévinas, "La trace de l'autre," in Lévinas, *En découvrant l'existence avec Husserl et Heidegger*, third edition (Paris, 1982), 187–202, here, 189–91.

82. Because freedom thus understood is at play between "me" and the other, one might want to determine them with a concept that goes back to Fichte and Hegel as "recognition." Yet with this concept, the understanding of freedom would be indicated based on those who are free, that is, me and the other. With the concept of recognition, freedom is subjectivized, or, more precisely, intersubjectivized, but in any case on the underlying basis of those who are free. Two subjects cognize one another and, in this, recognize themselves in their subjectivity. Axel Honneth, *Kampf um Anerkennung. Zur moralischen Grammatik sozialer Konflikte*, second edition (Frankfurt am Main, 1998), especially 63–92. It is true that no recognition exists without freedom, but according to its essence, it belongs in language. Cf. § 27, especially, 236–37.

83. Kant, *Grundlegung zur Metaphysik der Sitten*, AA IV, 428.

84. Ibid.

85. Ibid., 429.

86. Ibid., 435.

87. Ibid., 429.

88. Helmuth Plessner, "Grenzen der Gemeinschaft. Eine Kritik des sozialen Radikalismus (1924)," in *Gesammelte Schriften* (henceforth, *GS*), Vol. 5, ed. Günter Dux, Odo Marquard, and Elisabeth Ströker (Frankfurt am Main, 1981, reprinted Darmstadt, 2003). On Plessner's writing, cf. the volume edited by Wolfgang Eßbach, Joachim Fischer, and Helmut Lethen: *Plessner's "Die Grenzen der Gemeinschaft,"* (Frankfurt am Main, 2002). Moreover: Birgit Sandkaulen, "Helmuth Plessner: Über die 'Logik der Öffentlichkeit,'" in *Internationale Zeitschrift für Philosophie* (1994), 255–73.

89. Plessner, "Grenzen der Gemeinschaft," 62.

90. Ibid., 58.

91. Here, Plessner comes very close to the analysis of "the they" as Heidegger had provided it in *Being and Time*. Cf. Heidegger, *Sein und Zeit*, 153–73. On this, Figal, *Phänomenologie der Freiheit*, 133–53.

92. Plessner, "Grenzen der Gemeinschaft," 63.

93. Ibid.

94. Ibid., 71.

95. Ibid.

96. Ibid., 70.

97. Ibid., 72.

98. Ibid., 83.

99. Ibid., 84.

100. Ibid., 85.

101. Ibid., 83.

102. Ibid., 84.

103. Ibid., 82.

104. Ibid., 82.

105. Cf. on this Alasdair MacIntyre, *After Virtue: A Study in Moral Theory* (London, 1982), 30–31.

106. Plessner, "Grenzen der Gemeinschaft," 93–94.

107. Ibid., 94.
108. On this concept, cf. Hasso Hofmann, *Repräsentation. Studien zur Wort- und Begriffsgeschichte von der Antike bis ins 19. Jahrhundert* (Berlin, 1998); Carl Schmitt *Römischer Katholizismus und politische Form*, second edition (München, 1925).
109. Plessner, "Grenzen der Gemeinschaft," 95.
110. Ibid., 98.
111. Ibid., 99.
112. Walter Benjamin, "Zur Kritik der Gewalt," *Schriften* II.1, 179–203, here, 192.
113. Ibid., 191.
114. Ibid.
115. For a conceptual history, cf. Hannelore Rausch, *Theoria. Von ihrer sakralen zur philosophischen Bedeutung* (München, 1982).
116. Cf. § 18, 163–65.
117. Cf. § 5.
118. Plato, *Res publica* 514a–517a. Here, the "allegory of the cave" [*Höhlengleichnis*], as it is usually called in German, is actually signified as "picture" (εἰκών). On the effective history of the picture: Hans Blumenberg, *Höhlenausgänge* (Frankfurt am Main, 1989).
119. Aristotle, *Ethica Nicomachea* X, 8; 1178b 7–8, the talk is of θεωρητικὴ ἐνέργεια.
120. Ibid., 1178b 20–21: τῷ δὴ ζῶντι τοῦ πράττειν ἀφαιρουμένου, ἔτι δὲ μᾶλλον τοῦ ποεῖν, τί λείπεται πλὴν θεωρία.
121. Ibid., 1178b 17–18: τὰ περὶ τὰς πράξεις μικρὰ καὶ ἀνάξια θεῶν.
122. Ibid., 1177a 28–29.
123. Ibid., 1177a 30–33.
124. Ibid., I,4; 1095a 22–23.
125. Ibid., 1095a 23–30.
126. Hannah Arendt has made this idea the center of her conception of action. *Vita activa*, 164–71.
127. Considered on this basis, Kierkegaard's criticism of "aesthetic existence" has its justification in the fact that it uncovers the inappropriateness of carrying over presentation to action. Cf. Søren Kierkegaard, *Enten-Eller. Et Livsfragment (Entweder-Oder. Ein Lebensfragment)*, *SV* II (Kopenhagen, 1901), especially 143–60.

Notes to Chapter 5

1. Wilhelm von Humboldt, *Ueber die Verschiedenheit des menschlichen Sprachbaues und ihren Einfluss auf die geistige Entwicklung des Menchengeschlects (posthum 1836)*, cited in Wilhelm von Humboldt, *Werke in fünf Bände*, ed. Andreas Flitner and Klaus Giel, Vol. 3 (Schriften zur Sprachphilosophie), (Darmstadt, 1963), 418, (accords with the *Akadamie-Ausgabe*, ed. Albert Leitzmann, Vol. 7, 46; henceforth the page numbers of this edition are referred to).
2. Humboldt, *Sprachbau*, *Werke* 3, 418; Leitzmann 7, 46.
3. Ibid.; Leitzmann, 46.
4. Ibid.; Leitzmann, 46.

5. In Grimm's German dictionary, "language" signifies "the activity of speaking and the capacity to do so in general." Grimm, *Deutsches Wörterbuch*, Vol. 10, Part One (Leipzig, 1905), columns 2718–41, here, 2718.

6. Cf. here the following sketch by Paul Valéry: "Comme cela est commun qu'un même mot clair quand on l'emploie est obscur quand on le pèse. Cela tient à ce qu'on les emploie toujours avec leur définition momentanée, avec ce qui suffit à les maintenir. Quand isolés, on les regarde—on cherche à leur substituer l'ensemble indéterminé de leurs relations—au lieu qu'en composition cet ensemble est determiné." Paul Valéry, *Cahiers*, edition établiée, présentée et annotée par Judith Robinson-Valéry (Bibliothéque de la Pléiade), (Paris, 1973) Vol. 1, 386.

7. The lecture, "Der Weg zur Sprache," to which the following considerations above all refer, originate in the year 1959 (Heidegger, *GA* 12, 227–58).

8. Heidegger, "Der Weg zur Sprache," 232.

9. Ibid., 234.

10. Ibid., 235.

11. Cf. Donatella Di Cesare, "Einleitung" to Wilhelm von Humboldt, *Über die Verschiedenheit des menschlichen Sprachbaues und ihren Einfluß auf die geistige Entwicklung des Menschengeschlechts*, ed. Dontella Di Cesare (Paderborn/München/Wien, 1998), 11–128, here, 12.

12. Donatella Di Cesare comments that "Humboldtianism" in linguistics may be spoken of "better in reference to a few directions ... than to a few representatives." Ferdinand Saussure's conception, which is path breaking for the modern science of linguistics, appears to be influenced by Humboldt only indirectly through Steinthal's lectures. Cf. Di Cesare, *Sprachbau*, 15. In regard to de Saussure, cf. also Ludwig Jäger, *Zu einer historischen Rekonstruktion der authentischen Sprach-Idee F. de Saussures* (Düsseldorf, 1975).

13. Aristotle, *De interpretatione* 1; 16a 2-4: "Ἔστι μὲν...τὰ ἐν τῇ φωνῇ τῶν ἐν τῇ ψυχῇ παθημάτων σύμβολα. Cited in: *Aristotelis Categoriae et Liber de Interpretatione*, ed. L. Minio-Palvello (Oxford, 1949). For a more detailed commentary, cf. Aristotle, *Peri Hermeneias*, translated and elucidated by Hermann Weidemann (Werke in deutscher Überzetzung, begründet von Ernst Grumach, ed. Hellmut Flashar), Vol. 1, Part II (Berlin, 1994), 133–51. [I have made reference to Ackrill's translation of Aristotle in the *Complete Works of Aristotle* here. *The Complete Works of Aristotle, the Revised Oxford Translation*, ed. Jonathan Barnes, Vol. 1 (Princeton: Princeton University Press, fourth printing 1991), 25. —Trans.]

14. Humboldt, *Sprachbau*, Werke III, 426; Leitzmann, 53.

15. Cf. also Heinrich von Kleist, "Über die allmähliche Verfertigung der Gedanken beim Reden," *Sämtliche Werke und Briefe*, ed. Helmut Sembdner (München, 1952), Vol. 2, 321–27.

16. Heidegger, "Der Weg zur Sprache," 238.

17. Ibid.

18. Ibid.

19. On the relationship between Humboldt and Hegel, cf. Di Cesare, *Sprachbau*, 25–26 and the literature cited there.

20. Heidegger, "Der Weg zur Sprache," 239.

21. Ibid., 243.

22. Humboldt, *Sprachbau*, 555; Leitzmann, 166.

23. Ibid., 419; Leitzmann, 47.
24. Heidegger, "Der Weg zur Sprache," 243. Cf. in this context Manfred Riedel, *Hören auf die Sprache: die akroamatische Dimension der Hermeneutik* (Frankfurt am Main, 1990).
25. Heidegger, "Der Weg zur Sprache," 243.
26. Heidegger, "Logos (Heraklit, Fragment 50)," 219. [I use the translation by David Ferrell Krell and Frank A. Capuzzi. See Martin Heidegger, *Early Greek Thinking* (San Francisco, 1984), 65. —Trans.]
27. On searching for words, cf. in connection with Gadamer: Donatella Di Cesare, "Sein und Sprache in der philosophischen Hermeneutik," in *Internationales Jahrbuch für Hermeneutik* (2002) 21–38, here, 30–31.
28. Cf. Hans Magnus Enzensberger, "Die Entstehung eines Gedichts," in Enzensberger, *Gedichte. Die Enstehung eines Gedichts*, second edition (Frankfurt am Main, 1963), 55–82.
29. Heidegger, "Der Weg zur Sprache," 243.
30. Cf. Günter Figal, "The Doing of the Thing Itself: Gadamer's Hermeneutic Ontology of Language," in *The Cambridge Companion to Gadamer*, 102–25.
31. Plato, *Theaetetus* 190a: οὐ μέντοι πρὸς ἄλλον οὐδὲ φωνῇ, ἀλλὰ σιγῇ πρὸς αὑτόν. Cf. Plato, *Sophista* 263a.
32. Valéry, *Cahiers* I, 403. "Le langage associe trios éléments: un Moi, un Toi, un Lui ou chose—Queleu'un parle à quelqu'un de quelque chose." Cf. also Donald Davidson, *Subjective, Intersubjective, Objective* (Oxford, 2002). Cf. moreover Karl Bühler, *Die Darstellungsform der Sprache*, second edition (Jena, 1965) and Karl Bühler, *Die Axiomatik der Sprachwissenschaften* (Frankfurt am Main, 1969).
33. Grimm, *Deutsches Wörterbuch*, Vol. 6 (Leipzig, 1885), columns 1924–35, here, 1924.
34. Heidegger determined the function of philosophical concepts in this sense as formally indicating. They only draw attention to something, which they themselves are not. Cf. already the Jaspers-Rezension, "Anmerkungen zu Karl Jaspers 'Psychologie der Weltanschauungen' [1919/21]," 1–44, here, 10–11; moreover, *Einleitung in die Phänomenologie der Religion*, 55–65, and also *Die Grundbegriffe der Metaphysik*, 428–29. Concepts like "death, resoluteness, history, existence" are "*indications* for the fact that understanding" must "first be wrested from the vulgar constitution of what is and transform it specifically into the Da-sein in it" (*GA* 29/30, 428).
35. Cassirer mentions the belongingness of showing and grasping in the first volume of his *Philosophie der symbolischen Formen* and cites as evidence a passage from Wilhelm Wundt's folk psychology. Ernst Cassirer, *Philosophie der Symbolischen Formen, Erster Teil. Die Sprache*, in *Gesammelte Werke, Hamburger Ausgabe* (henceforth, *ECW*), Vol. 11, ed. Birgit Recki (Hamburg, 2001), 125–27.
36. Cassirer, *Philosophie der symbolischen Formen*, 126.
37. Hegel, *Phänomenologie des Geistes*, 65.
38. Ibid.
39. The concept is used differently here than in literary studies [Literaturwissenschaft], where it signifies the "comparisons of texts as results of an artificial process." Cf. Moritz Bassler, "Textur," in Jan Dirk Müller, ed., *Reallexikon der deutschen Literaturwissenschaft*, Vol. III (Berlin/New York, 2003), columns 618–19, here, 618.
40. Plato, *Sophista* 251a.

41. Ibid., 253b–c.
42. Aristotle, *De interpretatione* 4–5; 17a 2–9.
43. Ibid., 4; 16b 26.
44. Heidegger, "Der Weg zur Sprache," 242.
45. Aristotle, *De interpretatione* 4; 16b 32.
46. Ibid., 2 16a 19 and on occasion.
47. In Plato's dialogue *Cratylus*, this suspicion is the impetus for the whole discussion, and, with this point of departure, the dialogue only takes up what was the common property of the sophists.
48. Cf. Tilman Borsche, "Zeichentheorie im Übergang von den Stoikern zu Augustin," in *Allgemeine Zeitschrift für Philosophie* 19:2 (1994), 41–52.
49. Augustine, *Confessiones*, I, 8: cum ipse appellabant rem aliquam et cum secundum eam uocem corpus ad aliquid mouebant, uidebam, et tenebam hoc ab eis uocari rem illam, quod sonabant, cum eam uellent ostendere. Hoc autem eos uelle ex motu corporis aperiebatur tamquam uerbis naturalibus omnium gentium, quae fiunt uultu et nutu oculorum ceteroque membrorum actu et sonitu uocis indicante affectionem animi in petendis, habendis, reiciendis, fugiendisue rebus. The *Confessiones* is cited in: Sacti Augustini, *Confessionum Libri* XIII (Corpus Christianorum Series Latina XXVII) ed. Lukas Verheijen (Turnholt, 1981).
50. Wittgenstein, *Philosophische Untersuchungen* 32; *Schriften* I, 305.
51. Cf. Thomas Nagel, "What Is It Like To Be A Bat?" in Thomas Nagel, *Mortal Questions* (Cambridge, 1979), 65–180.
52. Heidegger, *Sein und Zeit*, 106. [I use Stambaugh's translation here. —Trans.]
53. Ibid., 107.
54. Ibid. [I use Stambaugh's translation here. —Trans.]
55. Ibid., 103.
56. Heidegger, "Logos (Heraklit, Fragment 50)" 215–17.
57. Ibid., 216. [Cf. Krell, 62. —Trans.]
58. Ferdinand de Saussure, *Cours de linguistique générale*. Édition critique préparée et éditée par Tullio de Mauro (Paris, 1972). The first edition was undertaken in 1915, two years after de Saussure's death, by his pupils Bally, Sechehaye and Riedlinger.
59. Intended is language in general in contrast to a determinate language (*language*).
60. De Saussure, *Cours de linguistique générale*, 166: "dans la langue il n'y a que des différences."
61. Ibid., 155: "Pyschologiquement, abstraction faite de son expression par les mots, notre pensée n'est qu'une masse amorphe et indistincte.... Prise en elle-même, la pensée est comme une nébuleuse où rien n'est nécessairement délimitée. Il n'ya a pas d'idées préétablies, et rien n'est distinct avant l'apparition de la langue."
62. Thus also, despite all qualifications, Umberto Eco, *Einführung in die Semiotik*, eighth edition (München, 1994), 28.
63. De Saussure, *Cours de linguistique générale*, 156: "il n'y a donc ni matérialisation des pensées, ni spiritualisation des sons, mais il s'agit de ce fait en quelque sorte mystérieux, que la 'pensée-son' implique des subdivisions que la langue élabore ses unités en se constituant entre deux masses amorphes."

64. Cf. Manfred Frank, *Was ist Neostrukturalismus?*, second edition (Frankfurt am Main, 1984), 89-90.
65. Gottlob Frege, "Über Sinn und Bedeutung (1892)," in Gottlob Frege, *Funktion, Begriff, Bedeutung*, ed. Günter Patzig (Göttingen, 1962), here, 44.
66. Frege, "Über Sinn und Bedeutung," 44.
67. Ibid., 48.
68. Ibid., 47. Frege's idea may thus also be reformulated, so that one identifies the significance of an expression with its conditions of truth. Besides Frege and others, this position was also forwarded by the Wittgenstein of the Tractatus, by Carnap, Tarski, and Davidson. Cf. the discussion in Ernst Tugendhat, *Vorlesungen zur Einführung in die sprachanalytische Philosophie* (Frankfurt am Main, 1976), 134-35. In any case, it is unclear why Tugendhat does not count Frege among the representatives of the "traditional constitution," according to which "linguistic expressions are generally used to stand for something" (134). Precisely this is said with Frege's understanding of significance. [For my translation of Frege's comment on Odysseus, I have borrowed from Max Black's translation in *Translations from the Philosophical Writings of Gottlob Frege*, ed. Peter Geach and Max Black (Oxford, 1952). —Trans.]
69. Frege, "Über Sinn und Bedeutung," 41.
70. Ibid., 42.
71. Ibid., 45.
72. Ibid.
73. Ibid., 46.
74. Edmund Husserl, *1. Logische Untersuchung*, II.1 § 15, 59.
75. Ibid.
76. Edmund Husserl, *6. Logische Untersuchung*, II.2, "Einleitung,"; *Husserliana* XIX.2, *Untersuchungen zur Phänomenologie und Theorie der Erkenntnis*, ed. Ursula Panzer (Den Haag, 1984), 538. Cf. to Husserl's theory of significance: Rudolf Bernet, "Bedeutung und intentionales Bewußtsein. Husserls Begriff des Bedeutungsphänomens," in *Studien zur Sprachphänomenologie. Phänomenologische Forschungen* 8 (Freiburg i. Br./München, 1979), 31-64. Moreover: Rolf Kühn, *Wort und Schweigen. Phänomenologische Untersuchungen zum originären Sprachverstandnis* (Hildesheim/Zürich/New York, 2005), 59-88.
77. Husserl, *1. Logische Untersuchung*, II.1, § 15, 61. [Cairnes suggests "illustration" for *Veranschaulichung*. See Cairnes, *Guide for Translating Husserl*, 122. —Trans.]
78. Humboldt, *Sprachbau*, 418; Leitzmann VII, 46.
79. Jacques Derrida, *La voix et le phénomène. Introduction du problème du signe dans la phénomenologie de Husserl* (Paris, 1967), 14-15: "Husserl a sans doute voulu maintenir... une couche originairement silencieuse, 'pré-expressive,' du vécu."
80. Wittgenstein, *Philosophische Untersuchungen* 40, 310.
81. Ibid., 43; *Schriften* 1, 311.
82. Ludwig Wittgenstein, *Philosophische Bemerkungen, zweiter Anhang; Schriften* 2, 327-28: "I cannot say: this is a pawn *and* validate this or that rule of play for this figure. Rather, the rules of play first *determine* this figure: the pawn *is* the sum of the rules, according to which it is moved."
83. Wittgenstein, *Philosophische Untersuchungen* 5, 291.

84. Ibid. 7, 293.

85. Ibid. 108, 342: "The question, 'What is a word?' is an analog of the question 'What is a chess piece?'" On the thesis, that Wittgenstein wanted to be free of the problem of significance [*Bedeutungsproblem*] with this idea, cf. Donatella Di Cesare, *Die Bedeutung dekonstruieren. Bemerkungen anhand des "Big Typescript,"* Manuscript. Moreover: Stefan Majetschak, *Ludwig Wittgensteins Denkweg* (Freiburg i. Br./München, 2000), 175–94.

86. Aristotle, *Metaphysica* VII, 13; 1038b 11–12: ὃ πλείοσιν ὑπάρχειν πέφυκεν.

87. Ibid., 1038b 18.

88. Ibid., 1038b 19.

89. Husserl, *Ideen I*, § 22, 47.

90. Ibid., § 23, 50.

91. Husserl, *2. Logische Untersuchung*, III.1, § 41, 222.

92. Ibid., 220.

93. Husserl, *6. Logische Untersuchung*, II.2, § 7, 563.

94. Husserl, *1. Logische Untersuchung*, II.1, § 15, 59.

95. Husserl, *6. Logische Untersuchung*, II.2, § 7, 564.

96. Ernst Jünger, "Die rote Farbe," in *Das abenteuerliche Herz*. Second edition. *Sämtliche Werke*, Vol. 9 (Stuttgart, 1979), 232–36.

97. As a prominent example, cf. Plato, *Symposium*, 211d, where it is said that if the life of the human being is worthwhile, then it is when one views the beautiful itself (θεωμένῳ αὐτὸ τὸ καλόν). In the same context, it is said that if Socrates were ever to look at the beautiful itself (ὅ ἐάν ποτε ἴδῃς), he will want to compare it with nothing that would now delight him to see (οὕς νῦν ὁρῶν ἐκπέπληξαι). Cf. also Plato *Res publica* 533c–d.

98. Husserl, *Ideen I*, § 3, 14. [N.B. that Cairns recommends "seeing an essence" for *Wesensershauung*. See Cairns, *Guide for Translating Husserl*, 137. —Trans.]

99. Ibid., § 24, 51.

100. Cf. above, 187–88.

101. Nietzsche, *Fröhliche Wissenschaft*, no. 374, 626. Cf. above, 53–55.

102. Cf. above, 108.

103. Plato, *Res publica* 338c: φημὶ γὰρ ἐγὼ εἶναι τὸ δίκαιον οὐκ ἄλλο τι ἢ τοῦ κρείττονος συμφέρον. A more friendly, although no less relativistic, understanding of shared human life is found in Richard Rorty, *Contingency, Irony, Solidarity* (Cambridge, 1989), as well as Richard Rorty, *Solidarität oder Objektivität?* (Stuttgart, 1988).

104. Cf. Jacques Derrida, *Épérons. Les styles de Nietzsche* (Paris, 1978).

105. Friedrich Nietzsche, *Über Nutzen und Nachtheil der Historie für das Leben*, § 9, 319. Cf. on this Günter Figal, *Nietzsche* (Stuttgart, 1999), 44–52.

106. Nietzsche, *Fröhliche Wissenschaft*, no. 355, 594: "how? is our need for knowledge [*Erkennen*] not just this need for the familiar [*Bekanntem*], the will to discover under everything foreign, unfamiliar, questionable something that no longer disquiets us? Should it not be the *instinct of fear*, which is called knowledge by us? Should not the gloating of the one who knows be precisely the gloating of the feeling of security once again achieved?"

107. Nietzsche, *Über Wahrheit und Lüge im außermoralischen Sinne*, § 1, 880.

108. Derrida does not take over this concept in order to avoid echoes of "destruction." This is elucidated in *De la grammatologie*: "la destruction, non pas la démolition, mais la dé-sedimentation." Jacques Derrida, *De la grammatologie* (Paris, 1967), 21. [I use Stambaugh's translation of Heidegger's *Destruktion* as "destructuring" —Trans.]
109. Heidegger, *Phänomenologische Interpretationen*, 368.
110. Ibid.
111. Jacques Derrida, "Sémiologie et Grammatologie," in Jacques Derrida, *Positions. Entretiens avec Henri Ronse, Julia Kristeva, Jean-Louis Houdebine, Guy Scarpetta* (Paris, 1972), 25–50.
112. Derrida, *Sémiologie et Grammatologie*, 28: "les deux faces d'une seule et même production."
113. Ibid.
114. Ibid., 29.
115. Derrida, *De la Grammatologie*, 107.
116. Derrida, *Sémiologie et Grammatologie*, 29.
117. Ibid., 30: "un concept signifée en lui-même."
118. Ibid.
119. In Heidegger, cf. above all the lecture *Platon: Sophistes. Winter 1924/25. GA 19*, ed. Ingeborg Schüßler (Frankfurt am Main, 1992), here 220–25, especially 222: "What is [Das Seinde] is what is present [*anwesend*] in the proper [*eigentlichen*] sense." Moreover, the lecture *Logik. Die Frage nach der Wahrheit*, 193.
120. Derrida, *Sémiologie et Grammatologie*, 30: "signifié transcendental."
121. Ibid., 29.
122. Derrida, *De la Grammatologie*, 108: "toujours déjà en position de signifiant." Cf. also the slightly, but significantly, differing formulation in *Sémiologie et Grammatologie*. There, it is said: "que tout signifié est *aussi* en position de signifiant." *Sémiologie et Grammatlogie*, 30, emphasis added.
123. So, too Josef Simon, *Philosophie des Zeichens* (Berlin, 1989).
124. Derrida, *De la Grammatologie*, 46–50.
125. Derrida, *Sémiologie et Grammatologie*, 32, "substance phonique."
126. Ibid., 32: "la substance signifiante qui *se donne à la conscience* comme le plus intimement unie à la pensée du concept signifié."
127. Ibid., 32: "la conscience elle-même."
128. Ibid., 32-33: "Quand je parle, non seulement j'ai conscience d'être présent à ce que je pense, mais aussi de garder au plus proche de ma pensée ou du 'concept' un signifiant qui ne tombe pas dans le monde, que j'entends aussitôt que je l'émets, qui semble dépendre de ma pure et libre spontanéité, n'exiger l'usage d'aucun instrument, d'aucun accessoire, d'aucune force prise dans le monde. Non seulement le signifiant et le signifié semblant s'unir, mais, dans cette confusion, le signifiant semble s'effacer ou devenir transparent pour laisser le concept se présenter lui-même, comme ce qu'il est, ne renvoyant à rien d'autre qu'à sa présence. L'extériorité du signifiant semble reduit."
129. Derrida, *De la Grammatologie*, 23.
130. Aristotle, *De interpretatione* 1; 16a 3: τὰ ἐν τῇ φωνῇ.
131. Derrida translates τὰ ἐν τῇ ψυχῇ παθήματα (Aristotle, *De interpretatione* 1; 16a 3–4) as "états d'âme." (*De la Grammatologie*, 21).

132. Derrida, *De la Grammatologie*, 21–22: "productrice des *premiers symboles*."
133. Ibid., 22: "[la voix] signifie 'l'état d'âme' qui lui-même reflète ou réfléchit les choses par ressemblance naturelle."
134. Heidegger, *Sein und Zeit*, 239–371.
135. Derrida, *De la Grammatologie*, 22. Cf. Martin Heidegger, "Nachwort" to "Was ist Metaphysik? (1943)," 303–12, here, 307.
136. Derrida, *De la Grammatologie*, 25: "*clôture*."
137. Derrida, *De la Grammatologie*, 25: "époque du signe."
138. Aristotle, *De interpretatione* 2; 16a 19: κατὰ συνθήκην. [Note that the Ackrill translation of this in the *Complete Works of Aristotle* reads "by convention." —Trans.]
139. Here I follow Gadamer's hint that the formula used by Aristotle may not be understood in the sense of an "instrumental theory of signs." "Rather," per Gadamer, "the agreement that signifies something in using enunciations or linguistic signs is not an arrangement about the means of agreement—language would always already presuppose such an arrangement. Rather, it is that having-come-to-agreement on which the community of human beings, their agreement in what is good and right, is grounded." Accordingly, one must see the "terminological expression" of *De interpretatione* "in the light of the 'Politics.'" Gadamer, *Wahrheit und Methode*, 435. Similarly, Wolfgang Wieland, *Die aristotelische Physik*, second edition (Göttingen, 1970), 163. Also in agreement, Hermann Weidemann, in *Aristoteles. Peri Hermeneias*, translated and elucidated by Hermann Weidemann (Berlin, 1994).
140. Derrida, *Sémiologie et Grammatologie*, 33.
141. Husserl, *1. Logische Untersuchung*, II.1, § 8, 42–43.
142. Ibid., 43.
143. For the translation of *La voix et la phénomène*, comparison was made to: Jacques Derrida, *Die Stimme und das Phänomen*. Translated from the French with a Preface provided by Jochen Hörisch (Frankfurt am Main, 1979) and Jacques Derrida, *Die Stimme und das Phänomen*. Translated from the French by Hans-Dieter Gondek (Frankfurt am Main, 2003).
144. Derrida, *La voix et le phénomène*, 46.
145. Husserl, *1. Logische Untersuchung*, II.1, § 7, 40.
146. Ibid., § 8, 42.
147. Derrida, *La voix et le phénomène*, 47–48: "des signes non existants *montrent* des signifiés (*Bedeutungen*) idéaux, donc non exisants, et certaines, car présents à l'intuition."
148. Husserl, *Cartesianische Meditationen*, 137 and on occasion.
149. Cf. Husserl, *Ideen I*, 104.
150. Derrida, *La voix et le phénomène*, 44.
151. Ibid., 85.
152. Ibid., 88.
153. Ibid.: "auto-affection." The concept goes back to Heidegger, who introduces it in the interpretation of Kant's conception of time. Time, says Heidegger, is "pure self-affection, not an effective affection, which" concerns "a present self"; rather, as "pure," it forms "something like self-address [*Sich-selbst-angehen*]." Martin Heidegger, *Kant und Das Problem der Metaphysik*, GA 3, ed. Friedrich-Wilhelm von Herrmann (Frankfurt

am Main, 1991), 189. Cf. by and large: Heidegger, *Kant und Das Problem der Metaphysik*, § 34; 338-47. To this, Derrida, *La voix et le phénomène*, 93. Cf. moreover: Heidegger, *Logik, Die Frage nach der Wahrheit*, here, 188-95, 344-47.

154. Derrida, *La voix et la phénomène*, 89.

155. In Heidegger, *Kant und das Problem der Metaphysik*, 189, it is said that it is "the essence of subjectivity."

156. Derrida, *La voix et le phénomène*, 92.

157. Ibid., 97: "supplément."

158. Ibid., 97: "manque." *Supplément* means in typical linguistic usage "a bonus for something that is in itself incomplete," in older linguistic usage, however, "supplementation [Ergänzung] of something incomplete to completeness." Cf. *Dictionnaire alphabétique et analogique de la langue françois* by Paul Robert (Le petit Robert), (Paris, 1972).

159. Derrida, *La voix et le phénomène*, 97: "une non-présence à soi originaire."

160. Programmatically on this, Derrida, *Sémiologie et Grammatologie*, 37-38.

161. In *De la Grammatologie*, 21-22, Derrida discusses this idea in regard to Aristotle.

162. Derrida, *La voix et le phénomène*, 95: "trace."

163. Derrida, *De la Grammatologie*, 108.

164. Derrida, *La voix et le phénomène*, 98: "l'opération du différer qui, à la fois, fissure et retarde la présence, la soumettant du même coup à la division et au delai originaires."

165. Derrida, *La voix et le phénomène*, 18: "vouloir-dire."

166. Derrida, *Sémiologie et Grammatologie*, 38: "le jeu systématique des différences." On the concept of play, cf. moreover, *L'Ecriture et la Différence* (Paris, 1967), 409-28.

167. Derrida, "La structure, le signe et le jeu," 423: "ce champ est en effet celui d'un jeu, c'est-à-dire de substitutions infinies das la clôture d'un ensemble fini."

168. Ibid., 423: "Le mouvement de la signification ajoute quelque chose, ce qui fait qu'il y a toujours plus, mais cette addition est flottante parce qu'elle vient vicarier, suppléer un manque du côté du signifié."

169. Ibid., 417-18.

170. Derrida, *Sémiologie et Grammatologie*, 38: "l'espacement par lequel les éléments se rapportent les uns aux autres."

171. Derrida, *Sémiologie et Grammatologie*, 38.

172. The concept already appears in Humboldt. Cf. above, 195. On the history of the word, cf. the article in the *Historical Dictionary of Philosophy*, ed. Karlfried Gründer and Joachim Ritter (Darmstadt, 1998), Vol. 10, columns 303-34, especially 303.

173. Derrida, *Sémiologie et Grammatologie*, 39: "le thème de la différance est imcompatible avec le motif statique, synchronique, taxinomique, ahistorique, etc. du concept de structure."

174. Ibid., 39: "[La différance] produit des transformations systématiques et réglées."

175. Ibid., 40: "la production d'un systeme de différences."

176. Cf. as an attempt to dissolve the aporia on the basis of Derrida: Rodolphe Gasché, *The Tain of the Mirror* (Cambridge, MA, 1986), 186.

177. Merleau-Ponty, *Le visible et l'invisible* and, in this, the chapter, "L'entrelacs-le chiasme," 178-204. This idea will be discussed more detail in § 36.

178. Merleau-Ponty, *Le visible et l'invisible*, 180: "chose parmi les choses."

179. Cf. Derrida's considerations on "s'adresser" in *Force de loi. Le 'fondement mystique' de l'autorité* (Paris, 1994).

180. This is the great theme of dialogic philosophy [*Dialogphilosophie*]. Cf. Michael Theunissen, *Der Andere* (Berlin, 1965). The fundamental idea is found already in Wilhelm von Humboldt, "Ueber die Verwandtschaft der Ortsadverbien mit dem Pronomen in einigen Sprachen," Leitzmann, VI, 58–75.

181. Cf. above, 196.

182. On the "face" (visage) in Emmanuel Lévinas cf. especially *La philosophie et l'idée de l'infini*. (Lévinas, "En découvrant l'existence avec Husserl et Heidegger," 165–78, here, 172–74). Moreover, Emmanuel Lévinas, *Totalité et infini. Essai sur l'extériorité* (Den Haag, 1961), 22 and on occasion.

183. John Burbidge indicates the fact that language is the "medium of recognition" also in the context of Hegel. Unfortunately, this indication is not developed far enough that the consequences that it would have for the clarification of Hegel's social philosophy can come into view. John Burbidge, "Sprache und Anerkennung," in Hans-Helmuth Gander, ed., *Anerkennung. Zu einer Kategorie gesellschaftlicher Praxis* (Würtzburg, 2004), 33–44, here, 37). By contrast, Lesaar, in the same volume, stresses the finitude of recognition, which is also central form my considerations. Cf. Henrik R. Lesaar, "Anerkennung als hermeneutischer Prozess," 45–62, here especially 60.

184. Cf. above, 58–59.

185. In Hannah Arendt, it is said in this sense: "the act is integrated into a context of significance first through the spoken word, whereby, however, the function of the speech is not, say, a matter of explaining what was done. Rather, it is to identify the actor and to announce that it is he who acts, namely, someone who can be called to other actions and decisions." It is in any case no coincidence that Hannah Arendt discusses this under the generic concept of action. In her, this occurs not in order to subordinate speech to action, but, rather, in order to show that self-showing is the essence of action.

186. The concept of speech act goes back to John L. Austin and became familiar from John Searle. Cf. John L. Austin, *How To Do Things With Words* (Cambridge, MA, 1962) and John Searle, *Speech Acts. An Essay in the Philosophy of Language* (Cambridge, MA, 1969). On the concept of communicative action, cf. Habermas, *Theorie des kommunikativen Handelns*.

187. Cf. Plato, *Gorgias*, 453a, where rhetoric is determined as "producer of conviction" (πειθοῦς δημιουργός).

188. In Cicero the significance of the presentation [*Vortrag*] of a talk (actio) is stressed in this sense. The greatest speaker can validate nothing without this significance, whereas the mediocre speaker who is trained in presentation can often defeat the greater one. Marcus Tullius Cicero, *De oratore* III, in: *Cicero in Twenty-eight Volumes*, Vol. 4, ed. G. P. Goold (London, 1982), LVI. 213: Actio, inquam, in dicendo una dominatur; sine hac summus orator esse in numero nullo potest, mediocris hac instructus summos saepe superare.

189. What Gadamer ascribes to the "inner word" also holds of what here is called the "pure word": It is the "substantive content" of what is said, the "substantive content, which is thought up to the end." Gadamer, *Wahrheit und Methode*, 426. On the "inner

word," cf. Jean Grondin, *Introduction à Hans-Georg Gadamer* (Paris, 1999), 191-97. German: *Einführung zu Gadamer* (Tübingen, 2000).

190. Cf. Sonja Dierks, "Musikalische Schrift," in *Adorno im Widerstreit*, 222-34.

191. Plato, *Res publica* 510d: τοῖς ὁρωμένοις εἴδεσι προσχρῶνται καὶ τοὺς λόγους περὶ αὐτῶν ποιοῦνται, οὐ περὶ τούτων διανοούμενοι, ἀλλ' ἐκείνων πέρι οἷς ταῦτα ἔοικε, τοῦ τετραγώνου αὐτοῦ ἕνεκα τοὺς λόγους ποιούμενοι καὶ διαμέτρου αὐτῆς, ἀλλ' οὐ ταύτης ἣν γράφουσιν.

192. Ibid., 510c: ὑποθέμενοι τό τε περιττὸν καὶ τὸ ἄρτιον καὶ σχήματα καὶ γωνιῶν τριττὰ εἴδη καὶ ἄλλα τούτων ἀδελφὰ καθ' ἑκάστην μέθοδον, ταῦτα μὲν ὡς εἰδότες, ποιησάμενοι ὑποθέσεις αὐτά, οὐδένα λόγον οὔτε αὑτοῖς οὔτε ἄλλοις ἔτι ἀξιοῦσι περὶ αὐτῶν διδόναι ὡς παντὶ φανερῶν.

193. Ibid., 511c.

194. Socrates can in fact describe talk of ideas as something hackneyed. Cf. Plato, *Phaedo* 100b.

195. Plato, *Res publica* 511b: ἅπτεται.

196. Ibid., 511d-e. [I borrow from Bloom's translation here. —Trans.]

197. Plato, *Phaedo*, 99e.

198. Plato, *Res publica* 511b: τῷ ὄντι ὑποθέσεις.

199. Ibid.: ἐπιβάσεις τε καὶ ὁρμάς.

200. Ibid.: μέχρι τοῦ ἀνυποθέτου ἐπὶ τὴν τοῦ παντὸς ἀρχήν.

201. Ibid., 505d: ἀγαθὰ δὲ οὐδενὶ ἔτι ἀρκεῖ τὰ δοκοῦντα κτᾶσθαι, ἀλλὰ τὰ ὄντα ζητοῦσιν, τὴν δὲ δόξαν ἐνταῦθα ἤδε πᾶς ἀτιμάζει.

202. Ibid., 505d-e: Ὃ δὴ διώκει μὲν ἅπασα ψυχὴ καὶ τούτου ἕνεκα πάντα πράττει, ἀπομαντευομένη τι εἶναι, ἀποροῦσα δὲ καὶ ἔχουσα λαβεῖν ἱκανῶς τί ποτ' ἐστὶν οὐδὲ πίστει χρήσασθαι μονίμῳ οἵᾳ καὶ περὶ τἆλλα.

203. The good is hidden in appearance. It is in this sense that the talk in the *Philebus* is of the flight of the good into the beautiful. Plato, *Philebus*, 64e.

204. Plato, *Res publica*, 510b: ἀρχὴν ἀνυπόθετον.

205. Ibid., 510c.

206. Cf. Ibid., 507a-09b.

207. Ibid., 511b: ἐχόμενος τῶν ἐκείνης ἐχομένων.

208. Ibid.: αἰσθητῷ παντάπασιν οὐδενὶ προσχρώμενος.

209. Ibid., 511c: εἴδεσιν αὐτοῖς δι' αὐτῶν εἰς αὐτά, καὶ τελευτᾷ εἰς εἴδη.

210. Plato, *Parmenides*, 135e-36a.

211. Based on this, dialectic may, with Petra Schmidt-Wiborg, be called a "dialectical conception of unity." Petra Schmidt-Wiborg, *Dialektik im Platons Philebus* (Tübingen, 2005), 115.

212. Plato, *Sophista*, 217a.

213. Plato, *Res publica*, 525c: φύσις.

214. Ibid., 525a: ἅμα γὰρ ταὐτὸν ὡς ἕν τε ὁρῶμεν καὶ ὡς ἄπειρα τὸ πλῆθος.

215. Dorothea Freda also stresses that in regard to dialectic the ideas are independent from individual things. Cf. Plato, *Philebus*. Translation and commentary by Dorothea Frede (Göttingen, 1997), 141.

216. Plato, *Philebus*, 14e: τό τε ἓν ὡς πολλά ἐστι καὶ ἄπειρα, καὶ τὰ πολλὰ ὡς ἓν μόνον.

217. Ibid., 16e: μεταξὺ τοῦ ἀπείρου τε καὶ τοῦ ἑνός.
218. Ibid., 16c–e: δεῖν οὖν ἡμᾶς ... ἀεὶ μίαν ἰδέαν περὶ παντὸς ἑκάστοτε θεμένους ζητεῖν - εὑρήσειν γὰρ ἐνοῦσαν - ἐὰν οὖν μεταλάβωμεν, μετὰ μίαν δύο, εἴ πως εἰσί, σκοπεῖν, εἰ δὲ μή, τρεῖς ἤ τινα ἄλλον ἀριθμόν, καὶ τῶν ἓν ἐκείνων πάλιν ὡσαύτως, μέχριπερ ἄν τὸ κατ' ἀρχὰς ἓν μὴ ὅτι ἓν καὶ πολλὰ καὶ ἄπειρά ἐστι μόνον ἴδῃ τις, ἀλλὰ καὶ ὁπόσα. τὴν τοῦ ἀπείρου ἰδέαν πρὸς τὸ πλῆθος μὴ προσφέρειν πρὶν ἄν τις τὸν ἀριθμὸν αὐτοῦ πάντα κατίδῃ τὸν μεταξὺ τοῦ ἀπείρου τε καὶ τοῦ ἑνός, τότε δ'ἤδη τὸ ἓν ἕκαστον τῶν πάντων εἰς τὸ ἄπειρον μεθέντα χαίρειν ἐᾶν.
219. It does not, then, concern a "many-sided determination of unity and diversity." Michael Hoffmann, *Die Entstehung der Ordnung: zur Bestimmung von Sein, Erkennen und Handeln in der späteren Philosophie Platons* (Stuttgart, 1996), 91.
220. Plato, *Philebus*, 16e: μεταξύ.
221. Ibid., 17a–18e.
222. Plato, *Phaedrus*, 274c–75d.
223. Cf. Cassirer's concept of symbolic pregnancy in the *Philosophie der symbolischen Formen* (EWC 13, 271). On this topic, Oswald Schwemmer, *Cassirer. Ein Philosoph der europäischen Moderne* (Berlin, 1997), 116–25.
224. This was worked out especially clearly by Adorno. Theodor Wiesengrund Adorno, *Ästhetische Theorie, Begriff der Komposition und der rationalen Vermittlung*, in *Gesammelte Schriften* 7, ed. Rolf Tiedemann (Frankfurt am Main, 1970), 86–97, 160–71. Cf. Günter Figal, *Theodor W. Adorno. Das Naturschöne als speculative Gedankenfigur* (Bonn, 1977), 51–63.
225. Nietzsche, *Jenseits von Gut und Böse*, no. 34, 53. [I have consulted Kaufmann's translation of Nietzsche here. —Trans.]
226. Hans Blumenberg, *Die Lesbarkeit der Welt*.

Notes to Chapter 6

1. Anaximander, VS 12 B 1: ἐξ ὧν δὲ ἡ γένεσίς ἐστι τοῖς οὖσι, καὶ τὴν φθορὰν εἰς ταῦτα γίγνεσθαι κατὰ τὸ χρεών· διδόναι γὰρ αὐτὰ δίκην καὶ τίσιν ἀλλήλοις τῆς ἀδικίας κατὰ τὴν τοῦ χρόνου τάξιν.
2. Martin Heidegger, "Der Spruch des Anaximander," GA 5, 321–73. Geoffrey S. Kirk and John E. Raven judge differently than Heidegger in *The Presocratic Philosophers* (Cambridge, 1962), 117–18.
3. Aristotle, *Physica* IV, 10; 218b 13: πανταχοῦ καὶ παρὰ πᾶσιν. [R. P. Harie and R. K. Gaye translate Aristotle's phrase as "everywhere and with all things." See Aristotle, *The Complete Works*, Vol. 2, 371, 218b13. Although this would also be a good English translation of the author's German *Überall und an Alles*, I have used the English "ubiquitous" for Aristotle's πανταχοῦ and Figal's *Überall*. —Trans.]
4. Heidegger, *Sein und Zeit*, 577.
5. Aristotle, *Ethica Nicomachea* I, 4; 1095b 2–3.
6. Kant, *Kritik der reinen Vernunft*, B 47, A 31; AA III, 58.
7. Ibid., B 49, A 31–33; AA III, 59.
8. Ibid., B 49, A 33; AA III, 60.

9. Ibid., B 50, A 33; AA III, 60.

10. Cf. Heidegger, *Sein und Zeit*, § 81, esp. 556. Moreover, Heidegger, *Grundprobleme der Phänomenologie*, GA 24, 327-69. As is shown in what follows, however, it would be of little help to reject this critique with the argument that the temporality of Dasein, which Heidegger distinguishes from the vulgar understanding of time, is already found in Aristotle. Enno Rudolph, *Zeit und Gott bei Aristoteles aus der Perspektive der protestantischen Wirkungsgeschichte* (Stuttgart, 1986), here, 14 and 87-88. The significance of the Aristotelian treatment of time lies precisely in the fact that it does not anticipate the Heideggerian perspective—which I go into later.

11. Heidegger, *Sein und Zeit*, 556. [I have consulted Stambaugh here. Cf. Stambaugh 386. —Trans.]

12. Aristotle, *Physica* IV, 11; 219b 2: ἀριθμὸς κινήσεως κατὰ τὸ πρότερον καὶ ὕστερον.

13. Ibid., IV, 11; 219b 6-9.

14. Ibid., IV, 12; 220b 20-22: τῷ μὲν γὰρ ἀριθμῷ τὸ τῶν ἵππων πλῆθος γνωρίζομεν, πάλιν δὲ τῷ ἑνὶ ἵππῳ τὸν τῶν ἵππων ἀριθμὸν αὐτόν. [Cf. Ross, *The Complete Works of Aristotle*, Vol. 2, 376. —Trans.]

15. Compared with the conception of determinate number as it is developed in the *Philebus* (see above, 246-50), the determination of time "as regards content" appears as being in agreement. Yet, whereas Plato thinks of a complex of equal moments, in Aristotle the concern is with the one in a plurality of states.

16. Aristotle, *Physica* IV, 11: 219b 7-8: ὁ δὴ χρόνος ἐστὶν τὸ ἀριθμούμενον καὶ οὐχ ᾧ ἀριθμοῦμα μεν.

17. Ibid., IV 10; 218b 10-20.

18. Ibid., IV 11; 218b 23: οὐ δοκεῖ ἡμῖν γεγονέναι χρόνος.

19. Ibid., IV 11, 218b 23-27.

20. Ibid., IV 14; 223a 30-33.

21. Aristotle himself also maintains that the two is the smallest possible number: Aristotle, *Physica* IV, 12; 220a 27.

22. Heidegger, *Sein und Zeit*, 557. Cf. also Figal, *Phänomenologie der Freiheit*, 307-12.

23. Aristotle, *Physica* IV, 11; 219b 12-15: τὸ δὲ νῦν ἔστι μὲν ὡς τὸ αὐτό, ἔστι δ' ὡς οὐ τὸ αὐτό· ᾗ μὲν γὰρ ἐν ἄλλῳ χαὶ ἄλλῳ, ἕτερον . . . , ὃ δέ ποτε ὄν ἐστι τὸ νῦν, τὸ αὐτό.

24. Ibid., IV, 11; 219b 22-23.

25. In this respect, Wolfgang Wieland goes too far with his thesis that "now" is "a predicate of the moved thing." Wieland, *Die aristotelische Physik*, 325. The now is thus understood as "of the now" [das Jetztig], 324. Walter Mesch also goes in the same direction, *Reflektierte Gegenwart* (Frankfurt am Main, 2003), 380.

26. On the understanding of this formula, cf. Franco Volpi, "Chronos und Psyche. Die aristotelische Aporie von Physik IV, 14, 223 a," 16-29, 26-62 and Hartmut Kuhlmann, " 'Jetzt?' Zur Konzeption des νῦν in der Zeitabhandlung des Aristoteles (Physik IV 10-14)," in Enno Rudolph, ed., *Zeit, Bewegung, Handlung. Studien zur Zeitabhandlung des Aristoteles* (Stuttgart, 1988), 63-96. Cf. moreover: Adolf Torstrik, " Ὁ ποτε ὄν: ein Beitrag zur Kenntnis des aristotelischen Sprachgebrauches," in *Rheinisches Museum* 12, 1857. The clarification developed here deviates from the mentioned one.

27. Aristotle, *Metaphysica* VII, 11; 1037a 29: τὸ εἶδος τὸ ἐνόν.
28. What is foundational can bear the movement because it is the "most familiar" in it: γνώριμον δὲ μάλιστα τοῦτ' ἔστιν. Aristotle, *Physica* IV, 11; 219b 29. One signifies the movements, of which Aristotle thinks, in that one initially says what it is that moves. What moves itself, as it is called (*Physica* IV, 11; 219b 30–31), is a "this there," the movement, however, not: τόδε γάρ τι τὸ φερόμενον, ἡ δὲ κίνησις οὔ.
29. Cf. Günter Figal, "*Substanz*," in *Religion in Geschichte und Gegenwart (RRG)*, fourth edition, Vol. 7, columns 1824–1827.
30. On the idea of the elementary in this sense cf. John Sallis, *Force of Imagination* (Bloomington, 2000), 147–83.
31. Aristotle, *Physica* IV; 221b 1–2; φθορᾶς γὰρ αἴτιος καθ' ἑαυτόν.
32. Ibid., IV; 221b 2–3.
33. Ibid., IV, 12; 211a 31–32.
34. Walter Mesch understood his book on *Reflektierte Gegenwart* as a case for the possibility of such a passing away of the present. Cf. also on this Kuhlmann "'Jetzt?' Zur Konzeption des νῦν in der Zeitabhandlung des Aristoteles (Physik IV 10–14)," 92.
35. Aristotle, *Physica* IV, 11; 219a 14–18.
36. Ibid., 219a 19–21: ἔστι δὲ τὸ πρότερον καὶ ὕστερον ἐν τῇ κινήσει ὃ μέν ποτε ὂν κίνησις.
37. Ibid., IV, 12; 221a 26–28.
38. Ibid., IV, 12; 223a 16–25. For a discussion of this passage in the tradition and in recent research, cf. Volpi, *Chronos und Psyche*. The clarification suggested in what follows deviates from everything discussed by Volpi.
39. Aristotle, *Physica* IV, 14; 223a 25–29: εἰ δὲ μηδὲν ἄλλο πέφυκεν ἀριθμεῖν ἢ ψυχὴ καὶ ψυχῆς νοῦς, ἀδύνατον εἶναι χρόνον ψυχῆς μὴ οὔσης . . . , ἀλλ' ἢ τοῦτο ὅ ποτε ὂν ἔστιν ὁ χρόνος, οἷον εἰ ἐνδέχεται κίνησιν εἶναι ἄνευ ψυχῆς. τὸ δὲ πρότερον καὶ ὕστερον ἐν κινήσει ἐστίν· χρόνος δὲ ταῦτ' ἐστὶν ᾗ ἀριθμητά ἐστιν. [I have consulted the Hardie/Gaye translation of the Greek here. See Ross, *Complete Works of Aristotle*, Vol. 1, 377. —Trans.]
40. Augustinus, *Confessiones* XI, 28, 38.
41. For this distinction, the significations "A-series" (for past, present, and future) and "B-series" (for earlier and later) have gained currency in connection with John Ellis McTaggart, *The Nature of Existence* (Cambridge, 1927, new edition 1968). I will not take up these significations since they do justice neither to the relationship of earlier and later as worked out in regard to Aristotle, nor the belonging together of past, present, and future. McTaggart's distinction begins from a dating of occurrences, which are each respectively understood as "occurring now." Then, one can say that an occurrence G1, if it is earlier than G2, is always earlier than G2. By contrast, an occurrence G is for someone first futural, then, by entering, present, and finally past. In the distinction of an earlier and a later now as they were found in Aristotle, however, the concern is not with two occurrences, but, rather, with the temporal stretch of a movement. It will be made clear in what follows why the connection of past, present, and future in Augustine's sense is not a series.
42. Augustinus, *Confessiones* XI, 28, 38.
43. Augustinus, *Confessiones* XI, 28, 37: Quis igitur negat futura nondum esse? Sed tamen iam est in animo expectatio futurorum. Et quis negat praeterita iam non esse?

Sed tamen adhuc est in animo memoria preateritorum. Et quis negat praesens tempus carere spatio, quia in puncto praeterit? Sed tamen perdurat attentio, per quam pergat abesse quod aderit.

44. On the typology of such fatherhood, cf. Hans-Peter Schütt, *Die Adoption des "Vaters der modernen Philosophie." Studien zu einem Gemeinplatz der Ideengeschichte* (Frankfurt am Main, 1998).

45. Edmund Husserl, *Vorlesungen zur Phänomenologie des inneren Zeitbewußtseins*, first printing in: *Jahrbuch für Philosophischen und phänomenologische Forschung* (1928) 368–490. The lectures are part of *Husserliana* X, ed. Rudolf Boehm (Den Haag, 1966), here, 3.

46. Husserl, *Zeitbewußtsein*, 4.

47. This according to Friedrich-Wilhelm von Herrmann, *Augustinus und die phänomenologische Frage nach der Zeit* (Frankfurt am Main, 1992), 9. Mesch also contradicts the Augustine-interpretation in the spirit of Husserl, *Reflektierte Gegenwart*, 327; Ernst A. Schmidt, *Zeit und Geschichte bei Augustin* (Heidelberg, 1985) and Kurt Flasch, *Was ist Zeit?* (Frankfurt am Main, 1993).

48. On this, Augustinus, *Confessiones* XI, 20, 26: tempora sunt tria, praesens de praeteritis, praesens de praesentibus, praesens de futuris. Sunt enim haec in anima tria quaedam et alibi ea non uideo, praesens de praeteritis memoria, praesens de praesentibus contuitus, praesens de futuris expectatio. On this also, Schmidt: "in the soul, the past (and future) are not a psychological reduction of the phenomenon of time in denial of its objective presence, rather, it is how the human being encounters objective time." Schmidt, *Zeit und Geschichte bei Augustin*, 25.

49. Augustinus, *Confessiones* XI, 28, 38: Et quod in toto cantico . . . hoc in tota uita hominis.

50. Ibid.

51. Ibid.

52. Ibid., 23, 30.

53. Ibid., 26, 33: Inde mihi uisum est nihil esse aliud tempus quam distentionem: sed cuius rei, nescio, et mirum, si non ipsius animi. What he still considers here as a possibility, Augustine confirms a little later, namely, in *Confessiones* XI, 29, 39: ecce distentio est uita mea, as well as again a little later: at ego in tempora dissilui. Cf. to this problematic the illuminating comments by Schmidt, *Zeit und Geschichte bei Augustin*, 23–24 as well as 43–44.

54. Ernst A. Schmidt draws attention to the fact that Augustine by no means discovers these forms. Talk is of them even already in Aristotle (*De memoria*), and they were familiar to Augustine from the "grammatical school tradition." Schmidt, *Zeit und Geschichte bei Augustin*, 21. In any case, Augustine made what was familiar to him in this way effective for philosophical reflection on time.

55. This according to Karen Gloy, "Die Struktur des Augustinischen Zeittheorie im XI. Buch des Confessiones," in *Philosophisches Jahrbuch* Vol. 95 (1988), 72–95.

56. Augustinus, *Confessiones* XI, 20, 26: tempora sunt tria, praesens de praeteribus, presens de praesentibus, praesens de futuris.

57. The foundations for the following debate with Husserl's philosophy of time are above all the *Vorlesungen zur Phänomenologie des inneren Zeitbewußtseins* edited by Heidegger. To the extent that material on the problematic of time was published from the

unpublished writings [Nachlaß], it is available in volumes X and XXXIII of *Husserliana*. On Husserl's conception of time, cf.: Rudolf Bernet, "Die ungegenwärtige Gegenwart. Anwesenheit und Abwesenheit in Husserls Analyse des Zeitbewusstseins," in Bernet, *Zeit und Zeitlichkeit bei Husserl und Heidegger (Phänomenologische Forschungen 14)* (Freiburg i. Br./München, 1983), 16–57. Moreover: Klaus Held, *Lebendige Gegenwart. Die Frage nach der Seinsweise des transzendentalen Ich bei Husserl, entwickelt am Leitfaden des Zeitproblematik (Phänomenologica 24)* (Den Haag, 1966).

58. Husserl, *Zeitbewußtsein*, 24.
59. Karl Ernst Georges, *Ausführliches Lateinisch-Deustsches Handwörterbuch*, seventh edition, 1880, Vol. 2, column 2111.
60. Husserl, *Zeitbewußtsein*, 30.
61. Ibid., 35.
62. Ibid., 29.
63. Ibid., 30. [N.B. "apprehension" is the translation of *Auffassung* here, although I have elsewhere used "apprehension" for *Vernehmung*. —Trans.]
64. Ibid., 29–30.
65. The determination of memory in the tenth book is also to be thought of here, where it is called an "aula ingens." *Confessiones* X, 8, 14).
66. As a differently posed critique of Husserl's orientation toward the now, cf. also Klaus Held, "Phänomenologie der 'eigentlichen Zeit' in Husserl und Heidegger," in *Internationales Jahrbuch für Hermeneutik* (2005), 251–72.
67. Husserl, *Zeitbewußtsein*, 31.
68. Ibid., 31–32.
69. Ibid., 31.
70. Ibid., 38. [I have consulted James Churchill's translation. See Husserl, *The Phenomenology of Internal Time Consciousness*, trans. James Churchill (Bloomington: Indiana University Press, fifth printing 1974), 60. —Trans.]
71. Ibid., 39.
72. Ibid., 38.
73. Ibid., 52. [N.B. Churchill uses "voidly" instead of "blankly" for *leer*, and "intercepts" instead of "collects" for *auffangen* here. Cf. Churchill, 76. —Trans.]
74. Edmund Husserl, "Die Bernauer Manuskripte über das Zeitbewußtsein (1917/18)," *Husserliana* XXXIII, ed., Rudolf Bernet and Dieter Lohmar (Dortrecht/Boston/London, 2001), 4. Husserl has become aware of the significance of protentions first later. The passages devoted to it in the *Vorlesungen* are introduced later. Cf. Husserl, *Zeitbewußtsein*, 52, editor's note.
75. Husserl, *Zeitbewußtsein*, 55. [I borrow from Churchill's translation here. Cf. Churchill, 79. —Trans.]
76. Ibid., 56. [I borrow from Churchill here. Cf. Churchill, 80. —Trans.]
77. Ibid.
78. When Augustine makes the experience of time clear in regard to an activity or "action," this does not mean that activity is as such exemplary for time. Cf. Rainer Enskat, "Zeit, Bewegung, Handlung und Bewußtsein im XI. Buch der 'Confessiones' des hl. Augustinus," in Enno Rudolph, ed., *Zeit, Bewegung, Handlung*, 193–222. If the focus were not on occurrence in activity, Augustine could not understand time as *distentio animi*.

79. In regard to this, Peter Bieri on unfreedom and time in *Handwerk der Freiheit*, here, 127–52.
80. Plato, *Timaeus*, 37d: καθ' ἀριθμόν.
81. Ibid., 37e: τό τ' ἦν τό τ' ἔσται.
82. Ibid.: μέρη χρόνου.
83. Blumenberg, *Lebenszeit und Weltzeit*.
84. Ibid., 86.
85. Pindar, 8. Isthmische Ode, Verses 14–15: δόλιος γὰρ αἰ - / ὢν ἐπ' ἀνδράσι κρέμαται, / ἑλίσσων βίου πόρον. Cited in: *Pindar. Siegeslieder*, ed., trans., and with introduction by Dieter Bremer (München, 1992).
86. Michael Theunissen, *Negative Theologie der Zeit* (Frankfurt am Main, 1991), 41. Cf. also, Michael Theunissen, *Pindar. Menschenlos und Wende Der Zeit* (München, 2000), esp. 79–122.
87. Friedrich Nietzsche, *Also Sprach Zarathustra* II, KSA 4, 103–90, here, 179–80. [I have consulted Hollingdale's translation here. Cf. Friedrich Nietzsche, *Thus Spoke Zarathustra*, trans. R. J. Hollingdale (New York: Penguin Books, 1961, reprinted 1969), 161. —Trans.]
88. This according to Friedrich Fulda against Theunissen: "the power that time has over us is not lordship but rather only force and its actio; strictly speaking, it is not even the power of time since it overwhelms our resistance which in any case also belongs to time." Fulda, "Das Konzept einer entfremdend über uns herrschenden Zeit. Erwägungen, Einsprüche, Fragen," in Emil Angehrn, et al, eds., *Der Sinn der Zeit* (Weilerswist, 2002), 85–97, here, 93.
89. Augustinus, *Confessiones* XI, 20, 26: in anima.
90. Aristotle, *Ars rhetorica* II, 1; 1378a 19–21: ἔστι δὲ τὰ πάθη δι' ὅσα μεταβάλλοντες διαφέρουσι πρὸς τὰς κρίσεις οἷς ἕπεται λύπη καὶ ἡδονή. Cited from: *Aristotelis Ars rhetorica*, ed. W. D. Ross (Oxford, 1959). [I have consulted and borrowed from the English translation here. See Ross, *Complete Works of Aristotle*, Vol. 2, p. 2195. —Trans.]
91. Ibid., II, 5; 1382a 21–22: ἔστω δὴ ὁ φόβος λύπη τις ἢ ταραχὴ ἐκ φαντασίας μέλλοντος κακοῦ φθαρτικοῦ ἢ λυπηροῦ.
92. Plato, *Philebus*, 32c.
93. Heidegger, *Sein und Zeit*, 428–29.
94. That fear is only an example and that other affects could be equally well founded by the analysis is explicitly emphasized: Heidegger, *Sein und Zeit*, 456–57.
95. Heidegger, *Sein und Zeit*, 451. [Cf. Stambaugh, 313. —Trans.]
96. Ibid., 452. [Cf. Stambaugh, 314, however, I have differed from her translation here. —Trans.]
97. Ibid.
98. Ibid. [Cf. Stambaugh, 314. —Trans.]
99. Ibid., 453.
100. The concept of anxiety discussed in what follows is not congruent with the conception of the Freiburg inaugural lecture which was discussed above, 33–35.
101. Heidegger, *Sein und Zeit*, 453.
102. Ibid., 248.
103. Ibid., 250.

104. Ibid., 248.
105. Ibid., 249.
106. In this regard, Heidegger's determination of anxiety is really a reversal of the Kierkegaardian one, according to which anxiety is the experience of being able to. Cf. Kierkegaard, *Begrebet Angest (Begriff Angst)*, SV IV, 315.
107. Heidegger, *Sein und Zeit*, 455. [Cf. Stambaugh, 316. —Trans.]
108. Ibid., 455.
109. Ibid., 250.
110. Ibid., 252.
111. Heidegger, *Die Grundbegriffe der Metaphysik*, 201.
112. Ibid., 207.
113. Ibid.
114. Ibid., 208.
115. Ibid., 221.
116. Ibid.
117. Ibid.
118. Friedrich Nietzsche, *Vom Nutzen und Nachtheil der Historie für das Leben*, 243–334.
119. On the concept of constellation, cf. Figal, "Die Komplexität philosophischer Hermeneutik," 22, 28–30.
120. Gadamer, *Wahrheit und Methode*, 129. Cf. also Gadamer, "Die Aktualität des Schönen," *GW* 8, 94–124, here, 132–33, as well as Gadamer, "Zur Phänomenologie von Ritual und Sprache," *GW* 8, 400–40, here, 414–15.
121. Søren Kierkegaard, *Gjentagelsen (Die Wiederholung)*, SV III (Kopenhagen, 1901), 169–264, 173.
122. Gilles Deleuze, *Différence et repetition*, first edition (Paris, 1968), 36: "pur mouvement créateur."
123. Ibid., 2. Cf. also Bernhard Waldenfels, "Die verändernde Kraft der Wiederholung," *Zeitschrift für Ästhetik und allgemeine Kunstwissenschaft*, 46 (2001), 5–17.
124. Nietzsche, *Die Fröhliche Wissenschaft*, no. 341, 570.
125. Marcel Proust, *A la recherche du temps perdu*. Édition publiée sous la direction de Jean-Yves Tadié, I–IV (Paris, 1987–1989), here, IV, 446.
126. This is the passage, to which the following considerations refer: "Chaque fois je refaisais rien que matériellement ce même pas, il me restait inutile; mais si je réussissais, oubliant la matinée Guermantes, à retrouver ce que j'avais senti en posant ainsi mes pieds, de nouveau la vision éblouissante et indistincte me frôlait comme si elle m'avait dit: 'Saisis-moi au passage si tu en as la force, et tâche à resoundre l'énigme de bonheur que je te propose.' Et presque tout de suite, je la reconnus, c'était Venise, dont mes efforts pour la décrire et les prétendus instantanés pris par ma mémoire m'avaient jamais rien dit, et que la sensation que j'avais ressentie jadis sur deux dalles inégales du baptisère de Saint-Marc m'avait rendue avec toutes les autres sensations jointes ce jour-là à cette sensation-là et qui étaient restées dans l'attente, à leur rang, d'où un brusque hasard les avait impérieusement fait sortir, dans la série des jours oubliés." Proust, *Temps retrouvé*, IV, 446.
127. Kierkegaard, *Begrebet Angest (Begriff Angst)*, 358.

128. Proust, *Temps retrouvé*, IV, 444.
129. Ibid.: "comme une exposition de photographies."
130. Ibid., 446. [Note that "sensations" is not an English translation here, but, rather, a transcription of the author's use of the French word. —Trans.]
131. Ibid., 457: "caractères hiéroglyphiques, qu'on croirait représenter seulement des objets matériels."
132. Ibid.: "Sans doute ce déchiffrage était difficile, mais seul il donnait quelque vérité à lire. Car les vérités que l'intelligence saisit directement à claire-voie dans le monde de la pleine lumière ont quelque chose de moins profond, de moins nécessaire que celles que la vie nous a malgré nous communiquées en une impression, matérielle parce qu'elle est entrée par nos sens, mais dont nous pouvons dégager l'esprit."
133. Ibid., 458: "un critérium de vérité."
134. Ibid., 457: "il fallait tâcher d'interpréter les sensations ... en essayant de penser, c'est-à-dire de faire sortir de la pénombre ce que j'avais senti."

Notes to Chapter 7

1. Heidegger, *Sein und Zeit*, 62.
2. Heidegger, *Die Grundprobleme der Phänomenologie,* 90.
3. Heidegger, *Sein und Zeit*, 83.
4. Cf. above all Lévinas, *En découvrant l'existence avec Husserl et Heidegger.*
5. Heidegger, *Grundprobleme der Phänomenologie,* 91.
6. Heidegger, *Sein und Zeit*, 18.
7. Aristotle, *Metaphysica* IV, 2; 1003a 33–34.
8. Heidegger, *Phänomenologische Interpretationen*, 352.
9. Ibid., 348. Cf. on this anti-ontological application Graf Paul Yorck von Wartenburg, *Bewußtseinsstellung und Geschichte. Ein Fragment aus dem philosophischen Nachlass,* intro. and ed. Iring Fetscher (Tübingen, 1956), 38; as well as the *Correspondence of Wilhelm Dilthey and Graf Paul Yorck von Wartenburg,* ed. E. Rothacker (Halle, 1923), 203.
10. Heidegger, "Mein Weg in die Phänomenologie," 81.
11. This is how Plessner characterizes the conception of life in the philosophy of life [*Lebensphilosophie*]. Helmuth Plessner, *Die Stufen des Organischen und der Mensch* [1928], 37.
12. Dilthey, *Der Aufbau der geschichtlichten Welt in den Geisteswissenschaften,* 261.
13. Ibid., 136.
14. Nietzsche, *Von Nutzen und Nachteil der Historie für das Leben,* 269.
15. Aristotle, *Ethica Nicomachea* I, 7; 1097b 24–1098a 18.
16. Plessner, *Die Stufen des Organischen und der Mensch,* 63.
17. Ibid., 115.
18. Ibid., 131.
19. Ibid., 129.
20. Ibid., 130.

21. Cf. above, 131–32. [In the context of Husserl's work, the term *Abschattung* translated here as "profile" is sometimes translated as "aspect," "adumbration," or another word. —Trans.]
22. Plessner, *Die Stufen des Organischen und der Mensch*, 130.
23. Ibid., 154.
24. Ibid.
25. Ibid., 184.
26. Ibid., 183.
27. Johann Gottlieb Fichte, *Grundlage des gesammten Wissenschaftslehre (1794)*, *Sämmtliche Werke*, I, 96: "The positing of the I through itself is the pure activity of the same. —The I *posits itself* and it *is* by force of this mere positing through itself; and, conversely: the I *is*, and it *posits* its being by force of its mere being."
28. Plessner, *Die Stufen des Organischen und der Mensch*, 187.
29. Ibid., 183.
30. Ibid., 184.
31. Merleau-Ponty, *Le visible et l'invisible*, in this: "L'entrelacs–le chiasme," 172–204.
32. As a concise overview cf. John Sallis, *Phenomenology and the Return to Beginnings*, second edition (Pittsburgh, 2003).
33. Merleau-Ponty, *Le visible et l'invisible*, 173.
34. Ibid.: "D'où vient que, les enveloppant, mon regard ne les cache pas, et, enfin, que, les voilant, il les dévoile?"
35. Ibid.: "incorporation du voyant au visible".
36. The model for this elucidation may, incidentally, be found in Husserl himself. Cf. Husserl, *Ideen II*, 144–45. In the context of his transcendental-philosophical approach, however, Husserl does not draw the consequence from his analyses of conceiving intentionality as such on the basis of the fold.
37. Merleau-Ponty, *Le visible et l'invisible*, 175: "Une variante remarquable."
38. Ibid., 176: "Rapport de principe, quelque parenté."
39. Ibid.
40. Ibid., 195: "hiatus entre ma main droite touchée et ma main droite touchante, entre ma voix entendue et ma voix articulée, entre un moment de ma vie tactile et le suivant."
41. Literally: "a two-sided being [un être à deux feuillets]." Ibid., 180.
42. Ibid., 317: "Le chiasme est cela: la réversibilité."
43. Ibid., 194.
44. Ibid., 319: "l'idée du *chiasme*, c'est à dire: tout rapport à l'être est *simultanément* prendre et être pris, la prise est prise, elle est *inscrite* et inscrite au même être qu'elle prend."
45. Ibid., 183: "je me sens regardé par les choses."
46. Ibid.: "du sorte que voyant et visible se réciproquent et qu'on ne sait plus qui voit et qui est vu." In *Le philosophe et son ombre* Merleau-Ponty has said that the difference of subject and object is obscured in my body. Merleau-Ponty, *Signes*, 211: "la distinction du sujet et de l'objet est brouillée dans mon corps."
47. Merleau-Ponty, *Le visible et l'invisible*, 183: "un narcissisme fondamental de toute vision."

48. Ibid.: "deux séries indéfinies d'images emboîtées qui n'appartiennent vraiment à aucune des deux surfaces, puisque chacune n'est que la réplique de l'autre, qui font donc couple, un couple plus réel que chacune d'elles."
49. Ibid., 184.
50. Merleau-Ponty says in this sense that space is known through my body. Merleau-Ponty, *signes*, 210–11: "que l'espace lui-même se sait à travers mon corps."
51. The following consideration would not be possible without Heidegger's treatment "Vom Wesen und Begriff der Φύσις. Aristoteles Physik B 1," 239–301. However, they follow Heidegger neither in his train of thought nor in his intention.
52. Aristotle, *Physica* II, 1; 192b 9–11.
53. Ibid., 192b13–14: ἐν ἑαυτῷ ἀρχὴν ἔχει κινήσεως καὶ στάσεως.
54. Ibid., 192b18–19: οὐδεμίαν ὁρμὴν ἔχει μεταβολῆς ἔμφυτον.
55. Heidegger, *Ursprung des Kunstwerks*, GA 5, 19.
56. Cf. above § 28, 245.
57. Aristotle, *Physica* II, 1; 192b 36–193a 1: τοῦτο γὰρ φύσις μὲν οὐκ ἔστιν οὐδ' ἔχει φύσιν, φύσει δὲ καὶ κατὰ φύσιν ἐστίν.
58. Aristotle, *Physica* II, 1; 192b 33–34: καὶ ἔστιν πάντα ταῦτα οὐσία· ὑποκείμενον γάρ τι, καὶ ἐν ὑποκεινένῳ ἐστὶν ἡ φύσις ἀεί.
59. Ibid., 193a 29: ἡ πρώτη ἑκάστῳ ὑποκειμένη ὕλη τῶν ἐχόντων ἐν αὑτοῖς ἀρχὴν κινήσεως καὶ μεταβολῆς.
60. Ibid., 193b 7.
61. Ibid., 193a 35–193b 2: οὔτ' ἐν τοῖς φύσει συνισταμένοις· τὸ γὰρ δυνάμει σὰρξ ἢ ὀστοῦν οὔτ ἔχει πω τὴν ἑαυτοῦ φύσιν, πρὶν ἂν λάβῃ τὸ εἶδος τὸ κατὰ τὸν λόγον, ᾧ ὁριζόμενοι λέγομεν τί ἐστι σὰρξ ἤ ὀστοῦν.
62. Martin Heidegger, *Phänomenologische Interpretationen*, GA 62, 374, 398.
63. This speaks against Aristotle, although likewise against Heidegger, who, in the *Beiträge zur Philosophie*, develops a kind of genealogy of the philosophical orientation of production out of the experience of φύσις. Cf. Martin Heidegger, *Beiträge zur Philosophie*, GA 65, ed. Friedrich-Wilhelm von Herrmann (Frankfurt am Main, 1989), 190–91.
64. Aristotle, *Physica* II, 1; 193b 7.
65. Ibid., 193b 1–2.
66. Aristotle, *Metaphysica* VII, 7; 1032b 1.
67. Aristotle, *Physica* II, 1; 193b 8, 12.
68. Ibid., 192b 30–31; 193a 6–7.
69. Ibid., 192b 15.
70. Cf. here the expositions on dialectic in § 28, esp., 246–50.
71. Cf. here Aristotle, *De anima* II, 1; 412b 10–11, where Aristotle identifies the οὐσία κατὰ τὸν λόγον—and this is tantamount to the εἶδος κατὰ τὸν λόγον—with the τί ἦν εἶναι. On this expression, cf. Curt Arpe, *Das τί ἦν εἶναι bei Aristoteles* (Hamburg, 1937); Wolfgang Wieland, *Die aristotelische Physik*, 174–75; Hermann Schmitz, *Die Ideenlehre des Aristoteles. Kommentar zum 7. Buch der Metaphysik* (Bonn, 1985), 13–22.
72. In the lexicon by Liddell and Scott, the discussed significance of φύσις is elucidated as "*the natural form or constitution* of a person or a thing *as the result of growth.*" Henry G. Liddell and Robert Scott, *A Greek-English Lexicon*, ninth edition (Oxford,

1940). Aristotle, *Politica*, 1252b 32 is referenced in evidence: οἷον γὰρ ἕκαστόν ἐστι τῆς γενέσεως τελεσθείσης, ταύτην φαμὲν τὴν φυσιν εἶναι ἑκάστου. Cited according to *Aristotelis Politica*, ed. W. D. Ross (Oxford, 1957).

73. Cf. in introduction to this W. K. C. Guthrie, *A History of Greek Philosophy*, Vol. III, Part 1: The World of the Sophists (Cambridge, 1969).

74. Heidegger, "Vom Wesen und Begriff der Φύσις. Aristoteles, Physik BI (1939)," 239–301, here, 300.

75. Ibid. 299.

76. Ibid., 300–01.

77. Ibid., 300.

78. Heraklit, VS 22 B 123: φύσις ... κρύπτεσθαι φιλεῖ.

79. Heidegger, "Vom Wesen und Begriff der Φύσις," 300.

80. Heraclitus, VS 22 B 30: πῦρ ἀείζωον.

81. Ibid., B 67: It is clear from the context in Hippolitos, who passes down the statement, that here κόσμος and not God (θεός) is intended. Diverging from the common version, the sentences are, then: κόσμος ἡμέρη εὐφρόνη, χειμὼν θέρος, πόλεμος εἰρήνη, κόρος λιμός..., ἀλλοιοῦται δὲ ὅκωσπερ <πῦρ>, ὁπόταν σιμμιγῆι θυώμασιν, ὀνομάζεται καθ' ἡδονὴν ἑκάστου. [For my translation of the passage cited, I have borrowed from Kirk and Raven. See Kirk and Raven, *The Presocratic Philosophers*, 190. —Trans.]

82. This also holds of philosophy. For the philosophical linguistic usage of the twentieth century, Helmut Holzhey maintains that, in it, "soul" has "extensively lost the status of a well-defined concept." Its use shows "a pull into the anachronistic," and, thus, the expression makes it possible "to transport and to hold indistinctly and emotionally present a 'substance' of faith, which is no longer rationally identifiable." Holzhey, "Soul," in *Historisches Wörterbuch der Philosophie*, Vol. 9, Columns 26–52, here, 50. On the recent theological rehabilitation of the concept of the soul, cf. Walter Sparn, "Fromme Seele, wahre Empfindung und ihre Aufklärung. Eine historische Anfrage an das Paradigma der Subjektivität," in D. Korsch and J. Dierken, eds., *Subjektivität im Kontext. Erkundungen im Gespräch mit Dieter Henrich* (Tübingen, 2004), 29–48; Ulrich Barth, "Selbstbewußtsein und Seele," in *Zeitschrift für Theologie und Kirche* (2004), 198–217.

83. On the analytic treatment of the them in the 'philosophy of mind,' cf. Erik Ostenfeld, *Ancient Greek Psychology and the Modern Mind-body Debate* (Aarhus, 1987). The concern here, however, is rather to fit Aristotle into the schemata of the recent discussions instead of to learn from him.

84. The concept is still used unspecifically here. It first becomes clear in the differentation of body and the body quick in § 39.

85. Bruno Snell, *Die Entdeckung des Geistes: Studien zur Entstehung als europäischen Denkens bei den Griechen*, fourth revised edition (Göttingen, 1975). As the still unsurpassed standard work on the significance of Psyché in art and religion: Erwin Rohde, *Psyche: Seelencult und Unsterblichkeitsglaube der Griechen*, third edition (Tübingen, 1903).

86. Aristotle, *De anima* II, 1; 412a 27–28: ἐντελέχεια ἡ πρώτη σώματος φυσικοῦ δυνάμει ζωὴν ἔχοντος.

87. Ryle, *The Concept of Mind*, 43: "To possess a dispositional property is not to be in a particular state, or to undergo a particular change; it is to be bound or liable

to be in a particular state, or to understand a particular change, when a particular condition is realized."

88. For the first time in Heidegger, "Anmerkungen zu Karl Jaspers 'Psychologie der Weltanschauung,'" 10. With particular clarity: Heidegger, *Einleitung in die Philosophie der Religion*, 55.

89. Aristotle, *De anima* II, 1; 412a 10–11.

90. Cf. the commentary by Theiler in: *Über die Seele*, trans. Willy Theiler, seventh edition, unaltered vis-à-vis the third, revised edition. (Darmstadt, 1994), 107, and the parallel passages provided there.

91. Aristotle, *De anima* II, 1; 412a 28–412b 1.

92. Ibid., 412b 10–11: οὐσία ... κατὰ τὸν λόγον.

93. Martin Heidegger, "Die Frage nach der Technik (1953)," 5–36, here, 31–32. Cf. above, 314–15.

94. If this holds for Aristotle, then there is no dualism of body and psyche in him. Cf. also on this theme: Annette Hilt, *Ousia-Psyche-Nous: Aristoteles' Philosophie der Lebendigkeit* (Freiburg i. Br./München, 2005), 36–37.

95. Heidegger, "Die Frage Nach der Technik (1953)," 32. [I have relied on Lovitt's translation of "The Question Concerning Technology" here. See Heidegger, "The Question Concerning Technology," in *The Question Concerning Technology and Other Essays*, trans. William Lovitt (New York: Harper and Row, 1977), 30. —Trans.]

96. Aristotle signifies ψυχή as εἶδος in *De anima* II, 1; 412a 19–20.

97. Aristotle, *De anima* II, 4; 415a 18–20: πρότεραι γάρ εἰσι τῶν δυναμένων αἱ ἐνέργειαι καὶ αἱ πράξεις κατὰ τὸν λόγον.

98. In any case, propagation is treated as if not at all in *De anima*.

99. Aristotle, *De anima* II, 1; 413a 23–24.

100. Ibid., 413a 25.

101. Ibid., II, 4; 416a 21–22.

102. Ibid., II, 5; 416b 33: κινεῖσθαί τε καὶ πάσχειν.

103. Ibid., 417b 20.

104. Ibid., 417b 23–24: ταῦτα δ' ἐν αὐτῇ πώς ἐστι τῇ ψυχῇ.

105. Ibid., III, 5; 430a 10–25.

106. Ibid., II, 4; 416a 33.

107. Ibid., II, 5; 417b 2–5: σωτηρία ... τοῦ δυνάμει ὄντος ὑπὸ τοῦ ἐντελεχείᾳ ὄντος, καὶ ὁμοίου οὕτως ὡς δύναμις ἔχει πρὸς ἐντελέχειαν. [I have consulted the Ross edition translation of this passage. Cf. Ross, *Complete Works of Aristotle*, Vol. 1, 664. —Trans.]

108. Ibid., III, 2; 425b 26–27: ἡ δὲ τοῦ αἰσθητοῦ ἐνέργεια καὶ τῆς αἰσθήσεως ἡ αὐτὴ μέν ἐστι καὶ μία, τὸ δ'εἶναι οὐ τὸ αὐτὸ αὐταῖς.

109. Ibid., 426a 10–11: ἡ τοῦ αἰσθητοῦ ἐνέργεια καὶ ἡ τοῦ αἰσθητικοῦ ἐν τῷ αἰσθητικῷ.

110. Ibid., 426a 20–26.

111. Ibid., 426a1: τὸ μὲν εἶναι ἄκουσιν τὸ δὲ ψόφησιν. [I have consulted the Ross edition here. See Ross, Vol. 1, 677. —Trans.]

112. Merleau-Ponty, *Le visible et l'invisible*, 180.

113. Aristotle, *Metaphyisca* IX, 6; 1048b 23–24.

114. Heidegger, "Vom Wesen und Begriff der Φυσις," 284.

115. Aristotle, *De anima* II, 3; 414b 3. It is not entirely clear whether this includes plants or not. Within the framework of the Aristotelian discussion the question can nevertheless only be whether one is prepared to ascribe the sense of touch to them or not. If yes, then everything fundamentally holds of them that is developed in what follows.

116. Ibid., III, 10; 433b 27–28: ᾗ ὀρεκτικὸν τὸ ζῷον, ταύτῃ αὑτοῦ κινητικόν. Cf. also ibid., III, 9; 432b 16–17.

117. Snell, *Die Entdeckung des Geistes*, 16.

118. Cf. Grimm, *Deutsches Wörterbuch*, Vol. 5, Column 1834.

119. By contrast, Waldenfels uses the concept as a superordinate concept that encompasses the "corporeal-thing" and the quick itself. Bernhard Waldenfels, *Das leibliche selbst. Vorlesungen zur Phänomenologie des Leibes*, ed. Regula Guiliani (Frankfurt am Main, 2000), 248–49.

120. Grimm, *Deutsches Wörterbuch*, Vol. 5, Column 580.

121. Husserl, *Ideen II*, § 18, 56.

122. Plato, *Res publica* 508b: τὰ περὶ τὰς αἰσθήσεις ὄργανα. Cf. also *Theaetetus* 184c–85e.

123. Aristotle, *De anima* II, 1; 412a 27–412b 1.

124. Heidegger, *Die Grundbegriffe der Metaphysik*, 319.

125. Ibid., 324. Cf. also *Sein und Zeit*, 217, as well as "Logos (Heraklit Fragment 50)," 220.

126. Heidegger, *Die Grundbegriffe der Metaphysik*, 327.

127. Cf. Aristotle, *Physica* VII, 3; 253b 34–254a 1: οἰκεῖος τόπος.

128. In this idea one can call on Merleau-Ponty, who also calls the body quick a place, though without explaining this further. Cf. Merleau-Ponty, "Kandidatur am College de France," in *Das Auge und der Geist* (Hamburg, 2003), 99–110, here, 101. French original: Merleau-Ponty, "Un inédit de Merleau-Ponty," in *Revue de Métaphysique et de Morale* 67 (1962), 401–409. Cf. also Schmitz, *System der Philosophie, zweiter Band, erster Teil: Der Leib*, esp. 6.

129. Heidegger takes up the idea that a place "always" opens "a vicinity" [Gegend] in this sense. Martin Heidegger, "Die Kunst und der Raum," *Aus der Erfahrung des Denkens 1910–976*, GA 13, ed. Hermann Heidegger (Frankfurt am Main, 1983), 203–10, here, 207.

130. This is an alternative to the conception of the body quick in Hermann Schmitz, which begins in the experience of the self in "feeling", *Der unerschöpfliche Gegenstand: Grundzuge der Philosophie* (Bonn, 1990), 115. Cf. also, Schmitz, *System der Philosophie, zweiter Band, erster Teil: Der Leib*.

131. Cf. above, 307–08.

132. Aristotle, *Metaphysica* I, 1; 980a 21–24.

133. Aristotle, *De anima* III, 4; 429a 15: ἀπαθές.

134. Ibid., 429a 18: ἀμιγῆ.

135. Ibid., 429a 22: δυνατός.

136. Aristotle, *Metaphysica* VII, 11; 1037a 29–30: τὸ εἶδος τὸ ἐνόν. Cf. above, 263.

137. Aristotle, *De anima* III, 4; 429b 14: τὸ σιμόν.

138. Ibid., 429b 10-11: τὸ μεγέθει εἶναι, ... τὸ ὕδατι εἶναι. [I have consulted an English translation here. See *Complete Works of Aristotle*, Vol.1, 683. —Trans.]
139. Ibid., III, 5; 430a 18: ἐνέργεια.
140. Ibid., 430a 16: ποιεῖν.
141. Aristotle, *De anima* III, 5; 430a 15: οἷον τὸ φῶς.
142. Plato, *Res publica*, 507b-09a.
143. Aristotle, *De anima* III, 5; 430a 16-17: τρόπον γάρ τινα καὶ τὸ φῶς ποιεῖ τὰ δυνάμει ὄντα χρώματα ἐνεργείᾳ χρώματα.
144. Ibid., II, 7; 418b9-10: φῶς δέ ἐστιν ἡ τούτου ἐνέργεια, τοῦ διαφανοῦς ᾗ διαφανές.
145. Ibid., 418a 26-27.
146. Ibid., 419a 13-15.
147. Ibid., III, 5; 430a 23: ἀθάνατον καὶ ἀΐδιον.
148. Aristotle, *De generatione animalium* 736b 28: λείπεται δὴ τὸν νοῦν μόνον θύραθεν ἐπεισιέναι καὶ θεῖον εἶναι μόνον. Cited from: *Aristotelis opera* ed. Academia Regina Borusica, Vol. 1 (Berlin, 1831).
149. Cf. Klaus Bussmann, ed., *Eduaro Chillida. Hauptwerke* (Mainz/München, 2003), photographs of the wind combs, 92–93; drawings of the hand, 148–49.
150 Cf. Figal, "Lebensverstricktheit und Abstandnahme."
151. Søren Kierkegaard, *Sygdommen til Døden. En christelig psychologisk Udvikling til Opbyggelse og Opvaekkelse af Anti-Climacus. (Die Krankheit zum Tode. Eine christliche physchologische Erörterung zur Erbauung und Erweckung von Anti-Climacus)*, SV XI (Kopenhagen, 1905), 111–241, here, 128.
152. Plato, *Res publica* 436b: Δῆλον ὅτι ταὐτὸν τἀναντία ποιεῖν ἢ πάσχειν κατὰ ταὐτόν γε καὶ πρὸς ταὐτὸν οὐκ ἐθελήσει ἅμα. [I use Paul Shorey's English translation of Plato's passage here, cited in Plato, *Collected Dialogues*, ed. Edith Hamilton and Huntingeon Cairns (New York: Pantheon Books, 1961, fourth printing, 1966), 678. Although I have relied on Shorey's translation because of its accuracy as well as its familiarity to the English reader, it should be noted that Shorey's English translation differs slightly from Figal's German formulation: *Es sei klar, daß dasselbe nicht gleichzeitig und in derselben Hinsicht oder auf das Selbe hin das Selbe hervorbringen oder erleiden kann* —Trans.]
153. Plato, *Res publica* 437b. [I have borrowed the phrase "to endeavor after" from the Shorey translation. See Plato, *Republic*, in *Complete Works of Plato*, 679. —Trans.]
154. Dihle elucidates the difference of ἐθέλειν and βούλεσθαι by determining the former as "being composed," "being ready," the latter as "the planning in accord with understanding, which goes ahead of action." Albrecht Dihle, *Die Verstellung vom Willen in der Antike* (Göttingen, 1985), 3. I hold this elucidation of βούλεσθαι to be weak. There is more to willing than only planning.
155. Plato, *Res publica* 437b-c.
156. Ibid., 439d.
157. Aristotle, *De anima* III, 9; 432b 5-6: ἔν τε τῷ λογιστικῷ γὰρ ἡ βούλησις γίνεται, καὶ ἐν τῷ ἀλόγῳ ἡ ἐπιθυμία.
158. Ibid., *De anima* II, 3; 414b 5-6.
159. Ibid., III, 10; 433b 5-8.

160. Plato, *Res publica*, 439e: τρίτον.
161. Ibid.
162. Ibid., 440e.
163. Snell points out the proximity of θυμός and ψυχή. Based on this, θυμός may also be translated with "liveliness." Cf. Snell, *Die Entdeckung des Geistes*, 19–21.
164. Plato, *Res publica* 440b: σύμμαχον τῷ λόγῳ.
165. Plato, *Res publica* 439d: τὰ δὲ ἄγοντα καὶ ἕλκοντα διὰ παθημάτων τε καὶ νοσημάτων παραγίνεται.
166. Plato, *Philebus* 31d: Λέγω τοίνυν τῆς ἁρμονίας μὲν λυομένης ἡμῖν ἐν τοῖς ζῴοις ἅμα λύσιν τῆς φύσεως καὶ γένεσιν ἀλγηδόνων ἐν τῷ τότε γίγνεσθαι χρόνῳ.
167. Ibid., 31d: Πάλιν δὲ ρμοττομένης τε καὶ εἰς τὴν αὑτῆς φύσιν ἀπιούσης ἡδονὴν.
168. Ibid., 32c: προσδόκημα.
169. Ibid.
170. Ibid., 27b: γεγενημένη οὐσία. [I have consulted the R. Hackforth translation of the *Philebus* here, in Plato, *Collected Works*, 1104. —Trans.]
171. On the interpretation of this determination cf. Michael Theunissen, *Das Selbst auf dem Grund der Verzweiflung* (Frankfurt am Main, 1991). Moreover: Figal, "Lebensverstricktheit und Abstandnahme"; Tilo Wesche, *Kierkegaard: eine philosophische Einführung* (Stuttgart, 2003).
172. Kierkegaard, *Sygdommen til Døden (Die Krankheit zum Tode)*, 139. The translation here follows the translation by Emanuel Hirsch in: Sören Kierkegaard, *Die Krankheit zum Tode. Der Hohepriester, der Zöllner, die Sünderin, Gesammelte Werke*, Part 24/25 (Düsseldorf, 1957), 1–134.
173. Figal, *Phänomenologie der Freiheit* § 8; 190–269.
174. Kierkegaard, *Sygdommen til Døden (Die Krankheit zum Tode)*, 133–34.
175. Heidegger, *Sein und Zeit*, 407.
176. F. W. J. Schelling, *Philosophische Untersuchungen über das Wesen der menschlichen Freiheit und die damit zusammenhängenden Gegenstände (1809), Sämmtliche Werke*, ed. K. F. A. Schelling, Part I, Vol. 7, 350.
177. Martin Heidegger, "Zu Ernst Jünger," *GA* 90, ed. Peter Trawny (Frankfurt am Main, 2004), 226.
178. Schelling, *Vom Wesen der menschlichen Freiheit*, 350.
179. Arthur Schopenhauer, *Die Welt als Wille und Vorstellung* § 34; *Arthur Schopenhauer's sämmtliche Werke*, ed. Julius Frauenstädt, second edition (Leipzig, 1877), Second Volume, *Die Welt als Wille und Vorstellung* (henceforth: *SW* II), 212.
180. Cf. the appendix "Socrates, Callicles, and Nietzsche," in Plato, *Gorgias. A Revised Text with Introduction and Commentary by E. R. Dobbs* (Oxford, 1959).
181. Schopenhauer, *Die Welt als Wille und Vorstellung* § 54; *SW* II, 336.
182. Martin Heidegger, Ἀγχιβασίη. *Ein Gespräch selbstdritt auf einem Feldweg zwischen einem Forscher, einem Gelehrten und einem Weisen*, in *Feldweg-Gespräche (1944/45), GA* 77, ed. Ingrid Schüßler (Frankfurt am Main, 1995), 1–159, here, 78, and also especially 106.

Bibliography

Abel, Günter. *Die Dynamik der Willen zur Macht und die ewige Wiederkehr.* Berlin/New York, 1984.
———. *Interpretationswelten. Gegenwartsphilosophie jenseits von Essentialismus und Relativismus.* Frankfurt am Main, 1993.
Adorno, Theodor Wiesengrund. *Ästhetische Theorie. Gesammelte Schriften* Vol. 7 Edited by Rolf Tiedemann. Frankfurt am Main, 1970.
———. *Negative Dialektik. Gesammelte Schriften* Vol. 6. Edited by Rolf Tiedemann. Frankfurt am Main, 1973.
Angehrn, Emil. *Interpretation und Dekonstruktion: Untersuchungen zur Hermeneutik.* Weilerswist, 2003.
Anz, Heinrich. "Hermeneutik und Individualität. Wilhelm Diltheys hermeneutische Position und ihre Aporien." In *Hermeneutische Position. Schleiermacher–Dilthey–Heidegger–Gadamer*, ed. Hendrik Birus, 59–88. Göttingen, 1982.
Apel, Karl-Otto. *Die Erklären-Verstehen-Kontroverse in transcendentalpragmatischer Sicht.* Frankfurt am Main, 1979.
Arendt, Hannah. *Vita activa oder vom tätigen Leben.* München, 1981.
———. *Vom Leben des Geistes. Band 1. Das Denken.* München, 1979.
Aristotle. *Ars rhetorica (Aristotelis Ars rhetorica).* Edited by W. D. Ross. Oxford, 1959.
———. *De anima (Aristotelis De anima).* Edited by W. D. Ross. Oxford, 1956.
———. *De arte poetica (Aristotelis De arte poetica liber).* Edited by I. Bywater. Oxford, 1897.
———. *De generatione animalium. Aristotelis opera.* Edited by the Academia Regina Borusica. Vol. 1. Berlin, 1831.
———. *De interpretatione (Aristotelis Categoriae et Liber de Interpretatione).* Edited by L. Minio-Paluello. Oxford, 1949.
———. *De motu animalium (Aristotle's De motu animalium).* Edited by Martha Craven Nussbaum. Princeton, 1978.
———. *Ethica Nicomachea (Aristotelis Ethica Nicomachea).* Edited by I. Bywater. Oxford, 1894.
———. *Metaphysica (Aristotle's Metaphysics).* Edited by W. D. Ross. Two Vols. Oxford, 1924.
———. *Peri Hermeneias, übersetzt und erläutert von Hermann Weidemann. Werke in deutscher Übersetzung, begründet von Ernst Grumach.* Edited by Hellmut Flashar, Vol. 1, Part II. Berlin, 1994.

———. *Physica (Aristotle's Physics)*. Edited by W. D. Ross. Oxford, 1936.
———. *Politica (Aristotelis Politica)*. Edited by W. D. Ross. Oxford, 1957.
———. *Über die Seele*, trans. Willy Theiler. Seventh edition, compared with the third edition, which was reviewed for accuracy and unaltered. Darmstadt, 1994.
Arpe, Curt. *Das τί ἦν εἶναι bei Aristoteles*. Hamburg, 1937.
Ast, Friedrich. *Grundlinien der Grammatik, Hermeneutik und Kritik*. Landshut, 1808.
Augustinus (Sancti Augustini). *Confessionum Libri XIII (Corpus Christianorum Series Latina XXVII)*. Edited by Lukas Verheijen. Turnholt, 1981.
Austin, John L. *How to do things with words?* Cambridge, Mass., 1962.
Barbarić, Damir. "Philosophie als Zurückgezogenheit–René Descartes." In *Denkweg 2*, 5–50. Tübingen, 2001.
Barth, Ulrich. "Selbstbewußtsein und Seele." *Zeitschrift für Theologie und Kirche* (2004). 198–217.
Bassler, Moritz. "Textur." In *Reallexikon der deutschen Literaturwissenschaft*, ed. Jan Dirk Müller, Vol. 3, Columns 618–19. Berlin/New York, 2003.
Benjamin, Walter. "Das Kunstwerk im Zeitalter seiner technischen Reproduzierbarkeit, zweite Fassung (1936–38)." In *Gesammelte Schriften*, ed. Rolf Tiedemann, Vol. I.2, 2nd ed., 471–508. Frankfurt am Main, 1978.
———. *Ursprung des deutschen Trauerspiels*. In *Gesammelte Schriften*, ed. Rolf Tiedemann, Vol. I.1. 2nd ed., 203–409. Frankfurt am Main, 1978.
———. "Zur Kritik der Gewalt." In *Gesammelte Schriften*, ed. Rolf Tiedemann, Vol. II.1, 179–203. Frankfurt am Main, 1977.
Bernet, Rudolf. "Bedeutung und intentionales Bewußtsein. Husserls Begriff des Bedeutungsphänomens." In *Studien zur Sprachphänomenologie. Phänomenologische Forschungen* 8. Freiburg i. Br./München, 1979. 31–64.
———. "Die ungegenwärtige Gegenwart. Anwesenheit und Abwesenheit in Husserls Analyse des Zeitbewusstseins." In *Zeit und Zeitlichkeit bei Husserl und Heidegger (Phänomenologische Forschungen 14)*, ed. Ernst Wolfgang Orth, 16–57. Freiburg i. Br./München, 1983.
Bieri, Peter. *Das Handwerk der Freiheit. Über die Entdeckung des eigenen Willens*. München/Wien, 2001.
Blumenberg, Hans. *Ästhetische und metaphorologische Schriften. Auswahl und Nachwort von Anselm Haverkamp*. Frankfurt am Main, 2001.
———. *Die Legitimät der Neuzeit*. Frankfurt am Main, 1966.
———. *Die Lesbarkeit der Welt*. Frankfurt am Main, 1981.
———. *Höhlenausgänge*. Frankfurt am Main, 1989.
———. *Lebenszeit und Weltzeit*. Frankfurt am Main, 1986.
———. *Paradigmen zu einer Metaphorologie (1960)*. Frankfurt am Main, 1998.
———. *Schiffbruch mit Zuschauer. Paradigma zu einer Daseinsmetapher*. Frankfurt am Main, 1979.
Boehm, Gottfried. *Bildnis und Individuum. Über den Ursprung des Porträtmalerei in der italienischen Renaissance*. München, 1985.
———. "Der stumme Logos." In *Leibhaftige Vernunft. Spuren von Merleau-Pontys Denken*, ed. Alexandre Métraux and Bernhard Waldenfels, 289–304. München, 1986.
Borsche, Tilman. "Zeichentheorie im Übergang von den Stoikern zu Augustin." In *Allgemeine Zeitschrift für Philosophie*. 19/2 (1994): 41–52.

Bühler, Karl. *Die Axiomatik der Sprachwissenschaften.* Frankfurt am Main, 1969.
———. *Die Darstellungsform der Sprache.* 2nd ed. Jena, 1965.
Burbidge, John. "Sprache und Anerkennung." In *Anerkennung. Zu einer Kategorie gesellschaftlicher Praxis*, ed. Hans-Helmuth Gander, 33–44. Würzburg, 2004.
Bussmann, Klaus, ed. *Eduardo Chillida. Hauptwerke.* Mainz/München, 2003.
Cassirer, Ernst. "Die Tragödie der Kultur." In *Zur Logik der Kulturwissenschaften. Fünf Studien*, 103–27. Darmstadt, 1961.
———. *Philosophie der symbolischen Formen, Erster Teil. Die Sprache. Gesammelte Werke*, Hamburg edition. Vol. 11. Edited by Birgit Recki. Hamburg, 2001.
Cicero, Marcus Tullius. *De oratore III.* In *Cicero in twenty-eight volumes.* Vol. 4. ed. G. P. Goold. London, 1982.
Claesges, Ulrich. *Edmund Husserls Theorie des Raumkontitution.* Den Haag, 1964.
Crescenzi, Luca. "Die Leistung des Buchstabens. Ein ungeschriebenes Kapitel zur Unverständlichkeitsdebatte in der deutschen Frühromantik." *Internationales Jahrbuch für Hermeneutik* (2002):81–133.
Dannhauer, Johann Conrad. *Hermeneutica sacra sive methodus exponendarum sacrarum literarum proposita et vindicita.* 1654.
Davidson, Donald. "Radical Interpretation." In *Inquiries into Truth and Interpretation*, 125–39. Oxford, 1984.
———. *Subjective, Intersubjective, Objective.* Oxford, 2002.
Deleuze, Gilles. *Différence et répétition.* 1st ed. Paris, 1968.
Deniau, Guy. *Cognitio imaginativa: la phénoménologie herméneutique de Gadamer.* Brüssel, 2003.
Derrida, Jacques and Gadamer, Hans Georg. *Der ununterbrochene Dialog.* Edited by Martin Gessmann. Frankfurt am Main, 2004.
Derrida, Jacques. *De la grammatologie.* Paris, 1967
———. *Die Stimme und das Phänomen*, trans. from French with Preface by Jochen Hörisch. Frankfurt am Main, 1979.
———. *Die Stimme und das Phänomen*, trans. from French by Hans-Dieter Gondek. Frankfurt am Main, 2003.
———. *Éperons. Les styles de Nietzsche.* Paris 1978.
———. *Force de loi. Le 'fondement mystique' de l'autorité.* Paris, 1994.
———. "La Pharmacie de Platon." In *Plato. Phèdre traduction inédite, introduction et notes par Luc Brisson.* Paris, 1989. 257–403.
———. "La structure, le signe et le jeu dans le discours des scienes humaines." In *L'Ecriture et la Différence*, 409–28. Paris, 1967.
———. *La voix et le phénomène. Introduction au problème du signe dans la phénomenologie de Husserl.* Paris, 1967.
———. "Sémiologie et Grammatologie." In *Positions. Entretiens avec Henri Ronse, Julia Kristeva, Jean-Louis Houdebine, Guy Scarpetta*, 25–50. Paris, 1972.
Descartes, René. *Discours de la méthode. Oeuvres de Descartes.* Edited by Charles Adam and Paul Tannery. Vol. VI. Paris.
———. *Meditationes de prima philosophiae 7–8. Oeuvres de Descartes.* Edited by Charles Adam and Paul Tannery. Vol. VII. Paris.
———. *Principia philosophiae I. Oeuvres de Descartes.* Edited by Charles Adam and Paul Tannery. Vol. VIII.1. Paris.

Di Cesare, Donatella. *Die Bedeutung dekonstruieren. Bemerkungen anhand des "Big Typescript."* Manuscript.
———. "Einleitung." Wilhelm von Humboldt. *Über die Verschiedenheit des menschlichen Sprachbaues und ihren Einfluß auf die geistige Entwicklung des Menschengeschlechts.* Edited by Donatella di Cesare. Paderborn/München/Zürich/Wien, 1998. 11–128.
———. *L'utopia del comprendere.* Genua, 2003.
———. "Sein und Sprache in der philosophischen Hermeneutik." *Internationales Jahrbuch für Hermeneutik*, 21–38. 2002
Diels, Hermann and Kranz, Walther. *Die Fragmente der Vorsokratiker.* 7th ed., Vol. 1–3. Berlin, 1954.
Dierks, Sonja. "Musikalische Schrift." In *Adorno im Widerstreit*, ed. W. Elte, G. Figal, R. Klein, G. Peters, 222–34. Freiburg i. Br./München, 2004.
Dihle, Albrecht. *Die Vorstellung vom Willen in der Antike.* Göttingen, 1985.
Dilthey, Wilhelm and Wartenburg, Graf Paul Yorck von. *Briefwechsel Wilhelm Dilthey und Graf Paul Yorck von Wartenburg.* Edited by E. Rothacker. Halle, 1923.
Dilthey, Wilhelm. "Das Wesen der Philosophie." In *Die geistige Welt. Einleitung in die Philosophie des Lebens. Erste Hälfte. Abhandlungen zur Grundlegung der Geisteswissenschaften. Gesammelte Schriften.* Vol. V, ed. Georg Misch. 4th ed., 339–416. Stuttgart, 1964.
———. *Der Aufbau der geschichtlichen Welt in den Geisteswissenschaften. Gesammelte Schriften.* Vol. VII, Edited by Bernhard Groethuysen. 2nd ed. Stuttgart, 1958.
———. "Die Entstehung der Hermeneutik (1900)." In *Die geistige Welt. Einleitung in die Philosophie des Lebens. Erste Hälfte. Abhandlungen zur Grundlegung der Geisteswissenschaften. Gesammelte Schriften.* Vol. V, ed. Georg Misch, 4th ed., 317–38. Stuttgart, 1964.
———. *Grundlegung der Wissenschaften vom Menschen, der Gesellschaft und der Geschichte. Ausarbeitungen und Entwürfe zum zweiten Band der Einleitung in die Geisteswissenschaften (ca. 1870–1895). Gesammelte Schriften.* Vol. XIX. Edited by Helmut Johach and Frithjof Rodi. Göttingen, 1982.
———. "Ideen über eine beschreibende und zergliedernde Psychologie (1894)." In *Die geistige Welt. Einleitung in die Philosophie des Lebens. Erste Hälfte. Abhandlungen zur Grundlegung der Geisteswissenschaften. Gesammelte Schriften*, Vol. V, ed Georg Misch, 4th ed., 139–240. Stuttgart, 1964.
———. *Weltanschauungslehre: Abhandlungen zu Philosophie der Philosophie. Gesammelte Schriften.* Vol. VIII. Edited by B. Groethuysen. 2nd ed. Berlin, 1960.
Dodds, E. R. "Socrates, Callicles, and Nietzsche." In Plato, *Gorgias. A Revised Text with Introduction and Commentary by E. R. Dodds.* Oxford, 1959.
Dostal, Robert, ed. *The Cambridge Companion to Gadamer.* Cambridge, UK, 2002.
Droysen, Johann Gustav. *Grundriß der Historik.* Leipzig, 1868.
Ebert, Theodor. "Praxis und Poesis. Zu einer handlungstheoretischen Unterscheidung des Aristoteles." *Zeitschrift für philosophische Forschung,* 30, (1976):12–30.
Eco, Umberto. *Einführung in die Semiotik.* 8th ed. München, 1994.
Enskat, Rainer. "Zeit, Bewegung, Handlung und Bewußtsein im XI. Buch des 'Confessiones' des hl. Augustinus." In *Zeit, Bewegung, Handlung, Studien zur Zeitabhandlung des Aristoteles*, ed. Enno Rudolph, 193–222. Stuttgart, 1988.

Enzenberger, Hans Magnus. "Die Entstehung eines Gedichts." In *Gedichte. Die Entstehung eines Gedichts* 2nd ed., 55–82. Frankfurt am Main, 1963.
Eßbach, Wolfgang, Fischer, Joachim, and Lethen, Helmut, eds., *Plessners "Die Grenzen der Gemeinschaft."* Frankfurt am Main, 2002.
Fichte, Johann Gottlieb. *Grundlage der gesammten Wissenschaftslehre (1794)*. In *Sämmtliche Werke*, ed. Immanuel Hermann Fichte, Vol. 1, 83–328. Berlin, 1845/46.
Figal, Günter. "Dekonstruktion und Dialektik." In *Platon über das Gute und die Gerechtigkeit*, ed. Damir Barbarić, 261–70. Würzburg, 2005.
———. "Die Gegenständlichkeit der Welt. Freiburger Antrittsvorlesung, 17. Juli 2003." *Internationales Jahrbuch für Hermeneutik* (2004): 123–35.
———. "Die Komplexität philosophischer Hermeneutik." In *Der Sinn des Verstehens*, ed. Günter Figal, 11–31. Stuttgart, 1996.
———. "Die Rekonstruktion der menschlichen Natur. Zum Begriff des Naturzustandes in Rousseaus 'Zweitem Discours.' " In *Rousseau und die Folgen. Neue Hefte für Philosophie* 29 (1989): 24–38.
———. "Die Wahrheit und die schöne Täuschung. Zum Verhältnis von Dichtung und Philosophie im Platonischen Denken." *Philosophisches Jahrbuch* 107 (2000): 301–15.
———. "Ethik und Hermeneutik." In *Hermeneutik als Ethik*, ed. Hans-Martin Schönherr-Mann, 117–33. München, 2004.
———. "Gadamer im Kontext. Zur Gestalt und den Perspektiven philosophischer Hermeneutik." *Gadamer verstehen / Understanding Gadamer*, eds. Mirko Wischke and Michael Hoffer, 141–56. Darmstadt, 2003.
———. "Leben als Verstehen." In *Leben. Verständnis, Wissenschaft, Technik. Kongressband des XI. Europäischen Kongresses für Theologie, 15–19. September in Zürich*, ed. Eilert Herms, 32–40. Gütersloh, 2005.
———. *Lebensverstricktheit und Abstandsnahme. "Verhalten zu sich" im Anschluß an Heidegger, Kierkegaard und Hegel*. Tübingen, 2001.
———. "Logos (philosophisch)." In *Religion in Geschichte und Gegenwart (RGG)*. 4th ed. Vol. 7. Columns 498–500.
———. *Martin Heidegger–Phänomenologie der Freiheit*. Vol. 3. Weinheim, 2000.
———. *Martin Heidegger zur Einführung*. 4th ed. Hamburg, 2003.
———. *Nietzsche*. Stuttgart, 1999.
———. "Recht und Moral als Handlungsspielräume." *Zeitschrift für Philosophische Forschung* 36 (1982): 361–77. Reprinted as: "Recht und Moral bei Kant, Cohen und Benjamin." In *Materialen zur Neukantianismus-Diskussion*, ed. Heinz-Ludwig Ollig, 163–83. Darmstadt, 1987.
———. "Selbstverstehen in instabiler Freiheit. Die hermeneutische Position Martin Heideggers." In *Hermeneutische Positionen. Schleiermacher–Dilthey–Heidegger–Gadamer*, ed. Hendrik Birus, 89–119. Göttingen, 1982.
———. "Substanz." In *Religion in Geschichte und Gegenwart (RRG)*. 4th ed. Vol. 7. Columns 1824–27.
———. "The Doing of the Thing Itself: Gadamer's Hermeneutic Ontology of Langauge." In *The Cambridge Companion to Gadamer*, ed. Robert Dostal, 102–25. Cambridge, UK, 2002.
———. *Theodor W. Adorno. Das Naturschöne als spekulative Gedankenfigur*. Bonn, 1977.

———. "Über das Nichtidentische." In *Adorno im Widerstreit. Zur Präsenz seines Denkens*, ed. Wolfram Ette, Günter Figal, Richard Klein, Günter Peters, 13–23. Freiburg i. Br./München, 2004.

———. "Verbindliche Freiheit. Überlegungen zu einer hermeneutischen Variante der morale par provision." 105–23. In *Conditio Humana–Dynamik des Wissens und der Worte. XVII. Deutscher Kongreß für Philosophie. Leipzig 23–27. September 1996. Vorträge und Kolloquien*, ed. Christoph Hubig, 95–105. Berlin, 1997.

———. "Welt (philosophisch)." In *Religion in Geschichte und Gegenwart (RGG)*. 4th ed. Vol. 8. Tübingen, 2005. Columns 1390–92.

———. "Weltbild (philosophisch)." In *Religion in Geschichte und Gegenwart (RGG)*. 4th ed. Vol. 8. Tübingen, 2005. Columns 1406–07.

———. "Zeit und Erinnerung. Überlegungen im Anschluß an Theunissen, Hegel, und Proust." In *Der Sinn der Zeit*, ed. Emil Angehrn, Christian Iber, Georg Lohmann, and Romano Pocai, 101–11. Weilerswist, 2002.

Flasch, Kurt. *Was ist Zeit?* Frankfurt am Main, 1993.

Frank, Manfred. *Was ist Neostrukturalismus?* 2nd ed. Frankfurt am Main, 1984.

———. *Stil in der Philosophie*. Stuttgart, 1992.

Fränkel, Hermann. *Dichtung und Philosophie des frühen Griechentums*. München, 1962.

Frege, Gottlob. "Über Sinn und Bedeutung (1892)." In Frege, *Funktion, Begriff, Bedeutung*, ed. Günter Patzig, Göttingen, 1962.

Fruchon, Pierre. *L'herméneutique de Gadamer: platonisme et modernité, tradition et intérpretation*. Paris, 1994.

Fulda, Hans Friedrich. "Das Konzept einer entfremdend über uns herrschenden Zeit. Erwärtungen, Einsprüche, Fragen." In *Der Sinn der Zeit*, ed. Emil Angehrn, Christian Iber, Georg Lohmann, Romano Pocai, 85–97. Weilerswist, 2002.

Gadamer, Hans-Georg. "Die Aktualität des Schönen. Kunst als Spiel, Symbol, und Fest (1974)." In *Ästhetik und Poetik I. Kunst als Aussage. Gesammelte Werke*. Vol. 8. 94–142. Tübingen, 1993.

———. "Die phänomenologische Bewegung (1963)." In *Neuere Philosophie I. Hegel, Husserl, Heidegger. Gesammelte Werke*. Vol. 3. 105–46. Tübingen, 1987.

———. "Die Wissenschaft von der Lebenswelt (1972)." In *Neuere Philosophie I. Hegel, Husserl, Heidegger. Gesammelte Werke*. Vol. 3. 147–59. Tübingen, 1987.

———. "Heideggers theologische Jugendschrift." In Martin Heidegger, *Phänomenologische Interpretationen zu Aristoteles. Ausarbeitung für die Marburger und Göttinger Philosophische Fakultät (1922)*, ed. Günther Neumann. 76–86. Stuttgart, 2002.

———. "Hermeneutik als praktische Philosophie." In *Rehabilitierung der praktischen Philosophie. Band 1, Geschichte, Probleme, Aufgaben*, ed. Manfred Riedel, 325–44. Freiburg i. Br., 1972.

———. *Hermeneutik I. Wahrheit und Methode: Gründzuge einer philosophischen Hermeneutik*. 5th ed. *Gesammelte Werke*. Vol. 1. Tübingen, 1986.

———. "Hermeneutik und ontologische Differenz (1989)." In *Hermeneutik im Rückblick. Gesammelte Werke*. Vol. 10. 58–70. Tübingen, 1995.

———. "Lob der Theorie (1980)." *Neuere Philosophie II. Probleme, Gestalten. Gesammelte Werke*. Vol. 4. 37–51. Tübingen, 1987.

---. "Praktisches Wissen (1930)." In *Griechische Philosophie I. Gesammelte Werke.* Vol. 5. 230-48. Tübingen, 1985.

---. "Text und Interpretation (1983)." In *Hermeneutik II. Wahrheit und Methode. Ergänzungen, Register. Gesammelte Werke.* Vol. 2. 2nd ed. Tübingen, 1993. 330-60.

---. "Vom Zirkel des Verstehens (1959)." In *Hermeneutik II. Wahrheit und Methode. Ergänzungen, Register. Gesammelte Werke.* Vol. 2. 2nd ed. 57-65. Tübingen, 1993.

---. "Zur Phänomenologie von Ritual und Sprache (1992)." In *Ästhetik und Poetik I. Kunst als Aussage. Gesammelte Werke.* Vol. 8. 400-40. Tübingen, 1993.

Gander, Hans-Helmuth. *Positivismus als Metaphysik. Voraussetzungen und Grundstrukturen von Diltheys Grundlegung der Geisteswissenschaften.* Freiburg i. Br./München, 1988.

---. *Selbstverständnis und Lebenswelt. Grundzüge einer phänomenologischen Hermeneutik im Ausgang von Husserl und Heidegger.* Frankfurt am Main, 2001.

Gasché, Rodolphe. *The Tain of the Mirror.* Cambridge, Mass., 1986.

Gloy, Karen. "Die Struktur der Augustinischen Zeittheorie im XI. Buch der Confessiones." *Philosophisches Jahrbuch* 95 (1988): 72-95.

Goodman, Nelson. *Ways of Worldmaking.* Indianapolis, 1978.

Greisch, Jean. *Hermeneutik und Metaphysik. Eine Problemgeschichte.* München, 1993.

Grondin, Jean. *Der Sinn für Hermeneutik.* Darmstadt, 1994.

---. *Einführung in die Philosophische Hermeneutik.* Darmstadt, 1991.

---. *Introduction à Hans-Georg Gadamer.* Paris, 1999.

Guthrie, W. K. C. *A History of Greek Philosophy, Vol. III, Part 1: The world of the Sophists.* Cambridge, 1969.

Habermas, Jürgen. *Erkenntnis und Interesse.* 11th ed. Frankfurt am Main, 1994.

---. *Theorie des kommunikativen Handelns.* Two Volumes. Frankfurt am Main, 1981.

---. Hahn, Lewis Edwin, ed. *The Philosophy of Hans-Georg Gadamer, Library of Living Philosophers.* Peru, Ill, 1997.

Hegel, G. W. F. *Grundlinien der Philosophie des Rechts oder Naturrecht und Staatswissenschaft im Grundrisse.* Werke 7. Frankfurt am Main, 1970.

---. *Phänomenologie des Geistes.* Wolfgang Bonsiepen and Reinhard Heede, historische-kritische edition. *Gesammelte Werke,* ed. Rheinisch-Westfälischen Akademie der Wissenschaften. Vol. 9. Hamburg, 1980.

---. *Vorlesungen über die Ästhetik I.* Werke 13. Frankfurt am Main, 1970.

---. *Wissenschaft der Logik I.* Historische-kritische edition. *Gesammelte Werke,* ed. Rheinisch-Westfälischen Akademie der Wissenschaften. Vol. 21. Hamburg, 1985.

Heidebrink, Ludger. "Intensität als Kategorie ästhetischer Erfahrung." In *Musik und Ästhetik.* 10 (1999): 5-27.

Heidegger, Martin. Ἀγχιβασίη. *Ein Gespräch selbstdritt auf einem Feldweg zwischen einem Forscher, einem Gelehrten und einem Weisen.* In Feldweg-Gespräche (1944/45). *Gesamtausgabe.* Vol. 77, ed. Ingrid Schüßler, 1-159. Frankfurt am Main, 1995.

———. "Anmerkungen zu Karl Jaspers 'Psychologie der Weltanschauungen' (1919–21)." In *Wegmarken. Gesamtausgabe*. Vol. 9, ed. Friedrich-Wilhelm von Herrmann, 1–44. Frankfurt am Main, 1976.

———. "Aus einem Gespräch von der Sprache. Zwischen einem Japaner und einem Fragenden (1953/54)." In *Unterwegs zur Sprache. Gesamtausgabe*. Vol. 12, ed. Friedrich-Wilhelm von Herrmann, 76–146. Frankfurt am Main, 1985.

———. *Beiträge zur Philosophie. Gesamtausgabe*. Vol. 65, ed. Friedrich-Wilhelm von Herrmann. Frankfurt am Main, 1989.

———. "Das Ding (1950)." *Vorträge und Aufsätze. Gesamtausgabe*. Vol. 7, ed. Friedrich-Wilhelm von Herrmann. Frankfurt am Main, 2000. 165–87.

———. "Das Ende der Philosophie und die Aufgabe des Denkens." In *Zur Sache des Denkens*. 61–80. Tübingen, 1976.

———. "Der Hinweis." In *Bremer und Freiburger Vorträge. Gesamtausgabe*. Vol. 79, ed. Petra Jaeger, 3–4. Frankfurt am Main, 1994.

———. "Der Satz vom Grund (1955–56)." *Gesamtausgabe*. Vol. 10, ed. Petra Jaeger. Frankfurt am Main, 1997.

———. "Der Spruch des Anaximander." In *Holzwege. Gesamtausgabe*. Vol. 5. Ed. Friedrich-Wilhelm von Herrmann, 321–73. Frankfurt am Main, 1977.

———. *Der Ursprung des Kunstwerks (1935/36)*. In *Holzwege. Gesamtausgabe*. Vol. 5, ed. Friedrich-Wilhelm von Herrmann, 1–74. Frankfurt am Main, 1977.

———. "Der Weg zur Sprache." In *Unterwegs zur Sprache. Gesamtausgabe*. Vol. 12, ed. Friedrich-Wilhelm von Herrmann, 227–58. Frankfurt am Main, 1985.

———. "Die Frage nach der Technik (1953)." In *Vorträge und Aufsätze. Gesamtausgabe*. Vol. 7, ed. Friedrich-Wilhelm von Herrmann, 5–36. Frankfurt am Main, 2000.

———. *Die Grundbegriffe der Metaphysik. Welt–Endlichkeit–Einsamkeit. Gesamtausgabe*. Vol. 29/30, ed. Friedrich-Wilhelm von Herrmann. Frankfurt am Main, 1983.

———. *Die Grundprobleme der Phänomenologie (Sommersemester 1927). Gesamtausgabe*. Vol. 24, ed. Friedrich-Wilhelm von Herrmann. Frankfurt am Main, 1975.

———. *Die Idee der Philosophie und das Weltanschauungsproblem (1919)*. In *Zur Bestimmung der Philosophie. Gesamtausgabe*. Vol. 56/57, ed. Bernd Heimbüchel, 1–117. Frankfurt am Main, 1987.

———. "Die Kunst und der Raum." In *Aus der Erfahrung des Denkens 1910–1976. Gesamtausgabe*. Vol. 13. Ed. Hermann Heidegger, 203–10. Frankfurt am Main, 1983.

———. "Die Sprache (1950)." In *Unterwegs zur Sprache. Gesamtausgabe*. Vol. 12, ed. Friedrich-Wilhelm von Herrmann, 7–30. Frankfurt am Main, 1985.

———. *Einführung in die phänomenologische Forschung. Gesamtausgabe*. Vol. 17, ed. Friedrich-Wilhelm von Herrmann. Frankfurt am Main, 1994.

———. *Einleitung in die Phänomenologie der Religion (1920/21)*. In *Phänomenologie des religiösen Lebens. Gesamtausgabe*. Vol. 60, ed. Matthias Jung and Thomas Regehly, 3–156. Frankfurt am Main, 1995.

———. "Einleitung zu 'Was ist Metaphysik?' (1949)." In *Wegmarken. Gesamtausgabe*. Vol. 9, ed. Friedrich-Wilhelm von Herrmann, 365–83. Frankfurt am Main, 1976.

———. *Grundfragen der Philosophie. Gesamtausgabe.* Vol. 45, ed. Friedrich-Wilhelm von Herrmann. Frankfurt am Main, 1984.
———. *Grundprobleme der Phänomenologie (1919/20). Gesamtausgabe.* Vol. 58, ed. Hans-Helmuth Gander. Frankfurt am Main, 1993.
———. "Hegels Begriff der Erfahrung. (1942/43)." In *Holzwege. Gesamtausgabe.* Vol. 5, ed. Friedrich-Wilhelm von Herrmann, 115–208. Frankfurt am Main, 1977.
———. *Kant und das Problem der Metaphysik. Gesamtausgabe.* Vol. 3, ed. Friedrich-Wilhelm von Herrmann. Frankfurt am Main, 1991.
———. *Logik. Die Frage nach der Wahrheit (1925/26). Gesamtausgabe.* Vol. 21, ed. Walter Biemel. Frankfurt am Main, 1976.
———. "Logos (Heraklit, Fragment 50)." In *Vorträge und Aufsätze. Gesamtausgabe.* Vol. 7, ed. Friedrich-Wilhelm von Herrmann, 211–34. Frankfurt am Main, 2000.
———. "Mein Weg in die Phänomenologie." In *Zur Sache des Denkens.* Tübingen, 1976. 81–90.
———. "Nachwort zu 'Was ist Metaphysik?' (1943)." In *Wegmarken. Gesamtausgabe.* Vol. 9, ed. Friedrich-Wilhelm von Herrmann, 303–12. Frankfurt am Main, 1976.
———. *Nietzsche: Der Wille zur Macht als Kunst. Gesamtausgabe.* Vol. 43, ed.Bernd Heimbüchel. Frankfurt am Main, 1985.
———. "Nietzsches Wort, 'Gott ist tot' (1943)." In *Holzwege. Gesamtausgabe.* Vol. 5, ed. Friedrich-Wilhelm von Herrmann, 209–67. Frankfurt am Main, 1977.
———. *Ontologie (Hermeneutik der Faktizität). Gesamtausgabe.* Vol. 63, ed. Käte Bröker-Oltmanns. Frankfurt am Main, 1988.
———. *Phänomenologische Interpretationen zu Aristoteles (Anzeige der hermeneutischen Situation). Ausarbeitung für die Marburger und Göttinger Philosophische Fakultät (1922).* In *Phänomenologische Interpretationen ausgewählter Abhandlungen des Aristoteles zu Ontologie und Logik, Frühe Freiburger Vorlesung Sommersemester 1922. Gesamtausgabe.* Vol. 62, ed. Günther Neumann. Frankfurt am Main, 2005. Single edition: *Phänomenologische Interpretationen zu Aristoteles. Ausarbeitung für die Marburger und Göttinger Philosophische Fakultät [1922].* ed. Günther Neumann. Stuttgart, 2002.
———. *Platon: Sophistes (Winter 1924/25). Gesamtausgabe.* Vol. 19, ed. Ingeborg Schüßler. Frankfurt am Main, 1992.
———. *Sein und Zeit. Gesamtausgabe.* Vol. 2, ed. Friedrich-Wilhelm von Herrmann. Frankfurt am Main, 1977.
———. "Vom Wesen der Wahrheit (1930)." In *Wegmarken. Gesamtausgabe.* Vol. 9, ed. Friedrich-Wilhelm von Herrmann, 177–202. Frankfurt am Main, 1976.
———. *Vom Wesen der Wahrheit. Zu Platons Höhlengleichnis und Theätet. Gesamtausgabe.* Vol. 34, ed. Hermann Mörchen. Frankfurt am Main, 1988.
———. "Vom Wesen des Grundes (1929)." In *Wegmarken. Gesamtausgabe.* Vol. 9, ed. Friedrich-Wilhelm von Herrmann, 123–75. Frankfurt am Main, 1976.
———. "Vom Wesen und Begriff der φύσις. Aristoteles, Physik B, 1 (1939)." In *Wegmarken. Gesamtausgabe.* Vol. 9, ed. Friedrich-Wilhelm von Herrmann. Frankfurt am Main, 1976. 239–301.
———. "Was ist Metaphysik? (1929)." In *Wegmarken. Gesamtausgabe.* Vol. 9, ed. Friedrich-Wilhelm von Herrmann, 103–22. Frankfurt am Main, 1976.

———. "Zu Ernst Jünger." *Gesamtausgabe*. Vol. 90, ed. Peter Trawny. Frankfurt am Main, 2004.

Held, Klaus. *Lebendige Gegenwart. Die Frage nach der Seinsweise des transzendentalen Ich bei Husserl, entwickelt am Leitfaden der Zeitproblematik (Phänomenologica 24)*. Den Haag, 1966.

———. "Phänomenologie der 'eigentlichen Zeit' bei Husserl und Heidegger." *Internationales Jahrbuch für Hermeneutik* (2005):251–72.

Herrmann, Heinrich-Wilhelm von. *Augustinus und die phänomenologische Frage nach der Zeit*. Frankfurt am Main, 1992.

Hesiod, *Opera et dies*. ed. Friedrich Solmsen. Oxford, 1970.

Hilt, Annette. *Ousia–Psyche–Nous: Aristoteles' Philosophie der Lebendigkeit*. Freiburg i. Br./München, 2005.

Hoffmann, Michael. *Die Entstehung von Ordnung: zur Bestimmung von Sein, Erkennen und Handeln in der späteren Philosophie Platons*. Stuttgart, 1996.

Hofmann, Hasso. *Repräsentation. Studien zur Wort-und Begriffsgeschichte von der Antike bis ins 19. Jahrhundert*. Berlin, 1998.

Holzhey, Helmut. "Seele." In *Historisches Wörterbuch der Philosophie*, eds. Joachim Ritter and Karlfried Gründer, Vol. 9, columns 26–52. Basel, 1995.

Honneth, Axel. *Kampf um Anerkennung. Zur moralischen Grammatik sozialer Konflikte*. 2nd ed. Frankfurt am Main, 1998.

Hossenfelder, Malte. "Einleitung." Sextus Empirikus. *Grundriß der phyrrhonischen Skepsis*. Frankfurt am Main, 1968.

Hufnagel, Erwin. *Einführung in die Hermeneutik*. St. Augustin, 2000.

Hühn, Lore. *Fichte und Schelling oder: Über die Grenzen menschlichen Wissens*. Stuttgart, 1994.

Humboldt, Wilhelm von. *Ueber die Verschiedenheit des menschlichen Sprachbaues und ihren Einfluss auf die geistige Entwicklung des Menschengeschlechts (posthum 1836). Werke in fünf Bänden*, eds. Andreas Filtner and Klaus Giel. Vol. III. (Schriften zur Sprachphilosophie). Darmstadt, 1963.

———. *Über die Verschiedenheit des menschlichen Sprachbaues und ihren Einfluß auf die geistige Entwicklung des Menschengeschlects (1830). Wilhelm von Humboldts Werke*, ed. Albert Leitzmann. Vol. 7. First half. Berlin, 1907.

———. "Ueber die Verwandtschaft der Ortsadverben mit dem Pronomen in einigen Sprachen." In *Wilhelm von Humboldts Werke*, ed. Albert Leitzmann, Vol. 6, 58–75. Berlin, 1907.

Husserl, Edmund. *Analysen zur passiven Synthesis (1918–1926). Husserliana* XI, ed Margot Fleischer. Den Haag, 1966.

———. *Cartesianische Meditationen*. In *Cartesianische Meditationen und Pariser Vorträge. Husserliana* I, ed. S. Strasser, 41–193. Den Haag, 1950.

———. *Die Bernauer Manuskripte über das Zeitbewußtsein (1917/18). Husserliana* XXXIII, ed Rudolf Bernet and Dieter Lohmar. Dordrecht/Boston/London, 2001.

———. *Die Idee der Phänomenologie. Husserliana* II, ed. Walter Biemel. Den Haag, 1950.

———. *Ideen zu einer reinen Phänomenologie und phänomenologischen Philosophie. Husserliana* III.1, ed. Karl Schuhmann. Den Haag, 1976.

———. "Kant und die Idee der Transzendentalphilosophie." In *Erster Philosophie (1923/24). Erster Teil. Husserliana* VII, ed. Rodolf Boehm, 230–87. Den Haag, 1956.

———. *Krisis der europäischen Wissenschaften und die transzendentale Phänomenologie. Husserliana* VI, ed. Walter Biemel. Den Haag, 1954.

———. *Logische Untersuchungen. Erster Band. Prolegomena zur reinen Logik. Husserliana* XVIII, ed. Elmar Holenstein. Den Haag, 1975.

———. *Logische Untersuchungen. Zweiter Band, Erster Teil. Husserliana* XIX.1, ed. Ursula Panzer. Den Haag, 1984.

———. *Logische Untersuchungen. Zweiter Band, Zweiter Teil. Untersuchungen zur Phänomenologie und Theorie der Erkenntnis. Husserliana* XIX.2, ed. Ursula Panzer. Den Haag, 1984.

———. "Pariser Vorträge." In *Cartesianische Meditationen und Pariser Vorträge. Husserliana* I, ed. S. Strasser, 1–30. Den Haag, 1950.

———. "Philosophie als strenge Wissenschaft." *Logos.* 1 (1910/11): 289–341.

———. *Vorlesungen zur Phänomenologie des inneren Zeitbewußtseins.* First printing in *Jahrbuch für Philosophischen und phänomenologische Forschung* (1928). 368–490. The lectures are part of *Husserliana* X, ed. Rudolf Boehm. Den Haag, 1966.

Ineichen, Hans. *Philosophische Hermeneutik.* Frieburg i. Br./München, 1991.

Jäger, Ludwig. *Zu einer historischen Rekonstruktion der authentischen Sprach-Idee F. de Saussures.* Düsseldorf, 1975.

Jaspers, Karl. *Psychologie der Weltanschauung.* Berlin, 1919.

Jünger, Ernst. "Die rote Farbe." In *Das abenteuerliche Herz.* 2nd ed. *Sämtliche Werke.* Vol. 9. 232–36. Stuttgart, 1979.

———. "Typus, Name, Gestalt." *Sämtliche Werke.* Vol. 13. 83–174. Stuttgart, 1982.

Kant, Immanuel. *Kritik der reinen Vernunft. Kant's gesammelte Schriften,* ed. Königlichen Preußischen Akademie der Wissenschaften. Vol. III. Berlin, 1911.

———. "Was heißt: sich im Denken zu orientieren?" In *Kant's gesammelte Schriften,* ed. Königlichen Preußischen Akademie der Wissenschaften. Band VIII. 131–47. Berlin 1923.

Kästner, Erhart. *Der Aufstand der Dinge. Byzantinische Aufzeichnungen.* Frankfurt am Main, 1973.

Kierkegaard, Søren. *Begrebet Angest (Begriff der Angst).* In *Samlede Værker,* ed. A. B. Drachmann. Vol. IV, 237–428. Kopenhagen, 1902.

———. *Die Krankheit zum Tode. Der Hohepriester–der Zöllner–die Sünderin,* trans. Emanuel Hirsch. *Gesammelte Werke,* Vol. 24/25, 1–134. Düsseldorf, 1957.

———. *Enten-Eller. Et Livsfragment (Entweder-Oder. Ein Lebensfragment). Samlede Værker,* ed. A. B. Drachmann. Vol. 2. Kopenhagen, 1901.

———. *Gjentagelsen (Die Wiederholung).* In *Samlede Værker,* ed. A. B. Drachmann. Vol. 3, 169–264. Kopenhagen, 1901.

———. *Philosofiske smuler (Philosophische Brocken).* In *Samlede Værker,* ed. A. B. Drachmann. Vol. 4, 171–272. Kopenhagen, 1902.

———. *Sygdommen til Døden. En christelig psykologisk Udrikling til Opbyggelse og Opvækkelse af Anti-Climacus. (Die Krankheit zum Tode. Eine christliche psychologische Erörterung zur Erbauung und Erweckung von Anti-Climacus).*

In *Samlede Værker*, ed. A. B. Drachmann. Vol. XI, 111–241. Kopenhagen, 1905.

Kirk, Geoffrey S. and Raven, John E. *The Presocratic Philosophers*. Cambridge, 1962.

Kisiel, Theodore J. "Das Entstehen des Begriffsfeldes 'Faktizität' im Frühwerk Heideggers." *Dilthey-Jahrbuch* 4 (1986/87):91–120.

Kleist, Heinrich von. "Über die allmähliche Verfertigung der Gedanken beim Reden." In *Sämtliche Werke und Briefe*, ed. Helmut Sembdner, Vol. 2. 321–27. München 1952.

Koller, Hermann. *Die Mimesis in der Antike. Nachahmung, Darstellung, Ausdruck*. Bern, 1954.

Kuhlmann, Hartmut. " 'Jetzt'? Zur Konzeption des νῦν in der Zeitabhandlung Aristoteles (Physik IV 10–14)." In *Zeit, Bewegung, Handlung, Studien zur Zeitabhandlung des Aristoteles*, ed. Enno Rudolph, 63–96. Stuttgart, 1988.

Kühn, Rolf. *Wort und Schweigen. Phänomenologische Untersuchungen zum originären Sprachverständnis*. Hildesheim/Zürich/New York, 2005.

Kuhn, Thomas, S. *The Structure of Scientific Revolutions*. Chicago, 1962.

Lambert, Johann Heinrich. *Neues Organon oder Gedanken über die Erforschung und Bezeichnung des Wahren und dessen Unterscheidung von Irrthum und Schein. Philosophische Schriften*, ed. Hans-Werner Arndt. Vols. 1 and 2. Leipzig, 1965.

Leibniz, Gottfried Willhelm. *Les principes de la philosophie ou la monadologie*. In *Gesammelte Werke*. Vol. 1, ed. Hans Heinz Holz. Darmstadt, 1965.

Lesaar, Henrik R. "Anerkennung als hermeneutischer Prozess." In *Anerkennung. Zu einer Kategorie gesellschaftlicher Praxis*, ed. Has-Helmuth Gander, 45–62. Würzburg, 2004.

Lévinas, Emmanuel. *En découvrant l'existence avec Husserl et Heidegger*. 3rd ed. Paris, 1982.

———. "La philosophie et l'idée de l'infini." In *En découvrant l'existence avec Husserl et Heidegger*. 3rd ed, 165–78. Paris, 1982.

———. "La trace de l'autre." In *En découvrant l'existence avec Husserl et Heidegger*. 3rd ed, 187–202. Paris, 1982.

———. *Totalité et infini. Essai sur l'exteriorité*. Den Haag, 1961.

Lorenzer, Alfred. *Sprachzerstörung und Rekonstruktion, Vorarbeiten zu einer Metatheorie der Pyschoanalyse*. 4th ed. Frankfurt am Main, 1995.

Lukács, Georg. *Geschichte und Klassenbewußtsein. Studien über marxistische Dialektik*. Berlin, 1923.

MacIntyre, Alasdair. *After Virtue. A study in moral theory*. London, 1982.

Majetschak, Stefan. *Ludwig Wittgensteins Denkweg*. Freiburg i. Br./München, 2000.

Makkreel, Rudolf A. *Dilthey. Philosoph der Geisteswissenschaften*. Frankfurt am Main, 1991.

Marquard, Odo. "Kompensation. Überlegungen zu einer Verlaufsfigur geschichtlicher Prozesse." In *Aesthetica und Anaesthetica. Philosophische Überlegungen*. Paderborn/München/Wien/Zürich, 1989. 64–81

Marx, Karl. *Das Kapital. Kritik der politischen Ökonomie. Erster Band. Buch I: Der Produktionsprozeß des Kapitels*. *Marx/Engels Werke (MEW)*. Vol. 23. Berlin, 1962.

———. *Thesen über Feuerbach*. *Marx/Engels Werke (MEW)*. Vol. 3. Berlin, 1958.

Matuschek, Stefan. *Über das Stauen. Eine ideengeschichtliche Analyse*. Tübingen, 1991.
McTaggart, John Ellis. *The Nature of Existence*. Cambridge, 1927.
Merleau-Ponty, Maurice. "Un inèdit de Merleau-Ponty." In *Revue de Métaphysique et de Morale* 67 (1962), ed. Martial Guéroult, 401–09. (German: "Kanditatur am Collège de France." In Merleau-Ponty. *Das Auge und der Geist. Philosophische Essays*, ed. Christian Bermes, 99–110. Hamburg, 2003.).
———. *L'Oeuil et l'esprit*. Paris, 1967.
———. "Le doute de Cézanne." In *Sens et non-sens*, 15–44. Paris, 1958.
———. "Le philosophe et son ombre." In *Signes*, 201–28. Paris, 1960.
———. *Le visible et l'invisible*. Paris, 1964.
———. *Phénoménologie de la perception*. Paris, 1945.
Mesch, Walter. *Reflektierte Gegenwart*. Frankfurt am Main, 2003.
Müller-Lauter, Wolfgang. *Nietzsche. Seine Philosophie der Gegensätze und die Gegensätze seiner Philosophie*. Berlin/New York, 1971.
———. "Nietzsches Lehre vom Willen zur Macht." *Nietzsche-Studien* 3 (1974):1–60.
Nagel, Thomas. "What is it like to be a bat?" In *Mortal Questions*, 65–180. Cambridge, UK, 1979.
Nielsen, Cathrin. *Die entzogene Mitte. Gegenwart bei Heidegger*. Würzburg, 2003.
Nietzsche, Friedrich. *Die fröhliche Wissenschaft*. In *Sämtliche Werke, Kritische Studienausgabe*, eds. Giorgio Colli and Mazzino Montinari. Vol. 3, 343–651. Berlin/New York, 1980.
———. *Jenseits von Gut und Böse*. In *Sämtliche Werke, Kritische Studienausgabe*, eds. Giorgio Colli and Mazzino Montinari. Vol. 5, 9–243. Berlin/New York, 1980.
———. *Nachlaß 1881*. In *Sämtliche Werke, Kritische Studienausgabe*, eds. Giorgio Colli and Mazzino Montinari. Vol. 9. Berlin/New York, 1980.
———. *Nachlaß 1885*. In *Sämtliche Werke, Kritische Studienausgabe*, eds. Giorgio Colli and Mazzino Montinari. Vol. 11. Berlin/New York, 1980.
———. *Nachlaß 1885–86*. In *Sämtliche Werke, Kritische Studienausgabe*, eds. Giorgio Colli and Mazzino Montinari. Vol. 12. Berlin/New York, 1980.
———. *Nachlaß 1886–87*. In *Sämtliche Werke, Kritische Studienausgabe*, eds. Giorgio Colli and Mazzino Montinari. Vol. 12. Berlin/New York, 1980.
———. *Nachlaß 1887–88*. In *Sämtliche Werke, Kritische Studienausgabe*, eds. Giorgio Colli and Mazzino Montinari. Vol. 13. Berlin/New York, 1980.
———. "Ueber Wahrheit und Lüge im aussermoralischen Sinne (1873)." In *Sämtliche Werke, Kritische Studienausgabe*, eds. Giorgio Colli and Mazzino Montinari. Vol. 1, 875–97. Berlin/New York, 1980.
———. "Vom Nutzen und Nachtheil der Historie für das Leben (Unzeitgemässe Betrachtung II)." In *Sämtliche Werke, Kritische Studienausgabe*, eds. Giorgio Colli and Mazzino Montinari. Vol. 1, 243–334. Berlin/New York, 1980.
———. *Zarathustra* II. In *Sämtliche Werke, Kritische Studienausgabe*, eds. Giorgio Colli and Mazzino Montinari. Vol. 4, 103–90. Berlin/New York, 1980.
———. *Zur Genealogie der Moral*. In *Sämtliche Werke, Kritische Studienausgabe*, eds. Giorgio Colli and Mazzino Montinari. Vol. 5, 245–412. Berlin/New York, 1980.
Ostenfeld, Erik. *Ancient greek psychology and the modern mind-body debate*. Aarhus, 1987.

Parmenides. *Vom Wesen des Seienden. Die Fragmente*, ed., trans., and elucidated by Uvo Hölscher. Frankfurt am Main, 1969.
Pindar. *Siegeslieder*, ed., trans., introduction by Dieter Bremer. München, 1992.
Plato. *Philebos. Übersetzung und Kommentar von Dorothea Frede*. Göttingen, 1997.
Plato's dialogues are cited from *Platonis Opera*. Edited by John Burnet. Oxford 1900-07.
Plessner, Helmuth. *Die Stufen des Organischen und der Mensch (1928). Gesammelte Schriften*. Vol. 4, ed. Günter Dux. Frankfurt am Main, 1981.
———. *Grenzen der Gemeinschaft. Eine Kritik des sozialen Radikalismus (1924)*. In *Macht und Menschliche Natur. Gesammelte Schriften*. Vol. 5, eds. Günter Dux, Odo Marquard, and Elisabeth Ströker. Frankfurt am Main, 1981. (Rpt Darmstadt, 2003)
Pöggler, Otto. *Heidegger und die hermeneutische Philosophie*. Freiburg im Breisgau/München, 1983.
Polanyi, Michael. *Personal Knowledge. Towards a post-critical philosophy*. London, 1973.
———. *The Tacit Dimension*. Garden City, NY.
Proust, Marcel. *A la recherche du temps perdu. Édition publiée sous la direction de Jea-Yves Tadié (Bibliothéque de la Pléiade)*, I–IV. Paris, 1987-89.
Quintilian. *Institutio Oratoria*. Book IV. Cf. The Institutio Oratoria of Quintilian edition in four volumes, trans. H. E. Buttler. Vol. III. Cambridge/London, 1921.
Rausch, Hannelore. *Theorie. Von ihrer sakralen zur philosophischen Bedeutung*. München, 1982.
Recki, Birgit. " 'Tragödie der Kultur' oder 'dialektische Struktur des Kulturbewußtseins'? Der ethische Kern der Kontroverse zwischen Simmel und Cassirer." *Internationale Zeitschrift für Philosophie* (2000):157-75.
———. *Aura und Autonomie. Zur Subjektivität der Kunst bei Walter Benjamin und Theodor W. Adorno*. Würzburg, 1988.
Rese, Freiderike. *Praxis und Logos bei Aristoteles. Handlung, Vernunft und Rede in Nikomachischer Ethik, Rhetorik und Politik*. Tübingen, 2003.
Ricoeur, Paul. *De l'interprétation. Essai sur Freud*. Paris, 1965.
———. "La fonction herméneutique de la distanciation." In *Du texte à l'action. Essais d'herméneutique II*, 101-17. Paris, 1986.
———. "Phénoménologie et herméneutique: en venant de Husserl." In *Du texte à l'action. Essais d'herméneutique II*, 39-73. Paris, 1986.
Riedel, Manfred, ed. Edited by *Die Rehabilitierung der praktischen Philosophie*. Freiburg i. Br., 1972.
———. *Für eine zweite Philosophie. Vorträge und Abhandlungen*. Frankfurt am Main, 1988.
———. *Hören auf die Sprache: die akromatische Dimension der Hermeneutik*. Frankfurt am Main, 1990.
———. *Verstehen oder Erklären? Zur Theorie und Geschichte der hermeneutischen Wissenschaften*. Stuttgart, 1978.
Ritter, Joachim. "Landschaft. Zur Funktion des Ästhetischen in der modernen Gesellschaft." In *Schriften der Gesellschaft zur Föderung der Westfälischen Wilhelms-Univeristät Münster*. Vol. 45. Münster, 1963. Rpt in Ritter. *Subjektivität. Sechs Aufsätze*. Frankfurt am Main, 1974. 141-63.

Rohde, Erwin. *Psyche: Seelencult und Unsterblichkeitsglaube der Griechen*. 3rd ed. Tübingen, 1903.
Rorty, Richard. *Contingency, Irony, Solidarity*. Cambridge, 1989.
———. *Philosophy and the Mirror of Nature*. Princeton, New Jersey, 1979.
———. *Solidarität oder Objektivität?* Stuttgart, 1986.
Rudolph, Enno. *Zeit und Gott bei Aristoteles aus der Perspektive der protestantischen Wirkungsgeschichte*. Stuttgart, 1986.
Ryle, Gilbert. *The Concept of Mind*. London, 1949.
Sallis, John. *Force of Imagination*. Bloomington, 2000.
———. *On Translation*. Bloomington, 2002.
———. *Phenomenology and the Return of Beginnings*. 2nd ed. Pittsburgh, PA, 2003.
Sandkaulen, Birgit. "Helmuth Plessner: Über die 'Logik der Öffentlichkeit.'" *Internationale Zeitschrift für Philosophie* (1994):255–73.
Saussure, Ferdinand de. *Cours de linguistique générale*. Edition critique préparée et éditée par Tullio de Mauro. Paris, 1972.
Schelling, F. W. J. *Die Weltalter. Fragmente, in den Urfassungen von 1811 und 1813*. Edited by Manfred Schröter. München, 1946.
———. *Philosophische Untersuchungen über das Wesen der menschlichen Freiheit und die damit zusammenhängenden Gegenstände (1809)*. *Sämmtliche Werke*, ed. K. F. A. Schelling. Part I, Vol. 7.
Schlegel, Friedrich. *Über das Studium der griechischen Poesie*. *Kritische Friedrich-Schlegel-Ausgabe*. Vol. 1, ed. Ernst Behler. 217–367. Paderborn/München/Wien, 1979.
———. "Über die Unverständlichkeit." In *Charakteristiken und Kritiken I (1796–1801)*. *Kristische Friedrich-Schlegel-Ausgabe*. Vol. 2, ed. Hans Eichner, 363–72. München/Paderborn/Wien, 1967.
Schleiermacher, F. D. E. *Hermeneutik und Kritik*. Edited by Manfred Frank. Frankfurt am Main, 1977.
———. *Hermeneutik. Nach den Handschriften neu herausgegeben und eingeleitet von Heinz Kimmerle*. Abhandlungen der Heidelberger Akademie der Wissenschaften, Philosophisch-historische Klasse, Jahrgang 1959, zweite Abhandlung. Heidelberg, 1959.
———. *Allgemeine Hermeneutik von 1809/1810*. Edited by Wolfgang Virmond. In *Internationaler Schleiermacher-Kongreß, Berlin 1984*, ed. Kurt-Viktor Selge. Vol. 2, 1270–310. Berlin/New York 1985.
Schmidt, Dennis J. "Words on Paper." In *Lyrical and Ethical Subjects. Essays on the Periphery of the Word, Freedom, and History*, 131–40. Albany, NY, 2005.
Schmidt, Ernst A. *Zeit und Geschichte nach Augustin*. Heidelberg, 1985.
Schmidt-Wiborg, Petra. *Dialektik in Platons Philebos*. Tübingen, 2005.
Schmitt, Carl. *Der Begriff des Politischen*. 2nd ed. Hamburg, 1932.
———. *Römischer Katholizismus und politische Form*. 2nd ed. München, 1925.
Schmitz, Hermann. *Der unerschöpfliche Gegenstand: Grundzüge der Philosophie*. Bonn, 1990.
———. *Die Ideenlehre des Aristoteles. Kommentar zum 7. Buch der Metaphysik*. Bonn, 1985.
———. *System der Philosophie, zweiter Band, erster Teil: der Leib*. Bonn, 1965.
———. *Der Ursprung des Gegenstands. Von Parmenides bis Demokrit*. Bonn, 1988.

Scholz, Oliver R. *Verstehen und Rationalität. Untersuchungen zu den Grundlagen von Hermeneutik und Sprachphilosophie*. Frankfurt am Main, 2001.
Schopenhauer, Arthur. *Die Welt als Wille und Vorstellung. Arthur Schopenhauer's sämmtliche Werke*. Edited by Julius Frauenstädt. 2nd ed. Leipzig, 1877. Vol. 2. *Die Welt als Wille und Vorstellung*.
Schultz, Walter. *Metaphysik des Schwebens. Untersuchungen zur Geschichte der Ästhetik*. Pfullingen, 1985.
Schütt, Hans-Peter. *Die Adoption des "Vaters der modernen Philosophie." Studien zu einem Gemeinplatz der Ideengeschichte*. Frankfurt am Main, 1998.
Schwemmer, Oswald. *Cassirer. Ein Philosoph der europäischen Moderne*. Berlin, 1997.
Searle, John R. *Speech Acts. An essay in the Philosophy of Language*. Cambridge, Mass., 1969.
Sextus Empiricus. *Pyrrhoniae Hypotyposes (Pyrrhonische Skepsis)*.
Simmel, Georg. *Der Begriff und die Tragödie der Kultur*. In *Das individuelle Gesetz. Philosophische Exkurse*. Edited by Michael Landmann. Frankfurt am Main, 1968.
———. *Die Religion*. Frankfurt am Main, 1912.
Simon, Josef. *Philosophie des Zeichens*. Berlin, 1989.
Snell, Bruno. *Die Entdeckung des Geistes, Studien zur Entstehung des europäischen Denkens bei den Griechen*. 4th rev. ed. Göttingen, 1975.
Sparn, Walter. "Fromme Seele, wahre Empfindung und ihre Aufklärung. Eine historische Anfrage an das Paradigma der Subjektivität." In *Subjektivität im Kontext. Erkundungen im Gespräch mit Dieter Henrich*, eds. D. Korsch and J. Dierken, 29–48. Tübingen, 2004.
Stegmaier, Werner. *Philosophie der Fluktuanz. Dilthey und Nietzsche*. Göttingen, 1992.
Steiner, George. *Real Presences. Is there anything in what we say?* London.
Szlezák, Thomas. *Platon und die Schriftlichkeit der Philosophie*. Berlin/New York, 1985.
Theunissen, Michael. *Das Selbst auf dem Grund der Verzweiflung*. Frankfurt am Main, 1991.
———. *Der Andere*. Berlin, 1965.
———. *Negative Theologie der Zeit*. Frankfurt am Main, 1991.
———. "Philosophische Hermeneutik als Phänomenologie der Traditionsaneignung." In *"Sein, das verstanden weden kann, ist Sprache." Hommage an Hans-Georg Gadamer*. 61–88. Frankfurt am Main, 2001.
———. *Pindar. Menschenlos und Wende der Zeit*. München, 2000.
Torstrik, Adolf. " "Ο ποτε ὄν: ein Beitrag zur Kenntnis der aristotelischen Sprachgebrauches." In *Rheinisches Museum* 12. 1857.
Tugendhat, Ernst. *Der Wahrheitsbegriff bei Husserl und Heidegger*. 2nd ed. Berlin, 1970.
———. *Vorlesungen zur Einführung in die sprachanalytische Philosophie*. Frankfurt am Main, 1976.
Valéry, Paul. *Cahiers, édition établiée, présentée et annotée par Judith Robinson-Valéry (Bibliothéque de la Pléiade)*. Vol. I. Paris, 1973.
Vattimo, Gianni. *La fine della Modernità*. Mailand, 1985.

Vigo, Alejandro G. "Die aristotelische Auffassung der praktischen Wahrheit." *Internationale Zeitschrift für Philosophie* (1998):285-308.
Volpi, Franco. "Chronos und Psyche. Die aristotelische Aporie von Physik IV, 14, 223 a 16-29." In *Zeit, Bewegung, Handlung, Studien zur Zeitabhandlung des Aristoteles*, ed. Enno Rudolph, 26-62. Stuttgart, 1988.
Waldenfels, Bernhard. *Antwortregister*. Frankfurt am Main, 1994.
———. *Das leibliche Selbst. Vorlesungen zur Phänomenologie des Leibes*, ed. Regula Guiliani. Frankfurt am Main, 2000.
———. "Die verändernde Kraft der Wiederholung." *Zeitschrift für Ästhetik und allgemeine Kunstwissenschaft* 46 (2001):5-17.
———. *In den Netzen der Lebenswelt*. Frankfurt am Main, 1985.
———. *Phänomenologie der Aufmerksamkeit*. Frankfurt am Main, 2004.
Wartenburg, Graf Paul Yorck von. *Bewußtseinsstellung und Geschichte. Ein Fragment aus dem philosophischen Nachlass*, ed., introduction Iring Fetscher. Tübingen, 1956.
Wesche, Tilo. *Kierkegaard: eine philosophische Einführung*. Stuttgart, 2003.
Wieland, Wolfgang. *Die aristotelische Physik*. 2nd ed. Göttingen, 1970.
Wittgenstein, Ludwig. *Philosophische Bemerkungen. Schriften* 2. Frankfurt am Main, 1970.
———. *Philosophische Untersuchungen. Schriften* 1. 279-544. Frankfurt am Main, 1960.
———. *Tractatus logico-philosophicus. Schriften* 1. 7-83. Frankfurt am Main, 1960.
———. *Wittgenstein und der Wiener Kreis. Schriften* 3. ed. from the unpublished writings B. F. McGuinness. Frankfurt am Main, 1967.
Wright, Georg Henrik von. *Explanation and Understanding*. London/Ithaca, NY, 1971.
Zahavi, Dan. "Husserl's Noema and the Internalism-Externalism Debate." *Inquiry* 47/1 (2004): 42-66.

Index of Names

Abel, Günter, 359, 371, 372
Adorno, Theodor W., xxvi, 115, 388
Anaximander, 253, 264
Anz, Heinrich, 364
Apel, Karl-Otto, 360
Arendt, Hannah, 362, 373, 377, 386
Aristotle, xvii, xix, xxii, xxv, 18–23, 71, 119, 124, 157–165, 171–172, 176, 183, 184, 186, 187, 194, 204–205, 211, 219, 226, 228, 254, 255, 259–270, 271, 273, 274, 286, 288, 300, 301, 303, 308–321, 324, 329, 330, 333, 334–336, 339–342, 347, 364, 367, 384
Arpe, Curt, 397
Ast, Friedrich, 362
Augustine, xxii, 206, 207, 269–273, 274, 278, 283, 284
Austin, John L., 386

Barbarić, Damir, 356
Barth, Ulrich, 398
Baßler, Moritz, 379
Benjamin, Walter, 25, 26, 31, 138, 183, 184
Bernet, Rudolf, 381, 392
Bieri, Peter, 374, 393
Blumenberg, Hans, 356–357, 368, 371, 372, 377, 388, 393
Boehm, Gottfried, 360, 368
Borsche, Tilman, 380
Bühler, Karl, 379
Burbidge, John, 386

Carnap, Rudolf, 381
Cassirer, Ernst, 109, 110, 112, 193, 200, 388

Cézanne, Paul, 115
Chillida, Eduardo, 337
Chladni, Ernst, 359
Cicero, Marcus Tullius, 386
Claesges, Ulrich, 369
Crescenzi, Luca, 365

Dannhauer, Johann Conrad, 349
Davidson, Donald, 358, 379, 381
Deleuze, Gilles, xvii, 295
Deniau, Guy, 349
Derrida, Jacques, xxi, xxii, 2, 216, 225–233, 237, 241, 247, 361, 386
Descartes, René, 32, 33, 36–39, 42, 137, 138, 185, 369
Dewey, John, xxv
Di Cesare, Donatella, 349, 378, 379, 382
Dierks, Sonja, 387
Dihle, Albrecht, 401
Dilthey, Wilhelm, 1, 6, 9, 80, 89–94, 96, 146, 395
Dostal, Robert J., 349
Droysen, Johann Gustav, 89

Ebert, Theodor, 373
Eco, Umberto, 380
Enskat, Rainer, 392
Enzensberger, Hans Magnus, 379

Fichte, Johann Gottlieb, 105, 305, 346, 358, 376
Figal, Günter, 352, 360, 361, 363, 366, 367, 371, 372, 373, 374, 375, 376, 379, 382, 388, 389, 390, 394, 401, 402
Flasch, Kurt, 391
Frank, Manfred, 364, 381

Frede, Dorothea, 387
Frege, Gottlob, xx, 213–218
Friedrich, Caspar David, 115
Fruchon, Pierre, 349
Fulda, Hans Friedrich, 393

Gadamer, Hans-Georg, xi, xii, xiv, xvi,
    xx, xxi, xxvi, 1–3, 5–17, 21–24, 39, 53,
    57, 59, 72–75, 77, 80, 81, 92, 94–96,
    103, 112, 196, 361, 372, 384, 386, 394
Gander, Hans-Helmuth, 350, 372
Gasché, Rodolphe, 385
Georges, Karl Ernst, 392
Gloy, Karen, 391
Goethe, Johann Wolfgang, 105, 114,
    118fn, 359
Gould, Glenn, 98
Greisch, Jean, 349
Grondin, Jean, 349, 352, 386–387
Guthrie, W. K. C., 398

Habermas, Jürgen, 1, 2, 363, 386
Hahn, Lewis E., 349
Hegel, G. W. F., 6, 7, 8, 10–14, 23, 51,
    75, 108, 109, 112, 124, 142, 194, 202,
    205, 346, 375, 376
Heidbrink, Ludger, 357
Heidegger, Martin, xiii, xiv–xvii, xxii–xxiv,
    xxvi, 1, 8–21, 23, 24, 30, 32–42, 44, 49,
    66, 80, 90–93, 101, 110–114, 123, 128,
    134–139, 142, 146–151, 160, 169–174,
    177, 178, 185, 193–197, 204, 205, 208,
    209, 211, 212, 226, 228, 230, 236, 253,
    254, 259, 261, 262, 286–292, 300–302,
    309, 312, 314, 315, 317, 318, 323, 329,
    345, 347, 359, 360, 376, 379, 391, 397
Held, Klaus, 392
Heraclitus, 60, 315
Herrmann, Friedrich-Wilhelm von, 391
Hesiod, 31
Hilt, Annette, 399
Hippolitos, 398
Hoffmann, Michael, 388
Hofmann, Hasso, 377
Hölscher, Uvo, 355
Holzhey, Helmut, 398

Homer, 316
Honneth, Axel, 376
Hossenfelder, Malte, 352
Hufnagel, Erwin, 349
Hühn, Lore, 358
Humboldt, Wilhelm von, 192–196, 212,
    216, 228, 385, 386
Husserl, Edmund, xiv, xvii, xx–xxii, xxiv,
    9, 11, 13, 16–17, 24, 39, 66, 110–112,
    123–133, 150, 151, 172, 215, 216, 218,
    220, 221, 223, 228, 230, 232, 270,
    272–278, 300, 304, 306, 329, 346, 351

Ineichen, Hans, 349

Jäger, Ludwig, 378
Jaspers, Karl, 371
Jünger, Ernst, 362, 382, 402

Kafka, Franz, 105
Kant, Immanuel, xvi, xvii, xxii, 105, 119,
    137, 141, 142, 147, 149, 150, 152, 166,
    168, 179, 258, 272, 353
Kästner, Erhart, 115
Kierkegaard, Søren, xviii, xxvi, 13, 155,
    295, 296, 339, 340, 345, 346, 377, 394
Kirk, Geoffrey S., 388
Kisiel, Theodore J., 351
Kleist, Heinrich von, 378
Koller, Hermann, 361
Kuhlmann, Hartmut, 389, 390
Kühn, Rolf, 381
Kuhn, Thomas, 28

Lambert, Johann Heinrich, 124
Leibniz, Gottfried Wilhelm, 53, 148, 346
Lesaar, Henrik R., 386
Lévinas, Emmanuel, 300, 376, 386
Lévi-Strauss, Claude, 231
Liddell, Henry G., 397
Lorenzer, Alfred, 363
Lukács, Georg, 366

MacIntyre, Alasdair, 376
Majetschak, Stefan, 382
Makkreel, Rudolf A., 364

Marquard, Odo, 355
Marx, Karl, 108, 360
Matuschek, Stefan, 357
McTaggart, John Ellis, 390
Merleau-Ponty, Maurice, xiii, xvii, 20, 115, 132–134, 233, 234, 306, 322, 324, 332, 368, 400
Mesch, Walter, 389, 390, 391
Minkowski, Ernst, 370
Molière, 71
Monet, Claude, 27, 138
Morandi, Giorgio, 116, 117
Mozart, Wolfgang Amadeus, 98
Müller-Lauter, Wolfgang, 359

Nagel, Thomas, 380
Newman, Barnett, 222
Nielsen, Cathrin, 374
Nietzsche, Friedrich, 37, 51–55, 87, 108, 148–150, 223, 225, 251, 281, 295, 302, 346, 347, 394

Ostenfeld, Erik, 398

Parmenides, 31, 32, 33, 37, 42, 129, 185, 255
Pindar, 281
Plato, xix, xxiv, xxv, 15, 18, 26, 35–37, 40, 42, 43, 46, 47, 59, 60, 68, 69, 72, 101, 106, 119, 121, 122, 124, 175–178, 185, 188, 197, 204, 223, 225, 226, 228, 240–250, 280, 286, 316, 329, 335, 340–344, 346, 347, 357, 360, 363, 380, 386, 389
Plessner, Helmuth, 180–183, 303–306, 308, 395
Pöggeler, Otto, 351
Polanyi, Michael, 363
Proust, Marcel, xxiii, 27, 295–298, 301, 334, 335

Quintilian, Marcus Fabius, 360

Rausch, Hannelore, 377
Raven, John E., 388
Recki, Birgit, 366, 370

Rese, Friederike, 373
Ricoeur, Paul, 1, 84, 361, 368
Riedel, Manfred, 17, 360, 379
Ritter, Joachim, 23
Rohde, Erwin, 398
Rorty, Richard, 1, 2, 382
Rudolph, Enno, 389
Ryle, Gilbert, 89, 374, 398

Sallis, John, 359, 390, 396
Sandkaulen, Birgit, 376
Saussure, Ferdinand de, xx, 211–213, 217, 226–228, 232, 249
Schelling, F. W. J., 10, 13, 346
Schiller, Friedrich, 182
Schlegel, Friedrich, 105
Schleiermacher, F. D. E., 1, 5, 80, 89, 95–97, 103, 105, 118, 243
Schmidt, Dennis J., 361
Schmidt, Ernst A., 391
Schmidt-Wiborg, Petra, 387
Schmitt, Carl, 43, 44, 377
Schmitz, Hermann, 366, 369, 397, 400
Scholz, Oliver R., 358
Schopenhauer, Arthur, 346, 347
Schulz, Walter, 358
Schütt, Hans-Peter, 391
Schwemmer, Oswald, 388
Scott, Robert, 397
Searle, John R., 386
Sextus Empiricus, 352
Shakespeare, William, 105
Simmel, Georg, 108, 109, 372
Simon, Josef, 383
Simonides, 35
Snell, Bruno, 398, 400, 402
Socrates, xxiv, 18, 37, 68, 69, 175–177, 340–342, 357, 382, 387
Sparn, Walter, 398
Stegmaier, Werner, 366
Steiner, George, 361
Szlesák, Thomas, 361

Tarski, Alfred, 381
Theiler, Willy, 399
Theunissen, Michael, 281, 352, 386, 402

Torstrik, Adolf, 389
Tugendhat, Ernst, 353, 381

Valéry, Paul, 378, 379
Vattimo, Gianni, 1, 2
Vigo, Alejandro G., 353
Volpi, Franco, 389, 390

Waldenfels, Bernhard, 360, 370, 394, 400

Wartenburg, Graf Paul Yorck von, 11, 15, 395
Weidemann, Herrmann, 384
Wieland, Wolfgang, 384, 389, 397
Wittgenstein, Ludwig, xx, 40, 45, 108, 207, 216–218, 362, 381
Wright, Georg Henrik von, 360

Zahavi, Dan, 367

Index of Subjects

ability to be otherwise [*Anders-sein-können*], 18–19
ability, being able to [*Können*], xviii, 19, 64, 90, 91, 103, 115, 318–319, 325, 346
  freedom as possibility of being able to [*Freiheit als Möglichkeit zu können*], 155
abstraction [*Abstraktion*], 111, 117
  in Husserl, 220
across from [*Gegenüber*], 115–116
action [*Handeln, Handlung*], 20–22, 45, § 17, 91
  communicative [*kommunikatives*], 2, 238
  elementary [*elementares*], 160–161
  enactment of [*Handlungsvollzug*], 167
  schema of [*Handlungsschema*], 166–168
activity [*Tun*], 18, 22, 65, 67, 74–75, 82, 93–94, 99, 144, 279
  mediatory [*vermittelndes*], 184
actuality [*Wirklichkeit*], 19, 67, 97–100, 158, 194, 321–322. *See also* reality
affect [*Affekt*], 54–55, 206
affection [*Widerfahrnis*], 6, 39, 43, 45, 194, 285–286, 292–294, 325–326
affirmation [*Zusprechung*], 204
agreement [*Verständigung*], 36, 37
aim [*Ziel*], 18
  of an action [*einer Handlung*], 156–159
aiming at [*Abzielen*], 158
alien, the [*Fremdes*], 14, 233–234
allegory [*Allegorie*], 84

also otherwise [*auch anders*], 18, 156, 159, 167, 184–185
announcement [*Kundgabe*], 10–11
answer [*Antwort*], 58–60
  and philosophy [*und Philosophie*], 44–45
anxiety [*Angst*], 34–35, 40, 41, 289–291, 345
appearance [*Erscheinung*], 29, 53, 117, § 14, 131, 151, 322
  in Plessner, 181
  of things [*der Dinge*], 51
  of things in time [*der Dinge in der Zeit*], 258
appearing, appearance [*Erscheinen*], 25, 117, § 14, 138–139, 151–152, 322
application [*Applikation*], 22
apprehension [*Vernehmen*], 88, 333. *See also* perception
appropriation [*Aneignung*], 49–51, 95, 134, 138
archetype [*Urbild*], 37, 74
arrival [*Ankommen*], 145, 253, 275–276
art [*Kunst*]
  as fine art [*schöne Kunst*], 6–8, 68, 75, 115, 117, 119, 138, 148
  as τέχνη, 19, 64, 103, 240, 242, 309
art, piece of [*Kunststück*], 19, 64, 115
articulation [*Artikulation*], 56, 202, 250
artifact [*Artefakt*], 309, 312–313
artwork, work of art [*Kunstwerk*], 11, 13, 23, 27, 75, 117–119
as, hermeneutical [*Als, hermeneutische*], 49–50
asserting [*Behaupten*], 198, 238

425

assimilation [*Assimilation*], 52, 65, 320
astonishment [*das Staunen*], 40
attentiveness [*Aufmerksamkeit*], 10–11, 40, 69–70, 242, 271, 284–285
  in listening [*beim Hören*], 195–197
  in showing [*beim Zeigen*], 201
attitude [*Einstellung*], 37, 42, 54, 152
  everyday [*alltägliche*], 24
  methodologically directed [*methodisch gelenkte*], 6–7
  natural [*natürliche*], 16, 125–126, 127–128, 150–151
  phenomenological [*phänomenologische*], 24
  shift of attitude [*Wechsel der Einstellung*], 184–185
  toward temporality [*zur Zeitlichkeit*], 284–285
aura [*Aura*], 138
authenticity [*Eigentlichkeit, Authentizität*], 14–15

becoming [*Werden*], 25–26
  and passing away [*und Vergehen*], 253–254
beholder [*Betrachter*], 16, 24. See also viewer
being [*Sein*], 4, 10–11, 20–21, 23, 26, 40, 41, 44, 90, 93, 111, 131, 146–147, 150, 314–323
  constitution of [*Seinsverfassung*], 137
  ethical [*sittliches*], 22
  historical [*geschichtliches*], 12, 14
  without self [*selbstloses*], 13
being able to [*Können*]. See ability
being directed toward [*Sich hinweisen auf*], 198. See also reference
being-there [*Dasein*], 40–41. See also Dasein; existence
being-withdrawn [*Entzogensein*], 25, 40, 43
being, understanding of [*Seinsverständnis*], 20, 301
beings [*Seiendes*], 18, 18fn, 31, 112, 134, 135–136. See also what is
  being [*Seiendheit*], 311
  as a whole [*im Ganzen*], 33–35

beings as beings [*Seiendes als Seiendes*] (ὄν ᾗ ὄν), 19, 172, 301
between [*Zwischen*], 40, 46–47
blink of the eye [*Augenblick*], 40. See also moment
body [*Körper*], xxv, 306, 316–318, § 39
body quick [*Leib*], xxv, § 39. See also movement of the body
book [*Buch*], 61–64, 72
boredom [*Langeweile*], 34, 291–292
boundedness [*Bindung*], 44, 148, 295
bringing forth [*Hervorbringen*], 157, 335
bringing into language [*zur Sprache bringen*]. See putting into language

caricature [*Karikatur*], 70
carrying over [*Übertragung*], 46 § 7, 72, 180–181
cave, allegory of [*Höhlengleichnis*], 377
certainty [*Gewißheit*], 6
  loss of [*Verlust an*], 6
  uncertainty [*Ungewißheit*], 39
change [*Veränderung*], 263, 286, 309. See also transformation
chiasmus (also fold [*Verschränkung*]), 99, 152, 233, 275, 306, 307, § 36, 322
Christianity [*Christentum*], 119, 147
circle, hermeneutical [*Zirkel, hermeneutischer*], 80, 81
claiming [*Ansprechen*], 8, 16, 236
clarification (i.e., in interpretation) [*Deuten*], xv, 5, 83, 86, 122
clarification [*Klärung*], 21, 23, 28, 35, 68
  and interpretation [*Interpretation*], 57–58
  self-clarification [*Selbstklärung*], 3
clearing [*Lichtung*], 128
clock [*Uhr*], 253, 261–262, 280
clockwise [*Uhrzeigersinn*], 61
cogito, 32, 127
  pure [*reines*], 9, 11
  of the thinking subject [*denkendes Subjekt*], 132
cognition [*Erkenntnis*], 17. See also knowledge; recognition
  theory of [*Erkenntnistheorie*], 5, 6

Index of Subjects 427

coming to the fore [*Hervorkommen*], 222, 319
commentary [*Kommentar*], 5, 85
communication [*Mitteilung*], 58, 233, 235
community [*Gemeinschaft*], 177, 180
complementarity [*Komplementarität*], 31, 86
completion [*Vollendung*], 18-19
  first [*erste*], 317
complexity [*Komplexität*], 56, 335
comprehension [*Nachvollzug*], 83, 84, 89, 90, 94, 100, 181
concept [*Begriff*], 14-15, 30, 49, 194
  and matter [*und Sache*], 39
  conceptual thinking [*Begriffsdenken*], 10
  formation of [*Begriffsbildung*], 16, 23
concern [*Fürsorge*], 176
condition [*Bedingung*], 25
conduct [*Verhalten*], 18, 27, 68-71, 72, 113-114, 116, 156, 209, 324
  mimetic [*mimetisches*], 69
  directed at oneself [*zu sich*], xxv, 337-339
connections [*Verbindungen*], 128, 133, 192-193, 204, 210
conscience [*Gewissen*], 228, 345-346
  call of [*Ruf des*], 228, 346
consciousness [*Bewußtsein*], 11, 17, 110-113, 121, 126-127, 191, 227
  as self-affection [*als Selbstaffektion*], 230
  contemporary [*zeitgenössiches*], 6-7
  disassociation of [*Dissoziationsbewußtsein*], 44
  ethical [*sittliches*], 21
  hermeneutical [*hermeneutisches*], 21-24
  historical [*geschichtliches*], 7
  immanence of [*Bewußtseinsimmanenz*], 110-111, 150
  life of [*Bewußtseinsleben*], 110
  of becoming other [*des Anderswerdens*], 14
constellation [*Konstellation*], § 34, 294
constitution [*Konstitution*], 130, 151, 278-279

constitutive capacity [*konstituierende Leistung*], 304
contemplation [*Betrachtung*], 85, 138-139, 165, § 21, 199
continuity [*Kontinuität*], 14, 15, 78-79, 80
continuum [*Kontinuum*], 274, 276
conversation [*Gespräch*], 1-2, 36-37, 46, 198, 237
corpus, 327
correlate [*Korrelat*], 18, 67, 126-128
correlation [*Korrelation*], 126-129, 152, 201, 284, 294, 301-303, 307-308
counter-point [*Gegen-wort*], 58, 58fn
course [*Verlauf*], 100, 257
cult [*Kultus*], 75, 118
  cultic action [*kultische Handlung*], 183

Dasein, 20-21, 34. See also being-there; existence
  in Heidegger, 9-12, 16, 17, 20, 21, 90, 92-93, 111-112, 134-138, 146-148, 300-301
  de-removing [*Ent-fernung*], 134fn, 134-136, 137-138, 142, 160, 184, 188
  in showing [*beim Zeigen*], 200
decision [*Entscheidung*], 162-163
  of violence [*Gewaltsentscheidung*], 183
deconstruction [*Dekonstruktion*], 2, 225, § 26
  and destructuring [*und Destruktion*], 226-227
deliberation [*Überlegen*], 20, § 18
denial [*Absprechen*], 204
dependency [*Abhängigkeit*], 174-176
destructuring [*Destruktion*], 12, 15, 24, 153
  and deconstruction [*und Dekonstruktion*], 226-227
desire [*Begehren*], 340-344
despair [*Verzweiflung*], 345-346
determinacy [*Bestimmtheit, das Bestimmte*], 18, 34, 145, 203-204
determination [*Bestimmung*], 203-204
  of human nature [*des menschlichen Natur*], 19
  of philosophy [*der Philosophie*], 28

development [*Entwicklung*], 25
devotion of attention [*Zuwendung*], 236
　freedom of [*Freiheit der*], 45–46
dialectic [*Dialektik*], 6, 109
　in Plato, 240–247
différance, 231–232
difference [*Differenz*], 231–232
　and self-presence [*und Selbstgegenwart*], 230
　in language [*in der Sprache*], 211
difference, diversity [*Verschiedenheit*], 7, 29, 31, 96–97, 206, 213
dignity [*Würde*], 179, 183
dimensionality [*Dimensionalität*], 232
dimensions [*Dimensionen*], 4, 137, 143–146, 152–153
direction [*Richtung*], 45, 61, 77
　directing oneself [*Sichrichten*], 199
disclosedness [*Erschlossenheit*], 21, 90
disconcertedness [*Befremdlichkeit*], 40
discovery [*Entdeckung*], 81
dismantling [*Abbau*], 12
　dismantling return [*abbauender Rückgang*], 14–16, 41, 226
　of opinions [*der Meinungen*], 33
disposition [*Disposition*], 279, 317–319
distance [*Abstand*], 3, 15–17, 24, 34, 35–36, 40, 42, 49, 50–51, 69, 95, 115, 128–129, 129fn, 131, 133–134, 137–141, 144–146, 153, 303–304
　as translation of [*Distanz*], 14, 138
　from everyday life [*Abstand vom alltäglichen Leben*], 39
　historical [*geschichtlicher Abstand*], 7
　in Plessner, 182
　in showing [*Abstand beim Zeigen*], 198–200, 209–210
distantiation [*Abstandsnahme*], 16–17
distensio, 271
diversity [*Verschiedenheit*]. See difference
divided line, analogy of [*Liniengleichnis*], 241–244
divination [*Divination*], 95–96
doubt [*Zweifel*], 36–38, 39–40, 43
drawing [*Zeichnen, Zeichnung*], 57, 337–338

dream [*Traum*], 18, 155
　daydream [*Wachtraum*], 31
dubitable, the [*Zweifelhafte, das*], 32
duration [*Dauer*], 26, 253, 278, 285, 294
dynamization [*Dynamisierung*], 225
　of the difference of signs [*der Zeichendifferenz*], 232

earlier [*Früher*], 255–259
　and later [*und Später*], 262–268
effect [*Wirken*], 238. See also work
effectiveness [*Wirkung*], 67
element [*Element*], 192–193, 197, 211, 231, 308–309, 310
elemental, the elementary [*Elementärische, das*], 197, 307–308, 320
embodiment [*Leiblichkeit*], 132, 332–333
emergence [*Hervortreten*], 24, 76, 114, 200–201, 250
enactment [*Vollzug*], 12, 14, 17, 24, 76, 86, 100–101, 257
　character of [*Vollzugscharakter*], 10
　of a reading [*Lesevollzug, Lektürevollzug*], 79–82
enactment, sense of [*Vollzugsinn*], xv, 10–11, 66–67, 91
encounter [*Begegnung*], 42, 44–46, 66–67, 332
end [*Zweck*], 179. See also purpose
　in itself [*an sich selbst*], 179
entering [*Eintreten*], 257, 278
epistemological [*erkenntnistheoretische*], 11. See also cognition: theory of
essence [*Wesen*], 25, 54, 314–315, 318
estimating [*Ermessen*], 142–143, 163–164
ethics [*Ethik*], 21, 23
event [*Ereignis*], 26
　occurrence of openness [*Geschehen des Offenheit*], 173
everydayness, the everyday [*Alltäglichkeit, das Alltägliche*], 16, 35–36, 37, 39–40, 42–45
　break with [*Bruch mit der Alltäglichkeit*], 39
　everyday thought [*alltägliches Denken*], 32

everyday world of things [*alltägliche Dingwelt*], 18
ex-sistence [*Ek-sistence*], 173
exhibit [*Vorzeigen*], 69, 199, 200
existence [*Dasein, Existenz*], 9, 40–41, 43, 53, 126. See also Dasein; being-there
expanse [*Weite*], 130, 135, 143
expectation [*Erwartung*], 269–273
  as experience of time [*als Zeiterfahrung*], 284
  of an answer [*einer Antwort*], 238
experience [*Erfahrung*], 6–7, 28, 32, 56, 64–65, 72, 125, 152, 261–262, 273, 274–275, 277–294
  aesthetic [*ästhetische*], 23
  hermeneutical [*hermeneutische*], 2, 47
  in Hegel, Gadamer, 6–8, 13, 16, 23, 39, 124
  of beings as a whole [*des Seienden im Ganzen*], 33
  of fading [*des Schwindens*], 276
  of space [*von Raum*], 129
  of the "as a whole" [*des "im Ganzen"*], 43
  of the new [*des Neuen*], 295
  of the nothing [*des Nichts*], 34
  of the objective [*des Gegeständlichen*], 2
  of the phenomenal [*des Phänomenalen*], 127–128
  of the world [*der Welt*], 149–150
  of time [*von Zeit*], 270
  philosophical [*philosophische*], 33
explication [*Auslegen*], xv, 5, 83–87, 122. See also interpretation
expression [*Ausdruck*], 215–216
  as voice [*als Stimme*], 234–235
  originary expressive functions [*ursprüngliche Ausdrucksfunktionen*], 15
  of the idea [*Gedankenausdruck*], 192
  in Husserl, 228–229
exterior, the [*Äußere, das*], 60, 65, § 10, 107–108, 112–113, 320
  of feelings and thoughts [*der Gefühle und Gedanke*], 208

exteriority [*Äußerlichkeit*], 52, 61, 65–66, § 10, 96, 107, 111–113, 140, 320
  of the voice [*der Stimme*], 233–234
  of things [*der Dinge*], 114, 116
  representation of [*Vorstellung der*], 141

fabric [*Gewebe*], 56, 61, 65, 76, 96, 98, 138–139
  as texture [*als Textur*], 203–204
  and logos, 204
face [*Anlitz*], 236
facial expression [*Miene*], 206, 234
familiar obviousness [*Selbstverständlichkeit*], 15–16, 24, 41–42. See also nontransparency
  of the everyday [*des Alltäglichen*], 36, 37
familiarity [*Vertrautheit*], 34, 40, 94–95, 102, 135–137
family resemblance [*Familienähnlichkeit*], 76
fear [*Befürchtung, Furcht*], 34, 207, 284, 286–289
festival [*Fest*], 16, 74–75, 294–295
flesh (*chair*) [*Fleisch*], 308
flow [*fluß*]. See also flux; stream
  of occurrence [*des Geschehens*], 281
  of time [*der Zeit*], 274
flux [*fluß*], 108. See also flow; stream
fold [*Verschränkung*]. See chiasmus
for-sake-of-which, the [*Worum-willen*], 171
force [*Kraft*], 25, 52
foreignness [*Fremdheit*], 25, 94, 137, 191
form [*Form*], 25, 27
  as εἶδος, 311–314
  in Kant, 258
  symbolic [*symbolische*], 193
freedom [*Freiheit*], xiii, xviii–xix, 4, 38, 42–43, 144–146, 152, §§ 17–21
  of devoting one's attention [*der Zuwendung*], 44–45
freeing [*Freigabe*], 170, 172, 184
from itself [*von selbst*], 157 [*as of itself*], 308, 319
fulfillment [*Erfüllung*], 65, 86, 88

fullness [*Fülle*], § 42
fundamental mood [*Grundstimmung*], 34–35, 36, 39–41
future [*Zukunft*], 145, 269, 284
   futural [*zukünftig*], 20–21, 283
game, play [*Spiel*], 74–75, 101, 196
   of signs [*Zeichenspiel*], 227
   rules of [*Spielregeln*], 133
geometry [*Geometrie*], 15–16
gesture [*Geste*], 202, 206–208
   as showing [*als Zeigen*], 203–204
   in texture [*in der Textur*], 203–204
God [*Gott*], 13, 46–47, 146
good, the [*Gute, das*], 164–165, 243–245
grasping [*Greifen*], 200
growth [*Wachstum*], §§ 35–42

handicraft [*Handwerkskunst*], 312
handiness [*Zuhandenheit*], 112–113
   what is handy [*Zuhandene, das*], 135–136
happening [*Sich ereignen*], 33. *See also* event
happiness [*Glück, Wohlergehen*], 158, 165
   and memory [*Glück und Erinnerung*], 297
hearing [*Hören*], 61–62, 63, 139, 195, 196
hermeneutical, fact of [*hermeneutischer Sachverhalt*], 3
hermeneutical, the [*Hermneutische, das*], 47, 61, 122, 144
hermeneutics [*Hermeneutik*], §§ 1–6
   of facticity [*der Faktizität*], § 2, 20–21, 110
   of suspicion [*des Verdachts*], 84
   modern [*moderne*], 89
   philosophical [*philosophische*], 89, 122
historicism [*Historismus*], 9, 11
history [*Geschichte*], 6–8, 11–15, 24, 147–148, 293
honor [*Ehre*], 187
hope [*Hoffnung*], 284
horizon [*Horizont*], 14, 151
   intentional [*intentionaler*], 130

horizons, fusion of [*Horizontverschmelzung*], 14, 94
human being [*Mensch*], xxiv, 18–19, 20, 22, 44, 194, 303
human, the [*Menschliche, das*], 5, 113

I [*Ich*], 94, 109–110, 112, 151, 197, 227, 235–236, 237
   cogito, 32
idea [*Gedanke, Idee*], 52, 124–125, 148, 192, 214, 242
   of the good [*Idee des Guten*], 243
   transcendental [*tranzendentale Idee*], 168
idealism [*Idealismus*], 13, 346
image [*Bild*], 18, 42. *See also* picture
   copy and original [*Abbild und Urbild*], 117
imitation (imitatio) [*Nachahmung*], 68–69
immanence [*Immanenz*], 66, 112, 300
   of consciousness [*des Bewußtseins*], 110–111, 150
   of the sense of enactment [*des Vollzugssinn*], 116
immemorial, the [*Unvordenklichkeit*], 10, 12
impartiality [*Unbefangenheit*], 38
in-a-state [*In-einem-Zustand*], 324–326
inaugural, the [*Anfängliche, das*], 15, 41
inauthenticity [*Uneigentlichkeit*], 150
indication [*Anzeichen, Anzeigen*], 30, 200, 203, 317
   indication and expression [*Anzeichen und Ausdruck*] in Husserl, 229
individual thing [*Einzelding*], 263, 267, 311, 334
individuality [*Individualität*], 94–96, 100, 118, 180–183
inheritance [*Überlieferung*], 12–15, 16, 22, 30
inner experience [*Erlebnis*], 11, 17, 110, 124–125, 130–133, 324–325, 362
inner life [*Seelenleben*], 89–90, 93, 96

Index of Subjects   431

insight [*Einsicht*], 6, 13, 15–16, 19, 31, 42, 50–51, 97, 340, 343–344
insistence [*Insistenz*], 173–174
intending [*Meinen*], 13, 86, 198, 202, 213
 as intentionality [*als Intentionalität*], 215
intensification [*Intensivierung*], 43, 70, 201, 327
intensity, degree of intensity [*Intensität, Intensitätsgrad*], 43–44, 47, 201, 284–285, 326–327
intention [*Absicht*], 160, 167, 314
intentionality [*Intentionalität*], 126–127, 215, 277–278, 301, 306
interest [*Befangenheit*], 333
interiority, interior [*Inneres*], 66, 93
internalization [*Verinnerlichung*], 339–340
interpretation [*Auslegung, Interpretation*], xiv–xv, 3, 5, 21, 47, § 7, 121–122, 139. See also explication
 art of [*Kunstlehre der Auslegung, Auslegungskunst*], 1, 10
 in need of [*Interpetationsbedürftig*], 56, 58
 philosophical [*philosophische Auslegung*], 14
 self-interpretation [*Selbstauslegung*], 14
interruption [*Unterbrechung*], 14
intuition [*Anschauung, Intuition*], 11, 16, 124, 221
 hermeneutical [*hermeneutische*], 24
 mantic [*mantische Intuition*], 96

jurisprudence [*Recht*], 178
justice [*Gerechtigkeit*], 35–38, 41, 43, 178, 225

knowledge, knowing [*Erkenntnis, Wissen*], 7, 20, 21–24, 31, 32, 47, 57, 76, 88, 124, 333–334. See also cognition; recognition
 absolute [*absolutes Wissen*], 12–13, 109
 knowing what is good for oneself [*Für-sich-wissen*], 55

 of enactment [*Vollzugswissen*], 89, 91
 possibility of [*Erkenntnismöglichkeit*], 28
 practical [*praktisches Wissen*], 21–23

lack [*Mangel*], § 42
language [*Sprache*], xiii, xviii, xix–xxii, 4, 5, 30, 36–37, 42, 45–46, 51, 62–63, 77, 88, 96, 144–146, 152, §§ 22–28
 thought on [*Sprachdenken*], 11
 language itself [*Sprache selbst*], 196
language game [*Sprachspiel*], 45, 108, 217–218
lassitude [*Gelassenheit*], 32, 39
later [*Später*], 255–259
 and earlier [*und Früher*], 262–268
law [*Gesetz*], 28, 178
leap [*Sprung*], 26, 51
Lebensphilosophie, xxiv, 302
leisure [*Muße*], 32, 36, 38, 42, 45
letting be [*Seinlassen*], 172–173
life [*Leben*], xxiv–xxv, 4, 10–11, 17–20, 22, 23, 44, 47, 53, 108–110, 116–117, 122, 132, 145–146, §§ 35–42
 alien [*fremdes*], 93
 factical [*faktisches*], 9–10, 14, 18, 19
 good [*gutes*], 19, 158, 165
 historical [*geschichtliches*], 13–17
 just [*gerechtes*], 225
 religious [*religiöses*], 146
 understanding of [*Lebensverständnis*], 28
 way of life and life experience [*Lebensführung und Lebenserfahrung*], 36
life force [*Lebenskraft*], 31. See also powers of life
life-world [*Lebenswelt*], 150–152, 208, 210, 300
life, enactment of [*Lebensvollzug*], 10, 66, 116–117
life, form of [*Lebensform*], 27, 315–316, § 38, 331
life, powers of [*Lebenskräfte*], 341, 342. See also life force
life, structure of [*Lebensgefüge*], 337, § 41

limit (πέρας) [Grenze], 26–27, 106–107, 246–247
limit, limitation [Grenze, Begrenzung], 8, 30, 129, 304–305
linguistic enactment [Sprachvollzug], 192
listening [Zuhören], 81–82, 236–238
liveliness [Lebendigkeit], 303, 317, 331
location [Ort], 256–257. See also place
logocentrism [Logozentrismus], 228
look, reciprocal [wechselseitiger Blick], 332
lucidity [Klarheit], 10–11, 23

material [Material, Stoff], 196, 311–312, 335
mathematics [Mathematik], 39
matter [Sache], 2, 6–7, 29, 39, 41–43, 45, 46–47, 55, 64–65, 72–73, 76, 99, 117, 121, 240–241. See also substantiveness; the matter itself
matter itself, the [Sache selbst], 6, 29, 47, 55, 121, 186. See also matter; substantivess
matter of fact [Sachverhalt], 30
meaning [Sinn], 19–20, 22, 24, 36, 150, 156, 198, 216, §34
  in Frege, 213–215
  expectation and fulfillment of [Sinnerwartung und -erfüllung], 80
meaningful, the [Bedeutsame, das], 151. See also significance
means [Mittel], 46, 176, 179, 184, 208, 329. See also medium
measure [Maß, Meßbarkeit], 47, 135, 138–140, 142
mediation [Vermittlung], 46–49, 73–74, 78
medium [Mittel], 133. See also means
memoria, 269, 274
memory [Erinnerung], 26–27, 269–274
  secondary [sekundäre], 277
  primary [primäre], 277
metaphor [Metapher], 30, 51–52, 225
metaphysics [Metaphysik], 2, 11, 33, 34–35, 41, 226, 228
method [Methode], 6, 23, 28, 38–39

mimesis, 68–72
mimetic expression [mimischer Ausdruck], 207
model [Modell], 19, 29–31, 35, 37–38, 42, 47
moment [Augenblick], 15, 17, 18, 20, 296. See also blink of the eye
monads [Monaden], 53–54, 148
mood [Stimmung], 33–34, 41
motility [Bewegtheit], 323–324
movement [Bewegung], 6, 17–18, 157, 309–310, 322–323
  and time [und Zeit], 260–262
  course of [Bewegungsverlauf], 273
  enactment of [Bewegungsvollzug], 272–273
  in space [im Raum], 132
  of all living beings [alles Lebendigen], 308
  of the body [des Leibes], 132–133. See also body quick
multiplicity [Vielheit], 57, 85, 106
  and unity [und Einheit], 246–247
music [Musik], 57, 77, 119, 138
  piece of [Musikstück], 58, 63–64, 71–72

name [Name], 213–214
nation [Nation] in Humboldt, 195
nature [Natur], 23, 27, 303, 314
  human [menschliche], 19
  state of [Naturzustand], 175
neediness [Bedürftigkeit], 175, 177
negativitiy of time [Negativität der Zeit], 275
noema, 111
nonlanguage [Nichtsprache], 240, 243
nonsuppositional [Nichtunterstelltes], 243–245
nontransparency [Unselbstverständlichkeit], 45. See also familiar obviousness
not being there [Nichtdasein], 257
not understanding [Nichtverstehen], 91, 102–104
nothing [Nichts], 34, 40–41, 42, 44

nothingness [*Nichtigkeit*], 16. See also nullity
now [*Jetzt*], 235, 260–265
now point [*Jetztpunkt*], 274
now-time [*Jetzt-Zeit*], 262
nullity [*Nichtigkeit*], 6. See also nothingness
number [*Zahl*], 56, 247–251, 280
   in Aristotle, 259–262
   in Plato, 246–247

object [*Gegenstand*], 10, 11, 22, 107, 107fn, § 13, 121, 139, 199, 213, 215–218, 240
   and [*Gegen-Stand*], 107, 117, 199
   as translation of [*Objekt*], 109–110
objectification [*Objektivierung, Vergegenständlichung*], 108, 110, 112
objective, the [*Gegenständliche, das*], 3, 107, § 13, 121, 138
objectivity [*Gegenständlichkeit*], xii–xiii, 2, § 13, 121, 138, 152, 220
   as translation of [*Objektivität*], 55, 214
occurrence [*Geschehen*], 6, 16, 22, 24, 26, 43, 65, 67, 74, 78, 114, 117–118, 148, 196, 255–258
ontology [*Ontologie*], 8, 10, 12, 19–20, 301
   elevation of the status of [*ontologische Aufwertung*], 23
   ontological basis [*ontologische Basis*], 9
   ontological critique [*ontologische Kritik*], 13
   ontological perspective [*ontologisiche Perspektive*], 41
openness, the open [*Offenheit, das Offene*], 1–3, 7, 10, 16, 20–21, 30, 41, 42, 44–45, 106, 128–129, 131, 143, 196–197, 204–205
   of action [*des Handelns*], 159–160
   of temporality [*der Zeitlichkeit*], 284
   of texture [*der Textur*], 212
opinion [*Meinung*], 6, 31
   everyday [*alltägliche*], 32
order [*Ordnung*], 44, 56, 82, 147, 253–254, 258–259, 343–344
   in language [*in der Sprache*], 198

organ [*Organ*], 33, 318, 329–330
organism [*Organismus*], 331
orientation [*Orientierung*], 19, 133, 137, 209–210
origin [*Ursprung*], 24–26, 31, 34–35, 37, 39, 41–43, 44–46, 245, 312
   moments of [*Ursprungsmomente*], 44–46
original impression [*Urimpression*], 274
originariness [*Ursprünglichkeit*], xiv, 24–31, 33–34, 35, 37–38, 40–41, 43–47, § 37
origination [*Entspringen*], 24–27, 28, 37, 42, 46, 357
otherness, the other [*Andersheit, Anderes*], 14, 46
   historical [*geschichtliche Andersheit*], 13
others [*Anderen, die*], 45, 87, 176–177, 178
outside [*Außen*], 40, 42, 45, 51, 52, § 10, 95, 141, 233–235, 304
outside of [*außerhalb*], 60–61

pacing out [*Ausmessen*], 142
pain [*Schmerz*], 286, 324, 343
painting [*Malerei*], 57, 221–222
paradigm [*Paradigma*], 28
parody [*Parodie*], 70
particular, the [*Besondere, das*], 95, 125
passing away [*Vergehen*], 25–27, 145
   what passes away [*Vergehende, das*], 18
   and becoming [*und Werden*], 253–254
past, the [*Vergangene, das, Vergangenheit*], 8, 14, 94, 269, 283–285
path [*Weg*], 32, 42, 77, 136–137, 142
pausing [*Innehalten*], 16, 38–39, 43, 161, 166, 178, 184, 310
peace [*Ruhe*], 38, 44. See also rest
perception [*Vernehmen, Wahrnehmung*], 20, 90, 125–126, 139–140, 159, 276–278, 319–323
   inner experiences of [*Wahrnehmungserlebnisse*], 131
   recognition and realization [*Erkennen und Realisierung*], 37

perfect, a priori [*Perfekt, a priori*], 59, 170
performance [*Aufführung*], 57–58, 62–63, 64–65, 68–69, 72, 73, 75, 77, 81, 97, 118–119
perspectival [*Perspektivische, das*], 53–54
perspective [*Perspektive*], 53–54, 131, 133, 140, 148–149, 314
perspectivity [*Perspektivität*], 53–54, 331
phasal moment [*Phasenmoment*], 14, 97, 117, 250
phenomenality [*Phänomenalität*], § 14, 201
phenomenology [*Phänomenologie*], 3, 9, 11, 16, 24, 111, 120, § 14
  of the hermeneutical [*des Hermeneutischen*], 153
phenomenon [*Phänomen*], 3, 21, 23, § 14, 151, 201, 220
philosophy [*Philosophie*], §§ 1–6, 110, 119, 121–123, 144
  hermeneutical [*hermeneutische*], xi, xiii–xvi, 146
  in Hegel, 194
  modern [*moderne*], 107–108, 346
  practical [*praktische*], § 3
  theoretical [*theoretische*], 17, 19, 23
phonocentrism [*Phonozentrizmus*], 228
picture [*Bild*], 63, 65, 117–118. See also image
place [*Ort*], 141, 330–332. See also location
  placeless [*ortlos*], 336
  placeless contemplation [*ortlose Betrachtung*], 187
play (i.e., theatrical) [*Schauspiel*], 57, 70, 72, 74
play [*Spiel*]. See game
pleasure [*Lust*], 286, 324, 340, 343
poetry, poesy, poem [*Dichtung, Gedicht*], 11, 27, 57, 68, 71, 88, 106, 118–119, 123, 148
pointing [*Zeigen*], 83. See also showing
pointing out, to [*Aufzeigen, Hinzeigen*], 69, 83, 86, 201, 204
political, the [*Politische, das*], 35, 43–44

position [*Position*], 199, § 27
positionality [*Positionalität*] in Plessner, 305
positivism [*Positivismus*], 51
possibility [*Möglichkeit*], 8, 18–21, 30, 36–37, 38, 42, 44, 90–92, 94, 97–98, 100, 106, 155–156, 188
power of deliberation [*Kraft zu überlegen*], 341
pregnancy [*Prägnanz*], 36, 251
prejudice [*Vorurteil*], 16, 39
presence [*Vorliegen*], 220
presence, presentness [*Gegenwärtigkeit*], 10, 230
  linguistic self-presence [*sprachliche Selbstgegenwart*], 227–228
presence, real presence [*Präsenz, Realpräsenz*], 64, 67–68, 74, 97, 204–205
present [*Gegenwart, das Gegenwärtige*], 7, 94, 264, 268, 283–285
present thing [*Vorhandenes*], 135
presentation [*Darstellung*], 67–68, 70–77, 81, 99–102, 106, 115–117, 121–122, 130–132, 139–140, 144, 152
  and contemplation [*Betrachtung*], 188
  and structure [*und Struktur*], 251
  as intensification of the phenomenal [*als Intensivierung des Phänomenalen*], 201
  pictoral [*bildliche*], 123
presentation, structure of [*Darstellungsgefüge*], 121–122, 138, 142–144, 152
presuppositionlessness [*Voraussetzungslosigkeit*], 30, 39, 45
presuppositions [*Voraussetzungen*], 3, 15–16
pretension [*Prätention*], 221
principle of contradiction [*Satz vom Widerspruch*], 340
production [*Herstellung*], 18–19, 101–102, 108–109, 157, 312–313, 335
  enactment of [*Herstellungsvollzug*], 82
profile [*Abschattung*], 131, 304
projection [*Entwurf*], 80
promise [*Versprechen*], 42
protention [*Protention*], 277–278

Index of Subjects 435

proximity [Nähe], 134-137, 138, 191
psychologism [Psychologismus], 125
public [Öffentlich, Öffentlichkeit], 87, 187
public surface [öffentliche Oberflach], 41
purpose [Zweck], 74. See also end
putting into language, bringing into language [zur Sprache bringen], 11, 63, 77, 145, 196

rational, the [Vernünftige, das], 336
reader [Leser], 62, 87
readiness to deal with [Umgangsbereitschaft], 21
reading [Lektüre, Lesen], 5, 58, 62, 63, 65-66, 72, 77-82, 83, 87, 102, 210-211, 298
readability [Lesbarkeit], 251
reality [Wirklichkeit], 51, 127, 128, 150. See also actuality
realization [Realisierung], 73-74, 115, 157
reason [Vernunft], 19, 20, § 40, 228
 exterior [äußere], 336
 in history [in der Geschichte], 11
 practical [praktische], 18-19, 20-21
 theoretical [theoretische], 21
recitation [Rezitation], 57, 62
recognition [Erkenntnis, Anerkennung], 49-50, 57, § 11, 97, 100-102, 116-117, 133, 236, 347. See also cognition; knowledge
recognizability [Erkennbarkeit], 70
recurrence, eternal [Wiederkunft, ewige], 148-149, 295
reduction, phenomenological [Reduktion, phänomenologische], 126
reference [Bezug, Hinweisen, Verweisung], 53, 55, 85, 100-101, 169, 203, 210, 296
 and temporality [Bezug und Zeitlichkeit], 282
 in showing [Bezug beim Zeigen], 201, 202-203
 of action toward its end [Bezug des Handelns auf sein Ziel], 158
 to a matter [Bezug auf eine Sache], 76

reference, making [Bezugnahme], 54, 129, 133
 in showing [beim Zeigen], 199
reference, sense of [Bezugssinn], xv, 10, 67, 101, 335
referred, being [Bezogensein], 126-127
reflection [Reflexion], 8, 16, 62-63, 121-122, 236-237
 circle of [Reflexionskreis], 100, 163
 hermeneutical [hermeneutische], 121-123
 of appearance [des Erscheinens], 128
 philosophical [philosophische], 119
reflectiveness [Reflektiertheit], 76
refusal [Verweigerung], 60
reification [Verdinglichung], 24, 111-112
relation that relates to itself [Verhältnis, das sich zu sich selbst verhält], 339, 345
relevance [Bewandtnis], 169-171, 107fn
reliability [Verläßlichkeit], 309
religion [Religion], 75, 118-119, 146
 and theology [und Theologie], 13
remaining [Bleiben], 253
remoteness [Entferntheit], 115, 129fn, 131, 138-140
removal [Entfernung], 49, 129, 129fn, 131, 133-142, 145
 between action and aim [zwischen Handlung und Ziel], 158
 between agents [zwischen Handelnden], 178
 in showing [beim Zeigen], 199, 200
 in time [in der Zeit], 262
remove [Ferne], 129fn, 131, 134-145, 152, 175
repetition [Wiederholung], xxiii, 62, 294-295
representation [Repräsentation, Vorstellung], 18, 61-62, 183, 194
representation [Vorstellung] in Frege, 213
responsibility [Verantwortlichkeit], 157, 236
rest [Ruhe], 310, 323. See also peace
retention [Retention], 273-277
reversibility [Umwendbarkeit], 306
rhetoric [Rhetorik], 239

rule [*Regel*], 5–6, 22, 27, 28, 38, 192–193, 217

said, the, what is said [*Gesagte, das*], 36–37, 56, 197, 215, 235, 239–240
saying [*Sagen*], 56, 195, 197–198, 223
schema [*Schema*], 28, 166–168
science [*Wissenschaft*], 4, 6, 11, 15–16, 23, 27–28, 30, 32–33, 75
  hermeneutical [*hermeneutische Wissenschaft*], 122
  human [*Geisteswissenschaft*], § 1, 22–23
  natural [*Naturwissenschaft*], 6, 148
science, normal, 28
score (i.e., musical) [*Partitur*], 57, 61
seeing [*Sehen*], 61, 71, 132, 139, 158, 225, 233
self-actualization [*Selbstverwirklichung*], 108–109
self-affection [*Selbstaffektion*], 230, 234
self-concealment [*Selbstverborgenheit*], 10
self-consciousness [*Selbstbewußtsein*], 109
self-identification (in language) [*Sichausweisen (in der Sprache)*], 238
self-knowledge [*Sichwissen*], 12–14
self-presence [*Selbstgegenwart*], 12, 16, 75, 230
self-presentation [*Selbstdarstellung*], 73–76, 77, 81
self-preservation [*Selbsterhaltung*], 319
self-showing [*Sichzeigen*], 122–124, 201, 204–205, 222–223
self-transparency [*Selbstdurchsichtigkeit*], 12–14, 21
self-understanding [*Selbstverstehen*], 12, 14, 21, 90, 93
self, care of [*Selbstsorge, Sorge um Sich*], 18, 114
self, knowing of [*Sich-wissen*], 22
self, loss of [*Selbstverlust*], 108
sensibleness [*Verständigsein*], 158
sentence [*Satz*], 50, 197, § 23
  indicative [*aufzeigender*], 204
setting in [*Einsetzen*], § 9, 77
shift [*Umschlag*], 25–26

showing [*Zeigen*], xx, 29, 69, 198–203, 204–206, 209, 223
sign [*Zeichen*], 42, 205, § 24, 212–213, 226–228, 229
significance [*Bedeutung*], xx–xxi, 35, 112, 135–136, 147, 212, § 25, 334–335
  fixed [*feste*], 224
  complex of [*Bedeutungskomplex*], 248, 335
signified and signifier [*Bezeichnetes und Bezeichnendes*], 213, 227–228
signifié/signifiant, 227–228
transcendental signified [*transcendentales Bezeichnetes*], 226, 232
silence [*Schweigen, Stille*], 60, 77, 191, 197, 257, 276
simultaneity [*Simultaneität*], 79–81, 209
skepticism [*Skepsis*]
  language of [*Sprache der*], 16
  hermeneutical [*hermeneutische*], 64
song [*Gesang*], 62, 240
sophistry [*Sophistik*], 225, 314, 321
soul [*Seele*], 53, 180, 194, 316
  affectio animi, 206–207
sound (i.e., in speech) [*Laut*], 192, 193–194
space [*Raum*], xvi–xvii, 119–120, 129, § 15
  hermeneutical [*hermeneutischer*], 3–4, 119, § 15, 144, 146, 152–153, 336
spatiality [*Räumlichkeit*], § 15, 326
speech [*Sprechen*], 63, 88, 145, § 22, 202–205, 211
speech act [*Sprechhandlung*], 238
sphere of ownness [*Eigenheitssphäre*], 229
spirit [*Geist*], 93–94, 124
  philosophy of [*Geistesphilosophie*], 12, 23
  spiritual power [*Geisteskraft*], 194
standpoint [*Standpunkt*], 49, 132–133, 139
state [*Zustand*], 147, 322–327
stream [*fluß*], 25, 323. See also flow; flux
  of historical life [*des geschichtlichen Leben*], 14
  of life [*des Lebens*], 58

of the occurrence of inheriting [*des Überlieferungsgeschehens*], 17
striving [*Streben*], 31, 160, 162–163, 324–325, 328, 332–333, 341–342
structure [*Struktur*], 152, 232, 250
  in Humboldt, 195
  ontological [*ontologische*], 171
  temporal [*zeitliche*], 258
style [*Stil*], 96, 98, 100
subject [*Subjekt*], 13, 51, 109, 132–133, 151–152, 194, 300
subjectivism [*Subjektivismus*], 51
  of perception [*der Wahrnehmung*], 321
subjectivity [*Subjektivität*], 13, 151–152, 194, 268, 300
substance [*Substanz*], 13–14, 53–54, 227, 263, 304
  desubstantialization of the sign [*Desubstanzialisierung des Zeichens*], 226
substantiveness [*Sachlichkeit*], 2, 42, 55–56. See also matter; matter itself
sudden, the [*Plötzliche, das*], 40
sun, simile of [*Sonnengleichnis*], 335
supposition [*Unterstellung*], 242, 244
surrounding [*Umgebung*], 134–135, 325–326
suspension [*Schwebe*], 34, 42, 44, 127, 323
symbol [*Symbol*], 228
system [*System*], 132–133
  of needs [*der Bedürfnisse*], 175
  of signs [*von Zeichen*], 211–212

tactile sensation [*Tastsinn*], 306
talk [*Rede*], 56–59, 96, 197
temporality [*Zeitlichkeit*], xxii, 281, § 33
tension [*Spannung*], 43, 44, 63–64, 106, 158, 328
text [*Text*], xv, 6, 13, 46, §§ 8–12, 224, 250–251
  eminent [*eminenter*], 57
  sacred [*heiliger*], 118–119
  theological [*theologischer*], 251
textuality [*Textualität*], 96, 97–98

texture [*Textur*], 203–205, 210, 212, 224
  of significances [*der Bedeutungen*], 222
theoretical, the [*Theoretische, das*], 10, 17, 21, 23–24
theory [*Theorie*], 18, 20, 23–24
  critical [*kritische*], 2
thing [*Ding*], 17, 20, 50, 112, 131–136, 146, 151–152, 210
  and body [*und Körper*], 327–328
  as significant phenomenon [*als bedeutsames Phänomen*], 218
  everyday [*Alltagsding*], 27
  human [*menschliches*], 21
  in itself [*an sich*], 51, 113–114
thing-world, world of things [*Dingwelt*], 18, 150, 300
  and freedom [*und Freiheit*], 249
thingliness [*Dingliche, das*], 112
thought, thinking [*Denken*], 31–32, 38, 47, 60–61, 63, 194, 228, § 28, 319
  apperceptive [*vernehmendes*], 158
  conceptual [*begriffliches*], 8
  hermeneutical [*hermeneutisches*], 2, 24, 61, 117
  philosophical [*philosophisches*], 8, 16
  spatial [*räumliches*], 3
three-dimensionality [*Dreidimensionalität*], 299–300
time [*Zeit*], xiii, xviii, xxii–xxiii, 4, 40–41, 144–146, 152, §§ 29–34
  measurement of [*Zeitmessung*], 260, 281
  of enactment [*Vollzugszeit*], § 32, 282
tool [*Werkzeug*], 26–27, 50, 194
totality [*Totalität*], 147–148, 152
  absolute [*absolute*], 147, 149–150
touching [*Berühren*], 233, 338
trace [*Spur*], 230
tradition [*Tradition*], 2, 4, 6–8, 11–13, 14–15, 22–23, 30, 35, 41
transcendence [*Transzendenz*], 34
  finite, xiv, xvi, xviii, xix, xxii
transformation [*Veränderung*], 25–27, 258. See also change

translation [*Übersetzung*], 46, 224–225
  translatability of language [*Übersetzbarkeit der Sprache*], 192
traverse [*Durchmessen*], 135, 136, 142–143
  traversing of openness in action [*Durchmessen der Offenheit im Handeln*], 159
truth [*Wahrheit*], 2, 6, 13–14, 17, 31–33, 75, 251, 298
  practical [*praktische*], 18
turn, the [*Kehre, die*], 11
typical, the [*Typische, das*], 71

unconcealment [*Unverborgenheit*], 41, 172
underlying, the [*Zugrundeliegende, das*], 311
understanding [*Verstehen*], xv–xvi, 2–3, 5, 10, 12, 14–15, 20, 22, 24, 88, § 12, 121–122, 197
  art of [*Kunstlehre des*], 5
  elementary [*elementares*], 97, 100
  explanation and [*Erklären und*], 89
  originary [*ursprüngliches*], 20
understanding, practical [*praktische Verständigkeit*], 164
unfamiliarity [*Unselbstverständlichkeit*], 40–41
unfreedom [*Unfreiheit*], 174, 177
unintelligibility [*Unverständlichkeit*], 104–105, 180
unity [*Einheit*], 27, 56–58, 65, 84–87, 106, 130, 148, 195
  and multiplicity [*und Vielheit*], 245–247
  of a world [*einer Welt*], 148
  of the text [*des Textes*], 84–87
  on the basis of presentation [*aus Darstellung*], 130
universal, the [*Allgemeine, das*], 22–23, 35–37, 71, 95, 219
universality [*Allgemeinheit*], 36
  of the word [*des Wortes*], 219–221
unlimitedness [*Unbegrenztheit*], 26, 106–107, 129

usage (i.e., linguistic) [*Sprachgebrauch*], 50, 103, 193
use [*Gebrauch*], 112–114, 216–217, 309
useful thing [*Gebrauchsding, Zeug*], 27, 49–50, 66, 111–116, 118, 134–135, 169–171, 208–209
utilitarianism [*Utilitarismus*], 119

value [*Wert*], 52, 55–56, 179
verba naturalia, 206–207
view, point of [*Sichtpunkt*], 53
viewer [*Betrachter*], 139. See also beholder
virtue [*Tugend*], 179
voice [*Stimme*], 63, 194, 205, 225, § 26, 233–234, 239–240

we [*Wir*], 146, 237–238
what is [*Seiendes*], 18fn, 31, 34, 41, 146–148, 149. See also beings
  insofar as it is what is [*sofern es Seiendes ist*], 301
what is in the future [*Zukünftige, das*], 283–285
wholeness [*Ganzheit*], 30, 33–35, 36–38, 43, 46, 79–83, 148, 245, 247
will [*Wille*], 52, 54, 168, 343–348
  metaphysics of [*Willenmetaphysik*], 346
will to power [*Wille zur Macht*], 52–54, 148–149, 177, 223–224
wishing [*Wünschen*], 168
withdrawal [*Entzogenheit*], 42, 44
word [*Wort*], 21, 42, 43, 46, 61–62, 192–193, 195, 221
  pure [*reines*], 243
work [*Arbeit, Werk, Wirken*], 19, 27, 57–58, 64, 73–74, 75, 97–100, 108, 158, 166, 192–194, 346
  of spirit [*Arbeit des Geistes*], 228
world [*Welt*], xvii–xviii, 3–4, 14, 28, 42, 45, 51, 53–54, §§ 14–16, 221
  as order [*als Ordnung*], 147
  as totality [*als Totalität*], 147–148
  of useful things and work [*Zeug- und Werkwelt*], 150
spiritual [*geistige*], 94

world of things [*Dingwelt*]. *See* thing-world
world order [*Weltordnung*], 147, 280, 315. *See also* χόσμος
world-formation [*Weltbildung*], 148–149
world, picture of [*Weltbild*], 146
worldview [*Weltanschauung*], 146
writing [*Schrift*], xxii, 21, 57, 230–231, 239–240
    as structure [*als Struktur*], 250
    pieces of [*Schriftstücke*], 56, 59–60
    study of (i.e., grammar) [*Schriftkunde, Grammatik*], 250

you (plural) [*Ihr*], 237–238
you (singular) [*Du*], 94, 110, 112, 236, 237–238
    in language [*in der Sprache*], 197

Index of Greek Terms

ἀρχή, 20, 243, 245, 309
ἄπειρον, 107
αἴσθησις, 20, 319
ἀλήθεια, 41, 123
   ἕξις ἀληθής, 164
   πρακτική, 18
ἀντικείμενον, 112
ἀνυπόθετον, 244
ἀπειρία, 26, 247
ἀρετὴ διανοητική, 166

βούλησις, 162, 341
   βουλεύεσθαι, 165

γραμματικός, 250

διάνοια, 68, 243
δύναμις, 19

ἑρμηνεύειν, 49
ἔργον, 19, 99, 303
   τοῦ ἀνθρώπου, 19
εἶδος, 101, 223, 241, 243, 244, 245, 268, 312, 313, 334
   κατὰ τὸν λόγον, 313-315, 334
εἴδη, 244, 245
ἐνέργεια, 19, 99, 158, 186, 322, 323
ἐντελέχεια, 312, 313
ἐπιθυμία, 341, 342
ἐπιστήμη, 318, 334
ἐποχή, 16, 17, 24, 39, 46, 111, 125, 126, 150, 151, 239, 241, 291, 346
εὖ ζῆν, 165

φαινόμενον, 123, 201
φρονεῖν, 158, 319
φρόνησις, 18, 20, 21, 164, 165
φυσικά, τά, 35
φύσις, 308-315, 317, 323, 325
φωνὴ σημαντική, 204-206

καθόλου, 219
κίνησις, 157, 260, 267, 322-324
κόσμος, 147, 280, 315
λογιστικόν, 341
λόγος, xv, 19, 56, 57, 60, 164, 204, 206, 219, 243, 250

μεταβολή, 25
μεταφέρειν, 49
μίμησις, 68, 101, 123
μορφή, 311

νοεῖν, 158, 319, 333
νοῦς, 20, 266, 333
νόησις, 243
νόμος, 314
νῦν, 260, 262, 268

ὂν ᾗ ὄν, 19, 172, 301
ὄργανον, 318
οὐσία, 311, 318
ὅ ποτε ὄν, 262, 266, 267

παράδειγμα, 29
πάθος, 33, 285
περιαγωγή, 121
πέρας, 26, 106, 247

πίστις, 244
πόλις, 35, 177
προαίρεσις, 162

θεωρεῖν, 165, 318, 334
θεωρία, 184
θυμοειδές, 342
θυμός, 342

σημεῖα, 211
σύμβολον, 194, 207, 211
σῶμα, 316, 327, 329

τέχνη, 19, 103, 242, 246, 311, 335
   διαλεκτικὴ τέχνη, 240
τό τι ἦν εἶναι, 314, 334

ὕλη, 311
ὑπάρχειν, 219
ὑποκείμενον, 173, 263, 300
ὑπόθεσις, 15, 242, 245

ψυχή, 267, 316–320, 324, 340

ζῷον, 309
ζωή, 158, 317

www.ingramcontent.com/pod-product-compliance
Lightning Source LLC
Chambersburg PA
CBHW020118240426
43673CB00038B/520